Korean
Grammar

Korean Grammar

THE COMPLETE GUIDE
TO SPEAKING
KOREAN NATURALLY

Soohee Kim, Emily Curtis and Haewon Cho

TUTTLE Publishing

Tokyo | Rutland, Vermont | Singapore

"Books to Span the East and West"

Tuttle Publishing was founded in 1832 in the small New England town of Rutland, Vermont [USA]. Our core values remain as strong today as they were then—to publish best-in-class books which bring people together one page at a time. In 1948, we established a publishing office in Japan—and Tuttle is now a leader in publishing English-language books about the arts, languages and cultures of Asia. The world has become a much smaller place today and Asia's economic and cultural influence has grown. Yet the need for meaningful dialogue and information about this diverse region has never been greater. Over the past seven decades, Tuttle has published thousands of books on subjects ranging from martial arts and paper crafts to language learning and literature—and our talented authors, illustrators, designers and photographers have won many prestigious awards. We welcome you to explore the wealth of information available on Asia at www.tuttlepublishing.com.

Published by Tuttle Publishing, an imprint of Periplus Editions (HK) Ltd.

www.tuttlepublishing.com

Copyright © 2017 Soohee Kim, Emily Curtis and Haewan Cho

Library of Congress Control Number: 2017949656

ISBN 978-0-8048-4921-0

24 23 22 21   10 9 8 7 6 5 4
2112VP

Printed in Malaysia

Distributed by

North America, Latin America & Europe
Tuttle Publishing
364 Innovation Drive
North Clarendon
VT 05759-9436 U.S.A.
Tel: 1 (802) 773-8930
Fax: 1 (802) 773-6993
info@tuttlepublishing.com
www.tuttlepublishing.com

Japan
Tuttle Publishing
Yaekari Building 3rd Floor 5-4-12 Osaki
Shinagawa-ku Tokyo 141 0032
Tel: (81) 3 5437-0171
Fax: (81) 3 5437-0755
sales@tuttle.co.jp
www.tuttle.co.jp

Asia Pacific
Berkeley Books Pte. Ltd.
3 Kallang Sector #04-01
Singapore 349278
Tel: (65) 6741-2178
Fax: (65) 6741-2179
inquiries@periplus.com.sg
www.tuttlepublishing.com

For My Beautiful Mother,
Insook Heo (1937 - 2017),
who taught me how to live
and how to leave

S.K.

Contents

Acknowledgments

We authors would like to thank all our students in Korean and linguistics classes, including heritage language learners who may be 1.5- or second-generation immigrants, adoptees, and thousands of non-heritage students who have taken Korean language courses at the University of Washington, University of Michigan, and University of Pennsylvania in the last decade and a half. This book would not exist without the authors' glance into their linguistic world.

We would like to gratefully acknowledge the support Haewon Cho received for romanization and proofreading in the form of a faculty research grant from the James JooJin Kim Program in Korean Studies at the University of Pennsylvania.

We also want to express appreciation of our families for their support of our work and careers, their patience with this project, and their help in discussing language use and providing examples.

Soohee Kim would like to thank Yonghee, Hyunjin, and Yongjae Kim, Dongho and Sieun Kim, Eunbi, Soyoung and Donghyun Lee for their unending moral support—especially Soyoung Lee and Sieun Kim for making this book one step more accessible with their happy and amazing artistic contribution; her co-authors, who have been the powerhouse with their knowledge and grit, and their gleeful collaboration; Mimi and Bug as well as E.K.J.C-K for bearing with her "absence" during the writing of this book. Special acknowledgment is due for Virginia Mueller Gathercole, who opened the author's eyes and heart to the world of linguistics.

Emily Curtis would like to thank Kathie Curtis, Jen, Colin and Maya Monks, and Amy and Keith Amano for their patience and support during the writing of this book over holidays and many moons. Sincere admiration and appreciation are also due her spouse, for unfailing support of all kinds and for brilliant ideas for this project.

Haewon Cho would like to give her heartfelt thanks to Jubum, her unbelievably supportive and loving husband, for always being there whenever she needs him. Special thanks go to her wonderful daughter, Seyoung, for adding such joy to her life and giving her the energy and strength to continue working on this project. Much appreciation goes to her parents, Soja Lee and Yong Rok Cho, who have at all times supported her with their love and best wishes. She would also like to thank her former and current colleagues at the University of Washington, University of Michigan, and University of Pennsylvania for their continued encouragement and inspiration.

Much gratitude is also due our colleagues for invaluable learning and community. Among the numerous colleagues and advisors, we would especially like to thank Sharon Hargus, Richard Wright, Ellen Kaisse, Manka Varghese and Julia Herschensohn for teaching us at the University of Washington; Olga Kagan, Maria Carreira, Maria Gillman, Alejandro Lee, Alegria Ribadeneira, Sybil Alexandrov, and Claire Chik for their guidance and happy collegiality at National Heritage Language Research Center (NHLRC) workshops; and the members of the American Association of Teachers of Korean

(AATK) for their fellowship. We'd especially like to thank our wonderful colleague Ross King of the University of British Columbia for his unfailing support over many years in the field and also for being an inspiration.

Lastly, our sincere thanks go to Sandra Korinchak and Eric Oey, who so willingly welcomed the blueprint of this book before Korean became such a popular language. Huge acknowledgment also goes to the professional and patient help of Nancy Goh and Su Yin Ngo as well as anonymous reviewers who provided valuable feedback on manuscripts. We greatly appreciate the kind and helpful folks at Periplus-Tuttle. Also many thanks go to Jen Ramos for comments and romanization assistance. This final product is greatly improved by their care and attention, and any remaining missteps are our own.

Introduction

Welcome to Korean grammar!

We're excited to help you put the pieces together and see the wonder of the Korean language. In this book, we'll cover all the basics—from the letters of the alphabet to parts of speech to sentence endings, connectors, honorifics and embedded sentences; from the little pieces to the big meaningful units and back down to the grammatical bits and pieces, nuance, and cultural meanings.

If you have background knowledge of Korean, this book should fill in any gaps and help organize your knowledge. If you are a new learner of Korean, rest assured that it's all laid out carefully to be useful and approachable for you, too. If you are a Korean teacher, you can gain insight into the potential pitfalls and confusions of learners and solidify your explicit knowledge of Korean grammar and use.

1. About the book

This book presents an overview of Korean grammar at the basic to intermediate levels. It includes grammatical forms and expressions that might be covered in the first two or three years of a college or high school course. The structure, meaning and function of words and expressions are carefully explained, and we provide example sentences to illustrate how each grammatical construction is used in various contexts. Summary charts are provided throughout for quick reference. And for those who want to practice and review the grammar patterns introduced, exercises are provided at the end of each chapter. The goal is to help organize and deepen learners' understanding of the language, whether it be a review of prior learning, a supplemental material used alongside a conversation course, a preview for a language course, a linguistic exploration, or a professional development tool.

While we respect the rules set forth by the *National Institute of the Korean Language* 국립국어원 kwuklipkwukewen and traditional grammarians of South Korea, we also recognize common usage, even when non-standard, and try to represent what Korean people say in real life, as languages are living, constantly evolving, dynamic beings. We are careful to note the instances where we use non-standard spelling or expressions to reach readers or to illustrate a point. Similarly, every effort is made to present complex linguistic phenomena and minute nuance differences in accessible ways and to provide explanations of necessary terminology. We chose to use Yale romanization in this book, as it most faithfully offers letter-to-letter correspondence with the Korean alphabet without pretending to approximate actual pronunciation. Romanization is provided for linguists, dilettantes and work-shy students. We trust that any serious learners of Korean can learn the alphabet with a few days of concentrated work and not rely on romanization.

This book should make a very effective learning tool for those who just started their journey of learning the Korean language. To help those learners, romanization, word-by-word gloss, sentence translations, and example sentences are ample. Learners who would like to go beyond their beginning level, teachers who are looking for ways to give explicit and wise instruction, and fledgling linguists who are interested in the workings of the language will all benefit from this book.

1.1. A message for language learners

You do not have to know how to change a flat tire on your car just because you want to know how to drive it. When the occasion arises, though, say you are on a long journey by yourself and get a flat tire in the middle of nowhere, then your knowledge and skill to change the tire may save your life. Knowing a little bit about how the engine works might help you understand how to drive it gently and maintain it, or how to not get swindled when it comes time for repairs. Similarly, if you want to learn how to speak or understand Korean a *little*, you do not want to bother yourself with learning all its rules. But then again, you may be able to say just enough to get you to a point where … you wish you knew more. You wish you understood *which* way to say something in a given instance or *why* it is said a certain way and not another. This book can help with that, organizing what you know so that you can build on it.

Having a good grammatical command of the language will not only give you a boost in self-esteem but will help you to communicate with Korean speakers and understand the warmth they shine on you because now you understand the nuances of the language.

As you work through this book, make connections between the concepts and expressions presented here and ones you know from previous Korean exposure or from another language. Think critically and formalize your understanding of Korean grammar. You can do it, and we think you'll be glad you did.

1.2. A message to teachers

The car analogy for teachers is that sometimes we know *that* the oil needs to be changed but we can't explain *why* it does or what benefits from changing it. Similarly with language, it is easy to know how to speak and write the language, and even to provide a model little by little for learners to imitate, but it is usually much harder to *explain* how even one expression works and why it is used and not another.

Explaining how a language works requires knowing what categories (e.g. parts of speech) are needed, which words fit in each category, and how each category works in relation to others. This book lays out the grammatical categories needed to explain how Korean grammar works and identifies basic examples of each category and how they function in the grammar at the beginning to intermediate levels. Nuance and usage differences are also explained and exemplified.

Teaching also requires an understanding of what students know and think. While this is a moving target, explanations and examples are aimed, based on our experience, specifically at the challenges and assumptions English speakers have in learning Korean. Comparisons with English are provided which we believe will be helpful for learners as well as teachers. This kind of instruction for deep learning helps to consolidate learners' knowledge and expand their understanding of the language, taking them beyond simply memorizing a few phrases or simple structures.

2. What's in the book and how is it all organized?

We start with the alphabet in chapter 1 and pronunciation rules in chapter 2. You may know how to read Hangul, and it is a very logical and relatively simple alphabet, but chapter 1 aims to round out your knowledge of Hangul—what makes it an **alphabet**, how it is organized, and how it came to be. Chapter 2 lays out the pronunciation rules that explain how Korean is pronounced sometimes a bit differently from how it is written.

In chapter 3 we show that Korean sentences are made up of subject, time, place, indirect object, direct object, negation and lastly, the verb or **predicate** adjective. You'll see how these ideas are expressed with nouns, **particles**, adverbs, and verbs (along with a couple other recognized **parts of speech**), how information is organized from macro-level to micro-level, and how the particles attached to nouns help make clear who is doing what in a sentence.

In chapter 4, you learn all about **particles**—one of the most important features of Korean grammar. Even though they are often dropped in casual, spoken Korean, they are required in more formal and written Korean, and they help prevent miscommunication when they are used. Particles are one of the most fascinating complexities of Korean grammar.

In chapter 5, we discuss nouns, including numerals, pronouns, **dependent nouns**, and their origins. There are fun aspects to numerals in Korean, such as that there are two sets, native Korean and Sino-Korean. Usage of pronouns in Korean is also intriguingly different from English, as you will see. You will witness the sociolinguistic and cultural intricacy of Korean in learning about pronouns.

Chapter 6 is about verbs and adjectives in Korean. They come at the end of the sentence and take suffix-like "endings" to show the **tense** and **aspect**, the speaker's relationship with the listener, and the level of formality. And they **conjugate**—change shape based on those suffixes. Chapter 6 covers all the conjugation basics for the most-often used speech style. We also introduce irregular and special-class verbs that have different forms which depend on what endings are attached.

Chapter 7 is about how to end sentences—that is, additional interesting verb suffixes that express **speech styles** (based on the relationship between the speaker and listener), **modality** (expressed in English with verbs like *can*, *should*, *will*), and myriad nuances of speaker attitude. Chapter 7 is where you become truly expressive in Korean.

In chapter 8, we show you how to make your sentences longer, more complex and more nuanced by connecting two sentences together using **connector suffixes** with meanings like *because*, *before*, and *if…then*, and also how to use a clause to modify a noun, as in a *chapter in which we explain complex sentences*.

Chapter 9 is about how new verbs, **honorific**, **passive** and **causative** verbs, are **derived**, how verbs are converted into adverbs, and how all the different types of verbal suffixes work together in tandem.

And finally, in chapter 10, we show how to embed sentences in two ways: making them into noun phrases to talk about activities and happenings, as in *Studying Korean is good for your mental health*, and reporting sentence-sized things that someone says, thinks, knows, or wonders (*I knew listening to K-POP would improve my dancing skills!*). By using these embedded clauses, you can expand and elaborate on your ideas just like Korean people do.

3. Overview of Contents

Chapter 1. 한글 The Korean Alphabet
is an explanation of Hangul letters, the reasoning behind their shapes, and the sounds
they represent.

Chapter 2. 발음 법칙과 철자법 Pronunciation Rules & Spelling
helps you understand spelling rules and how the pronunciation shifts slightly in some
cases.

Chapter 3. 품사와 문장구조 Parts of Speech & Sentence Structure
helps you understand the basic building blocks of Korean grammar and how sentences
are organized.

Chapter 4. 조사 Particles
tackles "tiny" but fundamental elements of Korean, which mark the role of nouns in
sentences and carry particular nuances.

Chapter 5. 명사 Nouns
explains different kinds of nouns recognized in Korean grammar along with their origins and usage, and also introduces the TWO number systems.

Chapter 6. 동사 Verbs
lays out the basics of verb types and conjugation, another absolute fundamental of Korean grammar, focusing on the most widely used speech style.

Chapter 7. 문장 종결 어미 Sentence Endings
lays out the speech styles that represent social roles and a variety of other sentence endings to really express yourself.

Chapter 8. 복문 만들기 Complex Sentences
introduces clause connectors and how to combine two sentences into a complex one,
including how to modify nouns using clauses.

Chapter 9. 동사의 파생 Verb Derivations
shows how to derive honorific, causative, and passive verbs, how to convert verbs into
adverbs, and how to use multiple verbal suffixes at once.

Chapter 10. 내포절 Embedded Sentences
wraps it all up with how to embed clauses into a sentence to comment on activities and
events and to quote people's utterances and thinking.

4. Before you start

Before we begin examining the specifics of Korean structure and usage, it will help to
have some basic and essential knowledge about the language.

4.1 Basics

Korean is spoken by over 77 million people worldwide, with nearly 50 million in South
Korea overall and 10 million in Seoul. Although there are dialects spoken in South Korea, including Kyeongkido (or Seoul), Chungcheongdo, Kyongsangdo, Jeollado, and

Jeju Island dialects, and there are also North Korean dialects, we'll focus on the "standard" language of South Korea, basically that of Seoul.

Another fun fact about Korean is that there is still debate about the language family that it may belong to. Many scholars consider Korean to be an **isolate**—a language having no linguistic relatives. Various versions of the "Altaic hypothesis," on the other hand, position Korean in a branch of the Altaic **language family** alongside Japonic languages (e.g. Japanese and Okinawan) as more distant cousins of languages like Turkish, Khalkha Mongolian, Manchu and even Hungarian in other branches (somewhat like Romance, Balto-Slavic, and Celtic branches of the Indo-European language family). The evidence is thus far inconclusive. There is still much to be studied about this language.

4.2 Essentials

Four fundamental characteristics of the language will be helpful to have in mind as you begin working with this book:

1. The Korean writing system is different from English, but it's an **alphabet**.
2. Korean is **predicate-final**: the verb comes last.
3. Korean is an **agglutinating** language; words are made up of roots and many suffixes.
4. Korean grammar reflects the social structure in obvious and obligatory ways.

Let's see what those mean in a little more detail.

4.2.1 The Korean writing system, Hangul, is an alphabet

That means that each consonant sound and each vowel sound is represented with a letter. It is not like the Chinese writing system, where each character represents a word or meaning, nor like Japanese syllabaries, where each SYLLABLE (*to, ka, da, mu, hi, ne*, and so on) is its own character. Korean letters are arranged into syllables, instead of being written in a linear sequence, but there are only 21 vowel letters and 19 consonant letters. It is simple, logical, and easy to learn. We highly recommend learning it, as it makes parts of the grammar more straightforward.

Nonetheless, we have provided **romanization** throughout the book. It is a way of writing Korean (or any language) using the Roman alphabet. No romanization system is "just like" English spelling, of course. So you'll have to learn what sounds are represented by the letters in whatever romanization system is used. We use the Yale system, and it is introduced alongside Hangul in chapter 1.

4.2.2 Korean is predicate-final, so the verb comes last

Unlike English, where the basic word order of a simple statement is SVO (Subject-Verb-Object), as in *Humans eat fruit*, Korean has SOV (Subject-Object-Verb) word order: *Humans fruit eat*. That is, the verb always comes last in the sentence. This also means that it is VERBS that end up being conjugated and getting suffixes tacked on for speech style, speaker attitude, and other meanings at the end of the sentence. The reason we say "**predicate**-final" instead of verb-final is just because adjectives also come last when they are predicate adjectives as in *this book is terrific*. And by the way, adjectives function as a kind of verb in Korean.

4.2.3 Korean is an agglutinating language, and the shape of verbs varies

Agglutinating languages are those whose words are made up of many smaller pieces. Certain kinds of **root words** MUST come with **affixes** and cannot stand alone as independent words like *go, book, cool*, and even *at, the* or *but* can in English. In Korean, it is usually suffixes that attach to verbs to make the verb sometimes hugely long. You can think of a comparable English word *transformationalizability* (*transform* (root)+*ation-al-ize-able-ity*) to imagine how Korean works, except in Korean, the meanings of suffixes are more like past tense or subject-verb agreement. Also, many kinds of meanings are expressed in affixes, including some distinctions we don't make or don't realize we make in English.

Many suffixes can stack up on Korean verbs. For example, in the sentence 벌써 저녁을 드시었겠지요? pelsse cenyekul tusiesskeyssciyo, the underlined verb is made up 드- tu the verb root *eat*, plus suffixes −시 -si *honorific*, −었− -ess- *perfective*, −겠− -keyss- *conjecture*, −지 -ci *presumptive*, and −요 -yo *politeness*.

벌써	저녁을	<u>드시었겠지요?</u>
벌써	저녁-을	<u>드-시-었-겠-지-요?</u>
pelsse	cenyek-ul	tu-si-ess-keyss-ci-yo
already	*dinner-object*	*eat-honorific-perfective-conjecture-presumptive-polite*

I guess he/she (someone to be honored) has already had dinner, don't you think?
(I am saying this to you politely)

And yes, there are many, MANY verb suffixes in Korean, expressing all kinds of meanings. We dedicate chapters 6-10 to different kinds. It will be helpful to have in mind when reading that, given the agglutinating nature of Korean and the innumerable verb suffixes, any single verb has multiple "forms." In explanations of grammar and usage, we will use the dictionary form to talk ABOUT verbs, but in example sentences, the forms of the verbs will vary, based on the different suffixes used. You will get better understanding of the suffixes as you progress through the chapters, but you can always recognize the root in a verb—it is the part that is left over when you take -다 -ta off of the dictionary form, and it will show up in all forms of the verb that you see in examples.

4.2.4 Korean is hierarchical: the social structure is expressed in the grammar

Now you know that verb roots always come with some suffix attached. Some of those suffixes express social hierarchy relationships and politeness. For example, when speaking to someone of similar age as with whom you are very close, you can tell them 먹어! meke! which means "*eat!*" but when speaking with someone you are a little less casual with, you should add the politeness suffix and say 먹어요 mekeyo in what we'll call the polite ordinary **speech style**. If that person is in a higher social position than you (age counts as social position) and needs to be "honored," you have to use a special **honorific** verb and an honorific suffix before -요 -yo and say 드세요 tuseyyo. Be aware that you need to learn how to use the socially appropriate suffixes on your verbs to speak Korean; it's not extra information, it's essential to communicating.

These four traits are where Korean differs most from English, and they combine to make the grammar tricky in some ways. We hope to make it less difficult and more intriguing.

5. On using this book

How you use the book is of course up to you and dependent on your goals. You may wish to read sequentially chapter-by-chapter, or use the book as a reference, searching topic-by-topic. You can also search the table of contents or headings for specific expressions.

English words and translations are written in *italics*, emphasis is indicated with SMALL CAPS, and romanization is in smaller font. Technical grammar terminology is in **bold** for those who wish to look it up for more thorough understanding. We explain the concepts as they apply to the Korean examples at hand. The goal is to learn about how Korean works!

CHAPTER 1

The Korean Alphabet

한글 hankul, the Korean alphabet, is simple and easy to learn. You may have already learned to read it, but here we give a holistic picture of the system to complete your knowledge and fill in any gaps.

한글 hankul was created in 1443 by 세종대왕 seycongtaywang, *King Sejong the Great*, the fourth king of the Joseon Dynasty. Korean scholars had been using Chinese characters for more than 1,500 years, but the majority of ordinary Korean people were illiterate. As Sejong was a compassionate king, he wanted to create a writing system for everyone, one that not just erudite scholars but everyone could learn with ease and put into daily use. 훈민정음 hwunmincengum, the first book published in the newly invented alphabet, claims that 한글 hankul is extremely easy to use, and it is! It has acquired fame as the world's most scientific and accessible alphabet. The manual that contains the philosophy and the mechanics of its invention, 훈민정음 해례 hwunmincengum haylyey, has been designated as Korea's National Treasure item number 70, and it was registered in 1997 as a UNESCO Memory of the World document.

한글 hankul is an alphabet, and each of its letters represents a consonant or vowel sound. The letters are arranged into blocks that represent syllables. It may look complicated at first, but rest assured that there are only 21 vowel letters and 19 consonant letters to learn, along with the basic writing conventions. Depending on how you count them, you could even say there are only 6 (or 8) basic vowel and 10 (or 5!) basic consonant letters to learn. In the olden days, 한글 hankul was read top-to-bottom, right-to-left, but the modern day convention is to read it left-to-right, top-to-bottom like English. The letter strokes and the positioning of the letters (syllable-blocks) are *written* basically left-to-right, top-to-bottom as well.

Say *ah* or *oh* out loud. Now try saying *p* or *ch* or *n* (without the help of a sound like *ee* or *uh*). You can feel your mouth getting more closed or blocked when you say *p* or *ch* or *n*. Sounds with more (or total) closure or "obstruction" in the mouth are called **consonants**, and sounds that don't have that closure are called **vowels**. The sound *y* (like in the word *you*) or *w* (like in the word *way*) are somewhere in between, which is why they are sometimes called **semi-consonants** or **semi-vowels**, but as you will see later, they are counted as part of "complex vowels" in Korean.

In this book, we are providing **romanization** for Korean words (that is, spelling in the Roman alphabet) for readers who do not know how to read Korean well. You might have noticed the romanization appearing in smaller font next to each Korean word. There are several romanization systems for Korean, but we chose the Yale romanization system because it has been around longer than others and is also relatively easy to get used to. Yale romanization represents the pronunciation of EACH HANGUL LETTER, so it may be easier to learn to switch between the two systems, too. Be aware that no romanization can reflect the actual pronunciation of words. If we need to emphasize the precise pronunciation of words, we will provide that either in IPA (International Phonetic Alphabet) symbols or in Korean letters in square brackets. Shall we begin with the vowel letters then?

1.1 Vowels (V)

A vowel is a sound that you can make and prolong with your mouth mostly open and unblocked. Vowels are called 모음 moum in Korean, which means "mother sound."

1.1.1 Basic vowels

Here are the basic vowels, along with the romanization in small font and an explanation of each sound.

아 a   *a* as in *father*

어 e   a mid back unrounded vowel [ʌ], somewhat like *au* in *caught* (as pronounced by those for whom it is different from *cot*); or somewhat like *uh* in *huh* and the vowel sound in *some*

오 o   *o* as in *tote*

우 wu   [u] as in *moo* said with both lips sticking really far out. Pretend to be a gorilla, and don't hold back!

으 u   a high central vowel [ɨ] not found in English. Try saying *good* while smiling. That's the vowel!

이 i   *ee* as in *see*

애 ay   *eh* as in *bed* [ɛ] (some say it is [æ] as in *bad*, but that sound does not exist in Korean)

에 ey   the first part of the vowel in *mate*, or, *ay* without the *y* sound; or *eh* as in *bed* [ɛ]

(Most Korean speakers do not distinguish the last two vowels 애 ay and 에 ey.)

Korean vowels are pronounced for a relatively long duration and DO NOT have **off-glides** like they do in English. When you pronounce 오 [o], 우 [u], 에 [ɛ], for example, you should not say them staccato or with a glottal stop at the end like you would when pronouncing Japanese short vowels. Nor should you slide into a *w* or *y* at the end like English *no*, *ew*, or *hey*. (Think about how it is possible to make the word *no* into two syllables using that off-glide *w* when you are insisting: *no-wuh!*) To make the Korean vowel 오 sound, for example, try to make a pure vowel sound, as in Spanish *taco*, *bueno*, *olé* (if you know how to): keep the shape of your lips and tongue constant, and prolong the vowel sound: *oooo~*. No *w* at the end!

Despite many claims otherwise, there is no clear pronunciation difference between 애 ay and 에 ey in the modern Seoul dialect, especially among young people. For this reason, many Koreans pronounce the second person pronoun *you*, 네 ney, as [니 ni] to avoid confusion between 내 nay *I* and 네 ney *you*. Just as in the case of *tuff* and *tough*, or *phish* and *fish*, you just have to memorize the spelling when encountering new words with ㅐ or ㅔ. Notice that 애 ay is made up of 아 a + ㅣ i and 에 ey is made up of 어 e + ㅣ i. This is one way to refer to the different vowels, and it might come in handy in memorizing spelling.

Korean vowels are, by convention, written with a placeholder 이응 iung (ㅇ) before them. The idea is that a well-formed syllable begins with a consonant, so the consonant letter ㅇ can hold the place of the expected consonant. (Here ㅇ has no sound value, so ㅏ is pronounced the same as 아 a, but 아 is the "correct" way to write it.) When writing, strokes are written left-to-right, top-to-bottom. If the vertical stroke of a vowel is long, the vowel is written to the right of the initial consonant (or ㅇ); if its horizontal stroke is long, it is placed UNDER the consonant:

Vowels highlighted in the light color in the box above, 아 a and 오 o (and 애 ay, which is based on 아 a), often behave alike in Korean grammar, and they are called **Yang vowels** (양성 모음 yangseng moum). These Yang vowels carry a sense of lightness, smallness, brightness, or intensity. Dark-colored vowels 어 e and 우 wu (and 에 ey, which is based on 어 e) can be clumped together into the **Yin vowel** group (음성 모음 umseng moum), and they carry a heavy, big, dark, or diffused nuance. There used to be what is called **Vowel Harmony** (모음 조화 moum cohwa) in the history of the Korean language whereby the vowels in a suffix had to match the vowels in the base word as all Yang or all Yin vowels. Although strict vowel harmony has more or less died away, the phenomenon remains in modern standard Korean in certain frozen forms of words and in verb conjugations as well as in onomatopoeic words (e.g., 반짝 panccak *twinkle, glint, glitter, sparkle* vs. 번쩍 penccek *glare, flash, gleam* or 깡충 kkangchong *hop* vs. 껑충 kkengchwung *jump, leap*). So, do remember that 아 a - 오 o (and vowels derived from these) and 어 e - 우 wu go together.

When a short stroke "-" is added to the basic vowels, it represents that the sound value [y] is also added; thus 아 [a] becomes 야 [ya], and 우 [u] becomes 유 [yu]. 얘 yay and 예 yey are pronounced the same since there is no pronunciation difference between 애 ay and 에 ey:

Lastly, many Korean dictionaries list vowel length differences between words: for example, 밤 pam is *night* and 밤: paam is *chestnut*. This is NOT like the English phonics concept of long and short vowels (*nape* versus *nap*), but was a difference in vowel DURATION found earlier in the history of Korean. The younger generation (as young as 50 or 60!) does not make the distinction now, although some vowels may sound long when they are contracted from 2 syllables and said fast (e.g., 마음 maum [마:ㅁ maam] *mind*). Some vowels also may sound long if they are from 2 different syllables, one being a root and the other a suffix (e.g., 달은 talun → 단 tan [다:ㄴ taan]). There is no true vowel length difference in Korean though. Ask your native speaker friends if they know which 말 mal should be long, *word* or *horse*? And do they make the distinction in their speech?

1.1.2 Complex vowels

Say *o* very quickly followed by *ah*. You will end up saying *wah*. The Korean complex vowels capture this intuition in writing. With the Yang vowel 오 o and the Yang vowels 아 a or 애 ay combined, the complex vowels 와 wa and 왜 way are created. The effect is adding the sound of [w] at the beginning. The same holds true for the Yin vowel 우 wu combined with the Yin vowels 어 e or 에 ey, producing the complex vowels 워 we and 웨 wey:

오	우
오 + 아 → 와 [o + ah = wah]	우 + 어 → 워 [u + aw = woh]
오 + 애 → 왜* [o + eh = wɛ]	우 + 에 → 웨* [u + eh = wɛ]

Also, when the neutral (neither Yin nor Yang) vowel 이 i is combined with 오 o, 우 wu, and 으 u, you get 외 oy, 위 wi, and 의 uy. The sound combination of 위 wi and 의 uy is quite simple and logical. 위 wi is a fast combination of 우 wu and 이 i, pronounced like the game Wii, and 의 uy is pronounced as a fast combination of 으 u and 이 i (but some Southern regions of Korea pronounce it as 으 u or 이 i).

오	우	으
오 + 이 → 외*	우 + 이 → 위	으 + 이 → 의
[o + eh = wɛ]	[u + I = wi]	[ɨ + I = ɨi]

Very unexpectedly, 외 oy is pronounced like 왜 way or 웨 wey by most Seoul dialect speakers these days. Remember the three (외 oy, 왜 way, 웨 wey). They are pronounced the same!

The **complex vowels** are graphically complex (with more than one written component), but it is important to memorize these vowels as single vowels in their own right. When 왜 way is spotted, it should be recognized and pronounceable right away as [wɛ], not as a combination of 오 + ㅐ, for example. Also, the WRITTEN vowel harmony in complex vowels is a must. In other words, Yang vowels combine with Yang vowels, and Yin vowels go with Yin vowels. Even computer programs will not allow combining vowels of mismatched categories and will not put them together (e.g., wrong 오ㅓ oe vs. correct 워 we, and wrong 우ㅐ wuay vs. correct 왜 way) so, learn to write them correctly. 오ㅓ or 우ㅐ are wrong!

1.1.3 Dictionary order of the vowel letters

Nowadays words can be looked up in online dictionaries so the order of consonants and vowels may not seem critical for you to know, but it could come in handy

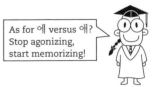

As for 에 versus 애?
Stop agonizing,
start memorizing!

and is culturally relevant, too. It is also interesting trivia that North and South Korean grammarians order the vowel letters differently. In South Korea, a basic vowel precedes ALL of its derivations before the next basic vowel set begins; in North Korea, basic vowels and their y-versions are given first, then 애 ay, 에 ey and their y-versions, followed by the w-versions of the vowels:

South Korea:	아 애 야 얘 / 어 에 여 예 / 오 와 왜 외 요 / 우 워 웨 위 유 / 으 의 / 이
North Korea:	아 야 어 여 / 오 요 우 유 으 이 / 애 얘 에 예 / 외 위 의 / 와 워 왜 웨

1.2 Consonants (C)

As noted before, a consonant is a sound you make by constricting some part of the mouth and obstructing the outward airflow. Try saying the word *porch*. You can feel your lips and your tongue block the airflow before you let it out, for *p* and *ch*, especially. Try saying *l* or *m* or *s* without the assistance of any vowel. Though the air is not completely blocked, it is still obstructed significantly somewhere in the mouth. These are all consonant sounds. 자음 caum *consonant* in Korean means "child sound" because they can't usually stand alone and are in need of a 모음 moum "mother sound" (vowel).

1.2.1 Basic consonants and double consonants

In the mid 15th century, when King Sejong the Great created the Korean alphabet, he came up with the five basic consonant shapes ㄱ, ㄴ, ㅁ, ㅅ, and ㅇ based on the shape of articulatory organs like the tongue, teeth, and the lips.

- ㄱ *k* or *g* as in "skill" shows the back of the tongue touching the back of the palate

- ㄴ *n* as in "nine" shows the tongue tip touching behind the upper teeth

- ㅁ *m* as in "mmmwah!" shows the shape of the mouth with the lips closed

- ㅅ *s* as in "sleeping" outlines the teeth seen from the side

- ㅇ *ng* as in "ring" shows the throat as a hole, closing for this sound

Then, onto the five core consonant shapes, King Sejong added extra strokes to create more consonant letters.

ㄱ *k/g*	→ ㅋ *kʰ* as in *cruise*		ㄱ → ㅋ (throat sounds)
ㄴ *n*	→ ㄷ *t/d* as in *still*	→ ㅌ *tʰ* as in a**tt**ack → ㄹ *l* or *r* as in **l**adde**r**	ㄴ → ㄷ → ㅌ, ㄹ (tongue tip sounds)
ㅁ *m*	→ ㅂ *p/b* as in **sp**ill	→ ㅍ *pʰ* as in **p**lease	ㅁ → ㅂ → ㅍ (lip sounds)
ㅅ soft *s*	→ ㅈ *j/ch* as in lun**ch** or lun**ge**	→ ㅊ *chʰ* as in **ch**ips	ㅅ → ㅈ → ㅊ (teeth sounds)
ㅇ *ng*	→ ㅎ *h* as in **h**at		ㅇ → ㅎ (throat sounds)

The letter ㄴ n (니은 niun) models the shape of the tongue making the [n] sound with the tip of the tongue touching the back of the upper teeth as the leftmost diagram below shows. The letter ㄷ t (디귿 tikut), which is pronounced like [t] or [d] as in *stop*, is produced in the same place in the mouth using the same tongue shape. The only difference is that air is completely stopped. The added stroke (top line) represents the blocking of the sound. ㅌ th (티읕 thiuth), which is pronounced like [tʰ] as in *attack*, adds another stroke to represent the very noticeable burst of air (called aspiration) that happens when the stoppage is released. ㄹ l (리을 liul), which represents the *r/l* sound, can be thought of as representing the tongue being sort of "folded." All these mentioned are produced in the same place with the same tongue position.

ㄴ → ㄷ → ㅌ, ㄹ (tongue sounds)

As for pronunciation, ㄱ k, ㄷ t, ㅂ p, and ㅈ c do not have a loud burst of air after them like English *k, t, p,* and *ch* often do. ㄱ k, ㄷ t, ㅂ p, and ㅈ c sound like *g, d, b,* and *j* (or *dg*) much of the time, especially when they are between vowels or other voiced sounds like ㅁ m, ㄴ n, and ㅇ ng. The other set of sounds ㅋ kh, ㅌ th, ㅍ ph, and ㅊ ch do have a loud and long burst of air after them (called "**aspiration**"), even more so than most English *k, t, p* and *ch* sounds. ㄱ k, ㄷ t, ㅂ p, and ㅈ c are called **plain** or **lax** consonants, and ㅋ kh, ㅌ th, ㅍ ph, and ㅊ ch are called **aspirated** consonants.

ㅅ s is a very soft-sounding [s]; try saying it as if there were an [h] sound before it (and after it).

ㄴ n, ㅁ m, ㅇ ng, and ㄹ l are called **sonorant** or **resonant** sounds (because the sounds resonate, as in singing). They do not participate in the plain/aspirated distinction.

At the beginning or in the middle of a word, ㄹ l is an *r* sound that is similar to that of Spanish or Japanese, or like the sound in the middle of *kitty* or *buddy* when said really fast. Don't curl your tongue or purse your lips as you would for English *r*. At the end of a word or syllable, it is a bit more like *l*. To correctly pronounce ㄹ l as in 알 al, stick your tongue out, between your teeth or against your upper lip. Do not swallow the back of your tongue as if to say *all* or *doll* in English. Or, say *lemon* very slowly. Use that *l* for final ㄹ l as in 알 al.

When ㅇ ng comes at the beginning of a syllable, it is not pronounced, and when it comes end of a syllable, it has the *ng* sound.

Although some of the original 한글 hankul letters have fallen out of use, 19 of the the original consonants are still going strong in the modern system. Of those, 14 BASIC consonants are shown here with approximate pronunciations and then romanization:

ㄱ	ㄴ	ㄷ	ㄹ	ㅁ	ㅂ	ㅅ	ㅇ	ㅈ	ㅊ	ㅋ	ㅌ	ㅍ	ㅎ
k/g	n	t/d	l/r	m	p/b	soft s	ng	ch/j	ch^h	k^h	t^h	p^h	h
k	n	t	l	m	p	s	*/ng	c	ch	kh	th	ph	h

*At the beginning of a syllable, where ㅇ ng is silent, it is not represented in the romanization.

Yet another set of consonant letters were created off of the plain consonants, and they are written as doublets of ㄱ k, ㄷ t, ㅂ p, ㅅ s, and ㅈ c, a little squished together. These are called **tense** or **reinforced** consonants, they have an extra build-up of air at the throat before they are released, and there is no burst of air:

ㄲ	ㄸ	ㅃ	ㅆ	ㅉ
kk	tt	pp	ss	jj
kk	tt	pp	ss	jj

A key point to note is that there is a three-way distinction in non-sonorant conso-nant sounds in Korean: PLAIN VS. ASPIRATED VS. TENSE. Only the ㅅ s lacks an aspirated counterpart:

Plain (lax)	Aspirated	Tense	Examples
ㄱ k	ㅋ kh	ㄲ kk	기 ki *flag,* 키 khi *height,* 끼 kki *artistic talent*
ㄷ t	ㅌ th	ㄸ tt	달 tal *moon,* 탈 thal *mask,* 딸 ttal *daughter*
ㅂ p	ㅍ ph	ㅃ pp	불 pwul *fire,* 풀 phwul *grass,* 뿔 ppwul *horn*
ㅅ s		ㅆ ss	사 sa *buys,* 싸 ssa *cheap*
ㅈ c	ㅊ ch	ㅉ cc	자 ca *sleeps,* 차 cha *kicks,* 짜 cca *salty*

If you are a beginner, the pronunciation of plain consonants such as ㄱ k, ㄷ t, and ㅂ p may seem elusive to you. You think they sound like the English [g], [d], and [b], and the next moment they sound like English [k], [t], and [p], although native Korean speakers may tell you that they are in fact "just like" English *g*, *d*, and *b*. The truth is that in the word-initial position, they do sound a little like English [k], [t], and [p], but slightly softer, with less aspiration. If you listen to Koreans say the sounds ㄱ k, ㄷ t, and ㅂ p, or the other plain consonants ㅅ s, and ㅈ c, you'll hear the puff of air is very small and gentle, and the pitch of the voice is low. (Though Korean is NOT a **tone lan-guage**, Korean speakers do use pitch differences to distinguish sounds.)

On the other hand, when the consonants ㄱ k, ㄷ t, and ㅂ p, come after sonorous sounds like ㄴ n, ㅁ m or ㅇ ng, they sound more like a soft version of English [g], [d] and [b]. So, when a Korean person says the word 바보 papo *a fool*, native English speakers will hear something like [pabo].

> This p~b alternation is not too terribly odd, as all languages do this sort of thing. Think about how you say the English *p* in a word like *pot* as opposed to *spot*. The same? Then say this made up word *sbot* to yourself. Did you just say *spot* or *sbot*? This time say *time, sty,* and *writer.* Did you use the same exact sounding *t*? Probably not. In this way, native speakers do subtle things they themselves are not aware of that make them sound native. Korean 바보 **papo** is one such case. So, if you want to sound like a native speaker, don't insist on using English sounds but try to mimic Koreans' pronunciation.

Practice these words or have a Korean friend say them:

고기 koki *meat*   비빔밥 pipimpap *rice and veggie mix dish*
자주 cacwu *frequently*   도도해 totohay *arrogant*

When you say the word *arrogant* 도도해 totohay, it should sound more like the English word *toe* (with a gentle puff of air, and low tone) and *doe* coming together and not *doe-doe* or *toe-toe*. Of course, you should use the simple vowel *o* and not *o-uw*.

Once the plain sounds are conquered, Korean aspirated and tense consonants are quite easy to master. Just remember these two tricks: Korean aspirated consonants require a whole lot more air than English *p, t, k* sounds, and the tense consonants should have neither voicing nor a puff of air in their burst. The tense consonant sounds do not require any tensing of the muscles in your face. The key to the tense consonants is that you produce no air burst and you do not vibrate your vocal chords (Adam's Apple) when you pronounce them. Think of how Homer Simpson says the *d* in "Doh!" This is a lot like a Korean 쌍디귿 ssangtikut, ㄸ tt. If you have trouble saying tense or aspirated consonants, make the following vowels longer and higher (in pitch), and that will trick native speakers.

Here are a couple more pronunciation tricks that will help you sound more like a native speaker:

In pronouncing syllables that have an ㅅ s, like 사 sa and 소 so, don't think of the English *s*. Think more like you are pronouncing an *h* with your tongue slightly raised, pretending to approximate an *s*.

In pronouncing 시 si, use the English word *she*, except you should not make your lips round or stick them out; smile the whole time.

Finally, the Korean consonants ㄴ n, ㄷ t, ㅌ th, and ㄸ tt are made further toward the front of the mouth than the English sounds *n, d,* and *t*. Try to feel the back of your upper teeth with the tip of your tongue. Slowly pull your tongue back and feel the bone (called the **alveolar ridge**—it's the spot you burn when you bite into pizza that is too hot). English *d* and *t* are made around there. Korean ㄷ t, ㅌ th and ㄸ tt are made almost with your tongue between your teeth like when you say *the*, except that you are saying it quicker.

1.2.2 Names of the consonant letters

The names of the consonant letters are given in the box below. The two columns show the names used in South Korea and in North Korea respectively, and names that look somewhat different from the rest are highlighted.

	South Korea	North Korea
ㄱ	기역 kiyek	기윽 kiuk
ㄴ	니은 niun	니은 niun
ㄷ	디귿 tikut	디읃 tiut
ㄹ	리을 liul	리을 liul
ㅁ	미음 mium	미음 mium
ㅂ	비읍 piup	비읍 piup
ㅅ	시옷 sios	시읏 sius
ㅇ	이응 iung	이응 iung
ㅈ	지읒 ciuc	지읒 ciuc
ㅊ	치읓 chiuch	치읓 chiuch

	South Korea	North Korea
ㅋ	키읔 khiukh	키읔 khiukh
ㅌ	티읕 thiuth	티읕 thiuth
ㅍ	피읖 phiuph	피읖 phiuph
ㅎ	히읗 hiuh	히읗 hiuh
ㄲ	쌍기역 ssangkiyek	된기윽 toynkiuk
ㄸ	쌍디귿 ssangtikut	된디읃 toyntiut
ㅃ	쌍비읍 ssangpiup	된비읍 toynpiup
ㅆ	쌍시옷 ssangsios	된시읏 toynsius
ㅉ	쌍지읒 ssangciuc	된지읒 toynciuc

The name of each consonant letter follows the pattern of 이응 iung (the name of the letter ㅇ ng). To make the name of ㄴ niun, replace the initial and last ㅇ ng in 이응 iung with ㄴ n. You get 니은 niun. Do the same for ㄹ l, and you get its name 리을 riul. The same works for all but three letter-names: ㄱ k is called 기역 kiyek, ㄷ t is called 디귿 ti-kut, and ㅅ s is called 시옷 sios.

For the tense consonants, you use 쌍 ssang, which means *pair* or *twin*, thus 쌍비읍 ssangpiup means "twin 비읍 piup" (ㅃ pp).

North Korean letter names do not have the exceptions mentioned, and instead of 쌍 ssang, tense consonants are named with 된 toyn which means *thick, rough*.

The 한글 hankul letters are written left to right, top to bottom. Some letters may look different depending on individuals' handwriting or computer fonts or even the make-up of the syllable. For example, the first letter ㄱ k has a more sideways-leaning down-ward stroke (like the Arabic number 7) when it is an initial consonant with a vowel to its right side (거 ke); it has a shorter downward stroke when the vowel is placed under-neath (especially with a consonant under THAT: 국 kwuk). The letters ㅈ c, ㅊ ch, and ㅎ h also have variant shapes:

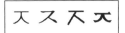  

If the vowel's vertical stroke is long, the vowel is written to the right of the initial consonant); if its horizontal stroke is long, the vowel is placed UNDER the consonant. Learn to distinguish 기 ki from 지 ci from 시 si!

1.2.3 Dictionary order of the consonant letters

It is useful to memorize the order of the plain consonants with the vowel ㅏ a attached, three or four syllables at a time. This is a typical poetry beat for Koreans, too. Here is the standard South Korean version, where the rhythmic pauses are indicated with a bracket "]":

가	나	다	라]	마	바	사]
ka	na	ta	la	ma	pa	sa]

아	자	차]	카	타	파	하
a	ca	cha	kha	tha	pha	ha

All vowel-initial words are listed under o ng plus the vowel, and you recall the order of vowels from section 1.1.3 (basically, 아 a, 어 e, 오 o, 우 wu, 으 u, 이 i).

In South Korea, the tense consonants come right after the corresponding plain letters in the dictionary reading order, while in North Korea, all tense consonants come at the end, after all of the basic letters. ㅇ ng, a letter with two sound values, is placed between the basic and the tense consonants in North Korea. Grammarians from both Koreas meet to discuss the order of the letters—perhaps a unified version can be expected in the near future. But in the meantime, here is the order of the consonants used in dictionaries in the two Koreas:

South Korea		North Korea	
ㄱ	ㅆ	ㄱ	ㅌ
ㄲ	ㅇ	ㄴ	ㅍ
ㄴ	ㅈ	ㄷ	ㅎ
ㄷ	ㅉ	ㄹ	ㅇ
ㄸ	ㅊ	ㅁ	ㄲ
ㄹ	ㅋ	ㅂ	ㄸ
ㅁ	ㅌ	ㅅ	ㅃ
ㅂ	ㅍ	ㅈ	ㅆ
ㅃ	ㅎ	ㅊ	ㅉ
ㅅ		ㅋ	

1.3 Putting It Together into Syllable Form

Korean consonants and vowels are grouped together as a single unit when written, a square block representing a syllable that can be said on one beat. The arrangement of consonants (C) and vowels (V) in each syllable-block depends on the particular letters that are in the syllable (e.g., *go*, *guy*, or *gap*) and on the shape of the vowels (vertical or horizontal lines).

1.3.1 Writing an open syllable (CV)

The simplest syllable in Korean is just a vowel (V) (like ㅏ a or ㅗ o), but it is written with a silent 이응 iung (ㅇ) at the beginning. The next level up in simplicity is a consonant (C) plus a vowel: CV. Because these types of syllable can be prolonged for a long time—try saying 아 a or 가 ka—they are called an **open syllable**. Still remember that vowels with long vertical strokes are written to the right of the preceding consonant, and those with long horizontal strokes are written under it? That is true no matter what consonant comes before the vowel.

Complex vowels are written more or less split with the first (horizontal) vowel under the consonant and the second (vertical) vowel to the right of EVERYTHING, as shown in the third schematic below. Since Korean speakers treat 이응 iung (the letter ㅇ ng) as a consonant, example words with it are included in the chart. (Tense consonants like ㅃ pp and ㅉ cc are treated as single consonants in the schema):

CV	다 ta *all*, 애 ay *kid*, 개 kyay *that kid*, 저 ce *I (humble)*, 게 key *crab*, 네 ney *yes*, 비 pi *rain*, 짜 cca *salty, to wring*
C̲V̲	소 so *cow*, 오 o *five*, 표 phyo *ticket*, 구 kwu *nine*, 부부 pwupwu *married couple*, 주소 cwuso *address*, 뽀뽀 ppoppo *kiss*
C̲V̲V̲	과 kwa *lesson*, 왜 way *why*, 최 choy *Choi (a last name)*, 쥐 cwi *mouse*, 뒤 twi *back*, 의 uy *'s*, 꿔 kkwe *to borrow, to dream*

Any consonant, single or double, can be an initial consonant, although some are much more rarely used than others. ㄹ, for example, is used as a word-initial consonant mainly in borrowed words (e.g., 라디오 latio *radio*, 러브 lebu *love*). ㄹ l is more common syllable-initially in the MIDDLE of words (e.g., 머리 meli *head*, 허리 heli *waist/lower back*, 다리 tali *bridge, leg*, 꼬리 kkoli *tail*, 소리 soli *sound*, 자리 cali *seat*, 하루 halwu *a day*, 도로 tolo *paved road*).

1.3.2 Writing a closed syllable (CVC)

When the syllable block contains a final consonant, it is called a CLOSED SYLLABLE—try saying 박 pak or 엄 em to feel how you are closing the syllable with the consonant sound. All consonant letters, except for the three doublets ㄸ tt, ㅃ pp, ㅉ cc, can come as the last consonant (known as 받침 patchim) to close a written syllable. When 이응 iung (ㅇ ng) is used as a final consonant, it is pronounced, and its sound value is *ng* like the last sound in the English word *song*. As you will soon see, whether or not a word ends in a consonant is serious business in Korean because it often decides which form of a particular suffix should be chosen. Practice paying attention to whether the word you see is an open syllable without a final consonant or a closed syllable with a final consonant. The final consonants will always come at the bottom of the syllable block regardless of whether the vowel is written to the right or under the initial consonant. It is possible to have two 받침 patchim consonants. But only single consonants come after complex vowels. A tense consonant like ㅆ ss is treated as a single consonant, but they do not combine with other 받침 patchim consonants.

Structure	Examples
C$\underset{C}{\overset{CV}{V}}$ C$\underset{CC}{\overset{CV}{V}}$	집 cip *house,* 턱 thek *chin,* 절 cel *temple,* 남 nam *others,* 잘 cal *well,* 값 kaps *price,* 삶다 salmta *to boil,* 짧다 ccalpta *short,* 앉다 ancta *to sit*
C$\underset{C}{\overset{V}{V}}$ C$\underset{CC}{\overset{V}{V}}$	눈 nwun *eye,* 숲 swuph *forest,* 끝 kkuth *end,* 공 kong *ball,* 돌다 tolta *to turn,* 곪다 kolmta *to fester,* (무릎을) 꿇다 (mwuluphul) kkwulhta *to kneel*
$\underset{C}{\overset{CVV}{}}$	꽉 kkwak *tight,* 된장 toyncang *soybean paste,* 훨씬 hwelssin *far (more),* 괌 kwam *Guam,* 왕 wang *king*

The following is the list of plain and complex final consonants permissible in *writing*, with examples. As you can see, among the doublets, only ㄲ kk and ㅆ ss are possible final consonants:

Single 받침 patchim *(CVC)*

ㄱ	각	kak	ㄹ	발	pal	ㅅ	옷	os	ㅊ	쫓	ccoch
ㄲ	꺾	kkekk	ㅁ	몸	mom	ㅆ	갔	kass	ㅋ	엌	ekh
ㄴ	만	man	ㅂ	밥	pap	ㅇ	휭	hwing	ㅌ	곁	kyeth
ㄷ	곧	kot	ㅃ			ㅈ	찾	chac	ㅍ	앞	aph
ㄸ						ㅉ			ㅎ	낳	naph

Complex 받침 patchim *(CVCC)*

ㄳ	삯	saks	ㄻ	젊	celm	ㄿ	읊	ulph
ㄵ	앉	anc	ㄼ	밟	palp	ㅀ	끓	kkulh
ㄶ	끊	kkunh	ㄽ	곬	kols	ㅄ	없	eps
ㄺ	읽	ilk	ㄾ	훑	hwulth			

Some of these are rarely used as final consonants (e.g., ㅋ kh, ㅌ th, ㄲ kk, ㄽ ls, ㄾ lth, ㄿ lph), and others are quite common (e.g., ㄱ k, ㅂ p, ㅅ s, ㅆ ss, ㄴ n, ㄹ l, ㅁ m, ㅇ ng). The pronunciation of the final consonants will be discussed later.

1.4 Reading Borrowed Words

Many foreign words are borrowed into Korean—that is, they are used by Korean speakers and become part of the Korean language—just as the words, *spaghetti, raccoon, coffee, moccasin, chic,* and *pajamas* were borrowed into English (and are now pronounced as English words and have somewhat altered meanings). When words are borrowed into Korean, they are written according to certain conventions so that Koreans can read and pronounce them.

Since Korean does not have some of the sounds that English has, those sounds have to be replaced with sounds that Korean does have. This creates situations where different English words are pronounced the same way in Korean. There are also conventions about how to handle SEQUENCES of sounds that don't occur in Korean. Let's see what the basic conventions are—and you can start getting used to Korean pronunciation and spelling. We've arranged the section in terms of "rules" of writing borrowed words, with examples for you to sound out.

1.4.1 Consonant clusters are broken apart with the vowel 으

guest 게스트 keysuthu   *task* 태스크 thaysukhu

ski 스키 sukhi   *dryer* 드라이어 tulaie

strike 스트라이크 suthulaikhu   *McDonald* 맥도날드 mayktonaltu

1.4.2 Final sounds s, z or ch, dg in English need a vowel inserted

bus 버스 pesu   *dance* 댄스 taynsu

jazz 재즈 caycu   *quiz* 퀴즈 khwicu

punch 펀치 phenchi   *touch* 터치 thechi

bridge 브리지 pulici

(For *s* and *z*, 으 is used, and for *ch* and *j* or *dg*, 이 is used.)

1.4.3 All *s*-borrowings are written with one ㅅ

box 박스 [박쓰, 빡스]   *bus* 버스 [버쓰, 뻐쓰]
paksu [pakssu, ppaksu]   pesu [pessu, ppessu]

Sam 샘 [쌤]   *stop* 스톱 [스톱]
saym [ssaym]   stop [suthop]

(They are all PRONOUNCED as ㅆ ss, though, unless they are part of a cluster as in the word *stop*.)

1.4.4 For a final *t*, the ㅅ s 받침 is used
That final ㅅ s 받침 patchim is pronounced as [t].

pet 펫 (not 펱 or 펜) pheys (not pheyth or pheyt)

Juliet 줄리엣 (not 줄리엩 or 줄리엔) cwullieys (not cwullieyth or cwullieyt)

Scott 스콧 (not 스콭 or 스콘) sukhos (not sukhoth or sukhot)

1.4.5 English initial b, d, g sounds are written with ㅂ, ㄷ, ㄱ; and p, t, k with ㅍ, ㅌ, ㅋ

boy 보이 poi

game 게임 keyim

team 팀 thim

doughnut 도넛 tones

pie 파이 phai

cleaner 클리너 khulline

1.4.6 For final consonants, both b and p are written with ㅂ; and g and k with ㄱ

Bob 밥 pap

Gap 갭 (not 걒) kayp (not kayph)

bag 백 payk

pop 팝 (not 팦) phap (not phaph)

cup 컵 (not 컾) khep (not kheph)

back 백 (not 백) payk (not paykh)

1.4.7 English ("short e") e is written as 에, and a is written as 아, 애 (short a) or 에이 (long a)

pen 펜 pheyn

iPad 아이패드 aiphaytu

and 앤드 ayntu

L.A. 엘에이 eyleyi

banana 바나나 panana

apple 애플 ayphul

J 제이 ceyi

These days, more and more personal names with an *a* are written with 에 ey (e.g., Amber 엠버 eympe, Albert 엘버트 eylpethu).

1.4.8 Lack of a vowel length difference in Korean also erases distinctions between English words

hill, heal 힐 hil

gin, Jean 진 cin

Tim, team 팀 thim

1.4.9 Distinctions between l-r, p-f, b-v, and z-j disappear in Korean

lane, rain 레인 leyin

pan, fan 팬 phayn

Jen, zen 젠 ceyn

lap, lab, rap, wrap 랩 layp

ban, van 밴 payn

1.4.10 A final r (even in a cluster) is not written, and a final l is written and pronounced as ㄹ

car 카 kha

hotel 호텔 hotheyl

silk 실크 silkhu

chart 차트 chathu

court 코트 (also for coat) khothu

1.4.11 An *r* sound between two vowels is written as one ㄹ, and an *l* as two ㄹ's

This is so even if the English words are written with two *r*'s or *l*'s, since only one *r* or *l* sound is pronounced in English, and it is the SOUND that makes the difference in how *r*'s and *l*'s are written in Korean.

Dora 도라 tola   *cherry* 체리 cheyli

jelly 젤리 ceylli   *Somalia* 소말리아 somallia

island 아일랜드 aillayntu   *vanilla* 바닐라 panilla

1.4.12 Some final consonants may vary unexpectedly

Final consonants are sometimes borrowed with an inserted vowel 으 u and other times not, depending on the route through which they have been borrowed into Korean in history. Newer borrowings tend to aim for pronunciation more similar to the original English words, and p-final words have a tendency to be used without the empty vowel 으 u.

(guitar) pick 픽 phik   *bag* 백 payk

peak 피크 phikhu   *Guinea pig* 기니피그 kiniphiku

hotdog 핫도그 hastoku   *bulldog* 불도그 pwultoku

GAP 갭 kayp   *job* 잡 cap

cup 컵 khep   *tip* 팁 thip

chip 칩 chip   *tape* 테이프 theyiphu

If the vowel 으 u is not inserted, the final consonant *d* or *t* is written with a ㅅ s (not ㄷ t or ㅌ th).

good shot 굿샷 kwussyas   *cut* 컷 *(print illustration)* khes

(hair)cut 커트 khethu   *pad* 패드 phaytu

What is "standard" is often a different matter from how people actually write certain words, especially foreign words. The standard spelling of *Washington* is 워싱턴 wesingthen, but you will see (and hear) 와싱턴 wasingthen or 워싱톤 wesingthon. What is "correct" is 달러 talle *dollar*, but you will see 달라 talla written (and [딸라] [ttalle] said).

When in doubt about the standard spelling, check the dictionary!

Exercises

1.1 Vowels (V)

Exercise 1. Re-write the following vowels with the silent ㅇ to the left or below as appropriate. Try to think of the sound each one represents.

ㅏ	ㅒ	ㅗ	ㅓ	ㅜ	ㅑ	ㅖ	ㅡ	ㅣ	ㅛ
아									

Exercise 2. Re-write the following vowels in dictionary order. Read them out loud.

여	아	야	우	이	요	유	으	어	오
아				요					

Exercise 3. Write the complex vowel made by combining the two vowels. Pronounce each vowel out loud and put a check next to the three complex vowels that are pronounced the same way.

1) | ㅗ | + | ㅏ | = | |

2) | ㅗ | + | ㅒ | = | |

3) | ㅗ | + | ㅣ | = | |

4) | ㅜ | + | ㅓ | = | |

5) | ㅜ | + | ㅖ | = | |

6) | ㅜ | + | ㅣ | = | |

7) | ㅡ | + | ㅣ | = | |

1.2 Consonants (C)

Exercise 4. Re-write the following consonant syllables in dictionary order. Read them out loud.

나	다	아	차	라	마	자	타	카	가	파	바	하	사
가							사						
아							하						

Exercise 5. Combine the consonant in the top row with the vowel in the second row to make a one-syllable word. One is done for you.

ㅊ	ㅎ	ㅋ	ㅍ	ㄷ	ㅁ	ㅎ	ㄴ	ㄸ	ㄱ
ㅏ	ㅐ	ㅗ	ㅛ	ㅓ	ㅜ	ㅕ	ㅔ	ㅣ	―
차									
car	sun	nose	ticket	more	radish	tongue	yes	belt	the/that

Exercise 6. Thinking about the meaning, read the following words out loud.

1) 기 flag, qi/chi   끼 artistic talent   키 height
2) 달 moon   딸 daughter   탈 mask
3) 불 fire   뿔 horn   풀 grass
4) 사 four, buy   싸 cheap, wrap
5) 자 sleep   짜 salty, wring   차 car, tea, kick

1.3 Putting it Together into Syllable Form

Exercise 7. Read the following words out loud, noting their spelling.

1) 아이 child   우유 milk   여우 fox   오이 cucumber   요요 yoyo
2) 애 child   예 yes   에이 "A" (letter)   얘 this kid   야호 hooray
3) 차 car   바다 ocean   아가 baby   자요 sleeps   이사 moving
4) 하마 hippo   사자 lion   나라 country   마차 carriage   타자 let's ride
5) 가게 store   얘기 story   치마 skirt   머리 head   새 bird, new
6) 코 nose   구 nine   아파 hurts   교과서 textbook   자유 freedom
7) 시계 clock   과자 snack   의사 doctor   가위 scissors   왜 why
8) 뭐 what   귀 ear   더워 hot   외워 memorize   돼지 pig

Exercise 8. Read the following words out loud, paying special attention to their spelling.

1) 꼬리 tail   꿈 dream   아까 a little while ago
2) 또 again   땀 sweat   따라와 follows me
3) 빵 bread   아빠 dad   나빠 bad
4) 싸워 fights   쌀 rice   써 bitter, write
5) 까 peels   가짜 fake   진짜 real

Exercise 9. Read the following words out loud. Try to memorize the spelling of the words.

1) 기차 train	자전거 bicycle	지하철 subway	비행기 airplane	버스 bus
2) 새벽 dawn	아침 morning	점심 lunch	저녁 evening	밤 night
3) 머리 head	손 hand	발 foot	어깨 shoulder	무릎 knee
4) 토끼 rabbit	호랑이 tiger	뱀 snake	말 horse	원숭이 monkey
5) 밥 rice	국 soup	찌개 stew	불고기 bulgogi	반찬 side dishes
6) 집 house	대학 college	도서관 library	서점 bookstore	가게 store
7) 오늘 today	내일 tomorrow	어제 yesterday	그저께 the day before yesterday	

Exercise 10. Guess the meaning of the following expressions. If you do not know their meaning, ask someone who does or look them up in a dictionary.

1) 하나, 둘, 셋, 넷, 다섯, 여섯, 일곱, 여덟, 아홉, 열
2) 일, 이, 삼, 사, 오, 육, 칠, 팔, 구, 십
3) 월, 화, 수, 목, 금, 토, 일
4) 안녕하세요? 제 이름은 김은지예요.
5) 안녕히 가세요. 안녕히 계세요.
6) 고맙습니다. 감사합니다.
7) 실례합니다.
8) 미안합니다. 죄송합니다.

Exercise 11. Choose the correct spelling for the given word. Check the answer key, and memorize the correct spelling of any words you missed.

1)	child	애	에	
2)	dog	개	게	
3)	this child	애	예	
4)	yes	애	예	
5)	yes	내	네	
6)	three	새	세	
7)	bird	새	세	
8)	above	위	의	
9)	why	왜	웨	외
10)	store	가개	가게	
11)	when	언재	언제	
12)	stew	찌개	찌게	
13)	doctor	으사	의사	
14)	chair	이자	의자	
15)	scissors	가이	가위	가의

16) please go   가새요   가세요
17) how is   어때요   어떼요
18) my name   내 이름   네 이름
19) your name   내 이름   네 이름
20) three people   새 사람   세 사람
21) new person   새 사람   세 사람

1.4 Reading Borrowed Words

Exercise 12. For each borrowed word, find the English counterpart from the box.

Switzerland radio love stress pie tire opera yoga coffee banana

1) 파이   6) 라디오
2) 바나나   7) 오페라
3) 요가   8) 러브
4) 타이어   9) 스위스
5) 커피   10) 스트레스

Exercise 13. For each borrowed word, find the English counterpart from the box.

bag film lunch jazz ice cream island bus pop quiz dryer

1) 백   6) 드라이어
2) 팝   7) 아이스크림
3) 필름   8) 재즈
4) 아일랜드   9) 퀴즈
5) 런치   10) 버스

Exercise 14. See if you can turn the following English words into Korean!

1) star   6) vanilla
2) coat   7) computer
3) fork   8) television
4) sandwich   9) New York
5) quiz   10) your own name

CHAPTER 2

Pronunciation Rules & Spelling

Mastering spelling can be daunting to a beginner because certain sets of letters may sound very similar to each other (e.g., 집 cip or 칩 chip for *house*?). You can soon overcome this difficulty by developing an ear for the sounds and memorizing the correct spelling, such as ㅈ c for 집 cip. Spelling may also be challenging because some pronunciation differences have disappeared but the distinct spelling remains (e.g., Is it 집에 cipey or 집애 cipay? for *at home/to the house*). Inevitably, there are going to be words whose spelling you have to memorize. This "problem" is much like having to accept the fact that the sound [f] is spelled many different ways in English, so you get used to the spelling of words like *fish*, *philosophy, enough* and *giraffe*.

One more important piece of knowledge will help you to be a master speller in Korean: words are not spelled the way they are said! This is true of all languages, but Korean can be more deceiving because we THINK Korean spelling is one-sound-to-one-letter, unlike English spelling, which we know is tricky. The fact is that the pronunciation of some of the letters in Korean changes depending on the surrounding sounds. (This is mostly true of CONSONANTS.)

To master Korean spelling, you need to learn the underlying, or "original," form of a word (this is how you spell it) and how and why the pronunciation changes in certain situations (this is how you say it). In this chapter, we will teach you the pronunciation rules that Korean kids learn in school so you can see how to pronounce words that you see written, how to think about the spelling of words that you hear, and very importantly, how to pronounce new vocabulary as you learn it. This knowledge will be indispensable in improving your pronunciation as well as your spelling!

2.1 One-spelling Principle

One of the main guiding principles to Korean spelling is that each word or part of a word (a root or a suffix, for example), is SPELLED the same way regardless of what sounds are around it. (It's the same in English where we spell *electric-* the same way, even though it is pronounced differently in the related words *electric* and *electricity*.)

To take a Korean example, the root word for eat is 먹- mek-. It is spelled the same way regardless of what suffix comes on it and how its pronunciation changes due to pronunciation rules. (The PRONUNCIATION of each word is given in square brackets [...]. When necessary, we'll use a dot "." to show where the syllable ends in the Korean spelling.)

Spelling	Pronunciation	Meaning
먹다 mek.ta	[먹따 mek.tta]	*to eat* (dictionary form)
먹어요 mek.e.yo	[머거요 me.ke.yo]	*eats, is eating* (polite ordinary style)
먹는다 mek.nun.ta	[멍는다 meng.nun.ta]	*I'm eating this!* (plain style)
먹고 가 mek.ko ka	[머꼬 가 me.kko ka]	*eat and then go* (intimate ordinary style)

Though it may SOUND right, you cannot spell (*I*) *am eating*, as 머거요 me.ke.yo (dots here indicate the syllable breaks); it has to be 먹어요 mek.e.yo to keep the root 먹- mek- in one piece.

2.2 Simple-syllable Principles

The simplest syllable is a single vowel, like 아 a. The next simplest (and a favorite in all languages) is a consonant plus a vowel, like 가 ka. Next simplest is perhaps consonant + vowel + consonant, like 간 kan. These syllable types are favored in Korean, and efforts are made (or "rules" are applied) to avoid more complex syllables when pronouncing them. That is the basis for several pronunciation rules: the general principle of creating the simplest possible syllable shape.

2.2.1 Plain 받침 seven representative principle

This core principle is, "if you're going to have a 받침 patchim, at least keep it as simple as possible (use a plain consonant)." And there are only seven consonants that are okay to be pronounced as final consonants.

ㄴ n, ㅁ m, ㅇ ng, or ㄹ l as 받침 patchim can be read as is (e.g., 돈 ton *money*, 삼 sam *three*, 강 kang *river*, 발 pal *foot*). The same is true for plain consonants ㄱ k, ㄷ t, ㅂ p; they are pronounced as usual, except that they are not **released**—that is, you don't open your mouth at the end: 속 sok *inside*, 곧 kot *right away*, 입 ip *mouth*).

If you have any other consonant—a tense or aspirated one, ㅎ h, ㅅ s, ㅈ c, ㅉ cc, or ㅊ ch—it is pronounced as one of the simple consonants, according to where in the mouth that original consonant is pronounced.

❖ ㄷ t, ㅅ s, ㅈ c, ㅌ th, ㅆ ss, ㅊ ch, ㅉ cc, and notably ㅎ h as well, are pronounced as ㄷ t (The PRONUNCIATION of each word is given in square brackets [...]):

낟 nat	[낟 nat] *grain*	낫 nas [낟 nat] *sickle*
났- nass-	[낟 nat] *came to be (verb root)*	낮 nac [낟 nat] *daytime*
낯 nach	[낟 nat] *face (derogatory)*	낱 nath [낟 nat] *each piece*
낳- nah-	[낟 nat] *give birth to (verb root)*	

❖   ㅂ p and ㅍ ph are pronounced as ㅂ p:

집 cip   [집 cip] *house*   짚 ciph   [집 cip] *straw*

❖   ㄱ k, ㄲ kk, and ㅋ kh are pronounced as ㄱ k.

박 pak   [박 pak] *Park (Korean last name)*
밖 pakk   [박 pak] *outside*
부엌 pwuekh [부억 pwuek] *kitchen*

> To show this schematically:
> ㄱ, ㄲ, ㅋ → [ㄱ]
> ㄷ, ㅅ, ㅆ, ㅈ, ㅊ, ㅌ, ㅎ → [ㄷ]
> ㅂ, ㅃ, ㅍ → [ㅂ]

2.2.2 Single 받침 principle

When a syllable is written with two final 받침 patchim consonants, typically only one of them is pronounced.

❖   The first consonant is pronounced in these clusters: ㄳ ks, ㄵ nc, ㄼ lp, ㄽ ls, ㅄ ps:

몫 mok   [목 mok] *share*
여덟 yetelp [여덜 yetel] *eight*
값 kaps   [갑 kap] *cost, price*
앉다 ancta [안따 antta] **to sit* (*tensing explained later on)
외곬 oykols [외골 oykol] *single-minded*

❖   The second consonant is pronounced in these clusters: ㄺ lk, ㄻ lm:

닭 talk   [닥 tak] *chicken*
삶다 salmta [삼따 samtta] *to boil (of food in liquid)* (tensing explained later on)

❖   Both consonants (or for some people, only the second consonants) are pronounced in these clusters: ㄺ lk, ㄼ lp, ㄿ lth, ㄿ lph:

읽다 ilkta   [읽따 ilktta] *to read* (tensing explained later on)
밟다 palpta [밟따 palptta] *to step on*
핥다 halthta [할ㄷ따 haldtta] *to lick*
읊다 ulphta [읊따 ulptta] *to recite (poetry)*

> Did you notice the contradiction between 여덟 yetelp *eight* [여덜 yetel] and 밟다 palpta *to step on* [밟따 palptta] and 닭 talk *chicken* [닥 tak] and 읽다 ilkta [읽따 ilktta]? You can think of the pronunciation of 여덟 yetelp and 닭 talk as exceptions to the general rule!

You can also see from how 낫 nas *sickle* [낟 nat] and 낯 nach *face* [낟 nat] are pronounced that final consonants in Korean are not **released**—there is no opening of the mouth or release of air, including *s* or *ch* "hissing"—and this is why Koreans insert the vowel 으 u or 이 i when pronouncing English words like bus [버스 pesu] or *punch* [펀치 phenchi]. (With the vowel there, the consonant can be released.) How do Koreans know which is which when they hear a [낟 nat], then? Is the interpretation all in the context? Not always. An easy solution is found in the next rule.

2.2.3 Liaison or spill-over principle

When a syllable with a 받침 patchim is followed by one that starts with a vowel, that 받침 patchim is pronounced as the beginning of the next syllable, instead of as a (SIMPLIFIED) 받침 patchim. This is because, as we said, Korean prefers [consonant + vowel] syllables to syllables with 받침 patchim.

We saw this very natural phenomenon in 먹어요 mekeyo *eats*, pronounced [머거요 me.ke.yo] (not [먹'어요 mek.'e.yo] with the glottal stop sound as in *uh-oh*). When it can be pronounced before a vowel like this, a consonant takes on its original characteristics, and that means it is possible to figure out the true nature of a 받침 patchim. You can think of English parallels where the *n* and *k* sounds come alive when they meet a vowel in *condemn → condemnation*, and *knowledge → acknowledge*. (We like to call this phenomenon the "revival of the suppressed!") In the following examples, notice how the 받침 patchim is simplified when there is no following vowel, and the pronunciation is restored to its true state (aspirated or tense, etc.) before a vowel. (This doesn't happen between words; it happens only between a root and a suffix, a noun and a particle, or within a root.)

국 [국] → 국은 [구근]
kwuk [kwuk] → kwuk.un [kwu.kun]
soup → soup-topic particle

부엌 [부억] → 부엌에 [부어케]
pwuekh [pwuek] → pwuekh.ey [pwu.e.key]
kitchen → kitchen-location particle

입 [입] → 입이 [이비]
ip [ip] → ip.i [i.pi]
mouth → mouth-subject particle

낫 [낟] → 낫으로 [나스로]
nas [nat] → nas.ulo [na.su.lo]
sickle → sickle-tool particle

낯 [낟] → 낯이 [나치]
nach [nat] → nach.i [na.chi]
face → face-subject particle

웃 [욷] + 옷 [옫] → 웃옷 [우돋]
wus [wut] → os [ot] → wus.os [wutot]
up + clothes → tops (shirts)

밖 [박] → 밖에서 [바께서]
pakk [pak] → pakk.eyse [pa.kkey.se]
outside → outside-location particle

앞 [압] → 앞에 [아페]
aph [ap] → aph.ey [a.phey]
side → side-location particle

값[갑] → 값을 [갑쓸]
kaps [kap] → kaps.ul [kap.ssul]
price → price-object particle

Use of [ㅆ ss] instead of [ㅅ s] here will be explained in a later rule!

낮[낟] → 낮에 [나제]
nac [nat] → nac.ey [na.cey]
daytime → daytime-time particle

있–어 [읻]–[어] → 있어 [이써]
iss-e [it]-[e] → iss.e [isse]
exist → exist-ordinary ending

As we mentioned, it is CRITICAL to learn the basic form of each word. For 앞 aph *front*, for example, once you have internalized that the base form is 앞 aph, the correct spelling naturally comes to you, regardless of what the following sound is (e.g., 앞에 aphe, 앞이 aphi, 앞은 aphun, 앞을 aphul, 앞에서 apheyse, 앞으로 aphulo, 앞도 aphto, 앞만 aphman, 앞문 aphmwun, etc.). Another way to use this rule to your advantage is to recognize that you hear the true form of a word with a 받침 patchim when it comes next to a suffix that starts with a vowel; listen carefully to those contexts and learn the spelling of the word.

This spill-over rule also creates a funny, often unrecognizable pronunciation of borrowed words that are written with a final ㅅ s to represent the [t] sound, as the ㅅ s "spills over," meeting vowel-initial particles (written here with hyphens):

팻	[팯]	→	팻-은	[패슨]
phays	[phat]		phays-un	[phaysun]
				Pat-topic particle

줄리엣	[줄리엗]	→	줄리엣-이	[줄리에시]
cwullieys	[cwullieyt]		cwullieys-I	[cwullieysi]
				Juliet-subject particle

커네티컷	[커네티컫]	→	커네티컷-에서	[커네티커세서]
kheneythikhes	[kheneythikhest]		kheneythikhes-eyse	[kheneythikheseyse]
				Connecticut-location particle

2.2.4 Look-ahead principle

Learning how to correctly read Korean words involves looking at least **one syllable ahead**. It is necessary to look ahead to do the spill-over rule, and it will be necessary, as you will learn in section 2.3, to see how the 받침 patchim of one syllable interacts with the first consonant of the next syllable.

In words like 신라 sinla *Silla (Kingdom)*, 학년 haknyen *school year*, for example, the pronunciation of the initial syllable changes because of the following syllable. 신 sin [신 sin] vs. 신라 sinla [실라 silla] and 학 hak [학 hak] vs. 학년 haknyen [항년 hangnyen], so you need to be looking ahead for correct pronunciation.

Turning this principle around 180 dgrees gives you a shortcut to spelling Korean words successfully: Know what you are hearing or saying. Take [실라 silla] or [항년 hangnyen], for example. Before writing the word as you hear or have been saying it, you will need to stop yourself and think about any other possible ways it might be spelled (based on pronunciation rules). If you are not sure about the spelling, look it up, and don't get stuck in wrong habits!

Even educated native Korean speakers often have to look up the correct spelling online, if nothing else, because spelling conventions occasionally change. For example, the most recent official change in spelling happened in 2011, when the National Institute of the Korean Language (국립국어원 kwuklipkwukewen) approved the spelling of 짜장면 ccacangmyen, for the Korean Chinese black-bean noodle dish, as standard. Previously, the approved spelling had been 자장면 cacangmyen only. Do not despair, though! Korean spelling is challenging, but not unconquerable!

2.2.5 Initial consonant simplification principle

When a syllable has a complex vowel with a w or y sound AND an initial consonant, that makes for a complex (double) onset to the syllable (consonant + w or consonant + y). This kind of syllable is often simplified in natural, casual speech by deleting the w or y sound. But since we are only talking about the pronunciation, it will be necessary to memorize the spelling of individual words—it might be 저 ce and might be 져 cye, for example.

Here are the individual rules:

❖ ㅕ ye is pronounced as [ㅓ e] after ㅈ c, ㅉ cc, ㅊ ch (but not ㅅ s):

가져	[가저]	*have*		쪄	[쩌]	*steam*
kacye	[kace]			ccye	[cce]	

다쳐	[다처]	*get hurt*	BUT! 마셔	[마셔]	*drink*
tachye	[tache]		masye	[masye]	

❖ ㅖ yey is pronounced as [ㅔ ey] after a consonant:

시계	[시게]	*clock*		계피	[게피]	*cinnamon*
sikyey	[sikey]			kyeyphi	[keyphi]	

계산서	[게산서]	*bill*	BUT! 예	[예]	*yes*
kyeysanse	[keysanse]		yey	[yey]	

실례합니다	[실레암니다]	*excuse me*
sillyeyhapnita	[silleyamnita]	

안녕히 계세요	[안녀~이 게세요]	*goodbye (to one who is staying)*
annyenghi kyeyseyyo	[annye~i keyseyyo]	

❖ After a consonant, ㅘ wa, ㅙ way are pronounced as [ᵂㅏ wa], [ᵂㅐ way] (with a hint of [w] on the consonant):

놔요	[ᵂ나요]	*let go*		괜찮아	[ᵂ갠차나]	*it's ok*
nwayo	[ᵂnᵂayo]			kwaynchanha	[kᵂaynchana]	

안 돼	[안ᵂ대]	*no, don't!*		전화번호	[저ᵂ나버노]	*phone number*
an tway	[an tᵂay]			cenhwapenho	[cenᵂapeno]	

봤어?	[ᵂ바써]	*did you see?*	BUT! 이리 와	[이리와]	*come here!*
pwasse	[ᵂpᵂasse]		ili wa	[ili wa]	

❖ ㅝ we and ㅚ oy are pronounced as [ᵂㅓ we] or [ᵂㅗ wo] and [ᵂㅔ wey] after a consonant:

뭐?	[ᵂ머, ᵂ모]	*what*		줘요	[ᵂ저요, ᵂ조요]	*give*
mwe	[ᵂmᵂe, ᵂmᵂo]			cweyo	[ᵂcᵂeyo, ᵂcᵂoyo]	

관둬   [ᵂ간ᵂ더, ᵂ간ᵂ도, ᵂ곤ᵂ도]   *forget it*
kwantwe   [kʷantʷe, kʷantʷo, kʷontʷo]

처음 뵙겠어요   [처:ㅁᵂ베께써요]   *nice to meet you*
cheum poypkeysseyo   [cheem pʷeykkeysseyo]

BUT! 워싱턴   **[워**싱턴]   *Washington*
    wesingthen   [wesingthen]

2.2.6 의 and 희

의 uy is pronounced as 의 uy only when at the beginning of a word in the Seoul dialect. Anywhere else in a word, it is pronounced as something between [의 uy] and [이 i]:

의사   [의사]   *doctor*   편의   [편이]   *convenience*
uysa   [uysa]   phyenuy   [phyenᵘⁱ]

의자   [의자]   *chair*   강의   [강이]   *lecture*
uyca   [uyca]   kanguy   [kangᵘⁱ]

> In the Southeast part of South Korea (e.g., in 경상 Kyengsang dialect), word-initial 의 uy is pronounced as [이 i], and in the Southwest part of South Korea (e.g., 전라 Cenla dialect), it is pronounced as [으 u].

❖ If 의 uy is the possessive particle (meaning '*s* (as in *Mom's*)), it is pronounced as [에 ey]:

꿈의 동산   [꿈에동산]   *a hill of dreams* (literally, *dreams' hill*)
kkwumuy tongsan   [kkwumey tongsan]

123-4567   [일리사메사오륙칠]   *(telephone number)*
ilisam-uy-saoywukchil   [ilisameysaoywukchil]

❖ If ㅢ comes with a consonant before it (which is usually ㅎ h), it is pronounced as [이]:

희망   [히망]   *hope*   흰색   [힌색]   *the color white*
huymang   [himang]   huynsayk   [hinsayk]

희소식   [히소식]   *good, happy news*   띄다   [띠다]   *to stand out, be visible*
huysosik   [hisosik]   ttuyta   [ttita]

2.2.7 ㅎ deletion

The best syllables are consonant + vowel. But ㅎ h is the weakest consonant in Korean, so, what happens is that ㅎ often gets dropped (from the pronunciation) when it does not begin a word and if the word is said fast. And, ㅎ never spills over to the following syllable as its lone initial consonant.

하나   [하나]   *one*   한글   [항글]   *the Korean alphabet*
hana   [hana]   hankul   [hangkul]

하루 종일 [하루종일] *all day long*
halwu congil [halwucongil]

일흔   [이른]   *seventy*
ilhun   [ilun]

좋아   [조아, 조와] *good*
coha   [coa, cowa]

안녕하세요 [안녕아세요]   *hello*
annyenghaseyyo [annyengaseyo]

많이   [마니]   *much, a lot*
manhi   [mani]

놓아요   [노아요, 놔요] *let go*
nohayo   [noayo, nwayo]

2.3 Interactions Between Consonants

Another set of pronunciation rules applies when a 받침 patchim comes in contact with a consonant that begins the next syllable—that is, when two (or more) consonants come in contact. Many of them will feel quite natural, but they mask the spelling of the word.

2.3.1 ㅎ-Combo rule

When ㅎ h comes next to a plain consonant, the two combine to yield an aspirated version of the consonant. The order of ㅎ h and the other consonant does not matter (just like the commutative math rule ($1 + 2 = 2 + 1 = 3$):

❖ ㄱ k + ㅎ h = [ㅋ kh]   ≈   ㅎ h + ㄱ k = [ㅋ kh]

백화점   [백콰점] *department store*   어떻게 [어떠케] *how*
paykhwacem [payk.khwa.cem]   ettehkey [e.tte.khey]

착하다   [착카다] *to be good (person)*   좋고   [조코]   *good and*
chakhata   [chakkhata]   cohko   [cokho]

❖ ㄷ t + ㅎ h = [ㅌ th]   ≈   ㅎ h + ㄷ t = [ㅌ th]

맏형   [마텽]   *eldest brother*   많다   [만타]   *tons!*
mathyeng   [mathyeng]   manhta   [mantha]

비슷해요   [비스태요] *similar*   넣도록   [너토록]   *in order*
pisushayyo [pisuthayyo]   nehtolok   [netholok]   *to put in*

못 해요   [모태요]   *can't do*   그렇지만 [그러치만] *but*
mos hayyo [mothayyo]   kulehciman [kulechiman]

❖ ㅈ c + ㅎ h = [ㅊ ch]   ≈   ㅎ h + ㅈ c = [ㅊ ch]

괜찮지   [괜찬치 or 갠찬치] *ok, right?*   그렇지만   [그러치만] *but*
kwaynchanhci [kwaynchanchi or kaynchanchi] kulehciman [kulechiman]

❖   ㅂ p + ㅎ h = [ㅍ ph]

법학   [법팍]   *study of law*   답답해   [답답패]   *frustrated, stir-crazy*
pephak   [pep.phak]   taptaphay   [tap.tap.phay]

In careful speech, ㅎ h + consonant combos are sometimes pronounced as long/double (as well as aspirated) when ㅎ h is the 받침 patchim: 넣도록 nehtolok [넏토록 nettholok] or 어떻게 ettehkey [어떡케 ettekkhey])

2.3.2 Nasalization

Nasalization refers to a phenomenon by which a sound becomes one of the nasal sounds ㄴ n, ㅁ m or ㅇ ng.

(1) Backward nasalization

When a 받침 patchim of the the non-sonorous sort (e.g., ㄱ k, ㄷ t, ㅂ p, ㅆ ss, ㅊ ch) comes before a **nasal** sound ㄴ n or ㅁ m in the following syllable, that 받침 patchim is pronounced as a nasal, for the sake of smoother pronunciation. "Throat sounds" ㄱ k, ㅋ kh and ㄲ kk become ㅇ ng, "lip sounds" ㅂ p and ㅍ ph become ㅁ m, and "tongue-tip" or "teeth sounds" sounds ㄷ t, ㅌ th, ㅅ s, ㅆ ss, ㅈ c, and ㅊ ch become ㄴ n.

OK, that was a mouthful. A list of examples will illustrate the point more clearly.

먹는 [멍는] *eating*
meknun [mengnun]

학년 [항년] *school year*
haknyen [hangnyen]

한국말 [한궁말] *the Korean language*
hankwukma [hankwungmal]

감사합니다 [감사함니다] *thank you*
kamsahapnita [kamsahamnita]

옆머리 [염머리] *side hair/sideburns*
yephmeli [yemmeli]

십만 [심만] *hundred thousand*
sipman [simman]

급모 [금모] *immediate hire*
kupmo [kummo]

못난이 [몬나니] *bumpkin*
mosnani [monnani]

앞문 [암문] *front gate*
aphmwun [ammwun]

못 먹어 [몬머거] *cannot eat*
mos meke [monmeke]

꽃망울 [꼰망울] *flower bud*
kkochmangwul [kkonmangwul]

잇몸 [인몸] *gums*
ismom [inmom]

(2) Forward nasalization

When ㄹ l follows a nasal sound (ㅁ m, ㄴ n, or ㅇ ng), that ㄹ l is pronounced as ㄴ n.

대통령 [대통녕] *president (of a country)*
taythonglyeng [taythongnyeng]

심리학 [심니학] *psychology*
simlihak [simlihak]

왕릉 [왕능] *royal tomb*
wanglung [wangnung]

공론 [공논] *pointless debate*
konglon [kongnon]

While turning into a nasal, the 받침 patchim nevertheless keeps its original PLACE of articulation in the mouth. Say 응 ung and quickly move to 윽 uk. Do the same with 은 un and 윽 uk. It is easy to feel that ㅇ ng and ㄱ k (but not ㄴ n and ㄱ k) are pronounced around the same place in the mouth, right?

This nasalization happens often in Sino-Korean words (한자어 hancae). Have you been to 독립문 toklipmwun *Dongnimmun Gate* or walked down 종로 conglo *Jongno (street)* in Korea? They are pronounced as [동님문 toklngnimmwun] and [종노 congno]. A key point for these words is that in 한자어 hancae, syllable-initial ㄹ l acts as if it were a ㄴ n. So it also forces the preceding final consonant (only the ㄱ, ㅂ sort) to be pronounced as a nasal:

백로 payklo [뱅노 payngno] *white heron*   급류 kuplyu [금뉴 kumnyu] *torrent*
섭리 sepli [섬니 semni] *provision, Providence*

Try learning the words that you hear frequently and memorize their spelling. You will learn about 한자어 hancae in a later chapter.

A Note on Using These Pronunciation Rules in Your Learning

The memorization required for spelling is quite minimal, if you know how to slow yourself down. Say you know that *Eat the rice* SOUNDS LIKE [밤머거 pammeke], and *Are you eating rice?* SOUNDS LIKE [밤멍니 pam mekni], and you know the word 밥 pap *rice/food*.

First, you can figure out that *rice/food* is spelled 밥 pap and that its pronunciation changes to [밤 pam] in the two phrases because of the nasalization rule. Next, you can figure out the same for *eat*, 먹- mek-, which changes to [멍 meng] before the ㄴ n in [밤멍니 pam mekni], but the base form is really 먹- mek- in [밤머거 pammeke]. So, for spelling, you have figured out 밥 먹- pap mek- so far. Then what you need is the command ending for *Eat the rice!* and the question ending for *Are you eating rice?* What is needed to complete the sentence to get [밤머거 pammeke]? Naturally, it is 어 e, yielding 밥 먹어 pap meke.

Likewise, if you have up to 밥 먹- pap mek-, what is needed to complete the sentence [밤멍니 pam mekni]? It must be -니 -ni, thus 밥 먹니 pap mekni. This deduction is only possible when you know there is such thing as a nasalization rule that might make 밥 pap and 먹- mek- sound different with certain sounds following. Once you can deduce this far, the rest is a piece of cake, as the endings and connectors are recurrent—and always spelled the same,—so you will soon recognize the repeated patterns of spelling.

The flip side, if you don't know how something is pronounced but you learned to spell all the pieces, is to "get" the pronunciation rules—this begins to happen naturally, if you 1) become aware of the sound-changing rules, and 2) keep practicing!

2.3.3 Place Assimilation

받침 patchim that are tongue-tip or teeth sounds (ㄷ t, ㅌ th, ㅅ s, ㅆ ss, ㅈ c, ㅊ ch, ㄴ n) take on the PLACE OF ARTICULATION of a neighboring consonant in fast speech—they become lip sounds before other lip sounds and throat sounds before other throat sounds. (The tensing that you see in the examples is explained later.)

얕보다가 [얍뽀다가] *look down on (something) and then*
yathpotaka [yapppotaka]

닫고 [닥꼬] *close and*
tatko [takkko]

친구 [칭구] *friend*
chinkwu [chingkwu]

This is also true of ㄷ t sounds that came about via the the Plain 받침 patchim Principle:

못 봐 [몹빠 or 몹빠] *can't see*
mos pwa [moppa or mopppwa]

English does something quite similar. Try pronouncing the word *congress* and *Vancouver* **fast**. Do you say *n* or *ng* before your *g* and *k*? Oftentimes it is *ng*, though we may think of it as an *n*. Similarly, if you say *hot-pot* fast, it might come out as *hop-pot* or, at least without the *t* in *hot*.

웃겨 [욱껴] *funny*
wuskye [wukkkye]

ㄴ n sounds that came about from the nasalization rule can also be assimilated to ㅁ m:

잇몸 → [인몸] → [임몸] *gums*
ismom → [inmom] → [immom]

Be careful! Throat sounds (ㄱ k, ㄲ kk, ㅋ kh, ㅇ ng) are not subject to this change:

국보 [국뽀] **not** [~~굽뽀~~ or ~~구뽀~~] *national treasure*
kwukpo [kwukppo] not [~~kwupppo~~] or ~~kwuppo~~]

각자 [각짜] **not** [~~갇짜~~ or ~~가짜~~] *each individual*
kakca [kakcca] not [~~katcca or kacca~~]

강북 [강북] **not** [~~감북~~] *Gangbuk (North of the River District)*
kangpwuk [kangpwuk] not [kampwuk]

강남 [강남] **not** [~~간남~~] *Gangnam (South of the River District)*
kangnam [kangnam] not [~~kannam~~]

2.3.4 Liquidization

When a nasal ㄴ n 받침 patchim meets a so-called "**liquid**" ㄹ l initial, the sequence is pronounced as ㄹㄹ ll; when ㄹ l 받침 patchim meets a ㄴ n initial, the sequence is also pronounced as long ㄹ ll—the liquid wins out. (Just like the ㅎ h-combo rule; the order doesn't matter.)

❖ ㄴ n + ㄹ l = [ㄹㄹ ll]

신라 [실라] *Silla Kingdom*
sinla [silla]

한라산 [할라산] *Mt. Halla*
hanlasan [hallasan]

연락 [열락] *contact, call*
yenlak [yellak]

편리 [펼리] *convenience*
phyenli [phyelli]

관리 [괄리] *management*
kwanli [kwalli]

곤란 [골란] *difficulty*
konlan [kollan]

❖ ㄹ l + ㄴ n = [ㄹㄹ ll]

달님 [달림] *moon-honorific*
talnim [tallim]

칼날 [칼랄] *blade of a knife*
khalnal [khallal]

월남 [월람] *Vietnam*
welnam [wellam]

물난리 [물랄리] *flood*
mwulnanli [mwullalli]

실내 [실래] *inside*
silnay [sillay]

발냄새 [발램새] *stinky feet smell*
palnaymsay [pallaymsay]

2.3.5 Tensing

Certain combinations of consonants cause the second to be pronounced as tense. In this section, we introduce the tensing that happens between particular sets of consonants, and later you will see some other rules of tensing in other special situations.

(1) Plain consonant + plain consonant

When a plain consonant (ㄱ k, ㄷ t, or ㅂ p) follows another plain consonant 받침 patchim in the previous syllable, that second one becomes tense. If the two abutting consonants are of the same place of articulation, the final consonant in the previous syllable may even disappear in fast speech (as shown in parentheses below). Remember—it is just the pronunciation; the SPELLING does not change!

ㄱ + ㄱ = [(ㄱ)ㄲ] k + k = [(k) kk]	ㄷ + ㄷ = [(ㄷ)ㄸ] t + t = [(t) tt]	ㅂ + ㅂ = [(ㅂ)ㅃ] p + p = [(p) pp]	ㅅ + ㅅ = [(ㄷ)ㅆ] s + s = [(t) ss]	ㅈ + ㅈ = [(ㄷ)ㅉ] c + c = [(t) cc]

So, if you have a sequence of syllables like 듣도록 tuttolok *so that you'll hear*, it will be pronounced as [듣또록 tut.tto.lok], with the ㄷ t 받침 patchim pronounced, but the following initial consonant "strengthened" to be pronounced as tense. In fast speech, you will hear [드또록 tu.tto.lok] with the ㄷ t 받침 patchim gone. But, of course, you should not write it that way! Here are some more examples:

학교 [학꾜 or 하꾜] *school*
hakkyo [hakkkyo or hakkyo]

찾지요 [찬찌요 or 차찌요] *looking for (it), right?*
chacciyo [chatcciyo or chacciyo]

As in simple math, you can get 4 from not just 2 + 2 but other combinations as well (e.g., 1 + 3 = 4). It works similarly with the tensing rule, so you get tensing of the second consonant even if the 받침 patchim consonant is not its twin sister. The 받침 patchim just has to be a plain consonant. Also, that plain consonant can have been derived through the Plain 받침 patchim Principle, as in the last example here:

ㅂ + ㄷ = [ㅂㄸ] p + t = [p tt]	ㄱ + ㅂ = [ㄱ뻬] k + p = [k pp]	ㄺ + ㄱ = [ㄹㄲ] lk + k = [l kk]	ㅆ + ㅈ = [ㄷㅉ], etc. ss + c = [t cc]

Here are some words to exemplify the rule. Practice saying them out loud to help you internalize the rule:

학생 [학쌩] *student*
haksayng [hakssayng]

읽고 [읽꼬] *read-and*
ilkko [ilkkko]

찼다 [찬따 or 차따] *kicked*
chassta [chattta or chatta]

> The fast speech pronunciation (dropping the 받침 patchim of the preceding syllable) will sound weird if your speech is not actually fast. Experiment with it, saying 듣고 tutko, for example. You can say [듣꼬 tutkko] carefully, and [드꼬 tukko] really fast. Hopefully you will gain the fluency to start using the fast-speech version soon!

(2) ㄹ + plain tongue-tip consonants ㄷ, ㅅ, ㅈ (but not ㄱ, ㅂ)

When a ㄹ l 받침 patchim meets another tongue-tip sound (or teeth sound) ㄷ t, ㅅ s, or ㅈ c, the second consonant is pronounced as tense. ㄱ k and ㅂ p are not tongue-tip sounds, so they are pronounced as they are written!

절대 [절때] *never*
celtay [celttay]

글자 [글짜] *letter/syllable/character*
kulca [kulcca]

얼굴 [얼굴] *face*
elkwul [elkwul]

일본 [일본] *Japan*
ilpon [ilpon]

홀수 [홀쑤] *odd number*
holswu [holsswu]

갈대 [갈때] *reed*
kaltay [kalttay]

달걀 [달걀] *egg*
talkyal [talkyal]

갈비 [갈비] *rib*
kalpi [kalpi]

(3) Prospective suffix -(으) ㄹ + plain consonants

When a plain consonant of any sort (including ㅂ p and ㄱ k) follows a ㄹ l with the prospective (≈ future) meaning, the plain consonant is pronounced (but not written) as tense.

내가 알 게 뭐야? [내가 알 께 뭐야]
nayka al key mweya? [nayka al kkey mweya]
How would I know?/It's no concern of mine.

내가 알 바 아니야. [내가 알 빠 아니야]
nayka al pa aniya [nayka al ppa aniya]
It's no concern of mine.

갈 데가 없어. [갈 떼가 업써]
kal teyka epse. [kal tteyka epsse]
There is no place to go.

비가 올지도 몰라. [비가 올찌도 몰라]
pika olcito molla [pika olccito molla]
It may rain.

먹을 수 있어. [머글 쑤 이써]
mekul swu isse [mekul sswu isse]
I can eat.

울 정도로 아파? [울 쩡도로 아파]
wul cengtolo apha? [wul ccengtolo apha?]
Does it hurt so much that it makes you cry?

2.4 Verb Root, Suffix and Word Boundaries

A few of the pronunciation rules apply only between roots and suffixes, or roots and other roots in compound words.

2.4.1 ㄷ- and ㅌ-softening

When a ㄷ t 받침 patchim comes before an 이 i suffix, it is "softened" to ㅈ c, and ㅌ th to ㅊ ch.

맏-이 [마지]   *the end-person suffix* → *the eldest*
mac.i [maci]

굳-이 [구지]   *hard-adverb suffix*   → *obstinately, insistently*
kwut.i [kwuci]

밭-이 [받치 or 바치] *field-subject particle*
path.i [patchi or pachi]

같-이 [가치]   *same-adverb suffix* → *together, alike*
kath.i [kachi]

If the 이 i sound is not a separate suffix but is part of the root, the pronunciation (and the spelling) stays intact:

마디 [마디] not [~~마지~~] *knot, joint*
mati [mati] not [~~maci~~]

부디 [부디] not [~~부지~~] *please*
pwuti [pwuti] not [~~pwuci~~]

코디 [코디] not [~~코지~~] *coordination*
khoti [khoti] not [~~khoci~~]

You may feel like the difference between 마디 mati [마디 mati] and 맏이 mati [마지 maci] is weird, but similar things happen in English, too! Consider *body* vs. *did you* ([didju] or [didja]) and *authority vs. Got ya!* The first *dy* and *ty* sequences in each set are pronounced as [di] and [ti], and the second *d y* and *t y* sequences are pronounced as *dj* and *ch*. The "softening" happens to take place across the word boundary in English.

2.4.2 Noun compounds

If you are good at subtracting and deducing, you will quickly get the hang of many Korean pronunciation rules. Similar "equations" work to derive tense consonants in noun compounds:

(1) Tensing

For example, if the first noun in a noun + noun compound (like *bedhead* or *pickpocket*) has a 받침 patchim, plain consonant initials ㄱ k, ㄷ t, ㅂ p, ㅅ s, ㅈ c in the second noun are pronounced as tense. The tensing usually happens for Native Korean noun compounds and when the first noun is an independent noun, which is the case for all the words before "vs." below. What is marked in bold after "vs." may have an independent meaning, but it works more like a prefix or suffix (such as *pre-* or *-ship* in English) and is not a separate word. (You will learn more about this in chapter 5). 자리 cali in the very last word 잠자리 camcali *dragonfly* also does not carry any meaning by itself.

금값 [금깝] kumkaps [kumkkap]	*cost for gold*	← 금 *gold* + 값 *price* kum + kaps
vs. **금**관 [금관] kumkwan [kumkwan]	**golden** *crown*	
장독 [장똑] cangtok [cangttok]	*crock for condiments*	← 장 *condiment* + 독 *crock* cang + tok
vs. **장**도 [장도] cangto [cangto]	**long** *sword*	
안방 [안빵] anpang [anppang]	*master bedroom*	← 안 *inside* + 방 *room* an + pang
vs. **안**경 [안경] ankhyeng [ankyeng]	**eye** *glasses*	
잠자리 [잠짜리] camcali [camccali]	*place for sleeping*	← 잠 *sleep* + 자리 *place* cam + cali
vs. 잠자리 [잠자리] camcali [camcali]	*dragonfly*	

금 kum *gold* (金) and 방 pang *room* (房) are Sino-Korean words, but they are totally nativized!

Also, if you look at the words, 금관 kumkwan *golden crown*, 장도 cangto *long sword* and 안경 ankhyeng *eye glasses*, all have a meaning boundary in them: *gold-crown*, *long-sword*, and *eye-mirror*. But 관 kwan, 도 to, and 경 khyeng are not considered independent nouns by Korean speakers, so these are not compound words, which explains the lack of tensing of the second syllable.

Some people insert an empty consonant before the suffix -님 nim and pronounce 아버님 apenim *father (honorific)*, 어머님 emenim *mother (honorific)* as [아번님 apennim, 어먼님 emennim], but the words are still written as 아버님 apenim and 어머님 emenim.

If you find this compound tensing rule overwhelming or confusing, keep it in mind for later use. Once you have accumulated some vocabulary, this rule will start making sense and become very handy!

(2) ㅅ- insertion and tensing

If the first noun in a noun + noun compound does not have a 받침 patchim, ㅅ s (사이 시옷 sai sios) is inserted IN THE WRITING and the initial consonant of the second noun is pronounced as tense. (The second pronunciation in square brackets below is the fast speech version.)

고춧가루 [고춘까루 or 고추까루] ← 고추 + 가루
kochwuskalwu [kochwutkkalwu / kochwutkkalwu] kochwu + kalwu
red pepper powder *red pepper + powder*

바닷가 [바닫까 or 바다까] *beach* ← 바다 *sea* + 가 *edge*
pataska [patatkka / patakka] pata + ka

김칫국 [김칟꾹 or 김치꾹] *kimchi soup* ← 김치 *kimchi* + 국 *soup*
kimchiskwuk [kimchitkkwuk / kimchikkwuk kimchi + kwuk

어젯밤 [어젣빰 or 어제빰] *last night* ← 어제 *yesterday* + 밤 *night*
eceyspam [eceytppam / eceyppam] ecey + pam

콧수염 [콛쑤염 or 코쑤염] *mustache* ← 코 *nose* + 수염 *beard*
khosswuyem [khotsswuyem / khosswuyem] kho + swuyem

We will risk sounding like a broken record here: the key to spelling better is to re-member how to spell the **base form** of each word. If you know how to spell the word that means *sleep(ing)* 잠 cam and also the word *room/space* 자리 cali, then you will have no problem with the spelling of 잠자리 camcali even if what you hear is [잠짜 리]. The same is true of 코 kho *nose* and 수염 swuyem *beard*. Although you will hear [코쑤염 khosswuyem] or [콛쑤염 khotsswuyem], you know the correct spelling is 콧수 염 khos.swu.yem, if you know the spelling of the individual parts 코 kho and 수염 swuy-em and the ㅅ-insertion rule. The magic works backwards as well. If you see 콧수염 khos.swu.yem written or hear [콛쑤염 khosswuyem] and you happen to know the mean-ing of 코 kho *nose* and the meaning of either 수염 swuyem or 콧수염 khosswuyem, you can probably guess the meaning of the remaining part. We make it sound so easy, but as you can imagine, spelling words correctly can be a challenging task even for Korean speakers. The best way is to learn to spell each new word correctly as you en-counter it. If you learn a word and are not sure about the spelling, double-check it.

(3) ㄹ- insertion

In a noun + noun compound, if the first noun ends in ㄹ l and the second noun be-gins with the vowel 이 i, which includes 야 ya (이 i + 아 a), 여 ye (이 i + 어 e), 요 yo (이 i + 오 o), or 유 yu (이 i + 우 wu), the ㄹ l gets doubled (only in pronunciation)—that is, you add one more ㄹ l sound (할일 halil below is not a noun compound, but it works the same way):

물약 [물략] *liquid medicine* ← 물 *water* + 약 *medicine*
mwulyak [mwullyak] mwul + yak

할일 [할릴] *things to do, chores*
halil [hallil]

← 할 *do-prospective* + 일 *work, job*
hal + il

구팔육칠 [구팔륙칠] *9, 8, 6, 7*
kwuphalyukchil [kwuphallyukchil]

(4) ㄴ- insertion

In a noun + noun compound, if the first noun ends in a consonant other than ㄹ l and the second noun begins with a vowel 이 i (야 ya, 여 ye, 요 yo, 유 yu), ㄴ n is inserted (only in pronunciation) (식용 sikyong below is not a noun, but it acts like one):

색연필 [생년필] *colored pencil*
saykyenphil [sayngnyenphil]

← 색 *color* + 연필 *pencil*
sayk + yenphil

중국 요리 [중궁뇨리] *Chinese cuisine*
cwungkwuk yoli [cwungkwunyoli]

← 중국 *China* + 요리 *cuisine*
cwungkwuk + yoli

식용유 [시콩뉴] *cooking oil*
sikyongyu [sikyongnyu]

← 식용 *eat-for* + 유 *oil*
sikyong + yu

깻잎 [깬닙] *sesame leaf*
kkaysiph [kkaynnip]

← 깨 *sesame* + ㅅ *s* + 잎 *leaf*
kay + s + iph

2.5 Natural Speech

Now you know all the pronunciation-changing rules. The next step is to use them in natural, flowing speech. Start by re-reading the examples throughout the chapter so that you begin to internalize the rules. As a last set of hints, this section shows how the rules are put together, along with some final quirks of pronunciation in fast and casual speech.

2.5.1 Same or different?

As a result of all the crazy sound rules, there are many word pairs with different spellings that are pronounced the same in Korean:

[소라 sola]   솔아 sol.a *pine tree-vocative particle*   소라 so.la *conch*

[보리 poli]   볼이 pol.i *cheek-subject particle*   보리 po.li *barley*

[밤만 pamman]   밥만 pap.man *rice-only*   밤만 pam.man *chestnut-only*

[밥또 paptto]   밥도 pap.to *rice-also*   밥 또 pap tto *rice again*

Also be careful with pairs that may sound VERY similar to you but make a world of difference to native speakers:

[노라 nola]   놀아 nol.a *play*
[놀라 nolla]   놀라 nol.la *surprised*

[파리 phali]   파리 pha.li *fly*, 팔이 phal.i *arm-subject*

[팔리 phalli]   팔리 phal.li *to be sold*

[다리 tali]   다리 ta.li *leg*, 달이 tal.i *moon-subject*

[달리 talli]   달리 tal.li *to run, be pended*

[노래 nolay]   노래 no.lay *song, yellow*

[노ː래 noolay]   놓으래 noh.u.lay *(someone says) let go*

[마나 mana]   많아 manh.a *be plentiful*

[마ʷ나 manʷa]   만화 man.hwa *comics*

[만나 manna]   만나 man.na *meet*

2.5.2 Emotional/habitual tensing

Even though plain and tense consonants must be differentiated when speaking Korean, some initial plain consonants are pronounced as tense just for emphasis. This happens mainly with words that have emotional weight. It's best not to use the tense versions with polite company or in formal situations. Here are some typical examples:

세다 [쎄다] *strong*
seyta [sseyta]

진하다 [찌ː나다] *thick, strong*
cinhata [ccinata]

생으로 [쌩으로] *raw*
sayngulo [ssayngulo]

공짜로 [꽁짜로] *for free*
kongccalo [kkongccalo]

버스 [뻐쓰] *bus*
pesu [ppessu]

줄었어 [쭈러써] *It shrank.*
cwulesse [ccwulesse]

작다 [짝따] *small*
cakta [ccaktta]

좀 [쫌] *a little bit*
com [ccom]

질기다 [찔기다] *tough, chewy*
cilkita [ccilkita]

내버려 둬 [냅뻐려ʷ도] *Leave it.*
naypelye twe [naypppelyetʷo]

닦아 [따까] *Wipe it! (Clean it up!)*
takka [ttakka]

잘렸나? [짤련나] *Was it cut?/Was he fired?*
callyessna [ccallyenna]

2.5.3 Vowel change

Because the vowels 애 ay and 에 ey sound the same to most speakers, Koreans have come up with a new way to distinguish them: pronounce the vowel 에 ey as 이 i! But this happens only in certain words, and in a more relaxed, casual setting. (In a formal situation, speakers tend to "fake" the distinction between 애 ay and 에 ey by making 애 ay longer or louder.)

예뻐 [이뻐] *pretty*
yeyppe [ippe]

베개 [비개] *pillow*
peykay [pikay]

네 거 [니꺼] *yours*
ney ke [nikke]

데었어 [디었어]
teyesse [tiesse]
I burned myself.

베었니? [비었니]
peyessni [piessni]
Did you cut yourself?

2.5.4 Fast speech

Certain pronunciation rules like 신라 sinla [실라 silla] *Silla* (Kingdom) and 십년 sipnyen [심년 simnyen] *ten years* ALWAYS apply, so you will definitely sound like a non-native speaker if you pronounce these words [신.라 sinla] and [십.년 sipnyen]. But there are also personal, regional and situational pronunciation tendencies as well. In general, when you speak in a casual environment with close friends, you are likely to speak fast, slur your words, and use short and contracted forms (e.g. 뭐 mwe *what* instead of 무엇 mwues). You also try to minimize your effort by making sounds similar (assimilating) to their neighboring sounds (친구 chinkwu [친구 chinkwu] *friend* → [칭구 chingkwu]); this happens even more in fast, casual speech. Practice the following words until they come to you naturally, if you want to sound like a native speaker!

마음 maum [마ː口 maam] *heart*

가을 kaul [가ː ㄹ kaal] *fall*

놓아 noha [나ː nwaa] *let go*

좋아 coha [좌ː cwa] *good*

구워 kwuwe [궈ː kwe] *broil*

추워 chwuwe [춰ː chwe] *cold*

좋은 cohun [조ː ㄴ coon] *good*

사은품 saunphwum [사ː ㄴ품 saanphwum] *freebie*

2.5.5 All together!

When two or more pronunciation rules come together, things get a little busier. See if you can figure out the pronunciation of the words below before looking at the right hand column.

못 먹어 mos meke *cannot eat*

[몬머거 mon meke, 몸머거 mom meke]

잤는지 cassnunci *whether you slept*

[잔는지 cannunci]

윗니 wisni *upper teeth*

[윈니 winni]

윗물 wismwul *water from the upstream*

[윈물 winmwul or 윔물 wimmwul]

몇 해 myech hay *how many years, few years*

[며태 myethay]

못 해 mos hay *cannot do*

[모태 mothay]

웃옷 wusos *top, shirt, upper garment*
  vs. [웃었어] *laughed*

[우돋 wutot]
  vs. [우서써 wusesse]

못 읽어 mos ilke *cannot read*

[모딜거 motilke or 몬닐거 monnilke]

옷 입어 os ipe *wear clothes*

[오디버 otipe or 온니버 onnipe]

갇히다 kathita *be locked up*

[가치다 kachita]

같이 kathi *together*

[가치 kachi]

People also speak quickly and slur their words, like English "gotcha!" and "didju?" Here are some common ones:

	Standard spelling	Pronounced	Meaning
1.	그런데 kulentey	[근데]* [kundey]	*but, however*
2.	그러면 kulemyen	[그럼, 금] [kulem, kum]	*if so*
3.	그렇지만 kulehciman	[그치만] [kuchiman]	*but, however*
4.	그러니까 kulenikka	[그니까, 그니깐, 긍까, 까] [kunikka, kunikkan, kungkka, kka]	*so*
5.	그래서 kulayse	[~서] [~se]	*so*
6.	갑니다 kapnita	[감니다, 감:다] [kamnita, kamta]	*go*
7.	놓는다 nohnunta	[논는다, 논:다] [nonnunta, nonta]	*put (sth.) on*
8.	귀여워 kwiyewe	[기여워] [kiyewe]	*cute*
9.	이리로 ililo	[이리루, 일루] [ililwu, illwu]	*this way*
10.	할머니이세요 halmeniiseyyo	[할머이세요] [halmeiseyyo]	*(she is) a grandmother*
11.	할머니는 halmeninun	[**할머닌**] [halmenin]	*grandmother*
12.	얼마인데 elmaintey	[**얼만데**] [elmantey]	*how much-and*
13.	얼마일까 elmailkka	[**얼말까**] [elmalkka]	*how much would it be*
14.	맛있다 masissta	[마시따] [masitta]	*delicious*
15.	재미있어 caymiisse	[재미써] [caymisse]	*fun*
16.	반가워 pankawe	[방가워] [pangkawe]	*glad to see*
17.	어디 있어요 eti isseyo	[어디써요] [etisseyo]	*where is it?*
18.	여기있어 yeki isse	[여긴써, 여기써] [yekitsse, yekisse]	*here it is*
19.	저기있어 ceki isse	[저기써] [cekisse]	*it's over there*

	Standard spelling	Pronounced	Meaning
20.	내버려둬 naypelye twe	[내비려둬, 내비도, 냅또] [naypilyetwe, naypito, nayptto]	*leave me/it*
21.	줄까 cwulkka	[죽까, 주까] [cwukkka, cwukka]	*shall (I) give it?*
22.	줄게 cwulkkey	[죽께, 주께] [cwukkkey, cwukkey]	*(I) will give*
23.	갈거야 kal keya	[갈꺼야, 각꺼야] [kalkkeya, kakkkeya]	*will go*
24.	먹으면 mekumyen	[머금:, 머그믄] [mekum, mekumun]	*if (sujb.) eats*
25.	일어나 ilena	[인나, 일라] [inna, illa]	*wake up; get up*
26.	같아 katha	[가태, 가터] [kathay, kathe]	*(it's) like*
27.	안돼 antoy	[안대] [antay]	*no way*
28.	이제는 iceynun	[**이젠**, 인젠] [iceyn, inceyn]	*any longer*
29.	이것은 ikesun	[**이건**] [lken]	*this thing*
30.	너는 nenun	[**년**] [nen]	*you-topic*
31.	나는 nanun	[**난**] [nan]	*I-topic*
32.	저는 cenun	[**전**] [cen]	*I (humble)-topic*
33.	여기에는 yekieynun	[**여기엔**, **여긴**] [yekieyn, yekin]	*here*
34.	여기에서는 yekieysenun	[**여기서는**, **여기선**] [yekisenun, yekisen]	*here*
35.	누구는 nwukwunun	[**누군**] [nwukwun]	*who-topic*
36.	거기인가봐 kekiinkapwa	[거긴가바, 거잉가바] [kekinkapa, keingkapa]	*seems like that's the place*
37.	비싸기는요 pissakinunyo	[**비싸긴요**] [pissakinyo]	*expensive? not at all!*
38.	어디를 etilul	[**어딜**] [etil]	*where-object*
39.	어디에다가 etieytaka	[**어디다가**, 얻따가, 어따가] [etitaka, etttaka, ettaka]	*to where*
40.	어디에서 etieyse	[**어디서**, 어:서] [etise, ese]	*from where*

	Standard spelling	Pronounced	Meaning
41.	며칠 myechil	[메칠] [meychil]	*how many days*
42.	몇시 myech si	[메씨] [meyssi]	*what time*
43.	제일 ceyil	[젤, 제:ㄹ] [ceyl, ceil]	*the best*
44.	내일 nayil	[낼, 내:ㄹ] [nayl, nayl]	*tomorrow*
45.	그냥 kunyang	[걍:, 갸~:] [kyang, kya]	*just*
46.	그거 kuke	[거:] [ke]	*that thing*
47.	한번 hanpen	[함, 하:ㅁ] [am, haam]	*once*
48.	부모님 pwumonim	[부몬님] [pwumonnim]	*parents*
49.	바르니까 palunikka	[발르니까] [pallunikka]	*apply so...*
50.	가려면 kalyemyen	[갈라면, 갈래면, 갈려면, 갈라믄, 갈래믄, 갈려믄] [kallamyen, kallaymyen, kallyemyen, kallamun, kallaymun, kallyemun]	*If (you) intend to go*
51.	정말 cengmal	[증말] [cungmal]	*really*
52.	큰일나 khunil na	[클라] [khulla]	*it'll be trouble*
53.	따뜻하다 ttattushata	[따:타다, 따드타다, 뜨드타다] [ttathata, ttatuthata, ttututhata]	*warm*
54.	나빠 nappa	[나뻐] [nappe]	*bad*

* Words in **bold** in brackets are contracted forms and accepted ways to spell the words casually, but they are not used in formal writing. The others you might see in facetious writings in social media.

As opposed to memorizing these pronunciation rules as such, we recommend that you 1) simply become aware that spelling differs from pronunciation in some cases, even in Korean, 2) practice reading the examples throughout the chapter and see if that helps you to INTERNALIZE the pronunciation rules, and 3) check back here and see if there is a rule to explain it whenever you wonder why a word is pronounced one way and spelled another in Korean.

One rule of thumb that might help you apply some of the rules without thinking too much is that Korean doesn't have glottal stops or hard stopping sounds. Never [몯' 먹'어 mot'mek'e] or [밥'먹'어 pap'mek'e]. Make it smooth [몸머거 mommeke] and [밤머거 pammeke].

Exercises

2.1 One-spelling Principle

Exercise 1. Fill in the blanks according to the one-spelling principle (which tells you that the roots in each column should be spelled the same and the suffixes in each row should be spelled the same).

eat	*mix*	*read*	meaning of the suffix:
먹다	_____다	읽_____	*to X* (dictionary form)
_____는다	섞는다	읽_____	*I'm Xing this!* (plain style)
_____어요	_____어요	읽어요	*Xs, is Xing* (polite ordinary style)
_____고 가	섞고 가	_____고 가	*X and then go*

2.2 Simple-syllable Principles

Exercise 2. One sounds different from the others. Which one?

1) a. 밖 *outside*
   b. 밤 *night*
   c. 박 *gourd*

2) a. 집 *house*
   b. 짚 *straw*
   c. 짖 *to bark (verb stem)*

3) a. 낮 *daytime*
   b. 납 *lead*
   c. 낯 *face*
   d. 낫 *sickle*

4) a. 잎 *leaf*
   b. 입 *mouth*
   c. 임 *Lim (Korean last name)*

5) a. 닥 *paper mulberry*
   b. 닫 *to close (verb stem)*
   c. 닦 *to wipe (verb stem)*

6) a. 곤 *soon*
   b. 곳 *place*
   c. 곡 *a piece of music*
   d. 곶 *cape, point*

Exercise 3. Read the following words out loud, applying the single-받침 rule.

1) a. 없다 *not to exist*
   b. 값 *price*

2) a. 괜찮다 *O.K.*
   b. 귀찮다 *feel bothered*
   c. 많다 *be a lot*

3) a. 앉다 *to sit down*
   b. 얹다 *to place on top*

4) a. 읽다 *to read*
   b. 늙다 *to get old*
   c. 맑다 *be clear*
   d. 밝다 *be bright*

5) a. 짧다 *be short*
   b. 넓고 *spacious-and*
   c. 얇지 *thin-right?*
   d. 여덟 *eight*

Exercise 4. Which syllable sounds the same as the one in bold?

1) 여**덟** *eight*:   a. 덜   b. 덥

2) **값** *price*:   a. 갑   b. 갓

3) **앉**다 *to sit*:   a. 안   b. 앚

4) **앓**다 *not*:   a. 안   b. 앟

5) **닭** *chicken*:   a. 달   b. 닥

6) **젊**다 *be young*:   a. 절   b. 점

Exercise 5. Which two sound the same?

1) a. 모래 *sand*
   b. 몰래 *stealthily*
   c. 모레 *the day after tomorrow*

2) a. 낯에 *in the face*
   b. 낮에 *during the daytime*
   c. 나체 *naked body*

3) a. 읽어 *read*
   b. 일거 *one effort*
   c. 익어 *ripen*

4) a. 안아 *hug*
   b. 안 자 *not sleeping*
   c. 앉아 *sit down*

5) a. 이 비 *this rain*
   b. 입이 *mouth-subject particle*
   c. 잎이 *leaf-subject particle*

6) a. 바글 *crowding over*
   b. 박을 *gourd-object particle*
   c. 밖을 *outside-object particle*

Exercise 6. Read the words aloud thinking about simplification of the initial consonant + w/y sequence in the syllable in bold.

1) a. **쳐** *hit*
   b. 가르**쳐** *teach*
   c. **여**자 *woman*

2) a. 시**계** *watch*
   b. **계**피 *cinnamon*
   c. **예** *yes*

3) a. 안 **돼** *no, don't*
   b. **괜**찮아 *it's ok*
   c. **왜** *why*

4) a. **뭐** *what*
   b. **줘**요 *give*
   c. **원** *circle*

Exercise 7. Read the following, paying attention to the pronunciation of 의 and 희.

1) **의**사 선생님의 의자
   a doctor's chair

2) 오늘 강의 시간에 만나서 **의**논하자.
   Let's meet and talk about it during the lecture.

3) 그 친구**의** 전화번호를 아세요?
   Do you know that friend's telephone number?

4) 제 전화번호는 123**의** 0987이에요.
   My phone number is 123-0987.

5) 은비가 오늘 **흰**색 옷을 입었네!
   Eunbi is wearing white clothes today!

6) 김**희**철은 슈퍼주니어 중의 하나야.
   Heechul Kim is one of the Super Junior members.

7) 김태**희**는 유명한 한국의 영화배우지.
   Tae-hee Kim is a famous Korean actress.

Exercise 8. Read the words out loud. Keep in mind that ㅎ in non-initial positions is not pronounced in fast speech.

1) a. 하루 *ond day*
   b. 지하철 *subway*
   c. 전화 *telephone*

2) a. 많은 *many*
   b. 좋아 *good*
   c. 넣어 *put in*

3) a. 해 *the sun*
   b. 이해 *understanding*
   c. 올해 *this year*

2.3 Interactions Between Consonants

Exercise 9. Read the following out loud applying the ㅎ-combo rule and minding the spelling.

1) a. 법학 *study of law*
   b. 백화점 *department store*
   c. 몇 해 *how many years*

2) a. 이렇게 *like this*
   b. 그렇게 *like it*
   c. 어떻게 *how*

3) a. 좋고 *good and*
   b. 그렇고 *it is so and*
   c. 많고 *a lot and*

4) a. 좋지요? *good, right?*
   b. 그렇지요 *it is so, right?*
   c. 많지요? *a lot, right?*

5) a. 밥하고 *rice and*
   b. 국하고 *soup and*
   c. 옷하고 *clothes and*

6) a. 답답해 *feel trapped*
   b. 착해 *docile, well-behaved*
   c. 비슷해 *be similar*

Exercise 10. Read the words out loud applying the nasalization rule and paying attention to the spelling of words that you know.

1) a. 갑니다 *goes*
   b. 옵니다 *comes*

2) a. 감사합니다 *thank you*
   b. 고맙습니다 *thank you*

3) a. 한국 남자 *Korean man*
   b. 한국말 *the Korean language*

5) a. 일학년 *freshman*
   b. 삼학년 *junior*
   c. 사학년 *senior*

4) a. 앞문 *front door*
   b. 옆문 *side door*
   c. 뒷문 *back door*

6) a. 돈 있니? *got money?*
   b. 돈 있네! *you have money!*
   c. 돈 있는 *having money*

Exercise 11. Read out loud. Then circle the syllable in bold if it is pronounced as it is spelled in natural speech.

1) a. **십**년 *ten years*
   b. **육**년 *six years*
   c. **팔**년 *eight years*

3) a. **봄**놀이 *spring picnic*
   b. 바**닷**물 *sea water*
   c. **윗**물 *the upper waters*

2) a. **백**만 *million*
   b. **참**말 *truth*
   c. **십**만 *hundred thousand*

Exercise 12. If you were to write the word as it is pronounced, which would it be?

1) 신라 *Silla Dynasty*   a. [신라]   b. [실라]   c. [신나]

2) 연락 *contact*   a. [연락]   b. [열락]   c. [연낙]

3) 난로 *stove*   a. [난로]   b. [날로]   c. [난노]

4) 편리 *convenience*   a. [편리]   b. [펼리]   c. [편니]

5) 달님 *moon-honorific*   a. [달님]   b. [달림]   c. [단님]

6) 실내 *indoors*   a. [실내]   b. [실래]   c. [신내]

Exercise 13. Which syllable in bold sounds different from the others?

1) a. 알**기** *knowing*
   b. 암**기** *memorization*
   c. 악**기** *musical instrument*

4) a. 금**지** *prohibition*
   b. 적**지** *enemy land*
   c. 반**지** *ring*

2) a. 글**자** *letter*
   b. 잡**자** *let's grab*
   c. 놀**자** *let's play*

5) a. 먹**다** *to eat*
   b. 없**다** *to not have*
   c. 잡**다** *to grab*
   d. 살**다** *to live*

3) a. 홍**수** *flood*
   b. 홀**수** *odd number*
   c. 적**수** *match*
   d. 맞**수** *rival*

6) a. 작**고** *small and*
   b. 잡**고** *grab and*
   c. 잦**고** *frequent and*
   d. 잔**고** *bank account balance*

2.4 Verb Root, Suffix and Word Boundaries

Exercise 14. Which of the following are pronounced the same?

1) a. 같이 *together (same-suffix)*
   b. 가치 *value*
   c. 갇히(다) *to be locked (lock-passive)*

2) a. 붙이(다) *to stick to*
   b. 부치(다) *to send*
   c. 부티 *the air of the rich*

3) a. 맏이 *the eldest*
   b. 마지 *horse fat*
   c. 마디 *knuckle*

4) a. 밭이다 *it's a field*
   b. 바치다 *to dedicate*
   c. 받히다 *to be hit (hit-passive)*

Exercise 15. Which of the two bold syllables sounds tense?

1) a. 잠**자**리 *dragonfly*
   b. 잠**자**리 *place for sleeping*

2) a. 술**잔** *a drinking glass*
   b. 한 **잔** *one glass (of drink)*

3) a. 내 **밥** *my rice*
   b. 술**밥** *rice used to make liquor*

4) a. 강**가** *Kang family*
   b. 강**가** *riverside*

5) a. 한**국** *Korea*
   b. 된장**국** *soybean paste soup*

6) a. 어젯**밤** *last night*
   b. 이 **밤** *this night*

Exercise 16. The following words have tricky pronunciation. Read them out loud and make sure you know how to say them.

1) **고춧가루** 넣으세요.　　　　　　　*Put some red peppers (in it).*

2) **어젯밤** 잘 잤어요?　　　　　　　*Did you sleep well last night?*

3) **물약** 주세요.　　　　　　　　　*Please give me liquid medicine.*

4) 오늘은 **할 일**이 없어요.　　　　　*I do not have anything to do today.*

5) **식용유**를 너무 많이 넣지 마세요.　*Don't put too much oil (in it).*

6) 요즘 **한국 요리**를 배워요.　　　　*I am learning Korean cooking nowadays.*

2.5 Natural Speech

Exercise 17. Read the following out loud and circle the ones that are pronounced similarly.

1) a. 많아 *a lot*
   b. 만화 *comic book*
   c. 만나 *meet*

2) a. 않아요 *be not*
   b. 안아요 *hold, hug*
   c. 안 나요 *doesn't come out*

3) a. 싫어 *dislike*
   b. 실어(증) *aphasia*
   c. 실로 *using a thread; truly*

4) a. 전화 *phone*
   b. 저나 *perhaps me (humble)*
   c. 전하 *Your Highness, Your Majesty*

5) a. 일흔 *seventy*
    b. 이른 *early*
    c. 일은 *job-topic particle*

Exercise 18. The following is a short conversation between Seyoung and Hyunwoo, who just met each other. Read it silently for the meaning. Then read it out loud, paying attention to spelling and pronunciation discrepancies. Practice each line until you feel comfortable saying it. The idea is to make these expressions your own! Finally, see if you can recall the dialogue (and the correct spelling) by writing the dialogue on a separate sheet of paper without looking at the original.

세영: 안녕하세요? 처음 뵙겠습니다. 저는 김세영이라고 해요.
현우: 저는 박현우라고 해요. 만나서 반가워요.
세영: 네, 정말 반갑습니다. 현우씨는 몇 학년이에요?
현우: 저는 이번 가을에 1학년이 돼요. 세영씨는요?
세영: 네, 저도 이번 가을에 1학년이 돼요. 같이 학교를 다니겠어요. 잘 됐죠?
현우: 네, 우리 친하게 지내요. 참, 세영씨 전화번호 좀 가르쳐 주실래요?
세영: 그럼요. 555의 5555예요.
현우: 내일 전화해도 괜찮아요?
세영: 물론이에요. 아, 지금 가야 돼요. 그럼 안녕히 계세요.
현우: 그래요? 그럼 안녕히 가세요. 나중에 얘기해요.

Translation 번역:
세영: Hello. Nice to meet you (*literally*, It's my first time meeting you). I am Seyoung Kim.
현우: I'm Hyunwoo Park. Nice to meet you.
세영: Very nice to meet you. What year are you?
현우: I will be a freshman this fall. How about you?
세영: I will be a freshman too. We'll be going to school together. Nice!
현우: Good! Let's be friends. Oh, can you tell me your phone number?
세영: Sure. It's 555-5555.
현우: May I call you tomorrow?
세영: Of course. Oh, I've got to run. Bye for now.
현우: OK. Good-bye, then. Talk to you later!

Exercise 19. The following is the script of a conversation between Amber and Tae-hee. Take special note of the discrepancy between how the underlined parts are written in standard Korean and how you might say them in natural, fast speech, which is written out for you, following the standard written version.

Standard written version:
엠버: 큰일 났어! 다음 주에 한국어 시험이 있는데 모르는 <u>것이</u> 너무 많아.
태희: 걱정 마. 내가 <u>제일</u> 잘 하는 과목이 한국어야. 내가 다 <u>가르쳐 줄게</u>.

엠버: 정말? 좋아, 좋아! 네가 도와준다니, 이제 마음이 놓인다. 정말 고마워.

태희: 그러니까 친구가 최고라는 거야.

엠버: 그러면 오늘 밤에 만나서 같이 공부할까?

태희: 좋은 생각이야! 우리 집에서 만나서 고기도 구워 먹고 공부도 하자.

엠버: 어! 어떻게 하지? 나는 고기를 못 먹어.

태희: 괜찮아. 다른 음식도 많아.

엠버: 좋아! 그런데 한국어를 잘 하려면 어떻게 해야 될까?

태희: 나같은 한국 친구들하고 한국어를 많이 해 봐.

엠버: 이제부터 그래야겠어. 정말 고마워! 내가 가기 전에 전화할게.

태희: 그래. 조금 이따 보자.

Fast speech pronunciation (Incorrectly spelled on purpose):

엠버: 클났어! 다음 주에 한국어 시험이 있는데 모르는 게 너무 많아.

태희: 걱정 마. 내가 젤 잘 하는 과목이 한국어야. 내가 다 갈쳐 주께.

엠버: 정말? 좌! 좌! 네가 도와준다니, 인제 맘이 놓인다. 증말 고마워.

태희: 그니까 친구가 최고라는 거야.

엠버: 금 오늘 밤에 만나서 같이 공바까?

태희: 존 생각이야! 우리 집에서 만나서 고기도 궈 먹고 공부도 하자.

엠버: 어! 어떡하지? 난 고길 몬먹어.

태희: 괜잔아. 딴 음식도 많아.

엠버: 좋아! 근데 한국어를 잘 할라면/할래면 어떻게 해야 되까?

태희: 나같은 한국 친구들하구 한국어를 많이 해 바.

엠버: 인제부터 그래야겠어. 증말 고마워! 내가 가기 전에 저날께.

태희: 그래. 쫌 이따 보자.

Translation 번역:

엠버: I'm in big trouble! I have a Korean test next week, but there are so many things I don't know!

태희: Don't worry. Korean is my best subject. I will teach you everything.

엠버: Really? Great! I feel relieved now, hearing that you will help me out. Thanks a lot!

태희: Don't they say "friends are the best thing ever"?

엠버: Then, shall we get together and study tonight?

태희: Good idea! Let's get together at my place and barbecue and study together.

엠버: Oh, no! Sorry… I don't eat meat.

태희: It's okay. I have a lot of other food besides meat.

엠버: Great! By the way, what should I do to get better at Korean?

태희: Try to speak Korean with Korean friends like me.

엠버: I should from now on. Thanks so much. I'll call you before coming over tonight.

태희: OK. See you soon!

Exercise 20. What is the standard spelling of the following expressions?

1) *Thank you.*
    (감사함니다   감사합니다   감사함미다)

2) *It's the teacher's book.*
    선생님(에   의) 책이에요.

3) *I am learning Korean.*
    (항구거   항국어   한국어) 배워요.

4) *Come here and let's watch a movie together.*
    여기 와서 (같이   가치) 영화 봐요.

5) *What time does the department store open?*
    (백하점   백카점   백화점)은 몇 시에 열어요?

6) *The bag is not in the room.*
    가방은 방에 (업써요   업서요   없어요).

7) *I do not have money now....*
    지금 돈이 (엄는데여   업는데요   없는데요).

8) *What year are you (in school)?*
    (몇 학년   며 탕년   몇 항년)이에요?

9) *I cannot go to school tomorrow.*
    내일은 학교에 (목   못) 가요.

10) *Nice to meet you.*
    만나서 (반가워요   방가워요).

11) *What's the date today?*
    오늘이 (며칠   몇일)이에요?

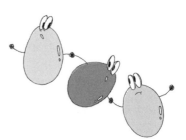

CHAPTER 3
Parts of Speech & Sentence Structure

To get you started with the grammar of Korean, this chapter lays out the sentence structure, explanation of which depends partly on parts of speech. What kinds of words are put in what order to make a sentence in Korean?

In English, the relationship between the words in a sentence (whether something is a subject, an object or a complement, etc.) is blueprinted by the verb and played out by the ORDER of the words. In Korean, the word relationships are likewise determined by the verb but made clear by the PARTICLES, the only unbreakable rule of WORD ORDER being that the verb comes last.

Three mantras for understanding Korean sentence structure are:

> *Korean is a pronoun-drop language.*
>
> *Korean is a predicate-final language.*
>
> *Korean uses particles to indicate subject, object, and so on.*

These three linguistic features are at the heart of Korean sentence structure, and to understand and manipulate them is to get a direct pass to the heart.

In more approachable terms, **pronoun-drop** means that you can leave out pronouns like *I* and *you* when it can be determined by context who is doing what. So, in Korean, you can say 지금 세 시예요 cikum sey siyeyyo for *It's 3 o'clock now* without the empty subject *it* that you would use in English. You will encounter missing subjects and objects more often in conversational context, but there will be some example sentences here and in later chapters where subject and object pronouns are dropped.

Predicate-finality means that the verb always comes last in a sentence. It comes after other information such as the subject, the direct object, the indirect object, the time, place, and reason for an action or event. Most often, if the subject and object are stated overtly, the subject comes first, then the object, then the verb is obligatorily last: so it's an SOV word order (Subject-Object-Verb). You'll learn that adjectives function like verbs (and come last in the sentence), so we call this PREDICATE-finality.

Lastly, though there are tendencies to keep a particular order of ideas in a sentence, it is **particles** that indicate unmistakably which is the subject, direct object, indirect object, location, and so on. Particles are something like suffixes that attach to nouns, and they are treated as part of speech in Korean grammar, alongside nouns and verbs. They are VERY IMPORTANT, so we will introduce them here and dedicate all of chapter 4 to exploring them in detail.

When putting a sentence together in Korean, or trying to understand one, these three pieces of knowledge will take you far, but it makes sense to review what pronouns, verbs, and particles (etc.) are to start with; that is, the **parts of speech** at work in Korean grammar. There are some differences between Korean and English parts of speech, so we'll start with that topic. Then we'll move on to sentence structure, reviewing concepts like **direct** and **indirect object** and demonstrating the basic order of such elements in the sentence before talking about how the basic word order can be manipulated for different pragmatic effects. We'll end the chapter with discussion of what is and isn't considered a word in Korean and thus where to leave spaces between words in your writing.

3.1 Parts of Speech

Perhaps you have heard the term **part of speech**. It refers to the kinds of words that sentences are made up of. English is generally said to have 8 parts of speech: noun, pronoun, verb, adjective, adverb, interjection, conjunction, and preposition, or depending on whose theory you follow, sometimes 9, including **determiners** (or **articles**) like *a*, *the*, and *such*. In Korean, there are 9 parts of speech (9품사 phwumsa), 6 of which are shared by English: 명사 myengsa **noun**, 대명사 tay-myengsa **pronoun**, 동사 tongsa **verb**, 형용사 hyengyongsa **adjective**, 부사 pwusa **adverb**, and 감탄사 kamthansa **interjection**. Two are not found in English: 조사 cosa **particle** and 관형사 kwanhyengsa **adnominal** (sometimes called *pre-noun*). Korean also counts 수사 swusa **numerals** as an independent part of speech. Let's take a quick whirlwind tour of what they are and what they do, then the following chapters get into the details—further explanations and lots of examples.

3.1.1 Parts of speech in Korean

Before reading about the parts of speech that are found in Korean, skim through the following chart, which gives an overview of the English (left side) and Korean (right side) parts of speech. You do not need to agonize over the details, but use it to remind yourself about the parts of speech and know that you have the chart as a reference point you can come back to when you want. The last three Korean parts of speech are highlighted because English counterparts do not exist. Also, the underlined words can belong to more than one part of speech in English, depending on how they are used in a given sentence.

영어 yenge **English**		한국어 hankwuke **Korean**	
Part of Speech (POS)	Example	품사 phwumsa	보기 poki
Noun Names!	school, flower, food, person, dog, <u>love</u>, <u>light</u>, beauty, <u>yesterday</u>, Korea, Sam Soon Kim…	명사 myengsa (Noun)	학교 hakkyo *school*, 꽃 kkoch *flower*, 음식 umsik *food*, 사람 salam *person*, 한국 hankwuk *Korea*, 김삼순 kimsamswun *Sam Soon Kim*…
Pronoun Names you can say without repeating yourself!	I, we, you, he, she, it, they; me, him, them; this, that…	**대명사** taymyengsa (Pronoun)	나/저 na/ce *I or me*, 우리/저희 wuli/cehuy *we or us*, 이것/이거 ikes/ike *this (thing)*, 여기 yeki *here*, 어디 eti *where*, 누구 nwukwu *who*, 무엇/뭐 mwues/mwe *what*…
Verb* for actions!	go, eat, die, live, cry, meet, tell, <u>love</u>, <u>light</u>, congratulate, <u>climb</u>, <u>build</u>…	**동사*** tongsa* Active Verb Existential Verbs	가다* kata *to go*, 먹다 mekta *to eat*, 앉다 ancta *to sit*, 기다리다 kitalita *to wait*, 자다 cata *to sleep*… 있다 issta, 없다 epsta
Adjective for descriptions!	heavy, small, pretty, <u>smart</u>, <u>light</u>, <u>calm</u>, yellow, interesting, <u>safe</u>, engaged, <u>quiet</u>…	**형용사** hyengyongsa Descriptive Verb Linking verb	예쁘다 yeypputa *pretty*, 무겁다 mwukepta *heavy*, 싫다 silhta *distasteful*, 무섭다 mwusepta *scared/scary*, 괜찮다 kwaynchanhta *OK*, 바쁘다 papputa *busy*, 많다 manhta *plenty*… 이다 ita
Adverb for the how, how much, how ~!	yesterday, fast, undoubtedly, barely, relatively, largely, slightly, fairly, amazingly, quite, merely, really, very…	**부사** pwusa (Adverb) Conjunctions, a.k.a. connectors, are adverbs in Korean!	아주 acwu *very*, 정말 cengmal *really*, 너무 nemwu *too*, 자주 cacwu *frequently*, 전혀 cenhye *(not) at all*, 깡총깡총 kkangchongkkangchong *hopping-hopping*, 반짝반짝 panccakpanccak *twinkle-twinkle*, 열심히 yelsimhi *diligently*, 과연 kwayen *indeed*, 결국 kyelkwuk *eventually*, 그리고 kuliko *and*, 그래서 kulayse *so*…

영어 yenge **English**		한국어 hankwuke **Korean**	
Part of Speech (POS)	Example	품사 phwumsa	보기 poki
Interjection basically, exclamations!	Oh! A-ha! Wow!	**감탄사** kamthansa (Interjection)	아이구 aikwu! *Oh, no!* 엄마 야 emmaya! *My golly!* 아야 aya! *Ouch!* 에이 eyi! *Fudge!* 참 cham! *Oh!* 아차 acha! *Oh, no! (I forgot!)* 어 e? *Huh?* 어 휴/에휴 ehyu/eyhyu... *Geeez...* 이런 ilen! *Dang!...*
Conjunction for connecting items in lists or contrasts	and, but, yet, so, or, nor...	**조사** cosa (Particle)	은/는 un/nun (*topic*), 이/가 i/ ka (*subject*), 을/를 ul/lul (*object*), 에/에서 ey/eyse *at,* 만 man *only,* 도 to *also...*
Preposition those little place words showing up before nouns!	in(side/to), to(ward), from, out, on, at, for, by, with, below, above, beyond, over, before, after, against, along, about...	**수사** swusa (Numeral)	하나/일 hana/il *one,* 둘/이 twul/i *two,* 셋/삼 seys/sam *three,* 첫 번째 ches penccay *first,* 두 번째 twu penccay *second,* 세 번째 sey penccay *third...*
Articles/ Determiners those tiny words that tell which and how many	a, an, the, another, some, which...	**관형사** kwanhyengsa (Adnominal)	새 say *new,* 헌 hen *old,* 첫 ches *first,* 옛 yeys *old,* 이 i *this,* 저 ce *that,* 무슨 mwusun *what kind of,* 그런 kulena *that kind of,* 아무 amwu *any...*

* Keep in mind here and throughout the book that when listing or talking about verbs, we use the dictionary form, made up of the verb root plus the suffix 다 ta, but when creating sentences, the verbs (and adjectives) must be conjugated to show tense, speech style and so on. The verbs at the end of sentences will have different suffixes.

Let's first talk about the elements that Korean and English have in common.

(1) Nouns

A **noun** is a word you use to name things in the world. You have a designated name, say, *Emma*, which is your own proper name (hence the term **proper noun**), but depending on the situation, you may be referred to as a *person, student, daughter, sister,* or *friend,* and those words are all common nouns, as are words referring to abstract things like *peace, joy, kindness, emancipation,* and *equality.*

Korean also has an interesting subcategory of nouns called **dependent nouns**. There aren't too many of them, but it is important to be aware of their existence. They are very short, usually only one syllable long, and they must have a descriptor in front of them, hence the name DEPENDENT noun. Native Korean speakers do not recognize dependent nouns as nouns that stand on their own with real noun-like meaning. If you walk into a room and say *love!* people will know what you are talking about. Likewise, if you yell out 책 chayk! *a book/books*, native Korean speakers will understand what you are talking about, but if you say 것 kes! *thing* or 데 tey! *place*, Koreans will have no idea what you are doing. You have to say 이 것 i kes *this thing* or 먹을 데 mekul tey *eating place/a place to eat*, for example.

Counters (also called **classifiers**) are a special kind of dependent noun that is used when talking about how many items there are. This will be explained in greater detail in another chapter, but be aware of the concept for now. To state the number of an item in Korean, you cannot simply use a number and then a noun, like *three cats*. In Korean, the noun comes first, then the number, and then it is necessary to use a counter that states the type of item. Here are some examples:

책	다섯	**권**	샀어요.
chayk	tases	kwen	sasseyo
book	*five*	*counter for books*	*bought-polite*

I bought five books.

개	다섯	**마리**	봤어요.
kay	tases	mari	pwasseyo
dog	*five*	*counter for animals*	*saw-polite*

I saw five dogs.

아기가	다섯	**명**	있어요.
aki-ka	tases	myeng	isseyo
baby-subj.	*five*	*counter for people*	*exist-polite*

There are five babies.

컴퓨터를	다섯	**대**	찾았어요.
khemphywuthe-lul	tases	tae	chacasseyo
computer-obj.	*five*	*counter for large machines*	*found-polite*

I found five computers.

We'll get into more detail about nouns and dependent nouns in chapter 4, but for now, long story short, these are what are called dependent nouns in Korean, and they are subpar in their noun muscle in that they must come with something describing them.

(2) Pronouns

A **pronoun** is a word you use in place of a noun or long noun phrase when you and your listener/reader already know what you are talking about. It doesn't matter whether you have already mentioned it or you both are so familiar that you just know it without having to mention it. Examples of pronouns are underlined here:

> <u>We</u>'ve been dreading <u>it</u> for a long time, but <u>it</u> finally happened last night.

> <u>I</u> bought a book yesterday, and <u>it</u> was so interesting that <u>I</u> finished reading <u>it</u> in 2 hours.

In Korean—especially spoken Korean, you will rarely hear pronouns. They are usually left out, and you are expected to understand who/what is being talked about based on the context or on the particles and suffixes. For example, if you say *I saw Jane yesterday* in English, your next sentence could be *She seemed busy*, but the same idea would look like this in Korean:

어제   제인을 봤어. 바빠 보이더라.
ecey   ceyin-ul pwasse. pappa poitela.
yesterday Jane-obj. saw. busy seemed-retrospection.
I saw Jane yesterday. She seemed busy. (Literally, *Saw Jane yesterday. Seemed busy.*)

In Korean, you say only *Saw Jane yesterday. Seemed busy.* Here is another example:

A: 어디   가?
   eti   ka?
   where go?
   Where are you going? (Literally, *Where go?*)

B: 아무   데도   안   가.
   amwu tey-to   an   ka.
   not-any place-even not go
   I'm not going anywhere (Literally, *Not go any place.*)

Another difference in the use of pronouns in Korean and English is that, if what you are referring to is not a specific item like *that thing you are looking at* or *what I just mentioned to you* but something more general such as *trees*, a Korean speaker will likely repeat the noun instead of using a pronoun. So, in English if you were to say something like *The trees were swaying in the wind. They, too, were weeping for their country*, this is how you would say it in Korean:

나무들이 바람에   흔들렸다.
namwutul-i palam-ey huntullyessta.
trees-subj. wind-in swayed-plain
The trees were swaying in the wind.

나무들도 조국을   위해   울고 있었다.
namwutul-to cokwuk-ul   wihay wulko issessta
trees-too country-obj. for was cry-ing-plain
They, too, were weeping for their country.
(Literally, *Trees in the wind swayed. Trees, too, for country, were crying.*)

Now you got the idea of the third mantra: Korean is a pronoun-drop language. Pronouns are truly RARELY used in Korean!

(3, 4) Verbs & adjectives/Active verbs and descriptive verbs

Our next stop is verbs and adjectives. Perhaps you have heard that a **verb** expresses an action, and an **adjective** describes a noun. That's a good start, but can you tell which of these are verbs and which are adjectives?

kick, sleep, sleepy, childish, guess, enjoy, resemble

What is expressed by the words *resemble, enjoy,* and even *sleep* may not feel quite like an action, though they are verbs. It is pretty much always true that adjectives describe nouns, but when in doubt about the odd verb, you can use the *be* trick in English. If the word needs the assistance of *be* to make a predicate (and is not trying to use the progressive *-ing*), then it is an adjective: *I resemble, I sleep, I guess, I enjoy* (verbs). Compare with these: *I am sleepy* or *You are childish* (adjectives). Another difference is that verbs come in different tenses and aspects, like *kicking, resembled,* and *eaten,* while adjectives generally do not (not ~~sleepying, sleepied,~~ etc.).

The same tricks do not work for Korean: Korean adjectives do not need a BE-verb and they conjugate for tense and aspect in the same ways active verbs do. Verbs and adjectives are very similar in Korean, such that adjectives are considered a type of verb, **descriptive verbs.** There are differences in how the two conjugate in some cases, so they need to be distinguished from active verbs in those cases—more on this in chapter 6.

Two basic points to remember about Korean verbs are: (1) they come at the very end of the sentence (this is the predicate-finality we mentioned), and (2) they **conjugate,** that is, they change shape and take on suffixes to express tense and other meanings. Adjectives, a.k.a. descriptive verbs, are similar to active verbs on these two counts in Korean. They come at the very end of the sentence to say something like *Sujin is very tall,* or, *Sujin is the tallest student in my class.* Compare these two sentences, one with an active verb and one with a descriptive verb as the predicate. You can see that both come at the end and are conjugated for past tense with (some form of) -었 -ess:

나무들이　바람에　**흔들렸다.**
namwutul-i　palam-ey　huntullyessta.
trees-subj.　wind-in　swayed-plain
The trees swayed/were swaying in the wind.

나무들이　아주　**예뻤다.**
namwutul-i　ajwu　yeyppessta.
trees-subj.　very　was pretty-plain
The trees were very pretty.

For adjectives that come BEFORE the nouns they describe, as in *the pretty trees,* the Korean equivalent also comes before the noun and has a special conjugation. The same works for active verbs used to describe nouns, to say, for example, *the trees that swayed.* This is another way in which descriptive verbs and active verbs are similar in Korean.

예쁜　　나무들　　　(*the*) *pretty trees*
yeyppun　　namwutul
pretty-modifier　trees

흔들린　　나무들　　　(*the*) *trees that swayed*
huntulin　　namwutul
sway-past modifier　trees

Be aware that not all English adjectives are descriptive verbs in Korean. Some English adjectives like *empty* 비다 pita, *full* 차다 chata, *sleepy* 졸리다 collita, and *late* 늦다 nucta are VERBS in Korean.

Lastly, Korean verbs (including descriptive verbs) ALWAYS come with a suffix. The verb roots do not stand alone as independent words in Korean. To talk ABOUT verbs, Koreans use their dictionary form, made up of the verb root plus the suffix -다 -ta. When a verb (or adjective) is used in a sentence, it MUST have other suffixes attached to show tense, speech style, and so on. We will follow this pattern, so be aware that the verbs used in example sentences will have different suffixes than those presented in explanations with -다 -ta. We will label the verb endings in the examples, but will explain more fully in chapter 6.

(5) Adverbs

An **adverb** is something that is "**add**ed" to a **verb** to qualify its meaning and provide information on how or how much, the degree to which or the way in which the verb is acted out: *I really love it*, *You are walking fast*, and *She slept a lot*. Adverbs also qualify adjectives: *It is quite expensive*, and *This painting is so beautiful*. Finally, (sentential) adverbs qualify whole sentences by expressing the speaker's attitude or general sentiment about the statement she is making: *Seriously, the driver was crazy. Unfortunately, he didn't make the cut.*

There are many, many, very descriptive adverbs in Korean. At this stage, it suffices to say that Korean adverbs work like English adverbs.

(6) Interjections

An **interjection** is what you occasionally throw in (inter- *between*, -ject *throw*) in a conversation, like *Eek!* 엄마야 emmaya! or *Gosh!* 이런 ilen! Interjections don't do much within sentence structure, but they exist in Korean, and function as in other languages.

(7) Particles

Now we turn to the elements that are classified as parts of speech in Korean and not in English, the most important of which, in Korean grammar, is the particles. A **particle** (조사 cosa), also called a **marker**, attaches to a noun and tells you what that noun does in the sentence (it's the **object**, or it's the **topic**) or adds meaning to the noun (e.g., *also, only, up to, including*).

They are sort of like suffixes in that they cannot be words on their own and must attach to a noun. There is no space or hyphen between the noun and the particle in Korean writing. (We will make them bold in the 한글 hankul examples when we're talking about them and use a hyphen in the romanization so that you can identify them when you need to.)

Particles are sometimes called *postpositions* because they come AFTER nouns and there is some overlap in the meanings of some particles and English prepositions. Some can be translated with English prepositions like *to*, *from*, or *at* in some of their usages, but the main (most frequently used) Korean particles, which mark the subject, object, and topic of sentences, have no equivalent prepositions.

Particles serve to indicate the role of words in the sentence—which is the subject and which is the object, and so on. Since Korean uses particles, it is possible to change the order of words and still have the same basic meaning. Nuances do change with changes to the basic order, as we'll discuss later in this chapter.

지훈**이**   피자를   만들었다.
cihun-i   phica-lul   mantulessta
Jihun-subj.   *pizza-obj.*   *made-plain*
Jihun made pizza.

피자를   지훈**이**   만들었다.
phica-lul   cihun-i   mantulessta
pizza-obj.   *Jihun-subj.*   *made-plain*
Jihun made the pizza.
(a little more emphasis that it was Jihun)

Chapter 4 is all about particles, but for now, check out how the particle tells the role of 지훈 cihun *Jihun* in the following sentences. (Particles are in bold in the 한글 hankul, following a hyphen in the romanization here and throughout the chapter.)

지훈**이**   피자를   먹었다.
cihun-i   phica-lul   mekessta
Jihun-subj.   *pizza-obj.*   *ate-plain*
Jihun ate the pizza. (subject)

There are two forms of the subject particle, -이 -i and -가 -ka , and two of the object particle 을 -ul and 를 -lul.

고양이**가**   지훈**을**   할퀴었다.
koyangi-ka   cihun-ul   halkhwiessta
cat-subj.   *Jihun-obj.*   *scratched-plain*
The cat scratched Jihun. (direct object)

고양이**가**   지훈**도**   할퀴었다.
koyangi-ka   cihun-to   halkhwiessta
cat-subj.   *Jinu-also*   *scratched-plain*
The cat scratched Jihun, too. (also)

고양이**가**   지훈**만**   할퀴었다.
koyangi-ka   cihun-man   halkhwiessta
cat-subj.   *Jihun-only*   *scratched-plain*
The cat scratched only Jihun. (only)

엄마**가**   지훈**한테**   피자를   줬다.
emma-ka   cihun-hanthey   phica-lul   cwuessta
Mom-subj.   *Jihun-to*   *pizza-obj.*   *gave-plain*
Mom gave the pizza to Jihun. = Mom gave Jihun the pizza. (indirect object)

There are changes in the shapes of some particles based on the word they attach to: the subject particle is -이 -i or -가 -ka, the object particle is -을 -ul or -를 -lul, the topic particle is -은 -un or -는 -nun. We'll explain more about this in chapter 6.

(8) Numerals

A **numeral** (수사 swusa) is any noun expressing a cardinal number like *one*, *two*, and *three* ... or ordinal number such as the *first*, *second*, *third*. There are two different cardinal number systems in Korean, Sino-Korean and Native, plus the ordinal numbers which are Native but a little different in shape from the cardinal numbers (like *one* versus *first*). You will learn about them in detail in the next chapter.

(9) Adnominals

An **adnominal** (관형사 kwanhyengsa) is something that is added to a noun to qualify it. How do you qualify a noun? By telling more about it. So, instead of just saying *a song*, if you say *a new song* or *this song*, you are making more specific what kind of song it is by qualifying or modifying it with the word *new* or *this*.

There are only a handful of adnominals in Korean, and they always appear before the noun they characterize. The word *new* in English is an adjective that can come before a noun to modify it (*This is a new book*) or after a noun (and the *be*-verb) to predicate it (*This book is new*). In Korean, the word that means *new* is 새 say, and it is an **adnominal**, that is, it is a modifier that can come ONLY before a noun (새 책 **say chayk** *a new book*), and it does not conjugate like descriptive verbs do in Korean (어책은 새 ichayk-un say *this book is new*). Adnominals are thus different from descriptive verbs in Korean, though English has only one category, adjective, that subsumes both functions.

So, how do you say *this book is new* in Korean? Since you always need a noun for 새 say to modify, you put in a sort of empty noun:

이	책은	새	**거**야	or	이건	새	**책**이야
i	chayk-un	say	keya		ike-n	say	chaykiya
this	*book-topic*	*new*	*thing-is*		*this-thing-topic*	*new*	*book-is*

This book is new (thing).　　　　　　　　　　*This (thing) is [a] new <u>book</u>.*

Other frequently used adnominals are 이 i *this*, 그 ku *that* (*close to you*), and 저 ce *that* (*not close to you or me*). They do not work like English PRONOUNS such as *this*, *that*, *these*, and *those* do, so to use them as such, again, you have to add the noun 거 ke *thing*: 이거 내 책이야 ike nay chaykiya *This (thing) is my book*, or 그거 먹지마 kuke mekcima *Don't eat that (thing)*.

3.1.2 English parts of speech not found in Korean

There are three parts of speech that English has that Korean doesn't have as such: articles, conjunctions and prepositions.

(1) Determiners/Articles

You may have noticed in the preceding examples that Korean common nouns, like *cat*, *book*, *tree*, and so on, do not need **articles** (or **determiners**), such as *a* and *the*. Common nouns are also rarely pluralized, using -들 -tul, unless referring to animate beings.

There are demonstrative articles, <u>this</u> (*cat/book/tree/thing*) and <u>that</u> (*cat/book/tree/thing*), but they are categorized as **adnominals** in Korean grammar.

(2) Conjunctions

A **conjunction** joins together two like elements: *this <u>or</u> that, fun <u>and</u> useful, I know of him, <u>but</u> I've never talked to him*. Korean does not have words that belong to a conjunction category. Nouns are conjoined using particles (e.g., -하고 hako *and*, -이나 ina *or*), sentences using conjunctive adverbs (e.g., 그리고 kuliko *and*, 그렇지만 kulehciman *but*, 그래도 kulayto *even so*), and clauses are conjoined into one sentence using suffixes we'll call **sentence connectors** on the verb at the end of the first clause. These last two look the same in English, but they have different shapes in Korean, and there are a very large number of connectors in Korean, which require conjugation of the verb to fit with the specific connector. Sentence connectors are covered in chapter 8, but here are examples of a conjunctive adverb (or, connector adverb) and a sentence connector (suffix).

나는　갔어.　**하지만**　걔는　안　갔어.
na-nun   kasse.   haciman   kyay-nun   an   kasse.
I-topic   go-past   But   s/he-topic   not   go-past
I went. But s/he didn't.

나는　갔**지만**　걔는　안　갔어.
na-nun   kassciman   kyay-nun   an   kasse.
I-topic   go-past-but   s/he-topic   not   go-past
I went, but s/he didn't.

(3) Prepositions

A **preposition** is a little element that is **preposed** (that is, placed in front of) a noun to express a location or direction with respect to the noun, as in *in the river* or *on the mountain*. Other relationships of nouns to the rest of the sentence are also expressed with prepositions: *with a pencil, for my mother, by a preposition*. Korean does not have prepositions. Those ideas are expressed by particles or noun + particle combinations; some are communicated by the verb itself (벗다 pesta *take off* (this is, strictly speaking, a particle verb in English, not a preposition)) and some are simply not needed in Korean the way they are in English (e.g. *listen to music*).

3.2 Korean Sentence Structure

The three mantras of Korean grammar should be clearer now that the parts of speech are laid out, and that gets you closer to FEELING Korean sentence structure. But let's do explore predicate-finality and how the meaningful elements of sentences are ordered in Korean. A quick review of those meaningful units, such as **subject** and **predicate**, is in order, then we'll need to think about different elements required by different kinds of verbs.

Not all verbs are born equal in their capacities as predicates (or predicate-builders). For starters, see if you can tell the differences between these types of English verbs:

sleep, yell	*be, seem*	*hold, mix*	*give, explain*	*paint, call*	*put, place*

These verbs are STRUCTURALLY different because you can simply *sleep* or *yell*, but you *seem happy* or you *are a teacher*. You can't just *hold* or *mix*; you need to *hold the bag* or *mix the drink*. While you *give me that* and *explain it to her*, you *paint it black* or *call me a genius* (and need two elements in the predicate).

In the floor plan of a sentence, the verb throws its weight around to determine how many and what kinds of elements are needed.

3.2.1 Basic elements of Korean sentences

When someone asks you *How's the weather today?* and you simply respond *Cold!*, you are uttering a single word and not a complete sentence. A complete sentence consists of a **subject** and a **predicate**. The predicate is headed by a verb and might contain an **object** or a **complement** in addition.

> SUBJECT does the action expressed in or is described by the rest of the sentence.
>
> PREDICATE expresses the subject's action (what it does) or its state (how it is) or identity (what it is).
>
> OBJECT is affected by the subject's action.
>
> COMPLEMENT completes the idea about (or describes) the subject or the object.

A few words of clarification first: The term SUBJECT has nothing to do with someone having a subjective opinion or certain tendency (as in *She is subject to laughing out loud in class*), and nor is it a target of any sort (as in *She was the subject of their admiration*). It is a grammatical concept that has a specific meaning *in a sentence*: *that which does or is*. The concept OBJECT, too, is not related to physical objects that you can see or touch, and it has no connection with a goal or an objective for a project (as in *The object of this lesson is…*). It is a grammatical concept that has a specific meaning in a sentence: *that which receives or undergoes the subject's action*. Some objects are directly acted upon or influenced by the subject's action, and this type is called a DIRECT OBJECT: *She kicked the ball*. Or, *That class enriched me*. If there happens to be another object in the sentence that is also affected by such an action (such as being given a book to), that object (usually a person) is an INDIRECT OBJECT: *I asked the teacher that question*. Or, *I handed the baby to my husband*. Finally, a COMPLEMENT completes an idea in a sentence by elaborating on the subject or the object as in *I named my cat Bunky* (object complement). or *It turned into a butterfly* (subject *complement*). It does not have to do with praising someone (which is spelled compliment). It will be easier if you think of the concepts presented in the box above as empty "positions" that hold varying words in different sentences.

The examples in the following table help you see at a glance how these new concepts fit in with each other. Also note how the order is always SOV (subject-object-verb) in Korean, the verb or predicate adjective always comes last, and the particles mark the subject, direct object, and indirect object position (each in its column). We put in hyphens to show the particles clearly, though this is not done in Korean spelling conventions. Particles are also in bold.

Subject 주어 cwue	Predicate 술어 swule				Translation 번역 penyek
	Indirect Object 간접 목적어 kancep mokceke	Direct Object 직접 목적어 cikcep mokceke	Complement 보어 poe	Verb/ Adjective 동사 tongsa/ 형용사 hyengyongsa	
1. 진우-**가** cinwu-ka Jinu-subj.				있어요. isseyo. exist-polite	*There is Jinu. (Jinu is here/exists.)*
2. 진우-**가** cinwu-ka Jinu-subj.	2 층-**에** I chung-ey 2-floor-loc.			있어요. isseyo exist-polite	*Jinu is upstairs.*
				올라갔어요. ollakasseyo. went up-polite	*Jinu went upstairs.*
3. 진우-**가** cinwu-ka Jinu-subj.				떠났어요. ttenasseyo left-polite	*Jinu left.*
				커요. kheyo tall-polite	*Jinu is tall.*
4. 진우-**가** cinwu-ka Jinu-subj.			제 친구 cey chinkwu *my friend*	-예요. -yeyyo. be-polite	*Jinu is my friend.*
5. 진우-**가** cinwu-ka Jinu-subj.			변호사-**가** pyenhosa-ka *laywer-subj.*	됐어요. twaysseyo. became-polite	*Jinu has become a laywer.*
6. 진우-**가** cinwu-ka Jinu-subj.		농구-**를** nongkwu-lul *basketball-obj.*		좋아해요. cohahayyo. like-polite	*Jinu likes basketball.*
7. 진우-**가** cinwu-ka Jinu-subj.		나-**를** na-lul *me-obj.*	바보-**로** papo-lo *fool-instr.*	봐요. pwayo. see-polite	*Jinu sees me as a fool.*
8. 진우-**가** cinwu-ka Jinu-subj.		손톱-**을** sonthop-ul *fingernail-obj.*	까맣-**게** kkamah-key *black-ly*	칠했어. chilhaysse. painted	*Jinu painted his fingernails black.*
9. 진우-**가** cinwu-ka Jinu-subj.	나-한테 na-hanthey *me-indir. obj.*	선물-을 senmwul-ul *gift-direct obj.*		사줬어요. sacwesseyo. buy-gave-polite	*Jinu bought me a gift.*
10. 진우-**가** cinwu-ka Jinu-subj.	집-에 cip-ey *home-loc.*	금송아지-를 kumsongaci-lul *gold cow-obj.*		보냈어요. ponaysseyo. sent-polite	*Jinu sent home a golden cow.*

It might seem confusing that we talk about both parts of speech and now these concepts of subject, and predicate, object and so on. If you ignore the double-duty played by the term **verb**, the simple explanation is that the subject-predicate concepts divide a sentence into big meaningful chunks, and the parts of speech categorize individual words. The parts of speech are the types of words, and the new structural concepts describe their roles and relationships in the sentence. Then we are able to say that nouns can be subjects, objects and indirect objects, for example; or ask which noun is the subject in a given sentence.

3.2.2 Transitive verbs

As we mentioned above, not all verbs are equal in terms of how they build predicate floor plans, or, require elements such as objects and complements. Transitive verbs are those that require objects.

   If the action expressed by the verb affects another entity (an **object**), as in *I hold the title* or *She mixes the two*, the verb is called **transitive**, because the action of the verb is **transferred** to another entity. Since the object is directly affected by the action, this kind of object is called a **direct object**.

(1) One-object verbs

Some verbs must have at least one such grammatical object. The verb in sentence #6 in the table above (진우가 농구를 좋아해요 cinwu-ka nongkwu-lul cohahayyo *Jinu likes basketball*) is of this type. Here are some more examples with a one-object transitive verb:

Subject	Object	Verb
민희는	공을	찼어요.
minhi-nun	kong-ul	chasseyo.
Minhee-topic	*ball-obj.*	*kicked-polite*

Minhee kicked the ball.

제니퍼가	문을	닫았습니다.
ceyniphe-ka	mwun-ul	tatassupnita.
Jennifer-subj.	*door-obj.*	*closed-formal*

Jennifer closed the door.

아기가	엄마를	닮았습니다.
aki-ka	emma-lul	talmassupnita.
baby-subj.	*mom-obj.*	*resembles-formal*

The baby looks like the mother.

You may notice that what we think of as a **subject** in English sometimes takes a **topic particle**. We'll study particles in the next chapter.

   The ends of the sentences are also variable (some are formal, some plain, some polite). These are the **speech styles** we mentioned in the introduction.

   Focus on sentence structure for now.

(2) Object-complement verbs

Some transitive verbs require an **object complement** in addition to the **direct object** as in *They painted the house gold* or *They called the man a liar*. Saying *They painted the house* is not the same as saying *They painted the house gold*; also, *They called the man* is quite different from *They called the man a liar*. The object complement embellishes the object noun saying something about its state, which results from doing the verb. By painting, the house became gold, for example; now the house is gold.

Example sentences #7 and 8 in the table above have object complements. Here are some more examples. Notice how the complement describes the object (indicated by the arrows).

Subject	Object	Complement	Verb
너는	나를	바보로	여기니?
ne-nun	na-lul	papo-lo	yekini?
you-topic	*I/me-obj.*	*fool-instr.*	*take-Q*

You take me for a fool?

Subject	Object	Complement	Verb
사람들이	벽을	빨갛게	칠했습니다.
salamtul-i	pyek-ul	ppalkah-key	chilhaysssupnita.
people-subj.	*the wall-obj.*	*red-ly*	*painted-formal*

People painted the wall red.

(3) Two-object verbs

Some transitive verbs need two objects, a **direct object** and an **indirect object**, one entity that is handled and the other that receives that first entity. In English, you say the direct object before the indirect object for verbs like *introduce* and *explain* AND you use the preposition *to* before the indirect object (e.g., *Explain that to me*), but for other verbs like *give* and *teach*, saying the indirect object before the direct object sounds more natural, especially in the spoken language (e.g., *Teach me Korean* rather than *Teach Korean to me*).

You have no such option in Korean. You ALWAYS say the indirect object first and use the indirect object particle attached to it. Sentence #9 in the table above is of this type. Here are some more examples. See how the words are ordered in Korean and English:

Subject	Indirect Object	Direct Object	Verb
그 친구가	나에게	윤아를	소개해 줬습니다.
ku chinkwu-ka	na-eykey	yuna-lul	sokayhay cwesssupnita.
that friend-subj.	*me-indirect obj.*	*Yuna-obj.*	*introduction gave-formal*

That friend introduced Yuna to me.

친구가	나에게	전화를	했습니다.
chinkwu-ka	na-eykey	cenhwa-lul	haysssupnita.
friend-subj.	*me-indirect obj.*	*phone-obj.*	*did-formal*

My friend gave me a call. (= My friend gave a call to me.)

친구는	고양이한테	우유를	먹여요.
chinkwu-nun	koyangi-hanthey	wuyu-lul	mekyeyo.
friend-topic	*cat-indirect obj.*	*milk-obj.*	*feed-polite*

My friend feeds the cat milk. (= My friend feeds milk to the cat.)

친구는	동생한테	케이크를	구워 줬어요.
chinkwu-nun	tongsayng-hanthey	kheikhu-lul	kwuwuecwuesseyo.
friend-topic	*sibling-indirect obj.*	*cake-obj.*	*baked-gave-polite*

My friend baked his sister a cake. (= My friend baked a cake for his sister.)

3.2.3 Intransitive verbs

On the other hand, there are verbs that can go with just the subject in a sentence and make sense, as in *I laughed* and *I win!* These verbs are called **intransitive** because the action expressed by the verb is NOT TRANSMITTED to anyone or anything else. Intransitive verbs are by definition no-object verbs, but they come in different types: namely, active verbs, descriptive verbs, existential verbs, linking verbs and locative verbs.

(1) Intransitive active verbs

The first type of intransitive verb is intransitive active verbs, where someone (or something) simply acts. The first example of sentence #3 in the table above (*Jinu left*) belongs to this type. Here are more examples with intransitive verbs:

Subject	Intransitive Verb	Subject	Intransitive Verb
아기가	자요.	달이	떠요.
aki-ka	cayo.	tal-i	tteyo.
baby-subj.	*sleeps-polite*	*moon-subj.*	*rises-polite*
The baby sleeps/is sleeping.		*The moon rises/is rising.*	

(2) Descriptive verbs

The second type of intransitive verb in Korean is the kind that tells *what someone (or something) is like*, **describing** the subject. These are the adjectives that come at the end of the sentence and conjugate, behaving like a kind of verb. Thus, they are considered descriptive verbs, and since they just serve to describe the subject, they are intransitive. The second option in #3 in the table above (*Jinu (is) tall*) belongs to this type. This type of sentence requires the verb *be* in English but not in Korean. Let's see a couple more examples with descriptive verbs.

Subject	Descriptive Verb	Subject	Descriptive Verb
날씨가	좋다.	기분이	나쁘다.
nalssi-ka	cohta.	kipwun-i	napputa.
weather-subj.	*good-plain*	*mood-subj.*	*bad-plain*
The weather (is) good.		*The mood (is) bad.*	

(3) Verbs of existence

Another type of verb that can make a complete sentence with just a subject is the verb of existence (or **existential verbs**). There are two in Korean: 있다 *issta there is/to exist* and 없다 *epsta there is no/not exist*. (Yes —there is an independent verb that means *there is no...* in Korean!) Sentence #1 in the table above is of this type.

Subject	Existential Verb	Subject	Existential Verb
돈이	있어요.	사랑이	없어요.
ton-i	isseyo.	salang-i	epseyo.
money-subj.	*exist-polite*	*love-subj.*	*not exist-polite*
There is money.		*There is no love.*	

Verbs of existence express location when there is a location word.

Location	Subject	Verb
주머니에	돈이	있어요.
cwumeni-ey	ton-i	isseyo.
pocket-loc.	*money-subj.*	*exist-polite*

There is (some) money in my pocket.

가슴에	사랑이	없어요.
kasum-ey	salang-i	epseyo.
heart-loc.	*love-subj.*	*not exist-polite*

There is no love in his/her/my heart.

(4) Linking verbs for equation

English verbs like *be, seem, become, appear,* and *look,* all LINK a complement to the subject or EQUATE the two in one way or another: *She is an engineer, He seems smart,* or *They became friends.* Since the linked element completes the idea about the **subject**, it is called a **subject complement**. These verbs are sometimes called **linking verbs**. You saw this type of verb in the table above in sentences #4 and #5.

<1> 되다, 아니다 *become, not be*

The structure of a sentence (floor-) planned for a verb of equation has the subject followed by the complement and then the verb. Since the two elements are linked, both are marked with a subject particle -이 -i or -가 -ka.

In Korean, 되다 toyta *to become,* 이다 ita *to be,* and 아니다 anita *to not be* belong to this type. (And, yes, Korean has a verb that means *not be!*)

Subject	Complement	Verb
수빈이가	의사가	됐습니까?
swupini-ka	uysa-ka	twaysssupnikka?
Subin-subj.	*doctor-subj.*	*became-formal question*

Has Subin become a doctor?

여기가	방이	아니에요.
yeki-ka	pang-i	anieyyo.
here-subj.	*room-subj.*	*not be-polite*

Here (This place) is not a room.

<2> 이다 *be*

The quintessential linking verb has to be *be,* right? That verb in Korean is 이다 ita *to be,* but unlike the other linking verbs, 이다 ita is written without a space between it and the noun that precedes it. It acts almost like a suffix. And that noun is not marked with a subject particle.

Subject	Complement+*be* Verb
여기**가**	부엌이에요.
yeki-ka	pwuekhieyyo.
here-subj.	*kitchen-polite*

Here/this place is the kitchen.

Subject	Complement+*be* Verb
그분**은**	선생님입니다.
kupwun-un	sensayngnimipnita.
That person-honorific-topic	*teacher-be-formal*

She is a teacher.

Do keep in mind the difference between 이다 ita *to be* and 있다 issta *there is/exists*: 있다 issta is a VERB OF EXISTENCE, AND 이다 ita is a VERB OF EQUATION.

3.2.4 Locative verbs

Finally, there are situations when you need to spell out WHERE. The usual kind of WHERE that you think of might be *where you do something,* like where you shop or where you sleep. That sort of WHERE is optional because you can just say *I shopped today* or *I slept* without specifying where the incidents occurred. The other kind of WHERE we are talking about is the kind without which the sentence is odd or ungrammatical. For example, if you say to your brother, *I put the bag,* he will instantaneously look at you expectantly and demand *Where?* This is because the verb *put* requires a direct object AND a location. Long story short, there are certain verbs, both transitive and intransitive, that need to come with information about WHERE. This type of verbs can be called **locative verbs**, and they were classified as #2 and #10 in the table above. Here are a couple of sentences with transitive verbs that require a location:

Subject	Location	Direct Object	Verb
언니**가**	은행**에**	돈**을**	넣었습니다.
enni-ka	unhayng-ey	ton-ul	nehesssupnita.
sister-subj.	*bank-loc.*	*money-obj.*	*put in-formal*

My older sister put the money in the bank.

창문	옆**에**	돈**을**	두었습니다.
changmwun	yeph-ey	ton-ul	tuesssupnita.
window	*side-loc.*	*money-obj.*	*placed-formal*

(I) left/placed the money next to the window.

Here are sentences with INTRANSITIVE locative verbs:

Subject	Locative	Intransitive Verb
고양이**가**	침대 위**에**	올라갔습니다.
koyangi-ka	chimtay wi-ey	ollakasssupnita.
cat-subj.	*bed on-loc.*	*went up-formal*

The cat got up on the bed.

동생**이**	의자**에**	앉았어요.
tongsayng-i	uyca-ey	ancasseyo.
younger sibling-subj.	*chair-loc.*	*sat down-polite*

My younger sibling sat on the chair.

You can try to argue that the verb 앉다 ancta *to sit* does not REQUIRE location information because you can simply say *He sat*, and the place where the sitting happens doesn't have to be spelled out. To express that meaning in Korean, another locative particle 에서 eyse would have been used, indicating that an action took place in the location (as opposed to the action ending up at a location or destination.) Then, the sentence sounds like your younger sibling squatted down with her feet on the seat of the chair instead of having sat down (normally) ONTO the chair; she was on the chair, and then she sat. You will learn more about these fun particles in detail in the next chapter.

Now you have gotten a taste of the structure of Korean sentences and some basic structural awareness. We now close this section with a fun yet cautionary set of English sentences with the verb *leave*. Based on the lessons from this chapter so far, see what you can make of them—can you find complements, objects, locations, and so on? The Korean translations are also food for thought…

진정한　　　학자가　　　떠났다.
cincenghan　hakca-ka　　ttenassta.
true　　　　*scholar-subj.*　*left-plain*
The true scholar left.

학계를　　　떠난　　　　것이다.
hakkyey-lul　ttenan　　　kesita.
academia-obj.　*left-modifier*　*thing-be-plain*
She left academia.

아픈　가슴을　　안고…
aphun　kasum-ul　anko...
pained　heart-obj.　hold-and...
She left the town heart-broken.

지역사회에는　　　　큰　　구멍을　　　남기며　　떠나
ciyeksahoy-ey-nun　khun　kwumeng-ul　namkimye　ttena
community-loc.-topic　large　hole-obj.　　left-and　　leaving
Leaving the community a huge hole,

동료들을　　　큰　　슬픔에　　　　잠기게　　했다.
tonglyotul-ul　khun　sulphum-ey　　camkikey　hayssta.
colleagues-obj.　large　sadness-location　dwell　　made-plain
She left the colleagues grief-stricken.

3.2.5 Negative sentences

There are several ways to make a sentence negative in Korean, but the structural chang-es are minimal: either add a negative adverb such as 안 an *not* right before the verb or use a suffix expression on the verb, such as -지 않다 -ci anhta *not.*

아기가   안   자요.
aki-ka   an   cayo.
baby-subj.   not   sleep-polite
The baby is not sleeping.

날씨가   좋지 않아요.
nalssi-ka   cohci anhayo.
weather-subj.   good-not-polite
The weather (is) not good.

제니퍼가   문을   안   닫았습니다.
ceyniphe-ka   mwun-ul   an   tatassupnita.
Jennifer-subj.   door-obj.   not   closed-formal
Jennifer did not close the door.

친구가   나에게   전화를   안   했습니다.
chinkwu-ka   na-eykey   cenhwa-lul   an   haysssupnita.
friend-subj.   me-indirect obj.   phone-obj.   not   did-formal
My friend didn't call me.

You also know about inherently negative verbs such as 없다 epsta *there isn't* and 아니다 anita *to not be*:

은행에   돈이   없어요.
unhayng-ey   ton-i   epseyo.
bank-loc.   money-subj.   not exist-polite
There is no money in the bank.

오늘은   수요일이   아니에요.
onul-un   swuyoil-i   anieyyo.
today-topic   Wednesday-subj.   not be-polite
Today is not Wednesday.

Negatives are discussed more fully in chapter 6.

3.3 Word Order

So, you got the general idea about the neutral order of Korean words in a sentence from reading Sentence Structure above. If we add in some elements like time and reason that are not REQUIRED but that embellish the sentence, the default order of informational units in a Korean sentence looks like this:

Subject-Time-Place-Reason-Accompaniment-Indirect Object-Direct Object-Manner-Verb

---

(나는) 어제 학교에서 바빠서 친구랑   선생님께   꽃을 아주 빨리 드렸어요.
(nanun) ecey hakkyo-eyse pappase chinkwulang senseyngnim-kkey kkoch-ul acwu ppalli tulyesseyo.
I-topic   yesterday school-loc. busy-so   friend-with teacher-ind.obj.   flower-obj. very quickly gave-humble-
                                                honorific   polite

I quickly gave the flower to my teacher at school yesterday with my friend because I was busy.

As long as the main verb comes last (i.e., **predicate finality**), it is possible to scramble words around in a Korean sentence. The particles will allow us to keep track of what role each word plays and which is subject, and so on. (This is quite unlike English where the word order makes a huge difference. Think about the two sentences *The mosquito bit the dog* and *The dog bit the mosquito*.)

Moving words around, though, does bring about some special effects in Korean as well. Let's see how that works.

3.3.1 Re-ordering for special attention

Although the basic meaning is maintained when words move out of their normal order (seen in the previous sections), nuances or implications may change. Compare the following sentences, as an example. The first one is neutral, where the speaker is just talking about what happened today, and the next two sentences sound like an answer to the question *Your friend gave WHOM a call?*:

친구가   나한테   전화를   했습니다.
chinkwu-ka na-hanthey   cenhwa-lul haysssupnita.
friend-subj.   me-indirect obj.   phone-obj.   did/called-formal
My friend gave me a call.

친구가   전화를   나한테   했습니다.
chinkwu-ka cenhwa-lul na-hanthey   haysssupnita.
friend-subj.   phone-obj.   I/me-indirect obj.   did/called-formal
My friend gave me a call.

나한테   친구가   전화를   했습니다.
na-hanthey   chinkwu-ka cenhwa-lul haysssupnita.
me-indirect obj.   friend-subj.   phone-obj.   did/called-formal
My friend gave me a call.

Let's try another pair. In the following case, you are just reporting what your naughty dog did. With an active verb, the location appears AFTER the subject by default. The first sentence is neutral, and the next sentence sounds like an answer to the question *The puppy pooped WHERE?*:

강아지**가** 침대**에**   똥을   쌌습니다.
kangaci-ka   chimtay-ey ttong-ul   ssasssupnita.
puppy-subj.   bed-loc.   poop-obj.   pooped-formal
The puppy pooped on the bed.

침대**에**   강아지**가** 똥을   쌌습니다.
chimtay-ey kangaci-ka   ttong-ul ssasssupnita.
bed-loc.   puppy-subj.   poop-obj. pooped-formal
It is <u>on the bed</u> that the puppy pooped.

But all bets are off if you raise the pitch of your voice on a word and say it a little louder. Then, that particular word is emphasized whatever position it is in!

침대에   강아지가 똥을 쌌습니다.
chimtay-ey kangaci-ka   ttong-ul ssasssupnita.
bed-loc.   puppy-subj.   pooped-formal
It is <u>the puppy</u> that pooped on the bed.

Here is another important pair to consider:

책상   위에   책이   있어요.
chayksang wi-ey   chayk-i   isseyo.
desk   top-loc. book-subj.   exist-polite
There is <u>a book</u> on the desk.

책이   책상   위에   있어요.
chayk-i   chayksang wi-ey   isseyo.
book-subj. desk   top-loc. exist-polite
<u>The book</u> is on the desk.

With an existential verb (있어요 isseyo), location first is the default order. Since the first sentence follows the normal order, it is interpreted with a simple existential meaning: that there is something somewhere. The second sentence makes the interpretation of the fronted 책 chayk **definite**, so 책 chayk is understood as *the book*.

In sum, there is a basic order of words in a sentence, which you follow when you are neutrally bringing up or reporting something in a plain, simple, declarative sentence, which is not a question, not a focused answer to a question, nor a contrasted situation. And when that order is disturbed, although the basic meaning relationships are the same, special attention should be drawn to the dislocated element, creating a slightly different interpretation from the normally-ordered sentence. Most often the focused element moves toward the front of the sentence. Lastly, raising the pitch on a word and saying it a little louder is the most powerful way to bring focus to that element.

3.3.2 Re-ordering for what's on my mind

To let you in on the truth … in spoken Korean, speakers actually say what's on their mind first and add on the rest as a sort of afterthought. So in fact, the verb may be said first, and topics (optionally marked with 은 un or 는 nun), subjects (optionally marked with 이 i or 가 ka), objects (optionally marked with 을 ul or 를 lul), or any other elements like time, place, and manner adverbs can all be added as an afterthought. In all the examples below, what appears after the comma is normally expected first:

나가요,　저(는).
nakayo,　ce-(nun).
go out-polite   I-humble-(topic)
(I'm) going out.

아파요,　어디(가)?
aphayo,　eti-(ka)?
hurts-polite   somewhere-subj.
Is anything hurting?/What hurts?

벌써　먹었어요,　점심(을)?
pelsse　mekesseyo,　cemsim(ul)?
already   ate-polite   lunch(-obj.)
Have you eaten already — lunch?

한국어　수업　들어요,　이번　학기(에).
hankwuke　swuep　tuleyo,　ipen　hakki(-ey).
Korean   class   take-polite   this time   term(-loc.)
I'm taking Korean this term.

파티해요,　여기에서?
phathihayyo,　yeki-eyse?
party-do-polite   here-at
Are you having a party here?

좋지 않아요,　날씨가.
cohci anhayo,　nalssi-ka
good not-polite   weather-subj.
The weather (is) not good.

왜　그래요,　자꾸!
way　kulayyo,　cakkwu!
why   do so-polite   repeatedly
Why do you keep bothering me!

어디　가요,　오늘?
eti　kayo,　onul?
where   go-polite   today
Where are you going today?

What about other elements not mentioned in these structures so far? What if there are two nouns in a row? Two adverbs? Which first? To quench your thirst for knowledge, here we offer some more simple guidelines to follow.

3.3.3 Macro to micro

In general, bigger concepts come before smaller concepts in Korean. What counts as bigger? Your last name as opposed to your first name does, and a city is bigger than a neighborhood. A month is bigger than a day. This is often the opposite way of presenting concepts from English:

김연아
kimyena
Yuna Kim

서울특별시	서대문구	신촌동	134
sewulthukpyelsi	setaymwunkwu	sinchontong	134
Special City of Seoul	*Seodaemun District*	*Sinchon Neighborhood*	*134*

134 Sinchon Neighborhood, Seodaemun District, Special City of Seoul

2019년	5월	10일
ichensipkwunyen	owel	sipil
2019-year	*May*	*10th*

May 10, 2019

3.3.4 Modifier before modified

If anything serves to limit, specify, describe or provide information about something else, it can be called a modifier, and it ALWAYS comes before the thing modified in Korean:

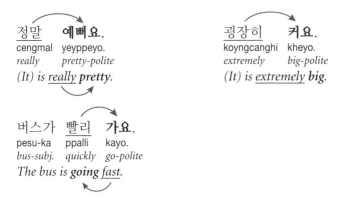

정말 **예뻐요**.
cengmal   yeyppeyo.
really   pretty-polite
(It) is _really_ **pretty**.

굉장히 **커요**.
koyngcanghi   kheyo.
extremely   big-polite
(It) is _extremely_ **big**.

버스가 빨리 **가요**.
pesu-ka   ppalli   kayo.
bus-subj.   quickly   go-polite
The bus is **going** _fast_.

It does not matter how long the modifier is. It *ALWAYS* comes before the modified:

저는 매운 **음식**이 좋아요.
ce-nun   maywun   umsik-i   cohayo.
I-topic   spicy   food-sub   good-polite
As for me, _spicy_ **food** is great.

저는 제 친구가 만드는 **음식**이 좋아요.
ce-nun   cey   chinkwu-ka   mantunun   umsik-i   cohayo.
I-topic   my   friend-subj.   make-ing   food-subj.   good-polite
As for me, **the food** _my friend makes_ is great.

And even the whole background clause typically comes before the main clause in Korean:

배가　　　　고파서　식당에　　　　갔어요.
pay-ka　　　　kophase　siktang-ey　　kasseyo.
stomach-subj.　*hungry-so*　*restaurant-loc.*　*went-polite*
I went to the restaurant, <u>*as I was hungry*</u>.

3.3.5 Adverbs

Adverbs can modify adjectives, as in <u>*very*</u> *cute*, verbs, as in *run <u>quickly</u>*, or sentences, as in <u>*luckily*</u>, *I can go*. In Korean, adverbs tend to come right before the word they modify:

한국은　　　여름에　　　아주　더워.
hankwuk-un　yelum-ey　　acwu　tewe.
Korea-topic　*summer-loc.*　*very*　*hot*
It's very hot in Korea in the summer.

매우　예쁜　　　　　나무들
maywu　yeyppun　　　namwutul
very　*pretty-modifier*　*trees*
(the) very pretty trees

버스가　빨리　　가요.
pesu-ka　ppalli　kayo.
bus-subj.　*quickly*　*go-polite*
The bus is going fast.

Adverbs like 이상하게 isanghakey *strangely* and 안타깝게도 anthakkapkeyto *unfortunately* are called sentential adverbs because they express the mood or attitude of the speaker toward the whole sentence. These sentential adverbs are usually said before the predicate in Korean, coming before or after the subject:

안타깝게도　　토니가　　시험에　　떨어졌어요.
anthakkapkeyto　thoni-ka　　sihem-ey　　ttelecyesseyo.
unfortunately　*Tony-subj.*　*exam-loc.*　*fell-polite*

토니가　　안타깝게도　　시험에　　떨어졌어요.
thoni-ka　anthakkapkeyto　sihem-ey　　ttelecyesseyo.
Tony-subj.　*untortunately*　*exam-loc.*　*fell-polite*
Too bad *Tony didn't make the cut on the exam/failed the exam.*

Rather than thinking of all these quirks or ordering and reordering of words as RULES in Korean, the best tactic is to learn them while speaking Korean with a real person in the right context. You'll gain the intuition right away!

3.4 Sentence Types

So far we've been talking only about STATEMENTS, but traditionally, grammarians talk about three sentence types for English: statements (indicative), questions (interrogative), and commands (imperative). To those, we'll add *let's* suggestions (propositive) in order to make the four Korean **sentence types**.

> We often talk about the different sentence types as if they were related, that is, as if they were based on the statement form. Then, to ask a question, what do you do in English? If it is a question, you pull the *wh*-word to the front of the sentence and add in the auxiliary verb *DO* (*do/does/did*). Do you agree? For *yes/no* questions, you use the auxiliary verb *do* and put that in front of the sentence. Isn't it so? But! If the first or only verb is *be* (or an auxiliary or modal verb, such as *have, can, will, should, would, could, shall, may,* or *might*), you don't need to add *do*; just switch the order of the subject and that first verb. Try it, and see! To make a command, take the subject out. Let's see how to make a suggestion in English: you just use the fixed expression *let's...* in front of the verb. Why don't we tackle negative sentences? How are they formed? Put the negative adverb NOT after the first verb if it is *be* (or an auxiliary or modal verb like *have, can, will, should, would, could, shall, may,* or *might*); otherwise, add *do not* before the verb. If the sentence is in the future or past tense, you'll need auxiliary verbs like *did* and *will*. You didn't realize how complex all these little rules are in English, did you?

Lucky for learners, making questions, commands, and suggestions in Korean is very simple, structurally-speaking. There are different suffixes to use at the end of sentences in various speech styles, discussed in chapter 6, but there is no need to rearrange the words or add auxiliary verbs. Let's check it out.

3.4.1 Statements

The main function of the statement is to transmit FACTUAL INFORMATION—to make a simple, informative statement. This is considered the basic sentence type and you know the basic order of elements, which depend on the verb.

지금 밥 먹어요.
cikum pap mekeyo.
now   rice eat-polite
I am eating now.

오늘은 날씨가 맑아요.
onul-un   nalssika   malkayo.
today-topic   weather-subj   clear-polite
The weather is clear today.

나, 내일 한국에 가.
na, nayil   hankwuk-ey   ka.
I,   tomorrow   Korea-loc.   go
I am going to Korean tomorrow.

저는 일주일에 한 번 편지를 써요.
cenun   ilcwuil-ey   han pen   phyencilul   sseyo.
I-humble-topic   one time   letter-obj.   write-polite   week-loc
I write a letter once a week.

3.4.2 Questions

There are two kinds of questions: *yes–no* questions that elicit an answer that is either a *yes* or a *no*, and *wh*-questions that involve a *wh*-question word (e.g. *who, what, where*).

(1) *yes-no* questions

To ask a *yes-no* question in Korean, you don't have to flip everything around and stand on your head like you do in English. Korean *yes-no* questions are very straightforward. For some speech styles, there is a special sentence-ending suffix on the verb for questions, but in general, you just need to write a question mark or make a sudden sharp rise in intonation at the end of the sentence:

아기가　자**요**? ↗
aki-ka　　cayo?
baby-subj.　sleep-polite question
Does the baby sleep?/Is the baby sleeping?

언니가　은행에　　돈을　　넓었습니**까**? ↗
enni-ka　unhayng-ey　ton-ul　　nehesssupnikka?
sister-subj.　bank-locative　money-obj.　put in-formal question
Did the older sister put the money in the bank?

To ask a simple **negative** question, add the negative adverb 안 an *not* immediately before the verb:

아기가　**안**　자요? ↗
aki-ka　an　cayo?
baby-subj.　not　sleep-polite question
Does the baby not sleep?/Is the baby not sleeping?

언니가　은행에　　돈을　　**안**　넓었습니까? ↗
enni-ka　unhayng-ey　ton-ul　an　nehesssupnikka?
sister-subj.　bank-locative　money-obj.　not　put in-formal question
Did the older sister not put the money in the bank?

To ask an *either-or* **question**, repeat the verb phrase with a negative, raising the last syllable of the positive phrase and optionally raising the last syllable of the negative phrase:

아기가　자, ↗　　안　자? (↗)
aki-ka　cayo,　an　cayo?
baby-subj.　sleep-polite　not　sleep-polite
Is the baby not sleeping or not?

은행에　　돈을　　넓었습니까, ↗　안　넓었습니까? (↗)
unhayng-ey　ton-ul　nehesssupnikka,　an　nehesssupnikka?
bank-loc.　money-obj.　put in-formal question　not　put in-formal question
Did you put the money in the bank or not?

(2) *wh*-questions

To make a *wh*-question, there is no need to pull the *wh*-question word to the beginning of the sentence and change the order of auxiliary verb and subject as in English. In Korean, you should put the question word where its answer would show up in a statement or answer.

나	어제	**학교에**	갔었어.
na	ecey	hakkyo-ey	kassesse.
I	*yesterday*	***school-loc.***	*had gone*

I was at <u>school</u> yesterday.

누가	어제	학교에	갔었어?
nwuka	ecey	hakkyo-ey	kassesse?
who	*yesterday*	*school-loc.*	*had gone*

<u>Who</u> was at school yesterday?

너	어제	**어디**	갔었어?
ne	ecey	eti	kassesse?
you	*yesterday*	***where***	*had gone*

<u>Where</u> were you yesterday?

너	**언제**	학교에	갔었어?
ne	encey	hakkyo-ey	kassesse?
you	***when***	*school-loc.*	*had gone*

<u>When</u> were you at school?

The following is the order in which the five *wh*- (and one *h*-) question words are memorized in Korean schools. It is also the normal order of the regular words and phrases in a sentence that would carry all this information. (We are leaving "why" out because it usually requires another clause):

누가	언제	어디에서	무엇을	어떻게	했나?
nwu-ka	encey	eti-eyse	mwues-ul	ettehkey	hayssna?
who-subj.	*when*	*where-loc.*	*what-obj.*	*how*	*did-plain*

What did who do when where how?

In Korean, asking a question using more than one *wh*-question word is OK, so the question above and the one following are totally legit!

Here's another example. The subject (누가 nwuka *who*) can go between almost any of the question words so long as it is before the object, and *how* and *why* tend to come immediately before the verb.

(너) 내일	(너) 몇 시에	(너) 어디에서	(너) 누구랑	(너) 무엇을	어떻게	해?
(ne) nayil	(ne) myechsi-ey	(ne) eti-eyse	(ne) nwukwulang	(ne) mwues-ul	ettehkey	hae?
(you) tomorrow	*(you) what time-loc.*	*(you) where-loc.*	*(you) with whom*	*(you) what-obj.*	*how*	*do?*

What are you doing tomorrow at what time, where, with whom, and how?

Likewise, in a regular non-question sentence, the same order of information pieces is expected.

3.4.3 Commands

There are special suffixes to use in making commands in the different speech styles, as you will learn about in chapter 6, but as with questions, there is little to change structurally about the sentence. Just like in English, Korean commands drop the subject. On the other hand, you can state the subject when you want to be a little more bossy or forceful both in English and Korean:

홍: 그럼, 좀 쉬어요.
hong: kulem, com swieyo.
Hong: Then, a little rest-polite
Hong: *Get some rest, then.*

최: 네, 그럴게요.
choy: ney, kulelkeyyo.
Choi: yes, do-promiste-polite
Choi: *Yes, I will.*

할머니: 얘들아, 들어와서 밥 먹어!
halmeni: yaytula, tulewase pap meke!
Grandma: Kids, come in and rice eat
Grandma: *You kids, come in for dinner!*

아이들: 네!
aitul: ney!
Kids: Yes!
Kids: *Okay!*

너 여기 앉아라.
ne yeki ancala.
You here sit-plain command
You *sit here.*

3.4.4 Suggestions

Finally, there are also ways to indicate *let's* suggestions in Korean through suffixes, which depend on the speech style, but the word order does not change. There is no word *let* or *let's* that is used (it's expressed by the verb suffix), and the subject 우리 wuli *we* may be used or dropped. If it is dropped, 나하고 같이 na-hako kathi *together with me* or just 같이 kathi *together* is often added to make it clear that it is an invitation.

나하고 같이 운동해요!
nahako kathi wuntonghayyo!
me-with together exercise
Why don't we exercise together?

우리 같이 가자!
wuli kathi kaca!
we together go-let's!
Let's go together!

(우리) 여기서 비빔밥 먹자!
(wuli) yeki-se pipimpap mekca
(we) here-at bibimbap eat-let's
Let's eat bibimbap here.

3.5 Spacing

Now that you know all the parts of speech and how to make up a sentence with the words in the right order, it will be good to learn how to write those words with spaces in the right places. Basically, Korean is written with spaces between words, but it gets a little more complicated with things like particles, dependent nouns, and linking verbs, so it is worth a closer look. Some of this may still be tricky, but try to get the gist now, and you can always use this section as a reference later on.

Spacing is as much a convention as spelling is, though, and to a large extent, what the contemporary users are accustomed to goes! This majority rule makes a little more sense when you consider the fact that King Sejong the Great, the creator of the Korean alphabet himself, also experimented with spelling and spacing, writing with the final consonants separated out from the syllable and with no spaces around words!

In some countries, writing conventions are directed by an institute in charge of language education, and 국립국어 연구원 kwuklipkwukeyenkwuwen *National Institute of the Korean Language* takes on that role on the lower half of the Korean peninsula. This institute lays out and updates a set of spelling and spacing guidelines, taking into account what native speakers do, and they revise their guidelines every so often.

Spelling and spacing matter most when they create ambiguity or confusion. One of the famous spacing examples is 아버지가방에들어가신다 apecikapangeytulekasinta, which can be understood in two different ways:

아버지가   ˅   방에   ˅   들어가신다.
apeci-ka   pang-ey   tulekasinta.
father-subj.   *room-loc.*   *enter-honorific-plain*
Father enters the room.

아버지   ˅   가방에   ˅   들어가신다.
apeci   kapang-ey   tulekasinta.
father   *bag-loc.*   *enter-honorific-plain*
Father enters (a) bag/Someone (honorable) enters Father's bag.

Both 방 pang *room* and 가방 kapang *bag* are words in Korean, and the subject particle -가 -ka can be omitted as in the second sentence (especially in spoken Korean), which creates an ambiguous situation in the sentence if it has no spacing. (The spaces in written language usually correlate with intonation phrasing in speaking.)

Since spacing plays an important part in effective written communication, and it is used in judging how educated the writer is in Korean, we introduce the guidelines below. How you use them is up to you!

3.5.1 No space

Spaces are inserted between words in Korean, but what counts as a word? We'll call your attention to some cases where it is important that NO space is left between units you may otherwise think of as words.

(1) No space between a noun and a particle, or a noun and 이다 *to be*

All Korean parts of speech are independent words except for the particles (조사 cosa) and the verb *to be*, 이다 ita. Since they are not considered independent words, particles and the 이다 ita verb are written attached to the preceding noun, leaving no space between. Once the <u>noun + 조사 cosa</u> or the <u>noun + 이다 ita</u> combination is written together as one word, if the sentence is continuing on, you should insert a space afterwards.

Particles and 이다 ita are in bold in the 한글 hankul below and are preceded by a hyphen in the romanization. Note that there is no space before either. The symbol "v" is inserted to emphasize spacing elsewhere:

이름은 ˅ 김데니이고 ˅ 나이는 ˅ 12 ˅ 살이에요.
ilum-un   kimteyni-iko   nai-nun   12   sal-ieyyo.
name-topic   KimDenny-is-and   age-topic   12   years-be-polite
The name is Denny Kim, and the age is 12.

아버지하고 ˅ 나
apeci-hako   na
father-and   I
(My) father and me

사과나 ˅ 배 둘 다 좋아요.
sakwa-na   pay   twul   ta   cohayo.
apple-or   pear   two   ta   good-polite
Apple or pear, either is fine.

(2) No space between first and last names, but yes, space between last names and titles

People's last names are written before their first names in Korean, with no space between the two, like 배용준 payyongcwun *YongJun Pae*. If one's position, job title, or family relationship title is written after his or her name, a space is needed:

김연아 ˅ 선수 (athlete)
kimyena senswu
Yuna Kim athlete/player

정경화 ˅ 누나 (older sister)
cengkyenghwa nwuna
Older sister Kyung Wha Chung

조수미 ˅ 여사 Mrs./Ms. (for the married)
coswumi yesa
Ms./Mrs. Sumi Jo

이병철 ˅ 할아버지 (grandfather)
ipyengchel halapeci
Old man/Grandpa Byung-chul Lee

배용준 ˅ 장관 *minister* (of a department)
payyongcwun cangkwan
Minister YongJun Pae

정주영 ˅ 회장 C.E.O.
chengcwuyeng hoycang
CEO Ju-yung Chung

임권택 ˅ 선생님 *(teacher)*
imkwenthayk sensayngnim
Dr./Professor Kwon-taek Im

김대중 ˅ 대통령 *President*
kimtaycwung taythonglyeng
President Dae-jung Kim

문익환 [∨] 목사 *Pastor/Reverend*
mwunikhwan moksa
Reverend Ik-hwan Moon

법륜 [∨] 스님 *Venerable*
peplyun sunim
Venerable Pomnyun

백남준 [∨] 씨 *Mr./Ms.*
payknamcwun ssi
Mr. Nam June Paik

김미현 [∨] 양 *Ms.* (for singles)
kimmihyen yang
Ms./Miss Mihyeon Kim

(3) Convention, convention, convention...

When a phrase takes on a new idiomatic or contextual meaning, it is often written with no space. It becomes a sort of compound word (like *bedhead*, or *stirfry*). 한번 han pen *one time*, for example, is written with a space when it is used with its original meaning *once, one time* but when it is used as an intensifier with the meaning *quite, truly,* or *just,* it is written with no space:

한 [∨] 번밖에 못 했어요.
han   penpakkey   mos   haysseyo.
one   time-only   can't   did-polite
I was able to do it only <u>one time</u>.

사람 [∨] 한번 착하네요.
salam   hanpen   chakhaneyyo.
person   once   good-surprise-polite
He is <u>truly</u> *a good man!*

한번 [∨] 해 보지요.
hanpen   hay pociyo.
once   give it a try-polite
I'll <u>just</u> *give it a try.*

> The same guideline holds for spelling. 국립국어연구원 kwuklip-kwukeyenkwuwen *National Institute of the Korean Language* creates a new spelling for a word when it takes on a new meaning and is considered to have obtained a new part of speech status:
>
> 넘어 nem.e *to go over* + connector
> → 너머 ne.me *over*
>
> 있다가 iss.ta.ka *to stay* + interrupted
> → 이따가 i.tta.ka *a little while later*

3.5.2 Yes, space

There are a few cases where it can be tricky in the other direction—where things may not seem like words, but they need spaces before and/or afterwards in Korean. Here we highlight four such cases.

(1) Yes, space between a modifier and a modified noun

Between modifiers and the modified, there is always a space. The first case is adjectives:

부지런한 [∨] 어린이 *a diligent child*
pwucilenhan   elini
diligent   child

멋진 [∨] 여자 *a cool woman*
mescin   yeca
cool   woman

착한 [∨] 남자 *a good man*
chakhan   namca
good-nature   man

Adnominals such as 헌 hen *old*, 무슨 mwusun *what* and 어떤 etten *what sort of* are also modifiers and need a space after them. Possessive adnominals (e.g., 나의 nauy *my*, 너의 neuy *your*, 저의 ceuy *my-humble*) are frequently contracted (e.g., 내 nay *my*, 네 ney *your-minor/peer directed*, 제 cey *my-humble*) and clumped together with the noun in SPOKEN Korean [내책] *my book*, but they, too, should be WRITTEN with a space:

제 [∨] 책이 어디에 있어요?
cey chayk-i eti-ey isseyo?
my (humble) *book-subj.* *where-loc.* *exist-polite*
Where is my book?

헌 [∨] 책이 더 좋아요.
hen chayk-i te cohayo.
old *book-subj.* *more* *good-polite*
I prefer used books./Used books are better for me.

어떤 [∨] 음악을 좋아해요?
etten umak-ul cohahayyo?
what kind of *music-obj.* *like-polite*
What kind of music do you like?

(2) Yes, space before dependent nouns

Dependent nouns, albeit short, pull their weight in terms of spacing: a space is needed between dependent nouns and their obligatory modifiers, even if they are close together when spoken:

예쁜 [∨] 것 *something pretty, the pretty thing*
yeyppeun kes
pretty *thing*

어제 먹은 [∨] 것 *things that I ate yesterday*
ecey mekun kes
yesterday *ate-modifier* *thing*

할 [∨] 수 있어요. *I can.*
hal swu isseyo.
to do *capability* *exist-polite*

점심 먹은 [∨] 지 오래 됐어요?
cemsim mekun ci olay twaysseyo?
lunch *ate* *since* *long* *has been-polite*
Has it been long since you had lunch?

갈 [∨] 거야. 좋은 [∨] 데 가?
kal keya. cohun tey ka?
go *will* *good* *place* *go?*
I'm going to go. *Are you going somewhere nice?*

(3) Yes, space after connecting suffixes

When any sort of grammatical suffix separates two verbs, a space is needed. (Suffixes are indicated in bold in the 한글 hankul and with hyphens in the romanization).

먹고 ᵛ 와.
mek-ko   wa.
eat-and   come
Eat before you come.

가기 ᵛ 싫어요.
ka-ki   silheyo.
going   distasteful-polite
I don't feel like <u>going</u>./I don't want to go.

와서 ᵛ 앉아요.
wa-se   ancayo.
come-and   sit-polite
Come 'n sit!

가지 ᵛ 마세요.
ka-ci   maseyyo.
don't   go-honorific-polite
Please don't go.

더 크게 ᵛ 말씀해 주세요.
te   khu-key   malssumhay cwuseyyo.
more   loudly   speak-honorific-polite
Please speak louder.

한번 놀러 ᵛ 오세요.
hanpen   nol-le   oseyyo.
once   play-in order to   come over-honorific-polite
Come over sometime!

(4) Yes, space before units and counters

Units such as *kilos* and *meters* or counters that are obligatory after numbers and counted nouns are written with a space before them. Numbers need a space after every 10,000. (Don't worry! You'll learn numbers in the next chapter.)

개 ᵛ 세 ᵛ **마리**   three dogs
kay   sey   mali
dog   three   animal-counter

사과 ᵛ 한 ᵛ **개**   one apple
sakwa   han   kay
apple   one   thing-counter

십오 ᵛ **년**   15 years
sipo   nyen
10-5   year

백 ᵛ **미터**   100 meters
payk   mithe
100   meter

이십칠**만** ᵛ 오천삼백이   275,302
isipchilman   ochensampayki
27-10,000   5-thousand-3-hundred-two

3.5.3 You have an option!

In some cases, the National Institute allows both ways of writing, with or without a space.

(1) Noun compounds

Non-personal proper nouns that are compounds (for example, school names or diseases) are written with spaces between the words, but they can also be written without a space without changing the meaning:

한국 ^V 사람 = 한국사람
hankwuk   salam = hankwuksalam
Korea   *people*
Korean person/people

과학 ^V 기술부 = 과학기술부
kwahak   kiswulpwu = kwahakkiswulpwu
science   *technology-department*
Ministry of Science and Technology

보건 ^V 복지 ^V 가족부 = 보건복지가족부
poken   pokci   kacokpwu = pokenpokcikacokpwu
health *welfare* *family-department*
Ministry of Health, Welfare, and Family Affairs

(2) Verbal compounds

When two verbs come together so the second verb can work as an auxiliary (= helping) verb, there is usually a space between the two verbs, although they can also be written as one long verb:

들어 ^V 오세요 = 들어오세요.
tule   oseyyo = tuleoseyyo.
enter *come-honorific-polite*
Please come in.

동생이   힘들어   ^V 해요 = 힘들어해요.
tongsayng-i   himtule   hayyo = himtulehayyo.
Younger sibling-subj. have a tough time-polite
My younger sister is having a tough time.

집이   비어   ^V 있습니다 = 비어있습니다.
cip-i   pie   issupnita = pieissupnita
house-subj. empty-formal
The house is empty.

(3) Shorties

One-syllable adnominals and dependent nouns can be written together:

저 ˅ 거 = 저거   *That (thing)*
ce ke = ceke
that thing

그 ˅ 때 = 그때   *at that time, then*
ku ttay = kuttay
the time when

이 ˅ 분 = 이분   *this honorable person*
i pwun = ipwun
this person-honored

(4) Frequent counters

Frequently used Sino-Korean numbers and units or **counters** can be written with no spaces between them:

일월 이일   *January 2nd*   일학년   *1st grade/freshman*
ilwel iil   ilhaknyen
1-month 2-day   *1-year-in-school*

열두시   *12 o'clock*   10개   *10 (items)*
yeltwusi   yelkay
12-hour   *10-things-counter*

100미터   *100 meters*   2019년   *the year 2019*
paykmithe   ichensipkwunyen
100-meter   *2019-year*

3.5.4 Getting fuzzy...

It is one thing to have rules and another to enforce them. Although the literacy rate is in the high 90's in Korea, speakers prefer certain spacing practices over others, typically not considering small words independent and thus clumping them together with subsequent words. The practice goes beyond what standard rules allow, and you should be aware of what Korean people's actual practices are.

Short words, even whole sentences, are sometimes written without a space in casual writing, such as emails and text messages:

헌책   *used book*   새옷   *new clothes*
henchayk   sayos
used books   *new-clothes*

다했다!   *All finished!*   못가?   *Can't you go?*
dahayssta!   moska?
all-did   *can't-go*

Sentence connectors and endings containing dependent nouns are often written without a space:

올테니까… *(They) will come so…*
oltheynikka…
will-come-so…

갈거예요. *I'm going./I'll go.*
kalkeyeyyo.
will go-polite

할수있어요. *I can do (it).*
halswuisseyo.
to-do-capability-exist-polite

Even the most educated Korean native speakers make frequent spacing and spelling mistakes, and those mistakes do not usually cause confusion. Most native speakers will GENERALLY follow the spacing guidelines, and even though they sometimes make mistakes, the intended meaning can usually be understood from the context!

Now you have an overview of the parts of speech and sentence structure. Korean grammar is fascinating, and yet, we're just getting started! In the next chapters, we'll go through the parts of speech one-by-one, and expression-by-expression. Here comes the fun part! Also, details of what is acceptable change quite frequently. When in doubt, check the 국립국어연구원 kwuklipkwukeyenkwuwen homepage or online dictionaries!

Exercises

3.1 Parts of Speech

Exercise 1. Can you identify the part of speech of the bold portion of each sentence? Choose the correct one.

Noun	Pronoun	Verb	Adjective	Adverb
Particle	Numeral	Adnominal	Interjection	

1) 날씨가 **추워요**. *The weather is cold.*   (Verb/Adjective/Adverb)
   weather-subect   cold-polite

2) 내 **방** *my room*   (Noun/Pronoun/Adjective)
   my   room

3) **맛있게** 드세요. *Bon appetite!*   (Adjective/Adverb/Verb)
   deliciously   eat-polite command

4) **새** 자동차 *new car*   (Adjective/Adverb/Adnominal)
   new   car

5) 같이 **먹어요**. *Let's eat together.*   (Verb/Adjective/Adverb)
   together   eat-polite

6) **네가** 예뻐. *You're pretty.*   (Noun/Pronoun/Adjective)
   you-subject   pretty

7) **하나**, 둘, 셋 *one, two, three*   (Noun/Pronoun/Numeral)
   one   two   three

8) 불고기를 **좋아해요**. *I like bulgogi.*   (Particle/Interjection/Verb)
   bulgogi-object   like-polite

9) **아야!** 아파요! *Ouch! It hurts!*   (Particle/Interjection/Verb)
   ouch!   (it's) painful-polite

3.2 Korean Sentence Structure

Exercise 2. Circle the verb in bold if it is TRANSITIVE.

1) 동생은 한국사를 **전공합니다.**
   younger sibling-topic   Korean history-object   major-formal
   My younger sibling is majoring in Korean history.

2) 한국어가 **좋아요.**
   Korean-subject   good/likeable-polite
   Korean is likeable (to me).

3) 한국어를 **좋아해요.**
   Korean-object   like-polite
   (I) like Korean.

4) 나는 김 선배를 형같이 **여깁니다.**
   I-topic   senior-object   brother-like   take-formal
   I think of upperclassman Kim as my brother.

5) 친구가 나에게 이메일을 **했습니다.**
   friend-subject   me-indirect obj.   email-object   did-formal
   My friend emailed me.

6) 언니가 은행에서 돈을 **찾았습니다.**
   sister-subject   bank-at   money-object   withdrew-formal
   My older sister withdrew money from the bank.

7) 여기가 내 방**이에요.**
   here-subject   my room-polite
   Here is my room.

8) 김치가 **매워요.**
   kimchi-subject   spicy-polite
   The kimchi (is) spicy.

9) 내일 학교에 **가요.**
   tomorrow   school-to   go-polite
   (I) go to school tomorrow.

Exercise 3. Circle any subjects and draw a box around any direct objects in these sentences. Keep in mind that not every sentence necessarily has an overt subject and an object.

1) 김치가 매워요. *The kimchi (is) spicy.*
   kimchi   spicy-polite

2) 내일 학교에 가요. *(I) go to school tomorrow.*
   tomorrow   school-to go-polite

3) 내일이 내 생일이에요. *Tomorrow is my birthday.*
   tomorrow-subject   my birthday-is polite

4) 김치를 매일 먹어요. *(I) eat kimchi everyday.*
   kimchi   everyday   eat-polite

5) 낚시가 아주 재미있어요. *Fishing is really fun.*
   Fishing   very   fun-polite

6) 엄마가 나한테 지갑을 줬어요. *Mom gave me a wallet.*
   Mom   me-to   wallet   gave-polite

Exercise 4. Make the following sentences negative using *not*, negative verbs, etc.

1) 나는 학생이에요. *I am a student.*

_____

2) 친구가 지금 방에 있어요. *My friend is in the room now.*

_____

3) 나는 오늘 학교에 가요. *I go to school today.*

_____

4) 비빔밥이 맛있어요. *Bibimbap is delicious.*

_____

5) 날씨가 좋아요. *The weather is nice.*

_____

3.3 Word Order

Exercise 5. How many different ways can you say the following sentence? Shuffle the words around and write at least five different versions!

오늘   친구하고   집에서   공부했습니다.
today   friend-and   home-location   studied -formal
I studied at home with a friend today.

1) _____

2) _____

3) _____

4) _____

5) _____

Exercise 6. Rewrite the following phrases according to Korean word order.

1) 필라델피아시,   펜실베니아주
   Philadelphia city   Pennsylvania State
   → 펜실베니아주 필라델피아시

2) 1월   2020년
   January   year 2020

   → _____

3) 5월   5일   2010년
   May   day five   year 2010

   → _____

4) 연아   김
   Yunah   Kim

   → _____

5) 시애틀시   킹카운티   워싱턴주
   Seattle City   King County   Washington State

   → _____

6) 종로구   서울시
   Jongno District   Seoul City

   → _____

Exercise 7. Where would the given modifier go in each sentence?

1) 정말: 아기가   예뻐요.
   really   baby-sub   pretty-polite
   The baby is very pretty.

   _____

2) 큰: 공원에서   나무가   넘어졌어요.
   big   park-at   tree-subject   fell-polite
   A big tree fell in the park.

   _____

3) 빨리: 인터넷에서   산   신발이   왔어요.
   quickly   internet-on   bought   shoes-subject   came-polite
   The shoes I ordered on the Internet came fast.

   _____

4) 무척: 선생님께서   나한테   잘   해 주세요.
   very   teacher-subj.-hon.   me-to   well   do-for-honorific-polite
   The teacher acts very well (kindly) toward me.

   _____

5) 꽤: 좋은   소식이네요.
   quite   good-modifier   news- is-polite
   That's very good news!

   _____

6) 아주: 오늘도   날씨가   추워요.
   very   today-also   weather-subject   cold-polite
   The weather is very cold today, too.

   _____

3.4 Sentence Types

Exercise 8. Identify each sentence as a S (statement), Q (question), C (command), or P (proposal/suggestion).

1) 가: 여기 앉으세요. _____ *Please sit here.*

   나: 네, 감사합니다. _____ *Thank you.*

2) 가: 오늘 같이 운동하자! _____ *Let's exercise together today.*

   나: 오늘 바쁜데 내일 어때? _____ *I am busy today, so how about tomorrow?*

3) 가: 누구세요? _____ *Who is it?*

   나: 제이미예요. _____ *It's Jamie.*

4) 가: 문 열어 주세요. _____ *Please open the door.*

   나: 잠깐만 기다리세요. _____ *Wait a minute.*

Exercise 9. What would be the questions to yield the following answers? Put the question word in parentheses in the right place to make the question in Korean.

1) _____

   언니가   국   먹어요. (뭐) ← *What is your sister doing?*
   sister-subject soup eat-polite

2) _____

   언니가   지금 자요. (누가) ← *Who's sleeping now?*
   sister-subject now   sleep-polite

3) _____

   언니가   방에서 자요. (어디에서) ← *Where is the sister sleeping?*
   sister-subject room-in sleep-polite

4) _____

   언니가   열 시에   자요. (언제) ← *When does the sister go to bed?*
   sister-subject ten o'clock-at sleep-polite

3.5 Spacing

Exercise 10. Rewrite each sentence below with appropriate spacing between words as shown in example #1!

1) 제이름은제이미예요.
   My name is Jamie.
   → 제 이름은 제이미예요.

2) 저는열아홉살이고대학교삼학년입니다.
   I am nineteen years old, and I am a junior at college.

   → _____

3) 제동생이름은진아예요.
   My sister's name is Jina.

   → _____

4) 진아는대학생이아니에요.
   Jina is not a college student.

   → _____

5) 동생은고등학교에다닙니다.
   My younger sibling goes to high school.

   → _____

6) 저는동생하고친해서매일전화합니다.
   I am close to my younger sibling, so I call her everyday.

   → _____

7) 우리가족은플로리다에삽니다.
   My family lives in Florida.

   → _____

8) 저는우리가족이보고싶습니다.
   I miss my family a lot.

   → _____

9) 그래서이번방학에플로리다에갈겁니다.
   So I will go to Florida this school break.

   → _____

Particles

In this chapter we'll explore in detail those particles mentioned in chapter 3 that demonstrate the intricacy and curiosity of Korean grammar at its best. You will see what variety in kind and richness of nuance they come in! If you can learn to manipulate particles and gain intuitions about them, you will be one step closer to obtaining a native speaker's finesse.

So what are particles? Particles are short, one- or two-syllable "words" that attach to nouns. They are sort of like English suffixes in that they cannot be words on their own and must attach to a "real" word, a noun. They are different in that they attach to ANY noun that they are meant for, unlike many English suffixes that can attach only to a handful of words (Think about how you can say *warmth* but NOT *coolth*, or *clarity* but NOT *strangity*).

What do particles do? Some particles tell us the grammatical role of the noun they attach to in the sentence, such as direct object or subject. Others add meanings comparable to English words. Some particles can also make a great difference in the nuance or implication of what you say.

It is sometimes difficult to determine whether a particle has a strictly grammatical function or some "larger" meaning, so we have simplified matters by putting particles into four categories: grammatical particles, lesser-grammatical particles, meaning-based particles, and context-based particles. This way of categorizing particles is different from standard grammar, and we hope you find it helpful and not overly technical. Let us begin with the grammatical particles. They can be tricky.

4.1 Grammatical Particles

Grammatical particles indicate what grammatical role the noun they attach to plays in the sentence, and the most important grammatical functions a noun can play are probably the roles of SUBJECT and OBJECT. You can tell the subject and the object of the sentence in English by the word order, and the same is largely true of Korean, as we saw in chapter 3: there is a default Subject-Object-Verb (SOV) word order in Korean sentences. Since this is true, grammatical particles are usually left out in everyday conversations. Here are example sentences with no grammatical particles:

강아지 침대 올라갔어요.
kangaci chimtay ollakasseyo.
puppy *bed* *got up-polite*
The puppy climbed onto the bed.

병곤이 의사 됐습니다.
pyengkoni uysa twayssupnita.
Byeong-Gohn *doctor* *became-formal*
Byeong-Gohn has become a doctor.

언니, 나   책   빌려줘.
enni,   na   chayk   pillyecwe.
sister   I/me   book   lend
Sis, lend me (a/the) book.

부침개   저   주려고   만드셨어요?
pwuchimkay   ce   cwulyeko   mantusyesseyo.
pancake   me-humble   give-for   made-honorific-polite
Did you make the pancake with me in mind?

By convention, however, particles are necessary in formally written Korean. In other words, you can freely leave out grammatical particles in your texts to your friends, but it would be more proper to use them in an email to your professor.

With some of the Korean sentences above you might have felt that it is not very clear who is the doer and who is the receiver of the action. This is because you don't have useful clues to make sense of what you are reading such as the larger context or intonation, pauses, and phrasing that help clarify the meaning in spoken language. Even in spoken Korean, the grammatical particles help illuminate the intended meanings, especially when words are scrambled around in the sentence.

There are also times when you HAVE TO use the particles. Besides formal speech situations such as business presentations or public lectures and when you want to avoid miscommunication and speak more "properly," there are situations that REQUIRE the use of particles; otherwise, the sentences would sound ungrammatical. So! It is a good idea to learn what the particles are and how to use them. Let's begin with three grammatical particles.

4.1.1 Subject-FOCUS particle: -이/가

Our first item of interest, the **subject-focus particle**, comes as a tag-team set of -이 -i and -가 -ka. For a noun that ends in a consonant, you need to use -이 -i, and for a vowel-final noun, you need to use -가 -ka.

Try saying these words: *Ta-da, city, Fido.* Now try these words: *dog-paw, CITGO, fight-king.* Which were easier to say? Definitely the first set, right? In general, it's harder to say sequences of consonants, as in the second set, than alternating consonants and vowels (in **open syllables**). Whether a word ends in a consonant or a vowel matters a lot in Korean grammar. The subject-focus particle -이/가 -i/ka attests to this sensitivity. The suffix -이 -i goes with a consonant-final noun and -가 -ka with a vowel-final noun to help achieve the desired alternation of consonants and vowels. That way, consonants do not come into contact, and pronunciation is smooth. Let's look at some examples. In general, the subject-focus particle is a marker of the **subject** of the sentence:

아기가   자요.
aki-ka   cayo.
baby-subj.   sleep-polite
The/a baby sleeps.

날씨가   나빠요.
nalssi-ka   nappayo.
weather-subj.   bad
The weather is bad.

그 학생이   숙제   안   했어요.
ku haksayng-i   swukcey   an   haysseyo.
that student-subj.   homework   not   did-polite
That student didn't do the homework.

Of the nouns in a sentence that you may deem the subject of the sentence, only certain kinds can be marked with the subject-focus particle -이/가 -i/ka. Let's see when you would use the subject particle.

(1) To add new information to the conversation

Use the particle -이/가 -i/ka when you introduce a new idea or information into the conversation:

잠깐!   어디서   개가   짖어요.
camkkan!   etise   kay-ka   ciceyo.
wait   somewhere   dog   bark-polite
Wait! A dog is barking somewhere.

어제   형이   왔었어요.
ecey   hyeng-i   wassesseyo.
yesterday   brother-subj.   came-polite
(My) big brother was here yesterday.

그런데 형이   직장   잡았대요.
kulentey hyeng-i   cikcang   capasstayyo.
and/but   brother-subj.   job-obj.   grabbed-they say-polite
And, he says he found a job.

In all these cases, the information shared is newly introduced. Let's take another example:

나: 오늘 숙제가   있어요?
na: onul   swukcey-ka   isseyo?
me: today   homework-subj.   exist-polite
Me: Is there homework today?

은수: 숙제가   없어요.
unswu: swukcey-ka   epseyo.
Eunsoo: homework-subj.   not exist-polite
Eunsu: There is no homework.

In this short exchange, the subject-focus particle is used in both sentences. Even though the word 숙제 swukcey is repeated, it is yet to become an established grammatical topic of the conversation. (Note that you can't refer to the *homework as "it"* even in English in 은수's unswu's answer. Also, 은수 unswu doesn't start talking about the nature of the homework in her answer.) So, if you are going to use a particle at all, it is going to be the subject-focus particle. In fact, most often when using the verbs of existence, you'll need to use -이/가 -i/ka because the existence or non-existence of something is new information, even in an answer to a question.

(2) To identify a particular individual that is the subject of the sentence

Another important function of the subject-focus particle is to pick out a particular individual from the rest:

이 책**이**   제 거예요.
i chaek-i   cey keyeyyo.
this book-subj.   *my-humble thing-be-polite*
This (particular/very) book (and not the others) is mine.

고추장**이**   안   맵네요.
kochwucang-i   an   maypneyyo.
hot pepper paste-subj.   *not*   *spicy-surprise-polite*
This (particular) pepper paste is not spicy (unlike others).

This is to say that the subject-focus particle is used when you are marking subjects that are **in focus**, which can be translated as "*It is … that/who*" or said with a little more emphasis on the word in English:

진: 내일   정호**가**   온댔어요?
cin: nayil   cengho-ka   ontaysseyo?
      tomorrow   *Jeongho-subj.*   *come-hearsay-polite*
Jin: Did you say Jeongho is coming tomorrow?

희: 정호는   안   와요.   상호**가**   와요.
huy: cengho-nun   an   wayo.   sangho-ka   wayo.
      Jeongho-topic   *not*   *come-polite*   *Sangho-subj.*   *come-polite*
Hee: Jeongho isn't coming. <u>Sangho</u> is coming.

In the short exchange above, 희 huy wants to make sure 진 cin understands that it is 상호 sangho who will be coming, so she FOCUSES on 상호 sangho by marking that noun with the subject-focus particle.

(3) To request and provide an answer that is the subject in focus

In general, *wh*-question words and the answers are in focus because people expect a specific answer to what they are asking about. This explains why you need to use the particle -이/가 -i/ka when asking for and providing specific information:

A: 내일   **누가**   와?
   nayil   nwuka   wa?
   tomorrow   *who-subj.*   *come*
   <u>*Who*</u> *is coming tomorrow?*

B: 학교   친구들**이**   놀러 와요.
   hakkyo   chinkwutul-i   nolle wayo.
   school   *friends-subj.*   *play-for-come-polite*
   (Some) <u>*school friends*</u> *are coming to play.*

X: 주머니에 **뭐가** 들었어요?
cwumeniey   mwe-ka   tulesseyo?
pocket-loc.   what-subj.   entered-polite
What is it that's in your pocket?

Y: **지갑이** 들었어요.
cikap-i   tulesseyo.
wallet-subj.   entered-polite
A wallet is in it.

You can also think of this usage as similar to the preceding usages: the fact that it is a wallet that is in the pocket is NEW INFORMATION, and it is a WALLET that is in focus.

(4) With the verbs 되다 and 아니다

So far, everything you saw marked with the subject-focus particle has been the subject of the sentence. What might not look like a subject in English, though, is sometimes considered a grammatical subject in Korean and marked with -이/가 -i/ka.

되다 toyta *to become* and 아니다 anita *to not be* are two verbs that demand the subject-focus particle.

은비가   (기자**가**   됐어요).
unpi-ka   (kica-ka   twaysseyo).
Eunbi-subj.   reporter-subj.   became-polite
Eunbi became/has become a reporter.

둘 다   (대학원생**이**   아니에요).
twul ta   (tayhakwensayng-i   anieyyo).
two all   graduate student-subj.   not-be-polite
Neither is a graduate student.

You can recall from chapter 3 that a complement, like *reporter* in the first sentence, is the same entity as the subject noun (*Eunbi*), so they both get the subject-focus particle. Or, you can simply memorize that before the verbs 되다 toyta and 아니다 anita, you normally use the subject-focus particle -이/가 -i/ka:

기자**가**   됐어요.
kica-ka   twaysseyo.
reporter-subj.   became-polite

Literally, *A reporter "has become."*

대학원생**이**   아니에요.
tayhakwensayng-i   anieyyo.
graduate student-subj.   not be-polite

Literally, *A graduate student "is not."*

(5) When not to leave out the subject-FOCUS particle in conversations

As mentioned before, the subject-focus particle can be left out in casually spoken Korean:

은비   기자   됐어요.
unpi   kica   twaysseyo.
Eunbi   reporter   became-polite
Eunbi became/has become a reporter.

둘   다   대학원생   아니에요.
twul   ta   tayhakwensayng   anieyyo.
two   all   graduate student   not be-polite
Neither is a graduate student.

In incomplete sentences, (that is, in sentence fragments), you can have the subject-focus particle in or not. The difference is that the subject particle emphasizes the agency of the doer (the fact that they did it):

A: 누가   까비 때렸어요?   *Who hit Gabi?*
   nwu-ka   kkapi ttaylyesseyo?
   who-subj. Gabi hit-polite

B: 은비가요.   *Eunbi (did).*
   unpi-ka-yo.
   Eunbi-subj.-polite

B': 은비요.   *(It's) Eunbi.*
   unpiyo.
   Eunbi-polite

Should the absence of the particle cause confusion, however, leave it in:

친구   선물   샀어요.
chinkwu   senmwul   sasseyo.
friend   gift   bought-polite
(I) bought a gift for my friend.(?) or My friend bought a gift.(?)

친구가   선물을   샀어요.
chinkwu-ka   senmwulul   sasseyo.
friend-subj. gift-obj.   bought-polite
My friend bought a gift.

To summarize, the subject-focus particle -이/가 -i/ka attaches to a noun to indicate that it is the subject of the sentence. Although it is often left out in casual conversations, it is recommended in formally spoken Korean, and using the subject-focus particle is a must in a complete, written sentence if (i) the subject itself or the information about the subject is new, (ii) the subject is the focus of the conversation, or (iii) the verb (such as 되다 toyta, 아니다 anita) requires it. Also, remember to leave the particle in if dropping it causes confusion.

4.1.2 Object-FOCUS particle: -을/를

The **object-focus particle** -을 ul/-를 lul attaches to a noun to signal that that noun receives or is somehow affected by the action expressed by the verb. Like the subject-focus particle, the object-focus particle is sensitive to whether the preceding noun ends in a consonant, for which -을 -ul is used, or in a vowel, for which -를 -lul is used.

So, when do you use the object-focus particle?

(1) To mark the grammatical object

You'll remember from chapter 3 that verbs like *bite* that "transfer" the subject's action onto the object are called transitive verbs; the object-focus particle marks the object of TRANSITIVE verbs:

개가 내 손**을** 물었어요.
kay-ka nay son-ul mwulesseyo.
dog-subj. my hand-obj. bit-polite
The dog bit <u>my hand</u>.

형이 개**를** 혼냈어요.
hyeng-i kay-lul honnaysseyo.
older brother-subj. dog-obj. scolded-polite
My older brother scolded <u>the dog</u>.

(2) When to use the object-FOCUS particle in conversations

You know that the subject-focus particle -이/가 -i/ka is omitted in casually spoken Korean. The object-focus particle -을/를 -ul/lul is even more likely to be left out in spoken Korean. The objects below (boldfaced in Korean, underlined in English translation) are easily identifiable from the context without the particle:

너 오늘 **아침** 꼭 먹어!
ne onul achim kkok meke!
you today breakfast definitely eat
Be sure to eat <u>breakfast</u> today!

그분 저 소개해 주실래요?
ku pwun ce sokayhaycwusillayyo?
that person-honorific me-humble introduce-honorific-wanna-polite
Could you introduce <u>her</u> to me?

나 **피아노** 안 칠래.
na phiano an chillay.
I/me piano not play-wanna
I don't wanna play <u>the piano</u>.

In formal situations, the object-focus particle tends to show up a little more often (along with any other intended particles) both in spoken and especially written Korean. If you want to emphasize or clarify (that is, grammatically put the **focus** on) the object, you want to use the particle. In English, this "focus" is comparable to *it is … that/who.* Or, you say the object noun a little louder with an exaggerated intonation:

나 채소 안 좋아해요. **과일을** 좋아해요.
na chayso an cohahayyo. kwai-lul cohahayyo.
I/me veggies not like fruit-obj. like-polite
I don't like veggies. It is <u>fruit</u> that I like.

뭐를/뭘   잃어버렸어? 카드를?
mwe-lul/mwe-l   ilhepelyesse?   khatu-lul?
what-obj.   *lost*   *card*

<u>*What*</u> *is it that you've lost?* <u>*A credit card?*</u>

(3) Translation mismatch

Choosing between the subject-focus and object-focus particles is straightforward as long as you know whether the noun they attach to is the subject or the object in the KOREAN sentence. There are situations where that might not be so easy, though. The following verbs are the infamous intransitive-transitive pairs. Depending on their transitivity, you need different particles. Learn them here and master them now. 좋다 cohta and 싫다 silhta are intransitive descriptive verbs that are used with a subject noun (with -이/가 -i/ka), while 좋아하다 cohahata and 싫어하다 silhehata are transitive active verbs that are used with an object (with -을/를 -ul/lul).

나는   비(가)   좋아.   *I like Rain.*
na-nun   pi(-ka)   coha.   (Literally, *As for me, Rain is good.*)
I/me-topic *rain-subj.* *good*

나는   비(를)   좋아해. *I like Rain.*
na-nun   pi(-lul)   cohahay.
I/me-topic *rain-obj.*   *like*

나는   그   치마(가)   싫어.   *I don't like that skirt.*
na-nun   ku   chima(-ka)   silhe.   (*I don't feel like wearing it.*)
I/me-topic *that* *skirt-subj.* *distasteful*

나는   그   치마(를)   싫어해. *I don't like that skirt.*
na-nun   ku   chima(-lul) silhehay.
I/me-topic *that* *skirt-obj.*   *dislike*

The particle use might also be confusing when the English translation does not quite match up with the transitivity of the Korean verb:

나는   돈(이)   필요해. *I need money.*
na-nun   ton(-i)   philyohay.
I/me-topic *money-subj.* *necessary*

나한테   현금(이) 좀   있어요. (*I*) *got a bit of cash.*
na   hyenkum(-i) com isseyo.   (Literally, *there is a little cash on me.*)
I/me-loc. *cash-subj.* *little* *exist-polite*

내가   현금(을) 좀   갖고 있어요. (*I*)*'ve got a bit of cash.*
nay-ka   hyenkum(-ul) com kacko isseyo.
I/me-sub. *cash-obj.*   *little* *carry-ing ("have")-polite*

4.1.3 Possessive particle: -의

While the other two grammatical particles tell you about the function of the noun in the sentence or its relationship to the verb, the possessive particle is about the relationship between two nouns.

(1) Possession relationship

If you own a car, it's *your* car, and if your sister owns it, it's *her* car. Words like *your* and *her* indicate who possesses what, so they are called **possessive pronouns** (some people call them **genitive**). Noun-to-noun possessive relationship in English is expressed with either an *apostrophe + s ('s)* or the preposition *of*. In Korean, the particle -의 -uy is added to a noun to show that that noun has ownership of the noun that follows it. -의 -uy is usually pronounced as [에 ey]:

선생님의	책	*a/the teacher's book*
sensayngnim-uy	chayk	
teacher-poss.	*book*	

사회의	역군	*a/the pillar of society (= society's pillar)*
sahoy-uy	yekkwun	
society-poss.	*worker, main force*	

But! -의 -uy, as in 선생님의 책 sensayngnim-uy chayk, is rarely used in real life, and when it is used, it is to contrast the teacher's book to someone else's or to emphasize that it is no one else's but the teacher's book. In spoken Korean, the possessive relationship is expressed by putting two nouns together, where the second noun belongs to the first noun: just 선생님 책 sensayngnim chayk. The order is always the same in Korean, whether you use *'s* or an *of* construction in English.

엄마	방	*Mom's room*
emma	pang	
mom	*room*	

가방	지퍼	*zipper of the bag (= bag's zipper)*
kapang	ciphe	
bag	*zipper*	

냄비	손잡이	*pot handle (= handle of the pot, pot's handle)*
naympi	soncapi	
pot	*handle*	

(2) Temporal and spatial relationship

Two location nouns or two temporal nouns also use this "NOUN'S NOUN" pattern.

학교	앞	*front of the school*
hak-gyo	ap	(*school's front*)
school	front	

둘	사이	(*the space/relationship*) *between the two*
twul	sai	(or, *the two people's relationship*)
two	between	

3 년	후	*three years later*
3 nyen	hwu	(Literally, *three years' afterward*)
3 years	after	

Korean speakers conceptualize the relationship in such a way, though no one really puts in the particle -의 -uy to express it.

(3) Other grammatical relationships

When two nouns are connected with the possessive particle 의 uy in literary or scholarly writings, the particle represents various grammatical relationships, being comparable to the English preposition *of*:

로마	제국의	패망	*the fall of the Rome Empire*
roma	ceykwuk-uy	phaymang	(*the Roman Empire falls/fell*)
Roman	Empire's	collapse, defeat	

도시의	파괴	*the destruction of the city*
tosi-uy	phakoy	(*the city is/was destroyed; someone destroyed the city*)
city's	destruction	

꽃의	계절	*the season of flowers*
kkoch-uy	kyeycel	(*the season in which flowers bloom*)
flower's	season	

일생일대의	실수	*the mistake of a lifetime*
ilsayngiltay-uy	silswu	
one lifetime's	mistake	

4.1.4 Summary of the grammatical particles

Particles	Function	Sample Sentences
subject-FOCUS particle: -이 (after a C-noun) -가 (after a V-noun)	To add new information to the conversation	어제 우리 집에 친구가 왔어요. *Yesterday, my friend came to my home.* 꽃이 예뻐요. *The flower is pretty.*
	To identify a particular individual that is the subject of the sentence	그건 제 게 아니에요. 이게 제 거예요. *(spoken)* 그것은 제 것이 아니에요. 이것이 제 것이에요. *(written)* *That's not mine. This is mine. (It is this that is mine.)*
	To request and provide an answer in *wh*-questions	A: 누가 왔어? *Who came?* B: 친구가 왔어요! *My friend came!*
	With the verbs 되다 and 아니다	A: 이름이 수미예요? 　*Is your name Sumi?* A: 아니요. 수미가 아니에요. 수민이에요. 　*No, my name is not Sumi. It's Sumin.*
object-FOCUS particle: -을 (after a C-noun) -를 (after a V-noun)	To mark the grammatical object	비빔밥을 좋아해요. *It is Bibimbap that I like.* 김치를 싫어해요. *It is Kimchi that I dislike.*
possessive particle: -의	To mark the first noun to show "ownership" of the second noun	친구의 가방 *a/the friend's bag*
	Temporal and spatial relationship	일 년 후 *one year later* 집 앞 *in front of the house*
	Other grammatical relationships	꽃의 계절 *the season of flowers; flower season*

4.2 Lesser-grammatical Particles

We have put six particles in the lesser-grammatical particle category. Like the grammatical particles, they also tell you something about the GRAMMATICAL FUNCTION the noun plays, but the lesser-grammatical particles add significant MEANING so they are usually not omitted. The concepts captured by lesser-grammatical particles in Korean appear mostly in the form of PREPOSITIONS in English.

4.2.1 Locative-CONTACT particle: -에

The first lesser-grammatical particle to introduce is the locative-CONTACT particle -에 -ey, which has various usages. Despite its versatility, its core meaning is comparable to the English preposition *onto* (or *into*), where either *on/in* or *to* can be highlighted depending on the kind of verb it appears with. It marks the noun as the DESTINATION or TARGET (that is, some sort of location), and the POINT OF CONTACT, so we call this particle a locative-CONTACT particle.

(1) -에 for point of contact

The core sense of the particle -에 -ey is that of contact, specifically, a POINT OF CONTACT (at some place).

If something exists, it is somewhere, making contact with some physical space. So the existential verbs 있다 issta *to exist/stay* and its negative counterpart 없다 epsta *to not exist* frequently show up with this particle:

지금	정류장에	있어.
cikum	cenglywucang-ey	isse.
now	*bus stop-loc.*	*exist*

(I'm) at the bus stop now.

잠깐	여기에	있어.
camkkan	yeki-ey	isse.
short while	*here-loc.*	*stay*

Stay here for a sec.

(2) -에 for target point of contact

The locative-CONTACT particle 에 ey is interpreted as *on(to)* or *in(to)* when it meets contact verbs (e.g. 앉다 ancta *to sit*, 눕다 nwupta *to lie down*, (손)대다 (son)tayta *to touch*, 넣다 nehta *to put in*, 놓다 nohta *to put down/release*, 담다 tamta *to hold (in a container)*, 두다 twuta *to leave (something somewhere)*, 얹다 encta *to place/set (on shelf)*, 싣다 sitta *to load up*, 올리다 ollita *to raise*, 풀다 phwulta *to release*, 감추다 kamchwuta *to conceal*, 숨기다 swumkita *to hide*, or 붙이다 pwuthita *to attach*). It marks the point of contact WHERE THE OBJECT ENDS UP AT/IN:

작품에	손대지	마시오.
cakphwum-ey	sontayci	masio.
artwork-loc.	*touch-comp.*	*don't-formal*

No touching the artwork.
(Literally, *Do not touch the artwork.*)

그	의자에	앉지	말아요.
ku	uyca-ey	ancci	malayo.
that	*chair-loc.*	*sit-comp.*	*don't-polite*

Please don't sit on that chair.

짐을	트럭에	실어.
cim-ul	thulek-ey	sile.
load-obj.	*truck-loc.*	*load*

Load the luggage in/onto the truck.

책	가방에	넣어요.
chayk	kapang-ey	neheyo.
book	*bag-loc.*	*put in-polite*

Put the book in the bag.

Of the physical contact verbs, RELEASE verbs that have the meaning of *putting away or releasing something* (e.g. 넣다 nehta *to put in*, 놓다 nohta *to put down/release*, 담다 tamta *to hold (in a container)*, 두다 twuta *to leave*, 얹다 encta *to set/place (on shelf)*, 싣다 sitta *to load up*, 올리다 ollita *to raise*, 풀다 phwulta *to release*, 감추다 kamchwuta *to conceal*, 숨기다 swumkita *to hide*, and 붙이다 pwuthita *to attach*) are often used with 에다 eyta or 에다가 eytaka in spoken Korean in order to emphasize the physical contact:

짐을   트럭에(다가)   실어.
cim-ul   thulek-ey(taka)   sile.
load-obj.   truck-loc.   load
Load the luggage into the truck.

가방   바닥에(다)   놓아요.
kapang   patak-ey(ta)   nohayo.
bag   floor-loc.   put down-polite
Put your bag (right) on/onto the floor.

(3) -에 for destination point of contact

The particle -에 -ey can also be attached to a DESTINATION noun, which is a target point that is just a bit farther than the physical target we just saw:

집에   늦게   와요.
cip-ey   nuckey   wayo.
house-loc.   late   come-polite
(I'm) coming home late.

부산에   운전해서   가요?
pwusan-ey   wuncenhayse   kayo?
Busan-loc.   driving   go-polite
Are you driving to Busan?

방금   공항에   도착했어요.
pangkum   konghang-ey   tochakhaysseyo.
just now   airport-loc.   arrived-polite
I just arrived at the airport.

Since the locative-CONTACT particle tells you about the destination, it is also used with (inanimate) entities that receive an action:

우리   집에   전화하자.
wuli   cip-ey   cenhwahaca.
we/us   home-loc.   call-suggestion
Let's call home. *(Let's make a phone call to the house.)*

벌써   경찰에   신고했어.
pelsse   kyengchal-ey   sinkohaysse.
already   police-loc.   reported
We/I already reported to the police.

그거   소 귀에   경   읽기야.
kuke   so kwi-ey   kyeng   ilkkiya.
that thing   cow ear-loc.   scripture   reading-be
That's (like) reading Buddhist scripts to cow's ears.
(They won't listen to you/They don't understand you.)

(4) -에 for time point

The locative-contact particle -에 -ey is also used to indicate a TIME POINT—you can abstractly think of this as temporal location.

우리   저녁에   만나자.
wuli   cenyek-ey   mannaca.
we/us   evening-loc.   meet-suggestion
Let's meet in the evening.

우리   월요일에   만나자.
wuli   welyoil-ey   mannaca.
we/us   Monday-loc.   meet-suggestion
Let's meet on Monday.

내일   세 시에   만나자.
nayil   sey si-ey   mannaca.
tomorrow   3 o'clock-loc.   meet-suggestion
Let's meet at 3 o'clock tomorrow.

Unlike English which requires all the various prepositions in a series of time expressions *(in the evening on Monday at 6 o'clock)*, Korean needs only one -에 -ey after the whole series of time expressions. And, the last time particle is never omitted:

토요일 아침   아홉 시에 만나자.
thoyoil   achim   ahop si-ey   mannaca.
Saturday   morning   9 o'clock-loc.   meet-suggestion
Let's meet at 3 o'clock in the morning on Saturday.

(5) -에 for point of measurement

The locative-CONTACT particle -에 -ey can also be used for counting or measuring, in which case -에 -ey takes on the *per unit* meaning, perhaps evolving from the metaphorical sense of a point <u>at</u> *that particular measurement* or *reaching that unit or standard*:

사과가   한 봉지에   얼마예요?
sakwa-ka   han pongci-ey   elmayeyyo?
apple-subj.   one paper bag-loc.   how much-be-polite
How much is the apple per/for a bag?

하루에 두 번   이를   닦아요.
halwu-ey   twu pen   i-lul   takkayo.
day-loc.   twice   teeth-obj.   brush-polite
I brush my teeth twice a day/for the day.

(6) -에 for cause of triggered event

One of the most interesting usages of the locative-CONTACT particle -에 -ey is to mark an **inanimate agent** (doer of things), or something that causes the event to happen. When -에 -ey is used this way, there is a sense of passivity in the predicate, whereby the person or thing that undergoes the event (the grammatical subject) has no control over it. (You may think of this as a "point" from which an event is instigated/set off.) The inanimate agent (or cause) is typically the subject in English sentences:

바람에 촛불이   꺼졌어요.
palam-ey   chospwul-i   kkecyesseyo.
wind-loc.   candle-subj.   turned off-polite
The wind blew out the candle.
(*The candle went out <u>the moment</u> the wind blew; the candle was blown out by the wind.*)

전화 소리에   깼어요.
cenhwa   soli-ey   kkaysseyo.
phone   sound-loc.   woke up-polite
The phone woke me up.
(*I woke up <u>when</u> the phone rang; I woke up from the phone noise.*)

친구	말에	슬퍼졌어요.
chinkwu	mal-ey	sulphecyesseyo.
friend	*word-loc.*	*became sad-polite.*

My friend's words saddened me.

(*I was saddened <u>on hearing</u> my friend's words; I was saddened at my friend's words.*)

(7) Omission of the particle -에

Can -에 -ey ever be left out? Yes—in the following two cases.

<1> After place adverbs

The particle -에 -ey can left out in spoken Korean after place adverbs, which are 어디 eti *where*, 여기 yeki *here*, 거기 keki *there (close to you)*, 저기 ceki *over there (far from both of us)*, and 요기 yoki *right here*, 고기 koki *right there*, or 조기 coki *right over there*:

어디(에)	앉아?
eti(-ey)	anca?
where-loc.	*sit*

Where am I to sit?

이거	요기(에)다	숨기자.
ike	yoki(-ey)ta	swumkica.
this thing	*here-loc.*	*hide-suggestion*

Let's hide this right here.

<2> After some destination nouns

The particle 에 ey can be omitted in REALLY casually spoken Korean after REALLY common place nouns that end in a vowel or a sonorant consonant. (But note that it DOESN'T get omitted after *house*!)

도서관(에)	가?
tosekwan(-ey)	ka?
library-loc.	*go*

Are you going to the library?

방금	공항(에)	도착했어요.
pangkum	konghang(-ey)	tochakhaysseyo.
just now	*airport-loc.*	*arrived-polite*

I just arrived at the airport.

집	가.
cip	ka.
home	*go*

(*I'm) going home.*

4.2.2 Locative-ORIGIN particle: -에서

The particle -에 -ey has an doppelganger, -에서 -eyse, that marks the location of an activity or where something (e.g., an item, some news) originates from. So we'll call this the locative-ORIGIN particle.

(1) -에서 for origin ("*from*")

The locative-ORIGIN particle -에서 -eyse marks the place where something comes from, with the "에" ey part denoting the location and the "서" se part the origin or source. The starting point can be a physical place, an action, or an abstract idea:

한국**에서**   왔습니다.
hankwuk-eyse   wasssupnita.
Korea-loc.   *came-formal*
I am/came from Korea.

회사**에서**   전화   왔었어요?
hoysa-eyse   cenhwa   wassesseyo?
company-loc.   *phone*   *came-polite*
Did someone call from work? (Did a phone call come from the company?)

어디**에서**   그걸   들었어요?
eti-eyse   kuke-l   tulesseyo?
where-loc.   *that thing-obj.*   *heard-polite*
Where did you hear that (from)?

자리**에서**   일어나세요.
cali-eyse   ilenaseyyo.
seat-loc.   *get up-honorific-polite*
Stand up/get up from your seat/bed.

전화소리에   잠**에서**   깼어.
cenhwasoli-ey   cam-eyse   kkaysse.
phone sound-loc.   *sleep-loc.*   *woke up*
I was awakened by a phone call. (I awoke from sleep at a phone call.)

운동부족**에서**   오는   피로감
wuntongpwucok-eyse   onun   philokam
exercise-deficiency-loc.   *coming*   *fatigue-sense*
Feeling of fatigue from lack of exercise

Since the -에 -ey part may be left out when used as a marker for certain destination nouns, -에서 -eyse is often reduced to -서 -se in casually spoken Korean:

거기**서**   어디까지   갔어?
keki-se   eti-kkaci   kasse?
there-loc.   *where-ending with*   *went*
Where did you end up going from there?

서울**서**   전주까지.
sewul-se   cencwukkaci.
Seoul-loc.   *Jeonju-ending with*
From Seoul to Jeonju.

(2) -에서 for location of activity

-에서 -eyse (and NOT -에 -ey) also marks a location where an event takes place (rather than where something is or ends up). Verbs that express actions like 춤추다 chwumch-wuta *dance*, 수영하다 swuyenghata *swim*, 산책하다 sanchaykhata *take a walk*, 노래를 부르다 nolaylul pwuluta *sing*, 먹다 mekta *eat*, 기다리다 kitalita *wait*, 달리다 tallita *run*, 걷다 ketta *walk*, 뛰다 ttwita *jump up and down*, and any other VERBS OF ACTIVITY (even 자다 cata *sleep!*) all call for a location WHERE THE ACTION TAKES PLACE FOR SOME AMOUNT OF TIME, and in these cases, -에서 -eyse must be used. If the verb describes where the action ends up at a certain moment in time (앉다 ancta *sit*, 서다 seta *stand*, 눕다 nwupta *lie down*, 넣다 nehta *put in*, 놓다 nohta *put down*, for example), use -에 -ey to mark the point of the arrival; if the verb describes an activity that lasts a while, use -에서 -eyse to mark the location of the activity that lasts.

공원에   뛰어갔다.   공원에서   뛰었다.
kongwen-ey   ttwiekassta.   kongwen-eyse   ttwiessta.
park-loc.   *run-went-plain*   *where-loc.*   *ran-plain*
I ran to the park.   I ran in the park.

공원에서   벤치에   혼자   앉아   있었다.
kongwen-eyse   peynchi-ey   honca   anca   issessta.
park-loc.   *bench-loc*   *alone*   *sat-plain*
I sat alone on the bench at/in the park.

You can think of the particle -에서 -eyse as something that expresses a combination of A LOCATION and AN ACTIVITY WITH DURATION, incorporating the concept *and there*:

지금   식당에   있어요.
cikum   siktang-ey   isseyo.
now   *restaurant-loc.*   *exist-polite*
I am at the/a restaurant now.

지금   집에서   저녁   먹어요.
cikum   cip-eyse   cenyek   mekeyo.
now   *home-loc.*   *dinner*   *eat-polite*
I am eating now, at home. (I am at home, <u>and there</u> I am eating.)

Here are some more examples:

오늘   공원에서   산책했어요.
onul   kongwen-eyse   sanchaykhaysseyo.
today   *park-loc.*   *walked-polite*
I took a walk at the park today. (I was at the park, <u>and there</u> I walked today.)

매일   도서관에서   잤어요.
mayil   tosekwan-eyse   casseyo.
everyday   *library-loc.*   *slept-polite*
I slept in the library every day. (I was at the library, <u>and there</u> I slept every day.)

Due to its dual function (origin and location of activity), the particle -에서 -ese introduces an interesting ambiguity of interpretation. In the following two sentences, the -에서 -ese question can seek an origin:

그 사람   어디에서   만났어?
ku salam   eti-eyse   mannasse?
that person   *where-loc.*   *met*
Where do you know the person from? (Where did you first meet the person?)

어디에서 한국어를 배웠어요?
eti-eyse   hankwuke-lul paywesseyo?
where-loc.   Korean-obj.   learned-polite
Where did you learn Korean from?

But the same sentences can have a slightly different interpretation, if the focus is on the LOCATION (of the ACTIVITY and not the ORIGIN):

그 사람   어디에서   만났어?
ku salam   eti-eyse   mannasse?
that person where-loc.   met
Where did you meet with the person?

어디에서   한국어를   배웠어요?
eti-eyse   hankwuke-lul paywesseyo?
where-loc.   Korean-obj.   learned-polite
Where did you learn/study Korean?

Two verbs 있다 issta and 살다 salta allow both particles -에 -ey and -에서 -eyse. They are used interchangeably with no great meaning difference to native speakers:

여기에 있다가   와.
yeki-ey isstaka   wa.
here-loc. stay-interruptive come
Stay put here – then come.

여기에서 있다가   와.
yeki-eyse isstaka   wa.
here-loc. live-interruptive come
Stay here a while before coming.

분당에   살아요.
pwuntang-ey salayo.
Bundang-loc. live-polite
I live in Bundang.

분당에서   살아요.
pwuntang-eyse salayo.
Bundang-loc. live-polite
My (current) residence is Bundang.
(I'm (currently) living in Bundang.)

(3) -에서 for an organization as an agent

When an organization such as 회사 hoysa *company*, 학교 hakkyo *school*, or -회 -hoy *association* (e.g. 학생회 haksaynghoy *student association*) is the agent (doer) of an action, it uses the -에서 -ese particle. Be careful not to interpret the organization as a PLACE of action, because it is the SUBJECT of the sentence; it just gets -에서 -ese as the subject-focus marker (instead of -이/가 -i/ka):

회사에서   보너스를   줬어요.
hoysa-eyse ponesu-lul   cwesseyo.
company-subj. bonus-obj.   gave-polite
The company gave (me) a bonus.
Not the intended meaning: *(Someone) gave (me) a bonus at the company.*

학교에서   연락을   드릴 거예요.
hakkyo-eyse yenlak-ul   tulil keyeyyo.
school-subj. contact-obj. will give-polite
The school will contact (you).
Not the intended meaning: *(Someone) will contact you at the school.*

4.2.3 Recipient particles: -한테 and -에게

The next lesser-grammatical are the recipient particles -에게 -eykey and -한테 -han-they. For formal and written Korean, the particle -에게 -eykey is used; for informally spoken Korean, -한테 -hanthey is used. Let's do a quick check on your grammar before moving on.

In English, the receiver of an item or a beneficiary of an action is normally placed before the item given. That is, the indirect object precedes the direct object:

I gave John a tie for his birthday; He made his mother a bottle of jam; She bought herself a nice laptop; I will give this project top priority.

If the recipient needs to be contrasted or happens to be a noun with a long modifier, the direct and indirect objects can be shuffled around with the use of the preposition *to* or *for*:

*I gave my old tie **to** some random person I saw on the street yesterday.*
*He made raspberry jam for his mother and blackberry jam **for** his next-door neighbor.*

In Korean, however, there is only one way to show who the recipient is, and that is by attaching the recipient particle to the **indirect object** noun. The indirect object also comes before the direct object.

나에게 전화해요.
na-eykey cenhwahay.
I/me-recipient call-polite
Give me a call/Call me.

나한테 공(을) 던져.
na-hanthey kong-(ul) tencye.
I/me-recipient ball-(obj.) throw
Throw me the ball/Throw the ball to me.

The recipient particle can be left out in casually spoken Korean only if the verb is 주다 cwuta *give*:

그거 나(**한테**) 줘.
kuke na(hanthey) cwe.
that thing I/me-recipient give
Give that to me.

걔가 나(**한테**) 잼(을) 만들어 줬어.
kyayka na(hanthey) caym(ul) mantule cwesse.
S/he-subj. me-recipient jam-obj. make-give
S/He made me jam/He made jam for me.

개(**한테**)　　　밥　　쥐.
kay(hanthey)　　pap　　cwe.
dog-recipient　　food　　give
Feed the puppy. (Give food to the puppy.)

금붕어(**한테**)　　　먹이　　　쥐.
kumpwunge(hanthey)　　meki　　cwe.
gold fish-recipient　　animal feed　　give
Feed the goldfish. (Give food to the goldfish.)

With verbs that have a sense of *giving* or directional verbs that express abstract giving, if the verb is other than 주다 cwuta, the particle usually cannot be omitted in spoken or written Korean. (And even if the verb is 주다, the particle cannot be omitted in formal written Korean.)

나**한테**　　　이메일　보내.
na-hanthey　　imeyil　ponay.
I/me-recipient　email　send
Send me an email/Send an email to me.

엄마**한테**　　　가.
emma-hanthey　　ka.
mom-recipient　go
Go to your mom.

개가　　나**에게**　　　덤벼들었어요.
kay-ka　　na-eykey　　tempyetulesseyo.
dog-subj.　I/me-recipient　lunged-polite
The dog lunged at/toward me.

내가　　그**에게**　　　넥타이를　줬다.
nay-ka　　ku-eykey　　neykthai-lul　cwessta.
I/me-subj.　he/him-recipient　necktie-obj.　gave-plain
I gave him a tie.

Plants do not make it into the animate category no matter how dear they might be to you. Neither do projects or other tasks. So for the same exact situation where you would use -한테 -hanthey or -에게 -eykey for people, -에 -ey is used if the recipients are inanimate beings. Again, the particle has to be there for formal registers:

꽃(**에**)　　물　　쥐.
kkoch(ey)　　mwul　　cwe.
flower-loc.　water　give
Water the flower. (Give the flower water.)

이 일**에**　　우선권을　　줄　　것입니다.
i il-ey　　wusenkwen-ul　　cwul　　kesipnita.
this job-loc.　priority-obj.　will　give-formal
I will give this project priority.

You have probably noticed great similarity between the recipient particle -에게 -eykey/ -한테 -hanthey and the locative-CONTACT particle -에 -ey. That's because the recipient particle is indeed an ANIMATE version of -에 -ey.

4.2.4 Animate source particles: -한테서 and -에게서

Much like the -에 -ey and -에서 -eyse pair, the animate recipient particle -한테 -hanthey/ -에게 -eykey comes with its spiritual twin -한테서 -hantheyse/-에게서 -eykeyse for marking an ANIMATE source from which an action or an item originates. Just as in the case of -에게 -eykey, -에게서 -eykeyse is used for more formal situations:

걔**한테서**	얘기	들었어?	*Did you hear the story from him/her?*
kyay-hantheyse	yayki	tulesse?	
he/she-source	*story*	*heard*	

친구**한테서**	받은	선물	*a gift (someone) received from a friend*
chinkwu-hantheyse	patun	senmwul	
friend-source	*received*	*gift*	

학생**에게서**	들은	소식	*news (someone) heard from a student*
haksayng-eykeyse	tulun	sosik	
student-source	*heard*	*news*	

Rather confusingly, the -서 -se part is often left out in spoken Korean, and the recipient particle -한테 -hanthey or -에게 -eykey will, as a result, carry the same meaning, leaving the correct interpretation up to the listener. In this case, the verb holds the key—this time it's the -서 -se part, not -한테 -hanthey or -에 -ey that is omitted, so be careful! Perhaps it will help if you think of -한테 -hanthey/-에게 -eykey as a point at which the transaction happens in EITHER DIRECTION:

걔**한테**	얘기를	했어?
kyay-hanthey	yayki-lul	haysse?
he/she-recipient	*story-obj.*	*did*

Did you tell the story to him/her (that child)?

걔**한테**	얘기를	들었어?
kyay-hanthey	yayki-lul	tulesse?
he/she-source	*story-obj.*	*heard*

Did you hear the story from him/her (that child)?

학생**에게**	전한	소식
haksayng-eykey	cenhan	sosik
student-recipient	*transmitted*	*news*

news (someone) transmitted to a student

학생**에게**	전해 들은	소식
haksayng-eykey	cenhay tulun	sosik
student-source	*transmit-heard*	*news*

news (someone) heard <u>through</u> a student

So, when a native Korean speaker hears someone say 친구한테 chinkwu-hanthey, she is likely to wait to hear the verb in order to interpret the direction of the transfer:

친구**한테**	준	선물	*a gift (someone) gave <u>to</u> a friend*
chinkwu-hanthey	cwun	senmwul	
friend-?	*gave*	*gift*	

친구**한테**	받은	선물	*a gift (someone) received <u>from</u> a friend*
chinkwu-hanthey	patun	senmwul	
friend-?	*received*	*gift*	

When the whole particle and not just -서 -se is omitted in casual speech with 주다 cwuta *to give*, the interpretation can only be recipient (TO *a person*):

친구	준	선물
chinkwu	cwun	senmwul
friend	*gave*	*gift*

a gift (I) gave to a friend/a gift a friend gave (to someone)

친구	받은	선물
chinkwu	patun	senmwul
friend	*gave*	*gift*

a gift (someone) received from a friend /a gift a friend received (from someone)

(this sentence is impossible, because the omitted particle can only mean *to*; one cannot *receive to*)

4.2.5 Companion particles: -(이)랑, -하고, and -와/과

The companion particle -(이)랑 -(i)lang is used in colloquial Korean, and its meaning and function are quite comparable to the English conjunction (*along, together*) *with*. It is sensitive to whether the noun ends in a vowel or consonant, so -랑 -lang attaches to a vowel-final noun, and -이랑 -ilang attaches to a consonant-final noun. There is another casual companion particle -하고 -hako, which has only one form. The companion particles frequently show up with the adverb 같이 kathi *together*:

동생**이랑**	(같이)	가.		나**랑**	(같이)	가.
tongsayngi-lang	(kathi)	ka.		na-lang	(kathi)	ka.
sibling-with	*(together)*	*go*		*sibling-with*	*(together)*	*go*
Go with your younger brother/sister.				*Go with me.*		

동생**하고**	(같이)	가.		나**하고**	(같이)	가.
tongsayng-hako	(kathi)	ka.		na-hako	(kathi)	ka.
sibling-with	*(together)*	*go*		*I/me-with*	*(together)*	*go*
Go with your younger brother/sister.				*Go with me.*		

There is yet another companion particle, which is mainly used in written and very formally spoken Korean: -와 -wa/-과 -kwa. We have said many times that certain particles are sensitive to whether the noun they attach to ends in a consonant or vowel, as you have seen in -(이)랑 -(i)lang, -을 -ul/-를 -lul, and -이 -i/-가 -ka. There is one particle that runs COUNTER to the general tendency to avoid two consonants in a row and create alternations of consonant and vowel, and it is -와 -wa/-과 -kwa. Contrary to expectation, -와 -wa attaches to a VOWEL-final noun, and -과 -kwa attaches to a CONSONANT-final noun. This particle frequently shows up with the adverb 함께 hamkkey *together*:

나**와**   (함께)   갑시다.
na-wa   (hamkkey)   kapsita.
I/me-with   *(together)*   *go-formal suggestion*
Let's go together. (Literally, *Let's go with me.*)

팀**과**   (함께)   하는   프로젝트
tim-kwa   (hamkkey)   hanun   pulocekthu
team-with   *(together)*   *do-rel.*   *project*
A project (I/we) work on with the/as a team

4.2.6 Instrument-WAY particle: -(으)로

The particle -(으)로 -(u)lo is usually called a TOOL or INSTRUMENT particle, but it is more than just for tools—its power is immense if you know how to control it. The unifying sense of -(으)로 -(u)lo is that of a *WAY* in which or with which something gets done, or an abstract MEANS by which something is accomplished. Depending on the context, it is translatable into such various English prepositions as *with, by, through, in, from, for, due to, toward, headed to, by means of, by way of,* and *via!*

-으로 -ulo is used after nouns ending in consonants, and -로 -lo is used after nouns ending in vowels AND nouns ending in ㄹ. The use of -로 -lo after nouns that end in ㄹ (서울 sewul, for example) is to avoid a string of ㄹ syllables that ends up as [서우르로 sewul<u>ulo</u>], which is rather difficult to pronounce!

(1) -(으)로 for means: *with, by*
The most concrete way -(으)로 -(u)lo is used is to mark MEANS or THE WAY/HOW something is done:

밥을   숟가락**으로**   먹어요.
pap-ul   swutkalak-ulo   mekeyo.
rice-obj.   *spoon-instr.*   *eat-polite*
You eat rice with a spoon.

버스**로**   가요,   지하철**로**   가요?
pesu-lo   kayo,   cihachel-lo   kayo?
bus-way   *go-polite*   *subway-instr.*   *go-polite*
Do we go by bus or subway?

끝내고   가벼운   마음**으로**   갔어요.
kkuthnayko   kapyewun   maum-ulo   kasseyo.
finish-and   *light*   *heart-instr.*   *went-polite*
I finished (it) and went with a light heart.

끈질긴 노력으로 엄마를 설득했다.
kkuncilkin nolyek-ulo emma-lul seltukhayssta.
persistent effort-instr. mother-obj. persuaded-plain
I convinced Mom with an unrelenting effort.

(2) -(으)로 for a reason: *with, by*

-(으)로 -(u)lo can indicate an inanimate REASON as the *way* or *how* something ends up happening. It is often translated as *with, from,* or *by*. Though some of these sentences may sound like they are providing causes in English, in Korean they have a strong sense of the speaker giving a reason for some other event or a larger context:

공사로 길이 막혔어요.
kongsa-lo kil-i makhyesseyo.
construction-instr. road-subj. is blocked-polite
The road was blocked by/from/with construction.
(The road was blocked because of the construction – that's why I am late.)

사람을 옷으로 판단해요?
salam-ul os-ulo phantanhayyo?
person-obj. clothing-instr. judge-polite
Do you judge people by/with their clothes?
(You judge people because of their clothes? – Are you that kind of a person?)

IMF 사태로 회사가 문을 닫게 됐어요.
IMF sathay-lo hoysa-ka mwun-ul tatkey twaysseyo.
IMF emergency-instr. company-subj. door-obj. was forced to close/ended up closing-polite
Suffering from an IMF crisis, the company closed.

(3) -(으)로 for pathway: *for, toward*

When that instrument-WAY particle -(으)로 -(u)lo marks a destination, it incorporates a sense of the pathway, like *toward* or *headed to*. This is because of the meaning *via path*. If the beginning of the pathway is called attention to, the English *toward* is a good parallel in English. If the final point of the route is focused, *headed for* is a good match:

이제 어디로 가요? *Now where (are you headed) to?*
icey eti-lo kayo?
now where-instr. go-polite

서울로 가는 비행기 *An/the airplane headed for Korea*
sewul-lo kanun pihayngki
Seoul-instr. go-ing airplane

이쪽으로 와. *Come (toward) this way.*
iccok-ulo wa.
this side-instr. come

To emphasize the pathway itself, a helping verb 하다 hata *to do* is often used. For good English translations of these phrases, *via*, *through*, and *by* are welcome choices:

저리로   (해서)   돌아.   *Make a turn that direction (around there).*
celi-lo   (hayse)   tola.
there-instr.   *doing-so*   *turn*

뒷길로   (해서)   왔어.   *I have come through/via the back route.*
twiskil-lo   (hayse)   wasse.
back road-instr.   *doing-so*   *came*

(4) -(으)로 for change or choice: *to, (go) with, toward*

The instrument-WAY particle -(으)로 -(u)lo can also indicate CHANGE, CHOICE, or DECISION, with the sense of *I end up here after having gone through or considered a different route*:

약속 시간을   세 시로   바꿨어요.
yaksok sikan-ul   sey si-lo   pakkwesseyo.
appointment. time-obj.   *3 o'clock-instr.*   *changed-polite*
We changed the appointment time to three o'clock. (We came around to make it 3 o'clock.)

어느 걸로 (=것으로) 살까?
enu   kel-lo (=kes-ulo)   salkka?
which   *thing-instr.*   *buy-wonder*
Which should I buy? (Which way should I go? Which one should I go with?)

이   신발   다른   걸로   주세요.
i   sinpal   talun   kel-lo   cwuseyyo.
this   *shoes*   *different*   *thing-instr.*   *give-honorific-polite*
Switch these shoes for others, please. (I'll go the other shoes' way.)

나는   갈비찜으로   먹을래요.
na-nun   kalpiccim-ulo   mekullayyo.
I-top.   *galbijjim-instr.*   *eat-wanna-polite*
I'll have galbijjim. (I'll go the galbijjim way.)

(5) -(으)로 for social position: *as*

The particle -(으)로 -(u)lo also marks A WAY in which one carries herself in a certain social position, like phrases with *as* (a noun). Such-and-such MANNER of behavior for the position is implied. This usually applies to **subject** or **object complements**:

나는   20 년   동안   외국인으로   살았다.
na-nun   20 nyen   tongan   oykwukin-ulo   salassta.
I-topic   *20 years*   *for/during*   *foreigner-instr.*   *lived-plain*
I lived as a foreigner for 20 years. (Living the foreigner's way of life)

미국에서　한국어 선생님으로　일하고 있다.
mikwuk-eyse hankwuk-e sensayngnim-ulo ilhako issta.
U.S.-loc.　*Korean teacher-instr.*　*work-ing-plain*
I'm working as a Korean teacher in the U.S.

네가　나를　바보로　생각하냐?
ney-ka na-lul papo-lo sayngkakhanya?
you-subj. I/me-obj. fool-instr. think-plain question
You think I'm a fool, huh? (You think of me as a fool [behaving in ways a fool would]?)

(6) Fine-tuning -에 vs. -(으)로

Both -에 -ey and -(으)로 -(u)lo can be used with a destination, but -에 -ey distinctly accentuates the end point whereas -(으)로 -(u)lo is interested in the entire passage experience. For this reason, verbs of destination like 도착하다 -tochakhata *to arrive* are used with -에 -ey, and verbs involving passageway or departure like 출발하다 chwulpalhata *to depart*, 떠나다 ttenata *to leave*, 돌다 tolta *to turn* and 이사하다 isahata *to move* are used with -(으)로 -(u)lo. Here, -(으)로 -(u)lo is translated as *for* or *toward*:

조카가　　　서울에 도착했어요.
cokha-ka　　　sewul-ey tochakhaysseyo.
niece/nephew-subj.　Seoul-loc. arrived-polite
My niece/nephew arrived in Seoul.

조카가　　　서울로　도착했어요.
cokha-ka　　　sewul-lo　tochakhaysseyo.
niece/nephew-subj.　Seoul-instr. arrived-polite
~~*My niece/nephew arrived at Seoul.*~~

조카가　　　서울로　출발했어요.
cokha-ka　　　sewul-lo　chwulpalhaysseyo.
niece/nephew-subj.　Seoul-instr. departed-polite
My niece/nephew departed for Seoul.

When the same verb (or verbs with a similar meaning) allow both -에 -ey and -(으)로 -(u)lo, the nuance difference is, again, destination vs. pathway:

누나가　서울에 갔어요.
nwuna-ka sewul-ey kasseyo.
sister-subj. Seoul-loc. went-polite
My sister went to Seoul.

누나가　서울로 갔어요.
nwuna-ka sewul-lo kasseyo.
sister-subj. Seoul-instr. went-polite
My sister headed for Seoul.

얼음이   물**이**   됐어요.
elum-i   mwul-i   twaysseyo.
ice-subj.   water-subj.   became-polite
Ice became water. (Focus on the identity of the entity in the final state)

얼음이   물**로**   변했어요.
elum-i   mwul-lo   pyenhaysseyo.
ice-subj.   water-instr.   changed-polite
Ice turned into water. (After going through the passage of time/change)

이쪽**에**   오세요.
iccok-ey   oseyyo.
this side-loc.   come-honorific
Come (right) here (don't go there), please. ('Here' as a destination point)

이쪽**으로**   오세요.
iccok-ulo   oseyyo.
this side-instr.   come-honorific
Come (toward) this way, please.
(From there toward this general area; you don't have to make a beeline.)

The instrument-WAY particle -(으)로 -(u)lo gives an explanation for the REASON why something has happened, much like the English *because of*, whereas the locative-CONTACT particle -에 -ey provides a CAUSE for the effect or result, much like the English *due to*. Because of this difference, -에 -ey is used for more factual and objective statements, while -(으)로 -(u)lo is used for incidents that one experiences:

감기로   결석했어요.
kamki-lo   kyelsekhaysseyo.
cold-instr.   was absent-polite
I was absent from (being sick with) a cold.

바람에   촛불이   꺼졌어요.
palam-ey   chospwul-i   kkecyesseyo.
wind-loc.   candle-subj.   turned off-polite
The candlelight went out due to the wind. (The candle went out at the wind.)

4.2.7 Summary of the lesser-grammatical particles

Particles	Function	Sample sentences
locative-CONTACT particle: -에	For point of contact	교실에 학생들이 있어요. *There are students in the classroom.* 교실에 학생들이 많아요. *There are a lot of students in the classroom.*
	For target point of contact	의자에 앉으세요. *Sit down on the chair.* 극장에 전화해서 물어보자. *Let's call the theater and ask.*
	For destination point of contact	내일 학교에 안 가요. *I am not going to school tomorrow.*
	For time point	세 시에 만나요. *Let's meet at three o'clock.*
	For point of measurement, *per*	사과가 한 개에 오백원이에요. *It is five hundred won per (one) apple.* 하루에 한 번 샤워해요. *I take a shower once a day.*
	For point of triggered event	바람에 문이 열렸다. *The door flew open from a gust of wind.*
locative-ORIGIN particle: -에서	For origin, *from*	서울에서 왔어요. *I am from Seoul.* 학교에서 전화가 왔어요. *The school called.*
	For location of activity	교실에서 공부를 해요. *We study in the classroom.* 집에서 저녁 먹어요. *I am eating now, at home.*
	For an organization as agent	회사에서 연락할 겁니다. *The company will contact (you).*
recipient particle: -한테 (spoken) -에게 (written)	To mark an animate recipient (IO)	친구한테 이메일을 보냈어요. *I sent an email to my friend.* 친구에게 이메일을 보냈다. *I sent an email to my friend.*
animate source particle: -한테서 (spoken) -에게서 (written)	To mark an animate source	친구한테서 이메일이 왔어요. *An email arrived from my friend.* 친구에게서 이메일이 왔다. *An email arrived from my friend.*
companion particle: -(이)랑, -하고 (spoken) -와/과 (written)	*With* animate object	내년에도 같은 룸메이트랑 살 생각이다. *I am thinking about living with the same room-mate next year.* 내년에도 같은 룸메이트하고 살 생각이다. *I am thinking about living with the same room-mate next year.* 내년에도 같은 룸메이트와 살 생각이다. *I am thinking about living with the same room-mate next year.*

Particles	Function	Sample sentences
instrument-WAY particle: -(으)로	For means	나무로 만든 의자 *A chair made of wood*
	For personally experienced cause/reason	감기로 결석했다. *I skipped class from a cold.*
	For pathway	서울로 가는 기차를 타세요. *Take a train headed for Seoul.*
	For change or choice	점원: 무슨 색으로 드릴까요? *Which color would you like?* 손님: 빨간색으로 주세요. *Red one, please.*
	For social position	내 동생은 고등학교에서 한국어 선생님으로 일하고 있다. *My younger sibling is working as a Korean teacher at a high school.*

4.3 Context-based Particles

Three Korean particles call for a context larger than just the sentence they appear in. Their interpretation is possible only in the context of some information previously made known. Two of them are like English adverbs (e.g., *also/too, only*), but the third one, the **topic-BACKGROUND particle**, is multi-functional and eludes pigeonholing. These particles replace the subject or the object-focus particles when they attach to a subject or an object noun.

4.3.1 Inclusive particle: -도

This particle means *also*, and as a particle, it attaches to the noun that is added or emphasized.

(1) -도 for newly added elements

The particle -도 -to works pretty much like the English adverb *also*; the assumption is that there is a previously mentioned like-element and you are telling about an additional item/person. While in English you can put *too* and *also* in many different places in a sentence and sometimes create ambiguity, in Korean, you add the particle directly to the element you want to mark as an addition:

현: 불고기를   먹었어요. 된장찌개도   먹었어요.
    pwulkoki-lul   mekesseyo.   toyncangccikay-to   mekesseyo.
    bulgogi-obj.   *ate-polite*   *doenjangjjigae-also*   *ate-polite*
Hyun: I ate bulgogi. I also ate doenjangjjigae.

(-도 tells you that the person has eaten something else: *doenjangjjigae*.)

경: 그래요?   나도   된장찌개   먹었어요.
    kulayyo?   na-to   toyncangccikay   mekesseyo.
    is it so-polite   *I/me-also*   *doenjangjjigae*   *ate-polite*
Kyoung: I, too, ate doenjangjjigae!

(-도 tells you there is someone else who ate *doenjangjjigae*: Hyun.)

나도   안   갈래.
na-to   an   kallay
I/me-also   not   go-wanna
I don't wanna go, either.

(-도 tells you that there is someone else who isn't going.)

Be careful not to confuse -도 -to with 또 tto, which is a free-standing adverb, meaning *again* or *in addition*. In *wh*-questions, 누가 또 nwuka tto is more commonly used than 누구도 nwukwu-to to mean *who else*, making two interpretations possible:

경: 누가   또   안   가?
nwu-ka   tto   an   ka?
who   else/again   not   go
Who else is not going?/Who is not going again?

누구도 nwukwu-to may be used in negative sentences to mean *nobody* (= *not anyone*) interchangeably with 아무도 amwu-to:

경: 동호는   왜   또   안   가?
tongho-nun   way   tto   an   ka?
dongho-topic   why   again   not   go
Why is Dongho not going? (What's the issue?)

진: 누구도 (=아무도) 몰라.
nwuku-to (=amwu-to)   molla.
anyone-also   not know
No one knows/Who knows why.

(2) -도 for anticipated lists

The particle -도 -to sometimes can "anticipate" what else is going to be listed. Even if it's the FIRST item you are mentioning as part of a new list (that is, not as an addition to some previous item), you can start out using the particle -도 -to. The following first example is a natural answer to the question 내일 누가 와? nayil nwu-ka wa? *Who is coming tomorrow?*:

지수도   오고   수빈이도   와.
ciswu-to   oko   swupini-to   wa.
Jisu-also   come-and   Subin-also   come
Both Jisu and Subin are coming. (In addition to Jisu, Subin, too, is coming.)

내일   운동도   하고   친구도   만날 거예요.
nayil   wuntong-to   hako   chinkwu-to   mannal keyeyyo.
tomorrow   exercise-also   do-and   friend-also   will meet-polite
Tomorrow, I will do exercise and also meet my friend.

(3) -도 for emphasis

If the particle -도 -to doesn't precede, follow or imply any other like items, it is interpreted as emphatic *even*:

초보자도 쉽게 할 수 있어요.
chopoca-to swipkey hal swu isseyo.
Novice-even easily can do-polite
Even a novice can easily do it.

아빠는 일요일에도 일하셔.
appa-nun ilyoil-eyto ilhasye.
Dad-topic Sunday-also work-honorific
Dad works even on Sundays.

(4) -도 replaces grammatical particles

All context-based particles, including -도 -to, REPLACE the subject and object-focus particles but STACK WITH the other particles:

나도 내일 책을 줄게.
na-to nayil chayk-ul cwulkey.
I/me-also tomorrow book-obj. give-promise
I, too, will give you a book tomorrow.

내가 내일 책도 줄게.
nay-ka nayil chayk-to cwulkey.
I/me-subj. tomorrow book-also give-promise
I'll give you a book as well tomorrow.

내가 내일 너(한테)도 책을 줄게.
nay-ka nayil ne-(hanthey)do chayk-ul cwulkey.
I/me-subj. tomorrow you-(to) also book-obj. give-promise
Tomorrow, I'll give a book to you too.

아침에(도) 운동하고 저녁에도 운동합니다.
achimey(to) wuntong-hako cenyek-ey-to wuntonghapnita.
morning-loc.-also exercise-and evening-loc.-also exercise-formal
I exercise in the morning and also in the evening.

집에서(도) 운동하고 헬스장에서도 운동합니다.
cipeyse(to) wuntong-hako heylsucang-eyse-to wuntonghapnita.
home-loc.-also exercise-and gym-place-also exercise-formal
I exercise at home and also at the gym.

혼자(도) 운동하고 친구하고도 운동합니다.
honca(to) wuntong-hako chinkwu-hako-to wuntonghapnita.
by oneself-also exercise-and friend-with-also exercise-formal
I exercise alone and also with my friend.

4.3.2 Exclusive particle: -만

(1) -만 for exclusiveness

-만 -man is a particle that means *only*, and it works very similarly to -도 -to, showing up in grammatical particles' stead and attaching to the noun that is the "only one." The assumption is that there exist like-elements, whether previously mentioned or not, out of which only this one thing is selected:

나**만**   내일   책을   줄게.
na-man   nayil   chayk-ul   cwulkey.
I/me-only   tomorrow   book-obj.   give-promise
I, only, will give you a book tomorrow. (*No one else will give you a book.*)

내가   내일   책**만**   줄게.
nay-ka   nayil   chayk-man   cwulkey.
I/me-subj.   tomorrow   book-only   give-promise
I'll give you just a/the <u>book</u> tomorrow. (*I won't give you other things.*)

내가   내일**만**   책을   줄게.
nay-ka   nayil-man   chayk-ul   cwulkey.
I/me-subj.   tomorrow-only   book-obj.   give-promise
I'll give you a book only <u>tomorrow</u>. (*And not on any other days.*)

내가   내일   너(한테)**만**   책을   줄게.
nay-ka   nayil   ne-(hanthey)man   chayk-ul   cwulkey.
I/me-subj.   tomorrow   you-(to) only   book-obj.   give-promise
I'll give the book only to you tomorrow. (*And not to anyone else.*)

내가   내일   너한테   책을   주기**만** 할게.
nay-ka   nayil   ne-hanthey   chayk-ul   cwukiman halkey.
I/me-subj.   tomorrow   you-recipient   book-obj.   giving-only do-promise
All I'll do tomorrow is to give you the book. (*And not do anything else.*)

(2) -만 as a softener

The particle -만 -man often works as a conversation softener, frequently used with the adverb 조금 cokum/좀 com *a little*. It does not mean *only* in that case but functions to soften the request:

만 원**만**   빌려 줘.
manwen-man   pillye   cwe.
10,000 won-only   lend   give
Can you lend me 10,000 Won?

이것**만**   끝내고   가자.
ikes-man   kkuthnayko   kaca.
this thing-only   finish-and   go-suggestion
Let's go soon—after wrapping up just this.

(3) -만 replaces grammatical particles

Like -도 -to, -만 -man replaces the subject and object-focus particles but is attached to the other particles:

나**만**	너를	사랑해.	*Only I love you.*
na-man	ne-lul	salanghay.	
I/me-only	*you-obj.*	*love*	

나는	너**만**	사랑해.	*I only love <u>you</u>.*
na-nun	ne-man	salanghay.	
I/me-topic	*you-obj.*	*love*	

아침**에만**	운동합니다.	*I exercise only in the morning.*
achim-e-man	wuntonghapnita.	
morning-time-only	*exercise-formal*	

헬스장**에서만**	운동합니다.	*I exercise only at the gym.*
heylsucang-eyse-man	wuntonghapnita.	
gym-place-only	*exercise-formal*	

친구**하고만**	운동합니다.	*I exercise only with my friend.*
chinkwu-hako-man	wuntonghapnita.	
friend-with-only	*exercise-formal*	

In SPOKEN Korean, however, -만 -man can be doubled up with the subject or the object particle for extra emphasis. Notice -만 -man comes BEFORE the grammatical particle in this case:

그 것만이		내 세상	*That alone is my world.*
ku kes-man-i		nay seysang	
that thing-only-subj.		*my world*	

당신만을	사랑해.	*I only love <u>you</u>.*
tangsin-man-ul	salanghay.	
you-only-obj.	*love*	

4.3.3 Topic-BACKGROUND particle: -은/는

The last context-dependent particle is -은/는 -un/nun, the **topic**-BACKGROUND **particle**. As you may have guessed, -은 -un marks nouns that end in a consonant, and -는 -nun those that end in a vowel.

The main function of this particle is to signal that *we both know this thing we are talking about* or *this is what we're talking about at the moment*. That is, -은 -un/-는 -nun marks a noun that has been established as a TOPIC of the conversation. An item or an idea can only be made a topic if those having the conversation share the same BACKGROUND knowledge about it. So we call this a topic-BACKGROUND particle. Also, once a topic is established, the conversation focus is on its characteristics—information about that topic, and the topic might be replaced by a pronoun in English.

You can think of a topic as a playing field with an established set of rules and an umpire-designated ball. We'll come back to this metaphor again below. Now, let's explore -은 -un/-는 -nun, which is probably the most enigmatic and fascinating particle in the Korean language.

(1) -은/-는 for established topic of conversation

People don't usually repeat every word the other person says in casual, everyday conversations, so a natural question-and-answer routine is something like this:

김: 학생회관   어디   있어요?
    haksaynghoykwan   eti   isseyo?
    student union building *where* *exist-polite*
Kim: *Where's the student union building?*

이: 저기   (있어)요.
    ceki   (isse)yo.
    over there *exist-polite*
Lee: *Over there.*

But! In written Korean, or even in spoken Korean when you want to sound a little more formal, you will want to use the particles. Once the question has been asked and what you are talking about is the *student union building*, it has become the established topic, so you will want to use the topic-BACKGROUND particle in your response:

김: 학생회관**이**   어디에   있어요?
    haksaynghoykwan-i   eti-ey   isseyo?
    student union building-subj. *there-loc.* *exist-polite*
Kim: *Where's the student union building?*

박: 학생회관**은**   저기에   있어요.
    haksaynghoykwan-un   ceki-ey   ksseyo.
    student union building-top. *over there-loc.* *exist-polite*
Pak: *It's over there.*

Did you notice that, in 박's sentence, the English translation uses the pronoun *it* while in Korean, the word 학생회관 haksaynghoykwan is repeated with the topic-BACKGROUND particle? We hope you have also taken note that in both the question and answer, the *student union building* is the grammatical subject. As you know, the subject-focus particle only marks a grammatical subject that is a NEW FOCUS of the conversation. Once something is established as the topic, understood by both the speaker and the listener, the item gets marked with the topic-BACKGROUND particle, EVEN IF it is a grammatical SUBJECT.

If you are supplying new information about the established subject noun, you are in a way beginning a new conversation about it and need to go back to using the subject-focus particle again:

김: 학생회관이   어디에   있어요?
haksaynghoykwan-i   eti-ey   isseyo?
student union building-subj.   where-loc.   exist-polite
Kim: *Where's the student union building?*

이: (학생회관은)   저기   있어요
(haksaynghoykwan-un)   ceki   isseyo.
student union building-top.   over there-loc.   exist-polite
Lee: *(It's) over there.*

김: (학생회관이)   아주   작네요.
(haksaynghoykwan-i)   acwu   cakneyyo.
Student union building   very   small-surprise-polite
Kim: *(It/this particular S.U. building) is very small!*

(2) -은/는 for understood NEW topic of conversation

The particle -은 -un/-는 -nun can also introduce a new topic. If you are thinking, "Wait! Aren't topics supposed to be already established in the conversation? How can you IN-TRODUCE a new topic??" your line of thinking is on the right track. For something to be a topic, it has to be something that has been previously mentioned OR something both parties can see in front of them or something that's familiar enough to both parties that the listener "gets it" as soon as the speaker mentions it.

Going back to the playing field metaphor, you can think of this situation as a person initiating a game that everyone knows how to play. If you are playing kickball and you want to switch to soccer, there is no need to explain the rules, so to speak; you just announce that the game is now soccer. For a language example: you could suddenly offer up someone (as a new topic) that hasn't been mentioned in the conversation you have been having:

진: 형진이는?
hyengcini-nun?
Hyeongjin-topic
Jin: *(And…) Hyeongjin?*

Since the topic-BACKGROUND particle engages the listener as the sharer of the information, the assumption is that the listener knows what to do with the ball just thrown to her—she knows how to talk about this new topic. 형진이는? hyengcini-nun might mean *Where's Hyeongjin?* if Hyeongjin is expected to be present but is currently absent, or *How about Hyeongjin?* if Hyeongjin has not been explicitly mentioned for the group trip you are planning, and he is a regular member of your group. It might mean *How is Hyeongjin?* if Hyeongjin has recently been sick and you want to know about how he is doing. The topic particle here introduces a new topic and basically says LET'S TALK ABOUT HYEONGJIN.

If someone doesn't know who Hyeongjin is, a natural follow-up question would mark the name Hyeongjin with the SUBJECT-FOCUS PARTICLE, because they are seeking new information—NOT taking Hyeongjin as a new topic:

장:　형진이**가**　　누구야?
　　hyengcini-ka　　nwukwuya?
　　Hyeongjin-subject　who-be

Jang:　*Who is Hyeongjin?*

If you are ready to play the same game (that is, PICK UP THE TOPIC and discuss it), you would continue on with the topic-BACKGROUND particle. Notice that a natural translation in English would use a PRONOUN, *he*, to carry on the same topic:

장:　형진이**는**　　아파서 못　왔어.
　　hyengcini-nun　aphase　mos　wasse.
　　Hyeongjin-topic　sick-so　can't　came

Jang:　*He was/is sick and wasn't able to come.*

장':　형진이**는**　　나중에　　올 거야.
　　hyengcini-nun　nacwungey　ol keya.
　　Hyeongjin-topic　later　will come

Jang:　*He'll join us later.*

You can also use the topic-BACKGROUND particle if you know Hyeongjin (and accept Hyeongjin as a new topic), but still don't know exactly what your friend is asking about him:

장:　형진이**는**　　뭐/왜?
　　hyengcini-nun　mwe/way?
　　Hyeongjin-topic　what/why

Jang:　*What <u>about</u> him?* (Why is he our conversation topic? Why did you bring him up?)

(3) -은/는 for new items under a topic

You can use the topic-BACKGROUND particle to bring a new item into the conversation, but the assumption again is that you are still playing the same game (that is, following the same thread of conversation under the same topic). Consider this conversation between 하 ha and 유 yu. 유 yu is a new employee at a company, and 하 ha is 유 yu rather picky boss. The two are trying to come up with a housewarming gift for a co-worker:

하:　집들이　　　선물로　　뭐**가**　　좋을까요?
　　ciptuli　　senmwul-lo　mwe-ka　cohulkka?
　　house warming　gift-for　what-subj.　good-wonder-polite

Ha:　*What would be good as a housewarming gift?* (New information-seeking question)

유:　성냥**이**　　어때요?
　　sengnyang-i　ettayyo?
　　matches-subj.　how-polite

Yu:　*<u>What about</u> matches?* (New information-seeking question)

하: 요즘   누가   성냥을   줘요?
   yocum   nwu-ka   sengnyang-ul   cweyo?
   these days   who-subj.   matches-obj.   give-polite
Ha: *Who gives matches nowadays?*

유: 그럼   세제는   어때요?
   kulem   seycey-nun   ettayyo?
   then   detergent-topic   how-polite
Yu: *Then, how about detergent?* (Same topic: housewarming gift. New item: detergent)

하: 세제도   좀   이상하다···
   seycey-to   com   isanghata...
   detergent-also   a little   strange-plain
Ha: *Detergent is a little weird, too…*

유: 휴지는요?
   hyuci-nun-yo?
   toilet paper-topic-polite
Yu: *How about toilet paper?* (Same topic: housewarming gift. New item: toilet paper)

After the first item 성냥 sengnyang *matches*, the other items that 유 yu introduces are simply "just another one of them" for the general topic "a good housewarming gift." 유 yu continues to play the game 하 ha is leading, suggesting items under the agreed-upon topic.

Compare the dialogue above with this one between friends:

민: 집들이   선물로   뭐가   좋을까?
   ciptuli   senmwul-lo   mwe-ka   cohulkka?
   house warming   gift-for   what-subj.   good-wonder
Min: *What would be good as a housewarming gift?*

방: 세제가   어때?
   seycey-ka   ettay?
   detergent-subj.   how
Pang: *What about detergent?*

민: 요즘   누가   세제를   줘?
   yocum   nwu-ka   seyceylul   cwe?
   these days   who-subj.   matches-obj.   give
Min: *Who's giving matches nowadays?*

방: 그럼   휴지가   어때?
   kulem   hyuci-ka   ettay?
   then   t.p.-subject   how
Pang: *Then, what about toilet paper?*

In this dialogue, 방 paŋ is COMING UP WITH NEW IDEAS and bringing them into the conversation using the subject-focus particle, whereas in the first dialogue, 유 yu is following along with the basic topic established by his/her boss by using the topic particle. What a difference a small particle can make, eh?

(4) -은/는 for overt and covert contrast

The topic-BACKGROUND particle can also be used to contrast items. This is natural because you may only compare or contrast what is in front of you, what is concrete, or what has been established as a topic:

그 건　　　크고　이건　　　작아.
ku ke-n　　khuko　ike-n　　caka.
that thing-topic　big-and　this thing-topic　small
That is big, and (in contrast) this is small.

왕:　너,　토마토　좋아해?
　　ne,　thomatho　cohahay?
　　you　tomato　like
Wang: Do you like tomatoes?

진:　딸기는 좋아하는데　토마토는　안　좋아해.
　　ttalki-nun cohahanuntey　thomatho-nun　an　cohahay.
　　strawberries-topic like-but　tomato-topic　not　like
Jin:　I like strawberries, but not tomatoes.

If an item is marked with the topic-BACKGROUND particle and the contrasted item is not explicitly mentioned, it is implied. (The mentioned element could be said with a high tone, but this is an odd response in English):

최:　너,　토마토　좋아해?
　　ne,　thomatho　cohahay?
　　you　tomato　like
Choi:　Do you like tomatoes?

변:　토마토는　안　좋아해.
　　thomatho-nun　an　cohahay.
　　tomato-topic　not　like

Byun: I don't like tomatoes.　(Not really. I am fine with other vegetables.)

Let's consider another wildly interesting case. Because "I" in 양's Yang's response is marked with the topic-BACKGROUND particle below, the implication is that "some other people are going/might be going."

송:　너　거기　가?
　　ne　keki　ka?
　　you　there　go
Song:　Are you going there?

양: 아니. 나는 안 가.
　　　ani.　　na-nun　an　ka.
　　　no　　*I-topic*　*not*　*go*

Yang: No. Ḭ am not going. *(but others might/are. – "I" said with a high tone)*

To give an answer without such an implication, the particle or the noun or pronoun itself is simply left out in spoken Korean. Note the use of the pronoun *them* in the English translation of 변 pyen's response:

최: 너, 토마토 좋아해?
　　　ne,　thomatho　cohahay?
　　　you　*tomato*　*like*

Choi: *Do you like tomatoes?*

변: (토마토) 안 좋아해.
　　　(thomatho)　an　cohahay.
　　　tomato　*not*　*like*

Byun: *I don't like* them.

송: 너 거기 가?
　　　ne　keki　ka?
　　　you　*there*　*go*

Song: *Are you going there?*

양: 아니. (나) 안 가.
　　　ani.　(na)　an　ka.
　　　no　*I*　*not*　*go*

Yang: *No. I am not (going).*

To close this section, let's entertain the possibility of saying the nouns with an object-focus or subject-focus particle. What would that sound like? The short answer is that it would be a very strange response because it doesn't make sense to put the nouns in focus (as if they were new information) in these cases.

최: 너, 토마토 좋아해?
　　　ne,　thomatho　cohahay?
　　　you　*tomato*　*like*

Choi: *Do you like tomatoes?*

변'': 토마토를 안 좋아해.
　　　thomatho-lul　an　cohahay.
　　　tomato-obj.　*not*　*like*

Byun'': ~~It is tomatoes that I don't like.~~

송:　너　거기　가?
　　ne　keki　ka?
　　you　there　go

Song:　*Are you going there?*

양'':　아니.　내가　안　가.
　　　ani.　nay-ka　an　ka.
　　　no　I-subj.　not　go

Yang":　~~*No, it is I who is not going.*~~

(5) -은/는 for subtle undertone

Once you understand what the topic-BACKGROUND particle does, the verbal play can begin, with hints and innuendos flying about in your everyday speech. Whenever you use the topic-BACKGROUND particle, the assumption is that there is an understood or contrasted element (that you have some background knowledge about) either stated or left unsaid. This sort of information is usually conveyed with intonation in English. Check out this terrible situation:

송:　너, 이름이　뭐니?
　　ne,　ilum-i　mweni?
　　you　name-subj.　what-(be) plain question

Song:　*What is your name?*

김:　(제　　　이름은)　김동호입니다.
　　ce　　　ilum-un　　kimtonghoipnita.
　　my-humble　name-topic　Kim Dongho-be-formal

Kim:　*(My name is/It's) Dongho Kim.*

송:　이름은　남자답다.
　　ilum-un　namcatapta.
　　name-topic　manly-plain

Song:　*Your <u>name</u> is manly.*

Since 남자답다 namcatapta *manly* is new information, the subject-focus particle -이 -i/-가 -ka is expected with its subject. By using the topic-BACKGROUND particle, however, 송 Song now presents a quite suspicious and potentially insulting situation. 송 Song marks the element 이름 ilum *name* with -은 -un, so that it gets pitted against an unstated other element. Unfortunately, in this case, Dongho is portrayed as less than manly because 송 Song is hinting at a contrast between the *name* and... something else!

If 송 Song didn't mean to insult 동호 tongho, how could this faux-pas be avoided? By using the subject-focus particle, which fits to offer up NEW INFORMATION about the name:

송:　이름이　남자답다.
　　ilum-i　namcatapta.
　　name-subj.　manly-plain

Song:　*Oh, your name is <u>manly</u>.*

(6) -은/는 for general truth statements

Because the topic-BACKGROUND particle marks something that "everyone" knows about, it has come to be used as a particle for GENERALIZED, TRIED-AND-TRUE, FACTUAL STATEMENTS:

개는   인간의   친구이다.   *Dogs are man's friend.*
kay-nun   inkan-uy   chinkwuita.
dog-topic   *human-possessive*   *friend-be-plain*

개는   짖는다.   *Dogs bark.*
kay-nun   cicnunta.   *(It is in the nature of dogs that they bark.)*
dog-topic   *barks-plain*

지구는   둥글다.   *The Earth is round.*
cikwu-nun   twungkulta.
earth-topic   *round-plain*

고추장은   맵다.   *Gochujang is spicy.*
kochwucan-gun   maypta.   *(What one knows as Gochujang is spicy.)*
pepper paste-topic   *spicy-plain*

If these statements were said in some larger context, then the sense of implied contrast that -은/는 -un/nun carries could come back. In that case, in both Korean and English, an emphasis is placed on the word. The emphasis falls on the particle and the noun begins with an unusually low tone in Korean):

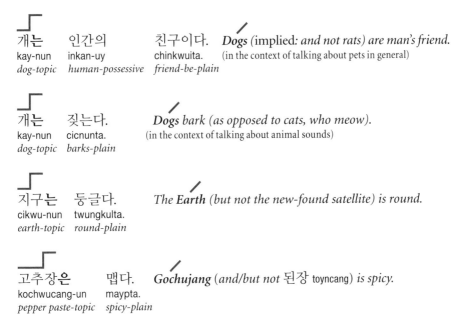

개는   인간의   친구이다.   **Dogs** (implied: *and not rats) are man's friend.*
kay-nun   inkan-uy   chinkwuita.   (in the context of talking about pets in general)
dog-topic   *human-possessive*   *friend-be-plain*

개는   짖는다.   **Dogs** *bark (as opposed to cats, who meow).*
kay-nun   cicnunta.   (in the context of talking about animal sounds)
dog-topic   *barks-plain*

지구는   둥글다.   *The* **Earth** *(but not the new-found satellite) is round.*
cikwu-nun   twungkulta.
earth-topic   *round-plain*

고추장은   맵다.   **Gochujang** *(and/but not* 된장 *toyncang) is spicy.*
kochwucang-un   maypta.
pepper paste-topic   *spicy-plain*

(7) Replacing vs. stacking of -은/는

As you have been seeing, the topic-BACKGROUND particle REPLACES subject-focus and object-focus particles. Most other particles, however, stay put, and the topic-BACK-GROUND particle ATTACHES TO them:

subject particle (replaced):

저는   안 먹어요.
ce-nun   an   mekeyo.
I-humble-topic   not   eat-polite
Me, I'm not eating.

object particle (replaced):

벌레는   싫어해.
pelley-nun   silhehay.
bug-topic   dislike
Bugs, I don't like.

other particles (stacked):

아침에(는)   운동하지만   저녁에는   운동 안 해요.
achim-ey(-nun) wuntonghaciman   cenyek-ey-nun   wuntong an hayyo.
morning-time   exercise-but   evening-time-topic   exercise not-polite
I exercise in the morning but not in the evening.

집에서(는)   운동하지만   헬스장에서는   운동 안 해요.
cip-eyse(-nun) wuntonghaciman   heylsucang-eyse-nun   wuntong an hayyo.
home-place-top. exercise-but   gym-place-topic   exercise not-polite
I exercise at home but not at the gym.

혼자서(는)   운동하지만   친구하고는   운동 안 해요.
honcase(-nun) wuntonghaciman   chinkwu-hako-nun   wuntong an hayyo.
along-topic   exercise-but   friend-with-topic   exercise not-polite
I exercise alone but not with my friend.

4.3.4 Fine-tuning -은/는 vs. -이/가

As you try to figure out which particles to use, the topic and the subject-FOCUS particles can be especially challenging. The rule of thumb is that if it's something you can walk up to a friend and say out of the blue, and if it's "news," you use the subject-FO-CUS particle. A noun marked with -이 -i/-가 -ka is emphasized with a high tone. If you are talking about something that you both have some shared background knowledge about, you use the topic-BACKGROUND particle. Now, here are some final words on the subject and topic particles.

(1) Characterize or identify?

In situations where the sentence CHARACTERIZES or further describes the thing you are talking about, use the topic-BACKGROUND particle. When the purpose is to IDENTIFY who, what, or which, use the subject-focus particle:

이   개는   내   개다.
i   kay-nun   nay   kayta.
this   dog-topic   my   dog-(be)-plain
This dog is my dog. ... (She is a Jindo dog, and is 6 years old. ...)
characterizing the topic

이 개**가**   내 개다.
i   kay-ka   nay   kayta.
this   dog-subj.   my   dog-(be)-plain
It is this dog that is mine. (Answering: *which is your dog?*)
identifying

개**는**   짖는다.
kay-nun   cicnunta.
dog-topic   barks-plain
(It is in the nature of) Dogs (that they) bark.
characterizing

개**가**   짖는다.
kay-ka   cicnunta.
dog-subj.   barks-plain
(I can hear) Some dog is barking/There is a dog barking.
identifying

고추장**은**   맵다.
kochwucang-un   maypta.
pepper paste-topic   spicy-plain
Gochujang (in general) is spicy.
characterizing

고추장**이**   안 맵다.
kochwucang-i   an   maypta.
pepper paste-topic   not   spicy-plain
(This) Gochujang is not spicy.
identifying

(2) The one or one out of many?

Remember that the subject-focus particle is only concerned about the ONE item, and topic-BACKGROUND particle always comes with some baggage in the mind of the speaker (that the listener also is expected to be aware of):

황: 은비**가**   안 왔어.
unpi-ka   an wasse.
Eunbi-subject   not came
Hwang: *Eunbi didn't come.*

황: 은비**는**   안 왔어.
unpi-nun   an wasse.
Eunbi-topic   not came
Hwang: *Eunbi didn't come.*
  (*Others were there, and I am making an issue of Eunbi's absence.*)

(3) The usual suspect

It is no secret to you that the verbs 되다 toyta *to become* and 아니다 anita *to not be* are typically found with the subject-focus particle. This can be seen as similar to IDENTIFYING:

시간**이**   됐어요.
sikan-i   twaysseyo.
time-subj.   became-polite
The time has (be)come/It's time.

그것**이**   아니에요.
kukes-i   anieyyo.
that thing-subj.   not be-polite
It's not <u>that</u>.

See how the interpretation can change with the topic-BACKGROUND particle when its sense of contrast (with something else) comes into play:

시간**은**   됐어요.
sikan-un   twaysseyo.
time-topic became-polite
It's time (but…) (They are not ready/I don't want to go, etc.)

그것**은**   아니에요.
kukes-un   anieyyo.
that thing-topic   not be-polite
Well, that's not it, (but …) (Anything else might be but not that.)

(4) *Wh*-question words in focus or not?

Whenever a *wh*-word is marked with the subject-focus particle, the answer has to be given with a subject-focus particle:

천: 누**가**   갔어?
      nwu-ka   kasse?
      who-subj. went
Chun: *Who went?*

하: 내**가**   갔어.
      nay-ka   kasse.
      I-subj.   went
Ha: *I went.*

오: 어디**가**   좋아?
      eti-ka   coha?
      where-subj.   good
Oh: *Where is good?*

백: 여기**가**   좋아.
      yeki-ka   coha?
      here-subj.   good
Paek: <u>*Here*</u> *is good/It's good here.*

If the *wh*-word is predicated by the linking verb 이다 ita *to be*, the *wh*-word is especially emphasized:

공: **뭐가**   문제야?
      mwe-ka   mwunceya?
      what-subj.   *problem-be*
Gohng: *What is it that's the problem?*

손: **네가**   문제야.
      ney-ka   mwunceya
      you-subj.   *problem-be*
Sohn: *It is you who is the problem.*

추: 언제**가**   생일이에요?
      encey-ka   sayngilieyyo?
      when-subj.   *birthday-be-polite*
Chu: *When is it that is your birthday?*

권: 내일**이**   생일이에요!
      nayil-i   sayngilieyyo!
      tomorrow-subj.   *birthday-be-polite*
Kweon: *It's tomorrow that's my birthday!*

However, it is more common to see *wh* -words showing up at the END of the sentence with the linking verb in Korean. When that happens, the subject noun gets the topic-BACKGROUND particle in the answer because that part is already established as a topic and known to the person giving the answer. The questions and answers below sound far more neutral and natural than the ones above:

신: 이름**이**   뭐예요?
      irum-i   mwueyyeyyo?
      name-subj.   *what-be-polite*
Shin: *What is (your) name?*

장: (제 이름**은**)   카일이에요.
      (ce irum-un)   kailieyyo.
      (my name-topic)   *Kyle-be-polite*
Jang: *(My name is/It's) Kyle.*

설: 생일**이**   언제예요?
      sayngil-i   enceyyeyyo?
      birthday-subj.   *when-be-polite*
Seol: *When is (your) birthday?*

여: (제 생일**은**)   내일이에요.
      (ce sayngil-un)   nayilieyyo!
      (my humble birthday-topic)   *tomorrow-be-polite*
Yeo: *(My birthday is/It's) tomorrow.*

(5) Has it been mentioned or not?

This is a dangerous generalization, but it tends to work in many cases. When a noun is first introduced in written Korean, it is marked with a subject-FOCUS particle. Once it is established as a topic and can be referred to with a pronoun like *she* or *it* in English, it is likely to show up with the topic-BACKGROUND particle. Here is how a character would be introduced and described in a story:

옛날   옛날,   빨간모자**가**   살았어요.
yeysnal   yeysnal,   ppalkanmoca-ka   salasseyo.
old days   old days   red hat-subj.   lived-polite
A long, long time ago, there lived a "Red Hat."

그 소녀**는**   엄마와   살고 있었어요.
ku sonye-nun   emma-wa   salko issesseyo.
That girl-topic   mother-with   live-ing-polite
She was living with her mother.

In the first sentence, 빨간모자 ppalkanmoca "(the) Red Hat" gets a subject-FOCUS particle. In the second sentence, *she*—the established subject—gets the topic-BACKGROUND particle. Some say that the topic-BACKGROUND particle -은 -un/-는 -nun marks OLD INFORMATION whereas the subject-FOCUS particle -이 -i/-가 -ka marks NEW INFORMATION. Let's end this section with a short story. You can check to see if that theory makes sense. The translation is given after the story:

1. 옛날   옛날에   콩쥐라고   하는   예쁜   소녀**가**   살았어요.
    yeysnal   yeysnal-ey   khongcwilako   hanun   yeyppun   sonye-ka   salasseyo.

2. 그 소녀**는**   어머니**가**   안   계셨어요.
    ku   sonye-nun   emeni-ka   an   kyeysyesseyo.

3. 콩쥐   어머니**는**   콩쥐**가**   어렸을   때   돌아가셨거든요.
    khongcwi   emeni-nun   khongcwi-ka   elyessul   ttay   tolakasyessketunyo.

4. 콩쥐   아버지**는**   콩쥐**가**   어렸을   때   새어머니**를**   맞아들였어요.
    khongcwi   apeci-nun   khongcwi-ka   elyessul   ttay   sayemeni-lul   macatulyesseyo.

5. 콩쥐**의**   새어머니**는**   팥쥐라고   하는   딸을   하나   데리고   아버지**가**
    khongcwi-uy   sayemeni-nun   phathcwilako   hanun   ttal-ul   hana   teyliko   wassnuntey
    새어머니**와**   팥쥐**는**   왔는데   계실   때**는**   콩쥐**한테**   잘해주는
    sayemeni-wa   phathcwi-nun   apeci-ka   kyeysil   ttay-nun   khongcwi-hanthey   calhaycwunun
    척 했지만   아버지**가**   밖에   나가시면   콩쥐**를**   구박하고   일을
    chek hayssciman   apeci-ka   pakk-ey   nakasimyen   khongcwi-lul   kwupakhako   il-ul
    많이   시켰어요.
    manhi   sikhyesseyo.

1. *A long, long time ago, there was a pretty girl named Kongjwi.*

2. *The girl did not have a mother.*

3. *It's because Kongjwi's mother had passed away when Kongjwi was little.*

4. *Kongjwi's father brought in a stepmother when Kongjwi was young.*

5. *Kongjwi's stepmother brought along a daughter named Patjwi, but the stepmother and Patjwi acted as though they were good to Kongjwi, but they abused her and made her work a lot when Kongjwi's father went out.*

(6) Double up!

You can use the topic and the subject-FOCUS particle in the same breath, and you can even use "double subjects" in the same sentence. Remember that the subject-FOCUS particle picks out the noun to FOCUS on:

박:　　요즘은　　　과일이　　뭐가　　좋아요?
　　　yocum-un　　kwail-i　　mwe-ka　　cohayo?
　　　these days-topic　*fruit-subj.*　*what-subj.*　*good-polite*
Pak:　*As for these days … what kind of fruit is good?*

정:　　요즘　　　과일은　　사과가　　괜찮아요.
　　　yocum　　kwail-un　　sakwa-ka　　kwaynchanhayo.
　　　these days　*fruit-topic*　*what-subj.*　*fine-polite*
Jeong:　*As for fruit these days, it is apples that are OK.*

(7) And, of course, idioms

너는　　　사람이　　왜　　그래?
ne-nun　　salam-i　　way　　kulay
you-topic　*person-subj.*　*why*　*do/be that*
What's wrong with you? (*Look at you… what kind of person acts like that?*)

4.3.5 Summary of the context-based particles

Particles	Function	Sample sentences
inclusive particle: -도	For newly added elements (*also*)	가: 시험이 있어요. 숙제도 있어요. *I have a test. I also have homework.* 나: 그래요? 저도요! *Is that right? Me, too!*
	For anticipated items (listing)	어제는 아주 바빴어요. 청소도 하고 설거지도 하고 장도 봤어요. *I was very busy yesterday. I cleaned, did dishes, and also did grocery shopping.*
	For emphasis (*even*)	주말에도 일해요. *I work even on weekends.*
exclusive particle: -만	For exclusiveness (*only*)	나만 너를 사랑해. *Only I love you.* 나는 너만 사랑해. *I love only you.*
	As a softner	하나만 주세요. *Please just give me one.*

Particles	Function	Sample sentences
topic-BACK-GROUND particle: after a consonant: -은 after a vowel: -는	Established topic of conversation	A: 세영씨가 왔어요? *Did Seyoung come?* B: 아니요. 세영씨는 안 왔어요. *No, she did not come.*
	For understood new topic	A: 저녁은 먹었어? *(By the way,) have you had dinner?* B: 네, 먹었어요. *Yes, I ate.*
	For new items under same topic	A: 오늘 시간 돼요? *Are you available today?* B: 좀 바쁜데요. *A little busy…* A: 내일은요? *How about tomorrow?* B: 내일도 바빠요. *Busy tomorrow, too.*
	For overt and convert contrast	비빔밥을 좋아해요. 그런데 볶음밥은 안 좋아해요. *I like Bibimbap. But I do not like fried rice.*
	For subtle undertones	이름은 예쁘네요. *Your <u>name</u> is pretty (but not your face, etc.)* 어제는 날씨가 좋았는데! *The weather was nice <u>yesterday</u> (the point: not so much today!)*
	For general truth statement	하루는 24시간이다. *One day is 24 hours.* 지구는 둥글다. *The Earth is round.*

4.4 Meaning-based Particles

Meaning-based particles say nothing about the noun's grammatical roles but simply add meaning or nuance. They are comparable to English adverbs (e.g., *just, merely, approximately*), conjunctions (e.g., *and, or*), or even intonation (how you move the pitch of your voice up and down). When you use these particles, you have to REPLACE the subject-FOCUS or the object-FOCUS particle. That is, you can't stack these particles.

4.4.1 *AND:* -(이)랑, -하고, and -와/과

Do you remember in Section 4.2.5, we learned companion particles, -(이)랑 -(i)lang, -하고 -hako, and -와 -wa/-과 -kwa? When they connect two nouns, these three particles -(이)랑 -(i)lang, -하고 -hako, and -와 -wa/-과 -kwa work like the English conjunction *and* to make a list of nouns. These connector particles can be used after every noun in the list, and commas are not typically used in Korean:

파랑	양파랑	마늘	*scallions, onions, and garlic*
pha-lang	yangpha-lang	manul	
scallion-and	*onion-and*	*garlic*	

마늘이랑	파	*garlic and scallions*
manul-ilang	pha	
garlic-and	*scallion*	

마늘하고 파   *garlic and scallions*
manul-hako   pha
garlic-and *scallion*

파와   마늘   *scallions and garlic*
pha-wa   manul
scallion-and *garlic*

마늘과   파   *garlic and scallions*
manul-kwa   pha
garlic-and *scallion*

Although Korean leaves many things to context, it also repeats certain things, and *and* is one of those concepts that can be marked redundantly. Redundancy is most prevalent in SPOKEN Korean. Check out this wildly redundant sentence!

마늘이랑   그리고   또,   파랑   가져와.   *Bring garlic and scallions.*
manul-ilang kuliko   tto   pha-lang   kacyewa.
garlic-and *and*   *also/again* *scallion-and* *bring*

4.4.2 OR, SOMETHING OF THAT SORT, and THAT MANY! -(이)나

There are several usages of the particle -(이)나 -(i)na, but the essence is MULTITUDE.

(1) Inclusive OR

Can you tell the subtle difference between the two *OR*s below?

Which do you want? This or that.

vs.

I can drink coffee or tea. Whichever is convenient for you.

In the first situation, one thing is to be chosen over the other. In the second situation, either would be OK. Teasing this out is quite unnecessary when using *or* in English (though it is sometimes necessary to figure it out in a given context), but the **exclusive** vs. **inclusive** nature of the word *or* makes a difference in Korean; the particle -(이)나 -(i)na functions as the **inclusive *or***, where either choice will do. Of course, -이나 -ina is used after consonant-final nouns and -나 -na after vowel-final nouns:

아침에   밥이나   빵   먹어요.   *I eat rice or bread in the morning.*
achim-ey   pap-ina   ppang   mekeyo.   *(inclusive" OR)*
morning-time *rice-or* *bread* *eat-polite*

이거나   저거나.   아무거나.   *This or that. Whatever/whichever.*
ike-na   ceke-na.   amwukena.   *(inclusive OR)*
this thing-or *that thing-or* *anything*

(2) Multiple options *OR (or something of that sort)*

The inclusiveness of the particle -(이)나 -(i)na extends to a sense of MULTIPLE ITEMS, thus, MANY OPTIONS. Even when only one or two options are explicitly mentioned, there is an implication that there are other options, and the ones that are listed do not HAVE TO be chosen; they are picked just as a sample:

오늘**이나**   내일   볼까?
onul-ina   nayil   polkka?
day-or   *tomorrow*   *see-wonder*
Shall we meet today or tomorrow (or something like that)?

영화**나**   볼까?
yenghwa-na   polkka?
movie-or   *watch-wonder*
Should I/shall we watch a movie (or something)? (e.g., unless you can think of a better option)

산책**이나**   하자.
sanchayk-ina   haca.
walk-or   *do-suggestion*
Let's take a walk or something. (e.g., that would be better than arguing at home)

(3) *ANY* + time/place/person/thing

The sense of selecting from many can also be found when -(이)나 -(i)na is used with question words to make *wherever, whoever, everything* and similar indefinite pronouns (more about these in Chapter 5). The idea is that there are many options of when/where/who, etc.:

언제**나** 웃는   얼굴
encey-na   wusnun   elkwul
when-or   *smiling*   *face*
an ever-smiling face; (Literally, *whenever smiling face*)
(*whenever you see it, the face is smiling*)

누구**나**   아는   사람
nwukwu-na   anun   salam
who-or   *knowing*   *person*
a person that everyone knows; (Literally, *person whoever knows*)
(*whoever it might be, he/she will know this person*)

어디서**나** 볼 수 있는   상품
eti-se-na   pol swu iss-nun   sangphwum
where-or   *see-can*   *product*
a product that one can see anywhere (wherever that might be, you'll see the product there)

거기 음식은 무엇**이나** 맛있어.
keki   umsik-un   mwues-ina   masisse.
there   *food*   *what-or*   *delicious*
The food there is delicious, regardless of what it is/whatever it is.
(*whatever it is, if it's their food, it's delicious.*)

(4) Approximation: *more or less how much, about how many*

When -(이)나 -(i)na is used with quantity question words like 얼마 elma *how much* and 몇 myech *how many*, you get the sense of *approximately*. The assumption is that there are many of what you are counting, and you are off-handedly picking some number (count) of them:

손님이   몇**이나**   왔어?
sonnim-i   myech-ina   wasse?
guest-subj.   *how many-or*   *came*
How many guests came? (Give me a rough number.)
(cf. 손님이 몇이야? *How many guests are there?—Give me the exact number.)*

노트북이   얼마**나**   해?
nothupwuk-i elma-na   hay?
laptop-subj.   *how much-or*   *go/do*
How much are laptops? (What's the range?)
(cf. 노트북이 얼마야? *How much is the laptop?—Give me the exact price.)*

(5) Exaggerated approximation: *that many, that much*

The sense of *many* extends to SURPRISE AT THE (LARGE) AMOUNT or NUMBER that -(이)나 -(i)na attaches to (*as many/much as that!*). Perhaps this meaning comes from the sense that, when you select a number from among many, the amount being *that* much is surprising:

20 불**이나**   해?   2 시간**이나**   걸렸어?
20 pwul-ina   hay?   2 sikan-ina   kellyesse?
20-dollars-that much *go/do*   *2-hours-that many* *took*
It cost (as much as) **20** *bucks?!*   *It took* **2** *(whole) hours?!*

(6) Exclusive *OR*

Finally, for an exclusive *or* that forces a choice between options, you can use 아니면 animyen, literally, *if not (that)*, for nouns or repeat the whole verb phrase (with a very distinct rising intonation on the final syllable of each option):

이거   **아니면**   저거?   거기 갔어, (**아니면**) 안 갔어?
ike   animyen   ceke?   keki   kasse,   (animyen)   an   kasse?
this thing *or (=if not)* *that thing*   *there* *went*   *or (if-not)*   *not* *went*
This or that?   *Did you go there or not (go there)?*

4.4.3 *START & FINISH*: -부터 and -까지

Korean has a special set of particles to express *starting with* and *ending with*.

(1) *Starting with* -부터

The pair -부터 -pwuthe and -까지 -kkaci are usually translated as *from* and *to* in various grammar books. To be more precise, though, -부터 -pwuthe picks out a beginning point in space or time, so a more fitting translation would be *starting with (that point)*:

너**부터** 시작해.
ne-pwuthe sicakhay.
you-starting with begin
Start with you.

이 책**부터** 읽자.
i chayk-pwuthe ilkca.
this book-starting with read-suggestion
Let's read this book first. (*Let's start with this book.*)

영화가 세 시**부터**야.
yenghwa-ka sey si-pwuthe-ya.
movie-subj. three o'clock-starting with-be
The movie starts at 3:00.

여기**부터**가 내 땅이야.
yeki-pwuthe-ka nay ttangiya.
here-starting with-subj. my land-be
Starting here is my land.

(2) Up to, including -까지

There are three different usages of -까지 -kkaci.

<1> Ending with

As a counterpart of -부터 -pwuthe, the particle -까지 -kkaci picks out a spatial or temporal point where something ends, and its interpretation usually INCLUDES the space or time that the noun it attaches to represents. So *ending with* or *up to and including* is a good way to understand this particle:

여기**까지**가 내가 할 일이야.
yeki-kkaci-ka nay-ka hal iliya.
here-ending with-subj. I-subj. to do-job-be
My job ends with this. (*Up to here, and including this piece, is my job.*)

이것**까지** 끝내자.
ikes-kkaci kkuthnayca.
this thing-ending with finish-suggestion
Let's finish this and call it done. (*Let's finish up to (and including) this.*)

<2> Even

Depending on the context, if the included portion is unexpected, the interpretation can be an exaggerative *even*:

너**까지** 갔어?
ne-kkaci kasse?
you-ending with went
You went, too? (*Even you went?*)

-조차 -cocha and -마저 -mace are two other particles with meanings similar to -까지 -kkaci. -조차 -cocha has the sense of *following everyone else, even you* but is used only in negative sentences (= *not even you*), and -마저 -mace has the sense of *as the last person to be added to the list, even you* and adds a little melodramatic nuance (= *as if that were not enough, even you*):

해가 진 후 새**조차** 울지 않았다.
hay-ka cin hwu say-cocha wulci anhassta.
sun-subj. set after bird-even didn't cry-plain
After the sun set, not even birds chirped.

새야! 이젠 너**마저** 우는구나!
sayya! iceyn ne-mace wununkwuna!
Bird! now you-even cry-plain exclamation
Oh, bird! Now even you are crying!

<3> By and *Until*

When used with time, -까지 -kkaci can mean *by* or *until* depending on the context. If the verb is durative (that is, it implies some duration), the meaning is *until*. Careful with contextual interpretation!

5 시**까지** 여기 올 거야.
5 si-kkaci yeki ol keya.
5 o'clock-ending with here will come
I'll be/come here by 5:00.

5 시**까지** 여기 있을 거야.
5 si-kkaci yeki issul keya.
5 o'clock- ending with here will stay
I'll be here until 5:00.

5 시**까지** 숙제 할 거야.
5 si-kkaci sukce hal keya.
5 o'clock- ending with homework will do
I'll do homework by/until 5:00.

4.4.4 *JUST, MERELY, BARELY:* -밖에

The particle -밖에 -pakkey is ALWAYS used with a NEGATIVE VERB to emphasize the meagerness or paucity of the noun it attaches to. Although it is historically developed from the noun 밖 pakk *outside*, it will help to just learn the meaning *merely, barely, just* or *only*, OR, *besides~ not/no/none/negative*. Don't forget to ALWAYS USE A NEGATIVE VERB (or the negative adverb 안 an)!

두 시**밖에** 안 됐어.
twu si-pakkey an twaysse.
two hours-merely not became
It's barely two o'clock.

십 불**밖에**   없어.
sip pwul-pakkey   epse.
ten dollars-merely   not exist
All I got is 10 bucks/I've only got 10 bucks.

맥주를   한 잔**밖에**   못   마셨어.
maykcwu-lul   han can-pakkey   mos   masyesse.
beer-obj.   one glass-merely   can't   drank
I was only able to drink one glass of beer.

4.4.5 *MORE THAN & AS ... AS*: -보다 and -만큼

The next meaning-based particle pair is the comparative -보다 -pota and -만큼 -mankhum which expresses an entire grammatical construction in English.

(1) *More than.../compared to* -보다

-보다 -pota marks the noun that is the comparison point (like *than*). -더 -te, meaning *more*, is usually added for emphasis:

쥐**보다** 다람쥐가 더   커.
cwi-pota   talamcwi-ka te   khe.
rat-than   squirrel-subj. more   big
A squirrel is bigger than a rat.

이거**보다**   저걸   더   빨리 쥐.
ike-pota   ceke-l   te   ppalli cwe.
this thing-than   that thing-obj.   more   fast   give
Give me that sooner than this.

To express *less than*, all you need to do is change 더 te to 덜 tel:

저게   이거**보다** 덜 빨라.
ceke-y   ike-pota   tel ppalla.
that thing-subj.   this thing-than   less   fast
That is slower (less fast) than this.

더 te and 덜 tel can also be used WITHOUT the comparative -보다 -pota:

좀   더   먹어.   *Eat a little more.*
com   te   meke.
a little   more   eat

좀   덜   먹어.   *Eat a little less.*
com   tel   meke.
a little   less   eat

When -보다 -pota is used without a comparative adverb (더 te or 덜 tel), then "더" te is assumed:

지하철이   택시**보다**   빨라.
cihachel-i   thayksi-pota   ppalla.
subway-subj.   taxi-than   fast
The subway is faster than a taxi.

-도 -to can be added to -보다 -pota for the meaning *even* (*more/less than*).

지하철이   택시보다도   빨라.
cihachel-i   thayksi-pota-to   ppalla.
subway-subj.   taxi-than-also   fast
The subway is <u>even</u> faster than a taxi.

(2) As ... as -만큼

-만큼 -mankhum attaches to a noun to mean *as (much) as* the noun, or when there is an adjective or adverb in the sentence, *as [adjective/adverb] as* the noun. The subject noun often gets the inclusive particle -도 -to:

그것도   이것**만큼**   먹었어.
ku kes-to   ikes-mankhum   mekesse.
that thing-also   this thing-as much   ate
I ate as much of that as I did of this.
I ate that as much as this.

택시도   지하철**만큼**   빨라.
thayksi-to   cihachel-mankhum   ppalla.
taxi-also   subway-as much   fast
A taxi, too, is as fast as the subway.

Take note of the following idiomatic expressions, especially with the particles -만 -man and -도 -to added. -도 -to ALWAYS appears with the negative:

그**만큼만**   줘.
ke-mankhum-man   cwe.
that-much-only   give
Give me just that much.

언니**만큼도**   안   했어?
enni-mankhum-to   an   haysse?
older sister-as much-also   not   did
You haven't even done as much as your sister?

4.4.6 EVERY/ALL & EACH: -마다 and -씩

What is the difference between *each*, *every*, and *all*? *Each* of course addresses individual items, while *all* clumps all the items together into a collective group. How about *every*? *Every* can be considered a combination of *all* and *each*, where you are addressing the collective whole without forgetting about each individual. Let's see how they are expressed in Korean.

(1) *Every*: -마다

The suffix -마다 -mata has a meaning closest to English *every*:

일요일**마다**　등산해요.
ilyoil-mata　tungsanhayyo.
Sunday-every　hike/climb mountain-polite
I go hiking every Sunday.

사람**마다**　취미가　달라요.
salam-mata　chwimi-ka　tallayo.
person-every　hobby-subj.　different-polite
Everybody has a different hobby/taste.

For *all*, there is no suffix in Korean; you just need to use the adverbs 모두 motwu and/ or 다 ta:

모기**가**　모두/다　죽었어요.
moki-ka　motwu/ta　cwukesseyo.
mosquito-subj.　all　died-polite
All (the) mosquitos are dead.

(2) *Each*: -씩

Then there is the particle -씩 -ssik. It is technically a suffix in Korean grammar, but it makes no great difference either way, so we'll call it a particle here. The function of -씩 -ssik is to separate people or things out one by one. It is fairly comparable to *each* in English, especially when dealing with MEASURABLE QUANTITIES:

한　분**씩**　들어오세요.
han　pwun-ssik　tuleoseyyo.
one　person-each　come in-honorific-polite
Please come in one by one. (Each person come in, please.)

하나**씩**　갖자.
hana-ssik　kacca.
one-each　have-suggestion
Let's have one each.

조금**씩**　열어.
cokum-ssik　yele.
little-each　open
Open (it) little by little.

The English sentence *Each person has a different hobby/taste* could be translated as 사람마다 취미가 달라요 salam-mata chwimi-ka tallayo (= *every* person has a different hobby/ taste); -씩 -ssik could not be used in this sentence in Korean. That is, you can't say 사람씩 취미가 달라요 because other than the adverb 조금씩 cokumssik *little by little*, -씩 -ssik only attaches to numbers and counters.

4.4.7 *JUST, AMONG, OF-THE-KIND*: -끼리

Some particles are just downright weird to non-Korean-speakers, and -끼리 -kkili probably takes the cake. It is a particle (well, technically it's categorized as a suffix by Korean grammarians) that attaches to nouns that can form a distinct, EXCLUSIVE CLASS to mean *among members of this group*. Naturally, the exclusive particle -만 -man often joins in to emphasize the exclusivity of the group to outsiders. Examples will speak more clearly than explanations:

우리**끼리**만　　가자.
wuli-kkili-man　　kaca.
we/us-group-only　go-suggestion
Let's just us go.

너희**끼리**만　여기서　뭐　　해?
nehuy-kkili-man　yeki-se　mwe　hay?
you-group-only　here　what　do
What are you guys doing here, just yourselves?

끼리끼리　모인다.
kkili-kkili　mointa.
group-group　gather-plain
Birds of a feather flock together.
(Literally, *gathering by kind*)

가족**끼리**　왜　이래?
kacok-kkili　way　ilay?
family-group　why　do/be like this
Why be that way among family members?
(*Why the fight/contention among family members?*)

4.4.8 *ABOUT, APPROXIMATELY:* -쯤

There are two more technical suffixes that behave like particles. One is -쯤 -ccum, expressing APPROXIMATION. It is usually used with measure words (numbers and counters) and frequently appears with the approximating adverb 한 han *more or less*:

한　　한　　시**쯤**에　　　　만나자.
han　han　si-ccum-ey　　　mannaca.
about　one　o'clock-approx.-loc.　meet-suggestion
Let's meet about one-ish tomorrow.

한　　한두　　　병**쯤**　　　시키자.
han　hantwu　pyeng-ccum　sikhica.
about　one-to-two　bottle-approx.　order-suggestion
Let's order about a bottle or two.

거기**쯤**　　앉아.
keki-ccum　anca.
there about　sit
Sit about there.

You may hear the noun 정도 cengto *extent/approximation* used synonymously with -쯤 -ccum:

한　　한　　시　　**정도**에　만나자.
han　han　si　cengto-ey　mannaca.
about　one　o'clock　extent-loc.　meet-suggestion
Let's meet about one-ish tomorrow.

4.4.9 *X's WORTH:* -짜리

The last meaning-based particle (also technically a suffix) that we will discuss is -짜리 -ccali. It attaches to a number + counter combination to reiterate the *worth* or *value* of the noun (even though it is already expressed in the number). It is very much like a hyphenated modifier in English, and it must be explicitly said in Korean:

세　　살**짜리**　아이가　　글을　　　알아요!
sey　sal-ccali　ai-ka　ku-lul　alayo.
three　year-worth　child-subj.　writing-obj.　know-polite
That three <u>year-old</u> child knows how to read!

이 수업은 5 학점**짜리**예요.
i   swuep-un 5 hakcem-ccali-yeyyo.
this class-topic 5 credit-worth be-polite
This is a _5-credit_ class. *(This class is 5 credits' worth.)*

우리는 방   두 개**짜리**   아파트에 살아.
wuli-nun pang twu kay-ccali   aphathu-ey sala.
we-topic room two rooms-worth apt.-loc. live
We live in a two-room apartment.
(We live in an apartment that's two rooms' worth/that comes with two rooms.)

If you do not use the particle -짜리 -ccali, the sentence is either ungrammatical or means something different:

너, 만   원짜리   있어?   cf.   너, 만   원   있어?
ne, man   wen-ccali isse?   ne, man   wen isse?
you 10,000 won-worth exist   *you 10,000 won exist*
Do you have a 10,000-Won bill?   **Do you have 10,000 Won?**

네   시간짜리 영화를   봤어요.
ney sikan-ccali yenghwa-lul pwasseyo.
four hour-worth movie-obj. watched-polite
I watched a four-hour movie.

cf. 네   시간 (동안) 영화를   봤어요.
ney sikan (tongan) yenghwa-lul pwasseyo.
four hour during movie-obj. watched-polite
I watched a movie for four hours.

그   시계 얼마짜리야?   cf.   그   시계 얼마야?
ku   sikyey elma-ccali-ya?   ku   sikyey elmaya?
that watch how much-worth-be   *that watch how much-be*
How expensive a watch is that?   **How much is that watch (exactly)?**

4.4.10 Summary of the meaning-based particles

Particles	Function	Sample sentences
-(이)랑, -하고 (spoken) -와/-과 (written)	Connect two nouns: and	언니**랑** 동생 *an older sister and a younger sister* 동생**이랑** 언니 *a younger sister and an older sister* 언니**하고** 동생 *an older sister and a younger sister* 언니**와** 동생 *an older sister and a younger sister* 동생**과** 언니 *a younger sister and an older sister*

Particles	Function	Sample sentences
-(이)나	Inclusive OR	커피**나** 차 주세요. *Please give me coffee or tea.*
	Multiple options (*or something of that sort*)	추운데 따뜻한 차**나** 한 잔 할까? *It's cold; shall we have hot tea (or…)?*
	Any time/place/ person/thing	어디**나** 다 좋아요. *Anywhere is fine with me.*
	Approximation	책이 몇 권**이나** 있어요? *How many books do you have?*
	Exaggerated approximation (*that many, that much*)	어제 열두 시간**이나** 일했어. *I worked (as many as) twelve hours!*
	Exclusive OR	이거 **아니면** 저거? *This or that?*
-부터	*Starting with*	수업이 오전 열 시**부터** 시작합니다. *The class begins at 10 AM.*
-까지	*Ending with*	이 영화는 두 시**까지** 합니다. *This movie goes until two o'clock.*
	Even	설거지**까지** 다 끝냈어요. *I even finished washing dishes.*
	By and *until*	두 시**까지** 오세요. *Come by two o'clock.*
-밖에	*Just, merely, barely*	바빠서 조금**밖에** 못 잤어요. *I was busy so I only slept a little.*
-보다	*More than, compared to*	동생이 나**보다** 더 커요. *My younger sibling is taller than I am.*
-만큼	*As much as*	동생도 형**만큼** 커요. *The younger brother is as tall as the older one.*
-마다	*Every*	일요일**마다** 등산을 가기로 했다. *I've decided to go hiking every Sunday.*
-씩	*Each*	한 사람에 두 개**씩** 먹을 수 있어. *Each person can have two.*
-끼리	*Just, among, of-the -kind*	우리 여자**끼리**만 가자. *Let's just us women go.*
-쯤	*About, approximately*	가: 몇 시**쯤** 만날까요? *About what time shall we meet?* 나: 두 시**쯤** 어때요? *How about around two o'clock?*
-짜리	*'s worth*	만원을 천 원**짜리**로 바꿔 줘. *Break this ₩10,000 bill into ₩1,000 bills.*

4.5 Choice of Particles

Let's look at some cases where you have a choice of which particles to use, and some cases where you need to be careful not to confuse particles with similar meanings.

4.5.1 Particle shift

Sometimes verbs become structurally complex, leading to a choice of particles. This happens when the verb meets an auxiliary (= helping) verb whose transitivity is different. In these sentences, the particle can match with either verb. Let's start with a normal sentence:

나는   학교에   가기   싫어요.
na-nun   hakkyo-ey   kaki   silheyo.
I/me   *school-loc.*   *going*   *distasteful-polite*
I don't want to <u>go to school</u>.

The default is to focus on *go to school*, and use the destination particle -에 -ey. The same idea can also be conveyed with the subject-focus particle, because -기 싫다 -ki silhta *(doing something is) distasteful* is a descriptive verb (so it takes only a subject), and here, the main subject, 나 na *I*, is marked as a topic. (We're calling this "shifting" the particle.)

나는   학교가   가기   싫어요.
na-nun   hakkyo-ka   kaki   silheyo.
I/me   *school-subj.*   *going*   *distasteful-polite*
I really don't want to go to <u>school</u>.

A similar situation arises with the helping verb (-고) 싶다 (-ko) siphta *be desired*, which is also a descriptive verb:

Default: 나는   엄마를   보고 싶어요.
na-nun   emma-lul   poko sipheyo.
I/me   *mother-obj.*   *want to see-polite*
I want to/would like to see Mom.

Shifted: 나는   엄마가   보고 싶어요.
na-nun   emma-ka   poko sipheyo.
I/me   *mother-obj.*   *want to see-polite*
I want to/would like to see Mom. (With alternative idiomatic meaning *I miss Mom*)

4.5.2 Fine-tuning here and there

The meaning of some of the particles is quite similar. Some paired examples will help to fine-tune your understanding.

(1) Which *from*?

The two particles -에서 -eyse *from* and -부터 -pwuthe *starting with* are very comparable and are used interchangeably for PLACES, -에서 -eyse focusing on a general origin and -부터 -pwuthe focusing on the POINT where a journey begins. The end point is always marked with -까지 -kkaci if the starting point is also mentioned. Because it is a more general particle, your safest bet is to use -에서 -eyse in most cases, unless you need to indicate a specific point:

서: 서울**에서** 부산까지   어떻게 갈 거야?
       sewul-eyse pwusan-kkaci   ettehkey kal keya?
       Seoul-from Busan-ending with how   will go
Seo: *How are we going from Seoul to Busan?*

안: 서울**에서** 부산까지는   기차로, 부산(에서)**부터**는   배로.
       sewul-eyse pwusan-kkaci-nun   kicha-lo, pwusan-(ese)-pwuthe-nun pay-lo.
       Seoul-from Busan-ending with-topic train-by Busan-starting with-topic boat-by
Ahn: *From Seoul to Mokpo by train, starting with Mokpo by boat.*

For TIME expressions, if you are talking about a general time frame *sometime between X and Y*, it is OK to use -에서 -eyse (usually with the word 사이 sai *between*), but if specific time points are are used to express the precise timing, -부터 -pwuthe and -까지 -kkaci have to be used:

양: 두 시**에서** 세 시 사이에   만나자.
       twu si-eyse sey si sai-ey   mannaca.
       2 o'clock-from 3 o'clock interval-loc. meet-suggestion
Yang: *Let's meet between two and three.*

문: 두 시**부터**   세 시까지   바빠.
       twu si-pwuthe   sey si-kkaci   pappa.
       2 o'clock-starting with 3 o'clock-ending with busy
Moon: *I'm busy starting from two until three.*

문': 두 시**에서** 세 시 사이에   바빠.
       twu si-eyse sey si sai-ey   pappa.
       2 o'clock-from 3 o'clock interval-loc. busy
Moon: *I'm busy (roughly) between two and three.*

배: 내일이나 모레   만나자.
       nayil-ina morey   mannaca.
       tomorrow-or the day after tomorrow meet-suggestion
Bae: *Let's meet tomorrow or the next day.*

노: 내일**부터**   모레까지   없어.
       nayil-pwuthe   moley-kkaci   epse.
       tomorrow-starting with the day after-ending with not exist
Noh: *I'm not (around) starting tomorrow until the next day.*

노': 내일에서   모레까지   없어.
       nayil-eyse   moley-kkaci   epse.
       tomorrow -from day after-tomorrow-until not exist.
Noh: *~~I'm not (around) between tomorrow and the following day.~~*
       (This is not a possible option because there is no such time!)

(2) Which *to*?

The particle -에 -ey marks a destination, and -까지 -kkaci marks an ending point. How do they compare with each other? The answer is that a simple destination is marked with -에 -ey, but if the PATH is in some way referred to or at least implicitly considered, -까지 -kkaci should be used:

주: 부산**에**   운전해서   가요?
pwusan-ey   wuncenhayse   kayo?
Busan-loc.   *driving*   *go-polite*

Ju: *Are you driving to Busan?*

주': 부산**까지**   운전해서   가요?
pwusan-kkaci   wuncenhayse   kayo?
Busan-ending with   *driving*   *go-polite*

Ju':   *Are you driving all the way to Busan?*

(3) For verbs of directional movement

When you have verbs of directional movement, you may expect to hear *to* a place or *from* a place: -에 -ey and -에서 -eyse. And yes, written and more formally spoken Korean prefer those particles:

학교(에) 가요.
hakkyo-(ey) kayo.
School-loc.   *go-polite*

(I) go to school.

열차가   서울역**에서**   떠납니다.
yelcha-ka   sewulyek-eyse   ttenapnita.
train-subj.   *Seoul Station-loc.*   *leave-formal*

The train is leaving from Seoul Station.

But in casually spoken Korean, the object-focus particle -을 -ul/-를 -lul is frequently used, if a particle is used at all, for emphasis. This is because -에 -ey and -에서 -eyse state the more distant destination and origin more factually, whereas -을 -ul/-를 -lul gives you an immediate feel, and we are more likely to talk about immediate surroundings in our day-to-day lives than factual events. The verbs of directional movement include 가다 kata *go*, 오다 ota *come*, 다니다 tanita *go to/attend*, 올라가다 ollakata *go up*, 내려오다 naylyeota *come down*, 들어가다 tulekata *go in*, 나오다 naota *come out*, 날아가다 nalakata *fly away*, 넘어오다 nemeota *climb over towards this way*, 떠나다 ttenata *leave*, and 출발하다 chwulpalhata *depart*:

학교(를) 가요.
hakkyo-(lul) kayo.
School-obj.   *go-polite*

I'm going to school (now).

기차가   역(을)   떠나요.
kicha-ka   yek-ul   ttenayo.
train-subj.   *station-obj.*   *leave-polite*

The train is leaving the station (soon).

Of course there are also idiomatic uses. 여행을 가요/떠나요 yehayng-ul kayo/ttenayo, for example, doesn't mean you leave FROM your travels, but rather you *go on a trip* or *embark on a journey.* 유학을 가요/떠나요 yuhak-ul kayo/ttenayo is another idiomatic case, meaning *go to/on study abroad.* You NEVER say 여행에 떠나요 yehayng-ey ttenayo or 유학에 떠나요 yuhak-ey ttenayo.

4.6 Idiomatic Particles

Some particles combine with a special verb to yield expressions that are overall comparable to simple English prepositions such as *through, about,* and *according to.* The verbs
대하다 tayhata *to face,* 비하다 pihata *to compare,* and 의하다 uyhata *to rely on* are combined
with -에 -ey, whereas 통하다 thonghata *to go through* and 위하다 wihata *to benefit/care for*
are combined with -을 -ul/-를 -lul to make these idiom-like particles (or particle-based
idioms). The point is that they seem simple in English, but there is no single particle
to express these meanings; they require a particle + a verb in a certain connector form.
But you can memorize them as single expressions. They are frequently used in writing
and formal speech.

4.6.1 *About:* -에 대해(서) and -에 관해(서)

-에 대해(서) -ey tayhay(se), literally, *facing to* and -에 관해(서) -ey kwanhay(se), literally,
connecting to, both mean *about* something. They are basically synonyms with no large
difference in meaning. Adding the -서 -se part makes them sound more colloquial:

한국**에 대해**　잘 알고 있다.
hankwuk-ey tayhay　cal alko issta.
Korea-about　*well know-ing*
I know a lot about Korea.

한국**에 관해서**　관심이　많다.
hankwuk-ey kwanhayse　kwansim-i　manhta.
Korea-about　*interest-sub.*　*a lot-plain*
I am highly interested in Korea.

4.6.2 *Compared to:* -에 비해(서) and -에 비하면

-에 비해(서) -ey pihay(se) literally means *being compared to,* and -에 비하면 -ey pihamyen
means *if compared to.* Sentences with -에 비해(서) -ey pihay(se) or -에 비하면 -ey pihamyen
are similar to comparative sentences with -보다 -pota (than), but they are more explicit
about and have more emphasis on the compared item. Note the slight difference in
meaning between -비해(서) -ey pihay(se) and -비하면 -ey pihamyen:

서울**에 비해**　아주　작은　도시이다.
sewul-ey pihay　acwu　cakun　tosiita.
Seoul-compared to　*very*　*small*　*city-be-plain*
<u>Compared to Seoul</u>, *it is a very small city.*

서울**에 비하면**　아주　작은　도시이다.
sewul-ey pihamyen　acwu　cakun　tosiita.
Seoul-compared to　*very*　*small*　*city-be-plain*
<u>If it is compared</u> *to Seoul, it is a very small city.*

4.6.3 *Based on, according to, by:* -에 의해(서) and -에 의하면

The core meaning of both -에 의해서 -ey uyhayse and -에 의하면 -ey uyhamyen is *to rely on.* The most natural translation of -에 의해서 -ey uyhayse is *by,* and -의하면 -ey uyhamyen *according to.* These two sound the most bookish among idiomatic particle expressions:

이 공원의 야생동물은 법에 의해 보호받고 있다.
i kongwen-uy   yasayngtongmwul-un   pep-ey uyhay   pohopatko issta.
this park's   wild animal-topic   law-by   protection receive-ing-plain
The animals at this park are protected by law.

일기예보에 의하면 내일은 더 춥대.
ilkiyeypo-ey uyhamyen   nayil-un   te   chwuptay.
weather forecast-based on   tomorrow-topic   more   cold-they say
According to the forecast, it will be colder tomorrow.

4.6.4 *Following, in accordance with, depending on:* -에 따라(서), -에 따르면

-에 따라(서) -ey ttala(se) and -에 따르면 -ey ttalumyen both come from the native verb 따르다 ttaluta, which means *to follow.* -에 따라(서) -ey ttala(se) most naturally translates into *depending on,* and you can think of -에 따르면 -ey ttalumyen as a more colloquial version of -에 의하면 -ey uyhamyen *according to:*

누가 가느냐에 따라(서) 내 대답이 달라져.
nwu-ka   kanunya-ey ttala(se)   nay taytap-i   tallacye.
who-subj.   go-Q-depending on   my answer-subj.   change
My answer depends on who is going. *(Depending on who is going, my answer differs.)*

일기예보에 따르면 내일은 더 춥다고 합니다.
ilkiyeypo-ey ttalumyen   nayil-un   te   chwuptako hapnita.
weather forecast-following   tomorrow-top   more   cold-they say
According to the forecast, it will be colder tomorrow.

4.6.5 *Through:* -을/를 통해(서)

-을 통해(서) -ul thonghayse means *through* (physically) or *by way of* in an abstract sense:

창문을 통해서 들어왔다.
changmwun-ul thonghayse   tulewassta.
window-through   came in-plain
I came in through the window.

동아리 모임을 통해서 많은 친구를 사귀었다.
tongali moim-ul thonghayse   manhun   chinkwu-lul   sakwiessta.
club meetings-through   many   friends-obj.made   friends-plain
I made many friends through club meetings.

4.6.6 *For:* -을/를 위하여 and -을/를 위해(서)

If you have heard of Koreans toasting with a loud 위하여! wihaye *In order to!*, you will have no problem with this particle. -을/-를 위해(서) -ul/-lul wihay(se) means *for (the benefit of)* the noun it attaches to. -을/-를 위하여 -ul/-lul wihaye is the older, stilted version of -을/-를 위해 -ul/-lul wihay. The final -서 -se of -을/-를 위해(서) -ul/-lul wihay(se) is used in spoken Korean:

너를 위해 준비했어.
ne-lul wihay   cwunpihaysse.
You-for   prepared
I prepared (this) for you.

4.6.7 Idiomatic particles in modifier forms

All these idiomatic particles are adverbial clauses in their ... 해서 ... hayse or -하면 -hamyen form. They also come with noun-modifying variants that can be used before a noun to mean, for example, *a book (that is) about Seoul.*

Although the English translation is the same (and the general meaning conveyed by the sentences is the same), the following two examples are structurally different. The relationship between elements in these sentences is indicated with a slash (/):

한국에 관해 /   관심이   많다.
hankwuk-ey kwanhay kwansim-i   manhta.
Korea-about   interest-subj. a lot-plain
I have a lot of interest / in Korea. (*What I have a lot of is interest, and it's in/about Korea.*)
(This might be an answer to "what are you interested in?")

한국에 관한   관심이 /   많다.
hankwuk-ey kwanhan kwansim-i   manhta.
Korea-about   interest-subj. a lot-plain
I have a lot of / interest in Korea. (*What I have a lot of is interest in Korea.*)

The "interest" pair may be difficult to tell apart, but the basic distinction is that the adverbial forms correspond with the verb, where as the noun-modifying forms go with a noun:

너를 위한 노래   *a song for you*
ne-lul wihan nolay
You-for   song

너를 위해 노래   ~~a song for you~~
ne-lul wihay nolay

너를 위해 노래하고파.   *I wish to sing for you.*
ne-lul wihay nolayhakopha.
You-for   sing-wish

이메일을 **통해** 바이러스를 유포했다. *(They) spread viruses through e-mail.*
imeyil-ul thonghay   pailesu-lul   yuphohayssta.
email-through   *virus-obj.*   *spread-plain*

이메일을 **통한** 바이러스를 ~~유포했다.~~ ~~*(They) spread viruses through e-mail.*~~
imeyil-ul thonghan   pailesu-lul   yuphohayssta.

4.7 Stacking & Ordering of Particles

As mentioned previously, some particles can "stack up" after a noun. The context-based particles -도 -to, -만 -man, and -은 -un/-는 -nun love to be added to other particles because of their context-dependent personality. The subject and the object-focus particles, however, are quite possessive and don't like to share their noun. They either disappear or exclude the other particles, so, no stacking with the grammatical particles -이 -i/가 -ka and -을 -ul/를 -lul (except in very colloquial cases):

현수**가**   떠났어.   *Hyeonsoo left.*
hyenswu-ka   ttenasse.
Hyeonsoo-subj.   *left*

정미**도**   떠났어.   *Jeongmi, too, left.*
cengmi-to   ttenasse.
Jeongmi-also   *left*

~~정미**가도**/정미**도가**~~   ~~떠났어.~~   *Jeongmi, too, left.*
cengmi-ka-to/cengmi-to-ka   ttenasse.
Jeongmi-subj.-also/-also-subj.   *left*

Lesser-grammatical particles happily accommodate any of the context-based particles:

이 건물**에만**   화장실이   없어요?
i kenmwul-ey-man   hwacangsil-i   epseyo?
this building-loc.-only   *restroom-subj.*   *not exist-polite*
Just this building doesn't have a restroom? *(Only in this building there is no restroom?)*

수요일**에는**   학교에   안 가?
swuyoil-ey-nun   hakkyo-ey   an ka?
Wednesday-loc.-topic   *school-loc.*   *not go*
Don't you go to school on Wednesday(s)?

빼앗긴   들**에도**   봄**은**   오는가?
ppayaskin   tul-ey-to   pom-un   onunka?
robbed   *field-loc.-also*   *spring-topic*   *come-plain question*
Does spring come even to the robbed fields?

음식**은**   이 방**에서만**   드세요.
umsik-un   i pang-eyse-man   tuseyyo.
food-topic   *this room-loc.-only*   *eat-honorific-polite*
Please eat only in this room.

그 거　　**나한테만**　　주세요.
ku ke　　na-hanthey-man　　cwuseyyo.
that thing　　I/me-recipient-only　　give-honorific-polite
Please give that only to me.

걔한테서는　　선물이　　없어.
kyay-hantheyse-nun　　senmwul-i　　epse.
that child-from-topic　　present-subject　　not exist
From him, there is no gift.

그　　사람**이랑은**　　데이트　안 해.
ku　　salam-ilang-un　　teyithu　an hay.
that　　person-with-topic　　dating　　not do
(If it's) with him/her, I'm not dating.

음식값은　　카드**로도**　　낼 수 있어.
umsikkaps-un　　khatu-lo-to　　nayl swu isse.
food cost-topic　　card-way-also　　pay can
You can pay for food with a card, too.

Idiomatic particles allow stacking only after the -서 -se form:

그 거**에 대해서만**　얘기하고　먹자.
ku ke-ey tayhayse-man　yaykihako　mekca.
that thing-about-only　　talk-and　　eat-suggestion
Let's talk about that only and then eat/Let's talk about that and then we eat.

이건　　**학교를 통해서만**　　얻을 수 있는　정보야.
ike-n　　hakkyo-lul thonghayse-man　etul swu issnun　cengpoya.
this thing-topic　　school-obj.-through-only　　obtain-can　　information-be
This is information you can only obtain through school.

That's a lot of little bits and pieces! That's why we said particles are one of the most powerful components of Korean grammar. They truly glue the pieces together. AND they add meaning and nuance. With this lesson on the essential particles, you are well on your way to natural and expressive Korean.

Exercises

4.1 Grammatical Particles

Exercise 1. Fill in the blank with the subject particle (-이/-가) or the object particle (-을/-를). Some translations are given to help you, but base your choice on the *Korean* sentence structure.

1) 세영: 김치찌개_____ 어때요?　　　*How is the kimchi stew?*

　　새라: 조금 매운데 맛있어요.　　　　*A little spicy, but delicious.*

2) 제니: 방에 누가 있어요?　　　　　　*Who is in the room?*

　　진우: 제 동생_____ 있어요.　　　*My younger sibling is there.*

　　제니: 동생이 지금 뭐 해요?　　　　*What is your younger sibling doing?*

　　진우: 책_____ 읽어요.　　　　　*S/he's reading a book.*

3) 민영: 여기가 영민 씨 방이에요?　　*Is this your room, Youngmin?*

　　영민: 아니요. 여기는 제 방_____ 아니에요. 저기_____ 제 방이에요.
　　　　No. This is not my room. That is my room over there.

　　민영: 어머, 방_____ 참 예뻐요.　*Wow, your room is really pretty.*

　　영민: 뭘요. 감사합니다!　　　　　*Nah. Thank you.*

4) 앰버: 오늘 시간_____ 있어요?　*Do you have time today?*

　　샘:　 미안해요. 오늘 바빠요. 내일 한국어 시험_____ 있어요.
　　　　Sorry. I'm busy today. I have a Korean test tomorrow.

　　앰버: 그럼 한국어_____ 같이 공부할래요? 내_____ 도와줄게요.
　　　　Then shall we study Korean together? I'll help you.

　　샘:　 정말요? 고마워요.　　　　　*Really? Thanks!*

5) 대한: 요즘 바빠요?　(Try these on your own!)

　　민국: 네. 돈_____ 필요해서 아르바이트_____ 세 개 하고 있어요.

6) 나는 만세하고 제일 친합니다. 만세하고 나는 대학교 때 친구_____됐습니다. 만세는 착합니다. 그리고 운동_____ 아주 잘 합니다. 만세는 한국 음식 _____ 좋아해서 우리는 한국 식당에 자주 갑니다. 나는 만세_____ 아주 좋습니다!

4.2 Lesser-grammatical Particles

Exercise 2. Take the challenge! Choose 에 or 에서 appropriately.

1) 종업원 (employee): 어서 오세요. 여기(에, 에서) 앉으세요.
   Welcome. Please sit here.

   손님 (customer):　　감사합니다.
   Thank you.

2) 혜나: 내일 학교(에, 에서) 가세요?
   Do you go to school tomorrow?

   진우: 네. 같이 갈까요?
   Yes. Shall we go together?

   혜나: 네, 그럼 세 시(에, 에서) 우리 집 앞(에, 에서) 만나서 같이 가요.
   Yes. Then let's meet in front of my house at three and go together.

3) 동수: 언니, 지금 어디(에, 에서) 있어? 왜 안 와?
   Sister, where are you now? Why are you not coming?

   동희: 도서관(에, 에서) 숙제하고 있었어. 끝났으니까 금방 갈게!
   I was doing my homework in the library. I am done, so I will come over soon!

4) 정숙: 그 사과를 어디(에, 에서) 샀어요?
   Where did you buy that apple?

   민주: 시장(에, 에서) 샀어요. 한 개(에, 에서) 2000원이었어요.
   I bought it at the market. It was 2,000 won each.

   정숙: 비싸네요!
   That's expensive!

5) 장희: 그 얘기를 어디(에, 에서) 들었어요?
   Where did you hear that from?

   세환: 라디오(에, 에서) 들었어요.
   I heard it on the radio.

Exercise 3. Which particle from those in parentheses would you choose? Some translations are given to help you, but base your choice on the *Korean* sentence structure.

1) 세영: 내일 콘서트에 버스(이, 가, 을, 를) 타고 갈까요?
   Are you taking the bus to tomorrow's concert?

   하린: 버스는 오래 걸려요. 같이 지하철(에, 에서, 로, 으로) 가요.
   The bus takes too long. Let's go together by subway.

세영: 그래요. 그럼, 우리 어디(에, 에서, 로, 으로) 만날까요?
Okay. Then where shall we meet?

하린: 10시까지 지하철 역 앞(이, 가, 을, 를, 로, 으로) 오세요.
Come to the front of the subway station by 10:00.

2) 점원: 고객님, 가방 색깔은 어느 것(이, 가, 로, 으로) 하시겠어요?
Customer Ma'am, what color bag would you like?

손님: 빨간 색(이, 가, 을, 를, 로, 으로) 할게요.
I'll go with red.

3) 룸메이트: 집(에, 에게, 까지) 전화해 봐. 아까 엄마한테서 전화 왔었어.
Try calling home. Mom called a while ago.

나: 응, 그럴게.
Okay, I will.

4) 엄마: 학교(에, 에서, 한테, 에게서) 전화왔다. 전화 받아라.

정우: 네!

5) 나: 커티스 선생님은 대학에서 한국어 선생님(으로, 로, 까지, 에게) 일하고
계셔.

친구: 대단하시구나!

6) 나: 저는 동생(을, 이랑, 와) 함께 살고 있어요.

선배: 그래? 동생이나 오빠(를, 랑, 과) 살면 재미있겠다.

Exercise 4. Which particle would you choose if you had to use a particle? If you wouldn't choose any, pick the Ø.

의	에서	부터	까지	한테/에게	한테서/에게서	Ø

1) 동생이 시애틀에 왔어요. 동생은 뉴욕 대학 학생_____이에요.
My younger sisbling came to Seattle. She is a student at NYU.

2) 빨리 친구_____ 이메일을 쓰세요.
Write an email to your friend right away.

3) 내 생일에 친구가 나_____ 선물을 줬어요.
On my birthday, my friend gave me a gift.

4) 그 이야기를 라디오_____ 들었어요
   I heard that story on the radio.

5) 어제_____ 동생_____ 전화가 왔어요.
   I got a phone call from my younger sibling yesterday.

6) 한국어 수업은 매일_____ 열 시_____ 열한 시_____ 해요.
   The Korean class runs from ten o'clock to eleven o'clock.

7) 서울_____ 부산_____ 기차로 다섯 시간쯤 걸려요.
   It takes about five hours from Seoul to Busan by train.

4.3 Context-based Particles

Exercise 5. See if you can pick the right particle from the ones in parentheses.

1) 재호: 만나서 반가워요. 이름이 뭐예요?

   지연: 네, 제 이름(은, 는) 최지연이에요.

   재호: 아, 그래요? 저(가, 는) 신재호라고 해요. 지연 씨(가, 는) 몇 학년이에요?

   지연: 이 학년이에요. 재호 씨(가, 는) 요?

   재호: 저(가, 는, 도) 이 학년이에요!

2) 정희: 필라델피아가 어디에 있어요?

   은영: 필라델피아(가, 는, 만, 도) 펜실베니아에 있어요.

3) 티나: 내 동생은 고기(가, 를) 안 먹어요. 채소하고 과일(이, 만, 도) 먹어요.

   토니: 생선(만, 도) 안 먹어요?

   티나: 네, 생선(만, 도) 안 먹어요.

4) 지미: 앗! 벌써 시간(이, 만, 도) 다 됐어. 이제 게임 그만 하고 집에 가자.

   제인: 벌써? 십 분(을, 만, 도) 더 하자.

5) 윤정: 혜성 씨는 어떤 영화(가, 를) 좋아해요?

   혜성: 저는 *공포 영화 빼고 다 좋아해요. 윤정 씨(가, 는) 요?
        *공포 영화: horror movie

   윤정: 저는 공포 영화(가, 를) 좋아요.

6) 콜린: 오늘은 냉면 먹을까요?

   케이: 미안해요… 냉면(이, 은) 별로 안 좋아해요. 비빔밥은 어떠세요?

7) 소영: 호영 씨 왔어요?

   은비: 종호 씨(를, 는) 왔는데 호영 씨(는, 도) 아직 안 왔어요.

8) 동호: 어? 고추장(이, 은, 을) 안 매워요!

   시은: 이상하지요? 고추장(은, 만, 도) 원래 매운 음식인데…?

Exercise 6. 미나 is talking about her family. Can you help her use appropriate particles? Which one from among -은/는, -만 and -도 would you use?

이건 우리 가족 사진이에요. 우리 가족＿＿＿＿ (1) 다섯 명이에요. 아버지는 선생님이세요. 어머니＿＿＿＿ (2) 회사원이세요. 저는 언니하고 오빠가 있어요. 언니는 대학생이이에요. 오빠＿＿＿＿ (3) 대학생이에요. 그래서 언니하고 오빠＿＿＿＿ (4) 부모님하고 같이 안 살아요. 저＿＿＿＿ (5) 부모님하고 같이 살아요.

4.4 Meaning-based Particles

Exercise 7. Do you have the finesse to pick the right particle?

나/이나	밖에	쯤	짜리	보다	만큼

1) 친구: 콘서트에 수영이도 같이 데려 갈까요?

   나:　그러고 싶은데 표가 두 장＿＿＿＿ 없어요.

   친구: 그래요? 그럼 수영이랑은 다음에 같이 가지요. 참, 공연은 몇 시간 동안 해요?

   나:　여덟 시부터 열두 시까지 해요.

   친구: 네 시간＿＿＿＿ 해요? 너무 길어요!

2) 동생: 얼마＿＿＿＿ 표를 샀어?

   나:　50달러.

   동생: 와, 비싸네.

   나:　아니야. 콘서트 표는 보통 다 50 불＿＿＿＿ 해.

3) 남친: 우리, 늦었으니까 거기까지 택시 타고 가요.

　　여친: 지하철로 타요. 지하철도 택시＿＿＿＿＿ 빨라요.

　　남친: 아니에요. 지금은 차가 안 막혀서 택시가 지하철＿＿＿＿＿ 더 빨라요.

Exercise 8. Can you guess what these people are trying to say? Choose a particle from the box.

보다	마다	와/과	나/이나	끼리	씩

1) 찬진:　주말에 바빠요?

　　호영:　네, 요즘은 일요일＿＿＿＿＿ 첼로를 연습해요.

　　찬진:　그래요? 재미있겠어요. 참, 호영 씨는 운동도 잘 좋아하지요?

　　호영:　아니요. 저는 운동＿＿＿＿＿ 음악을 더 좋아해요.

2) 미림:　미나 씨, 셰익스피어의 "로미오＿＿＿＿＿ 줄리엣"을 읽어 봤어요?

　　미나:　네, 그럼요. 요즘은 톨스토이의 "전쟁＿＿＿＿＿ 평화"(War and Peace)를 읽고 있어요.

3) 재호:　영지 씨, 우리 맥주 한 잔 하러 가요.

　　영지:　그래요, 재호 씨. 준성 씨! 준성 씨도 우리랑 같이 가요.

　　준성:　미안해요. 저는 술을 못 마셔요.

　　재호:　그래요? 그럼 영지 씨, 그냥 우리＿＿＿＿＿ 마셔요.

　　영지:　음… 준성 씨가 술을 못 마시니까 오늘은 다 같이 그냥 커피＿＿＿＿＿ 마시러 가요.

4) 학생들: 똑똑! 선생님, 인터뷰하러 왔습니다.

　　선생님: 네, 그럼 한 사람＿＿＿＿＿ 들어오세요.

4.5 Choice of Particles

Exercise 9. Choose the particle that CANNOT be used in the sentence.

1) 나는 동생(이, 을, 에) 보고 싶어요.

2) 오늘(부터, 에서) 모레까지 아주 바빠요.

3) 집(에, 에서, 까지) 걸어서 가요.

4.6 Idiomatic Particles

Exercise 10. Choose the appropriate expression from the box.

-에 대해   -에 비해   -에 의해   -에 따르면   -을/를 통해   -을/를 위해

1) 이번 발표는 한국의 문화_____ 하려고 합니다.

2) 실수_____ 많이 배울 수 있습니다.

3) 어머니 생신에 어머니_____ 요리를 만들었어요.

4) 시애틀은 다른 도시_____ 겨울에 비가 많이 와요.

5) 이 동물은 법_____ 보호되고 있습니다.

6) 최근 뉴스_____, 서울 인구가 늘고 있다고 합니다.

4.7 Stacking & Ordering of Particles

Exercise 11. Fill in the blanks with an appropriate marker. You may need more than one marker!

1) 나는 주중_____ 운동을 안 해요. 주말_____ 운동을 해요.
   I don't exercise on weekdays. I exercise only on weekends.

2) 나는 클래식 음악_____ 들어요. 그리고 팝 음악_____ 들어요.
   I listen to classical music. I also listen to pop music.

3) 나는 외식_____ 안 해요. 집_____ 먹어요.
   I don't eat out. I eat only at home.

4) 나는 친한 친구들_____ 술을 마셔요. 안 친한 친구들_____ 술을 안 마셔요.
   I drink only with close friends. I don't drink with not-so-close friends.

5) 나는 서울_____ 가고 싶어요. 그리고 부산_____ 가고 싶어요.
   I want to go to Seoul. And I also want to go to Busan.

6) 생일에 부모님하고 친구들_____ 선물을 받았어요. 그런데 동생
_____ 선물을 못 받았어요.

I got presents from my parents and friends on my birthday. But as for my younger sibling, I did not get any gift from her/him.

7) 경복궁에 지하철_____ 갈 수 있지만 버스_____ 갈 수 있어요.

You can go to Gyeongbok Palace by subway, but you can also go there by bus.

CHAPTER 5

Nouns

Nouns are the *whats, whos, whens,* and *wheres* of the sentence. This chapter is about three major categories of noun—basic nouns, numerals, and pronouns. In English, numerals are just nouns that are numbers, but in traditional Korean grammar they are considered a separate part of speech. Korean numerals show up with dependent nouns called **counters**. **Dependent nouns** are nouns that can't stand alone but must come with a modifier before them. Following nouns in 5.1 and numerals in 5.2, counters and dependent nouns are explained in 5.3. **Pronouns** are little words like *it* and *them*, which stand in for full nouns or noun phrases. We will cover pronouns last in 5.4.

Let's see what peculiarities all these nouns and numerals have in Korean.

5.1 Nouns

Nouns in Korean are quite similar to those in many other languages as they act as the subject, the direct object, and the indirect object of the verb in a sentence. One big difference, though, is that Korean nouns come with particles (조사 cosa) that tell the function of each noun in a sentence, especially in written and formal language—this part you already know. Here we will take a look at other important features of Korean nouns that you may not be familiar with.

5.1.1 Characteristics of Korean nouns

(1) Expressing definiteness and specificity

In English, many nouns (called **count nouns**) have to show up with *a, the,* or the plural marker *-s. A* (or *an*) is an **indefinite article**, so *a* book means some unspecified book, and only one book is being talked about. On the other hand, *the* book refers to a specific book that the speaker and the listener both know of. If there is more than one unspecified book, you use the plural *books,* and to speak of more than one specific book, you say *the books.* When you refer to a specific book, its existence becomes **definite**.

The Korean language does not have articles like the English *a* and *the,* so Korean speakers normally do not pay attention to the definiteness that English speakers are concerned about. When a Korean person says 책 chayk, she may mean *a book, books, the book* or *the books.* The context decides which is meant, and in many situations, it won't matter.

The definiteness and specificity of the noun can be expressed in Korean with the **demonstrative adnominals** 이 i *this,* 그 ku *that* and 저 ce *that over there.* 이 책 i chayk means *this book* and 그 책 ku chayk can mean *the book* as well as *that book.* An adnominal or a relative clause modifier can also specify what kinds of items (nouns) you are talking about. **헌** 양말 hen yangmal *worn-out socks* and 내가 **먹은** 빵 nayka mekun ppang (*the*) *bread that I ate* are two such examples. While **헌** 양말 hen yangmal *old socks* is somewhat more limited (to socks that are old or used), it can still be *any* old worn-out socks. To be more specific, and in fact, DEFINITE, add 그 ku to get **그** 헌 양말 ku hen yangmal *those old socks*.

(2) Expressing plurality

Korean doesn't usually pluralize inanimate nouns, but has the plural suffix -들 -tul to express plurality of people. (There is a growing tendency to use -들 -tul for everything in younger generations, though.) Even with animate nouns, -들 -tul is not REQUIRED, especially if plurality can be guessed from the context:

주말에는   공원에   **사람**이 많아요.
cwumaleynun   kongweney   salami   manhayo.
There are a lot of people in the park on weekends.

주말에는   공원에   **사람들**이 많아요.
cwumaleynun   kongweney   salamtuli   manhayo.
There are a lot of people in the park on weekends.

There are some differences in how the suffix -들 -tul is used and interpreted with sub-jects versus objects. When -들 -tul is used to indicate the plurality of an animate SUBJECT noun, the suffix can go pretty much anywhere in the sentence:

너희들   왔구나!
nehuy-tul   wasskwuna!
you guys-plural   came-I see
You guys are here!

뭐들   먹을래?
mwe-tul   mekullay?
what-plural   eat-want
What do y'all want to eat?

왜들   그래요?
way-tul   kulayyo?
why-plural   do like that
Why are you all doing that? (*What's wrong?*)

여기들   앉아라.
yeki-tul   ancala.
here-plural   sit-command
Y'all sit here.

안녕들   하셨어요?
annyeng-tul   hasyesseyo?
peaceful-plural   did-polite
How have you all been?

빗자루   하나씩들   가지고   나오세요.
piscalwu   hanassik-tul   kaciko   naoseyyo.
broom   one-each-plural   bring   come out-polite command
Everyone, come out with a broom each.

If the OBJECT is animate, it has to be marked with -들 -tul to be understood as plural. If the object noun is not animate, the interpretation of -들 -tul is associated with the SUB-JECT, even if it is attached to the object itself!

나 없이 걔들   언제 만났어?
na epsi   kyay-tul   encey mannasse?
When did you (sg. or pl.) meet them without me?

차들   타자!
cha-tul   thaca!
Let's everyone get in the car!

여태   술들   얼마나   마셨어?
yethay   swul-tul   elmana   masyesse?
How much (booze) have you guys drunk so far?

여태   술을   얼마나들   마셨어?
yethay   swulul   elmana-tul   masyesse?
How much (booze) have you guys drunk so far?

Again, only when the object noun is animate can the suffix -들 -tul be associated with it. When both are animate, the interpretation is potentially ambiguous—both subject and object might be plural:

오늘   누나들   봤어?
onul   nwuna-tul   poasse
Did you (singular) see the older sisters today?
or Did you (plural) see the older sister today?
or Did you (plural) see the older sisters today?

Similarly, when using a companion particle (-하고 -hako *with*) on an animate object, that object is only interpreted as plural if it is DIRECTLY marked with -들 -tul BEFORE -하고 -hako. If -들 -tul comes AFTER -하고 -hako, it is interpreted as a free-floating -들 -tul that indicates a plural SUBJECT.

나 없이 걔들하고   언제 만났어?
na epsi   kyay-tul-hako   encey mannasse?
When did you meet them without me?

나 없이 걔하고들   언제 만났어?
na epsi   kyay-hako-tul   encey mannasse?
When did you all meet him/her without me?

The long and short of it is that -들 -tul prefers to indicate a plural subject, even though it can hop around in the sentence. It rarely means the object is plural—only when the object is animate and has -들 -tul directly affixed.

To indicate plurality in questions in spoken Korean, you can reduplicate (or double up) the question-word (without any particles):

내일 **누구   누구**   와? (누가 누가 와?)
nayil   nwukwu   nwukwu   wa? (nwuka nwuka wa?)
Who all are coming tomorrow?

너, **뭐 뭐** 샀어? (뭘 뭘 샀어?)
ne, mwe mwe sasse? (mwel mwel sasse?)
What all did you buy?

5.1.2 Types of Korean nouns

Korean nouns have several different origins. A great number are of **Sino-Korean** origin, "**borrowed**" from Chinese languages or created based on Chinese words over centuries. Also more and more words are recent **loanwords** from other languages. Of course, many are of the native Korean stock. We will call this last category Haan (韓) vocabulary, named after the Korean peninsula for want of a better term. Each of these categories is a significant resource for increasing your vocabulary. Our adventure continues now into the variety of Korean nouns.

(1) Sino-Korean vocabulary

Sino-Korean vocabulary is a translation of the term 한자어 hancae, literally *Chinese character word*, and these words have come into Korean through various routes. The word 예 yey (禮) *proprieties*, for example, is a word that came from Classical Chinese hundreds and hundreds of years ago, whereas the word 공항 konghang (空港) *airport* was put together in Japanese using Sino-origin root words for *air* and *port* in the earlier part of the 20th century and then made its way into Korean. On the other hand, 한류 hanlyu (韓流) *the Korean Wave*, was borrowed from the modern Chinese language during the last decade. Many Sino-Korean words are being created in the modern day Korean language, and they sometimes compete with other Sino-based words with the same meaning. A good example pair would be 이동전화 itongcenhwa (移動電話) which Koreans created for the English word *mobile phone* using Sino-Korean roots, and 휴대전화 hyutaycenhwa (携帯電話) *portable phone*, which was made up in Japanese and then borrowed into Korean with Korean pronunciation of the Sino-Korean roots. Although they use Sino-Korean roots, these are not Chinese words nor Japanese words recognizable to speakers of those languages. They are fully Korean words now, just with some historical origin in Chinese.

Because Sino-Korean words are so integrated into the language, Korean speakers often cannot distinguish Sino-Korean words from native Haan words—and most of the time, there is no need to distinguish them! Can you guess which of the following words are Sino-Korean?

그저께	어제	오늘
kecekkey	ece	onul
the day before yesterday	*yesterday*	*today*

내일	모레
nayil	moley
tomorrow	*the day after tomorrow*

배	귤	감	사과	딸기
pay	kyul	kam	sakwa	ttalki
pear	*tangerine*	*persimmon*	*apple*	*strawberry*

Answer: (tomorrow) tangerine, and apple are Sino-Korean words!

Even though Koreans spoke Korean, Chinese characters were an important, and before the 15th century the only, medium for written communication in Korea for over two millennia. This means that for centuries, literary (or Classical) Chinese enjoyed high prestige among the Korean nobility and elite—those who could read and write. This literary tradition and its elitism continued even after the invention of the Korean alphabet 한글 hankul by King Sejong the Great in the mid-15th century, which allowed greater access to literacy for Korean commoners. The situation began to change only when Nativist elites used 한글 hankul as a vehicle for resistance movements during the Japanese colonial rule from 1910 to 1945.

Long-held traditions of prestige die hard, though. Koreans continued to rely heavily on Chinese characters for decades even after liberation. Although the use of Chinese characters saw a sharp decrease when the (South) Korean government announced a 한글 hankul-only policy in 1970, the Korean Ministry of Education repeatedly reversed its policy on Chinese character education, and Koreans' love affair with Chinese characters has continued for a number of reasons. For one, most of Korea's history is recorded in Chinese characters. Also, Korea's younger generations have become interested in China's econo-political might, and this has reignited interest in Chinese characters.

Whether written in Chinese characters (한자 hanca) or in the Korean alphabet (한글 hankul), the Sino-Korean VOCABULARY has been fully incorporated into the Korean language, hence the term "Sino-KOREAN." Much like the way English speakers feel comfortable saying *anti-depressant* or *elevator* as English words (even though they are of Latin origin), Sino-Korean words (한자어 hancae) are an integral part of Korean speakers' everyday vocabulary. Thus it behooves you to learn the characteristics of Sino-Korean, which we turn to now. We will mix in the word 한자어 hancae for Sino-Korean (words or vocabulary) below.

<1> "Same" meaning, different registers

In English, Latinate (and Greek) vocabulary tends to enjoy a higher status than the native Germanic stock as it was tied to the "high culture" of education and religion in the olden days (and, amazingly, the high status still remains). Which of the following sounds more educated, formal, written, or posh to you?

He seems pretty fatherly.   vs.   *He displays a paternal demeanor.*

You get the idea. Although some 한자어 hancae, like 방 pang *room*, 창문 changmwun *window*, and 양말 yangmal *socks* are so basic to the language that no linguistic prestige is noticeable, the majority of 한자어 hancae, especially abstract vocabulary, is considered learned and upscale. Using 한자어 hancae will make you sound more technical, precise, learned, sophisticated, erudite, and even pompous.

When sets of 한자어 hancae and synonymous native Haan words coexist, the 한자어 hancae versions are likely to be used in writing or more formal occasions. (Think of *edifice* versus *building* in English.) The nouns in the table below are such examples, where the Haan Korean words sound more colloquial and 한자어 hancae more formal. Some really mean exactly the same thing, and their usage depends only on the **register** (the formality of the situation); others have a narrower or broader sense than their counterparts and different grammatical restrictions:

Meaning	Haan Korean	Sino-Korean
person; human	사람 salam	인간 inkan
father	아버지 apeci	부친 puchin
mother	어머니 emeni	모친 mochin
eldest daughter	맏딸 matttal	장녀 cangnye
second son	둘째 아들 tulccay atul	차남 chanam
place	곳, 데 kos, tey	장소 cangso
front door	앞문 apmwun	정문 cengmwun
back door	뒷문 twismwun	후문 hwumwun
entrance	들어가는 곳 tulekanun kos	입구 ipkwu
exit	나가는 곳 nakanun kos	출구 chwulkwu
store	가게 kakey	상점 sangcem
customer	손님 sonnim	고객 kokayk
price	값 kaps	가격 kakyek

Meaning	Haan Korean	Sino-Korean
month (counter)	달 tal	개월 kaywel
year (counter)	해 hay	년 nyen
last year	지난 해 cinan hay	작년 caknyen
this year	올해 olhay	금년 kumnyen
next year	다음 해 taum hay	내년 naynyen
today	오늘 onul	금일 kumil
name	이름 ilum	성명 sengmyeng
age	나이 nai	연령 yenlyeng
place one lives	사는 곳 sanun kos	주소 cwuso
age (counter)	살 sal	세 sey
house	집 cip	주택 cwutayk
kitchen	부엌 pwuekh	주방 cwupang
meal	밥 pap	식사 siksa

Because 한자어 hancae is a valuable resource for gaining proficiency in advanced Korean, we will go over some useful roots and words below.

<2> Homophonic Sino-Korean root words

The first thing to learn about 한자어 hancae is that not all that sound the same mean the same. (Think of the *bank* you go to in your neighborhood to withdraw money and the river *bank* that you go to to catch fish.) In Korean, you eat 국 kwuk *soup* at mealtime, but this Haan Korean word 국 kwuk is not the same 국 kwuk you see in 우체국 wucheykwuk (郵遞局) *post office* or the 국 kwuk in 외국 oykwuk (外國) *foreign country*. That's right — sometimes even Haan Korean words can sound the same as Sino-Korean roots! You do not need to memorize which words are 한자어 hancae and which are native, but do be mindful that words that sound the same (called **homophones**) may have different meanings. Also keep in mind the CONTEXT of the word you encounter. (Did it appear in written Korean? Was it used in the formal register?)

한자어 hancae roots are one-syllable long. We'll give you homophonous roots with their original Chinese characters in parentheses and an example word below each one. (Koreans used classical Chinese characters like Taiwanese and Japanese, rather than the simplified characters used in mainland China.) Those without Chinese characters can be considered native Haan words. (The words with asterisks can be used with the *do* verb, 하다 hata, to make a verb. This will be explained further in section <4> below):

Root	Meaning 1	Meaning 2	Meaning 3	Meaning 4	Meaning 5
곤 kon	곤 (困) *fatigued, sleepy* 피**곤*** (疲困) *tired*	곤 (棍) *stick, club* **곤**봉 (棍棒) *club, cudgel*			
식 sik	식 (食) *eat, food* **식**사* (食事) *eating, meal*	식 (式) *ritual* 결혼**식** (結婚式) *wedding*	식 (識) *know* 지**식** (知識) *knowledge*		
남 nam	남 *(the) others* **남**모르는 슬픔 *hidden sorrow*	남 (南) *south* **남**대문 (南大門) *Great South Gate*	남 (男) *boy, man* **남**자 (男子) *man, male*	남 (藍) *dark blue* **남**색 (藍色) *dark blue*	
해 hay	해 *the sun* **해** 질 녘 *dusk, sunset*	해 (海) *sea, ocean* **해**산물 (海產物) *seafood*	해 (解) *solve, undo* **해**결* (解決) *resolving*	해 (害) *harm* 손**해** (損害) *damage, loss*	
장 cang	장 (裝) *costume, dress* 포**장*** (包裝) *packaging*	장 (將) *general* 대**장** (大將) *captain*	장 (醬) *sauce, paste* 간**장** (간醬) *soy sauce*	장 (腸) *intestine* 위**장** (胃腸) *stomach*	장 (長) *long, elder* 총**장** (總長) *university president*
수 swu	수 *way, method* 할 **수** 없이 *without a choice*	수 (輸) *deliver* **수**출* (輸出) *export*	수 (數) *number* 산**수** (算數) *arithmetic*	수 (水) *water* 냉**수** (冷水) *cold water*	수 (手) *hand* **수**화* (手話) *sign language*
기 ki	기 (機) *machine* **기**계 (機械) *machine*	기 (氣) *energy, air* 감**기** (感氣) *cold*	기 (旗) *flag* 국**기** (國旗) *national flag*	기 (記) *write, record* 일**기** (日記) *journal, diary*	기 (基) *base* **기**본 (基本) *basic, base*

Root	Meaning 1	Meaning 2	Meaning 3	Meaning 4	Meaning 5
고 ko	고 *that right there*	고 (高) *high*	고 (考) *test, investigate*	고 (苦) *bitter, painful*	고 (古) *old*
	고 거 뭐냐? *What's that little thing?*	고교 (高校) *high school*	고사 (考査) *exam*	고생* (苦生) *hard time(s)*	고대 (古代) *ancient times*
주 cwu	주 (週) *week*	주 (主) *main, primary*	주 (酒) *liquor*	주 (住) *live*	주 (注) *feed*
	주말 (週末) *weekend*	주인 (主人) *master, owner*	음주* (飲酒) *drinking*	주소 (住所) *address*	주유소 (注油所) *gas station*
대 tay	대 (對) *opposite, to*	대 (代) *replace, substitute*	대 (大) *big*	대 (待) *wait*	대 (隊) *team, squad*
	상대 (相對) *the other party*	대신* (代身) *instead (of)*	특대품 (特大品) *XX-large size*	기대* (期待) *anticipate*	군대 (軍隊) *military*
연 yen	연 (年) *year*	연 (連) *connect*	연 (延) *drag*	연 (煙) *smoke*	연 (演) *to act*
	연말 (年末) *year's end*	연결 (連結) *connection*	연기* (延期) *postpone*	연기 (煙氣) *smoke*	연기* (演技) *act(ing)*

Look at the last three words in the table. The pronunciation (and the Korean spelling) is the same, 연기 yenki, but there are three different meanings. if someone says 연기 yenki, you can only find out the meaning from the larger context:

약속을 내일로 **연기**하자.
yaksokul nayillo yenkihaca.
Let's <u>postpone</u> our meeting till tomorrow.

연기가 많이 나서 눈물이 난다.
yenkika manhi nase nwunmwuli nanta.
There is so much <u>smoke</u>, my eyes are watering.

그 배우 **연기** 참 잘 한다.
ku paywu yenki cham cal hanta.
That actress is very good at <u>acting</u>. (She is a good actress)

You have probably guessed by now that Sino-Korean roots come in recognizable bits much like Latinate prefixes or suffixes (e.g., *pre-, in-, re-, -ity, -ism*). Sino-Korean roots are rarely used alone as independent words. They usually show up in two-syllable (two-character) words, as you saw in the chart above. This can help you in figuring out the meaning of new Sino-Korean words or homophone roots. 외 oy (外), for example, means *outside*, and 국 kwuk (國) means *country*. Putting them together will get you 외국 oykwuk (外國) *foreign country*. If you happen to know the word 한국인 hankwukin (韓

國人) *Korean person*, you can guess the meaning of 외국인 oykwukin! Let's take another example, 색맹 saykmayng (色盲) *color-blind*. If you know the part 색 sayk *color*, you can deduce that 맹 mayng probably means *blind*, right? And it does! Now, knowing that 한국인 hankwukin means *Korean person*, can you guess the meaning of the word 맹인 mayngin?

Here is another collection of amazingly useful basic 한자어 hancae roots. How many of them do you know already?

국 kwuk (國 *country*)	국산 *domestically produced*, 한국 *Korea*, 미국 *U.S.*, 중국 *China*
자 ca (自 *self*)	자제력 *self control*, 자신감 *confidence*, 자영업 *private business (self-running business)*
인 in (人 *person*)	인구 *population*, 한국인 *Korean*, 미국인 *American*, 외국인 *foreigner*
어 e (語 *language, word*)	어휘 *vocabulary*, 언어 *language*, 한국어* *Korean*, 영어* *English*
학 hak (學 *study*)	학기 *a school term*, 일학년 *freshman, 1st-grader*, 방학* *school vacation*, 학장 *university dean*
내 nay (內 *inside*)	내복 *thermal underwear*, 내용 *content*, 실내 *indoor*, 안내책자 *guide, pamphlet*
외 oy (外 *outside*)	외국어* *foreign language*, 외신 *foreign press*, 과외활동 *extracurricular activity*
고 ko (高 *high*)	고등학생 *high school student*, 고급 *high-level, high class*, 최고 *the best*
대 tay (大 *big*)	대한민국 *Republic of Korea*, 대가족 *extended family*, 확대* *enlarge*
수 swu (水 *water*)	수요일 *Wednesday*, 수영장 *swimming pool*, 냉수 *cold water*, 음료수 *beverage*
교 kyo (教 *teach*)	교수 *professor*, 교과서 *textbook*, 교재 *learning materials*
교 kyo (校 *school*)	교장 *school principal*, 교육* *education*, 학교 *school*
기 ki (機 *machine*)	기계 *machine*, 세탁기 *washing machine*, 청소기 *vacuum cleaner*, 복사기 *copier*
구 kwu (球 *ball*)	구심점 *pivot*, 축구* *soccer*, 미식축구* *football*, 농구* *basketball*, 지구 *the Earth*
장 cang (場 *ground, space*)	장소 *location*, 야구장 *baseball field*, 시장 *(open) market*, 직장 *workplace*
점 cem (店 *store*)	점원 *clerk*, 서점 *bookstore*, 백화점 *department store*, 편의점 *convenience store*

식 sik (食 eat, food)	식사* meal, 식당 restaurant, 식초 (edible) vinegar, 음식 food
서 se (西 West)	서양 the West, the Occident, 대서양 the Atlantic, 서해 the Western Sea
양 yang (洋 ocean)	양파 onion, 양동이 bucket, 양초 candle, 태평양 the Pacific, 동양 the Orient
색 sayk (色 color)	색맹 color-blind, 색연필 color pen, 색종이 colored folding paper, 청색 dark blue
일 il (日 day)	일요일 Sunday, 매일 every day, 내일 tomorrow, 생일 birthday, 일주일 one week
주 cwu (週 week)	주중 mid-week, 주말 weekend, 주급 weekly pay, 매주 every week
월 wel (月 month)	월말 end of the month, 월급 salary, 유월 June, 매월 every month
남 nam (男 male)	남자 man, 남학생 male student, 남매 brothers and sisters, 미남 good-looking man
여/녀 ye/nye (女 female)	여자 woman, 미녀 beautiful woman, 손녀 granddaughter
연/년 yen/nyen (年 year)	연세 age, 연봉 annual salary, 작년 last year, 금년 this year, 내년 next year
노/로 no/lo (老 old)	노인 elderly person, 장로 elders, 경로석 seats reserved for the elderly
노/로 no/lo (路 road)	노선 (e.g. bus) route, 노상 of the street/road, 도로 paved road, 경로 route

* These nouns can be used as verbs with the 하다 hata verb.

<3> Peculiar pronunciation traits of some Sino-Korean roots

If you look again at the last four roots in the box above, you'll see there is an alternative way to spell them (여/녀 ye/nye *female*, 연/년 yen/nyen *year*, 노/로 no/lo *old*, and 노/로 no/lo *road*). A set of 한자어 hancae rules concerning the consonants ㄹ and ㄴ is responsible for this. The spelling and pronunciation of these two consonants can be puzzling, some ㄹ being pronounced as soft ㄹ, some as long ㄹ, and yet others as ㄴ. Some are even re-WRITTEN as ㄴ or ㅇ! We explain the relevant spelling and pronunciation rules here.

Let's begin with a quick review of the pronunciation of single ㄹ, and the liquidization rule from chapter 2.

a. Word-medially, a single ㄹ between vowels is (written and) PRONOUNCED as soft ㄹ:

고려 (高麗)   [고려]
kolye   [kolye]
Koryeo Dynasty

대리판사 (代理判事)   [대리판사]
tayliphansa   [tayliphansa]
deputy judge

b. **Word-medially, when** ㄴ **meets** ㄹ **or** ㄹ **meets** ㄴ, **the sequence is** PRONOUNCED **(not spelled) as long** ㄹ.

This is the liquidization rule you learned in chapter 2. It is the pronunciation of ㄴ that changes here.

신라 (新羅)	[실라]	한라산 (漢挐山)	[할라산]
sinla	[silla]	hanlasan	[hallasan]
Shilla Dynasty		*Halla Mountain*	
실내 (室內)	[실래]	월남 (越南)	[월람]
silnay	[sillay]	welnam	[wellam]
indoors		*Vietnam*	

Note that there are also words with a ㄹㄹ sequence that are originally spelled and pronounced that way:

철로 (鐵路)	[철로]	말로 (末路)	[말로]
chello	[chello]	mallo	[mallo]
railroad, track		*one's last days, the end*	
설립 (設立)	[설립]	탈락 (脫落)	[탈락]
sellip	[sellip]	thallak	[thallak]
founding		*being eliminated, failing*	

This means that you need to pay close attention to whether a Sino-Korean noun with a long ㄹ pronunciation is written as ㄴㄹ, ㄹㄴ, or ㄹㄹ.

c. **Word-medially,** ㄹ **that follows a nasal consonant other than** ㄴ **becomes** ㄴ **in the** PRONUNCIATION **(only):**

심리학 (心理學)	[심니학]	대통령 (大統領)	[대통녕]
simlihak	[simnihak]	taythonglyeng	[taythongnyeng]
psychology		*president*	
왕릉 (王陵)	[왕능]	염려 (念慮)	[염녀]
wanglung	[wangnung]	yemlye	[yemnye]
royal tomb		*concern*	
봉루 (烽樓)	[봉누]	경로 (敬老)	[경노]
ponglwu	[pongnwu]	kyenglo	[kyengno]
beacon tower		*respect for the elderly*	

This is the nasal assimilation rule you learned in chapter 2. The condition "a nasal consonant other than ㄴ" is important because a ㄴ would give you a ㄹㄹ pronunciation sequence by rule <b>. It is only ㅁ and ㅇ that trigger the ㄹ to turn into ㄴ here.

d. Word-medially, in fact, ㄹ that follows ANY consonant other than ㄴ or ㄹ will become ㄴ in PRONUNCIATION (only); and the triggering 받침 is PRONOUNCED (but not spelled) as a nasal (ㄴ, ㅁ, or ㅇ).

급류 (急流)	[금뉴]	섭리 (攝理)	[섬니]
kuplyu	[kumnyu]	sepli	[semni]
torrent		*provision*	
육류 (肉類)	[융뉴]	백로 (白鷺)	[뱅노]
yuklyu	[yungnyu]	payklo	[payngno]
meat		*white heron*	

The rule sounds rather convoluted, but the core is simple. ㄹ turns itself into ㄴ in pronunciation following a consonant. Then this ㄴ turns the proceeding consonant into a nasal sound due to backward nasal assimilation.

> Only ㄱ and ㅂ matter as final consonants here.
> In Sino-Korean words, only six 받침 patchim are possible in writing: ㄱ, ㅂ, ㄴ, ㄹ, ㅁ, ㅇ. These are the consonants that are allowed by the 'Plain 받침 patchim 7 representative principle' from chapter 2, minus ㄷ. That is to say, in native Haan Korean, only seven simple final consonants are pronounceable in isolation, and for writing down Sino-Korean words, only six of them are used.
> For this rule, only ㄱ and ㅂ matter because ㄴ would give you a ㄹㄹ pronunciation sequence by rule <b>, ㅁ and ㅇ are already nasals, and ㄷ doesn't occur as a 받침 patchim in Sino-Korean words.

e. Word-initially, all ㄹ are PRONOUNCED and SPELLED as ㄴ.

The spelling and pronunciation of ㄹ-roots change depending not only what they show up next to but on where in the word they show up. The same Sino-Korean root can be spelled with ㄹ in the middle of a word, but with ㄴ at the beginning of a word. The pronunciation follows the spelling.

루 lwu (樓) (storied) floor:

누각 (樓閣)	[누각]	경회루 (慶會樓)	[경회루]
nwukak	[nwukak]	kyenghoylwu	[kyenghoylwu]
pavilion		*Pavilion in Kyeongbok Palace*	

로 lo (老) old:

노인 (老人)	[노인]	해로 (偕老)	[해로]
noin	[noin]	haylo	[haylo]
elderly person		*married couple aging happily together*	

f. Word initially, 녀, 뇨, 뉴, 니 and 려, 료, 류, 리 are PRONOUNCED and SPELLED as 여, 요, 유, 이.

This is to say ㄴ and ㄹ simply disappear before the *i-* or *y-* vowels at the beginning of Sino-Korean words:

녀 nye (**女**) female:

여자 (女子)	[여자]	효녀 (長女)	[효녀]
yeca	[yeca]	hyonye	[hyonye]
female		*filial daughter*	
숙녀 (淑女)	[숭녀]	열녀 (烈女)	[열려]
swuknye	[swungnye]	yelnye	[yellye]
cultured lady		*woman of (chastity) virtue from Joeon Dynasty*	

뇨 nyo (**尿**) urine:

요도염 (尿道炎)	[요도염]	비뇨기과 (泌尿器科)	[비뇨기과]
yotoyem	[yotoyem]	pinyokikwa	[pinyokikwa]
urethritis		*urology*	
당뇨병 (糖尿)	[당뇨뼝]	혈뇨 (血尿)	[혈료]
tangnyopyeng	[tangnyoppyeng]	hyelnyo	[hyellyo]
diabetes		*hematuria*	

리 li (**理**) reason, logic, morally proper governance:

이유 (理由)	[이유]	의리 (義理)	[의리]
iywu	[iywu]	uyli	[uyli]
reason		*fidelity between friends*	
공리 (公理)	[공니]	순리 (義理)	[술리]
kongli	[kongni]	swunli	[swulli]
common good		*reason, laws of nature*	

레 lyey (**禮**) propriety, courtesy, rite, ritual:

예의 (禮儀)	[예이]	차례 (茶禮)	[차례]
yeyui	[yeyi]	chalyey	[chaley]
etiquette		*commemorative rites for ancestors*	
경례 (敬禮)	[경네]	결례 (缺禮)	[결례]
kyenglyey	[kyengney]	kyellyey	[kyelley]
respectful salute		*discourtesy, bad manners*	

Let's recap using a Sino-Korean root 리 li (理) *reason, logic, natural order*. This particular Sino-Korean root may be written as 리 li or 이 i and pronounced as soft (single) 리 li or long 르리 lli, and even 니 ni or 이 i.

expected ㄹ

무리 (無理)	[무리]	물리적 (物理的)	[물리적]
mwuli	[mwuli]	mwullicek	[mwullicek]
irrational pushing,		*physical (of*	
overextension		*phenomena)*	

after ㄴ, ㄹ → ㄹ

원리 (原理)	[월리]	관리 (管理)	[괄리]
wenli	[welli]	kwanli	[kwalli]
principle		*manage(ment)*	

after final consonant other than ㄴ, ㄹ → ㄴ

총리 (總理)	[총니]	합리 (合理)	[함니]
chongli	[chongni]	hapli	[hamni]
prime minister		*rational*	

word-initially before ㅣ → ∅

이유 (理由)	[이유]	이해 (理解)	[이해]
iyu	[iywu]	ihay	[ihay]
reason		*comprehension*	

The root 리 li (理) will never be WRITTEN as 니 ni. Also, a Sino-Korean root such as 로 lo (老) *old*, on the other hand, will NEVER become 오, because the initial ㄹ and ㄴ only disappear before the ㅣ (and *y-*) vowels.

Some of these pronunciation rules exist in the South Korean dialect varieties but not in North Korean, so if you hear a South Korean comedian say 리해 lihay *understanding* or 녀자 nyeca *woman*, you know it is a satire about North Korean pronunciation.

<4> Sino-Korean nouns + 하다

Sino-Korean words, even those that denote actions or states, are nouns, grammatically speaking, and can be used as such in a sentence:

구입은 쉽지만 유지가 어렵다.
kwuipun swipciman yucika elyepta.
Purchasing is easy, but maintaining (it) is hard.
(*Purchase is easy, but maintenance is hard.*)

If a 한자어 hancae has intrinsic verbal meaning (either descriptive or active), it can be used as a grammatical verb with the addition of 하다 hata, which is otherwise an independent verb that means *do* or *speak*. The asterisked words in the charts and tables (in section <2> above) are roots that can be used with 하다 hata; not all Sino-Korean words can, though. 하다 hata comes mostly with abstract nouns such as 운동 wuntong *exercise* (e.g., 운동하다 wuntonghata *to exercise*) and 가능 kanung *possibility* (e.g., 가능하다 kanunghata *possible*), although you will see concrete daily activity nouns with 하다 as well. Below are some 한자어 hancae frequently used as noun + 하다 hata. We left out 하다 hata but translated the VERBAL 하다 hata meanings. Can you figure out the meaning of the base NOUN?

> 공부 kongpu *to study,* 숙제 swukcey *to do homework,* 전화 cenhwa *to call/talk on the phone,* 문자 mwunca *to text,* 연락 yenlak *to contact,* 인사 insa *to greet,* 축하 chwukha *to congratulate,* 세수 seyswu *to wash (one's face),* 목욕 mokyok *to take a bath,* 운동 wuntong *to exercise,* 야구 yakwu *to play baseball,* 축구 chwukkwu *to play soccer,* 농구 nongkwu *to play basketball,* 청소 chengso *to clean,* 산책 sanchayk *to take a walk,* 정리 cengli *to put in order,* 선택 sentayk *to choose,* 피곤 phikon *tired,* 어색 esayk *awkward,* 상쾌 sangkway *refreshing*

There have been on-going controversies about the make-up of the Korean lexicon, but more than 60% of Korean words are believed to be Sino-Korean, 35% native Haan Korean, and about 2%–5% words borrowed from other languages. An estimated 57% of the entries in the unabridged Korean dictionary recently published by 국립국어연구원 kwuklipkwukeyenkwuwen *National Institute of the Korean Language* are reported to be Sino-Korean words. Although the number drops to 35% for FREQUENTLY USED VOCABULARY, it is a solid fact that native Korean speakers use Sino-Korean words on a daily basis.

(2) Loanwords and Konglish

Starting at the turn of the 20th century, the Korean language saw an influx of words from languages other than Chinese and incorporated them into daily use. Here are just a few examples that seem to have stuck it out for daily or literary uses:

English:	미디어 mitie *media,* 컴퓨터 khemphyuthe *computer,* 디스크 자키 tisuku cakhi *disc jockey*
Japanese:	우동 wutong *udon,* 가방 kapang *bag,* 구두 kwutwu *dress shoes,* 냄비 naympi *pot with ears*
French:	뷔페 pwiphey *buffet,* 발레 palley *ballet,* 란제리 lanceyli *lingerie,* 고무 komwu *eraser*
Spanish:	게릴라 keylilla *guerilla,* 메리야스 meyliyasu *cotton undershirt (medias)*
Portuguese:	담배 tampay *tobacco,* 빵 ppang *bread*
German:	히스테리 histheyli *hysteria,* 아르바이트 alupaithu *part-time work (arbeit)*
Russian:	아지트 acithu *hideout (agitpunkt),* 빨치산 ppalchisan *communist guerrilla (partizan)*

Now, due to globalization and the use of the Internet, the number of words coming in and going out of use is almost impossible to keep track of. Sometimes loanwords are borrowed when Haan or Sino-Korean words already exist, and other times grammarians who try to control the traffic of the language come up with native versions of new borrowings. In the beginning, when both native words and loanwords co-exist, the loanword tends to be used for a trendier feel. Then, if the borrowed word doesn't die out, it gets settled into the language, oftentimes with a slightly changed meaning or nuance. Older people or those who do not regularly use the Internet may not even be aware of new loanwords (e.g., the plus-marked examples below). No one knows how long recent technology-related or other trendy loanwords will stay around.

Haan/Sino-Korean	New loanwords	Haan/Sino-Korean	New loanwords
치마 chima	스커트 sukhethu *skirt*	머리방, 미장원 melipang, micangwen	헤어숍/헤어샵 heyesyop/heyesyap *hair shop*
춤, 무용 chwum, mwuyong	댄스 taynsu *dance*	밥집, 식당 papcip, siktang	레스토랑 lesutholang *restaurant*
닭고기 talkkoki	치킨 chikhin *chicken*	과자 kwaca	스낵 sunayk *snack*[+]
사랑 salang	러브 lepu *love*	국수 kwukswu	누들 nwutul *noodle*[+]
사탕 sathang	캔디 khaynti *candy*	사기 전화 saki cenhwa	보이스피싱 poisuphising *voice phishing*[+]
길라잡이, 안내원 killacapi, annaywen	가이드 kaitu *guide*	댓글 tayskul	리플 liphul *reply*[+]

Korean also has many so-called Konglish words that are Korean-style English words. Some are original borrowings that settled into the language with a mismatched meaning, and others are Korean speakers' ingenious creations. Here we give just a few examples. Can you think of more?

Konglish	Meaning	Konglish	Meaning
핸드폰 hayntuphon *"hand phone"*	*cell phone*	아이쇼핑 aisyophing *"eye shopping"*	*window shopping*
컨닝 khenning *"cunning"*	*cheating*	핸들 hayntul *"handle"*	*steering wheel*
미팅 mithing *"meeting"*	*group blind date*	사이다 saita *"cider"*	*lemon-lime soda*
프림 phulim *(product name)* *"Prima"*	*creamer*	화이팅! hwaithing *"fighting"*	*You can do it!/Go, team!*
깁스 kipsu *"gips"*	*(arm/leg) cast*	OT othi *"orientation"*	*freshman orientation*
MT *"membership training"*	*class retreat*	에이에스 (A/S)/ 애프터 서비스 eyieysu/eyphuthe sepisu *"after service"*	*after-sales service, warranty/customer service*
모닝콜 moningkhol *"morning call"*	*wake-up call*	사인 sain *"sign"*	*autograph, signature*
렌즈 leyncu *"lens"*	*(contact) lenses*	볼펜 polpheyn *"ball pen"*	*(ball-point) pen*
아르바이트 alupaithu *"arbeit"*	*part-time job*	폴라티 phollathi *"polar T"*	*turtleneck*
비닐하우스 pinilhausu *"vinyl house"*	*greenhouse*	콘센트 khonseynthu *"concent(ric plug)"*	*outlet, socket*

5.2 Numerals

Now we turn to numerals, which are not considered a kind of noun in Korean grammar, but a distinct part of speech. Numbers and counting work rather differently in Korean and English. We mentioned in chapter 3 that talking about the number of items requires a counter. That will come up in section 5.3 on counters. More fundamentally, it is important to know that there are two number systems used in Korean. One is the Sino-Korean system that was borrowed from the Chinese language long ago, and the other is the native system. A good general rule of thumb is that Sino-Korean numbers are used for naming things (Page Ten, Grade Three, etc.) and Haan Korean numbers are used for counting (ten pages, three months, seven people).

5.2.1 Sino-Korean numbers

Sino-Korean numbers are used also in math. The system is simple as long as you learn numbers up to ten (십 sip), then, *eleven* is 10 + 1 (십일 sipil), and *twenty* is 2 x 10 or two tens (이십 isip).

0	영, 공	yeng, kong	8	팔	phal	
1	일	il	9	구	kwu	
2	이	i	10	십	sip	
3	삼	sam	11	십일	sipil	
4	사	sa	19	십구	sipkwu	
5	오	o	20	이십	isip	
6	육	yuk	30	삼십	samsip	
7	칠	chil	99	구십구	kwusipkwu	

(1) How to read large Sino-Korean numbers

Large Sino-Korean numbers are not too difficult either. In fact, they are much simpler than English numbers as long as you know your number at every place: 십 sip *ten*, 백 payk *hundred*, and 천 chen *thousand*. The increments work like lower numbers, so 111 (100 + 10 + 1) is 백십일 payksipil, and 900 is 9 x 100 or *nine hundreds*, 구백 kwupayk.

1	*one*	일	il
10	*ten*	십	sip
100	*hundred*	백	payk
1,000	*thousand*	천	chen

If there is a 0 in a number, that digit is skipped (…) when reading:

25 이십오
isipo

408 사백(…)팔
sapaykphal

3084 삼천(…)팔십사
samchenphalsipsa

One difficulty arises with really big numbers. The difficulty stems from the fact that the number 10,000 has its own name in Korean, 만 man. In English, because there is no name beyond *thousand* (until *million*), you have to use *ten X* or *hundred X* for numbers that go beyond 1,000, and *ten X* begins with 10,000 (*ten thousand, hundred thousand, … ten million, hundred million, …*). In Korean, since there is a name for 10,000, the 십 sip X or 백 payk X begins with 100,000 sipman (literally, *ten ten-thousands*, or *ten* 만 man) and includes 천 chen X. This makes for a mismatch between naming units in the two languages. So 10,000 is 만 man in Korean and *ten thousand* in English. 100,000 is 십만 (literally *ten 10,000*) in Korean whereas it is *hundred thousand* in English, and so on. Some more comparisions are given in the chart below with the Korean way of reading underlined and the English given in bold:

10,000	***ten** thousand*	(일)만	(il)man
100,000	***hundred** thousand*	(일)십만	sipman
1,000,000	*million*	(일)백만	paykman
10,000,000	***ten** million*	(일)천만	chenman

The mismatch between naming units in English and Korean continues into larger numbers beyond 10,000,000 because there is a separate unit name for 100,000,000 *hundred million*, namely 억 ek, in Korean (but *million, billion, trillion,* etc. in English). Again, the correlation between the numbers is noted below with the Korean way of reading underlined and the English given in bold:

100,000,000	***hundred** million*	(일)억	(il)ek
1,000,000,000	*billion*	(일)십억	sipek
10,000,000,000	***ten** billion*	(일)백억	paykek
100,000,000,000	***hundred** billion*	(일)천억	chenek
1,000,000,000,000	*trillion*	(일)조	(il)co

It will be easier to read numbers in Korean if you disregard the comma which breaks up numbers every three places (1,000,000,000). Instead, remember that the name of 10000 is 만 man, and going upwards, you need to increase 십 sip, 백 payk, 천 chen before you switch to another unit (억 ek).

So, when you encounter a large number, count how many digits there are, working backwards, or practice this way at least until you become fluent with number reading. One digit corresponds to 일 il, two digits 십 sip, three digits 백 payk, four digits 천 chen, and five digits 만 man. Then start the 십 sip - 백 payk - 천 chen cycle again until you would get to 만 man - 만 man, which is 억 ek.

See if you can read the numbers below without looking at the Korean reading. For your practice, the Arabic numbers are given with the comma dividing the number at ten thousand. For the Korean reading, each unit is separated with a dash here. When writing, put a space after every four digits, such as 만 man, 억 ek, and 조 co:

2763,2195   이천-칠백-육십-삼만-이천-백-구십-오
ichen-chilpayk-yuksip-samman-ichen-payk-kwusip-o

이천칠백육십삼만   이천백구십오
Ichenchilpaykyuksipsamman   ichenpaykkwusipo

401,5938   사백-(⋯)-일만-오천-구백-삼십-팔
sapayk-ilman-ochen-kwupayk-samsip-phal

사백일만   오천구백삼십팔
sapaykilman   ochenkwupayksamsipphal

39,5104   삼십-구만-오천-백-(⋯)-사   삼십구만   오천백사
samsipkwuman-ochen-payk-sa   samsipkwuman   ochenpaykisa

1,3672   (일)만-삼천-육백-칠십-이   만 삼천육백칠십이
man-samchen-yukpayk-chilsip-i   man samchenyukpaykchilsipi

5790   오천-칠백-구십-(⋯)   오천칠백구십
ochen-chilpayk-kwusip   ochenchilpaykkwusip

Counting coins and paper money also makes use of Sino-Korean numbers, where the number represents the face value, as if it were the NAME of that coin or bill:

만 원
man wen
10,000 won, a 10,000-won bill

십칠만 원
sipchilman wen
170,000 won

(2) Labeling and naming

In addition to math calculations and monetary transactions, Sino-Korean numbers are used to LABEL things, DESIGNATING A PARTICULAR NUMBER VALUE such as *Contestant Number One* or *Room Number 5*. They specify a particular page in a book (face value or name of that page), a floor (in a building), an address (apartment complex), and phone numbers:

사십칠 번
sasipchil pen
Number 47

오백육 호(실)
opaykyuk ho(sil)
Room 506

십 페이지
sip peyici
Page 10

오 층
o   chung
5th Floor

종로 3 가
conglo sam ka
3rd Street of Jongno

(206) 123-4567
ikongyuk ilisam sao(l)yukchil
phone number

아파트 12동
aphathu sipi tong
12th building in an apartment complex

Since Sino-Korean numbers name things, they are also used for time expressions such as ages, years, months, dates, and interestingly for minutes and seconds (but NOT hours):

Jan.	1월	일월	ilwel	July	7월	칠월	chilwel
Feb.	2월	이월	iwel	Aug.	8월	팔월	phalwel
Mar.	3월	삼월	samwel	Sept.	9월	구월	kwuwel
Apr.	4월	사월	sawel	Oct.	10월	시월*	siwel
May	5월	오월	owel	Nov.	11월	십일월	sipilwel
June	6월	유월*	yuwel	Dec.	12월	십이월	sipiwel

(*Pay attention to *June* and *October* which drop the final consonant for ease of pronunciation; they are written as 유월 yuwel and 시월 siwel without spacing between the two words. The month suffix 월 wel may be written with or without a space.)

2021년 (이천이십일 년)
ichenisipil nyen
(the year) 2021

5분 27초 (오분 이십칠 초)
opwun isipchil cho
five minutes twenty-seven seconds

63세 (육십 세)
yuksip se
60 years of age

3주일 (삼 주일)
sam cwuil
three weeks

30분 (삼십 분)
samsip pwun
thirty minutes

6개월 (육 개월)
yuk kaywel
six months

제 생일은 양력 유월 삼십 일이에요.
cey sayngilun yanglyek yuwel samsip ilieyyo.
My birthday is 6/30 by the solar calendar.

음력으로 팔 월 십오 일은 추석입니다.
umlyekulo phal wel sipo ilun chwusekipnita.
8/15 by the lunar calendar is the Full Moon Festival.

Finally, for Sino-Korean ORDINAL NUMBERS (*first, second*, etc.), simply add 제 ce:

제1 과
ceil kwa
Lesson 1 (literally, *the first lesson*)

제2 기숙사
cei kiswuksa
the second dormitory

5.2.2 Native Haan numbers

Native Haan numbers are used for COUNTING things; that is, talking about how many. There are distinct number words for *one* through *ten*, and for each of the tens, but no Haan number beyond 99, so Sino-Korean numbers have to be used for 백 payk *hundred,* 천 chen *thousand,* 만 man *ten thousand* and 억 ek *hundred thousand* (e.g. 아흔아홉

개 ahun ahop kay, 백 개 payk kay, 백한 개 payk han kay, 백두 개 payk twu kay...). In fact, these days, Koreans tend to use Sino-Korean numbers starting with 40 or 50 in most counting situations. Here is a chart of the Haan numbers:

	Noun form		Adnominal form				Noun form		Adnominal form	
0	공/영	kong/yeng				10	열	yel		
1	하나	hana	한	han		20	스물	sumwul	스무	sumwu
2	둘	twul	두	twu		30	서른	selun		
3	셋	seys	세	sey		40	마흔	mahun		
4	넷	neys	네	ney		50	쉰	swin		
5	다섯	tases				60	예순	yeyswun		
6	여섯	yeses				70	일흔	ilhun		
7	일곱	ilkop				80	여든	yetun		
8	여덟	yetelp				90	아흔	ahun		
9	아홉	ahop								

In isolation, the NOUN forms (하나 hana, 둘 twul, 셋 seys, etc.) are used, and when the numbers modify what they are counting or when they come before a counter, their ADNOMINAL FORMS are used. Only five numbers have an adnominal form, namely 1, 2, 3, 4, and 20; they basically drop the final consonant (e.g., 둘 twul → 두 twu) or merge two syllables into one (e.g., 하나 hana → 한 han). *Twenty* gets back its full form when counting beyond 21, however: 스무 개 sumwu kay *twenty (of something)*, but 스물 다섯 개 sumwul tases kay *twenty-five (of something).*

When the number 한 han emphasizes unspecificity, it means *some certain unidentified (individual):*

한 번은 이런 일이 있었어요.
han penun ilen ili issesseyo.
There was this (one) time when this thing happened...

한 학생이 왔었어요.
han haksayngi wassesseyo.
Some certain student stopped by.

One of the main ways Haan numbers are used, which in fact doesn't seem much like counting, is for telling time. As you know, Sino-Korean numbers are used for minutes and seconds, but for reading off the hour part of the time, HAAN KOREAN numbers have to be used:

2:35	**두**	시	삼십오	분	7:19	**일곱** 시	십구	분
	twu	si	samsipo	pwun		ilkop si	sipkwu	pwun

4:18   **네** 시 십팔 분
ney si sipphal pwun

8:02   **여덟** 시 이 분
yetelp si i pwun

For *A.M.* and *P.M.*, 오전 ocen and 오후 ohwu can be used, respectively, but in Korean, these words come BEFORE the time. You can consider 오 o to mean *noon* (it really refers to the time between 11:00 AM and 1:00 PM); 오전 ocen covers the time between dawn and noon-ish, and 오후 ohwu refers to the time from noon-ish until the sunset.

For the *half-hour*, 반 pan (literally *half*) can be used. (*A quarter hour* is not used in Korean):

5:30 A.M.   오전 다섯 시 **반** ocen tases si pan

And, to express *till* or *before*, 전 can be used:

6:45 P.M.   오후 일곱 시 십오분 **전** ohwu ilkop si sipo pwun cen

A day can also be divided into two: 낮 nac *during the day/day time* and 밤 pam *night time*, but for telling time, more specific time concepts are used: 새벽 saypyek *dawn hours*, 아침 achim *morning*, 점심 cemsim *noon-time*, and 저녁 cenyek *evening*. The last three words can also refer to the three meals of the day.

10:15 in the morning   아침 열 시 십오 분 achim yel si sipo pwun

7:30 in the evening   저녁 일곱 시 반 cenyek ilkop si pan

11:20 at night   밤 열한 시 이십 분 pam yelhan si isip pwun

Finally, for ORDINAL NUMBERS, the suffix -(번)째 (pen)ccay is attached to Haan numbers, and number one has a special form, 첫 ches:

첫째, 둘째, 셋째, 넷째, 다섯째, 여섯째, 일곱째, 여덟째, 아홉째, 열째…, 몇 째
chesccay, twulccay, seysccay, neysccay, tasesccay, yesesccay, ilkopccay, yetelpccay, ahopccay, yelccay…, myech ccay
first, second, third, fourth, fifth, sixth, seventh, eighth, ninth, tenth…, (Which place?)

첫 번째, 두 번째, 세 번째, 네 번째, 다섯 번째… 열 번째…, 몇 번째
ches penccay, twu penccay, sey pensccay, ney pensccay, tases penccay… yel penccay…, mye penchccay
first (time), second time), third (time), fourth (time), fifth (time)…, tenth (time)…, (Which time around?)

첫째 딸   *the oldest ("first") daughter*
chesccay ttal

매달 첫째 일요일 *the first Sunday of each month*
maytal chesccay ilyoil

셋째 주 *the third week*
seysccay cwu

두 번째 여행 *the second-time travel, the second trip*
twu penccay yehayng

5.3 Counters and Dependent Nouns

You know from previous chapters that dependent nouns are grammatical nouns that are subpar in their size and function compared to full nouns. There is not a huge number of dependent nouns in Korean. Some dependent nouns have meanings that are hard to translate on their own, but they are at the heart of very useful idiomatic expressions. Many of the dependent nouns are **counters**, words used to express the number of things (and people, etc.). The reverse is not true: not all counters are dependent nouns. We will look at the details of how counters work and then some of the most frequently used dependent nouns that are not counters.

5.3.1 Counters

When you count most items in English, you just say "number + noun": *one book, two books, four friends, or ten bucks*. Or, if it so happens that what you want to count cannot be counted individually, like *sugar*, you find other ways to count them by using countable units that show the amount (e.g., *two kilos of sand*), or, COUNTERS: *two cups of sugar, three bags of sand*. When you say *two cups of sugar*, you want to know how much sugar there is rather than the number of cups, so *cups* is really a work-around for "counting" sugar. Some English nouns, although they appear countable on their own, require counters to be counted: *five sheets of paper, three pairs of jeans*.

In Korean, if you want to count ANYTHING, you have to use a counter. Counters are sometimes called **classifiers**, because the choice of counter depends on the specific item being counted, and the criterion is usually the semantic category the item belongs to (e.g., Is it a long thin object like a pencil or is it a flat sheet like a CD?). Here we'll show the grammar of counters, which counters are used with which nouns, which counters are used with which NUMBERS, and overlaps in the usage of counters and regular nouns.

(1) Grammar of counters

When you use a counter, the typical word order is noun-number-counter. There should be a space between the number and counter, according to standard orthography, although many native speakers ignore the practice in casual writing:

포도 두 **송이**를 샀어요.
photo twu songilul sasseyo.
I bought two bunches of grapes.

발렌타인데이에 장미 한 **송이**를 받았어요.
palleynthainteyiey cangmi han songilul patasseyo.
I received a rose on Valentine's Day.

The PARTICLES may come after the entire noun-number-counter phrase as you have just seen. They can also come after the noun before the number, breaking the phrase up:

포도를 두 **송이** 샀어요.
photo-lul twu songi sasseyo.
I bought two bunches of grapes.

발렌타인데이에 장미를 한 **송이** 받았어요.
palleynthainteyiey cangmilul han songi patasseyo.
I received a rose on Valentine's Day.

If you want to use the English counter structure (number-counter-*of*-items being counted), it is possible to say 세 잔의 커피 sey canuy khephi *three cups of coffee*, but perhaps only as the title of a book. 커피 세 잔 khephi sey can *three cups of coffee* is the natural way.

When speaking casually, just the noun form of the number (that is, without the counter) can be used, but not all nouns can be counted this way, just really frequent ones:

입장료가 얼마예요? 성인 **다섯**, 소인 **둘**입니다.
ipcanglyoka elmayeyyo? sengin tases, soin twulipnita. (명 myeng is the expected counter here.)
How much is the entrance fee? Five adults and two minors.

펜 **하나** 가져와라.
peyn hana kacye wala. (자루 calu is the expected counter here.)
Bring me a pen.

맥주 **둘** 주세요.
maykcwu twul cwuseyyo. (병 pyeng is the expected counter here.)
Give us two (bottles of) beer, please.

(2) Which counter?

As we mentioned, the choice of which counter to use with which nouns is based on some characteristic of the items, such as their shape and size. Some items are counted by the same counter because they look similar, or because they achieve similar functions. For example, because they are a thin layer, 종이 congi *paper*, 시디 siti *CD*, and 엽서 yepse *postcard* are counted with 장 cang. Because they all carry messages, 편지 phyenci *letter*, 이메일 imeyil *email*, 전화 cang *phone call* all share the same counter 통 thong. You may soon realize, though, what belongs to what category might seem artibrary, as musical instruments like 기타 kitha *guitar* or 피아노 phiano *piano* and machines or electronic appliances like a car or TV are all counted with the same counter 대 tay. In some cases, a particular counter is used to count only a few items in the whole world. 켤레 khyelley, for example, is used only for footwear (pairs of shoes), and 척 chek is used only to count boats! Since you can't just select the counters willy-nilly based on what you imagine to form a category and instead you have to follow conventions, the best way to conquer the counters is to just memorize them as they occur with particular objects being counted.

(3) Nouns used as counters

Some regular nouns function as counters with their original meaning (e.g., 접시 cepsi *plate*, 병 pyeng *bottle*, 컵 khep *cup*, 잔 can *glass*, 그릇 kulus *bowl*, 상자 sangca *box*, 통 thong *container*). When these full, regular nouns are used as counters, the meaning is fairly transparent, just like with uncountable nouns in English (e.g., *three bags of sand*), but the thing whose amount is being expressed has to be stated FIRST in Korean:

밥　한　**그릇** *one bowl of rice*
pap　han　kulus
rice　one　bowl

커피　두　**잔** *two cups of coffee*
khephi　twu　can
coffee　two　cup

(4) Counters that are the things being counted

Some counters do not require you to spell out what is being counted. Unlike other counters that can count a whole array of items in a particular category, these counters tend to count one very specific item, or, you could say that the counters themselves are being counted (e.g., 해 hay *sun/year*, 달 tal *moon/month*, 시간 sikan *time/hour*, 번 pen *times*). Since there is no need to prepose what you are counting, this sort of counting is most similar to how regular count nouns are counted in English.

한 **해** *one year*
han hay

두 **달** *two months*
twu tal

세 **시간** *three hours*
sey sikan

네 **번** *four times*
ney pen

너 (몸무게가/체중이) 몇 **킬로**야?
ne (mommwukeyka/cheycwungi) myech khilloya?
How many kilograms are you/is your body weight?

(5) Purely functional counters

There is another group of counters that can be tricky for native English speakers. Their meaning is not very clear by themselves, and they don't serve any function other than just being a counter (e.g., 끼 kki for meals, 그루 kulwu for trees):

가난해서 하루에 밥 한 **끼** 먹기도 힘들었다.
kananhayse halwuey pap han kki mekkito himtulessta.
They were so poor that even one daily meal was a luxury.

식목일이라 나무 한 **그루** 심었다.
sikmokilila namwu han kulwu simessta.
Since it's Arbor Day, I've planted a tree.

Of this functional counter group, the most widely used is 개 kay, which can be used in unrefined, spoken language for almost any small, inanimate, individual object:

펜 한 **개** (자루 is expected here.) 가져와라.
peyn han kay (calwu) kacye wala.
Bring me a pen.

개 is also the counter to use to count those regular nouns that are used as counters (that is, you are interested in counting the actual CONTAINERS and not what might go in them):

병 세 **개**만 가져와라.   상자 두 **개**가 필요해요.
pyeng sey kayman kacyewala.   sangca twu kayka philyohayyo.
Bring me three (empty) bottles.   *I need two (empty) boxes.*

(6) Which numbers?

It is true that counters are used for counting (and not labeling), so you may assume that Haan Korean numbers alone are used with counters and not Sino-Korean numbers. Interestingly, both sets of numerals are used with counters, and the numbers need to AGREE, in a sense, with the counters, so what type of word the counter is (Sino-Korean or Haan-Korean) matters as well.

<1> Counters used with Haan Korean numbers

Since the primary function of Haan Korean numbers is counting, Haan numbers show up with a lot of different counters.

Recall that the ADNOMINAL forms 한 han, 두 twu, 세 sey, 네 ney, and 스무 sumwu are used in phrases like the following for the numbers 하나 hana, 둘 twul, 셋 seys, 넷 neys, and 스물 sumwul:

학생 한 **명** *one student*   고양이 두 **마리** *two cats*
haksayng han myeng   koyangi twu mali

커피 세 **잔** *three cups of coffee*   종이 네 **장** *four sheets of paper*
khephi sey can   congi ney cang

책 다섯 **권** *five books*   맥주 스무 **병** *twenty bottles of beer*
chayk tases kwen   maykcwu sumwu pyeng

The following are some of the most frequently used counters. Approximate English translations are in italics, and items counted are in plain font:

List of most common counters used with Haan Korean numbers

Categories	Counters
containers	잔 can *glass*, 컵 khep *cup*, 병 pyeng *bottle*, 그릇 kulus *bowl*, 접시 cepsi *plate* 상자 sangca *box*, 통 thong *container; can*

Categories	Counters
time	해 hay years, 달 tal months, 시간 sikan hours, 번 pen times
clothing	벌 pel suits, 장 cang t-shirts/sheets, 켤레 khyelley *pair* – socks/shoes
stationery	자루 calu pencils/brooms, 장 cang *sheets* – paper/blankets, 권 kwen *volumes* – books 통 thong letters/emails/calls, 부 pwu newspapers/books
animals, plants, vegetables, fruit	사람 salam person, 명 myeng person, 분 pwun person-honorific 그루 kulwu trees, 송이 songi *bunch* – grapes/flower blooms/snow flakes 통 thong watermelons/melons, 단 tan *bunch* – veggies/firewood, 모 mo *cube* – tofu 묶음 mwukkum *tied up bunch* – firewood, 뿌리 ppwuli *root* – ginseng 알 al *pill/egg* – chestnuts/gingko nuts/potatoes, 포기 phoki *head* – cabbages, clumps of grass 조각 cokak *piece, slice* 덩어리 tengeli *lump, clump* – bread loaves, meat, dirt, gold
machines, instruments	대 tay cars, electronics, musical instruments, 척 chek boats
buildings	채 chay houses/buildings
abstract artifacts	곡 kok songs (written or sung), 가락 kalak songs (only when sung), 마디 mati *a word*, 편 phen poems/films/novels, 수 swu poems, 판 phan *round* – games (e.g., board games)
general items	개 kay objects
others	끼 kki meals, 줌 cwum *a fistful*, 모금 mokum *a gulp*, 방울 pangwul *a drop*, 개비 kaypi *stick* – cigarettes/matches, 갑 kap *packet* – cigarettes

<2> Counters with Sino-Korean numbers

Under normal circumstances, HAAN Korean numbers appear with the counters, be-cause they are the numbers used for counting, whereas SINO-KOREAN numbers usually have the function of naming something. In many cases when SINO-KOREAN NOUNS are counted, though, it tends to be SINO-KOREAN NUMBERS that are used. You can think of this as a kind of grammatical category agreement.

Some counters are used with both Sino- and Haan Korean numbers. When that happens, the Sino-Korean numbers (the 일, 이, 삼 version of numbers) put a LABEL or name to the item, and the Haan Korean numbers (the 한, 두, 세 kind) COUNT the quantity:

십 **페이지** sip peyici *Page 10*	vs.	열 **페이지** yel peyici *10 pages*
삼 **번** sam pen *Number 3*	vs.	세 **번** sey pen *3 times*
오 **과** o kwa *Chapter 5*	vs.	다섯 **과** tases kwa *five chapters*

This is of course only a generalization. Some deeply nativized Sino-Korean counters use Haan numbers, and relatively new Western counters use Sino-Korean numbers.:

이 킬로그램 i khillokulaym *2 kg*   vs.   두 근 twu kun (斤) *1200 grams*

Did you know that how much 근 measures is different depending on what is weighed? When weighing meat or traditional medicinal herbs, one 근 amounts to 600 grams; when weighing fruit or vegetables, a 근 is 375 grams, which is one tenth of one 관 kwan (貫)!

When, although very occasionally, both Sino-Korean number + Sino-Korean counter and Haan number + Haan counter convey the same meaning, the native version is likely to sound more poetic or romantic and the Sino-Korean version more factual and pragmatic. This is because Haan vocabulary is closer to the heart of the speakers:

Sino-Korean   Haan Korean

일 년 il nyen *one year*   vs.   한 해 han hay *one year*
이 개월 i kaywel *two months*   vs.   두 달 twu tal *two months*

The following is a table of Sino-Korean counters that are used with Sino-Korean numbers. Though this list is not exhaustive, there are notably fewer than are used with Haan Korean (counting) numbers. You will also notice that the items being counted involve typical Western or scientific measurements and delimitations of living or governing quarters. Some of them are more frequently used than others, but it will be helpful to learn all of them:

List of most common counters used with Sino-Korean numbers and Western units

Categories	Counters
time	년 nyen *years,* 개월 kaywel *months,* 일 il *days,* 분 pwun *minutes,* 초 cho *seconds*
money	원 wen *KRW,* 불 pwul *dollars,* 전 cen *cents*
weight	킬로그램 khillokulaym *kilograms,* 그램 kulaym *grams*
length/distance	킬로미터 khillomithe *kilometers,* 미터 mithe *meters,* 센티미터 seynthimithe *centimeters*
portion	인분 inpwun *serving portions*
family relations	삼촌 samchon *uncle,* 사촌 sachon *cousin,* 오촌 ochon *first cousin once removed,* 육촌 yukchon *second cousin*
other numbered systems	학년 haknyen *year in school,* 동 tong *buildings in a complex,* 층 chung *floors,* 호 ho *rooms,* 번 pen *numbers,* 과 kwa *chapters*

(7) Use of counters in sentences

The following examples show how the counters are used in sentences:

한 시간 동안 친구하고 채팅했어요.
han sikan tongan chinkwuhako chaythinghaysseyo.
I chatted with my friend for an hour.

지난 주말에 책을 **두 권** 읽었어요.
cinan cwumaley chaykul twu kwen ilkesseyo.
I read two books last weekend.

선물로 운동화를 **세 켤레**나 받았어.
senmwullo wuntonghwalul sey khyelleyna patasse.
I got three (!) pairs of sneakers for a present.

그 집은 차가 **세 대** 있지만 다 걸어 다녀.
ku cipun chaka sey tay issciman ta kele tanye.
They have three cars, but everyone walks to work.

나는 오늘 돈이 **일 원**도 없는데?
nanun onul toni il wento epsnuntey?
I don't even have a single penny today.

술 **한 잔** 하고 들어갈까?
swul han can hako tulekalkka?
Shall we have a drink before going home?

펜 **한 자루**만 빌려줄래?
pheyn han calwuman pillyecwullay?
Can I borrow a pen?

모두 **몇 분**이세요?
motwu myech pwuniseyyo?
How many of you in all?

여기 불고기 2 인분만 주세요!
yeki pwulkoki i inpwunman cwuseyyo!
Bulgogi for two here, please!

노래방에 왔는데 **한 곡** 부르셔야죠.
nolaypangey wassnuntey han kok pwulusyeyacyo.
We are here at noraebang; you gotta sing a song.

Appropriate use of counters will make your Korean sound much more natural and sophisticated.

5.3.2 Dependent Nouns

Now on to dependent nouns that are not counters. As introduced in chapter 3, **dependent nouns** are not recognized by Korean speakers as full-blown, stand-alone nouns. However, they are useful and highly frequent in everyday language. Many of them are counters, and some have a normal noun meaning, but most importantly, they all must have some sort of a modifier before them, which is why they are called dependent nouns. We'll talk about two sets here. The first set translates well as normal nouns in English, and the second set translates well only within a set expression.

(1) Useful dependent nouns: 것, 일, 곳, 데, 때

The four most useful dependent nouns are 것 kes *thing*, 일 il *matter/business/happening/task*, 곳 kos (formal) and 데 tey (casual) both meaning *place*, and 때 ttay *time when*. Although 일 il and 때 ttay are considered full nouns in standard grammar, we will treat them as dependent nouns here. These dependent nouns must always have a modifier before them, but they are written with a space.

단 **것**	큰 **일**	바쁜 **때**
tan kes	khun il	pappun ttay
a sweet thing, something sweet	*a big deal, matter, problem*	*a busy time*

조용한 **곳**	조용한 **데**
coyonghan kos	coyonghan tey
a quiet place, some place quiet	*a quiet place, some place quiet*

한 **때**는 우리도 젊었었다.
han   ttaynun   wulito   celmessessta.
We, too, were young at some point. (at one time we, too, were young)

When 것 kes, 곳 kos/데 tey, and 때 ttay are modified by a sentence, they can be translated as *what*, *where*, and *when* without the interrogative (question) meaning, that is, *what/a thing that…*, *a place where…*, *a time when…*:

어제 거기서 같이 본 **것**
ecey kekise kathi pon kes
what we saw there together yesterday

우리가 작년에 항상 만나던 **데**
Wulika caknyeney hangsang mannaten tey
where we always met last year

이제는 아무도 모르는 버려진 **곳**
icenun amwuto molunun pelyecin kos
somewhere deserted where no one knows

The noun 때 ttay is typically modified by a sentence adorned with -었을 -essul, thus -었을 때 -essul ttay *the time when I did (something)*:

어제 내가 너를 봤을 **때**
ece nayka nelul pwassul ttay
when I saw you yesterday

네가 울면서 방을 뛰쳐 나갔을 **때**
neyka wulmyense pangul ttwichye nakassul ttay
when you burst out of the room, crying

(2) Dependent nouns in idiomatic phrases: 때문, 적, 수, 지, 체, 뻔

There are also a number of dependent nouns that are used only in idiomatic phrases. For now, let's learn 때문 ttaymwun (*for the*) *reason* (*that*), 적 cek *experience*, 수 swu *capability*, 지 ci *since* (*the time*), 체 che *pretense*, and 뻔 ppen *almost* (these don't all translate as nouns in English). We recommend learning the whole idiomatic phrase and just noting from this discussion that it is based around a dependent noun. Each expression is spelled out in parentheses. We will revisit the them in later chapters:

감기 **때문에** 학교에 안 갔어요.
kamki ttaymwuney hakkyoey an kasseyo.
Because of a cold, I didn't go to school. (noun 때문에 ttaymwuney)

한국에 가 본 **적**이 있어요?
hankwukey ka pon ceki isseyo?
Have you ever been to Korea? (-(으)ㄴ 적이 있다 -(u)n ceki issta)

할 **수** 있어요!
hal swu isseyo!
I can do it! (-(으)ㄹ 수 있다 -(u)l swu issta)

이사온 **지** 일 년 됐어요.
isaon ci il nyen twaysseyo.
It's been a year since we moved (here). (-(으)ㄴ 지 됐다 -(u)n ji twaysta)

아는 **체** 좀 그만해.
anun chey com kumanhay.
Stop acting like a know-it-all. (verb+는/adjective -은 체 -nun/-(u)n chey)

큰일 날 **뻔**했어.
khunil nal ppenhaysse.
That was a narrow escape/close call. (Something bad almost happened.)
(-(으)ㄹ 뻔 했다 -(u)l ppen haysta)

5.4 Pronouns

The word **pronoun** literally means *in place of nouns*, and that's indeed how they work! For example, instead of using the same name *Mary* over and over again, you can use the pronouns *she* or *her*. You also probably want to sometimes refer to something as *this* instead of calling it *the thing that is closer to me than you*. If you don't know the person's name, you will want to use *who*, and if you don't have specific information, you may need to say *something/somewhere*, etc. These are personal, demonstrative, interrogative, and indefinite pronouns in English, respectively, and Korean has comparable pronouns.

5.4.1 Demonstrative adnominals and pronouns

In English, there is a two-way distinction between *here* and *there*, and the demonstrative adnominals and pronouns *this* and *that*. In Korean, there is a THREE-WAY distance distinction, with *that over there (far from me and you)* in the system.

(1) 이, 그, 저 and 이거, 그거, 저거

The **demonstrative** ADNOMINALS 이 i *this (close to me)*, 그 ku *that (close to you)*, and 저 ce *that over there (close to neither of us)* come before nouns to modify them. There is no difference in demonstratives before singular and plural nouns, unlike in English (*this* vs. *these*). These adnominals are written with a space before a regular noun and without a space before a dependent noun; they always must be followed by a noun.

> 저분 cepwun *that (honorable) person*　　　그쪽 kuccok *that side*
>
> 그 학생들 ku haksayngtul *those students*　　이 방들 i pangtul *these rooms*
>
> 저 사람들 ce salamtul *those people*

In English, the demonstrative adnominals *this* and *that* can also be used as demonstrative PRONOUNS, substituting for nouns (as in *I like this* and *Give me that*). In Korean, however, demonstrative adnominals 이 i, 그 ku, and 저 ce can only function as MODIFIERS, so if there is no other full noun you want to use, you need a filler noun, 것 kes or 거 ke *thing*, to make them pronouns: 이것 ikes, 그것 kukes, and 저것 cekes, or 이거 ike, 그거 kuke, and 저거 ceke. Of the two options, 것 kes is the full form and is used in formal or written language (or in spoken Korean to be facetiously pompous):

> 이 집 i cip *this house*
>
> 이거 언제 샀어? *When did you buy this (one)?*
> ike encey sasse?
>
> 이 ~~언제 샀어?~~ ~~*When did you buy this?*~~
> encey sasse?

저거 주세요.
ceke cwuseyyo.
Give me that, please/I would like that one, please.

그는 그 어느 것도 성에 차지 않았다.
kunun ku enu kesto sengey chaci anhassta.
He wasn't satisfied with any of them.

It is important to learn one special aspect of the pronoun 그것 kukes/그거 kuke *that*. In addition to referring to an object physically close to the listener, it plays double-duty and refers to something previously mentioned or at least understood by both the listener and the speaker, pretty much like the English pronoun *it*. It works for abstract "things" and whole sentences or facts. The other *that* in Korean (저것 cekes/저거 ceke), on the other hand, can only refer to physical things that you are looking or pointing at (unless you are a speaker of a non-standard dialect):

나한테 왜 그거 말 안 해 줬어?
nahanthey way kuke mal an hay cwesse?
Why didn't you tell me that?

그거 어디 있어?
kuke eti isse?
Where is it?

그것들도 봤나요?
kukestulto pwassnayo?
Did you see them, too?

저거 어디 있어?
ceke eti isse?
Where is it?

With the topic, subject, and object particles attached, the demonstrative forms used in spoken Korean become quite contracted:

Demonstrative Adnominals	Demonstrative Pronouns	+ Topic	+ Subject	+ Object
이 i *this*	이거 ike *this thing*	이것은 ikesun → **이건** iken	이것이 ikesi → **이게** ikey	이것을 ikesul → **이걸** ikel
그 ku *that*	그거 kuke *that thing*	그것은 kukesun → **그건** kuken	그것이 kukesi → **그게** kukey	그것을 kukesul → **그걸** kukel
저 ce *that over there*	저거 ceke *that thing over there*	저것은 cekesun → **저건** ceken	저것이 cekesi → **저게** cekey	저것을 cekesul → **저걸** cekel

이 i/그 ku/저 ce and 거 ke (or 것 kes) come from two separate words, but the combination is considered ONE pronoun so they are all written without a space (with or without a particle):

이건 또 뭐예요?
iken tto mweyeyyo?
And, what is this?

그건 두고 이걸 옮겨 주세요.
kuken twuko ikel olmkye cwuseyyo.
Leave that and move this for me, please.

In colloquial speech, you may hear Korean speakers say 이거 ike/그거 kuke/저거 ceke where you expect 이 i/그 ku/저 ce, referring to the same object redundantly:

저거 빨간 거 (instead of 저 빨간 거) 주세요.
ceke ppalkan ke   ce ppalkan ke cwuseyyo.
Give me that red thing. ("Give me that thing, red thing.")

DEMONSTRATIVE ADVERBS (e.g. *here, there*) also fall into the same three-way pattern. As a mnemonic trick, you might imagine a hypothetical noun 어기 eki *place* that combines with이 i, 그 ku, and 저 ce:

Demonstrative Adnominals	Demonstrative Pronouns	Demonstrative Adverbs
이 i *this*	이거 ike *this thing*	(이 *어기 i eki) → **여기** yeki *this place/here*
그 ku *that*	그거 kuke *that thing*	(그 *어기 ku eki) → **거기** keki *that place/there*
저 ce *that over there*	저거 ceke *that thing over there*	(저 *어기 ce eki) →**저기** ceki *that place over there/over there*

Here are some examples.

여기가 어디지?   거기 앉아
yekika etici?   keki anca
Where am I?   *Sit over there.*

(2) 요, 고, 조

If what you are referring to is small and if you want to give the hearer the impression that it is within a really close range, you can use the diminutive versions of the demonstratives 요 yo, 고 ko, and 조 co. This comes from the vowel harmony we talked about in chapter 1, where the two vowels 아 a and 오 o are light vowels and give you the sense of bright, light, and small.

Spatial Relationship	Diminutive Demonstrative Adnominals	Diminutive Demonstrative Pronouns	Diminutive Demonstrative Adverbs
from the speaker's point of view	요 yo *this very/small...*	요것 yokes, 요거 yo ke *this very/small (thing)*	요기 yoki *right here*
from the listener's point of view	고 ko *that very/small...*	고것 kokes, 고거 ko ke *that very/small (thing), it*	고기 koki *right there*
far away from the listener and speaker	조 co *that very/small... over there*	조것 cokes, 조거 co ke *that very/small (thing) over there*	조기 coki *right over there*

Extended to abstract nouns, the diminutive 요 yo, 고 ko, 조 co emphasize the insignificance or lightness of a task. For example,

요게 다야?
yokey taya?
This (tiny bit) is all?

고게 어딨지?
kokey etissci?
Where is that (little) thingy?

조것들만 끝내 주세요.
cokestulman kkuthnay cwuseyyo.
Please finish just those (swiftly, and then you'll be done).

5.4.2 Personal pronouns

Though pronouns are often dropped in natural Korean, they do exist and they express the same first, second and third person singular (*I, you,* and *he/she/it*) and plural (*we, you-all,* and *they*) as English does. To achieve the case distinctions (subject vs. object (*I* vs. *me*), and so on) and possessive adjectives, Korean uses particles on the pronouns just as it uses particles on regular nouns. For the possessive NOUNS and *it*, 것 kes/거 ke *thing* is used. Gender distinctions are almost non-existent.

The system is simpler than that of English, but one important complication to be aware of is the additional dimension of **honorifics**. Social relationships are demonstrated in the Korean language in a number of ways, and one of those ways is by choosing pronouns to honor the right people and to humble oneself when talking to certain others. This is done through **honorific** and **humble pronouns**, as opposed to what we will call "familiar" pronouns. **Familiar pronouns** are used when talking to close friends, peers and children. **Humble pronouns** show the lower social status of the person being referred to (and usually to show respect for someone else with a higher social status), and **honorific pronouns** are used to show respect for the person referred to, who has a higher social status (such as older people, bosses, etc.).

(1) The first person pronouns

Here is a table for the first person pronouns that is comparable to the English "*I, my, me, mine*" and plural "*we, our, us, ours*" table. Here we need to distinguish the familiar forms from humble form, which are used to recognize one's own lower social status with respect to the listener (and likewise, the listener's honored status). Notice that there is no honorific form of *I/we* because ONE NEVER, EVER honors oneself. In a polite context, or when talking to someone "equally" honored, the humble pronouns are used.

1st Person	Familiar			
	Subject Pronoun	Possessive Adjective	Other Cases	Possessive Pronoun
Singular	내 nay + 가 ka *I*	내 nay *my*	나 na + particles *me*	내 것 nay kes 내 거 nay ke *mine*
Plural	우리(들) wuli(tul) + particles *we/us/our*			우리(들) 것 wuli(tul) kes 우리(들) 거 wuli(tul) ke *ours*

1st Person	Humble			
	Subject Pronoun	Possessive Adjective	Other Cases	Possessive Pronoun
Singular	제 cey + 가 ka *I*	제 cey *my*	저 ce + particles *me*	제 것 cey kes 제 거 cey ke *mine*
Plural	저희(들) cehuy(tul) + particles *we/us/our*			저희(들) 것 cehuy(tul) kes 저희(들) 거 cehuy(tul) ke *ours*

For the singular first person FAMILIAR PRONOUN, 나 is the base form to which any particle can be attached (e.g., 나는 nanun, 나만 naman, 나도 nato, 나를 nalul, 나한테 nahanthe, and 나와 nawa), except for subjects.

나는 오늘 바빠. *I'm busy today.*
nanun onul pappa.

나도 오늘 바빠. *I'm also busy today.*
nato onulpappa.

나를 사랑해 줘. *Please love me.*
nalul salanghay cwue.

For the SUBJECT particle, the base form is 내, so you say 내가 nayka (and not 나가 naka unless you are a speaker of a southern dialect):

내가 왔어요.   *I'm here!*
nayka wasseyo.

Since 내 nay is the base form for the subject particle only, you do not say 내도 nayto *I too* or 내만 nayman *I alone* (unless you are a speaker of a southern dialect).

The possessive form is a shortened form of the expected 나 na + 의 uy: 내 nay *my*. So, for *my book*, you say 내 책 nay chayk, which is a contracted version of 나의 책 nauy chayk. The form 내 nay looks like the base subject pronoun, so do not get confused about the meaning.

For *mine*, you can simply use 내 nay plus the word 것 kes (formal) or 거 ke (informal), which means *thing*. The pronunciation of this word after the possessive 내 nay is [꺼 kke]. By convention, the space is observed after possessive pronouns, even though the words 내 and 것/거 are both short:

그거 내 거야.   *That's mine.* (Literally, *that thing is my thing.*)
kuke nay keya.

The humble forms, used when speaking to someone to be honored, work quite similarly. The base form is 저 ce, and particles are added as usual, except for the subject and possessives. The base form of the humble subject is 제 cey, not 저 ce, so with the subject particle, the form is 제가 ceyka. Also, as with the familiar possessive 내 nay, be careful with the humble possessive 제 cey, which is a contracted version of 저 ce + 의 uy *my* (humble). Don't get it confused with the base form of the humble subject 제 cey—they are spelled and pronounced the same. Finally, use 거 ke or 것 kes to make the possessive pronoun, and pronounce it as [꺼 kke] and [껟 kket]:

저를 보세요.
celul poseyyo.
Look at me, please.

이게 제 거예요.
ikey cey keyeyyo.
This is mine.

저도 갑니다.
ceto kapnita.
I'm going, too.

그것도 제 것입니다.
kukesto cey kesipnita.
That, too, is mine.

제가 그랬어요.
ceyka kulaysseyo.
I did that/It was me who did that.

내가 and 나 (+ other particles) are what you would use when referring to yourself as you talk to your peers or CLOSE acquaintances of similar age. They can be used in relatively polite situations (that is, with the polite ending -요 yo). *But!* 나 na or 내 nay will sound VERY RUDE if you are talking to someone older than you or to an adult you don't know very well, so be extremely careful! To be on the safer side, use the **humble** forms 제가 ceyka and 저 ce + (other particles) whenever you speak to anybody older.

For the plural *we, our, us, ours* pronouns, you do *not* say 나들 or 저들, but instead use the plural forms 우리(들) wuli(tul) and 저희(들) cehuy(tul), either with -들 -tul or without it:

우리(들)끼리 가자.
wuli(tul)kkili kaca.
Let's just us go. (said to a peer or a younger person)

저희는/저희들은 잘 몰라요.
cehuynun/cehuytulun cal mollayo.
We don't know (it) very well. (said to an older person)

Using these PLURAL possessives is a polite way to express *my* when talking about **communal property** such as one's house and one's family members. In this case, the forms WITHOUT -들 are used:

그분이 저희 할머니예요.
kupwuni cehuy halmeniyeyyo.
That's my grandmother. (said humbly)

그거 저희 거예요.
kuke cehuy keyeyyo.
That's ours/mine. (said humbly of communal property)

그거 우리 거야.
kuke wuli keya.
That's ours/mine. (said to a peer or a younger person)

Finally, when referring to oneself, the first person pronoun *I* (나 na, 저 ce) is most frequently used, if the pronoun is going to be used at all. If the speaker is older than the listener, or if the speaker wants to sound more affectionate to the listener, however, kinship terms or titles can be used instead of 나 na:

할아버지는 안 먹어.
halapecinun an meke.
I (your grandpa) won't be eating.

엄마도 갈 거야.
emmato kal keya.
I (your mother) will be going, too.

선생님도 몰라요.
sensayngnimto mollayo.
I (your teacher) don't know either.

(2) The second person pronouns
Here are the forms comparable to the English *you, your, you, yours.* Notice that there is no humble form of *you.* There are many ways to refer to honored people face-to-face, taking the place of any pronoun system.

2nd Person					
Familiar (peer/minor-directed)				Humble	Honorific and Other Various Levels
Subject Pronoun *you*	Possessive Adnominal *your*	Other Cases *you*	Possessive Pronoun *yours*		
Singular 네 ney + 가 ka	네 ney	너 ne + particles	네 것 ney kes 네 거 ney ke	∅	그쪽 kuccok, 자기 caki, 그대 kukay, 당신 tangsin, 자네 caney, 댁 tayk, *etc.* + particles
Plural 너희(들) nehuy(tul) + particles			너희(들) 것 nehuy(tul) kes 너희(들) 거 nehuy(tul) ke		그쪽들 kuccoktul, 그대들 kukaytul, 당신들 tangsintul, 자네들 caneytul, 댁들 tayktul, *etc.* + particles

<1> Familiar (peer/minor-directed)

Much like the first person pronouns, 너 ne is the base form to which any particle can be attached for the second person familiar *you* (e.g. 너는 nenun, 너만 neman, 너도 neto, 너를 nelul, 너한테 nehanthey, 너와 newa, etc.), except that 네 ney is used with the subject particle, and 네 ney is a contraction of 너 ne + 의 uy for the possessive adnominal:

너도 가니?
neto kani?
You are going, too?

네가 불렀어?
neyka pwullesse?
You called me?/Is it you who called me?

The possessive 네 거/네 것 ney ke/ney kes are shortened forms of 너의 것 neuy kes, but the full form is nearly never used. 네 ney of the possessive 네 거 ney ke and of 네가 neyka (with the subject particle attached) is pronounced as [니 ni]:

그거 네 거지? [그거 **니** 꺼지]
kuke ney keci? [kuke nik keci]
It's yours, isn't it?

네가 그걸 몰라? [**니**가 그걸 몰라]
neyka kukel molla? [nika kukel molla]
(Of all people,) you don't know that?

Unlike the first person familiar 나 na, which can be used in some polite situations (with the polite ending -요 yo), you can only use second person 너 ne and 네 ney with peers you've known from childhood, people who are much younger than you, or peers you are really close to, and it is normally restricted to casual situations. If you mix 너 ne with the polite -요 yo ending, it is downright ungrammatical.

너 어디 가요?
ne eti kayo?
Where are you going? (politeness intended)

그거 네 거지요?
kuke ney keciyo?
It's yours, isn't it? (politeness intended)

네가 그걸 몰라요?
neyka kukel mollayo?
(Of all people,) you don't know that? (politeness intended)

Now to the familiar PLURAL *you*: 너희(들) nehuy(tul) tends to be used in slightly formal situations because it is the standard form. 너네(들) neney(tul), and by some people 니네 (들) niney(tul), are contracted versions of 너희네(들) nehuyney(tul) and are used in more casual situations. (The suffix -네 ney gives the sense of household, community, or an entity larger than an individual.)

너희가 불렀어?
nehuyka pwullesse?
You called me?/Is it you who called me? (Plural)

네가 불렀어?
neyka pwullesse?
You called me?/Is it you who called me? (Singular)

<2> Honorific and other various levels

There are numerous words that are comparable to the English *you*. Words like 그대 kutay, 당신 tangsin, 자기 caki, 그쪽 kuccok, 자네 caney, and 댁 tayk are all listed as personal pronouns, and each one calls for a highly specific context, some of which are quite odd, to say the least! Let's take a look at these pronouns and the contexts in which they are used. Some have a plural form, and some do not:

그쪽(들): kuccok(tul)	young adults with unclear social relationship	그쪽들도 가요? kuccoktulto kayo?	*You all are going, too?*
자기: caki	affectionate, unmarried couples to each other	자기야! 사랑해! cakiya! salanghay!!	*Honey, I love you~*
그대(들): kutay(tul)	poetic, song lyrics	별에서 온 그대 pyeleyse on kutay	*You (my love) from the stars*
당신(들): tangsin(tul)	poetic; between spouses; unfamiliar adults	당신들의 천국 tangsintuluy chenkwuk	*Heaven of yours*
자네(들): caney(tul)	older to younger adult (with respect)	자네, 또 올텐가? caney, tto oltheynka?	*Will you come again?*
댁(들): tayk(tul)	elder to elder	댁은 뉘시오? taykun nwisio?	*Who are you?*

So, which second person pronoun you choose to use depends on an intricate web of social status and relationships—whether the person you are talking to is close to you, older (or younger) than you, married to you, or whether it is unclear how to define your social relationship with the other party.

In your Korean learning career, the last two pronouns on the list may not enter your everyday vocabulary any time soon because they are used by people older than 50 or so. 자네 caney, especially, is used by older people to address a younger person with some respect (like a mother-in-law calling her son-in-law or an older professor addressing her married graduate student). 댁 tayk is used by elderly people to address an older adult stranger of equal age or social status.

Continuing back up the list from the bottom, if you are a love song writer, you may use 그대 kutay, and if you are married to a Korean person, you may use 당신 tangsin. You may hear any of these in TV dramas. There is one thing to be careful of, though. 당신 tangsin actually has three usages. One is the poetic, romantic *you* in poems and songs that is used along with 그대 kutay. Another is the *you* used by a married couple. The last one is the oddball—this *you* is the rude one you can use when you have an altercation with a stranger, and it can be pluralized:

당신들이 뭐야?
tangsintuli mweya?
Who the heck are you all?/Who do you all think you are?

Before leaving the second person pronouns, let's re-revisit a couple of pronouns that might become immediately useful to you. 그쪽 kuccok can be used with peers that you are not terribly family with. 그쪽 kuccok literally means *that side*, referring to where *you* (the other person) is. You may sometimes even hear 거기 keki *there* as well:

그쪽은 오늘 뭐 해요?
kuccokun onul mwe hayyo? kekinun
What are you doing today?

거기는 벌써 점심 먹었어요?
pelsse cemsim mekesseyo?
You already had lunch?

Finally, if you begin a romantic relationship, you may use 자기 caki. 자기 caki as the second person pronoun, *you*, is not pluralized because, presumably, if you are in a relationship, it is with one person.

If you can't find the right second person pronoun for *you*, there are other options, namely, use a title. Until you get to know your boy/girlfriend or spouse, you may address your partner with a kinship term (!) such as 오빠 oppa *older brother (of a female)*, 누나 nwuna *older sister (of a male)*, or just his or her name. And it is good to use titles when possible, such as 할머니 halmeni *grandmother*, 할아버지 haapeci *grandfather*, 아주머니 acwumeni *aunt*, 아저씨 acessi *uncle* (all used for elder folks outside the family as well), 선생님 sensayngnim *teacher*, 목사님 moksanim *pastor*, 사장님 sacangnim *president (of company)*, 부장님 pwucangnim *section chief*, and so on. Another tip for navigating the second-person pronouns is to remember that it is possible to drop them much of the time.

(3) The third person pronouns

Now let's turn to the the third person pronouns for *he/she, him/her, his/her, his/hers* and *they, them, their, theirs*. Notice that there is no humble form here either because you can't really "humble" others:

3rd person	Singular *he/she, him/her, his/her*	Plural *they, them, their*
Literary Pronoun	그 ku *he*, 그녀 kunye *she* + particles	그들 kutul + particles
Adult-neutral	그 사람 ku salam + particles	그 사람들 ku salamtul + particles
Honorific Pronoun	그분 kupwun + particles	그분들 kupwuntul + particles
High Honorific Pronoun	당신 tangsin + particles	당신들 tangsintul + particles
Familiar (peer/minor-referenced)	(그 아이 ku ai) → 걔 kyay + particles	(그 아이들 ku aitul) → 걔(네)들 kyay(ney)tul + particles
Inanimate Pronoun *it/that (thing), its*	그것 kukes, 그거 kuke + particles	그것들 kukestul + particles

Technically speaking, Korean does not really have third person pronouns that amount to the English *he, she, it,* and *they* (or their possessive counterparts). Just like the inanimate third person 그것 kukes /그거 kuke *it/that (thing),* all "pronouns" (except 당신 tangsin) given in the table here are a combination of 그 ku and a (full or dependent) noun. *Bona fide* third person pronouns 그 ku *he,* 그녀 kunye *she,* and 그들 kutul *they* are also based on the demonstrative adnominal 그 ku, and they are all limited to literary usage. Interestingly, the pronoun 그 ku can be used for both male and female characters, although its predominant use is for males:

그가 모른 장소
kuka molun cangso
the place (s)he didn't know

덕암에는 왜 간다는 걸까, 그녀는?
tekamenun way kantanun kelkka, kunyenun?
Why is she set on going to Deogam?

Now, let's work through the table towards the right along the row, starting with 그 사람 ku salam. If you see a stranger leaving your house and want to find out who it was, you will probably use the generic noun 사람 salam *person*. You'd better make sure the stranger was not old(er) and did not particularly look to be of a high social status, or at least didn't hear you; you don't want to be caught being rude behind someone's back! For older people and people of a high social status, the honorific pronoun 그분 kupwun should be used. For both 그분 kupwun and 그 사람 ku salam, the suffix -들 -tul makes them plural:

그분이 누구세요?
ku pwuni nwukwuseyyo?
Who is he/she ("the honorable person")?

그 사람들이 누구였어?
ku salamtuli nwukwuyesse?
Who were they?

Along with 그 사람 ku salam, the gendered noun set 그 남자 ku namca *that male* and 그 여자 ku yeca *that female* are also highly useful:

그 여자 누구야?
ku yemca nwukwuya?
Who is she? (Literally, *Who is that woman*)

그 남자 누구야?
ku namca nwukwuya?
Who is he? (Literally, *Who is that man*)

Look at the pronoun 당신 tangsin in the next column. To be highly honorific, referring to (grand)parents or older professors in a highly respectful way, 당신 tangsin should be used—yes, indeed, for the third person (in addition to its three different uses with the second person):

당신께서 오늘도 못 오신다셔요.
tangsinkkeyse onulto mos osintasyeyo.
The venerable says he/she cannot come today, either.

Korean grammarians do not count 걔 kyay and 그 사람 ku salam as official pronouns, but we are including them here because they are far more useful than literary pronouns 그 ku and 그녀 kunye. 걔 kyay and its plural 걔(네)들 kyay(ney)tul are categorized as nouns by standard grammar, contracted from 그 아이 ku ai *that kid* (*he/she*) and 그 아이들 ku aitul *those kids* (*they*). 걔 kyay and 걔(네)들 kyay(ney)tul can be used to refer to the same folks you would use 너 ne *you* to talk to directly, that is, children or adults you are very close to or have known since childhood:

걔는 요즘 뭐 해요?
kyaynun yocum mwe hayyo?
What does he/she ("that kid") do these days?

For inanimate *it*, you already know the pronoun is 그거 kuke. For its plural versions, you have to use 그것들 kukestul (not 그거들 kuketul):

그것들은 이쪽으로 놓아 주세요.
kukestulun iccokulo noha cwuseyyo.
Please put them/those down over this way.

For all animate possessives, simply add the particle -의 -uy for written language, and otherwise just place the owned noun after the pronoun. (Since 그(들) ku(tul) is a literary pronoun, -의 -uy never gets omitted after it.)

그들만의 잔치
kutulmanuy canchi
a party of their own (written)

그 사람의 아내도 왔다.
ku salamuy anayto wassta.
His wife was also there. (written)

그분(의) 성함이 뭐죠?
kupwun(uy) senghami mwecyo?
What is his name? (spoken)

Before leaving this section, let's talk briefly about very colloquiual (almost vulgar) pronouns and nouns that are used like pronouns. We are including them here because it is more likely that people gossip in the absence of others (that is, using the third person pronouns), and it may be interesting for you to see what kinds of derogatory nouns are in use that are not swear words. We have picked out 자식 casik, 녀석 nyesek, 작자 cakca and 그치 kuchi, 그것 kukes, and 그놈 kunom, where the latter three are classified as legitimate pronouns (and 그 ku is written without a space after it):

그 자식/그 녀석 똑똑한데!
ku casik/ku nyesek ttokttokhantey!
He/That chum is pretty smart!
(speaking of a close male friend or someone of the same age/younger)

그치 대단한데!
kuchi taytanhantey!
He/that fella is something else!
(speaking of a male acquaintance/peer with some social distance)

그게/그 작자가 그런 말까지 했어?!!
kukey/ku cakcaka kulen malkkaci haysse?!!
He/That lowlife even said such a thing?!! (with disdain and contempt)

그것들도 봤나요?
kukestulto pwassnayo?
Did those jerks see (it), too? (OR) *Did you see those jerks, too?*

고놈 참 귀여워!
konom cham kwiyewe!
He/that little squirt is so cute! (speaking of a child you know well)

(4) General *you, they* and *one*

When English proverbs and general statements of advice make use of pronouns like *you* or *they*, there is no specific referent. These statements are supposed to mean PEOPLE *do this*, or *everybody should do this*. In Korean, the subject is simply left out in statements about "people in general":

피라미를 놓쳐야 큰 물고기를 잡을 수 있다.
philamilul nohcheyya khun mwulkokilul capul swu issta.
To catch a salmon, you must sacrifice a minnow.

한국에서는 집에 들어가기 전에 신발을 벗어야 한다.
hankwukeysenun cipey tulekaki cecey sinpalul peseya hanta.
You're supposed to take your shoes off before entering a Korean house.

(대)학교 옆에 새 병원 건물을 짓고 있다.
(tay)hakkyo yepey say pyengwen kenmwulul cisko issta.
They're building a new hospital next to the university.

More old-fashioned-sounding proverbs and statements that use *those who*, and *one* or *he* in English require an explicit subject in Korean, typically expressed as ...는 사람 nun salam or its Sino-Korean version (...는) 자 (者) (nun) ca:

마지막에 웃**는 사람**이 최후의 승자다/마지막에 웃**는 자**가 최후의 승자다.
macimakey wusnun salami choyhwuuy sungcata/macimakey wusnun caka choyhwuuy sungcata.
He who laughs last, laughs best.

없**는 사람**이 더 너그럽다/빈**자**(貧者)가 더 후(厚)하다.
epsnun salami te nekulepta/pincaka te hwuhata.
Those who have little are usually the most generous.

When the general statement comes with a reflexive pronoun, 자신 casin *(one)self*, the subject is optionally said explicitly, which in most cases is 사람 salam or 사람들 salamtul, but the subject should be mentioned only once:

서른이 넘으면 (**사람**은) **자신**의 얼굴을 책임져야 한다.
seluni nemumyen (salamun) casinuy elkwulul chaekimcyeya hanta.
Beyond 30, one should be responsible for one's own face.

(**사람**은) 서른이 넘으면 **자신**의 얼굴을 책임져야 한다.
(salamun) seluni nemumyen casinuy elkwulul chaekimcyeya hanta.
Beyond 30, one should be responsible for one's own face.

(5) Reflexive pronouns

For all persons, there is only one reflexive pronoun 자기 caki 自己 *(one)self*/자기들 cakitul *themselves* and its redundant form 자기 자신(들) caki casin(tul) for emphasis. This Sino-Korean word literally means "self-body," and its variation, 자신 casin 自身 (with the same meaning), is used in written Korean.

너 **자신**을 알라.
ne casinul alla.
Know thyself.

"아무든지 나를 따라오려거든 **자기**를 부인하고 십자가를 지고 나를 좇으라."
"amwutunci nalul ttalaolyeketun cakilul pwuinhako sipckalul ciko nalul cochula."
*Whoever wants to follow me must deny **themselves** and take up their cross and follow me.*

However, 자기 caki is not necessarily used in all the cases where a reflexive pronoun might be used in English.

그냥 혼잣말 하고 있었어.
kunyang honcasmal hako issesse.
I was just talking to myself.
(Literally, *I was doing an alone-talk.*)

거울로 네 모습을 좀 봐라.
kewullo ney mosupul com pwala.
Look at yourself in the mirror.
(Literally, *Look at your appearance in the mirror.*)

The most typical use of reflexive pronouns in Korean is for EMPHASIS, for meanings such as *one's own*. (The pronunciation of 것 kes in *one's own* is tense [자기 껀 caki kket]):

자기 것만 챙기세요.
caki kesman chayngkiseyyo.
Everyone just take care of your own belongings.

그는 꿈인가 싶어 **자기** 얼굴을 꼬집어 보았다.
kunun kkwuminka siphe caki elkwulul kkocipe poassta.
He pinched himself to see if he was dreaming. (Literally, "his own" face)

그 여자가 **자기** 자랑을 많이 했다니...
ku yecaka caki calangul manhi haysstani...
It's hard to believe that she bragged about herself so much!

It may seem strange, but the "reflexive" pronoun 자기 caki can anticipate itself and the subject it is supposed to refer to can show up in the reflexive form:

자기가 **자기** 칭찬을 그렇게 많이 하다니...
cakika caki chingchanul kulehkey manhi hatani...
I can't believe one can praise one's own self so much!

To emphasize reflexivity or the sense of *by oneself*, the adverb 스스로 susulo can be added even without the pronoun:

(**자기**) 스스로가 하는 발 마사지 *a massage one gives her own feet*
(caki) susuloka hanun pal masaci

(**자기**) 스스로에게 주는 사랑의 메시지 *a message of love one gives herself*
(caki) susuloekey cwunun salanguy meysici

In colloquial talk 자기 caki can be drastically contracted to 저 ce, or even 지 ci, usually for pejorative purposes. Don't get this confused with the humble *I* or determiner *that* 저 ce (the three words are just accidental homophones):

걔는 **저**만 알아.
kyaynun ceman ala.
He only knows himself.

For third person inanimate *itself*, referring to abstract concepts, (그) 자체 (ku) cachey *itself* or *in and of itself* is used. You will also see 자체 내 cachey nay, referring to (the "inside" of) an organization:

겪어가는 과정 **그 자체**를 즐겨라.
kyekkekanun kwaceng ku cacheylul culkyela.
Enjoy the experience itself that you are living.

거기 가고 싶어 한다는 것 **자체**가 문제야.
keki kako siphe hantanun kes cacheyka mwunceyya.
You wanting to go there is an issue in and of itself.

페북 **자체 내**에(서) 문제가 생겼어.
pheypwuk cachey nayey(se) mwunceyka sayngkyesse
There was a problem within Facebook itself.

Because 자기 caki is an umbrella reflexive pronoun for all persons in Korean, and also because it is mainly used for emphasis, AND because there is usually no obvious subject in the sentence, it may sometimes be difficult to interpret it. Context helps, but savor the meaning of the following sentences:

자기들은 안 가면서!
cakitulun an kamyense!
While they themselves/you yourselves are not going! (They/you are trying to make us!)

(너) **자신**만 모르고 있어.
(ne) casinman moluko isse.
Only you (yourself) don't know. (You are the only one that does not know.)

(그) **자신**만 모르고 있어.
(ku) casinman moluko isse.
Only he (himself) doesn't know. (He is the only one that does not know.)

You may have noticed that the reflexive pronoun does not have to be and rarely is the object of reflexive sentences in Korean. This is partly because at least SINO-KOREAN verbs often incorporate the *self* part (자 ca 自) in them. This is the same 자 ca you see in 자기 (자신) caki (casin) 自己 (自身) and (그) 자체 自體 (ku) cachey:

너무 **자책**(自責)하지 마.
nemwu cachaykhaci ma.
Don't blame yourself too much.

동물은 **자살**(自殺)을 하지 않는대.
tongmwulun casalul haci anhnuntay.
I hear that animals don't kill themselves.

너무 **자만**(自慢)하지 마세요.
nemwu camanhaci maseyyo.
Don't be so conceited/full of yourself.

왜 그랬나 **자문**(自問)해 보니 참 부끄럽네요.
way kulayssna camwunhay poni cham pwukkulepneyyo.
I have asked myself why I behaved that way, and I feel so embarrassed.

It will be helpful for you to learn the multiple interpretations of the *self* (자 ca 自) root, whether they show up in verbs (with 하다 hata) or nouns. Some words with this root have the meaning *on one's own* or *by oneself*, others *by one's own strength* or *of one's own accord*, and yet others *self-inflicted* or *self-directed*. Here are a few "self" words—keep an eye out for more!

자습하고 있으세요.
casuphako issuseyyo.
Study by yourself/yourselves. (Do self-study.)

학생자치기구가 새로 생겼다면서요?
haksayngcachikikwuka saylo sayngkyesstamyenseyo?
I hear that a self-governing student organization has formed anew – is that true?

자원봉사는 원래 보수가 없는 일 아니에요?
cawenpongsanun wenlay poswuka epsnun il anieyyo?
Isn't volunteering ("self-want" service) supposed to not have any pay?

자기 연민에 빠지는 건 소용없는 짓이에요.
caki yenminey ppacinun ken soyongepsnun cisieyyo.
It's no use wallowing in self-pity.

(6) Reciprocal pronoun

서로 selo in Korean is comparable to English *each other*. It can be used as a reciprocal pronoun or as an adverb:

아이들이 서로를 껴안았다.　　　　우리는 서로 선물을 교환했다.
aituli selolul kkyeanassta. wulinun selo senmwulul kyohwanhayssta.
The children hugged each other.　　*We exchanged gifts with each other.*

For *one another*, or to emphasize *each other*, 서로 can be reduplicated:

서로 서로 사랑하세요.
selo selo salanghaseyyo.
Love one another/Love each other.

(7) Using pronouns in Korean

As we mentioned in chapter 3, Korean is a pronoun-drop language. This means that subjects and objects are usually left out and simply understood from the context and that pronouns are used less often than in English. Instead of pronouns (regardless of person), NOUNS can be repeated or omitted especially in spoken language. In some cases, you may be able to omit the pronouns in English; in others, you may not.

진: 김 선생님 어디 계세요?
      kimsensayngnim eti kyeyseyyo?
Jin: *Where is Teacher Kim?*

우: (김 선생님) 오늘 안 오셨어요.
      (kimsensayngnim) onul an osyesseyo.
Wu: *She did not come today.*

선: 내 가방 어디 있어?
      nay kapang eti isse?
Seon: *Where is my bag?*

주: (네 가방) 저기 있어.
      (ney kapang) ceki isse.
Ju: *(It's) over there.*

김: 한국의 **하늘은 가을에** 왜 유난히 파랄까요?
      hankukuy hanulun kauley way yunanhi phalalkkayo?
Kim: *Why is the Korean sky exceptionally blue in the fall?*

      그건 **가을에 하늘이** 특히 맑고 깨끗하기 때문입니다.
      kuken kauley hanuli thukhi malkko kkaykkushaki ttaymwunipnita.
Kim: *Because it is especially clear and clean then.*

To summarize the pronouns discussion, the best practice would be to use the familiar pronouns (나 na, 너 ne) only when you are speaking to a minor or a peer that you have known since childhood, or a peer that you have gotten really close to. Use the humble first person pronoun (저 ce) when talking to those who look older than you by 4–5 years or more. Since second person pronouns are tricky even for native speakers of Korean, use titles instead (or leave out the reference to the person altogether). The same is somewhat true when referring to someone not present (that is, use titles), although 걔 kyay can be used among young peers in less formal situations, and 그 사람 ku salam and 그분 kupwun are widely used. The following sentences can have two different interpretations because titles can refer to second or third persons. First persons are a little easier to discern, as the verb would not have honorific endings and the title would not have the honorific suffix -님 nim:

사장님 어디 가세요?
sacangnim eti kaseyyo?
Where are you going, boss?/Where is the boss going?

아버님께서는 어떻게 생각하세요?
apenimkeysenun ettehkey sayngkakhaseyyo?
What do you think, father?/What does father think?

엄마는 지금 나가요.
emmanun cikum nakayo.
Mom is going out. (said politely, not honoring mom)*/I am going out.* (said by mom)

The best way to conquer the pronouns? Listen for what Koreans do!

5.4.3 Interrogatives

Many Korean question words correspond to English words, but there are a few additional words for making fine distinctions that English doesn't have. Here is a table of the Korean question words including those distinctions:

	Question Words	
(1)	누구 nwukwu, 누가 nwuka	*who*
(2)	언제 ence	*when*
(3)	어디 eti	*where*
(4)	왜 way	*why*
(5)	무엇 mwues, 뭐 mwe; 무슨 mwusun	*what; what kind of*
(6)	어느 enu	*which*
(7)	어떻게 ettehkey; 어떤 etten	*how* (manner); *which*
(8)	어찌- ecc-	*how (how on earth)*
(9)	몇 myech	*how many*
(10)	얼마 elma	*how much ($ value), price*
(11)	얼마큼 elmakhum (얼만큼 elmankhum)	*for how much's worth*
(12)	얼마나 elmana	*how much, how (degree)*

As you know, Korean question words do not have to start the question sentence. 톰이 **언제** 와요? thomi ence wayo? *When is Tom coming?* is a fine sentence that respects the subject-first default word order. "**언제** 톰이 와요?" ence thomi wayo? also works with a little more emphasis on 언제 ence *when*. Generally, the question word fits into the sentence where the missing information would be. When you answer *wh*-questions, you simply replace *wh*-words with the new information sought by the question word.

Some question words work as both nouns and adverbs. For example, 언제 ence is an adverb in 톰이 언제 와요? thomi ence wayo? *When is Tom coming?*, but it functions as a noun with the particle attached in 언제부터 방학이에요? encepwuthe panghakieyyo? *When does the vacation start?* (Literally, *starting when is it vacation?*) Let's take a look at each question word.

(1) 누구, 누가 *who*

누구 nwukwu is the base form that means *who*, and 누가 nwuka is the form with the subject particle incorporated into it. 누구 nwukwu usually comes at the end of the question with the verb 이다 ita to ask for identity (*who is…?*).

누가 nwuka asks for the **agent** of an action and usually comes at the front of the question as a subject. When the answer needs a particle, it is always the subject-focus particle -이 -i/-가 -ka:

천: 김형규가 **누구**야?
     kimhyengkyuka nwukwuya?
Chun: *Who is Kim Hyeongkyu?*

송: 제 친구예요.
     cey chinkwuyeyyo.
Song: *(He) is my friend.*

김: 제가 김형규입니다.
     ceyka kimhyengkyuipnita.
Kim: *I am (Kim Hyeongkyu).*

전: 창문 **누가** 깼어?
     changmwun nwuka kkaysse?
Juhn: *Who broke the window?*

지: 제가요.
     ceykayo.
Ji: *I did.*

현: **누가** 누구야?
     nwuka nwukwuya?
Hyun: *Who is who?*

계: 저도 몰라요!
     ceto mollayo!
Gye: *I don't know, either!*

Because it is the base form, other particles can be used only with 누구 nwukwu (and not with 누가 nwuka): 누구하고 nwukwuhako, 누구를 nwukwulul, 누구부터 nwukwupwuthe.

누구하고 갔어요?
nwukwuhako kasseyo?
With whom did you go?

누구부터 시작할래?
nwukwupwuthe sicakhallay?
Who would like to begin?

누구 nwukwu can be used with or without the particles -의 -uy or -를 -lul and often is used without them, since there is no confusion with 누가 nwuka. When it comes with 것 kes/거 ke to mean *whose (thing)*, 것 kes/거 ke is pronounced as tense:

어제 **누구**(를) 만났어?
ecey **nwukwu**(lul) mannasse?
Whom did you meet yesterday?

이거 **누구**(의) 가방이에요?
ike **nwukwu**(uy) kapangieyyo?
Whose bag is this?

한: 이거 **누구** 거예요? [꺼예요]
　　ike **nwukwu** keyeyyo? [kkeyeyyo]
Han: *Whose is this?*

고: 제 거예요. [꺼예요]
　　ce keyeyyo. [kkeyeyyo]
Goh: *Mine.*

(2) 언제 *when*

언제 encey is used to ask for a time, *when*. For a specific time, adnominal 몇 myech *how many* + 시 si *hour* can be used as well:

김: 생일이 **언제**예요?
　　sayngili **encey**yeyyo?
Kim: *When is your birthday?*

삼: (내 생일은) 3월 3일이에요.
　　(nay sayngilun) samwel samilieyyo.
Sahm: *(My birthday) is March 3rd.*

김: 파티가 **몇 시**에 시작하지요?
　　phathika **myech siey** sicakhaciyo?
Kim: *What time does the party begin?*

(3) 어디 *where*

어디 eti means *where*, but given the important role of particles in Korean, you can imagine it is not always used on its own. You need particles: 어디에 etiey is used to ask about a "landing" location; for the location of an activity with some DURATION, use 어디에서/어디서 etieyse/etise; and, for *where* with more emphasis on the path or trajectory than the destination, 어디로 etilo is used. -에 -ey, however, is often left off of 어디에 etie in spoken Korean.

손: **어디**(에) 앉아요?
　　eti(ey) ancayo?
Sohn: *Where do/shall we sit?*

이: 여기(에).
　　yeki(ey).
Yi: *Here.*

김: **어디**(에)서 먹어요?
　　eti(ey)se mekeyo?
Kim: *Where are we eating?*

이: 집에서.
　　cipeyse.
Yi: *At home.*

박: **어디**로 가세요?
　　etilo kaseyyo?
Pak: *Where are you headed?*

정: 집으로 가요.
　　cipulo kayo.
Jung: *I'm heading home.*

To identify an event venue, that is, the place used for a specific purpose such as 수업 swuep *class*, 은행 unhayng *bank*, or 화장실 hwacangsil *restroom*, you can use the 어디 eti +이 다 ita *(it is)* structure, but to inquire about the location of an ITEM, you must use 어디 eti and 있다 issta *(exists, there is)*:

파티가 **어디**예요?
phathika etiyeyyo?
Where is the party?

화장실이 **어디**예요?
hwacangsili etiyeyyo?
Where/which is the restroom?

한국어 책이 **어디**예요?
~~hankwuke chayki etiyeyyo?~~
Where is the Korean book?

수업이 **어디**예요?
swuepi etiyeyyo?
Where is the class?

화장실이 **어디**에 있어요?
hwacangsili etiey isseyo?
Where is the restroom located?

한국어 책이 **어디**에 있어요?
hankwuke chayki etiey isseyo?
Where is the Korean book located?

(4) 왜 *why*

A question using 왜 way (the *why* adverb) is straightforward—it asks the reason or cause, *why*. In spoken Korean, answers to *why* questions often begin with 왜냐면 waynyamyen (shortened from 왜냐하면 waynyahamyen *if you ask me why*) and may include one of these endings: -기 때문 -ki ttaymwun, -(으)니까 -(u)nikka, -어서 -ese (or -(이)라서 -(i) lase), or -거든 -ketun to express a reason. The various endings express nuanced intentions of the speaker. It is difficult to give precise English translation of these endings, but let's see if we can convey the attitude of the speaker for each answer:

한: 길이 **왜** 이렇게 막히지?
　　kili way ilehkey makhici?
Han: *Why is the traffic so bad?*

권: (왜냐면) 이 근처가 공사 **중이라서** (그래).
　　(waynyamyen) i kuncheka kongsa cwungilase (kulay).
Kwon: *This area is under construction; so that's why.*

대: (왜냐면) 이 근처가 공사 중**이거든**.
(waynyamyen) i kuncheka kongsa cwungiketun.
Tae: *This area is under construction, you see.*

장: (왜냐면) 이 근처가 공사 중**이니까** (그래).
(waynyamyen) i kuncheka kongsa cwunginikka (kulay)
Jang: *Because this area is under construction.*

금: (왜냐면) 이 근처가 공사 중**이기 때문이야**.
(waynyamyen) i kuncheka kongsa cwungiki ttaymwuniya.
Geum: *Because of this area being under construction.*

These endings are discussed in chapter 8.

Finally, 왜 way can also be used with a particle (that is, as a noun) when talking about *asking why*:

왜를 왜 물어?
waylul way mwule?
Why ask why?

(5) 무엇, 뭐; 무슨 *what*

무엇 mwues is the full, written form of *what*, and 뭐 mwe is its spoken version. It is frequently pronounced as [모 mo] or [머 me] in sloppy speech, and it can even sound like [보 po] or [버 pe] to English speakers. 무슨 mwusun is the adnominal version of the word (that is, the version that comes before a noun to mean *what [noun]*):

사랑이란 **무엇**입니까?
salangilan mwuesipnikka?
What is so-called love?

이름이 **뭐**예요?
ilumi mweyeyyo?
What's (your) name?

무슨 음식 좋아해요?
mwusun umsik cohahayyo?
What (kinds of) foods do you <u>like</u>?

오늘 **무슨** 요일이에요?
onul mwusun yoilieyyo?
What day is it today?

(6) 어느 *which*

어느 enu is very much like the English *which*. It comes with the condition that more than one choice has to exist, out of which the selection is to be made.

어느 분이 짬뽕 시키셨어요?
enu pwuni ccamppong sikhisyesseyo?
Which one of you has ordered 짬뽕?

어느 길로 갈까?
enu killo kalkka? enu
Which road shall we take?

어느 날이 좋아?
nali coha?
Which day is better?

Just like the demonstrative adnominals 이 i, 그 ku, and 저 ce, Korean *which* 어느 enu can only be used as an adnominal (not a pronoun), so it cannot substitute for a noun and requires a filler noun 것 kes or 거 ke *thing*:

어느 거 살까?
enu ke salkka?
Which (one) should I buy?

어느 ~~거~~ 살까?
enu salkka?
Which (one) should I buy?

어느 건 좋고, 어느 건 싫고…
enu ken cohko, enu ken silhko...
You/I like certain things and not others…

In the context of story telling, 어느 has an idiomatic sense of *some certain*:

어느 날 한번은…
enu nal hanpenun...
One day, (this happened…)

(7) 어떻게; 어떤 *how, in what specific way; what specific type of*
어떻게 ettehkey is a question adverb that asks about the manner in which things are done or how things are done, just like how English *how* would be used. 어떻게 ettehkey is frequently used where *what* would be used in English, though. It is also pronounced [어터케] [ethehkey] or [어트게] [ethuhkey]:

이거 **어떻게** 해요?
ike ettehkey hayyo?
How do I do this?/What am to do with this?

어떻게 오셨어요?
ettehkey osyesseyo?
How did you get here?/What brings you here? (*How can I help you*)

연세가 **어떻게** 되세요?
yenseyka ettehkey toyseyyo?
What is your (honorable) age? How old are you?

그 사람 **어떻게** 생각해요?
ku salam ettehkey sayngkakhayyo?
What do you think of her?

어떤 etten is the adnominal version of 어떻게 ettehkey, always coming before a noun to mean something like *what kind of noun* or *a noun like what*. 어떤 etten is usually used once a topic is introduced to ask for specific descriptions of the item, while for more general inquiries, 무슨 mwusun is used:

어떤 경우에 그게 가능해요?
etten kyengwuey kukey kanunghayyo?
In what (specific type of) case is that possible?

무슨 말이야?
mwusun maliya?
What are you talking about?

어떤 etten can also idiomatically mean *some random choice (of an item)*, pretty much the same usage as 어느 enu when it means *(some) certain*:

어떤 날은 손가락도 움직이기 싫어.
etten nalun sonkalakto wumcikiki silhe.
Some days I don't even want to lift a finger.

어떤 건 먹고 **어떤** 건 왜 안 먹어?
etten ken mekko etten ken way an meke?
How come you eat certain things and not others?

(8) 어쯔- *how on earth; in some way*

어쯔- ecc- is a variant form of 어뜨- ett- as in 어떻게 ettehkey. 어찌 ecci (from 어떻게 ette-hkey) and 어쩌- ecce- (from 어떻게 하- ettehkey ha-) show up in many fixed expressions. While 어떻게 ettehkey has a factual sense of *in what* manner, 어쯔 ecc is more nuanced, adding exaggerated senses like *what on earth* or *by fluke*. There are only a handful of frozen 어쯔- ecc- words.

아이가 **어찌나 (어떻게나)** 시끄럽게 떠들던지..!
aika eccina (ettehkeyna) sikkulepkey ttetultenci..!
How noisily the child yapped!

넌 **어찌 (어떻게)** 그리 덤벙대?
nen ecci (ettehkey) kuli tempengtay?
How on earth can you be so hare-brained and careless?

어째서 (어떻게 해서) 이리 늦었어?
eccayse (ettehkey hayse) ili nucesse?
Why the heck are you this late?

어쩌면 (어떻게 하면) 이렇게 예쁠 수가!
eccemyen (ettehkey hamyen) ilehkey yeyppul swuka!
How could it be this pretty!

이걸 **어쩌나 (어떻게 하나)**?
ikel eccena (ettehkey hana)?
Oh, no! What am I going to do (with this)?

어쩌면 (어떻게 하면) 갈 수 있을 수도 있어.
eccemyen (ettehkey hamyen) kal swu issul swuto isse.
It might turn out to be possible for me to go.

어쩔 (어떻게 할) 수 없지, 뭐.
eccel (ettehkey hal) swu epsci, mwe.
Nothing can be done/No other way.

어쩐지 (어떻게 된 일인지) 이상하더라.
eccenci (ettehkey toyn ilinci) isanghatela.
I knew somehow something was off.

어쩌다 (어떻게 하다) 보니 그렇게 됐어.
ecceta (ettehkey hata) poni kulehkey twaysse.
I don't know how; it just happened by fluke.

(9) 몇 *how many*

몇 myech is a question word used for a COUNTABLE QUANTITY, *how many*. It is always used with a counter:

송: 모두 **몇 개**예요?
motwu myech kayyeyyo?
Song: *How many in all?*

정: 스물다섯 개예요.
sumwultases kayyeyyo.
Jung: *(All) is twenty five.*

장: **몇 살**이야?
myech saliya?
Jang: *How old are you?*

홍: 열아홉 살이야.
yelahop saliya.
Hong: *(I) am nineteen years old.*

선우: 지금 **몇 시**예요?
cikum myech siyeyyo?
Sunwu: *What time is it now?*

남궁: 네 시예요.
ney siyeyyo.
Namkung: *(It) is four.*

강: 생일이 **몇 월**이에요?
sayngili myech welieyyo?
Kang: *When is your birth month?*
(What (number) is your birth month)

양: 10월이에요.
siwelieyyo.
Yang: *(It) is October.*

When 몇 myech comes with 일 il *date/day of the month* (as well as *how many days*), the spelling becomes 며칠 myechil:

백: 거기 며칠 있었어요?
keki myechil issesseyo?
Paik: *How many days were you there?*

왕: 사흘 있었어요.
sahul issesseyo.
Wang: *(I) was (there) for three days.*

권: 오늘이 며칠이에요?
onuli myechilieyyo?
Kwon: *What's the date today?*

성: 2월 5일이에요.
iwel oilieyyo.
Sung: *(It) is February 2nd.*

(10) 얼마 *how much ($)*

얼마 elma is a noun and asks for an exact amount, referring to money:

변: 이거 **얼마**예요?
ike elmayeyyo?
Byun: *How much is this?*

천: 10,000원이에요.
manwenieyyo.
Chun: *(It) is 10,000 won.*

민: **얼마**를 주고 샀어요?
elmalul cwuko sasseyo?
Min: *How much did you pay to buy (it)?*

진: 10,000원 주고 샀어요.
manwen cwuko sasseyo.
Jin: *(I) paid 10,000 won.*

손: **얼마면 돼요?**　　　　　　　　　문: 10,000원이면 돼요.
　　　elmamyen twayyo?　　　　　　　　　　manwenimyen twayyo.
Sohn: *How much (money) will do?*　　Mun: *10,000 won will do.*

(11) 얼마큼 (얼만큼) *how much* (specific amount)

얼마 elma can be used with the particle -만큼 -mankhum *as … as.* So the combined form 얼마만큼 elmamankhum or its shortened form 얼마큼 elmakhum means *for how much's worth*, asking for UNCOUNTABLE quantities, *how much.* Although the current standard form is 얼마큼 elmakhum, many speakers use 얼만큼 elmankhum:

윤: **얼마큼** 먹었어?　　　　　　　　심: 한 공기 다 먹었어요!
　　　elmakhum mekesse?　　　　　　　　　han kongki ta mekesseyo!
Yun: *How much did you eat?*　　　　Shim: *I finished all of one bowl (of rice)!*

한: **얼만큼** 필요해요?　　　　　　　임: 20달러만 주세요.
　　　elmankhum philyohayyo?　　　　　　isiptalleman cwuseyyo.
Han: *How much do you need?*　　　　Lim: *Please give me (just) 20 dollars.*

(12) 얼마나 *how* (+ adjective/adverb)

얼마 elma can also be combined with the particle -(이)나 -(i)na *that many* and yields a new question word 얼마나 elmana *how much*, also referring to uncountable quantities. It is often used with an adjective or adverb to ask about a degree (e.g., *how fast, how heavy*):

장: 토끼가 **얼마나** 빨라요?　　　　　성: 거북이보다 빨라요.
　　　thokkika elmana ppallayo?　　　　　kepwukipota ppallayo.
Jang: *How fast is a hare?*　　　　　Seong: *It is faster than a tortoise.*

When there is no adjective or adverb after 얼마나 elmana, you can just assume 많이 manhi *much* or 오래 olay *long (time)* is left out:

차: **얼마나** (많이) 드릴까요?
　　　elmana (manhi) tulilkkayo?
Cha: *How much would you like?*

주: 500 그램만 주세요.
　　　opayk kulaymman cwuseyyo.
Ju: *Please give (me) 500 grams (only).*

김: 서울에서 **얼마나** (오래) 걸려요?
　　　sewuleyse elmana (olay) kellyeyo?
Kim: *How long does it take from Seoul?*

이: 비행기로 12시간쯤 걸려요.
　　　pihayngkilo yeltwusikanccum kellyeyo.
Lee: *It takes about twelve hours by air.*

Idiomatically, 얼마(나) 하다 elma(na) hata asks for the going rate:

박: 이런 노트북은 **얼마(나) 해요**?
ilen nothupwukun elmana hayyo?
Pak: What is the going rate for a laptop like this?

최: 한 500불 해요.
han opaykpwul hayyo.
Choi: It is about 500 hundred dollars.

(13) Fine-tuning

With the basics of the interrogatives under your belt, you are ready to consider some sticky areas. Here, we try to clarify what can be be some stumbling blocks for learners.

<1> 무슨, 어떤 and 어느 which "which" is what?

The three words for *what/which* have some differences in Korean. 무슨 mwusun assumes no background knowledge and poses a vague general question, *what (thing)*. On the other hand, 어떤 etten is the adnominal version of 어떻게 ettehkey, which means *like what/in what manner*, thus it demands the specifics or descriptions of the answer. A lukewarm English translation is *what kind of* or *what sort of*. 어떤 etten is used for conceptual choices, alluding to the characteristics of items (*one that is like what*) while 어느 enu refers to a handful of visible items from which you have to choose one. 어떤 etten is used in the same way (to choose one from a few) in colloquial speech:

무슨 일 있었어?
mwusun il issesse?
What happened?

어느 거 샀어?
enu ke sasse?
Which (one of them) did you buy?

어떤 거 먹을래?
etten ke mekullay?
What sort of food do you wanna eat? (Which do you wanna eat?)

Though each has a particular meaning and usage, 어떤 etten can be used casually in place of 무슨 mwusun:

오늘 **무슨** 옷 입지?
onul mwusun os ipci?   etten os ipci?
What should I wear today?

어떤 옷 입지?

Which kind of clothes should I wear?

그 사탕은 **무슨** 맛이 나요?
ku sathangun mwusun masi nayo?
What does that candy taste like?

그 사탕은 **어떤** 맛이 나요?
ku sathangun etten masi nayo?
What sort of taste does that candy have? (Fruit? Chocolate?)

무슨 일 하세요?
mwusun il haseyyo?
What do you do for living?

어떤 일 하세요?
etten il haseyyo?
What kind of work do you do for a living?

<2> Spacing and pronunciation of 거/것 after wh-words

By convention, a space is used after all interrogative pronouns. The pronunciation of the dependent noun 거/것 kes/ke after the *wh*-words is a little trickier because it changes depending on the (rather idiomatized) meaning of each *wh*-word. 어느 거 enu ke *which one* and 어떤 거 etten ke *which one/what sort of thing* maintain the regular pronunciation of the dependent noun, where as 누구 nwuku, 언제 ence, and 어디 eti trigger tensing on 것/거 kes/ke. The generalization is that거/것 kes/ke after an ADNOMINAL *wh*-word maintains its regular pronunciation. 거/것 kes/ke after a NOUN *wh*-word becomes tense because of the compound boundary or in place of the understood 의 uy:

그게 **어느 거**야? [어느 **거**]
ike enu keya? [enu ke]
Which one is that?

이거 **어떤 거**야? [어떤 **거**]
ike etten keya? [etten ke]
What kind is this?

이거 **누구 거**야? [누구 **꺼**]
ike nwukwu keya? [nwukwu kke]
Whose is this?

이 피자 **언제 거**야? [언제 **꺼**]
i pica encey keya? [encey kke]
When is this pizza from?

이 차 **어디 거**야? [어디 **꺼**]
i cha eti keya? [eti kke]
Where is this car from (what make of car)?

Since 무엇 mwues/뭐 mwe already means *what thing*, 무엇 mwues and 무슨 mwusun NEVER come with 거 ke. That is, 무슨 거 mwusun ke, 뭐 거 mwu ke or 무엇 거 mwues ke do not mean *what thing*; they do not make any sense.

5.4.5 Indefinite pronouns and adverbs

Imagine you run into your Korean friend and she says **어디에** 가요? etie kayo? to you. You might wonder why she is curious about your whereabouts. In this case, however, **어디에** 가요? etie kayo is a way to say *hello*, and your friend is asking not *where are you going?* but *going somewhere?* just as a greeting. So you can answer, 네, 어디 가요. ney, eti kayo *Yes, I am going somewhere.* In this interaction, 어디 eti means *somewhere*, not *where?* It functions as an **indefinite pronoun**.

Indefinite pronouns are pronouns that stand in for nouns—not for any noun in particular, but for indefinite (non-specific or unknown) ones. There are also indefinite adverbs, but we will use the umbrella term "indefinite pronouns," unless it really matters to make the distinction.

In English, indefiniteness is expressed by modifiers like *any, some, every, no, another,* and *few,* and they serve two different functions. Or, you might even think of there being two different kinds of indefinite pronouns. When you say *Does anyone want this bag?* you have NO DEFINITE PERSON in mind. This is one kind. When you say *I saw my cousins during that trip, and some are already married,* you are more interested in conveying an INDEFINITE NUMBER of people rather than UNSPECIFIC people. (We will call the second kind "indefinite number nouns," as they are NOUNS in Korean).

In these last sections, you will learn about Korean pronouns that express *some, any* and *every*, and then move on to the unmeasured or unlimited number expressions.

(1) Indefinite pronouns: *some-X*

The indefinite pronouns are quite simple in Korean because the question words (interrogatives) can function as indefinite pronouns (and adverbs in cases like 어떻게 ettehkey).

Here is the list of *wh*-words that do double-duty as question words and indefinite pronouns:

	Interrogatives	Indefinite/Unspecified
누구, 누가 nwukwu, nwuka	*who*	*somebody*
언제 encey	*when*	*sometime*
어디 eti	*where*	*somewhere*
무엇/뭐 mwues/mwe	*what*	*something*
어떻게 ettehkey	*how*	*somehow, by some means*
몇 myech	*how many*	*some number, a few*
얼마 elma	*how much*	*some amount*

<1> Question words vs. indefinite pronouns and adverbs

How do you know when a *wh*-word is acting as a question word and when it is an indefinite pronoun? In written language, if there is no question mark at the end, the interpretation is always going to be that of the indefinite. In spoken language, if the first syllable of the VERB is said with a special low tone, the word gets the indefinite (not question) interpretation (e.g., *sometime*). Also, the intonation at the end of the sentence will shoot up, as it is a Yes-No question. You might also hear a slight pause after the *wh*-word.

지: 그 사람이 거기 언제 ^V 갔어?   우: 응.
    ku   salami   keki   encey   kasse?   ung.
Gee: *Did she go there sometime?*   Woo: *Yes.*

If the first syllable of the QUESTION WORD is said with an emphatic LOW tone, the word is interpreted as a question word asking for a definite time, place, or person (e.g., *when?*).

허: 그 사람이 거기 **언제** 갔어?   노: 아까 갔어.
    ku   salami   keki   encey   kasse?   akka   kasse.
Huh: *When did she go here?*   Noh: *She went there a while ago.*

Here are some more examples contrasting the two, *wh*-usage appearing first in each set:

채: **어디**(에) 가니?
eti(ey)   kani?
Chae: *Where are you going?*

서: 집에 가.
cipey ka.
Suh: *(I) am going home.*

고: 어디(에) [∨] **가니**?
eti(ey)   kani?
Goh: *Are you going somewhere?*

류: 응.
ung.
Ryu: *Yes.*

조: 집에 지금 **누가** 있어요?
cipey cikum nwuka isseyo?
Jo: *Who is at home now?*

권: 어머니가 계세요.
emenika   kyeyseyyo.
Gweon: *(My) mother is.*

백: 집에 지금 **누가** [∨] 있어요?
cipey cikum nwuka isseyo?
Baek: *Is someone/anyone at home now?*

심: 네, 있어요.
ney, isseyo
Shim: *Yes, there is.*

구: **뭐** 읽을래?
mwe ilkullay?
Gu: *What do you wanna read?*

변: 신문 읽을래.
sinmwun ilkullay
Byun: *I wanna read newspapers.*

채: **뭐** 읽을래?
mwe ilkullay?
Chae: *Do you wanna read something?*

천 : 응.
ung.
Chun: *Yes.*

Here are a couple more examples. Note where the dip is in the intonation.

좀 **어떻게** 해 봐!
com ettehkey hay pwa!
Do something!

친구 **몇**이랑 여행 가려고 해.
chinkwu myechilang yehayng kalyeko hay.
I'm thinking about going on a trip with a few friends.

기름이 **얼마** 안 남았어.
kilumi elma an namasse.
We don't have much gas left.

Indefiniteness does not have to assume lack of knowledge. That is to say, a statement like *Someone is home* doesn't necessarily mean you don't know who is home. It could be that, because the exact information is not important or because you don't want to reveal the information, you are intentionally being unspecific.

진: **언제** 한번 만나자.
      encey hanpen mannaca.
Jin: *Let's get together sometime.*

엄: 그래, 그러자.
      kulay, kuleca.
Yum: *Yes, let's do that.*

송: **어디** 가세요?
      eti kaseyyo?
Sohng: *Are you going somewhere?*

황: 네, **어디** 좀 다녀 오려고요.
      ney, eti com tanye olyekoyo.
Hwang: *Yes, I am going somewhere (for business).*

황보: **누가** 오셨어요?
       nwuka osyesseyo?
Hwangbo: *Did someone come?*

선우: 네, **누가** 오셨네요.
       ney, nwuka osyessneyyo.
Seonu: *Yes, someone is here (we have a visitor).*

<2> Indefinite pronouns + 인가

To give a stronger sense of indefiniteness, especially from LACK OF KNOWLEDGE OR LACK OF COMMITMENT, you can use the -인가 -(i)nka (or shorter -ㄴ가 -nka) versions of the indefinite pronouns. These are a little like English *some-X* with emphasis on the *some* part:

Interrogatives		Non-committal Indefinite/Unspecified	
누구, 누가 nwukwu, nwukwa	who	누구인가/누군가 nwukwuinka/nwukwunka	*some*body
언제 encey	when	언제인가/언젠가 enceyinka/enceynka	*some*time
어디 eti	where	어디인가/어딘가 etiinka/etinka	*some*where
무엇/뭐 mwues/mwe	what	무엇인가/ 뭔가 mwuesinka/mwenka	*some*thing

Here are some examples:

언제 한번 만나자.
encey hanpen mannaca.
Let's get together sometime.
(in the near future)

언젠가 한번 만나자.
enceynka hanpen mannaca.
Let's get together sometime.
(I don't know when that would be.)

집에 지금 **누가** 있어요.
cipey cikum nwuka isseyo.
(Yes,) someone's home at this time.

집에 지금 **누군가** 있어요.
cipey cikum nwukwunka isseyo.
I don't know who, but someone's home.

뭔가 이상하다.
mwenka isanghata.
Some*thing is wrong (but I am not sure what it is).*

어쩌 ecce and 왜 way show up with the ending -인지 -(i)nci and -ㄴ지 -nci (instead of -인 가 -(i)nka and -ㄴ가 -nka) for a similar sense of *I am not sure*. -인지 -(i)nci is a clipped suffix that comes from -인지 모르다 -(i)nci moluta *to not know whether*:

	Non-committal Indefinite/Unspecified
어쩐지 eccenci	*No wonder … (I didn't know why/how but I knew there must be some reason)*
왜인지/왠지 wayinci/waynci	*I'm not sure why but for some unknown reason*

어쩐지 춥더라니. 창문이 열려 있구나.
eccenci cuptelani, changmwuni yellye isskwuna.
No wonder I was cold – the window is open!

그 사람이 **왠지** (모르게) 짜증난 거 같아.
ku salami waynci (molukey) ccacungnan ke katha.
I don't know why, but he seems/seemed peeved.

(2) Indefinite pronouns: *any-X* and *no-X*

And then there are words like *anyone*. The difference between the *some-* kind of words that we just went over and the *any-* kind is subtle but palpable in English. While *some-one* speaks of some certain unidentified individual, *anyone* highlights the INDISCRIMINATE RANDOMNESS ("it doesn't matter") of the individual chosen. To express concepts like *anywhere* and *not anywhere* (*nowhere*) in Korean, you use the **adnominal** 아무 amwu with a dependent noun of place or time. For *any random X you pick*, you can use 아무 amwu + Noun + (이)나 (i)na in positive statements or questions. For *no X that you randomly pick*, you can use 아무 amwu + Noun + 도 to in negative sentences. 싫다 silhta *distasteful* grammatically acts like a positive verb in other situations, but in this case that focuses on meaning, it counts as negative:

태: 이거 어디에 놓을까?
　　　 ike etiey nohulkka?
Tae: *Where should I put this down?*

진: **아무 데나** 놔.
　　　 amwu teyna nwa.
Jin: *Put it down anywhere.*

구: 휴가 때 어디 가요?
　　　 hyuka ttay eti kayo?
Koo: *Where are you going during the vacation?*

팽: 피곤해서 **아무 데도 안** 갈 거예요.
　　　 phikonhayse amwu teyto an kal keyeyyo.
Paeng: *I'm tired, so I'm not going anywhere.*

김: 우리 **아무 거나** 먹을까?
　　　 wuli amwu kena mekulkka?
Kim: *Shall we eat anything?*

박: **아무 것도** 먹기 **싫어**.
　　　 amwu kesto mekki silhe.
Bak: *I don't want to eat anything.*

When 아무 refers to a person, it can function as a noun by itself. That is, you do not say 아무 사람 for *anyone/anybody*, just 아무 amwu + 나 na; use a negative verb with 아무 amwu + 도 to for *no one/nobody*:

아무나 시간 있으면 나 도와주세요!
amwuna sikan issumyen na towacwuseyyo!
Whoever has time, please help me! (*Anyone who has time, please help me*)

어제 파티에는 **아무도** 안 왔어요.
ecey phathieynun amwuto an wasseyo.
No one came to yesterday's party.

Whereas in English you use *no-* words in the subject position and negative *any-* words after the verb, you conveniently have only one option (the 아무 amwu word) in Korean:

아무도 그와 음식을 나누어 먹지 않았다.
amwuto kuwa umsikul nanwue mekci anhassta.
<u>*No one*</u> *shared (their food) with him.*

그는 **아무하고도** 나누어 먹지 않았다.
kunun amwuhakoto nanwue mekci anhassta
He didn't share (his food) with <u>*anyone*</u>.

아무 **데서도** 이렇게 매운 김치는 안 팔아.
amwu teyseto ilehkey maywun kimchinun an phala.
<u>*Nowhere*</u> *sells kimchi this spicy.*

그거 **아무 데서도** 살 수 없어.
kuke amwu teyseto sal swu epse.
You can't buy it anywhere.

Here is the *any* chart for your review:

Indiscriminate Inclusive Indefinite		Negative Indefinite	
아무 때나 amwu ttayna	*any time, any random time*	한번도, 절대(로) 안/못, 전혀 hanpento, celtay(lo) an/mos, cenhye	*(never)*
아무 데나 amwu teyna	*anywhere, any random place*	아무 데도 안/못 amwu teyto an/mos	*nowhere*
아무 거나 amwu kena	*anything, any random thing*	아무 것도 안/못 amwu kesto an/mos	*nothing*
아무나 amwuna	*anyone, any random person*	아무도 안/못 amwuto an/mos	*no one*

Note that 아무 amwu does not usually come with 때 ttay for negative sentences, 아무 때
도 안··· ~~amwu ttayto an~~... to mean *never*. In fact, English *"never"* has many meanings, and
not all of them translate with a "never" sentence in Korean. Two of the English meanings correspond well to Korean adverbs 한 번도 han pento and 절대(로) celtay(lo). Both
are used with a negative verb like 없어 epse, or with 안 an/못 mos, -지 않아 -ci anh and
-지 마라/마 -ci mala/ma.

한 번도 han pento literally means *not even one time* so it is used when the action can be
done some number of times:

거기 한번도 못 갔어/가지 못했어.
keki han pento mos kasse/kaci moshaysse.
I never went there/I've never been there.

오징어는 (한 번도) 안 먹어 봤어.
ocingenun (han pento) an meke pwasse.
I (have) never tried squid (even one time).

한국에 한 번도 안 갈 거야?
hankukey han pento an kal keya?
Aren't you going to Korea even once?

한 번도 물을 주지 않았기 때문에 꽃이 죽었어.
han pento mwulul cwuci anhasski ttaymwuney kkochi cwukesse.
The flower died because I never watered it.

절대(로) celtay(lo) means *absolutely not*. It has a very ominous sense that, for Koreans,
has little to do with time or times and more to do with emphasizing *under no circumstances*. It is often used for INSISTING in negative promises, predictions, or commands:

거기에 절대 가지 마세요.
kekiey celtay kaci maseyyo.
Do not ever go there/Never go there.

당신을 절대로 버리지 않을게.
tangsinul celtaylo pelici anhulkey.
I will never leave you.

절대 그 차를 안 사주실 걸.
celtay ku chalul an sacwusil kel.
They're never going to buy you that car, I'm pretty sure.

절대 그런 일은 없어/없을 거야.
celtay kulen ilun epse/epsul keya.
That's never gonna happen. (That sort of thing never happens/will never happen.)

With verbs that don't happen some countable number of TIMES, you can't use 한 번도 han pento; so the equivalent Korean sentence will be flipped around to use *always* instead of *never* (That is, *never rich* = *always poor*). Or you can use the adverb 전혀 cenhye to emphasize *not at all*:

"We never had a lot of money growing up."

→ 어렸을 때 항상 가난했어.
elyessul ttay hangsang kananhaysse.
We were always poor when I was young.

→ 어렸을 때 항상 돈이 부족했어.
elyessul ttay hangsang toni pwucokhaysse.
Money was always scarce when I was young.

"I never have time."

→ 시간이 전혀 없어요.
sikani cenhye epseyo.
I have no time at all.

→ 항상 바빠요.
hangsang pappayo.
I am always busy.

"That student never turns in homework on time."

→ 그 학생은 숙제를 항상 늦게 내요.
ku haksayngun swukceylul hangsang nuckey nayyo.
That student always turns in homework late.

In cases where you might answer "never" to a question about HOW OFTEN you do something, or to make a generalization about your habits, you'd just say that you DON'T do it, and perhaps add the adverb 전혀 cenhye *not at all* in Korean:

"How often do you wash your car? – Never."

→ 세차를 전혀 안 해요.
seychalul cenhye an hayyo.
I never wash my car/I don't wash my car at all.

→ 세차를 (보통) 안 해요.
seychalul (pothong) an hayyo.
I don't (usually) wash my car.

For *have never done*, you can use the idiomatic expression -(으)ㄴ 적이 없다 -(u)n ceki epsta, which emphasizes that you have not had the experience of doing something. You can add 한 번도 han pento, but don't have to:

홍길동을 읽어 본 적이 있어요?
hongkiltongul ilke pon ceki isseyo?
Have you ever read Hong-gil Dong?

네, (한 번) 읽은/읽어 본 적이 있어요.
ney, (han pen) ilkun/ilke pon ceki isseyo.
Yes, I have tried it (once) before.

아니오, (한 번도) 읽어 본 적이 없어요.
anio, (han pento) ilke pon ceki epseyo.
No, I have never read it.

Or, you can simply flip it around and say *This is the first time...*:

아니오, 처음 읽어 봤어요.
anio, cheum ilke pwasseyo.
No, this is (my) first time reading it.

(3) Indefinite pronouns: *every-X*

Wh-question words with the right suffixes in Korean can also convey the concepts of indefinite *any* and *every*. One the one hand, -든(지) -tun(ci), the **selection suffix**, turns question words into *any-(thing)* words. Suffixed with -든(지) -tun(ci), the words take on the sense of *whichever you choose*:

언제든(지) 놀러 오세요.
enceytun(ci) nolle oseyyo.
Come and visit us any time. (*Whichever time/Whenever you choose to visit, you are welcome*)

On the other hand, -(이)나 -(i)na, the **inclusive suffix**, turns question words into *every-(thing)* words. Suffixed with -(이)나 -(i)na, the question word *when*, for example, takes on the sense of *any time it happens... (it is the same)*, thus, EVERY *time*/ALL *the time*:

언제나 웃는 얼굴이 예뻐요.
enceyna wusnun elkwuli yeyppeyo.
Her ever-smiling face is pretty. (*It smiles any/every time you see it/Her face smiles all the time*)

Since -(이)나 -(i)na is a marker of multitude and choice, as you saw in chapter 4, it can also be understood and translated as *any* in Engish. So the difference between -든(지)

-tun(ci) and -(이)나 -(i)na is really in the nuance, where -든(지) -tun(ci) emphasizes *any random choice*, and -(이)나 -(i)na *every case* and *all the cases* involved:

그런 건 어디든(지) 있어.
kulen ken etitun(ci) isse.
You can find stuff like that anywhere/wherever (you go).

그런 건 어디에나 있어.
kulen ken etieyna isse.
You can find stuff like that anywhere/everywhere.

Here is a complete chart of the *wh*-words suffixed with -든(지) -tun(ci) and -(이)나 -(i)na:

Selective Indefinite		Inclusive Indefinite	Meaning
언제든(지) enceytun(ci)	*whenever;* *any time*	언제나 enceyna	*any time;* *every time, all the time*
어디든(지) etitun(ci)	*wherever;* *anywhere*	어디(에)나 eti(ey)na	*anywhere;* *everywhere*
누구든(지) nukwutun(ci)	*whoever;* *anyone*	누구나 nwukwuna	*anyone;* *everyone*
무엇이든(지); mwuesitun(ci); 뭐든(지) mwetun(ci)	*whatever;* *anything*	무엇이나 mwuesina	*anything;* *everything*
어떻게든(지) ettehkeytun(ci)	*(anyhow,* *how~ever)*	어떻게나/어찌나 ettehkeyna/eccina	*(everyhow, in every way)*

In most cases either type of indefinite pronoun can work, but since the two types carry different nuances, they may not always be interchangeable. See if you can get the sense:

누구든지 오면 알려줘.
nwukwutunci omyen allyecwe.
If anyone ever comes, let me know.

~~**누구나** 오면 알려줘.~~
nwukwuna omyen allyecwe.
~~*If everyone ever comes, let me know.*~~

누구든지 환영입니다.
nwukwutunci hwanyengipnita.
We welcome whoever/anyone.

누구나 환영입니다.
nwukwuna hwanyengipnita.
We welcome anyone/everyone.

뭐든지 보면 읽고 싶어져.
mwetunci pomyen ilkko siphecye.
I feel like reading whatever I see/anything I see.

~~**뭐나** 보면 읽고 싶어져.~~
mwena pomyen ilkko siphecye.
~~*I feel like reading everything-ever I see.*~~

무엇이든 다 대답할 수 있어!
mwuesitun ta taytaphal swu isse!   mwuesina
I can answer anything – whatever I'm asked!

무엇이나 다 대답할 수 있어!
ta taytaphal swu isse!
I can answer anything and everything!

어떻게 ettehkey *how* behaves somewhat erratically in Korean (just like it does in English *however*), and so it is with indefinite pronoun versions. 어떻게든지 ettehkeytunci may show up as 어떻게(해서)든지 ettehkey(hayse)tunci:

어떻게(해서)든지 갈게.
ettehkeytunci kalkey.
I'll go however – no matter what means I need to adopt.

어떻게나 ettehkeyna is used IDIOMATICALLY with -든지 -tunci elsewhere in the sentence:

어떻게나 아프든지 죽는 줄 알았어.
ettehkeyna aphutunci cwuknun cwul alasse.
It hurt ever so badly—I thought I was dying.

You may recall from the previous chapter the particle -마다 mata *all/every*. -마다 -mata highlights individuality, namely, *each-and-every-single one* under consideration:

오는 사람**마다** 울고 간다.
onun salammata wulko kanta
Every single person that comes, leaves crying.

날**마다** 책을 읽는 게 좋아.
nalmata chaekul ilknun key coha.
It's good to read a book every single day.

(4) Fine-tuning 아무...나 and -든(지); 아무 데 and 어디

Because the meaning is so similar, the 아무 amwu … -나 na and … -든(지) -tun(ci) indefinite pronouns tend to be used interchangeably. The key point to remember is that 아무 amwu … -나 na tends to be used with a dependent noun, while … -든(지) -tun(ci) attaches to a *wh*-question word:

염:　　아무 때나 와도 돼요?
　　　amwu ttayna wato twayyo?
Yum:　*May I stop by any time?*

어:　　아무 때나 상관 없어요.
　　　amwu ttayna sangkwan epseyo.
Uh:　*Anytime (you pick) will do.*

어':　　언제든지 상관 없어요.
　　　enceytunci sangkwan epseyo.
Uh':　*Anytime is fine.*

왕: 어디에서 밥 먹을까?
etieyse pap mekulkka?
Wang: *Where should we eat?*

음: 아무 데나 괜찮아.
amwu teyna kwaynchanha.
Eum: *Anywhere (you pick) will work.*

음': 어디든지 괜찮아.
etitunci kwaynchanha.
Eum: *Anywhere will work.*

형: 너, 정말 아무 거나 먹어도 돼?
ne, cengmal amwu kena meketo tway?
Hyung: *You really don't care what you eat?*

홍: 응, 아무 거나 줘.
ung, amwu kena cwe.
Hong: *Yes, give me whatever. It doesn't matter.*

홍': 응, 뭐든지 줘.
ung, mwetunci cwe.
Hong': *Yes, give me anything.*

Finally, let's explore an interesting difference between 어디 가자 eti kaca *Let's go some-where* and 아무 데나 가자 amwu teyna kaca *Let's go anywhere.* 어디 eti as an indefinite pronoun underscores the UNSPECIFICITY OF THE LOCATION as in *Let's go to some place (and we'll figure out where as the conversation unfolds)*, whereas 아무 데나 amwu teyna emphasizes the IRRELEVANCE OF THE SPECIFIC LOCATION as in *Let's go SOMEwhere – ANYwhere.* These distinctions may seem crazy and minute, often correlating only with intonation in English, but we are introducing them so you can avoid miscommunication caused by these nuanced differences. It is not just Korean that is so crazy. Think of the difference between these two English questions:

Are you going somewhere this summer? vs. *Are you going anywhere this summer?*

The LITERAL translation into Korean would be 이번 여름에 어디 가요? ipen yelume eti kayo? The first question expects or assumes *yes* and the second question leans toward expecting *no* as an answer, so a more contextually relevant translation in Korean for the second question would be 이번 여름에도 어디 안 가요? ipen yelumeto eti an kayo? *Are you not going anywhere this summer, either?*

(5) Indefinite number nouns

So far you learned how to say such vague and inclusive sorts of indefiniteness as *It doesn't matter who, anyone,* and *whoever* in Korean. There is another kind of indefiniteness that we talked about earlier. In English, you refer to vague or approximate NUM-BERS OF people or items using words like *a few, some, most, all,* and *no.* (You may feel like *all* and *no* are pretty definite numbers, but grammatically they work like the others here.) These words can come before a noun as in _some_ coins, _most_ children, _all_ the food, or _no_ cats, or can stand in for nouns as a pronoun as in _I have some_ (_of them_), _most_ (_of them_), _one_ (_of them_), or _another_ (_of them_).

<1> A few, a portion, and all

A basic way to express indefinite quantities like _a few_ is to use the native Korean expressions 몇(몇) myech(myech) _some number_, 모두 motwu _all_ (_all of them, every one_), and 다 ta _all_. These expressions work somewhat like counters and require the noun they are quantifying to precede them.

사람들 **모두** 갔어?
salamtul motwu kasse?
Has everyone left?/Did everyone go (there)?

새 **몇** 마리가 푸드득 날아갔다.
say myech malika phwututuk nalakassta.
A few birds flitted away.

너희들 **다** 신분증 가져왔지?
nehuytul ta sinpwuncung kacyewassci?
You all brought your ID, right?

모두 motwu _all_ also has an ADNOMINAL version 모든 motun _all_:

사람들 모두 갔어?
salamtul motwu kasse?
Have all (of them) left?

세상의 모든 음악
seysanguy motun umak
all the music of the world

Indefinite number ideas can also be expressed with Sino-Korean nouns using the roots 수 swu _number_ or 부분 pwupwun _part_:

극소수 kuksoswu	極少數	_only a small number_
소수 soswu	少數	_a few in number_
다수 taswu	多數	_many or several in number_
대다수 taytaswu	大多數	_the majority, many in number_
일부(분) ilpwu(pwun)	一部(分)	_some of; one (small) part or section (of the whole)_
대부분 taypwupwun	大部分	_most part (of the whole)_
전부 cenpwu	全部	_all, literally all parts, in its entirety_

These Sino-Korean quantity terms also function somewhat like counters and require the noun they are quantifying to precede them, just as the Haan quantity terms:

배달품 **일부**가 파손되어 있었다.
paytalphwum ilpwuka phasontoye issessta.
Some (part) of the shipment was damaged.

사람들 **몇**이 아직 안 왔어.
salamtul myechi acik an wasse.
A few people haven't come yet.

Most of these words can also function as adverbs, and words meaning *all* are most often used as adverbs and cannot be marked with particles:

숙제(가) **전부** 다(~~가~~) 끝났어?
swukcey(ka) cenpwu ta(~~ka~~) kkuthnaysse?
Is your homework finished in its entirety?

그거(를) **다** 읽었어?
kuke(lul) ta ilkesse?
Did you read it all?/Have you finished reading it all?

Some of these Sino-Korean quantity words may also show up with the [number + 의 uy + noun] structure in more formal writings:

극소수의 사람들만 부유층에 속한다.
kuksoswuuy salamtulman pwuyuchungey sokhanta.
Only the extreme minority belongs to the rich class.

대다수의 임원들이 반대표를 던졌다.
taytaswuuy imwentuli pantayphyolul tencyessta.
The majority of the board members cast a "no" vote.

대부분의 사람들은 침묵했다.
taypwupwunuy salamtulun chimmwukhayssta.
Most people kept their silence.

<2> Some

The English word *some* can be used to refer to a type or group without really referring to the NUMBER of people at all, as in *Some (people) like coffee and some (people) don't.* In that case, you would use the adnominal 어떤 etten *certain* in Korean:

어떤 사람들은 커피를 더 좋아해.
etten salamtulul khephilul te cohahay.
Some people like coffee better.

When the word *some* just means *a little bit*, regardless of whether it is referring to an indefinite number or an indefinite (uncountable) amount, you can use the generic word 좀 com or 조금 cokum *a little bit* in Korean:

돈이 **좀** 있어. 동전이 **조금** 있어.
toni com isse. tongceni cokum isse.
I have some money. There are some coins.

케이크를 **조금** 먹었어. 다 먹지는 않았어.
kheyikhulul cokum mekesse. ta mekcinun anhasse.
I ate some cake, but I didn't eat it all.

<3> Another one

The indefinite pronouns *one* and *another* really mean *one* and *an + other*, and the Korean language respects that etymology with the words 하나 hana and 하나 더 hana te *one more*:

나 하나 줘. 맛있다! 하나 더 줘.
na hana cwe. masissta! hana te cwe.
Give me one. This is delicious! Give me another.

갑자기 한 사람이 더 걸어들어왔다.
kapcaki han salami te keletulewassta.
Then, suddenly, another person walked in.

And when the word *another* means *a different one*, you can use 다른 talun:

나 하나 줘. 상했다! 다른 거 줘.
na hana cwe. sanghayssta! talun ke cwe.
Give me one! …This is bad. Give me a another/different one.

We have taken a headlong tour of Korean nouns and pronouns that are definite, indefinite, or interrogative. You have seen some intensely interesting and very Korean expressions in this chapter. As we move into later chapters of this book, you will taste more nuanced expressions, and that's where the fun is!

Exercises

5.1 Nouns

Exercise 1. The following two words have the same meaning. Which of the two is more scholarly?

1)	사람	인간	5)	가게	상점
2)	정문	앞문	6)	값	가격
3)	나이	연령	7)	금일	오늘
4)	식사	밥	8)	이름	성명

Exercise 2. Can you guess the meaning of the boldface syllable common to each set of words? Look up any unfamiliar words in the dictionary.

1) 외**국**   한**국**   중**국**   미**국**   국: _____

2) **학**교   **학**기   **학**년   방**학**   학: _____

3) **주**말   **주**중   일**주**일   매**주**   주: _____

4) **남**자   **남**매   **남**녀   **남**학생   남: _____

5) **식**당   **식**사   외**식**   한**식**   식: _____

6) **수**영   냉**수**   음료**수**   **수**요일   수: _____

Exercise 3. Can you guess the meaning of the Sino-Korean noun in bold, based on its verb usage in the sentence?

1) 나는 한 달에 한 번 방을 **청소**해요
   I clean my room once a month.

2) 결국 우리는 진돗개를 **선택**했다.
   Finally, we chose a Jindo dog.

3) 할머니께서는 매일 **산책**하세요.
   My grandmother takes a walk every day.

4) 집에 도착하면 **전화**하세요.
   Please call me when you get home.

5) 할머니, 할아버지께서 오시면 **인사**드려라.
   Greet your grandparents when they visit.

Exercise 4. Can you guess the meaning of the following "Konglish" words? If not, try searching online and then figure out what English words they come from.

1) 에이에스: _____   5) 아이쇼핑: _____

2) 사이다: _____   6) 핸들: _____

3) 미팅: _____   7) 원룸: _____

4) 핸드폰: _____   8) 셀카: _____

Exercise 5. Where would you put 들 to make the correct plural meaning? If 들 cannot be used, write "X".

1) 아이가 자요.   *The children are sleeping.*

2) 친구하고 같이 바닷가에 갔어요.   *I went to the beach with (my) friends.*

3) 여기 앉으세요.   *Please you all sit here.*

4) 너희, 거기서 뭐 하고 있어?   *What are you kids doing there?*

5) 친구가 과자를 세 개 먹었다.   *The friend ate three cookies.*

5.2 Numerals

Exercise 6. Fill in the blanks with the right number words. The lower cells are Sino-Korean while the upper cells are native Korean.

0	1	2	3	4	5
공/영			셋		
	일			사	

6	7	8	9	10
	일곱			열
		팔		

10	20	30	40	50	60
열	스물			쉰	
십		삼십			

70	80	90	100	1,000	10,000	1 million
칠십						

Exercise 7. Spell out the underlined numbers in Korean!

(예) 현충일은 <u>6</u> 월 <u>6</u> 일입니다. → **유월 육** 일

1) 한글날은 <u>10</u> 월 <u>9</u> 일입니다. _____

2) 우리 집 전화 번호는 <u>234-5910</u> 입니다. _____

3) 지금은 <u>12</u> 시 <u>45</u> 분입니다. <u>1</u> 시 <u>30</u> 분에 점심을 먹을 겁니다.

_____

4) 하루는 <u>24</u> 시간이고 일년은 <u>365</u> 일입니다. _____

5) 나는 <u>2015</u> 년에 학교를 졸업했습니다. _____

6) 이 차는 <u>23,000</u> 달러입니다. _____

7) 한국에는 <u>48,000,000</u> 명의 사람이 삽니다. _____

8) 미국에는 <u>320,000,000</u> 명의 사람이 삽니다. _____

Exercise 8. Fill in the blanks with the appropriate Sino-Korean or Native numbers.

1) 가을 학기는 (예: **구**) 월에 시작합니다. 이번 학기에 한국어 수업을 듣습니다.

a. 9
   한국어 교실은 _____ 층에 있고, 교실의 방 번호는 _____ 호입니다. 교실

b. 3   c. 305
   에 학생이 _____ 명있습니다. 수업은 매일 _____ 시 _____ 분에 있는

d. 20   e. 8   f. 30
   데 _____ 분 동안 합니다.

g. 50

2) 한국어 수업에 교과서가 _____ 권 필요합니다. 교과서는 별로 안 비쌉니다.

h. 2
   _____ 권에 _____ 달러입니다. 교과서에는 모두 _____ 과가 있습니다.

i. 1   j. 55   k. 10
   그리고 지금은 _____ 과를 공부하고 있습니다. 그런데 _____ 주일 후에

l. 5   m. 2

시험이 있습니다. 그래서 오늘은 _____ 시간 동안 한국어를 공부했습니다.
n. 3
저녁에는 친구들하고 커피를 _____ 잔 마시러 나갈 겁니다. 아직 _____
o. 1   p. 21
살이 안 돼서 술은 안 마십니다.

5.3 Counters & Dependent Nouns

Exercise 9. Fill in the blanks with the appropriate counter.

1) 나는 기숙사에 살아요. 내 방은 삼 _____ 에 있고 내 방 번호는 307 _____
a.   b.
예요. 룸메이트 두 _____ 하고 같이 방을 써요. 내 룸메이트 수빈은 아주
c.
재미있는 친구예요. 밥을 좋아해서 매일 저녁 밥을 두 _____ 이나 먹어요.
d.
매일 운동도 세 _____ 이나 해서 건강해요. 예쁜 구두도 많아요. 스물세
e.
_____ 나 있어요. 또 다른 룸메이트 지예는 커피를 좋아해서 매일 커피를
f.
일곱 _____ 이나 마셔요. 피아노를 잘 쳐서 피아노 *대회에서 일 _____ 을
g.   h.
했어요. 방에 텔레비전이 한 _____ 있지만 별로 안 봐요. 그냥 룸메이트들
i.
하고 얘기해요. 나는 우리 룸메이트들이 좋아요!

*대회: competition

2) 나는 한국 노래를 아주 좋아합니다. 부를 수 있는 한국 노래가 모두 열
_____ 이나 됩니다! 그리고 한국 가수 시디도 스무 _____ 이나 있습니
j.   k.
다. 그리고 한국 영화도 아주 좋아해서 지난 여름 방학에 한국 영화를 다
섯 _____ 이나 봤습니다. 그 중에서 *"과속스캔들"이 너무 재미있어서 세
l.
_____ 이나 봤습니다. 한국어도 배워서 한국 책도 많이 읽습니다. 이번 달
m.
에는 벌써 두 _____ 이나 읽었습니다.
n.

*과속스캔들: Scandal Makers

5.4 Pronouns

Exercise 10. 이? 그? 저? Choose the right one.

1) 고객 (customer): _____ 가방 얼마예요?

   점원 (clerk): 3만원입니다.

2) 고객: _____ 가방은 얼마예요?

   점원: 2만원입니다.

3) 고객: _____ 가방은 얼마예요?

   점원: 4만원입니다.

Exercise 11. Choose the most appropriate personal pronoun from the parentheses.

1) 선생님: 김세영 학생이 누구예요?
   학생: (나, 저, 내, 제)가 김세영이에요.

2) 학생: 처음 뵙겠습니다. (나, 저, 내, 제)는 김세영이라고 합니다.
   선생님: 반가워요. 환영합니다~! (나, 저, 내, 제)는 조은지예요.

3) 학생 1: (우리, 저희) 집은 필라델피아예요.
   학생 2: 그래요? (나, 저, 내, 제)도 필라델피아에서 왔어요!

4) 학생 1:   (우리, 저희) 한국어 선생님은 조은지 선생님이에요.

   학생 2:   아! 그래요?

5) 손녀: (우리, 저희) 한국어 선생님은 조은지 선생님이세요.
   할아버지: 아, 그래?

6) 친구 1:   (나, 너, 내, 네) 가방에 뭐가 들어있어?

   친구 2:   책이 있어.

   친구 1:   좀 보여줘 봐. 그거 (나, 너, 내, 네) 책 아니야?

   친구 2:   아니야. 내 책이야.

Exercise 12. Pick the appropriate reflexive pronoun for the following proverbs!

자기	자신	자체	스스로

1) 너 _____ 을 알라. (소크라테스)
   Know thyself (Socrates).

2) 하늘은 _____ 돕는 자를 돕는다.
   Heaven helps those who help themselves.

3) 남의 것이 _____ 것보다 더 좋아 보인다.
   The grass is always greener on the other side.

4) 돈은 행복의 조건이 될 수 있지만 행복 _____ 는 될 수 없다.
   Money may be a necessary condition for happiness but cannot be happiness itself.

Exercise 13. 정빈 and 연우 are having a conversation. Help them pick out the right question word. You can use the hints in the box.

언제	어디	누구	누가	뭐	어떻게	왜
무슨	어느	어떤	몇	얼마나	얼마	

1) 정빈: 연우야, 얼굴 좀 보자. _____ 요일에 시간이 돼?

   연우: 수요일에 시간 있어.

2) 정빈: 그럼 오늘이네! 지금 _____ 하고 같이 있어?

   연우: 혼자 있어.

3) 정빈: 오늘 만나자! _____ 에서 만날까?

    연우: 너희 기숙사로 갈게.

4) 정빈: 지금 올 수 있어? _____ 만날래?

    연우: 지금은 운전 중이니까 두 시까지 갈게.

    = 오후 두 시에 기숙사에서 =

5) 민영: _____ 오셨어요?

    연우: 정빈 씨 만나러 왔어요.

6) 연우: _____ 방에 정빈씨가 있어요?

    민영: 저 방에 있어요.

7) 정빈: 민영 씨, 지금 _____ 왔어요?

    연우: 내가 왔어!

8) 정빈: 너, 어디 있었어? 여기 오는 데 _____ 걸렸어?

    연우: 가까운 데 있어서 별로 안 걸렸어.

9) 연우: 민영 씨는 누구야? _____ 사람이야?

    정빈: 룸메이트인데 재미있는 사람이야.

10) 연우: (민영 씨는) _____ 학년이야?

    정빈: 삼학년이야.

11) 정빈: 우리, 점심 먹은 다음에 _____ 할까?

    연우: 영화 보자!

12) 정빈: 영화 표가 _____ 야?

    연우: 십 달러 정도 해.

    = 영화관에서 =

13) 연우: _____ 그렇게 웃어?

    정빈: 영화가 재미있어서.

Exercise 14. Choose the correct indefinite pronoun from the words in parentheses. There may be more than one possible answer!

1) 집에 (누군가, 누구나, 누구든지, 아무나, 아무도) 있는 것 같아요.

2) 집에 (누군가, 누구나, 누구든지, 아무나, 아무도) 없어요.

3) 벌써 2 시인데 (뭐든지, 무언가, 아무거나, 아무것도) 못 먹었어.

4) 빨리 밥 먹으러 가자. 배 고파서 (뭐든지, 무언가, 아무거나, 아무것도) 다 먹을 수 있어!

5) 저희 집에 (언제든지, 아무 때나, 아무 때도) 오세요!

6) (누구든지, 누군가, 아무나, 아무도) 다 환영합니다!

7) 찾아 오는 길을 모르시면 (언제든지, 언젠가, 아무 때나, 아무 때도) 전화하세요.

8) (어디에선가, 어디에서나, 어디에서든지, 아무 데서나, 아무 데서도) 김치를 안 판다.

9) 그 사람을 (언젠가, 언제나, 언제든지, 아무 때나, 아무 때도, 한 번도) 만난 적이 있어요.

Exercise 15. Choose the appropriate word to fill in the blanks for the boldface word in the English translation.

다른	더	몇	모두	어떤	좀

1) 초대한 친구들이 _____ 다 왔어요. *All the friends that I invited came.*

2) 친구들 _____ 은 지금 수영하고 있어요. *A few friends are swimming now.*

3) _____ 사람들은 김치를 안 먹어요. *Some people don't eat kimchi.*

4) 밥을 _____ 먹었는데 아직 배가 고파요.
I ate some rice, but I am still hungry.

5) 밥 한 그릇 _____ 주세요. *Please give me another bowl of rice.*

6) 이거 말고 _____ 색 바지로 주세요.
Not this. Please give me pants in a different color.

Exercise 16. Choose the most appropriate word to fill in the blanks. Use each word only once.

전혀	절대로	항상	한번도

1) 친구 1: 비행기 안에서는 담배는 _____ 피우면 안 돼.

   친구 2: 나도 알아.

2) 친구 1: 김치 피자 먹어 봤어?

   친구2: 아니, _____ 안 먹어 봤어.

3) 친구1: 아침에 시간 있어?

   친구 2: 아니, 아침에는 _____ 운동을 해. 저녁 때 만나자.

4) 친구 1: (showing a picture to her friend) 이 사람 알아?

   친구 2: 아니, _____ 모르는 사람이야. 만난 적이 없거든.

Exercise 17. Can you figure out the right word based on the translation?

1) *Most students come to class on time.*
   (대부분, 전부, 다소, 소수) 의 학생들은 제 시간에 수업에 온다.

2) *A few people haven't shown up.*
   사람들 (다소, 일부분, 몇몇) 이 아직 안 왔습니다.

3) *Sorry, but everything is incorrect.*
   미안하지만 (전부, 대부분, 소수) 다 틀렸어요.

4) *What I ordered arrived somewhat damaged.*
   주문한 게 (다소, 대부분, 소수) 파손돼서 도착했어요.

CHAPTER 6

Verbs

In this chapter, we will cover probably the most important category of all: the verbals, which include verbs and adjectives. We said Korean particles are rich in their variety, but Korean verbal suffixes come with a much greater degree of variety and intricacy than particles. And a single consonant in the suffix, -(으)ㄴ -(u)n vs. -(으)ㄹ -(u)l, to take an example, may result in as huge a difference in meaning as past versus future.

All kinds of information is encoded in the suffixes of Korean verbs, including whether the sentence is a statement, question, command, suggestion, or exclamation (the **sentence type**); how formal or polite the speaker is being (the **speech style**); whether something has happened or will happen (the **tense**); whether an action has been completed or is on-going (the **aspect**); and what the mental and emotional attitude of the speaker might be when she uttered the sentence. Enmeshed with these various and sundry suffix types and functions is verb **conjugation**, namely, how the roots change shape to connect with different suffixes.

Before we get started, it is important to know that, in Korean, both adjectives and active verbs come at the end of the sentence in order to function as the **predicate**, and both conjugate and attach with most of the same kinds of suffixes. There are some differences in how the two behave, but there are also many similarities, such that ADJECTIVES ARE CONSIDERED A KIND OF VERB IN KOREAN, called **descriptive verbs**.

Unlike English verbs, all verbs in Korean must be conjugated and have at least one suffix in any utterance. There is no "bare verb," like *be* that works as a word in Korean. To talk about the word itself or the verb without any tense, speech style, etc., the DICTIONARY FORM is used. The dictionary form consists of the verb **root** and the suffix 다 ta. Throughout this book, we will use the dictionary form when we are speaking about verbs in general terms, but we will use their conjugated forms with necessary suffixes in the example sentences to show their natural usage. Little by little, you will learn the conjugations and suffixes.

We will begin by explaining the two types of verb (active and descriptive) in 6.1, then move on to how they conjugate for the ordinary speech style (6.2), with different tenses and aspects (6.3), and then on to how to make a sentence **negative** (6.4). Lastly, in section 6.5, we will summarize verbal SUFFIXES into three basic conjugation categories and introduce classes of verbs that have special conjugations.

Verbs are truly where the action is in Korean sentences. Shall we begin?

6.1 Korean Verbs

It is the verb that is the boss of the entire sentence. Verbs dictate the relationship between words—which is the doer of the action and which is done to, etc. So the most important thing you should remember about any verb is its **transitivity**. That is, is this verb **transitive** (does it take an object?) or **intransitive**? The distinction between transitive and intransitive is essential to good particle use as well, so let's devote a bit of space here for a quick review.

If the verb is **intransitive** like 일어나다 ilenata *to get up* or 자다 cata *to sleep*, it CANNOT appear with an object, a noun that could potentially be marked with the object particle -을/를 -ul/lul. When the verb is intransitive, any elements besides the subject and the verb may be omitted (indicated with parentheses here):

아기가 (또) (마루에서) 자요.
akika (tto) (malwueyse) cayo.
The baby sleeps/is sleeping (on the floor) (again).

On the other hand, as you learned when we talked about grammatical particles in chapter 4, verbs such as 먹다 mekta *to eat*, 마시다 masita *to drink*, 읽다 ilkta *to read*, and 듣다 tutta *to listen*, are transitive verbs, and they an object in the sentence. Unlike English transitive verbs, Korean transitives tend to NOT allow leaving out the object unless it is already mentioned or retrievable from the context. One such case is if the sentence is an answer to a question specifically asking for the subject, then the object is not an important element, so it can be left out:

제가 원래 분식을 좋아해요.
ceyka wenlay pwunsikul cohahayyo.
I always liked flour-based food.

제가 원래 좋아해요.
ceyka wenlay cohahayyo.
I always liked (something).

민우가 점심을 먹어요.
minwuka cemsimul mekeyo.
Minu eats lunch/Minu is having lunch.

민우가 먹어요.
minwuka mekeyo.
Minu is eating.

동생이 책을 읽어요.
tongsayngi chaykul ilkeyo.
My younger sibling reads/is reading a book.

동생이 읽어요.
tongsayngi ilkeyo.
My younger sibling reads/is reading.

Compare:

누가 점심을 먹어요?
nwuka cemsimul mekeyo?
Who is having lunch?

민우가 먹어요.
minwuka mekeyo.
Minu eats (lunch)/Minu is (having lunch).

Certain verbs like 멈추다 memchwuta *to stop* and 내리다 naylita *to bring/come down* can act as both transitive and intransitive verbs:

차가 멈췄어요.

chaka memchwesseyo.

The car stopped.

차를 멈추세요.

chalul memchwuseyyo.

Stop the car.

비가 내려요.

pika naylyeyo.

The rain is coming down.

가격을 내렸어요.

kakyekul naylyesseyo.

They brought down the price.

6.1.1 Active verbs & descriptive verbs

The next thing to know about a Korean verb is whether it is an **active verb** or a **descriptive verb**. Korean adjectives and verbs behave very similarly; they both change shape to **conjugate** for different suffixes, and they both serve as the **predicate** at the end of the sentence.

What you would typically think of as verbs—those that express an ACTION by a doer—are called **active verbs**, and what you may think of as adjectives—the type that DESCRIBES what an entity is like—are called **descriptive verbs** in Korean. We will refer to both active and descriptive verbs in Korean as simply "verbs" and distinguish the two types when necessary. Whereas adjectives that are used as the predicate in English require a linking verb, such as *be*, Korean descriptive verbs are verb-like and do not require a linking verb to be the predicate:

미나는 수학을 **공부해요**.

minanun swuhakul kongpwuhayyo.

Mina studies math. (Active verb)

미나는 **똑똑해요**.

minanun ttokttokhayyo.

Mina is smart. (Descriptive verb)

미나가 **바빠요**.

minaka pappayo.

Mina is busy. (Descriptive verb)

You can consider all Korean **descriptive verbs** to be **intransitive**. Because the main function of the descriptive verbs is to DESCRIBE the subject, they can never show up with a noun marked with the OBJECT particle -을/를 -ul/lul:

저 방은 너무 작아요.

ce pangun nemwu cakayo.

That room is too small.

파란색도 예뻐요.

phalansaykto yeyppeyo.

Blue, too, is pretty.

시험이 너무 길었어요.

sihemi nemwu kilesseyo.

The test was too long.

~~시험을 너무 길었어요~~.

sihemul nemwu kilesseyo.

The test was too long.

Be aware that not all English adjectives are descriptive verbs in Korean. Also, descriptive verbs conjugate differently from active verbs with certain suffixes, as you will see in later chapters.

6.1.2 Existential verbs 있다 and 없다

For the funky English structure *there is*, which expresses existence, Korean uses the verb 있다 issta, which means *to exist* or *be present* or *be located (at some place)*. The negative counterpart of the existential verb 있다 issta is 없다 epsta *there is no/is lacking*. The thing whose existence is expressed by these existential verbs never appears with the object particle -을/를 -ul/lul but instead with the subject marker; a sentence with the 있다 issta verb basically means [*subject*] *exists*.

The location is marked with -에 ey, and if the location happens to be animate, that is, if a person "has" the item, it is indicated with -한테 -hanthey or -에게 -eykey, in a sense saying *the item exists at/on the person*. Although these sentences are best translated into English with the verb *have*, they use the Korean verbs 있다 issta and 없다 epsta, so the item owned is marked with the subject particle -이/가 -i/ka:

내 방에 텔레비전**이 있어요**.
nay pangey theylleypiceni isseyo.
There is a television in my room.

내 방에 침대**가 없어요**.
nay pangey chimtayka epseyo.
There is no bed in my room.

나한테 돈**이** 조금 **있어요**.
nahanthey toni cokum isseyo.
I have a little bit of money.

나한테는 동생**이 없어요**.
nahantheynun tongsayngi epseyo.
I do not have a younger sibling.

You may turn the location (or person who has) into a TOPIC of the sentence, but you still should NOT use an object particle:

내 방은 바퀴벌레**가** 있다.
nay pangun pakhwipelleyka issta.
My room has roaches.

나는 돈**이** 땡전 한 푼 없다.
nanun toni ttayngcen han phwun epsta.
I don't have a red penny.

있다 issta can also function as an active verb, meaning *to stay (at a place)*:

잠깐 여기에 있어.
camkkan yekiey isse.
Stay here for a sec.

Either way, 있다 issta and 없다 epsta can NEVER be used with an object with the object particle -을/를 -ul/lul.

6.1.3 Linking verbs 이다 and 아니다

The Korean linking verb 이다 ita *to be* functions as a link between the subject and the **complement** noun in the predicate in sentences such as 저분들은 선생님이에요 cep-wuntulun sensayngnimieyyo *They are teachers*. 이다 ita *to be* conjugates for tense and speech style at the end of the sentence. It is rather parasitic in that it cannot be a predicate on its own: it is attached to a noun to form one word (that is, with no space between them). 아니다 anita *to not be*, the negative counterpart of 이다 ita *to be*, does not work that way. It acts as a fully independent verb, following the complement noun which is marked with the subject marker -이/가 -i/ka:

나는 학생이에요.
nanun haksayngieyyo.
I am a student.

나는 선생님이 아니에요.
nanun sensayngnimi anieyyo.
I am not a teacher.

여기가 부엌이에요.
yekika pwuekhieyyo.
This ("Here") is the kitchen.

여기는 내 방이 아니에요.
yekinun nay pangi anieyyo.
This ("Here") is not my room.

English uses the verb *be* to express EXISTENCE or PRESENCE *(There is a book/The book is on the table)* and to LINK two nouns *(It is a book)*, but keep in mind that Korean has two distinct verbs for these functions: 있다 issta *there is* (as in 책이 있다 chayki issta *There is a book)* and 이다 ita (as in 그건 책이다 kuken chaykita *It is a book)*. Think of the final consonant of 있다 issta and memorize it as the verb *exist*, and think of the one with no final consonant 이다 ita as *equal* (A = B). For either 이다 ita/아니다 anita or 있다 issta/없다 epsta, you will NEVER need the object particle -을/를 -ul/lul.

6.1.4 Restrictions on descriptive verbs

In addition to the conjugation differences we keep alluding to, there are also some restrictions on how descriptive verbs function in Korean. For example, descriptive verbs cannot in general be made into commands or suggestions in Korean. This is because descriptive verbs do not include any sense of intentional behavior themselves, and there is no *be* verb that could take on a meaning of *act* or *behave*:

착해라!   *Be nice!*
chakhayla!

예쁘자!   *Let's be pretty!*
yeyppuca!

Similarly, descriptive verbs cannot be made **progressive** (like English *is doing* or *is being*), generally because they cannot be made to happen dynamically—there is an IN-HERENT duration in them to begin with. Even for states that are temporary, Korean descriptive verbs cannot be expressed in the progressive aspect with -고 있다 -ko issta; just use the present tense, and, if necessary, an adverb like 요즘 yocum *these days* or 지금 cikum *now*. Otherwise, you need to make use of an active verb and make the descriptive verb into an ADVERB with -게 -key, for example:

나는 지금 바쁘고 있어.
nanun cikum pappuko isse.
~~I am being busy.~~

나는 바쁜 중이야.
nanun pappun cwungiya.
~~I am in the middle of being busy.~~

나는 지금/요즘 바빠.
nanun cikum/yocum pappa.
I am busy now/these days.

나는 바쁘게 일하고 있어.
nanun pappukey ilhako isse.
I am working busily.

나는 바쁘게 일하는 중이야.
nanun pappukey ilhanun cwungiya.
I am in the middle of working busily.

무례하고 있어.
mwulyeyhako isse.
He is being rude.

무례하**게** 굴고 있어.
mwulyeyhakey kwulko isse.
He is being rude/He is acting rudely.

무례하**게** 행동하고 있어.
mwulyeyhakey hayngtonghako isse.
He is being rude/He is acting rudely.

6.1.5 Descriptive to active conversion

Another important point about descriptive verbs in Korean is that you can't use them
AS IS to talk about a third party's feeling or mood (because you can't know what they
really feel). You can ASK about other people's emotions, but unless you are a writer
describing a character from a bird's-eye view or are a very close friend or relative, you
need a way to state the other's emotions "objectively."

나 요즘 슬퍼.
na yocum sulphe.
I'm sad these days.

걔 요즘 우울해?
kyay yocum wuwulhay?
Is s/he down these days? (said by a close friend or sibling)

지니 요즘 피곤해.
cini yocum phikonhay.
Jinny is tired these days. (said by a close friend or sibling)

그는 너무 심심했다.
kunun nemwu simsimhayssta.
He was so bored. (written from a bird's-eye view)

You can achieve "objective" reporting of a third person's emotions by attaching the auxiliary verb -어 하다 -e hata to descriptive verbs of emotion. If this objectification doesn't
happen, certain descriptive verbs may sound like they are describing what the person
makes YOU feel rather than their feelings:

걔가 요즘 **피곤해해요**.
kyayka yocum phikonhayhayo.
He is (acting like he is/feeling) tired these days.

그 사람 좀 피곤해.
ku salam com phikonhay.
He makes me tired. (He is a tiring kind of person.)

그 여자가 좀 기분 **나빠해요**.
ku yecaka com kipwun nappahayo.
She is (acting/feeling) a little upset.

그 여자 좀 기분 나빠.
ku yeca com kipwun nappa.
She kinda makes me upset.

When you use the -어 하다 -e hata ending, you are grammatically turning descriptive verbs into active verbs, which can then also be made progressive with -고 있다 -ko issta. The English translation would still be adjectival:

할 게 없어서 아이가 심심해하고 있어.
hal key epsese aika simsimhayhako isse.
There is nothing to do, so he is bored. (from what I can tell).

Here are some more descriptive verbs and their conversion pairs:

기쁘다 kipputa *happy*	기뻐하다 kippehata *act happy*	심심하다 simsimhata *bored, boring*	심심해하다 simsimhayhata *find (it) boring*
슬프다 sulphuta *sad*	슬퍼하다 sulphehata *act sad*	피곤하다 phikonhata *tired, tiring*	피곤해하다 phikonhayhata *act tired*
재미있다 caymiissta *fun*	재미있어하다 caymiissehata *find (it) fun*	춥다 chwupta *cold*	추워하다 chwuwehata *act cold*
우울하다 wuwulhata *depressed*	우울해하다 wuwulhayhata *act depressed*	기분 나쁘다 kipwun napputa *in a bad mood*	기분 나빠하다 kipwun nappahata *find (it) upsetting*

The -어하다 -ehata conversion (descriptive verb to active verb) is also needed for DE-SIRES expressed by the auxiliary verb -고 싶다 -ko siphta *want to* (more on this in chapter 7). Because one cannot truly know what others (especially the third person) desire, it has to be expressed objectively as -고 싶어하다 -ko siphehata. -고 싶다 -ko siphta is a descriptive verb and turns into an active verb when -어하다 -ehata is attached:

나는 한국에 가고 싶어.
nanun hankwukey kako siphe.
I want to go to Korea.

너도 한국에 가고 싶어?
neto hankwukey kako siphe?
Do you want to go to Korea, too?

동생은 한국에 가고 싶어.
tongsayngun hankwukey kako siphe.
My younger brother wants to go to Korea.

동생은 한국에 가고 **싶어해**.
tongsayngun hankwukey kako siphehay.
My younger brother wants to go to Korea.

동생은 한국에 가고 **싶어하고 있어**.
tongsayngun hankwukey kako siphehako isse.
My younger brother (currently) wants to go to Korea.

One more situation calls for descriptive verbs to be converted into active verbs, and that is with the change-of-state suffix -어 지다 -e cita *go/come into such-and-such state* as in 슬퍼지다 sulphecita *to become/turn sad*. The suffix -어 지다 -e cita attaches to descriptive verbs, but with this suffix attached, the whole word is an active verb, so it can also be made progressive:

요즘 날이 **춥지**?
yocum nali chwupci?
It's cold these days, isn't it?

요즘 날이 **추워진다**.
yocum nali chwuwecinta.
It's getting cold these days.

요즘 날이 (점점) **추워지고 있다**.
yocum nali (cemcem) chwuweciko issta.
Recently, days are getting colder and colder.

6.1.6 Active vs. descriptive 하다 verbs

A quintessential TRANSITIVE verb in Korean would be 하다 hata *to do* because you always *do SOMETHING*, so the object particle -을/를 -ul/lul will likely appear with this verb. When the particle is left out, as it often is in spoken Korean, 하다 hata is sort of "suffixed" to the preceding noun. In writing, 하다 hata with an object particle before it will have a space between, and the "suffixed" 하다 hata that is attached to the noun will be written with no space:

인터넷을 했어요.
intheneysul haysseyo.
I used the Internet.

인터넷했어요.
intheneyshaysseyo.
I used the Internet.

When the object noun is **incorporated** into the verb like this, you can have a new object noun marked with the object particle:

공부해요.
kongpwuhayyo.
I study./ I am studying.

한국어를 공부해요.
hankwukelul kongpwuhayyo.
I study Korean.

내 방을 청소해요.
nay pangul chengsohayyo.
I clean my room.

The added object can also form a compound with the original object and take an object marker, leaving 하다 hata as a stand-alone verb:

한국어 공부를 해요.
hankwuke kongpwulul hayyo.
I study Korean. (Literally, *I do "Korean study."*)

내 방 청소를 해요.
nay pang chengsolul hayyo.
I clean my room. (Literally, *I do "(my) room cleaning."*)

As discussed in chapter 5 (5.1.2), the 하다 hata verb attaches to many Sino-Korean words, but it can also attach to a handful of native Haan words and most loanwords that denote actions:

Haan words:

밥하다 paphata *cook rice*, 설거지하다 selkecihata *to do the dishes*, 빨래하다 ppallayhata *to do laundry*, 사랑하다 salanghata *to love*, 뽀뽀하다 ppoppohata *to kiss*, 일하다 ilhata *to work*, 말하다 malhata *to speak/say*, 이야기하다 iyakihata *to talk*, 생각하다 sayngkakhata *to think*, 절하다 celhata *to bow*

Loanwords:

데이트하다 teyithuhata *to date*, 키스하다 khisuhata *to kiss*, 프로포즈하다 phulophocuhata *to propose (marriage)*, 드라이브하다 tulaipuhata *to go for a drive*, 테스트하다 theysythuhata *to test*, 컴퓨터하다 khemphyuthehata *to use a computer*, 인터넷하다 intheneyshata *to be on the Internet*, 게임하다 keyimhata *to play a game*, 메일하다 meyilhata *to email*, 파마하다 phamahata *to get a perm*, 린스하다 linsuhata *to condition (hair)*, (헤어)커트하다 (heye) khethuhata *to get a haircut*, 카피하다 khaphihata *to copy*, 리포트하다 liphothuhata *to report*, 다운로드하다 tawunlotuhata *to download*, 프린트하다 phulinthuhata *to print*, 체크하다 cheykhuhata *to check*, 채팅하다 chaythinghata *to chat*, 미팅하다 mithinghata *to have a meeting*, 쇼핑하다 syophinghata *to do shopping*, 드라이클리닝하다 tulaikhullininghata *to dryclean*

 BE AWARE, AND BEWARE!   하다 hata also makes DESCRIPTIVE verbs (out of nouns and borrowed roots of various kinds)!

These descriptive 하다 hata verbs can NEVER show up with the object particle -을/를 -ul/lul, as they are INTRANSITIVE:

용돈이 더 **필요해요**.
yongtoni te philyohayyo.
I am in need of more pocket money.

그 친구들은 아주 **쿨해요**.
ku chinkwutulun acwu khwulhayyo.
They are such cool friends.

As we said, the 하다 hata words come in Sino-Korean, Haan Korean, and loanword varieties. Native speakers don't always know the origin of these words, but they know which ones are active verbs and which are descriptive verbs which cannot be made progressive (and so on). Here are some DESCRIPTIVE (thus INTRANSITIVE) 하다 hata verbs that will be useful for you:

행복하다 *happy* hayngpokhata	조용하다 *quiet* coyonghata	피곤하다 *tired* phikonhata
친절하다 *kind* chincelhata	깨끗하다 *clean* kkaykkushata	이상하다 *weird* isanghata
복잡하다 *complicated or congested* pokcaphata	따뜻하다 *warm* ttattushata	미안하다 *sorry* mianhata

편하다 phyenhata	comfortable	심심하다 simsimhata	boring	섹시하다 seyksihata	sexy
필요하다 philyohata	necessary	씩씩하다 ssikssikhata	energetic	터프하다 thephuhata	tough
편리하다 phyenlihata	convenient	답답하다 taptaphata	stuffy	시원하다 siwenhata	cool
불편하다 pwulphyenhata	uncomfortable or inconvenient	똑똑하다 ttokttokhata	smart	쿨하다 khwulhata	cool
뚱뚱하다 ttwungttwunghata	fat	쌀쌀하다 ssalssalhata	chilly	핫하다 hashata	hot

Unlike 하다 hata ACTIVE verbs, 하다 hata DESCRIPTIVE verbs cannot be broken into two parts, even with the subject marker:

행복이 했어요.   *I was happy.*   행복했어요.   *I was happy.*
hayngpoki haysseyo.   hayngpokhaysseyo.

6.1.7 좋아요 and 싫어요 vs. 좋아해요 and 싫어해요. Which particles?

There is often confusion around the verbs that are used to express *liking* and *disliking* in Korean. In simplest terms, 좋아요 cohayo and 싫어요 silheyo are DESCRIPTIVE (INTRANSITIVE) verbs, no matter how they are translated into English, and 좋아해요 cohahayyo and 싫어해요 silhehayyo are active (transitive) verbs. You can think of the descriptive verbs 좋아요 cohayo as *good* (*to be liked*) and 싫어요 silheyo as *icky* (*to be disliked*), *distasteful, dispreferred*, etc., and the active verbs 좋아해요 cohahayyo and 싫어해요 silhehayyo as the "real" verbs of liking and disliking. Luckily, you CAN use 좋아하다 cohahata and 싫어하다 silhehata or 좋다 cohta and 싫다 silhta to describe your own likes and dislikes and ask about the second person's. For a third person's likes and dislikes, though, you can ONLY use 좋아하다 cohahata and 싫어하다 silhehata, unless you are writing as an omniscient author.

Do whatever it takes to learn the following patterns along with the particles used:

나는 K-pop이 좋아.
nanun K-popi coha.
As for me, K-pop is good. (= I like K-pop.)

너도 K-pop이 좋아?
neto K-popi coha?
As for you, too, is K-pop is good? (= Do you like K-pop?)

나는 K-pop을 좋아해.   너도 K-pop을 좋아해?
nanun K-popul cohahay.   neto K-popul cohahay?
I like K-pop.   *Do you like K-pop, too?*

나는 시험이 싫어요.
nanun sihemi silheyo.
As for me, tests are icky. (= I don't like tests.)

학생들은 시험을 싫어해요.
haksayngtulun sihemul silhehayyo.
Students don't like tests.

경희는 시험이 싫어요.
kyenghuynun sihemi silheyo.
Kyunghee doesn't like tests. (written from a bird's-eye view)

> This last sentence is possible only if a bird's-eye view author is writing about a protagonist named 경희 Kyunghee.

6.1.8 English adjectives that are active verbs in Korean

Be aware that some English adjectives are ACTIVE VERBS in Korean. They are used in the present tense for generalizations or **habitual** aspect in Korean, but where English would use an adjective to describe a present state, these Korean verbs are used in the PAST TENSE. You can think of this as an action that took place sometime in the past whose effect is now felt or whose resulting state continues. It's not too different from the situation in English in which you are and have been *interested* in something since the moment something *interested* you!

그 강의는 수강신청 첫날 정원이 다 **차요**.
ku kanguynun swukangsincheng chesnal cengweni ta chayo.
That class fills up on the first day of registration.

욕조가 다 **찼어요**.
yokcoka ta chasseyo.
The bathtub is <u>full</u>. (Literally, *The tub has filled.*)

세 시가 되면 강당이 **비어요**.
sey sika toymyen kangtangi pieyo.
The assembly hall empties out at 3:00.

물컵의 반이 **비었어요**.
mwulkhepuy pani piesseyo.
The water glass is <u>half-empty</u>. (Literally, *The glass has half-way emptied.*)

아침에 못 일어나서 수업에 **늦어요**.
achimey mos ilenase swuepey nuceyo.
I can't get up in the morning and am late for class.

오늘도 수업에 **늦었어요**.
onulto swuepey nucesseyo.
I am/was <u>late</u> for class today again. (Literally, *I have become late.*)

요즘은 많이들 서른이 넘어서 결혼을 **해요**.
yocumun manhitul seluni nemese kyelhonul hayyo.
Many get married past their 30s these days.

그 사람은 결혼**했어요**.
ku salamun kyelhonhaysseyo.
He's married. (Literally, *He got married.*)

샌프란시스코에서는 안개가 많이 **껴요**.
saynphulansisukhoeysenun ankayka manhi kkyeyo.
In San Francisco, it gets so foggy.

오늘은 안개가 많이 꼈어요.
onulun ankayka manhi kkyesseyo.
It's foggy *today.* (Literally, *Fog has gathered.*)

곰은 겨울에 살이 찌고 여름에는 **말라요**.
komun kyewuley sali cciko yelumeynun mallayo.
Bears gain weight in the winter and "shrivel" in the summer.

모델이 너무 **말랐어요**.
moteyli nemwu mallasseyo.
The model is too skinny. (Literally, *The model has dried up.*)

가게가 몇 시에 문을 **열어요**?
kakeyka myech siey mwunul yeleyo?
What time does the store open (its doors)?

도서관이 문을 **열었어요**.
tosekwani mwunul yelesseyo.
The library is open. (Literally, *The library opened (its doors.)*)

면역력이 떨어져서 자주 감기에 걸려요.
myenyeklyeki ttelecyese cacwu kamkiey kellyeyo.
My immunity is weak, so I frequently catch a cold.

감기에 **걸렸어요**.
kamkiey kellyesseyo.
I have a cold. (Literally, *I have caught a cold.*)

세수를 잘 안 하면 여드름이 생겨요.
seyswulul cal an hamyen yetulumi sayngkyeyo.
If you don't wash your face often, pimples appear.

아기가 참 잘 생겼어요.
akika cham cal sayngkyesseyo.
The baby is really good-looking! idiomatic (Literally, *appeared well.*)

물건을 험하게 다루면 빨리 **낡아요**.
mwulkenul hemhakey talwumyen ppalli nalkayo.
If you are rough with stuff, it wears down quickly.

건물이 많이 **낡았어요**.
kenmwuli manhi nalkasseyo.
The building is quite worn-down. (Literally, *The building has worn down.*)

날이 더워서 **지쳐요**.
nali tewese cichyeyo.
Because the day is hot, I feel enervated.

이제 너무 **지쳤어요**.
icey nemwu cichyesseyo.
I'm so worn out now. (Literally, *I have become enervated.*)

첫째는 보통 아빠를 **닮아요**.
chesccaynun pothong appalul talmayo.
The first child usually resembles the father.

저는 아빠를 **닮았어요**.
cenun appalul talmasseyo.
I resemble my father. (Literally, *I have taken after my father.*)

6.2 Conjugating for the ORDINARY Speech Style

Now, we know how descriptive and active verbs differ, but that all verbs come at the end of the sentence as the predicate. There, they are also conjugated for tense and other information about the social situation of the sentence.

A person does not exist in a vacuum. She finds herself in a web of social relationships as soon as she is able to walk or talk. In Korea, a child has to learn how to address people in different positions and relationships as early as 3 or 4 years old. Once merely a daughter or a granddaughter, a child suddenly becomes a pupil to a teacher or a friend to other little ones upon entering kindergarten. Who you are talking to and about matters greatly in the Korean language. Honoring elders, respecting your superiors, and giving proper distance between yourself and an acquaintance are all encoded in Korean grammar, where **speech styles** that express the social relationships between speaker and listener are shown in **sentence-final endings** (suffixes). The complete set of styles is discussed in a later section, but for now, we'll start with the **ordinary speech style** (일상체 ilsangchey) and see how verb conjugations work.

The style a Korean child will hear first is the ordinary speech style. It is also the style she will use the most in her lifetime and the one style used by all kinds of people in the most kinds of social situations. There are two variations on this basic style—polite and intimate. Let's see how speech style works.

6.2.1 Polite ordinary style

If you hear someone say the polite suffix -요 -yo at the tail end of her sentences, you know that the person is being polite to you. This **polite ordinary style** (공손한 일상체 kongsonhan ilsangchey or "해요"체 "hayyo"chey, as traditional grammarians call it, from the style's command ending) can be used with anyone you are trying to be polite to, except for little children (although school teachers may speak to their little students using this style as a way of teaching them).

6.2.2 Intimate ordinary style

Taking the -요 -yo suffix off makes the speech less polite, and thus, shows that the speaker and the listener are very close. This **intimate ordinary style** (친밀한 일상체 chinmilhan ilsangchey) is the way most family members speak to each other these days. Koreans call this style 반말 panmal *half-talk*, because formality and politeness suffixes are omitted, leaving "half" the verb.

As you can imagine, the intimate ordinary style is a double-edged sword. While it can cut the awkward distance between you and the other person, it can also cut a little too close, sounding rude. Cultured families, or families that are more on the conservative side with their children's upbringing, expect their children to use the polite ordinary style in the presence of non-family members, who might include family friends, visitors, or people at stores or on the street. Some families teach their children to switch to the polite speech style as they grow older. Especially when they reach their mid teens and definitely when they enter college, at least a mixture of 반말 panmal and polite speech is expected from adult children. Strict families do not allow young children to use 반말 panmal at all to address elders, even within the family.

If you do not belong to a Korean family and are learning Korean as an older adult, chances are that you will use the intimate style only to young children in Korea. It can sound rude to use the intimate speech style, even to those who are younger than you if they are past puberty, and it is definitely rude to use it with adults you do not know very well.

If you use the polite speech style as an an older adult, you may hear younger adults pleading with you with 말씀 낮추세요 malssum nacchwuseyyo, 말씀 낮춰서 하세요 malssum nacchwese haseyyo, or 말씀 편하게 하세요 malssum phyenhakey haseyyo—they are saying, *Please speak informally with me, Ma'am/Sir.* If you are a young adult, you will likely use 반말 panmal to friends you get to know really well. You can expect Koreans to initiate the intimate style with 우리, 말 놓아요/놔요 wuli, mal nohayo/nwayo, 우리, 말 놓읍시다 wuli, mal nohupsita, 우리, 말 놓자 wuli, mal nohca, 우리, 말 놓을까? wuli, mal nohulkka? or any version of the wall-breaker, *Shall we speak informally with each other?*

In either case, the implicit message is that we are close enough to not be so formal with each other, so let's let go (놓다 nohta) of our careful speech.

One final word of warning about the use of pronouns before leaving this section: the familiar first-person pronouns 나 na and 내 nay can be used with either polite or intimate ordinary styles, with 나 na giving a more intimate flare than 저 ce when it is used in polite style:

내 친구는 오늘 기분이 좋아요.
nay chinkwunun onul kipwuni cohayo.
My friend is in a good mood today.

나는 한국 사람이에요.
nanun hankwuk salamieyyo.
I am Korean.

내 친구는 오늘 기분이 좋아.
nay chinkwunun onul kipwuni coha.
My friend is in a good mood today.

나는 한국 사람이야.
nanun hankwuk salamiya.
I am Korean.

The humble first-person pronouns 저 ce and 제 cey, on the other hand, are ONLY used with the POLITE ordinary style:

저는 한국 사람이에요/~~저는 한국 사람이야~~.
cenun hankwuk salamieyyo./cenun hankwuk salamiya.
I am Korean.

제가 사진을 찍을게요/~~제가 사진을 찍을게~~.
ceyka sacinul ccikulkeyyo/ceyka sacinul ccikulkey.
I'll take a picture.

And on the flip side, the familiar (peer/minor-directed) *you*, 너 ne, can ONLY be used in the intimate style:

너, 오늘 기분이 좋아?/~~너, 오늘 기분이 좋아요~~?
ne, onul kipwuni coha?/ne, onul kipwuni cohayo?
Are you in a good mood today?

Learn to swiftly switch back and forth between the pronouns when you leave the politeness marker out.

Now then! Let's learn how verbs conjugate in the present tense for the ordinary speech style.

6.2.3 Regular consonant-final verbs

In conjugating verbs in Korean, it often makes a difference whether the verb root ends in a consonant (e.g. 읽다 ilkta) or in a vowel (e.g. 쓰다 ssuta). We will refer to roots that end in a consonant as **consonant-final** and those that end in a vowel as **vowel-final** verbs or verb roots. In this section, we'll show you how the consonant-final roots conjugate for the present tense ordinary speech style. Then you will see what happens when a vowel-final root meets the vowel of the suffix in 6.2.4.

The present tense ending of the ordinary speech style, is achieved by the simple addition of -어(요) -e(yo) or -아(요) -a(yo) to the root of the verb. -요 -yo indicates POLITE ordinary style, and dropping it makes the INTIMATE ordinary style.

The choice of which vowel the suffix should have (-어 or -아?) is based on the vowel in the verb root. If the LAST VOWEL in the root (regardless of any final consonant) is a bright vowel ㅏ or ㅗ, the suffix uses the bright vowel -아; for all other roots, the suffix uses the default dark vowel -어. (This is the yang-with-yang and yin-with-yin **vowel harmony** from chapter 1.) Here is a summary for the INTIMATE ordinary style conjugation:

The last vowel in the root is a **BRIGHT VOWEL** ㅏ or ㅗ
→ Use the **BRIGHT VOWEL** 아 suffix

The last vowel in root is **ANY OTHER VOWEL** → Use the default 어 suffix

---

Below are some consonant-final verbs conjugated for the INTIMATE ordinary style. The first few verbs call for the suffix 아, and the last few verbs call for the suffix -어. Notice that the final consonant in the verb root plays no role in the choice of suffix vowel. Although we show the intimate ordinary forms here, you need only add 요 yo at the end to make the polite ordinary form. This is probably the most important conjugation pattern in Korean, so pay special attention!

Meaning in English	Dictionary Form	Which Suffix Vowel?	Conjugated Form	Example
to sit	앉다 ancta	앉+아 anc+a	앉아 anca	이 의자에 앉아. i uycaey anca. *Sit on this chair.*
to take by force	빼앗다 ppayasta	빼앗+아 ppayas+a	빼앗아 ppayase	동생 장난감을 빼앗아. tongsayng cangnankamul ppayasa. *(He always) takes (his) brother's toys.*
to wipe clean	닦다 takkta	닦+아 takk+a	닦아 takka	이를 닦아. ilul takka. *I brush (my) teeth.*
to let go of, put (down)	놓다 nohta	놓+아 noh+a	놓아, 놔 noha, nwa	책을 책상 위에 놓아/놔. chaykul chayksang wiey noha/nwa. *I put books on the desk.*
to be good	좋다 cohta	좋+아 coh+a	좋아 coha	내 친구는 성격이 좋아. nay chinkwunun sengkyeki coha. *My friend has a good personality.*
to eat	먹다 mekta	먹+어 mek+e	먹어 meke	밥을 먹어. papul meke. *I eat rice.*
to bite	물다 mwulta	물+어 mwul+e	물어 mwule	모기가 자꾸 물어. mokika cakkwu mwule. *Mosquitos keep biting me.*

Meaning in English	Dictionary Form	Which Suffix Vowel?	Conjugated Form	Example
to exist	있다 issta	있+어 iss+e	있어 isse	오늘 시간이 좀 있어. onul sikani com isse. *I've got some time today.*
to be distasteful	싫다 silhta	싫+어 silh+e	싫어 silhe	공부가 싫어. kongpwuka silhe. *I do not like studying.*
to spit (out)	뱉다 paythta	뱉+어 payth+e	뱉어 paythe	껌을 뱉어. kkemul paythe. *Spit out the gum.*
to take by force	뺏다 ppaysta	뺏+어 ppays+e	뺏어 ppayse	동생 장난감을 뺏어. tongsayng cangnankamul ppayse. *I snatch my brother's toys.*
to make	만들다 mantulta	만들+어 mantul+e	만들어 mantule	지금 빵을 만들어. cikum ppangul mantule. *I am making bread now.*
to caress, pet	쓰다듬다 ssutatumta	쓰다듬+어 ssutatum+e	쓰다듬어 ssutatume	강아지를 쓰다듬어. kangacilul ssutatume. *I'm petting a dog.*

If you look at the last two verbs, 만들다 mantulta and 쓰다듬다 ssutatumta, you see that they have both kinds of vowels (dark and bright) in their roots. Remember that it is the LAST vowel in the root that picks the color of the suffix. In both cases, that vowel is —, so you pick the default suffix -어.

One caveat about verb conjugation is that what people say in real life could be different from how you are supposed to spell the words. All 아-root verbs, including the two you see in the chart above 앉다 ancta and 닦다 takkta, are usually pronounced with 어 (e.g., [안저요 anceyo] and [따꺼요 ttakkeyo]) in everyday Seoul speech, and you might be tempted to write 앉어요 anceyo and 닦어요 takkeyo, but using 어 in the suffix is only okay in the pronunciation of these words. Standard spelling rules strictly observe vowel harmony, and you do have to spell the conjugated forms 앉아요 ancayo and 닦아요 takkayo.

Also note that 놓다 nohta allows an alternate conjugation 놔 nwa with contracted vowels and the ㅎ dropped—even in the spelling!

6.2.4 Regular vowel-final verbs

For verbs with no final consonant, the main vowel harmony principle is the same as for consonant-final verbs:

The verb root ends in **BRIGHT VOWEL** ㅏ or ㅗ
→ Use the **BRIGHT VOWEL** 아 suffix

The verb root ends in **OTHER VOWELS** → Use the default 어 suffix

But, when root vowels meet suffix vowels, the two may get fused or one may even disappear. Exactly what happens at the root-suffix boundary depends on the particular vowel at the end of the root.

(1) 아 and 어 vowel-final roots

For verb roots that end in the vowels ㅏ and ㅓ, what you need to do is… nothing! There is no need to add a suffix vowel that is identical to the neighboring root vowel, so in the end, the root form of the verb looks just like the conjugated form.

In the table below, the first verbs have the ㅏ vowel in the root, and the last verbs have ㅓ. The column in gray shows how the verbs look before the vowels fuse:

Meaning in English	Dictionary Form	Which Suffix Vowel?	Conjugated Form	Example
to go	가다 kata	가+아 ka+a	가 ka	집에 가. cipey ka. *Go home.*
to burn; to ride	타다 thata	타+아 tha+a	타 tha	버스를 타. pesulul tha. *Ride a bus.* 뭐가 타. mweka tha. *Something is burning.*
to wrap, pack; to be cheap	싸다 ssata	싸+아 ssa+a	싸 ssa	책을 싸. chaykul ssa. *Pack the book(s).* 책이 싸. chayki ssa. *The book is cheap.*
to be expensive	비싸다 pissata	비싸+아 pissa+a	비싸 pissa	정보가 비싸. cengpoka pissa. *Information is dear.*
to stand, stop	서다 seta	서+어 se+e	서 se	여기 서. yeki se. *Stop/stand here.*
to step out, come forward	나서다 naseta	나서+어 nase+e	나서 nase	동생이 자꾸 나서. tongsayngi cakkwu nase. *The little brother keeps butting in.*
to cross	건너다 kenneta	건너+어 kenne+e	건너 kenne	길을 건너. kilul kenne. *Cross the street here.*

(2) 오 and 우 vowel-final roots

If the verb root ends in the vowel ㅗ, which color suffix vowel do you need? The bright one, -아! If the verb root ends in ㅜ? The dark one, -어, of course! There is one caveat to this generalization about conjugating 오- final and 우- final roots. That is, that some frequently used verbs MERGE the root vowel with the suffix vowel, yielding ㅘ (from ㅗ + ㅏ) and ㅝ (from ㅜ + ㅓ). Less frequently used verbs tend to merge the vowels in the pronunciation only, while the written forms keep the vowels separate. Lastly, the vowel merging is REQUIRED for verbs that have no consonant at the beginning of the 오 or 우 syllable, like **오다** ota *to come* and 배우다 paywuta *to learn*, but not for 멈추다 memchuta *to stop*.

In the table below, the first five verbs have the ㅗ vowel in the root, and the next few verbs have ㅜ. Conjugated forms that appear in parentheses on the left are likely to be seen only in print materials; those in square brackets on the right are likely to be pronunciation only:

Meaning in English	Dictionary Form	Which Suffix Vowel?	Conjugated Form	Example
to come	오다 ota	오+아 o+a	와 wa	사람들이 이리로 와. salamtuli ililo wa. *People are coming this way.*
to see, watch	보다 pota	보+아 po+a	(보아), 봐 (poa), pwa	내일 영화를 봐. nayil enghwalul pwa. *We watch a movie tomorrow.*
to peck, chisel	쪼다 ccota	쪼+아 cco+a	쪼아, [쫘] ccoa, [ccwa]	병아리가 콩을 쪼아. pyengalika khongul ccoa. *The chick is pecking at the beans.*
to shoot	쏘다 ssota	쏘+아 sso+a	(쏘아), 쏴 (ssoa), sswa	활을 쏴. hwalul sswa. *Shoot the arrow.*
to twist, cross	꼬다 kkota	꼬+아 kko+a	(꼬아), 꽈 (kkoa), kkwa	나는 항상 다리를 꽈. nanun hangsang talilul kkwa. *I always cross my legs.*
to learn	배우다 paywuta	배우 + 어 paywu+e	배워 paywe	한국어를 배워. hankwukelul paywe. *Study Korean.*
to give	주다 cwuta	주+어 cwu+e	(주어), 줘 (cwue), cwe	꽃에 매일 물을 줘. kkochey mayil mwulul cwe. *I water the flower every day.*
to dream	꾸다 kkwuta	꾸+어 kkwu+e	(꾸어), 꿔 (kkwue), kkwe	꿈은 크게 꿔. kkwumun khukey kkwe. *Dream big.*

Meaning in English	Dictionary Form	Which Suffix Vowel?	Conjugated Form	Example
put (on), *place*	두다 twuta	두+어 twu+e	(두어), 뒤 (twue), twe	거기에 뒤. kekiey twe. *Leave it there.*
to stop	멈추다 memchwuta	멈추+어 memchwu+e	(멈추어), 멈춰 (memchwue), memchwe	K-pop 들을 때는 시간이 멈춰. K-POP tulul ttaynun sikani memchwe. *Time stops when I listen to K-pop.*

(3) Complex vowel-final roots 애, 에, and 외, 위, 웨

If the root vowel is complex (letter or sound), the suffix vowel for the ordinary style is always the default 어.

Roots with ㅐor ㅔact more like ㅏ and ㅓ roots these days, and leave the suffix vowel out altogether. In older written materials or forms with certain connector suffixes, you may see the long versions (e.g. 내어 naye, 매어서 mayese, 새어도 sayeto, 세어야 seyeya). The conjugated forms below that are in parentheses are only seen in print materials.

ㅚ roots tend to merge with the suffix vowel (to make 왜), especially in pronunciation, although less frequently used words like 뇌다 noyta *to repeat to oneself over and over* are written in their original, unmerged forms. The ones in square brackets in the table below are pronunciations and not traditional spelling, although recently the *National Institute of the Korean Language* began to accept them as written forms.

All 위 and 웨 roots are written without vowel-merging, even though their PRONUN-CIATION is always contracted.

Meaning in English	Dictionary Form	Which Suffix Vowel?	Conjugated Form	Example
to put forth	내다 nayta	내+어 nay+e	(내어), 내 (naye), nay	숙제를 내. swukceylul nay. *Hand in the homework.*
to tie (up), *fasten (up)*	매다 mayta	매+어 may+e	(매어), 매 (maye), may	안전벨트를 매. ancenpeylthulul may. *Fasten your seatbelt.*
to leak	새다 sayta	새+어 say+e	(새어), 새 (saye), say	지붕이 새. cipwungi say. *The roof is leaking.*
to count	세다 seyta	세+어 sey+e	(세어), 세 (seye), sey	돈을 세. tonul sey. *Count the money.*
to hand over	건네다 kenneyta	건네+어 kenney+e	(건네어), 건네 (kenneye), kenney	그 수건을 건네 줘. ku swukenul kenney cwe. *Hand over that towel to me.*

Meaning in English	Dictionary Form	Which Suffix Vowel?	Conjugated Form	Example
to tighten	죄다 coyta	죄+어 coy+e	죄어, [좨] coye, [cway]	나사를 좨. nasalul cway. *Tighten the screw.*
to get exposed to wind or sunlight	쐬다 ssoyta	쐬+어 ssoy+e	쐬어, [쐐] ssoye, [ssway]	머리 아프면 바람을 좀 쐐. meli aphumyen palamul com ssway. *Get some cold air if your head hurts.*
to get exposed to sun/fire warmth	쬐다 ccoyta	쬐+어 ccoy+e	쬐어, [쫴] ccoye, [ccway]	추우면 불을 좀 쫴. chwuwumyen pwulul com ccway. *Warm yourself up by the fire if you are cold.*
to humbly see	뵈다 poyta	뵈+어 poy+e	뵈어, [봬] poye, [pway]	선생님을 매일 봬. sensayngnimul mayil pway. *I see the teacher every day.*
to become	되다 toyta	되+어 toy+e	(되어), 돼 (toye), tway	공부가 잘 돼. kongpwuka cal tway. *My studies are going well.*
to rest	쉬다 swita	쉬+어 swi+e	쉬어 [ᵂ셔] swie [wsye]	집에서 쉬어. cipeyse swie. *Rest at home.*
to run	뛰다 ttwita	뛰+어 ttwi +e	뛰어 [ᵂ뗘] ttwie [wtye]	빨리 뛰어. ppalli ttwie. *Run fast.*
to thread	꿰다 kkweyta	꿰+어 kkwey+e	꿰어 [꿰] kkweye, [kkwey]	바늘을 꿰어. panulul kkweye. *Thread a needle.*

(4) 으 vowel-final roots

For 으 roots, the first thing to do is to lose that vowel. (으 is the weakest link in the vowel world.) Then, check the next root vowel back from the end, and pick the suffix vowel that is in color harmony with it. If there is no vowel available other than the 으 you just got rid of, simply use the default suffix vowel 어.

Meaning in English	Dictionary Form	Which Suffix Vowel?	Conjugated Form	Example
to write, use, to be bitter	쓰다 ssuta	쓰+어 ssu+e	써 sse	편지를 써. phyencilul sse. *I'm writing a letter.* 커피가 써. khephika sse. *The coffee is bitter.*

Meaning in English	Dictionary Form	Which Suffix Vowel?	Conjugated Form	Example
to be big	크다 khuta	크+어 khu+e	커 khe	나는 키가 커. nanun khika khe. *I am tall.*
to lock	잠그다 camkuta	잠그+아 camku+a	잠가 camka	문을 잠가. mwunul camka. *Lock the door.*
to be sad	슬프다 sulphuta	슬프+어 sulphu+e	슬퍼 sulphe	오늘 아주 슬퍼. onul acwu sulphe. *Today, I am very sad.*
to be painful	아프다 aphuta	아프+아 aphu+a	아파 apha	가슴이 아파. kasumi apha. *My heart aches.*
to be pretty	예쁘다 yeypputa	예쁘+어 yeyppu+e	예뻐 yeyppe	내 친구는 마음이 예뻐. nay chinkwunun maumi yeyppe. *My friend has a good heart.*

Recall from the previous section that complex vowels call for the default dark vowel 어, so 예쁘다 yeypputa, as in the chart above, is conjugated as 예뻐 yeyppe.

Verbs like 써 sse and 서 se may seem very similar in their conjugated form, but their dictionary forms are distinct: 쓰다 ssuta *to write, use, be bitter* and 서다 seta *to stop, stand*. So, it is of utmost importance that you learn the dictionary form of each new word you come across. All kinds of different conjugations will refer to the dictionary form of the verbs, so recite this new mantra: "Verb roots are the key!"

(5) 이 vowel-final roots

For ㅣ roots, you just need to use the default vowel 어 and merge it with ㅣ (ㅣ + 어) to make 여.

Meaning in English	Dictionary Form	Which Suffix Vowel?	Conjugated Form	Example
to strike	치다 chita	치+어 chi+e	쳐 chye	테니스를 쳐. theynisulul chye. *I play tennis.*
to be sour	시다 sita	시+어 si+e	셔 sye	김치가 너무 셔. kimchika nemwu sye. *This kimchi is too sour.*
to push into tight space	끼다 kkita	끼+어 kki+e	껴 kkye	팔짱을 껴. phalccangul kkye. *I cross my arms.*

Meaning in English	Dictionary Form	Which Suffix Vowel?	Conjugated Form	Example
to drink	마시다 masita	마시+어 masi+e	마셔 masye	주스를 마셔. cwusulul masye. *I drink juice.*
to touch, fiddle with	만지다 mancita	만지+어 manci+e	만져 mancye	장난감을 만져. cangnankamul mancye. *She is fiddling with the toy.*
to throw	던지다 tencita	던지+어 tenci+e	던져 tencye	공을 던져. kongul tencye. *I throw the ball.*

(6) Vowel-final root conjugation summary

Whew! Having gone through this fundamental verb conjugation, now you are 200% smarter in Korean! Here is a chart with all vowel-final roots conjugated in the intimate ordinary style. See if the conjugated forms make sense to you.

Root Vowel	Sub-type	How to Conjugate	Example	Meaning
아 or 어	아	Do nothing. Use verb root as is.	타다 → 타 thata → tha	*to burn; to ride*
	어		서다 → 서 seta → se	*to stand, stop*
오 or 우	오	Check the root vowel. Pick the agreeing suffix vowel. (Merge the vowels.)	쏘다 → 쏘아, 쏴 ssota → sswa	*to shoot*
	우		감추다 → 감추어, 감춰 kamchwuta → kamchwe	*to hide*
Complex vowels	애	Do nothing. Use verb root as is. (If unsure, add the default 어.)	재다 → 재(어) cayta → cay(e)	*to gloat, boast; to measure*
	에		건네다 → 건네(어) kenneyta → kenney(e)	*to hand over*
	외	Add the default 어. (For frequently used ㅚ verbs, merge the vowels into ㅙ.)	되어요 → 돼 toyeyo → tway	*to become; to be OK*
	위		뛰다 → 뛰어 ttwita → ttwie	*to hop; to run*
	웨		꿰다 → 꿰어 ttwita → ttwie	*to string (beads)*

Root Vowel	Sub-type	How to Conjugate	Example	Meaning
ㅡ		Drop ㅡ. Check previous root vowel. Pick the agreeing suffix vowel.	잠그다 → 잠가 camkuta → camka	*to lock*
			슬프다 → 슬퍼 sulphuta → sulphe	*to be sad*
ㅣ		Add default suffix 어. Merge ㅣ + ㅓ into ㅕ.	이기다 → 이겨 ikita → ikye	*to win*

6.2.5 Irregular anomalies

There is a small handful of verbs whose conjugation has become irregular over time.

(1) Linking verb pair 이다, 아니다

A pair of verbs that has become irregular in modern-day Korean is the linking verb pair 이다 ita *to be* and 아니다 anita *to not be*. In older printed materials, you can still find these words conjugated for the polite ordinary speech style as regular verbs, 이어요 ieyo and 아니어요 anieyo, and these forms are still accepted as correct by the *National Institute of the Korean Language* (국립국어원 kwuklipkwukewen). In real life, however, 이에요 ieyyo and 아니에요 anieyyo are unrivaled in use.

There are two additional points to remember about these linking verbs. First, for 이다 ita, the root vowel 이 i and the suffix vowel 에 ey merge to 예 yey when the preceding noun ends in a vowel:

제 이름은 김현진**이에요**.
cey ilumun kimhyencinieyyo.
My name is Hyunjin Kim.

만나서 반가워요. 제 이름은 이은비**예요**.
mannase pankaweyo. cey ilumun iunpiyeyyo.
Nice to meet you. Mine is Eunbi Lee.

The second important point about 이다 ita and 아니다 anita is that, for the INTIMATE ordinary style, the suffix vowel changes to -야 -ya, which means that you cannot simply drop the politeness marker -요 -yo from the polite ordinary form to get the intimate ordinary form as you can with other verbs, nor can you add the politeness marker -요 -yo to the intimate ordinary form (이)야 (i)ya. As in the polite ordinary form, the verb root 이 drops out after vowel-final nouns:

내 이름은 김현진**이야**.
nay ilumun kimhyenciniya.
My name is Hyunjin Kim.

~~내 이름은 김현진**이에**.~~
nay ilumun kimhyenciniey.
My name is Hyunjin Kim.

만나서 반가워. 내 이름은 이은비**야**.
mannase pankawe. nay ilumun iunpiya.
Nice to meet you. Mine is Eunbi Lee.

~~만나서 반가워. 내 이름은 이은비**에**.~~
mannase pankawe. nay ilumun iunpiyey.
Nice to meet you. Mine is Eunbi Lee.

(2) The verb 하다

The verb 하다 hata does not follow the expected conjugation patterns, and thus, it is considered irregular, too. You have seen it used throughout this book, conjugated for the ordinary speech style present tense as 해(요) hay(yo).

Here are some examples of 하다 hata used in ordinary speech style:

같이 교외로 드라이브 좀 **해요**.
kathi kyooylo tulaipu com hayyo.
Let's go for a drive into the suburbs.

요즘에는 주말에 뭐 **해요**?
yocumeynun cwumaley mwe hayyo?
What do you do on weekends these days?

나는 숙제를 항상 미리 **해**.
nanun swukceylul hangsang mili hay.
I always do my homework in advance.

Due to its literary and rather archaic conjugation 하여 haye, used with connector suffixes and in archaic writings, the official name for the 하다 hata verb is 여 불규칙 -ye pwulkyuchik (여 ye-irregular).

피곤**하여** 곧 자려고 한다.
phikonhaye kot calyeko hanta.
Feeling tired, I'm thinking of sleeping soon.

(3) The verb 푸다

푸다 phwuta *to scoop up* (e.g., *rice, soup*) is a randomly irregular verb. Instead of the expected 푸어 phwue or 풔 phwe, it conjugates as 퍼 phe.

지금 밥을 **퍼요**.
cikum papul pheyo.
Dish up/I'm dishing up rice (into a bowl) now.

(4) The verbs 이르다, 다다르다, 푸르다

As you will see in the next section on special-class verbs, nearly all verbs that end in the syllable -르 -lu conjugate specially. A few exceptions to this special conjugation include 이르다 iluta *to reach*, 다다르다 tataluta *arrive at, come to*, and 푸르다 phwuluta *to be of the deep, unpolluted color of the ocean or sky-blue*. They conjugate by dropping the weak vowel and adding either 아 or 어, depending on the preceding root vowel. In a sense, they are not irregular, as they follow the expected conjugation patterns. Interestingly, because most 르 lu-verbs conjugate irregularly, these are called 러 le-irregular verbs in traditional grammar:

산 정상에 **이르러** 맑은 공기를 깊게 들이 쉬었어.
san cengsangey ilule malkun kongkilul kiphkey tuli swiesse.
We breathed in the fresh air when we reached the mountain top.

가을 하늘이 끝없이 **푸르러** 눈이 시렸어요.
kaul hanuli kkuthepsi phwululu nwuni silyesseyo.
The endless deep blue of the sky almost hurt my eyes.

곧 산 정상에 다다랐어요.
kot san cengsangey tatalaseyo.
We soon arrived at the top of the mountain.

(5) Irregular verb conjugation summary

Here is a chart summarizing the verbs that conjugate irregularly:

Dictionary Form	Meaning	Conjugated Form	Example
이다 ita	to be (POLITE)	이어요 → 이에요 ieyo → ieyyo	수지는 학생이에요. swucinun haksayngieyyo. *Susie is a student.*
		예요 yeyyo (after a vowel-final noun)	내 친구 이름은 수지예요. nay chinkwu ilumun swuciyeyyo. *My friend's name is Susie.*
	to be (INTIMATE)	이야 iya	수지는 학생이야. swucinun haksayngiya. *Susie is a student.*
		야 ya (after a vowel-final noun)	내 친구 이름은 수지야. nay chinkwu ilumun swuciya. *My friend's name is Susie.*
아니다 anita	to not be (POLITE)	아니에요 anieyyo	수지는 중국 사람이 아니에요. swucinun cwungkwuk salami anieyyo. *Susie is not Chinese.*
	to not be (INTIMATE)	아니야 aniya	수지는 중국 사람이 아니야. swucinun cwungkwuk salami aniya. *Susie is not Chinese.*
하다 hata	to do	하여(요) → 해(요) haye(yo) → hay(yo)	수학 공부를 해(요). swuhak kongpwulul hay(yo). *I am studying math.*
푸다 phwuta	to scoop up (e.g, rice, soup)	퍼(요) phe(yo)	밥을 퍼(요). papul phe(yo). *Dish up the rice.*
푸르다 phwuluta	to be of a deep, ocean blue	푸르러(요) phwulule(yo)	한국의 하늘은 정말 푸르러(요). hankwukuy hanulun cengmal phwulule(yo). *Korea's skies are really blue.*

6.2.6 False-irregular verbs

In everyday speech, and most often in everyday informal writing as well, Korean speakers conjugate 같다 kathta *to be alike, the same* and 바라다 palata *to expect, yearn for* as 같애 kathay and 바래 palay. The *National Institute of the Korean Language* (국립국어원 kwuklipkwukewen) suggests 같아 katha and 바라 pala as the standard forms, but people usually conjugate them "irregularly."

오늘은 비가 올 것 같아.
onulun pika ol kes katha.
It looks like it will rain today.

그럼 연락 주기 바라.
kulem yenlak cwuki pala.
I look forward to hearing from you, then.

6.3 Tense and Aspect

Now that you have learned to maneuver the basics of the most useful speech style in Korean, let's see how you can handle verbs with various tenses and aspects. **Tense** is a grammatical term that refers to the time when an action takes place with respect to the time of recounting. Tenses include past, present and future. **Aspect** concerns whether an action has been completed (**perfective**) or not yet (**prospective**), is currently on-going (**progressive**) or is a repeated, **habitual** activity. In English, the past tense is marked on the verb (e.g., *walk vs. walked*), and the future tense with the auxiliary verb *will* (e.g., *I will walk*). Progressive aspect is expressed with auxiliary verb *be* and the suffix *ing* (*I am walking*), and perfective aspect is expressed with the auxiliary verb *have* and a suffix *ed/-en* (e.g., *I have walked*). In Korean, tense and aspect are indicated by suffixes on the verb, and the expression of tense and aspect overlap differently from the English system.

6.3.1 Past and perfective: -었

The past tense suffix is a combination of a vowel -어 or -아 and the final consonant -ㅆ. Its vowel changes in the same way the intimate speech style suffix does (it disappears after -어 or -아 vowel in the verb root, and otherwise follows vowel harmony to match the last vowel of the verb root). We will use -었 -ess to refer to the past tense suffix. Once the suffix attaches to the verb root to create a new past tense stem, then other suffixes can be added for speech style.

Let's take the verb 읽다 ilkta *to read* as an example. The root form is 읽- ilk-, the **past tense stem** is 읽었- ilkess- and is ready for another suffix to make a complete, usable verb. For the past tense ordinary speech style only the yin-vowel suffix -어(요) -e(yo) should be used after the past tense -었 -ess, so you get 먹었어(요) mekesse(yo) *ate*. That is, there is no redundant vowel harmony necessary after the past tense -었 -ess, so you will NEVER see 갔아(요) kassa(yo) or 작았아요 cakassa(yo). They are incorrect. The correct forms are 갔어(요) kasse(yo) and 작았어(요) cakasse(yo).

Let's look at another example with 쓰다 ssuta *to write*. The root form is 쓰- ssu-, and you drop the ㅡ vowel to get the past tense stem, 썼- ssess-. If you conjugate it for the past tense ordinary speech style by adding the suffix -어(요) -e(yo), you get 썼어(요) ssesse(yo) *wrote*.

The same suffix works to express **perfective aspect** in Korean. For example, the question 책 읽었어? chaek ilkesse? may be understood in two ways, depending on the context. If you come across a friend at school, and it is nearly class time for which you have to read a book, you may ask 책 읽었어? chayk ilkesse? to mean *Have you read the book (yet)?* Here, the suffix -었 -ess is used as a perfective aspect marker, indicating a COMPLETED action. Now, say you are talking to a friend who went to a local library yesterday to read a book assigned for a class, and you know that it happened to have been checked out. This time, if you say (어제 거기서 ecey kekise) 책 읽었어? chayk ilkesse? to your friend, you mean a simple past tense, *Did you read the book (over there yesterday)?*

This dual interpretation of the same sentence (책 읽었어? chayk ilkesse?) is possible because the suffix -었 -ess can function either as a tense marker (past) or as an aspect marker (perfective to indicate completed events), although native Korean speakers are not keenly aware of which purpose -었 -ess is being used for in a given instance. For simplicity's sake, we will refer to -었 -ess as the **past tense** most of the time. There will likely be cases where you may be surprised to hear a past tense suffix in Korean, some of which will have to do with a completed action, not tense *per se*. So, let's remember this:

Past or perfective: | Verb Root + -었 -ess |

Also remember that the verb needs a speech style suffix after the past tense suffix!

6.3.2 Remote and disconnected past: -었었

In casually spoken Korean, -었 -ess is frequently repeated as -었었 -essess to emphasize the remoteness of the past event (*long, long ago*), discontinuation of the event (*it was once so back then, but it is no longer the case*), or the isolation of the experienced incident (*I remember that it was the case then*):

초등학교 때 바니를 좋아했었어요.
chotunghakkyo ttay panilul cohahayssesseyo.
I used to like Barney when I was in elementary school.

그 두 사람 사귀었었다면서?
ku twu salam sakwiessesstamyense?
I hear that the two were dating once?

그 사람 한때 조금 뚱뚱했었어.
ku salam hanttay cokum ttwungttwunghayssessesse.
He was once (wa~y back when) a bit chubby.

Verbs that are conjugated for the past when expressing a state of affairs connected to the present, such as 전화 왔어 cenhwa wasse *there is a phone call (a phone call has come)* and as introduced in 6.1.8 above, usually make use of the doubled -었었 -essess marking to indicate an event in the past:

전화 왔어.
cenhwa wasse.
There is a phone call for you/You've got a phone call. (Literally, *a call (just) came/has come.*)

전화 **왔었어**.
cenhwa wassesse.
There was a phone call for you (while you were out). (Literally, *a call had come.*)

하나가 한국 갔어요.
hanaka hankwuk kasseyo.
Hannah went/has gone to Korea.

한국에 **갔었어요**.
hankwukey kassesseyo.
I was in Korea/I had gone to (and came back from) Korea.

결혼했어요?
kyelhonhaysseyo?
Are you married? (Literally, *did you marry/have you married?*)

결혼**했었어요**?
kyelhonhayssesseyo?
Have you been married (and are not any more)? (Literally, *had you married?*)

왜 이렇게 말랐어?
way ilehkey mallasse?
How come you are/have gotten so skinny?

전에도 **말랐었어**.
ceneyto mallassesse.
I was skinny before, too.

문을 안 열었어요.
mwunul an yelesseyo.
It is not/they are not open. (Literally, *the door didn't open.*)

아까는 **열었었는데**…?
akkanun yelessessnuntey…?
The library was/had been open a while ago…? (*It is currently not.*)

Remember:

Remote and disconnected past: | **Verb Root + -었었** -essess |

6.3.3 Progressive: -고 있다

Certain English verbs like *sleep, rot, rain, study*, and *eat* conceptualize events that have INHERENT DURATION. We will call them **durative** verbs, 지속동사 cisoktongsa. Other verbs like *kick, burst, turn off*, and *stand up* encode actions that are rather instantaneous and momentary. We will call them **punctual** verbs, 순간동사 swunkantongsa. With durative verbs, you can focus on the on-going action using the **progressive** construction (e.g., *I am sleeping*, or *It is raining*). With punctual verbs, the progressive construction expresses a REPEATED action (e.g., *He is kicking the car (over and over)*), a slow or imminent approach toward the action (e.g., *The plant is dying*), or an exaggerated expansion of a moment, as if you were using a slow motion re-play (e.g., *I am standing up (and it's taking so long to do so because of my rheumatism)*).

Progressives in Korean are expressed with the suffix -고 -ko, followed by the auxiliary verb 있다 issta. We will call this -고 있다 -ko issta construction a progressive **ending**.

아기가 **자고 있어요**.
akika cako isseyo.
The baby is sleeping.

꽃에 물을 **주고 있어요**.
kkochey mwulul cwuko isseyo.
I am watering the flower.

아이들이 공을 **차고 있어요**.
aituli kongul chako isseyo.
The kids are kicking the ball.

Remember:

Present progressive (dictionary form): | Verb Root + -**고 있다** -ko issta

An action that was in progress in the past is expressed with -고 있었다 -ko issessta:

머리에서 열이 많이 **나고 있었어요**.
melieyse yeli manhi nako issesseyo.
Her head was burning hot.

어제 책방 옆에서 뭐 하고 **있었어요**?
ecey chaykpang yepheyse mwe hako issesseyo?
What were you doing yesterday by the bookstore?

Remember:

Past progressive (dictionary form): | Verb Root + -**고 있었다** -ko issessta

In English, ADJECTIVES can also be made progressive with the meaning of temporarily behaving or acting in a certain way (e.g., *He is being crazy, or I'm being nice*). This doesn't work in Korean:

난 ~~착하고 있어요~~.
nan chakhako isseyo.
I'm being good.

아기가 ~~귀엽고 있어요~~.
The baby is being cute.
akika kwiyepko isseyo.

6.3.4 Resultative: -어 있다

There is another ending that looks very similar to the progressive -고 있다 -ko issta in Korean, and it is -어 있다 -e issta. (We are using the 어 here as shorthand to indicate that the verb conjugates like the intimate ordinary style.) When the ending -어 있다 -e issta is attached to a verb root, it tells you two things: the action was COMPLETED AT SOME POINT IN THE PAST, and the RESULTING STATE CONTINUES since that point in time and affects the present. This "state" would normally be expressed by an adjective in English:

밖에 새가 한 마리 죽**어 있**어.
pakkey sayka han mali cwuke isse.
A bird is dead (lying) outside.

Let's explore a little more closely how the resultative is used in Korean.

(1) Verb types and the resultative construction
Different types of verbs function differently with the resultative construction.

<1> Instant punctual verbs
Any ACTIVE verb may work with the PROGRESSIVE aspect; however, only **punctual verbs** that encode events that happen INSTANTANEOUSLY may be used with the RESULTATIVE ending -어 있다 -e issta. In colloquially spoken Korean, the -어 있다 -e issta construction is often reduced to the past tense -었다 -essta with these verbs to express a resulting state:

꽃이 피고 있어.
kkochi phiko isse.
The flower is blooming/starting to bloom.

꽃이 피**어 있**어/꽃이 피었어.
kkochi phie isse/kkochi phiesse.
The flower has bloomed/is in the state of bloom.

화가 나고 있어.
hwaka nako isse.
I am getting (more and more) upset.

화가 **나 있**어/화가 났어.
hwaka na isse/hwaka nasse.
I am upset/I got upset (and am still staying upset).

아기가 잠들고 있어.
akika camtulko isse.
The baby is falling asleep.

아기가 잠들**어 있어**/아기가 잠들**었어**.
akika camtule isse/akika camtulesse.
The baby is asleep/The baby fell asleep (and thus is asleep).

일어나고 있어.
ilenako isse.
I am in the process of getting up.

일어**나 있어**/일어**났어**.
ilena isse/ilenasse.
I am up/I got up/have gotten up (and currently am up).

눕고 있어.
nwupko isse.
I am in the middle/process of lying down.

누**워 있어**/누**웠어**.
nwuwe isse/nwuwesse.
I am lying down/I lay down (and am lying down).

지금 의자에 앉고 있어.
cikum uycaey ancko isse.
I am taking a seat now.

나는 앉**아 있어**/앉**았어**.
nanun anca isse/ancasse.
I am sitting/I sat (and am sitting).

Other verbs that are frequently used in this construction are 서다 seta *to stand,* 들다 tulta *to enter,* 붙다 pwuthta *to stick,* 비다 pita *to be empty,* 숨다 swumta *to hide,* 붓다 pwusta *to become swollen,* 켜다 khyeta *to light up,* 얼다 elta *to freeze,* and 녹다 nokta *to melt.*

<2> Durative verbs

Active verbs that are durative cannot be used in the resultative -어 있다 -e issta construction. To express COMPLETION of a durative verb, you can use the adverb 다 ta *all* and the past tense. Without the adverb 다 ta, the sentence simply says the event (has) happened at some point in the past:

책을 읽고 있어.　　　vs.　　책을 읽었어.
chaykul ilkko isse.　　　　　chaykul ilkesse.
I'm reading a/the book.　　*I (have) read a/the book.*

~~책을 읽어 있어.~~　　vs.　　책을 다 읽었어.
~~chaykul ilke isse.~~　　　　chaykul ta ilkesse.
~~I am read the book.~~　　　*I've finished reading the book.*

CHAPTER 6

점심을 먹고 있어. vs. 점심을 먹었어.
cemsimul mekko isse.   cemsimul mekesse.
I am eating lunch.   *I ate/I have eaten.*

~~점심을 먹어 있어.~~ vs. 점심을 **다 먹었**어.
cemsimul meke isse.   cemsimul ta mekesse.
~~*I am eaten lunch.*~~   *I'm done eating lunch.*

아기가 자고 있어. vs. 아기가 잤어.
akika cako isse.   akika casse.
The baby is sleeping.   *The baby (has) slept.*

~~아기가 자 있어.~~ vs. 아기가 **다 잤**어.
akika ca isse.   akika ta casse.
~~*The baby is slept.*~~   *The baby is done sleeping (has slept enough/is awake now).*

망치질을 하고 있어.   vs. 망치질을 했어.
mangchicilul hako isse.   mangchicilul haysse.
I am hammering.   *I (have) hammered.*

~~망치질을 해 있어.~~   vs. 망치질을 **다 했**어.
mangchicilul hay isse.   mangchicilul ta haysse.
~~*I hammered and remain all hammered.*~~   *I'm done hammering.*

페인트를 긁고 있어.   vs. 페인트를 긁었어.
pheyinthulul kulkko isse.   pheyinthulul kulkesse.
I am scraping the paint (off).   *I (have) scraped off the paint.*

~~페인트를 긁어 있어.~~   vs. 페인트를 **다 긁었**어.
pheyinthulul kulke isse.   pheyinthulul ta kulkesse.
~~*I am scraped (of?) the paint.*~~   *I'm done scraping the paint.*

<3> Clothing verbs

Clothing verbs in Korean are peculiar because, although they are punctual verbs, they also have some durative-ness in their meaning and behavior. Just like other punctual verbs, they can be interpreted resultatively when in the past tense, but like durative verbs, they cannot be used in the resultative -어 있다 -e issta construction. For this reason, sometimes they are better translated as the English punctual verb *put on* and other times as the English durative verb *wear*. Peculiarly, when they are in the PROGRESSIVE, the interpretation can be RESULTATIVE as well (e.g. 잠옷을 입고 있어 camosul ipko isse *I put on pajamas, thus I have them on*). The verb 타다 thata *get on/ride*, too, works like clothing verbs:

긴소매를 입고 **있어**.
kinsomaylul ipko isse.
I am putting on long sleeves; I am wearing long sleeves.

긴 바지를 입**었**어.
kin pacilul ipesse.
I (have) put on long pants; I am wearing long pants.

신발을 신고 **있어**.
sinpalul sinko isse.
I am putting on shoes; I am wearing shoes.

양말을 신**었어**.
yangmalul sinesse.
I (have) put on socks; I am wearing socks.

모자를 쓰고 **있어**.
mocalul ssuko isse.
I am putting on a hat; I am wearing a hat.

안경을 **썼**어.
ankyengul ssesse.
I (have) put on glasses; I am wearing glasses.

반지를 끼고 **있어**.
pancilul kkiko isse.
I am putting on a ring; I am wearing a ring.

장갑을 **꼈**어.
cangkapul kkyesse.
I (have) put on gloves; I am wearing gloves.

버스를 타고 **있어**.
pesulul thako isse.
I am getting on a bus; I am riding (on) a bus.

기차를 **탔**어.
kichalul thasse.
I (have) gotten on a bus; I am riding (on) a train.

Because they are fundamentally punctual verbs, clothing verbs and the verb 타다 thata *to get on/ride* need to be combined with a secondary verb 가다 kata *to go* or 오다 ota *to come* to express the meaning of putting something on and then going or coming somewhere, or getting on a vehicle and then going or coming.

거기에 우비를 입고 **가**세요.
kekiey wupilul ipko kaseyyo.
<u>Wear</u> *your raincoat there. (Put on a raincoat and go there.)*

여기로 버스를 타고 **오**세요.
yekilo pesulul thako oseyyo.
<u>Ride</u> *the bus over here. (Take the bus and come here.)*

(2) Transitive verbs and the resultative construction

Transitive verbs may not be made resultative, either. (Progressive form works fine, however.)

곰이 나무에 등을 긁어 있어.
komi namwuey tungul kulke isse.
~~The bear is all scratched its back on a tree.~~

곰이 나무에 등을 **긁고 있어.**
komi namwuey tungul kulkko isse.
The bear is scratching its back on a tree.

When the verb is made into its PASSIVE form (and, thus, loses its transitivity), then it can take the resultative construction. (The extra syllable (typically 여 ye) inserted in the main verb as you see in the second, resultative sentence in each pair is a passive marker. You will learn about passive verbs in chapter 9.)

십 년째 수를 놓고 있어.
sip nyenccay swulul nohko isse.
I've been doing embroidery for 10 years now.

테이블에 ~~수저를 놓아~~/수저가 놓**여 있어.**
theyipuley ~~swucelul noha~~/swuceka nohye isse.
The silverware has been put on the table.

난방기기가 고장나서 두꺼운 담요를 덮고 있어.
nanpangkikika kocangnase twukkewun tamyolul tephko isse.
The heater broke, so I have a thick blanket on.

온 산이 눈으로 ~~덮어 있어~~/덮**여 있어.**
on sani nwunulo tephe isse/tephye isse.
The whole mountain is covered with snow.

곰이 나무에 등을 긁고 있어.
komi namwuey tungul kulkko isse.
The bear is scratching its back on a tree.

~~유리를 긁어 있어~~/유리가 긁**혀 있어.**
yulilul kulke isse/yulika kulkhye isse.
The glass is/has been scratched.

펜대신 연필로 쓰고 있어.
pheyntaysin yenphillo ssuko isse.
I'm writing with a pencil instead of a pen.

화장실 벽에 낙서가 ~~낙서를 써~~/낙서가 쓰**여 있어.**
hwacangsil pyekey nakseka nakselul sse/nakseka ssuye isse.
Graffiti is written on the restroom wall.

지금 가게 문을 열고 있어.
cikum kakey mwunul yelko isse.
They are opening the store (door) now.

그 집 문은 항상 **열어/열려 있어.**
ku cip mwunun hangsang yele/yellye isse.
The gate of that house is always open.

Other passive verbs and verbs with a passive sense that are frequently used in this construction are 닫히다 tathita *to be closed*, 나뉘다 nanwita *to be divided*, 꺼지다 kkecita *to be turned off*, 떨어지다 ttelecita *to fall*, and 이어지다 iecita *to be connected*.

(3) Verbs with idiomatic usages

The verbs 살다 salta *to live*, 죽다 cwukta *to die*, (들어/나)가다 (tule/na)kata *to go (in/out)*, and (들어/나)오다 (tule/na)ota *to come (in/out)* can be used in both the progressive and resultative constructions, and the resultative is interpreted somewhat idiomatically (underlined here):

그 가족은 작은 집에 살**고 있어요.**
ku kacokun cakun cipey salko isseyo.
The family lives/is living in a small house.

아직도 살**아 있어!**
acikto sala isse!
It's still underline{alive}!

인문학이 죽**고 있어.**
inmwunhaki cwukko isse.
The humanities are dying.

인간애는 벌써 죽**어 있어.**
inkanaynun pelsse cwuke isse.
Humanity is already underline{dead}.

조금만 더 기다려. 지금 들어가**고 있어.**
cokumman te kitalye. cikum tulekako isse.
Wait a minute longer. I'm almost home.

추우니까 들어**가 있어.**
chwuwunikka tuleka isse.
It's cold; go in (and be underline{inside}).

어디야? 난 지금 가**고 있어.**
etiya? nan cikum kako isse.
Where are you? I'm on my way.

응. 와 있어.
ung. wa isse.
I'm underline{here}.

달이 구름 사이에서 나오**고 있어.**
tali kwulum saieyse naoko isse.
The moon is peeking out from the clouds.

왜 입이 나**와 있어?**
way ipi nawa isse?
Why the long face?
(Literally, *Why is your mouth underline{out}?*)

Remember:

Resultative (dictionary form): | **Verb Root + -어 있다** -e issta |

6.3.5 Future and Prospective

As with the **past tense** and **perfective aspect**, there are similarities in how Korean expresses the future tense and the prospective aspect.

(1) Future -(으)ㄹ 것이다

English verbs do not conjugate for the future tense; instead, the auxiliary verb *will* is needed to talk about FUTURE EVENTS or PLANS (e.g., *The party will be at 3:00*, or *The plane will leave in 3 minutes*). The auxiliary verb *will* can also express the speaker's VOLITION (or, their WILL), mainly just for the first person *I* (e.g., *I will not back down*), as well as strong ASSERTION about future events (e.g. *It'll rain*, or *If you wash your car, it'll (surely) rain.*). To express one's INTENTION, IMMEDIATE PLANS, or CONJECTURE, *be going to* is used in English (e.g., *I'm going to buy you a new bag*, or *It's going to rain*). Let's call all these situations "future" as shorthand.

Korean has an ending that is quite comparable to the English *be going to* future (and certain uses of *will*) to talk about one's intention or immediate plans. It is a combination of the suffix -(으)ㄹ -(u)l and a noun 것 kes *thing* with the 이다 ita verb: -(으)ㄹ 것 이다 -(u)l kesita. In this expression, 것 kes doesn't mean *thing*, but rather an abstract notion, and the ending translates literally as *it is (something) to...(happen)*.

In spoken Korean, a shorter version -(으)ㄹ 거다 -(u)l keta is used, and -(으)ㄹ 것이 다 -(u)l kesita is reserved for stodgy, written, "textbook" Korean. And of course, the 이다 ita verb at the end of this expression will conjugate for whatever speech style is needed:

주말에 테니스를 **칠 거야**.
cwumaley theynisulul chil keya.
I am going to play tennis this weekend.

오늘은 여기에 앉을 **거야**.
onulun yekiey ancul keya.
I'll sit here today.

내일은 아마 비가 **올 거예요**.
nayilun ama pika ol keyeyyo.
It will probably rain tomorrow.

이제는 **쉬워질 거다**.
iceynun swiwecil keta.
It's going to get easier from now on.

식목일에 사과 나무를 심을 **거예요**.
sikmokiley sakwa namwulul simul keyeyyo.
I am going to plant an apple tree on Arbor Day.

이 책을 떼고 한국어 문법 박사가 **될 거예요**.
i chaykul tteyko hankwuke mwunpep paksaka toyl keyeyyo.
With this book finished, I'll be a Korean grammar wiz.

A little more young-sounding, light-hearted GUESS about a future event can end in -(으)ㄹ걸(요) -(u)lkel(yo) with a high tone on the last syllable:

이제는 **쉬워질 걸요**.
iceynun swiwecil kelyo.
It's going to get easier now, I predict!

그렇지 **않을 걸**.
kulehci ahnul kel.
I don't think so.

And in fact, this ending can be used to express STRONG CONJECTURES about CURRENT events as well. This is similar to English conjectures like *He'll (surely) be on his way now*:

밖에는 지금 비가 **올 거예요**.
pakkeynun cikum pika ol keyeyyo.
I'm quite certain that it's raining outside now.

걔는 **알 걸**.
kyaynun al kel.
I'm pretty sure she knows.

Here is how this future tense conjugation works for the ordinary style, where ^{V} is a reminder to leave a space:

C-final verb root + 을 거다 ul keta	읽다 *to read* → 읽을 거예요, 읽을 거야 *be going to read* ilkta → ilkul keyeyyo, ilkul keya
V-final verb root + ㄹ 거다 l keta	쓰다 *to write* → 쓸 거예요, 쓸 거야 *be going to write* ssuta → ssul keyeyyo, ssul keya
ㄹ-*final verb root* + ^{V} 거다 keta	알다 *to know* → 알 거예요, 알 거야 *be going to know* alta → al keyeyyo, al keya

(2) Prospective -(으)ㄹ

The -(으)ㄹ -(u)l part of -(으)ㄹ 것이다 -(u)l kesita is an **aspect** suffix that indicates that an event is yet to happen or an action is yet to be completed. That aspect is called "**prospective**." It is not surprising then that this suffix is used to express conjecture or plans about unknown future events. In fact, the noun does not have to be 것 kes (or 거 ke) to talk about future events:

내일 걔를 만날 **계획**이야.
nail kyaylul mannal kyeyhoykiya.
I'm planning to meet her tomorrow.
It's my *plan* to...

내일 걔를 만날 **테**야.
nayil kyaylul mannal theyya.
I'm intending to meet her tomorrow.
I'm (in) a *place* to...

내일 걔를 만날 **지도 몰라**.
nayil kyaylul mannal cito molla.
I may get to meet him/her tomorrow.
I don't know if it is the *case* that...

내일 걔를 만날 **수가 있어**.
nayil kyaylul mannal swuka isse.
I can meet him/her tomorrow.
I have *means/ways* to...

거기에서 만날 **약속**이 있어.
kekieyse mannal yaksoki isse.
I will see her there.
I have an *appointment* to...

이건 오늘 밤 안으로 다 할 **작정**이야.
iken onul pam anulo ta hal cakcengiya.
I'm determined to finish this by tonight.
It's my *determination* that...

내년에는 한국으로 여행갈 **생각**이에요.
naynyeneynun hankwukulo yehayngkal sayngkakieyyo.
I am thinking of traveling to Korea next year. It's my *thought* to...

There are three more extremely useful endings that make use of the prospective suffix -(으)ㄹ -(u)l. They all have something to do with immediate future or prospective events but with a slightly different flavor. In what follows, we will introduce -(으)ㄹ까 -(u)lkka, -(으)ㄹ게 -(u)lkey and -(으)ㄹ래 -(u)lay. Two important points to keep in mind about them are, first, unlike -(으)ㄹ 것이다 -(u)l kesita, the other endings have no space after the prospective marker -(으)ㄹ -(u)l; second, unlike -(으)ㄹ 것이다 -(u)l kesita, which is a rightfully versatile future ending that can be used with all speech styles (which you will learn more about in chapter 7), its three sisters can ONLY be used for the ordinary style, typically by family members and close acquaintances. Let's see how they work!

<1> -(으)ㄹ래 *I wanna; I feel like doing...*

Whereas -(으)ㄹ 것이다 -(u)l kesita expresses *bona fide* future, -(으)ㄹ래 -(u)llay is an ending that expresses what the speaker feels like doing NOW, and a good translation for this is *wanna*:

너: 영화 보러 **갈래**?
ne: yenghwa pole kallay?
You: *Do you wanna go see a movie?*

나: 피곤해서 집에 **있을래**.
na: phikonhayse cipey issullay.
Me: *I'm tired; I wanna be home today.*

너: 같이 시험 **공부할래**?
ne: kathi sihem kongpwuhallay?
You: *Do you wanna study for the test together?*

나: 그래. 우리 집에서 **할래**?
na: kulay. wuli cipeyse hallay?
Me: *OK. Do you wanna study at my place?*

너: 우리 사진 **찍을래**?
ne: wuli sacin ccikullay?
You: *Do you wanna take pictures?*

나: 아니. 안 **찍을래**. 화장 안 했어.
na: ani. an ccilullay. hwacang an haysse.
Me: *No, I don't wanna. I didn't put on make-up.*

<2> -(으)ㄹ게 *I will*—offering, promising, or seeking consent

When you say *I will open the door for you* in English, you are not so much talking about the FUTURE as offering or promising to do something. This offering/promising sense is expressed in Korean with the ending -(으)ㄹ게 -(u)lkey. You can remember -(으)ㄹ게 -(u)lkey as *I'LL do it (for you), OK?*

Because you can only offer or promise your own actions and not those of others, this ending only works with a first-person subject (*I*). It is also NOT used as a QUESTION (like *shall I?*). For that, use -(으)ㄹ까 -(u)lkka, which is coming up in the next section.

모르는 사람: 누가 문 좀 열어 주세요.
molunun salam: nwuka mwun com yele cwuseyyo.
Stranger: *Somebody please open the door for me.*

나: 제가 열어 **드릴게요**.
na: ceyka yele tulilkeyyo.
Me: *I'll open it for you.* (offer)

엄마: 방 청소했니?
emma: pang chengsohayssni?
Mother: *Did you clean your room?*

나: 조금 있다가 **할게**!
na: cokum isstaka halkey!
Me: *I'll do it later.* (promise)

김: 죄송하지만 먼저 일어**날게요**.
kim: coysonghaciman mence ilenalkeyyo.
Kim: *Sorry, but I have to get going.* (consent-seeking)

이: 저도 가려고 했어요. 같이 갑시다.
i: ceto kalyeko haysseyo. kathi kapsita.
Lee: *I was about to leave, too. Let's go together.*

<3> -(으)ㄹ까 *shall we...? should I...?*

The last of the three prospective-not-future sister expressions is -(으)ㄹ까 -(u)lkka. It is used to make a suggestion directed to the second person *you* with a sense of *shall I...?*, *shall we...?*, or *do you want to?* Notice in the examples below—and think about—some of the other natural translations for this ending. (Korean endings do not always have a single equivalent in English!)

조: 오늘 밤에 영화 **볼까요**?
co: onul pamey yenghwa polkkayo?
Cho: *Shall we/Would you like to see movie tonight?*

문: 그래, 좋아요!
mwun: kulay, cohayo!
Moon: *Sure!*

엄마: 문 닫**을까**?
emma: mwun tatulkka?
Mother: *Do you want me/Do you think it's a good idea to close the door?*

나: 네!
na: ney!
Me: *Yes, please!*

For musing to oneself, or as a self-directed question, -(으)ㄹ까 -(u)lkka better translates as *should* (but without the sense of moralistic obligation):

청소할까? 늦잠 잘까?
chengsohalkka? nuccam calkka?
Should I (do I wanna) clean my room or sleep in? Hmmm…

-(으)ㄹ까 -(u)lkka is NOT used for other *shall* meanings, such as statements and commands (e.g. *You* SHALL NOT *pass!*). For very certain predictions or for stating your convictions, use -어야만 되다 -eyaman toyta *have to*, and for *should not*, use -(으)면 안 되다 -(u)myen an toyta *mustn't* (see more on these endings in chapter 7):

거기 꼭 가야만 돼.
keki kkok kayaman tway.
You shall go there.

오늘은 나가면 절대 안 돼.
onulun nakamyen celtay an tway.
You shall not go out today.

여기로 지나갈 수 없어!
yekilo cinakal swu epse.
You shall not pass through here!

With the third person (*he/she/it* and *they*), *I wonder* is a most apt translation for -(으)ㄹ까 -(u)lkka:

곧 비가 그칠까?
kot pika kuchilkka?
I wonder if the rain will stop soon.

내일 지나가 올까?
nayil Cinaka olkka?
I wonder if Gina is coming tomorrow.

(3) Intentional future 겠

-겠 -keyss is another ending often associated with "future" in Korean grammar books and sometimes translated as *will* or *would*. The meaning of -겠 -keyss is comparable to the prospective -(으)ㄹ -(u)l, but rather than conveying an objective temporal something-yet-to-happen notion like -(으)ㄹ -(u)l, -겠 -keyss comes with more SUBJECTIVITY, as URGENCY and WILLINGNESS. -겠 -keyss can have several different interpretations, but for "future," the main idea is that it expresses the speaker's intention:

내일 세상이 끝나도 난 한 그루의 사과 나무를 심겠다.
nayil seysangi kkuthnato nan han kulwuuy sakwa namwulul simkeyssta.
Even if the end of the world were to come tomorrow, I will plant an apple tree.

While -(으)ㄹ 것이다 -(u)l kesita talks about a future plan that has been set, -겠 -keyss expresses INTENTIONS, sometimes from decisions made on the spot, that could be carried out any time. Because of its WILLINGNESS component, -겠 -keyss is used interchangeably with -(으)ㄹ게 -(u)l key. It is used in this way with first and second-person subjects (*I* and *you*):

나:	식당 예약했어요?
na:	siktang yeyyakhaysseyo?
Me:	*Have you made a reservation at the restaurant?*

동료:	다음 주말에 **할 거예요**.
tonglyo:	taum cwumaley hal keyeyyo.
Co-worker:	*Im going to do it next weekend.*

나:	더 기다리면 자리가 없을 텐데…
na:	te kitalimyen calika epsul theyntey...
Me:	*There won't be space if you wait longer, I'm afraid.*

동료:	그럼 이번 주에 **하겠어요**/할게요.
tonglyo:	kulem ipen cwuey hakeysseyo/halkeyyo.
Co-worker:	*I'll do it this week, then.*

<1> Conjecture

Let's explore a little more about the suffix -겠 -keyss. If we are interested in describing the events in the world objectively, we want to use the objective future marker -(으)ㄹ 거다 -(u)l keta and express set plans or predictions based on factual data. If we are interested in a CONSTRUCTED WORLD, that is, a subjective interpretation of events in the head of the speaker, then we want to use the intentional future marker -겠 -keyss. In the following examples, you can see how -겠 -keyss is used to express one's subjective opinion based on situational evidence. Since the speaker's interpretation is emphasized, it does not make as strong a prediction as -(으)ㄹ 거다 -(u)l keta:

나:	보아 하니 그 사람, 미팅에 안 **오겠어요**.
na:	poa hani ku salam, mithingey an okeysseyo.
Me:	*It looks like he is not coming to the meeting; I don't think he will come to the meeting.*

동료:	아직도 안 왔으면 오늘 미팅에 안 **올 거예요**.
tonglyo:	acikto an wassumyen onul mithingey an ol keyeyo.
Co-worker:	*If he hasn't shown up by now, he won't be coming to the meeting today, I'd wager.*

<2> Empathy

-겠 -keyss is also used in expressing conjecture about a situation with a tone of caring or concern. For example, if you see someone fall down and scrape their knee, you might say, 아프겠어 aphukeysse. A good translation is *that's gotta hurt* or *that must hurt*; -겠 -keyss here expresses an imaginable world based on the speaker's life experience. Here are some more examples.

엄마: 와서 떡볶이 먹어라!
emma: wase ttekpokki mekela!
Mother: *Come and eat tteokbokki!*

경아: 와, **맛있겠다**! 엄마, 잘 먹겠습니다!
kyenga: wa, masisskeyssta! emma, cal mekkeyssssupnita!
Kyung-a: *Wow, it looks delicious!* (*It's gonna be good!*) *Thanks, Mom!*

곽: 현주가 남자 친구하고 헤어졌대요!
kwak: hyencwuka namca chinkwuhako heyecyesstayyo!
Kwak: *HyunJu just broke up with her boyfriend, I hear.*

최: 저런, **속상하겠다**.
choy: celen, soksanghakeyssta.
Choi: *Oh, no! She must feel terrible.*

오: 한국어를 5년 동안 배웠어요.
o: hankwukelul 5nyen tongan paywesseyo.
Oh: *I've been learning Korean for five years.*

현: 그럼 한국어 잘 **하시겠어요**.
hyen: kulem hankwuke cal hasikeysseyo.
Hyun: *You must be good at Korean.*

Notice that an apt translation uses *gotta* or *must*—not to express someone's obligation, but the speaker's CONJECTURE.

<3> Politeness

Because -겠 -keyss communicates *I'm only guessing*, it has come to convey POLITENESS in many greetings, official announcements, and other set expressions.

선생님: **알겠어요**?
sensayngnim: alkeysseyo?
Teacher: *Does that make sense?/Do you understand? /Okay?*

학생들: 네, **알겠습니다**.
haksayngtul: ney, alkeyssssupnita.
Students: *Yes, (we) got it.*

처음 **뵙겠습니다**.
cheum poypkeyssssupnita.
Nice to meet you.

또 **뵙겠습니다**.
tto poypkeyssssupnita.
I will see you again./Until next time.

말씀 좀 **묻겠습니다**.
malssum com mwutkeyssssupnita.
Would you mind me asking you a question?

잘 **먹겠습니다**.
cal mekkeyssssupnita.
Thank you for the food.

실례하겠습니다.
sillyeyhakeyssssupnita.
Please excuse me for a moment. (Literally, *I'll be briefly rude!*)

내일은 바람이 많이 불고 **춥겠습니다.**
nayilun palami manhi pwulko chwupkeysssupnita.
It will be windy and cold tomorrow. (Weather forecast)

승객 여러분께 안내 말씀 **드리겠습니다.**
sungkayk yelepwunkkey annay malssum tulikeysssupnita.
Attention, passengers. (Literally, *We would like to inform you…*)

It is also used in polite requests, where it translates well as *would you* (*like to*):

종업원: **주문하시겠습니까?**
congepwen: cwumwunhasikeysssupnikka?
Server: *Would you like to order?*

할머니 좀 모시고 **가시겠어요?**
halmeni com mosiko kasikeysseyo?
Would you mind taking Grandma with you?

저 소금 좀 집어 **주시겠어요?**
ce sokum com cipe cwusikeysseyo?
Could you pass/would you mind passing me the salt?

6.3.6 Using tense and aspect markers together

Sometimes you will see a verb marked -었 -ess and -을 together as -었을 -essul. This is not a typo or the writer's indecision about past or future. In this case, -(으)ㄹ -(u)l is used as a prospective marker for conjecture (guessing about something that the speaker is not certain about) and -었 -ess is a perfective marker (something has been completed), allowing you to express something you GUESS to HAVE HAPPENED. So, using these two suffixes in one breath with -었을 거다 -essul keta gives you *must have*:

어젯밤 서울에는 비가 **왔을 거예요.**
eceyspam sewuleynun pika wassul keyeyyo.
It probably rained in Seoul last night.

지금 그 사람 한국에 도착**했을 거예요.**
cikum ku salam hankwukey tochakhayssul keyeyyo.
I'm guessing that he has probably arrived in Korea.

You can also combine other tenses and aspects:

내년 이맘때쯤에는 뭘 **하고 있을 거예요?**
naynyen imamttayccumeynun mwel hako issul keyeyyo?
What <u>will</u> you <u>be</u> <u>doing</u> around this time next year?

그 사람 지금 시청쯤 **가고 있을 거예요.**
ku salam cikum sichengccum kako issul keyeyyo.
He is probably (<u>going</u>) near City Hall now.

걔는 그 때 자고 **있었을** 거예요.
kyaynun ku ttay cako issessul keyeyyo.
He was probably sleeping then.

Finally, it works similarly for -었겠 -esskeyss, except that the guessing is rather weak and personalized:

걔는 그 때 자고 **있었겠어요**.
kyaynun ku ttay cako issesskeysseyo.
It looks to me like he was sleeping then.

6.3.7 Summary charts

For a grand summary of this section, we present you with summary charts that show the present, past, progressive, and future conjugations for the ordinary speech style. Only prospective (not intentional) future is included.

(1) Conjugation chart for consonant-final verbs (for intimate ordinary style)

Dictionary	Meaning	Present	Past/Perfective	Progressive	Future/Prospective
Active Verbs					
앉다 ancta	*to sit*	앉아 anca	앉았어 ancasse	앉고 있어 ancko isse	앉을 거야 ancul keya
놓다 nohta	*to let go, put (down)*	놓아 noha	놓았어 nohasse	놓고 있어 nohko isse	놓을 거야 nohul keya
먹다 mekta	*to eat*	먹어 meke	먹었어 mekesse	먹고 있어 mekko isse	먹을 거야 mekul keya
뺏다 ppaysta	*to take by force*	뺏어 ppayse	뺏었어 ppaysesse	뺏고 있어 ppaysko isse	뺏을 거야 ppaysul keya
만들다 mantulta	*to make*	만들어 mantule	만들었어 mantulesse	만들고 있어 mantulko isse	만들 거야 mantul keya
Descriptive Verbs					
많다 manhta	*to be many*	많아 manha	많았어 manhasse	–	많을 거야 manhul keya
있다 issta	*to exist*	있어 isse	있었어 issesse	–	있을 거야 issul keya
싫다 silhta	*to be dislikable*	싫어 silhe	싫었어 silhesse	–	싫을 거야 silhul keya

(2) Conjugation chart for vowel-final verbs (for intimate ordinary style)

Dictionary	Meaning	Present	Past/Perfective	Progressive	Future/Prospective
Active Verbs					
타다 thata	to burn, ride	타 tha	탔어 thasse	타고 있어 thako isse	탈 거야 thal keya
서다 seta	to stand, stop	서 se	섰어 sesse	서고 있어 seko isse	설 거야 sel keya
재다 cayta	to measure	재 cay	쟀어 caysse	재고 있어 cayko isse	잴 거야 cayl keya
건네다 kenneyta	to hand over	건네 kenney	건넸어 kenneysse	건네고 있어 kenneyko isse	건넬 거야 kenneyl keya
쏘다 ssota	to shoot	쏴 sswa	쐈어 sswasse	쏘고 있어 ssoko isse	쏠 거야 ssol keya
감추다 kamchwuta	to hide	감춰 kamchwe	감췄어 kamchwesse	감추고 있어 kamchwuko isse	감출 거야 kamchwul keya
되다 toyta	to become	돼 tway	됐어 twaysse	되고 있어 toyko isse	될 거야 toyl keya
뛰다 ttwita	to hop	뛰어 ttwie	뛰었어 ttwiesse	뛰고 있어 ttwiko isse	뛸 거야 ttwil keya
꿰다 kkweyta	to string	꿰어 kkweye	꿰었어 kkweyesse	꿰고 있어 kkweyko isse	꿸 거야 kkweyl keya
잠그다 camkuta	to lock	잠가 camka	잠갔어 camkasse	잠그고 있어 camkuko isse	잠글 거야 camkul keya
이기다 ikita	to win	이겨 ikye	이겼어 ikyesse	이기고 있어 ikiko isse	이길 거야 ikil keya
Descriptive Verbs					
아프다 aphuta	to be sick	아파 apha	아팠어 aphasse	–	아플 거야 aphul keya
슬프다 sulphuta	to be sad	슬퍼 sulphe	슬펐어 sulphesse	–	슬플 거야 sulphul keya

(3) Conjugation chart for irregular verbs (for polite ordinary style)

Dictionary	Meaning	Present	Past/Perfective	Progressive	Future/Prospective
하다 hata	*to do*	해요 hayyo	했어요 haysseyo	하고 있어요 hako isseyo	할 거예요 hal keyeyyo
이다 ita	*to be*	이에요 ieyyo	이었어요 iesseyo	–	일 거예요 il keyeyyo
푸다 phwuta	*to scoop up*	퍼요 pheyo	펐어요 phesseyo	푸고 있어요 phwuko isseyo	풀 거예요 phwul keyeyyo
푸르다 phwuluta	*to be blue*	푸르러요 phwululeyo	푸르렀어요 phwululesseyo	–	푸를 거예요 phwulul keyeyyo

6.4 Negative Sentences

So far we have talked only about positive sentences. Besides adding 안 an *not* in the right place, there are some other ways to make a sentence negative in Korean. There are verbs that are inherently negative, another negative adverb (못 mos *cannot*), and a "**long-form**" auxiliary verb structure for making negatives. Let's see how these work.

6.4.1 Short negatives 안 and 못

The simplest way to negate sentences predicated with verbs other than 있다 issta, 이다 ita, and 알다 alta is to add the negative adverb 안 an *not* before the verb. The 안 an negative sentence can either state that something is not the case or express a negative volition (reluctance):

오늘은 학교에 안 가요.
onulun hakkyoey an kayo.
I'm not going/I don't go to school today.

방이 별로 안 커요.
pangi pyello an kheyo.
The room is not that big.

거기 안 앉아.
keki an anca.
I'm not sitting there/I don't wanna sit there.

While 안 an is comparable to (*will/do*) *not*, 못 mos expresses *can't*; thus you should not use 못 mos with volitional endings:

오늘은 학교에 못 갔어요.
onulun hakkyoey mos kasseyo.
I wasn't able to go to school today.

오늘은 학교에 못 갈 거야.
onulun hakkyoey mos kal keya.
I won't be able to go to school today.

오늘은 학교에 못 갈래.
onulun hakkyoey mos kallay.
I cannot want to go to school today.

On the other hand, 못 mos is used in many cases in Korean where we would use *don't* in English. The effect is to avoid sounding like one is WILLFULLY not doing something (because 안 an carries with it a sense of volition):

피망을 **못** 먹어요. 소화가 잘 **안** 돼요.
phimangul mos mekeyo. sohwaka cal an twayyo.
I don't/can't eat bell peppers; I don't digest them well.

피망은 **안** 먹어요. 맛을 별로 **안** 좋아해요.
phimangun an mekeyo. masul pyello an cohahayyo.
I don't eat bell peppers; I don't like the taste much. (I choose not to.)

사장님은 오늘 같이 **못** 가세요.
sacangnimun onul kathi mos kaseyyo.
The boss isn't going/can't come with me tonight.

사장님은 오늘 같이 **안** 가세요.
sacangnimun onul kathi an kaseyyo.
The boss isn't going to (decided not to) come with us tonight.

6.4.2 Negative verbs

The three verbs 있다 issta *to exist*, 이다 ita *to be*, and 알다 alta *to know* have negative counterparts, and their negatives can ONLY be expressed using those negative counterparts. The negative of 있다 issta *to exist* is 없다 epsta *to not exist*; the negative of 이다 ita *to be* is 아니다 anita *to not be*; and the negative of 알다 alta *to know* is 모르다 moluta *to not know*. These verbs are not used with 안 an *not* or other ways of making negatives. 있다 issta can be used in the "long form negative" discussed in 6.4.4, but only when contradicting, to say *no, it isn't ... .* It cannot be used with 안 an or 못 mos. This holds for compound verbs that end in 있다 issta, too, such as 맛있다 masissta *to be delicious* and 재미있다 caymiissta *to be fun.*

오늘은 시간이 **없어요**.   ~~오늘은 시간이 안 있어요~~.
onulun sikani epseyo.   onulun sikani an isseyo.
I don't have time today.   *I don't have time today.*

내 동생은 고등학생이 **아니에요**.
nay tongsayngun kotunghaksayngi anieyyo.
My younger sister is not a high school student.

~~내 동생은 고등학생 안 이에요~~.
nay tongsayngun kotunghaksayng an ieyyo.
My younger sister is not a high school student.

중국어를 **몰라요**.   ~~중국어를 안 알아요~~.
cwungkwukelul mollayo.   cwungkwukelul an alayo.
I don't know Chinese.   *I don't know Chinese.*

영화가 재미**없어요**.
yenghwaka caymiepseyo.
The movie is not fun.

~~영화가 재미 안 있어요~~.
yenghwaka caymi an isseyo.
The movie is not fun.

The negative of 있어요 isseyo is 없어요 epseyo in helping verbs only when 있어요 isseyo retains its original sense "there exists." Otherwise, the regular negative 안 an or -지 않 -ci anh has to be used:

그거 읽을 수 없어요.
kuke ilkul swu epseyo.
I can't read it.

요즘 신문을 안 읽고 있어요.
yocum sinmwunul an ilko isseyo.
I am not reading newspapers these days.

요즘 신문을 읽지 않고 있어요.
yocum sinmwunul ilkci anhko isseyo.
I am not reading newspapers these days.

6.4.3 Negation of 하다 verbs

NOUN-하다 hata verbs are a kind of compound verb that have particular patterns of negation. They work differently from other 하다 hata verbs.

(1) Noun-하다 verbs

For NOUN-하다 hata verbs, the negative adverbs 안 an and 못 mos have to come BETWEEN the noun and 하다 hata:

평일에는 운동을 **못** 해요.
phyengileynun wuntongul mos hayyo.
I can't exercise on weekdays.

~~평일에는 못 운동해요~~.
phyengileynun mos wuntonghayyo.
I can't exercise on weekdays.

룸메이트는 설거지를 **안** 해요.
lwummeyithunun selkecilul an hayyo.
My roommate doesn't do the dishes.

~~룸메이트는 안 설거지해요~~.
lwummeyithunun an selkecihayyo.
My roommate doesn't do the dishes.

이번에는 파마를 **안** 했어.
ipeneynun phamalul an haysse.
I didn't get a perm this time.

~~이번에는 안 파마했어~~.
ipeneynun an phamahaysse.
I didn't get a perm this time.

아직 사진 다운로드를 **못** 했어.
acik sacin tawunlotulul mos haysse.
I haven't been able to download the picture(s).

~~아직 사진을 못 다운로드했어~~.
acik sacinul mos tawunlotuhaysse.
I haven't been able to download the picture(s).

One way to check whether the word before 하다 hata is a noun (and therefore does negation in this way) is to see if it can be used with a particle in any sentence. Another way is to see if it can be used as a noun without 하다 hata in another sentence structure.

이번에는 파마를 할 거에요?
ipeneynun phamalul halkeeyyo?
Are you going to get a perm this time?

파마는 비싸요.
phamnun pissayo.
Perms are expensive.

(2) Other 하다 verbs

You can negate any OTHER 하다 hata verb, including 좋아하다 cohahata and 싫어하다 silhehata, by placing 안 an and 못 mos in front of the whole verb string. You saw earlier that a particle may NOT break up 하다 hata verbs like these (피곤아 해요 phikoni hayyo). Negative adverbs may not do so either:

커피를 **안** 좋아해요.
khephilul an cohahayyo.
I don't like coffee.

~~커피를 좋아 안 해요.~~
khephilul coha an hayyo.
I don't like coffee.

오늘은 별로 **안** 피곤해요.
onulun pyello an phikonhayyo.
I am not all that tired today.

~~오늘은 별로 피곤 안 해요.~~
onulun pyello phikon an hayyo.
I am not all that tired today.

아니야. 나, 감 **안** 싫어해. 좋아해.
aniya. na, kam an silhehay. cohahay.
No, I don't not like persimmon. I like it.

~~아니야. 나, 감 싫어 안 해. 좋아해.~~
aniya. na, kam silhe an hay. cohahay.
No, I don't not like persimmon. I like it.

6.4.4 Long-form negatives

In a formal setting where your writing or speaking might be judged for its appropriateness and learnedness, you will want to use long-form negatives. Descriptive verbs especially might sound childish or much too colloquial, even in spoken Korean, if you use the short-form negative (adverbs).

(1) -지 않다 *not*, -지 못하다 *cannot*

The long-form negative that takes the place of 안 an statements uses the connector suffix -지 -ci followed by the verb 않다 anhta:

오늘은 학교에 가**지 않**아요.
onulun hakkyoey kaci anhayo.
I'm not going/I don't go to school today.

거기 앉**지 않**을래.
keki ancci anhullay.
I'm not sitting there/I don't wanna sit there.

방이 별로 크**지 않**아요.
pangi pyello khuci anhayo.
The room is not that big.

The long-form negative that takes the place of 못 mos statements uses the suffix -지 -ci followed by 못하다 moshata:

오늘은 학교에 가지 못했어요.
onulun hakkyoey kaci moshaysseyo.
I wasn't able to go to school today.

오늘은 학교에 가지 못할 거야.
onulun hakkyoey kaci moshal keya.
I won't be able to go to school today.

(2) -지 말다 *do not* (command)

To make a negative COMMAND, use -지 말다 -ci malta, which has a special negative verb, 말다 malta, just for negative commands, *don't do*. It is conjugated as -지 말아요 -ci malayo for the polite speech style. For the intimate style, use -지 마 -ci ma (instead of -지 말아 -ci mala):

너무 늦었으니까 가지 말아요.
nemwu nucessunikka kaci malayo.
It's too late; don't go.

너무 늦었으니까 가지 마.
nemwu nucessunikka kaci ma.
It's too late; don't go.

학교 가지 말고 쉬어.
hakkyo kaci malko swie.
Don't go to school; take a rest.

6.5 Conjugating Special Verb Classes

You might have already figured it out, but conjugating a Korean verb really means changing the end of the verb appropriately when it comes in contact with a particular suffix.

Suffixes express all kinds of meanings, but in terms of conjugating, there are three patterns based on the suffix shapes: consonant-initial suffixes, 어-type suffixes, and 으-type suffixes. You have seen how examples of these three types work in the previous sections, but we'll review and generalize in this section.

There are also different types of verb. We talked about consonant- and vowel-final verbs and some irregular verbs and how they conjugate differently for the ordinary speech style in 6.2. Alas, there are some other CLASSES of verbs that conjugate a little differently as well. In this section, after talking about the three basic suffix categories, we'll tackle the special verb classes.

6.5.1 Three types of suffixes

As we said, there are three suffix types: consonant-initial suffixes, 어-type suffixes, and 으-type suffixes. The progressive ending -고 있다 -ko issta begins with a **consonant-initial suffix** 고 -ko, the present tense ending for the ordinary style -어(요) -e(yo) is an -**어-type suffix**, and the future tense/prospective aspect endings -(으)ㄹ 거다 -(u)l keta and -(으)ㄹ게(요) -(u)l key(yo) are -**으-type suffixes**.

Korean is all about suffixes and conjugations, so it will be helpful to keep these classifications in mind and start to get an ear for how verbs conjugate with each one. Don't worry about the meanings of the example suffixes for now; just focus on the conjugation patterns. (You can refer back to this section as you learn more suffixes, too.) The different suffix types are also essential distinctions for learning how special-class verbs conjugate.

(1) Conjugation for consonant suffixes

When a verb root meets a consonant-initial suffix, nothing further needs to happen to the verb root, whether the root belongs to a regular, irregular, or special class and whether the verb root itself ends in a consonant or a vowel. Simply use the root of the dictionary form of the verb, and add the consonant-initial suffix.

Here is a summary of the conjugation of the verbs 읽다 ilkta *to read* (consonant-final) and 쓰다 ssuta *to write* (vowel-final) for the consonant-initial suffixes -고 -ko, -기 -ki, -지 -ci, -네 -ney, -니 -ni, and -다가 -taka. (Nevermind the suffix meanings for now, as some are part of more complex endings that will be explained later.)

Consonant-final verb root

읽고 ilkko, 읽기 ilkki, 읽지 ilkci, 읽네 ilkney, 읽니 ilkni, 읽다가 ilktaka

Vowel-final verb root

쓰고 ssuko, 쓰기 ssuki, 쓰지 ssuci, 쓰네 ssuney, 쓰니 ssuni, 쓰다가 ssutaka

(2) Conjugation for 어-type suffixes

어-type suffixes are really suffixes that attach to the -어/아 verb stem, but they are commonly taught and memorized treating the -어 as part of the suffix. You already know how to make the -어/아 verb stem, that is, the intimate ordinary form of the verb (by selecting the suffix vowel and merging or fusing root and suffix vowels as necessary).

Here is a review of the conjugation of the verbs 읽다 ilkta *to read* and 쓰다 ssuta *to write* for the suffixes -어(요) -e(yo), 어서 -ese, 어도 -eto, and -어야 -eya.

Consonant-final verb root

읽어(요) ilke(yo), 읽어서 ilkese, 읽어도 ilketo, 읽어야 ilkeya

Vowel-final verb root

써(요) sse(yo), 써서 ssese, 써도 sseto, 써야 sseya

(3) Conjugation for 으-type suffixes

으-type suffixes are those that start with an empty vowel 으 when the verb root ends in a consonant and drop the 으 when it ends in a vowel. Many -으-type suffixes involve the prospective marker -(으)ㄹ -(u)l. See how 읽다 ilkta *to read* and 쓰다 ssuta *to write* conjugate for the 으 u-type suffixes (으)ㅂ시다 -(u)psita, -(으)니까 (u)nikka, -(으)시 -(u)si, -(으)면 -(u)myen, and -(으)ㄹ게 -(u)lkey:

Consonant-final verb root

읽읍시다 ilkupsita, 읽으니까 ilkunikka, 읽으시 ilkusi, 읽으면 ilkumyen, 읽을게 ilkulkey

Vowel-final verb root

씁시다 ssepsita, 쓰니까 ssenikka, 쓰시 ssesi, 쓰면 ssemyen, 쓸게 sselkey

6.5.2 Special verb classes

This section is about the conjugation of special verb classes that do not follow the regular conjugation patterns of the ordinary speech style. These verbs conjugate differently with respect to (usually) the vowel-initial suffixes (both 어-type and 으-type). We will begin with the ㄹ-final verbs. They are not truly a special class, but they have some odd behaviors, so it is worth beginning the section on special classes with them.

(1) ㄹ-final verbs & disappearance of ㄹ

ㄹ-final verbs are not truly a special class, but ㄹ has some odd behaviors in Korean. You know that ㄹ-final nouns change the pronunciation of ㄴ-initial syllables in NOUNS (e.g. 신라 sinla is pronounced as [실라 silla]). You also know that ㄹ-final nouns act vowel-final when it comes to the tool particle -(으)로 -(u)lo and don't need the empty vowel 으 (e.g. 연필로 yenphillo *with a pencil*, 지하철로 cihachello *by the subway*). ㄹ-final VERBS also behave oddly.

There are two key points about ㄹ-final verbs that are very important in getting a grip on conjugation. The first point is that 으 of 으-type suffixes and -(으)ㄹ of -(으)ㄹ suffixes are NEVER used after ㄹ-final verbs. In a sense, you can say ㄹ-final verbs also act vowel-final in these cases.

날(다) + -(으)면   becomes **날면**   (NOT ~~날으면 nalumyen~~) *if (I) fly*
nal(ta)   -(u)lkey   nalmyen

날(다) + -(으)러   becomes **날러**   (NOT ~~날으러 nalule~~) *in order to fly*
nal(ta)   -(u)le   nalle

날(다) + -(으)ㄹ 거야   becomes **날 거야**   (NOT ~~날을 거야 nalulkeya~~) *I am going to fly*
nal(ta)   -(u)l keya   nalkeya

날(다) + -(으)ㄹ게   becomes **날게**   (NOT ~~날을게 nalulkey~~) *I'll fly (I promise)*
nal(ta)   -(u)lkey   nalkey

The second is that when a ㄹ-final verb meets a ㅂ, ㄴ, or ㅅ-initial suffix (disregarding 으), such as -(으)ㅂ시다 -(u)psita, -니 ni, or (으)시 (u)si, it loses its final ㄹ. You can remember this trick with the mnemonic "when a BoNuS comes, your LOAN goes away." (The letters in bold represent ㅂ, ㄴ, or ㅅ, and ㄹ.) Here is how 날다 nalta *to fly* conjugates before BoNuS examples:

날(다) + -(으)ㅂ시다   becomes **납시다**   (NOT ~~날읍시다 nalupsita~~) *let's fly*
nal(ta)   -(u)psita   napsita

날(다) + -니   becomes **나니?**   (NOT ~~날으니 naluni~~) *do you fly?*
nal(ta)   -ni   nani

날(다) + -(으)시   becomes **나시**   (NOT ~~날으시 nalusi~~) *fly (honorific)*
nal(ta)   -(u)si   nasi

With consonant-initial and 어-type suffixes, ㄹ-final verbs conjugate normally:

날고 nalko *fly-and*   날지만 nalciman *fly-but*   날아서 nalase *by way of flying*

(2) Special-ㅎ class

Verbs of the special-ㅎ class are descriptive verbs from a very limited pool whose root ends in ㅎ. Basically, three semantic (meaning) groups of verbs belong to the special-ㅎ class, all from the native Haan vocabulary stock.

<1> Deictic verbs

Three deictic (pointing) words and two *how* words that end in ㅎ are of the special-ㅎ class in Korean:

이렇다 ilehta *to be this way*, 그렇다 kulehta *to be that way*, 저렇다 celehta *to be that way* (close to neither speaker nor listener), 어떻다 ettehta *to be how*, 아무렇다 amwulehta *to be anyhow, to be in some way*

<2> Color verbs

There are five core native Haan color terms and numerous color terms derived from them in Korean. (All other color terms are borrowed from other languages.) The five native color verbs and their derived relatives belong to the ㅎ class:

빨갛다 ppalkahta *red*, 노랗다 nolahta *yellow*, 파랗다 phalahta *blue*, 까맣다 kkamahta *black*, 하얗다 hayahta *white*

The dark-vowel version of the colors, denoting less intense or more dispersed colors (e.g. *reddish*), also belongs to this category:

뻘겋다 ppelkehta, 누렇다 nwulehta, 퍼렇다 phelehta, 꺼멓다 kkemehta, 허옇다 heyehta

<3> Physical and spatial verbs (with the -다랗 suffix)

A limited number of verbs that describe the physical and spatial quality of objects can be extended with a special-ㅎ -h suffix, -다랗 -talah (sometimes realized as -따랗 -ttalah):

가늘다	kanulta	→	가느**다랗**다	kanutalahta	*thin*
크다	khuta	→	커**다랗**다	khetalahta	*large*
길다	kilta	→	기**다랗**다	kitalahta	*long*
짧다	ccalpta	→	짤**따랗**다	ccalttalahta	*short*
굵다	kwulkta	→	굵**다랗**다	kwulktalahta	*thick (girth)*
높다	nophta	→	높**다랗**다	nophtalahta	*high*
넓다	nelpta	→	널**따랗**다	nelttalahta	*wide*

좁다 copta → 좁**다랗**다 coptalahta *narrow*

얇다 yalpta → 얄**따랗**다 yalttalahta *thin*

조금 cokum → 조그**맣**다 cokumahta *small* (-앟 -ah suffix):

<4> Conjugating special-ㅎ verbs

Here are the mechanics of the special-ㅎ class conjugation:

- Before the 어- and 으-type suffixes and those beginning with a ㄴ, the final ㅎ in this class DISAPPEARS.
- For the 어-type only the root vowel changes to **애** ay (or 얘 yay).
  (There is no vowel harmony! Even 그렇다 kulehta becomes 그래(요) kulay(yo), NOT 그레(요) kuley(yo).)

Here is a table comparing the conjugation of the special-ㅎ-class verbs 그렇다 kulehta *to be so* and 하얗다 hayahta *to be white* with REGULAR-ㅎ-class verbs 넣다 nehta *to put in* and 좋다 cohta *to be good* with respect to the consonant-initial suffix -지 않다 ci anhta and the 어 and 으 vowel-initial suffixes. The last two rows show how ㅎ drops out before ㄴ:

		Special-ㅎ Verbs		Regular-ㅎ Verbs	
		그렇다 kulehta *to be so*	**하얗다** hayahta *to be white*	**넣다** nehta *to put in*	**좋다** cohta *to be good*
C-type suffix	-지 않아요 -ci anhayo *not*	그렇지 않아요 kulehci anhayo	하얗지 않아요 hayahci anhayo	넣지 않아요 nehci anhayo	좋지 않아요 cohci anhayo
어-type suffix	어요 -eyo	그래요 kulayyo	하애요 hayayyo	넣어요 neheyo	좋아요 cohayo
으-type suffix	-(으)ㄹ 거예요 -(u)l keyeyyo *will*	그럴 거예요 kulel keyeyyo	하얄 거예요 hayal keyeyyo	넣을 거예요 nehul keyeyyo	좋을 거예요 cohul keyeyyo
	-(으)면 -(u)myen *if*	그러면 kulemyen	하야면 hayamyen	넣으면 nehumyen	좋으면 cohumyen
ㄴ-initial suffix	-네 -ney *oh!*	그러네 kuleney	하야네 hayaney	넣네 nehney	좋네 cohney
	-니? -ni *?*	그러니 kuleni	하야니 hayani	넣니 nehni	좋니 cohni

Note that double-받침 patchim ㅎ- final verbs (like 많다 manhta and 싫다 silhta) do NOT belong to the special class, so their conjugation is regular. Here are some examples with both regular and special-ㅎ verbs:

최:　이 꽃 식탁에 놓기에 너무 **빨강**지 않아요?
choy:　i kkoch sikthakey nohkiey nemwu ppalkahci anhayo?
Choi:　*Aren't these flowers too red to put on the table?*

한:　**그래**요? 너무 **빨개**요? 좋지 않아요?
han:　kulayyo? nemwu ppalkayyo? cohci anhayo?
Han:　*You think so? Are they too red? Don't you like them?*

최:　**그럴** 거예요. 너무 **빨가**면 안 돼요.
choy:　kulel keyeyyo. nemwu ppalkamyen an twayyo.
Choi:　*I think so. Too red isn't good.*

한:　**아무래도 그렇**지요?
han:　amwulayto kulehciyo?
Han:　*No matter how you look at it, it is (too red), isn't it?*

(3) Special-ㅂ class

Three groups of native Haan verbs belong to the special-ㅂ class of verbs whose roots end in ㅂ and conjugate in a special way.

<1> Sensory and sensation verbs (descriptive)

Most Haan Korean ㅂ-final verbs that describe sensory or emotional reactions are of the special-ㅂ class:

춥다	chwupta	*cold weather*	차갑다	chakapta	*cold-to-touch*
덥다	tepta	*hot weather*	뜨겁다	ttukepta	*hot-to-touch*
맵다	maypta	*spicy*	싱겁다	singgepta	*bland*
무겁다	mwukepta	*heavy*	가볍다	kapyepta	*light*
가깝다	kakkapta	*close*	쉽다	swipta	*easy*
어렵다	elyepta	*difficult*	더럽다	telepta	*dirty*
아름답다	alumtapta	*beautiful*	밉다	mipta	*ugly/detestable*
얄밉다	yalmipta	*unlikable*	무섭다	mwusepta	*scary/scared*
안타깝다	anthakkapta	*what a shame*	아쉽다	aswipta	*what a pity*
징그럽다	cingkulepta	*gross, repulsive, shudder-causing, creepy*			

<2> ㅂ-suffixed descriptive verbs

All descriptive verbs derived with -답다 -tapta as well as -스럽다 -sulepta and -롭다 -lopta are of the special-ㅂ class:

Displaying the characteristics of, matching the title of, behaving like NOUN (-답다 -tapta):

학생답다 haksayngtapta *studently (studentlike)*　　군인답다 kwunintapta *soldierly*

인간답다 inkantapta *humanly*　　부모답다 pwumotapta *parently*

Giving the air of NOUN, *feeling the sense of* NOUN (-스럽다 -sulepta):

자연스럽다 cayensulepta *natural*   갑작스럽다 kapcaksulepta *sudden*

사랑스럽다 salangsulepta *lovely*   만족스럽다 mancoksulepta *satisfactory*

Full of NOUN (-롭다 -lopta):

향기롭다 hyangkilopta *fragrant*   평화롭다 phyenghwalopta *peaceful*

경이롭다 kyengilopta *wonderous*   이롭다 ilopta *advantageous*

감미롭다 kammilopta *sweet and lingering*

<3> Basic active verbs

Just a handful of one-syllable native Haan Korean ㅂ-final verbs are of the special-ㅂ class:

굽다 kwupta *to broil*   돕다 topta *to help*

줍다 cwupta *to pick up*   눕다 nwupta *to lie down*

깁다 kipta *to mend/patch up clothing*

Take note. Most ㅂ-final VERBS, including some descriptive verbs, conjugate REGULARLY.

업다 epta *to piggy-back*   입다 ipta *to put on clothes*

잡다 capta *to hold/grab*   씹다 ssipta *to chew*

접다 cepta *to fold*   꼽다 kkopta *to count, point to*

뽑다 ppopta *to pluck/pick*   굽다 kwupta *to bend*

좁다 copta *to be narrow*   수줍다 swucwupta *to be shy*

헤집다 heycipta *to make way/ransack*

<4> Conjugating special-ㅂ verbs

Here are the mechanics of the the special-ㅂ class conjugation:

- Before the 어- and 으-type suffixes, the final ㅂ in this class changes to ㅜ.
- Before the 어-type suffix, the final ㅂ of the one-syllable, bright vowel verbs (돕다 topta, 곱다 kopta) changes to ㅗ.

Here is a table comparing the conjugation of the special-ㅂ class verbs 굽다 kwupta *to grill, bake,* 돕다 topta *to help,* and 춥다 chwupta *to be cold* with the regular-ㅂ class verbs 입다 ipta *to put on (clothing)* and 잡다 capta *to grab:*

		Special-ㅂ+			Regular-ㅂ	
		굽다 kwupta *to grill, bake*	돕다 topta *to help*	춥다 chwupta *to be cold*	입다 ipta *to wear*	잡다 capta *to hold*
C-type	-고 있어 -ko isse *-ing*	굽고 있어 kwupko isse	돕고 있어 topko isse	—	입고 있어 ipko isse	잡고 있어 capko isse
	-지 않아 -ci anha *not*	굽지 않아 kwupci anha	돕지 않아 topci anha	춥지 않아 chwupci anha	입지 않아 ipci anha	잡지 않아 capci anha
어-type	-어 -e	구워 kwuwe	도와 towa	추워 chwuwe	입어 ipe	잡아 capa
	-었어요 -esseyo *-ed*	구웠어 kwuwesse	도왔어 towasse	추웠어 chwuwesse	입었어 ipesse	잡았어 capasse
으-type	(으)면 -(u)myen *-if*	구우면 kwuwumyen	도우면 towumyen	추우면 chwuwumyen	입으면 ipumyen	잡으면 capumyen
	(으)ㄹ 거야 -(u)l keya *will*	구울 거야 kwuwul keya	도울 거야 towul keya	추울 거야 chwuwul keya	입을 거야 ipul keya	잡을 거야 capul keya

+ Speakers from the southeastern part of the Korean peninsula (for example, Busan) do not treat these verbs as special, conjugating them just like regular-ㅂ words (e.g. 추워라 chwuwela would be 추버라 chwupela or 추바라 chwupala according to these speakers.)

Here are some examples with both regular and special-ㅂ verbs. In the end, you may need to simply memorize which are special-ㅂ and which are regular verbs, but you will likely get an ear for the frequent ones.

박: 지금 생선을 **굽고** 있어?
pak: cikum sayngsenul kwupko isse?
Park: *Are you grilling fish?*

손: 아니. 아직 한 마리도 못 **잡았**어.
son: ani. acik han malito mos capasse.
Sohn: *No. I haven't caught even one yet.*

박: 그래? **잡은** 생선은 **구울 거야**?
pak: kulay? capun sayngsenun kwuwul keya?
Park: *Yeah? Will you be grilling what you catch?*

손: 석쇠에 **구우려고** 그래.
son: seksoyey kwuwulyeko kulay.
Sohn: *I'm thinking about grilling it on the gridiron.*

박: 내가 **도와** 줄게. 태우지 않고 잘 **구워**.
pak: nayka towa cwulkey. thaywuci anhko cal kwuwe.
Park: *I'll help. I grill it well without burning it.*

손: 그래. **고마워**.
son: kulay. komawe.
Sohn: *OK. Thanks.*

(4) Special-ㄷ class

Special-ㄷ class verbs are few in number and are all active verbs. You can probably memorize them on the spot right now:

걷다 ketta *to walk*   듣다 tutta *to listen*

알아듣다 alatutta *to get/understand*   묻다 mwutta *to ask*

싣다 sitta *to load up*   깨닫다 kkaytatta *to realize*

Here are the (simple!) mechanics of the conjugation:

> • For the -어 and -으 vowel-type suffixes, the final ㄷ in this class changes to ㄹ.

Here is a table comparing the conjugation of the special-ㄷ class verbs 듣다 tutta *to listen* and 걷다 ketta *to walk* to the regular-ㄷ class verbs 닫다 tatta *to close* and 걷다 ketta *to fold away*. We have used different endings to help show a variety, and verbs are conjugated for the intimate ordinary speech style this time. To prevent possible confusion, the ㄹ-final word 걸다 kelta *to hang* is also compared in the chart:

		Special-ㄷ		Regular-ㄷ		ㄹ-Final
		듣다 tutta *to listen*	걷다 ketta *to walk*	닫다 tatta *to close*	걷다 ketta *to fold away*	걸다 kelta *to hang*
C-type	-다가 -taka *in mid-act*	듣다가 tuttaka	걷다가 kettaka	닫다가 tattaka	걷다가 kettaka	걸다가 keltaka
	-지 마! -ci ma! *Don't!*	듣지 마 tutci ma	걷지 마 ketci ma	닫지 마 tatci ma	걷지 마 ketci ma	걸지 마 kelci ma
어-type	-어서 -ese *consequently*	들어서 tulese	걸어서 kelese	닫아서 tatase	걷어서 ketese	걸어서 kelese
	-었어 -esse *-ed*	들었어 tulesse	걸었어 kelesse	닫았어 tatasse	걷었어 ketesse	걸었어 kelesse
으-type	-(으)니까 -(u)nikka *because*	들으니까 tulunikka	걸으니까 kelunikka	닫으니까 tatunikka	걷으니까 ketunikka	거니까 kenikka
	-(으)ㄹ까? -(u)lkka? *I wonder*	들을까 tululkka	걸을까 kelulkka	닫을까 tatulkka	걷을까 ketulkka	걸까 kelkka

Here are some examples with both regular and special-ㄷ verbs:

이: 나랑 한 바퀴 **걷고** 싶어?
i: nalang han pakhwi ketko siphe?
Lee: *Do you want to walk around with me?*

김: 지금 빨래를 걷고 있어.
kim: cikum ppallaylul ketko isse.
Kim: *I am gathering up the (dry) laundry now.*

이: 좀 이따 **걸어**도 돼. 같이 가자.
i: com itta keleto tway. kathi kaca.
Lee: *We can go (walk) a little later. Let's.*

김: 조금 바쁜데. 소영이한테 **물어** 봐.
kim: cokum pappuntey. soyengihanthey mwule pwa.
Kim: *I am a bit busy. Ask Soyoung. (and see if she wants to go).*

It will be good to remember that the special- ㄷ verbs often create homophones (words that sound alike) with ㄹ-final verbs, and the meaning becomes clear only when you have the context:

그거 어디에 **걸었어**?
kuke etiey kelesse?
Where did you hang it?

어제 어디에서 **걸었어**?
ecey etieyse kelesse?
Where did you walk yesterday?

Finally, do be careful with the forms like 들을 tulul and 걸을 kelul. Because the root-final ㄹ comes from ㄷ and not ㄹ, it does not disappear before the -(으)ㄹ -(u)l suffixes. That is, the special- ㄷ verb conjugation will yield a syllable that is pronounced [르 lu], although this is avoided with ㄹ-final verbs.

누구한테 **물을**까? 걔는 **알**까?
nwukwuhantey mwululkka? kyaynun alkka?
Who shall I ask? I wonder if she knows.

(5) Special-ㅅ class

The final consonant ㅅ of this special-ㅅ class does not simply change to a different consonant when meeting the vowel suffixes as happens with other special class verbs. It disappears altogether. But, it ACTS LIKE IT IS STILL THERE, requiring the empty vowel 으 in 으 suffixes, which is normally needed only after a consonant-final root. For the 어 conjugation, the final ㅅ of the verb root drops, but the suffix 어 vowel is ALSO used. If you were to conjugate 지다 cita *to lose* for the ordinary present tense, you would come out with 져(요) cye(yo). For the special-ㅅ class verb 짓다 cista, the final product would be 지어 cie NOT 짓어 cise nor 져 cye. Thus, one could say that ㅅ alternates with its own ghost.

In speech, 지어 cie is pronounced like 져 cye, making it indistinguishable from the vowel-final verb. The same holds for 지을 거야 (지:ㄹ) ciel keya (ci:l) *will build*, which may be almost identical in length with 질 거야 cil keya *will lose.*

Like the special-ㄷ class, there are only a handful of special-ㅅ class verbs (mostly active verbs). You can probably memorize them now:

짓다 cista *to build/make*   붓다 pwusta *to pour/swell*   긋다 kusta *to draw (a line)*
낫다 nasta *to get/be better*   잇다 ista *to connect (points)*

Here are the mechanics of the conjugation:

- Before the 어- and 으-type suffixes, the final ㅅ disappears.
- Interacting with 어- and 으-type suffixes, verbs act as though the deleted ㅅ were still there.

The following is a table comparing the conjugation of the special-ㅅ class verbs 낫다 nasta *to be/get better* and 짓다 cista *to build/make* to the regular ㅅ-final verbs, 빗다 pista *to comb (hair)* and 웃다 wusta *to smile/laugh*:

		Special-ㅅ		Regular-ㅅ	
		낫다 nasta *to get better*	**짓다** cista *to build*	**빗다** pista *to comb*	**웃다** wusta *to laugh*
C-type	-다가 -taka *in mid-act*	낫다가 nastaka	짓다가 cistaka	빗다가 pistaka	웃다가 wustaka
	-지 마! -ci ma! *Don't!*	낫지 마 nasci ma	짓지 마 cisci ma	빗지 마 pisci ma	웃지 마 wusci ma
어-type	-어서 -ese *consequently*	나아서 naase	지어서 ciese	빗어서 pisese	웃어서 wusese
	-었어 -esse -*ed*	나았어 naasse	지었어 ciesse	빗었어 pisesse	웃었어 wusesse
으-type	-(으)니까 -(u)nikka *because*	나으니까 naunikka	지으니까 ciunikka	빗으니까 pisunikka	웃으니까 wusunikka
	-(으)ㄹ까? -(u)lkka *I wonder*	나을까 naulkka	지을까 ciulkka	빗을까 pisulkka	웃을까 wusulkka

Here are some examples with both regular and special-ㅅ verbs:

공: 독감 다 **나았어**? 약은 **지어** 먹었어?
kong: tokkam ta naasse? yakun cie mekesse?
Kong: *Did you get over the flu? You had medicine?*

천: 독감은 다 **나았**는데 이젠 몸살이 났어.
chen: tokkamun ta naassnuntey iceyn momsali nasse.
Chun: *Yes. I got over the flu, but now I have body aches.*

공: 몸살이 독감보다 **낫지**.
kong: momsali tokkampota nasci.
Kong: *Body aches are better than the flu.*

As a final check-up, let's compare the conjugations of 날다 nalta *to fly*, 나다 nata *to come to exist*, 낫다 nasta *to be/get better* (special-ㅅ class), 낳다 nahta *to give birth* (regular), and 낮다 nacta *to be low*. Those that are pronounced similarly are marked with matching symbols below:

Types	Suffixs/ Endings	날다 nalta *to fly*	나다 nata *to come to exist*	낫다 nasta special-ㅅ *to get better*	낳다 nahta *to give birth*	낮다 nacta *to be low*
C-type	-고 -ko *and*	날고 nalko	나고 nako	낫고$ nasko	낳고 nahko	낮고$ nacko
어-type	-었어 -esse *-ed*	날았어 nalasse	났어 nasse	나았어% naasse	낳았어% nahasse	낮았어 nacasse
으-type	-(으)ㄹ 거야 -(u)l keya *will*	날 거야^ nal keya	날 거야^ nal keya	나을 거야° naul keya	낳을 거야° nahul keya	낮을 거야 nacul keya
	-(으)니까 -(u)nikka *because*	나니까-- nanikka	나니까-- nanikka	나으니까+ naunikka	낳으니까+ nahunikka	낮으니까 nacunikka

Many of these words are pronounced the same way or are distinguished only by the slight vowel length difference (e.g., 날 거야 nal keya *will fly, will come to exist*, 나을 거야 naul keya *will get better*, 낳을 거야 nahul keya *will give birth*, and 나았어 naasse *got better* vs. 낳았어 nahasse *gave birth*). They can be told apart by their spelling or from the context:

아기 낳을 거야.
aki nahul keya.
They'll give birth to a baby.

vs.

이게 나을 거야.
ikey naul keya.
This will be better.

여기서 날 거야.
yekise nal keya.
It is probably produced here.

vs.

여기까지 날 거야.
yekikkaci nal keya.
It'll fly up to here.

(6) Special-르 conjugation

While most special class verbs show their alternate verb root form with both the -어 and -으 suffixes, 르-verbs are peculiar in that they use an ALTERNATE ROOT FORM ONLY BEFORE 어-type suffixes. And, unlike other special classes that have a small number of words, almost all 르-verbs conjugate specially. (You saw earlier that 따르다 ttaluta *to follow* conjugates regularly to become 따라 ttala; you also saw that 이르다 iluta *to arrive* and 푸르다 phwuluta *blue* are two 러 irregulars with the forms 이르러 ilule and 푸르러 phwulule.) Since most 르-verbs conjugate in this special way, we can't list all of them, but here are some common verbs, both active and descriptive:

모르다 moluta *to not know*

마르다 maluta *to get dry, to be skinny*

고르다 koluta *to choose*

누르다 nwuluta *to press down*

이르다 iluta *to tell, to be early*   다르다 taluta *to be different*

게으르다 keyuluta *to be lazy*   빠르다 ppaluta *to be fast*

자르다 caluta *to cut*   조르다 coluta *to tighten*

Here are the mechanics of the conjugation:

> • ONLY before -어 suffixes, 르-verbs lose the vowel 으 and double up the consonant 르.

Here is a table showing the conjugation of the 르 lu-verbs 고르다 koluta *to pick out, choose*, 누르다 nwuluta *to press down*, 빠르다 ppaluta *to be fast*, and 이르다 iluta *to tattle, to be early*. For comparison, we also included the 러-irregular verb 이르다 iluta *to reach* and 르-regular verb 따르다 ttaluta *to follow; pour*:

		Special-르				러-irregular	Regular-르
		고르다 koluta *to choose*	누르다 nwuluta *to press down*	빠르다 ppaluta *to be fast*	이르다 iluta *to be early*	이르다 iluta *to reach*	따르다 ttaluta *to follow*
C-type	-고 -ko *and*	고르고 koluko	부르고 pwuluko	빠르고 ppaluko	이르고 iluko	이르고 iluko	따르고 ttaluko
	-지 마! -ci ma! *Don't!*	고르지 마 koluci ma	부르지 마 pwuluci ma	—	이르지 마 iluci ma	이르지 마 iluci ma	따르지 마 ttaluci ma
어-type	-어서 -ese *consequently*	**골라서** kollase	**불러서** pwullese	**빨라서** ppallase	**일러서** illese	이르러서 ilulese	**따라서** ttalase
	-었어 -esse *-ed*	**골랐어** kollasse	**불렀어** pwullesse	**빨랐어** ppallasse	**일렀어** illesse	이르렀어 ilulesse	**따랐어** ttalasse
으-type	-(으)니 -(u)ni *because*	고르니 koluni	부르니 pwuluni	빠르니 ppaluni	이르니 iluni	이르니 iluni	따르니 ttaluni
	-(으)ㄹ까? -(u)lkka? *I wonder*	고를까 kolulkka	부를까 pwululkka	빠를까 ppalulkka	이를까 ilulkka	이를까 ilulkka	따를까 ttalulkka

In casually spoken Korean, speakers often insert another ㄹ for all conjugations. So, you may hear people say 불를 거니까 pwullul kenikka and 빨를 거니까 ppallul kenikka instead of 부를 거니까 pwulul kenikka and 빠를 거니까 ppalul kenikka, or 불를까요 pwullulkkayo and

불르지 마 pwulluci ma insead of 부를까요 pwululkkayo and 부르지 마 pwuluci ma. Here are some example sentences:

동현: 까비가 내 머리를 막 **눌렀어**!
tonghyen: kkapika nay melilul mak nwullesse!
Tonghyun: *Gabi totally pressed my head down!*

은비: 그래서 엄마한테 **일렀어**?
unpi: kulayse emmahanthey illesse?
Eunbi: *So, did you tell Mom?*

동현: 아니. 너무 **일러서** 엄마가 자.
tonghyen: ani. nemwu illese emmaka ca.
Tonghyun: *No. It's too early, so Mom's still asleep.*

은비: 엄마 일어나시면 **이를** 거야?
unpi: emma ilenasimyen ilul keya?
Eunbi: *Are you going to tell on him?*

동현: 좀 생각해 보고.
tonghyen: com sayngkakhay poko.
Tonghyun: *Let me think about it a little.*

은비: **이를** 거 없이 너도 **눌러** 주고 끝내.
unpi: ilul ke epsi neto nwulle cwuko kkuthnay.
Eunbi: *No need to tell. Push his head down and be done.*

(7) Conjugation summary chart for special verbs (for polite ordinary style)

Finally, see if you can conjugate all special verbs for various tenses and aspects.

Dictionary Form	Meaning	Present	Past/ Perfective	Progressive	Future/ Prospective
팔다 phalta	*to sell*	팔아요 phalayo	팔았어요 phalasseyo	팔고 있어요 phalko isseyo	팔 거예요 phal keyeyyo
그렇다 kulehta	*to be so*	그래요 kulayyo	그랬어요 kulaysseyo	—	그럴 거예요 kulel keyeyyo
돕다 topta	*to help*	도와요 towayo	도왔어요 towasseyo	돕고 있어요 topko isseyo	도울 거예요 towul keyeyyo
낫다 nasta	*to get better*	나아요 naayo	나았어요 naasseyo	낫고 있어요 nasko isseyo	나을 거예요 naul keyeyyo
기르다 kiluta	*to raise*	길러요 killeyo	길렀어요 killesseyo	기르고 있어요 kiluko isseyo	기를 거예요 kilul keyeyyo

Whew! This chapter has quite a lot to digest, but once it settles in, you are ready to go with the trickiest but most widespread speech style. That's a giant leap forward in Korean grammar!

Exercises

6.1 Korean Verbs

Exercise 1. Fill in the blanks with the appropriate verbs from the box below.

있어요	없어요	이에요/예요	아니에요

1) A: 안녕하세요? 제 이름은 박은지 _____. 저는 워싱턴 대학교 학생

   _____.

   B: 반갑습니다. 저는 에이미 브라운 _____. 저도 워싱턴 대학교 학생

   _____.

2) A: 여기가 은지 씨 방 _____?

   B: 아니요. 여기는 내 방이 _____. 저기가 내 방 _____.

3) A: 오늘 시간이 _____?

   B: 미안해요. 오늘은 바빠요. 그래서 시간이 _____. 그렇지만 내일은
   시간이 _____.

4) A: 은지 씨는 동생이 _____?

   B: 네. 한 명이 _____. 내 동생 이름은 은수 _____.

Exercise 2. Which underlined verbs are active verbs and which are descriptive verbs? Write A for active verbs and D for descriptive verbs.

1) 친구가 <u>자요</u>.   _____

2) 오늘은 날씨가 <u>나빠요</u>.   _____

3) 지금 <u>전화해요</u>.   _____

4) 시간이 더 <u>필요해요</u>.   _____

5) 오늘은 <u>피곤해요</u>.   _____

6) 동생이 아주 <u>피곤해해요</u>.   _____

7) 날씨가 <u>따뜻해요</u>.   _____

8) 날씨가 아주 <u>따뜻해졌어요</u>. _____

9) 그 노래를 <u>좋아해요</u>. _____

10) 그 노래가 <u>좋아요</u>. _____

Exercise 3. Underline the appropriate word in parentheses to complete the sentence.

1) 내 동생은 비디오 게임을 아주 (좋아요, 좋아해요). 그래서 저하고 같이 비디오 게임을 자주 해요. 동생은 비디오 게임에 지면 아주 (슬퍼요, 슬퍼해요). 동생이 너무 (귀여워요, 귀여워해요)!

2) 나와 내 친구는 성격이 아주 달라요. 나는 할 일이 많으면 우울한데 친구는 (즐거워요, 즐거워해요). 나는 집에 혼자 있는 것이 (좋은데, 좋아하는데) 친구는 나가서 사람들하고 (만나고 싶어요, 만나고 싶어해요). 친구하고 나는 서로 다르지만 우리는 (친해요, 친하고 있어요).

Exercise 4. Underline the appropriate word in parentheses to complete the sentence naturally.

1) A: 아, 목이 (말라요, 말랐어요)! 물 좀 주세요.
    B: 물도 마시고 빵도 좀 먹어. 요즘 너무 (말라, 말랐어).

2) A: 쓰레기통이 다 (차, 찼어).
    B: 알았어. 내가 비울게.

3) A: 오늘 날씨가 어때?
    B: 별로 안 좋아. 안개가 많이 (껴, 꼈어). 운전 조심해.

4) A: 오늘 도서관 (닫아, 닫았어)?
    B: 아니, (열어, 열었어).

5) A: B씨는 아버지를 많이 (닮아요, 닮았어요).
    B: 네, 다들 그렇게 얘기해요.

6) A: 오늘 왜 수업에 (늦어요, 늦었어요)?
    B: 죄송합니다. 버스가 안 와서 그랬어요.

7) A: 와, 네 동생 정말 잘 (생겨, 생겼어).
    B: 그래? 나는 잘 모르겠어.

8) A: 어머, 감기에 (걸려요, 걸렸어요)?
    B: 네, 그런 것 같아요.

6.2 Conjugating for the Ordinary Speech Style

Exercise 5. Complete the table to practice the intimate ordinary style.

Verb	Intimate ordinary style	Verb	Intimate ordinary style
공부를 하다	공부를 해	버스를 타다	
점심을 먹다		버스가 서다	
이를 닦다		커피를 마시다	
친구하고 놀다		테니스를 치다	
저녁을 만들다		돈을 내다	
선물을 주다		집에서 쉬다	
학교에 오다		친구가 되다	
동생이다		이메일을 쓰다	
친구이다		머리가 아프다	

Exercise 6. Conjugate the underlined verbs for the polite ordinary style, "-어요."

1) 나는 지금 대학교 1학년<u>이다</u>. 이름은 민지이다. 대학교 생활은 <u>재미있다</u>. 친구들도 많고 룸메이트도 <u>괜찮다</u>. 학교 캠퍼스가 <u>넓다</u>. 체육관하고 도서관도 *시설이 <u>좋다</u>.

   *시설: facilities

2) 기숙사에는 부엌이 없어서 음식을 못 <u>만들다</u>. 그래서 보통 학교 식당에서 아침하고 점심을 <u>먹다</u>. 가끔 한국 식당에도 <u>가다</u>. 영화를 좋아해서 친구하고 영화도 자주 <u>보다</u>. 그리고 테니스도 가끔 <u>치다</u>.

3) 매일 공부 때문에 <u>바쁘다</u>. 숙제도 매일 <u>내다</u>. 그리고 시험 때에는 하루 종일 도서관에서 <u>살다</u>. 잠도 잘 못 <u>자다</u>. 그렇지만 시험이 끝나면 기숙사 방에서 <u>쉬다</u>. 그리고 친구하고 같이 만나서 <u>놀다</u>. 시내에 나가서 커피도 <u>마시다</u>.

4) 한국의 가을은 정말 아름다워요. 가을 하늘은 참 <u>푸르다</u>. 가을에는 또 나뭇잎에 빨갛고 노랗게 <u>되다</u>. 나는 가을을 정말 <u>좋아하다</u>.

6.3 Tense & Aspect

Exercise 7. Fill in the chart to practice tense endings in the polite ordinary style, "-어 요."

Verb	Past	Present	Future
공부를 하다	했어요	해요	할 거예요
점심을 먹다		먹어요	
이를 닦다	닦았어요		
친구하고 놀다			놀 거예요
저녁을 만들다	만들었어요		
선물을 주다		줘요	
학교에 오다	왔어요		
커피를 마시다			마실 거예요
돈을 내다	냈어요		
이메일을 쓰다		써요	
집에서 쉬다	쉬었어요		
친구가 되다			될 거예요
친구이다	친구였어요		
동생이다		동생이에요	

Exercise 8. Conjugate the underlined verbs for the polite ordinary style. Pay attention to the tense.

1) 옛날 옛날에 신데렐라는 새엄마와 언니 두명과 <u>살다</u>. 새엄마와 언니들은 신데렐라를 <u>싫어하다</u>. 그래서 매일 많은 일을 <u>시키다</u>. 불쌍한 신데렐라는 매일 요리하고 빨래하고 <u>청소하다</u>. 어느 날, 새엄마와 언니들은 신데렐라를 집에 두고 파티에 <u>가다</u>. 신데렐라는 파티에 가고 싶었지만 예쁜 옷이 <u>없다</u>. 그리고 할 일도 <u>많다</u>. 신데렐라는 너무 슬퍼서 <u>울다</u>.

2) 신데렐라는 파티 갈 준비가 <u>끝나다</u>. 파티에 가서 춤을 <u>추다</u>. 그리고 사람들하고 <u>얘기하다</u>. 맛있는 케이크도 <u>먹다</u>. 그렇지만 새엄마하고 언니들은 안 <u>만나다</u>. 그리고 12시 전에 집에 <u>돌아오다</u>.

3) 다음 주말은 아주 <u>바쁘다</u>. 학교 풋볼 시합이 있어서 경기를 보러 <u>가다</u>. 경기를 보고 나서 친구들하고 맥주 한 잔 <u>마시다</u>. 그리고 같이 노래방에서 노래를 <u>하다</u>. 다음 주 일요일에는 친구 생일 파티가 있다. 그래서 생일 파티에 <u>가다</u>. 친구 선물은 벌써 <u>사다</u>. 친구한테 선물을 <u>주다</u>. 친구가 <u>좋아하다</u>.

4) 나는 어제 티셔츠를 사러 학교 서점에 <u>가다</u>. 빨간 티셔츠가 아주 마음에 <u>들다</u>. 그래서 빨간 티셔츠를 <u>사다</u>. 오늘 학교 티셔츠를 <u>입다</u>. 친구가 선물로 준 모자도 <u>쓰다</u>. 그 모자는 디자인이 <u>예쁘다</u>. 그래서 요즘 자주 <u>쓰다</u>.

5) 우리 형은 아주 키가 크고 잘 <u>생기다</u>. 그리고 착하고 머리도 <u>좋다</u>. 형은 3년 전에 <u>결혼하다</u>. 그래서 나는 귀여운 조카가 한 명 <u>있다</u>. 이번 추수감사절 방학 때 형네 가족을 만나러 시카고에 <u>가다</u>. 다음 달이 11월이니까 곧 <u>만나다</u>. 빨리 형네 가족을 보고 <u>싶다</u>.

Exercise 9. Underline the word in parentheses that best completes the sentence.

1) A: 점심 (먹어요, 먹었어요)?
   B: 아니요. 아직이요.

2) A: 언제부터 여기에 (살아요, 살았어요)?
   B: 태어나서 지금까지요.

3) A: 꽃이 (죽어요, 죽었어요).
   B: 꽃에 물을 너무 자주 주면 꽃이 (죽어요, 죽었어요). 조심하세요.

4) A: 와! 일년 동안 키가 많이 (커요, 컸어요)!
   B: 네, 지금은 친구들 중에서 키가 제일 (커요, 컸어요).

5) A: (일어나, 일어났어)! 벌써 8시야.
   B: 걱정 하지 마. (일어나, 일어났어).

6) A: 영화가 언제 (시작해요, 시작했어요)?
   B: 벌써 (시작해요, 시작했어요). 빨리 오세요.

Exercise 10. Underline the word in parentheses that completes the sentence more colloquially.

1) A: 지금 비 와.
   B: 어? 조금 전까지 날씨가 (맑았는데, 맑았었는데)?

2) A: (looking at her friend's family photo) 와, 네 오빠 정말 잘 (생겼어, 생겼었어).
   B: 고등학교 때는 더 잘 (생겼어, 생겼었어).

3) A: 왜 지금 와! 아까 네 여자친구가 너 만나러 (왔어, 왔었어).

B: 아이구, 그랬구나! 여자 친구가 언제 (갔어, 갔었어)?

4) A: 어렸을 때에는 많이 (아팠는데, 아팠었는데) 지금은 건강해요.

B: 저도 그래요.

Exercise 11. Underline the expression in parentheses that best completes the sentence.

1) A: 아기가 (자고 있어요, 자 있어요). 조용히 하세요.

B: 네.

2) A: 동생 깨워라.

B: 안 깨워도 돼요. 동생이 아까부터 (일어나고 있어요, 일어나 있어요)

3) A: 집 앞에 빨간 차가 (서고 있어요, 서 있어요). 누구 차예요?

B: 그거 내 차예요. 어제 차를 샀거든요.

4) A: 지금 어디에 (살고 있어요, 살아 있어요)?

B: 할아버지 댁에요.

A: 할아버지께서 아직 (살고 계세요, 살아 계세요)? 좋겠어요.

5) A: 가방에 뭐가 (들고 있어요, 들어 있어요)?

B: 책이요.

6) A: 실례합니다. 문이 (열고 있어서, 열려 있어서) 그냥 들어왔어요.

B: 아, 괜찮습니다.

7) A: 누가 언니예요?

B: 언니는 빨간 옷을 (입고 있어요, 입어 있어요). 그리고 안경을 (끼고 있어요, 껴 있어요).

Exercise 12. Underline the word in parentheses that best completes the sentence.

1) A: 순두부 드세요. 고춧가루를 많이 넣어서 좀 (매울, 매웠을) 거예요.

B: 잘 됐네요! 저는 매운 음식을 아주 좋아해요.

2) A: 순두부 어땠어요? 고춧가루를 많이 넣어서 좀 (매울, 매웠을) 거예요.

B: 하나도 안 맵고 맛있었어요. 정말 잘 먹었습니다.

3) A: 세영 씨가 아직 아직 안 왔어요?

B: 한 시간 전에 출발했으니까 금방 (올, 왔을) 거예요.

4) A: 세영 씨가 왔을까요?

   B: 열 시에 출발했으니까 한 시간 전쯤에 (올, 왔을) 거예요.

5) A: 어제 열 시쯤에 뭐 하고 있었어요?

   B: 아마 룸메이트하고 얘기하고 (있을 거예요, 있었을 거예요).

6) A: 내일 열 시쯤에 뭐 하고 (있을 거예요, 있었을 거예요)?

   B: 글쎄요. 아직 계획이 없어요.

Exercise 13. Underline the word in parentheses that best completes the sentence.

1) A: 이 커피 제가 (마실게요, 마실 거예요).

   B: 네, 그러세요.

2) A: 누가 책 좀 빌려 주세요.

   B: 내가 (빌려 줄게요, 빌려 줄 거예요, 빌려 줄래요).

3) A: 다음 학기에 수업을 일곱 과목 들으면 너무 힘들까요?

   B: 아마 (힘들게요, 힘들래요, 힘들 거예요).

4) A: 내일 세영씨가 파티에 올까요?

   B: 네, 아마 (올게요, 올 거예요, 올래요).

5) A: 내일 몇 시 비행기를 (탈게요, 탈래요, 탈 거예요)?

   B: 7시 비행기를 탈 거예요.

6) A: 같이 영화 봐요! 무슨 영화 (볼게요, 볼래요)?

   B: 아무거나 좋아요.

Exercise 14. Answer the question using -(으)ㄹ게(요).

1) A: 누가 여기를 청소할래요?

   B: 제가 _____.

2) A: 오늘 저녁에 저희 집에 오실래요?

   B: 네, 좋아요. 아홉 시쯤 _____.

3) A: 건강을 위해서 매일 1 시간씩 걸으세요.

   B: 네, 매일 _____.

4) A: (to daughter) 식탁 위 좀 닦아라.

   B: 네, 곧 _____.

5) A: 아직 샌드위치 안 만들었어요?

   B: 바빠서 그랬어요. 지금 곧 _____.

Exercise 15. Underline the appropriate answer in the parentheses to complete the conversation most naturally.

1) A: 내일 날씨가 (어떨까요, 어떨래요)?

   B: 내일은 따뜻할 거예요.

2) A: 겨울이 언제 (끝날까요, 끝날래요)? 빨리 봄이 오면 좋겠어요!

   B: 네, 저도 그래요.

3) A: 뭐 마실래요?

   B: 커피 (마실까요, 마실래요).

4) A: 동생이 벌써 (도착할까, 도착했을까, 도착할래)?

   B: 글쎄. 전화해 보자.

Exercise 16. Complete the dialogue using -겠습니다/-겠습니까 and one of the verbs from the box.

드리다	먹다	묻다	뵙다	오다	주문하다

1) (회사에서)

   고객 (client): 처음 _____. 김영우라고 합니다.

   나: 네, 반갑습니다.

2) (친구 집에서)

   나: 잘 _____!

   친구 엄마: 차린 건 없지만 많이 먹어요.

3) (식당에서)

   종업원 (server): _____?

   손님 (customer): 아직 한 사람이 안 왔어요. 조금 있다가 주문할게요.

4) (길에서)

A: 실례합니다. 말씀 좀 _____. 여기 근처에 지하
철 역이 어디 있습니까?

B: 저기 사거리에 있어요.

5) (비행기에서)

승객 여러분께 안내 말씀 _____.

6) (일기예보 weather forecast)

내일은 춥고 눈이 많이 _____.

Exercise 17. Choose the appropriate expression to complete the dialogues. Be sure to conjugate the given verb appropriately and use the same speech style as the person you are speaking with. Use each sentence ending only once.

-(으)ㄹ게요	-(으)ㄹ까요	-(으)ㄹ 거예요	-(으)ㄹ래요

1) A: 제가 음료수를 사 올게요. 누가 접시랑 컵을 가져 올래요?

B: 제가 _____. (가져가다)

A: 고마워요.

2) A: 자, 약 먹자.

B: 싫어! 안 _____. (먹다)

3) A: 내일 우리 몇 시에 _____? (만나다)

B: 세 시에 만나요.

4) A: 언니, 내일 뭐 _____. (하다)

B: 내일은 수업이 없어서 집에서 쉴 거야.

6.4 Negative Sentences

Exercise 18. Make the following sentences negative.

1) 나는 학생이에요. 그래서 바빠요. 숙제가 있어요. 시험도 있어요.

_____

2) 내 방은 커요. 그리고 조용해요. 나는 내 방이 좋아요.

_____

3) 나는 운동을 좋아해요. 그래서 매일 아침에 운동해요. 그리고 샤워해요.

_____

4) 주말에 학교에 가요. 그리고 친구들을 만나요. 같이 점심을 먹어요.

_____

5) 나는 일본어를 알아요. 중국어도 알아요.

_____

6) 밤에는 기숙사에 보통 있어요. 12시까지 공부해요. 그리고 자요.

_____

Exercise 19. Complete the sentence using 못.

1) 내일 바빠요. 그래서 영화를 _____. (보다)

2) 내 방은 안 깨끗해요. 그래서 내 방에서 파티를 _____. (하다)

3) 감기에 걸렸어요. 그래서 수업에 _____. (가다)

4) 닭고기 알레르기 있어요. 그래서 닭고기를 _____. (먹다)

5) 옆 방에서 시끄럽게 음악을 들어요. 그래서 _____. (공부하다)

Exercise 20. Change the underlined parts to make long-form negative statements.

1) 주말에는 학교에 안 가요.   _____

2) 오늘은 수업에 못 갔어요.   _____

3) 내일도 수업에 못 갈 거예요.   _____

4) 요즘은 바빠서 못 쉬어요.   _____

5) 그 친구하고는 더 이상 연락 안 해요.   _____

6) 그 동네는 안 조용해요.   _____

6.5 Conjugating Special Verb Classes

Exercise 21. Conjugate the verb for the suffix provided.

	Consonant suffix	어-type suffix	으-type suffix
	-고 있어요	-어요	-을 거예요
닦다			
치다			
주다			
뛰다			
재다			
공부하다			

Exercise 22. Label the underlined connectors and sentence-endings as A (어-type), B (으-type), or C (consonant-type).

(예) 어제 밤에는 방에서 책을 읽<u>고</u> 있었어요.
　　　　　　　　　　　　　　　　C

저는 이번 학기에 한국어 수업을 <u>들어요</u>. 한국어 수업에는 매일 <u>가요</u>. 수업이 많<u>으니까</u> 숙제도 아주 <u>많아요</u>. 그래서 주말에도 놀지 못 <u>하고</u> 공부를 해야 <u>돼요</u>. 지난 주말에도 못 <u>놀고</u> 계속 공부만 <u>하고</u> 있었어요. 이번 주말에는 시간이 좀 <u>있어서</u> 친구하고 쇼핑도 <u>하고</u> 영화도 볼 <u>거예요</u>. 재미있<u>을 거예요</u>!

Exercise 23. Conjugate the verbs using the given suffixes.

	Consonant suffix	으-type suffix	어-type suffix
	-지 않아요	-을까요	-어요
으-final: 크다			
ㄹ-final: 놀다			
Special-ㅎ: 그렇다			
Special-ㅂ: 덥다			
Special-ㄷ: 묻다			
Special-ㅅ: 짓다			
Special-르: 빠르다			

Exercise 24. Fill in the blanks with the special-class verb forms to fit with the given connectors and endings.

1) A: 지금 무슨 음악 _____요? (듣다)

    B: 한국 음악 _____고 있어요. (듣다)

2) A: 우리 같이 좀 _____까요? (걷다)

    B: 추워요. 나중에 _____요. (걷다)

3) A: 오늘 빵 _____거예요? (굽다)

    B: 아니요. *밀가루가 없어서 오늘 빵 못 _____요. (굽다) *밀가루: flour

4) A: 오늘 날씨가 정말 _____지요? (춥다)

    B: 아니요. 별로 안 _____요. (춥다)

5) A: 이 옷 색깔 _____요? (어떻다)

    B: 글쎄요. 입으면 너무 _____거예요. (빨갛다)

6) *백설공주는 머리가 _____고 얼굴이 _____요. (까맣다, 하얗다)

    *백설공주: Snow White

7) A: 어디 가세요?

    B: 약국에 약을 _____러 가요. (짓다)

8) A: 감기가 다 _____요? (낫다)

    B: 아니요. 아직 기침을 해요.

9) A: 샤워할 때 노래를 _____지요? (부르다)

    B: 네, 항상_____요. (부르다)

10) A: 오늘 더워서 아이들이 목이 _____거예요. 물을 준비하세요. (마르다)

    B: 네, 그럴게요.

Exercise 25. 르-verbs: Conjugate the verbs for the suffixes given.

	-고 있어요	-어요	-을 거예요	-습니다	-으세요	-네요
살다	살고 있어요					사네요
만들다		만들어요			만드세요	
달다			달 거예요	답니다		

Exercise 26. Special-ㄷ, regular ㄷ, and ㄹ: Fill in the blank with the given verb conjugated correctly.

1) 한국 음악을 _____까요?   (듣다)

2) 이 가방 좀 같이 _____까요?   (들다)

3) 모르니까 _____지 마세요.   (묻다)

4) 이 강아지는 _____지 않아요.   (물다)

5) 앞으로 매일 한 시간씩 _____거예요.   (걷다)

6) 내일 친구한테 전화를 _____거예요.   (걸다)

7) 일요일에는 도서관이 문을 _____요.   (닫다)

8) 케이크가 정말 _____요!   (달다)

Exercise 27. Special-르 and regular ㄹ-final verbs: Underline the correct conjugated forms.

1) 노래방에서 노래를 (불어요, 불러요).

2) 바람이 아주 많이 (불어요, 불러요).

3) 머리를 많이 (길었네요, 길렀네요).

4) 머리가 정말 (길어요, 길러요)!

5) 김밥을 많이 (말았어요, 말랐어요).

6) 동생이 아주 (말았어요, 말랐어요)!

Exercise 28. Conjugate the verbs in parentheses for the polite ordinary style.

어제는 11월 20일이었어요. 겨울이지만 날씨가 별로 안 _____ (춥다). 그래서 친구하고 같이 시내에 나가서 쇼핑도 하고 영화도 봤어요. 어젯밤에는 눈이 와서 온 세상이 _____ (하얗다). 추웠지만 기분이 좋아서 친구하고 계속 _____ (걷다). 그래서 감기에 걸렸어요. 오늘 아침에 일어났는데 목이 많이 _____ (붓다). 그래서 아침의 음악 수업 시간에 노래를 못 _____ (부르다). 그리고 지금은 기침도 나고 열도 많이 _____ (나다). 감기 때문에 오늘 오후에 병원에 갈 거예요. 병원이 학교에서 좀 _____ (멀다). 그래서 택시를 탈 거예요. 저녁에 약을 먹고 푹 잘 거예요. 약을 먹으면 감기가 다 _____ (낫다). 감기가 나으면 이번 주말에 친구하고 또 _____ (걷다). 그리고 _____ (놀다).

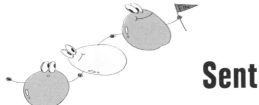

CHAPTER 7

Sentence Endings

You are now well versed in the kinds of verbs that Korean has, and you know much of what happens to those verbs. In chapter 6, you learned how verbs conjugate and take suffixes for tense, aspect and negation in the ordinary speech style (intimate and polite). In this chapter we continue the verbs saga, since verbs come last, in talking about how to end a sentence.

We have been using the term "suffix" to refer to the parts that attach to verb roots. We also used the term "ending" when we were looking at tense and aspect. Some endings are simple suffixes (e.g., -겠 -keyss), but others are strings of suffixes (e.g., -었었 -essess or -었을 -essul). Yet others you will encounter are even longer, sometimes having connector suffixes like -어 -e or -지 -ci AND a helping verb in them (e.g., -어 가다 -e kata *progressing toward*, -지 않다 -ci anhta *not*). Some endings might even contain a dependent noun AND a helping verb (e.g., -(으)ㄴ 적 있다 -(u)n cek issta *have -ed*). You can think of it this way: things that attach to a verb can be considered suffixes and those that come attached to the verb to end a sentence are endings, and yes, that means there is no hard and fast distinction between the two terms. Suffixes like -었 -ess -겠 -keyss, -었었 -essess, and -었을 -essul cannot end a sentence by themselves, but we will still refer to them as **endings**. If you want to make a distinction between the endings that can and cannot end a sentence, you can call them **final** and **pre-final endings**.

Some final endings are speech style endings, comparable to the ordinary speech style endings you learned in chapter 6. In 7.1, you will learn more speech style endings closely tied to age and social hierarchy.

Other final endings are uniquely Korean, some matched only by **intonation patterns** (how the pitch of your voice goes up and down) in English. That is what section 7.2 is about: endings that don't always have a clear translation in English. Among the concepts communicated in these endings are degrees of surprise, added explanation or reasoning, that some information is assumed, and that one has seen or experienced something first-hand. These endings carry a heavy cognitive and emotional as well as informational load in Korean. They are responsible for expressing speakers' attitudes, including surprise, accusation, and assertion.

In 7.3, we will explore Korean **helping verbs** that are comparable to English **modal** expressions (e.g., *will, could, must*, etc.), followed by more Korean helping verbs that express idiomatic or fixed expressions in English (e.g. *have -ed, used to, end up -ing*, etc.)

Now, let's try out the endings rollercoaster!

7.1 Speech Style Endings

How formal the speech situation is, how familiar you are with the person you are speaking with, how old you are, and how old the person you are talking to all matter greatly in Korean—not just in a general, common sensical, one-needs-to-respect-one's-elders way, but in a way that is rigidly dictated by the grammar of the language. The conjugation patterns you have seen so far have been based on the ordinary speech style that Korean grammarians call "해(요)"체 "hay(yo)"chey. We purposefully introduced this style first because it can be used in most situations by most people and because its conjugation patterns are the most complex. (The hardest part is over!) Once you know how to conjugate verbs for this style, you have the basis for conjugating anything. The formal and plain styles that you will learn in this section are also quite common. We will present them first and then briefly touch upon other speech styles that you may encounter.

If you remember, the ordinary style uses the -어(요) -e(yo) ending for questions and commands as well as statements and sometimes even for suggestions/proposals. For every style discussed below, however, there can be additional **sentence types** with differing sentence endings:

- 평서형 phyengsehyeng is a statement (indicative sentence)
- 의문형 uymwunhyeng is a question (interrogative sentence)
- 명령형 myenglyenghyeng is a command (imperative sentence)
- 청유형 chengyuhyeng is a suggestion, proposal, or invitation (propositive sentence)
- 약속형 yaksokhyeng is a promise (promissory sentence)
- 의도형 uytohyeng is a desire or intention (intentional sentence)
- 감탄형 kamthanhyeng is an interjection (exclamatory sentence)
- 허락형 helakhyeng is permission (permissive sentence)
- 경계형 kyengkyehyeng is a warning (adminotory sentence)

We will focus on the first four types, as they are the most widely used and useful types. Let's start now with the formal style.

7.1.1 FORMAL speech style

Contrasted with the ordinary style is the formal style, 격식체 kyeksikchey. (Traditional Korean grammar calls it "하십시오" or "합쇼" 체 "hasipsio" or "hapsyo" chey, using the style's command ending.) It is adopted when the speakers are aware of making conspicuous the social structure they are part of. We will distinguish two usages of this style: institutional usage and humble usage.

(1) INSTITUTIONAL usage

Children start to enjoy membership in a community greater than their family when they enter school. There, they begin institutional ways of behaving, and this includes language; they begin to read and hear the formal speech style. For Koreans, schooling takes up more than half of their waking life until they graduate college, so it makes sense that they use the ordinary -어(요) -e(yo) style mixed with the formal style.

With this style, you can go beyond your close family and out into formal territory in the larger society. This is also a style that is used toward customers and clients, as well as those who are older or "above" you in work situations. The formal style of speech is more rigorously adopted in the military and in companies because of the inherent hierarchical structure of these organizations. Thus, male college students' speech style changes drastically by the time they have finished their obligatory military service. Some traditional families, especially those with extended family members, also insist on teaching their young this style as a way to recognize the household as a social institution. Thus, we call this the **institutional usage** (조직사회 어법 cociksahoy epep) of the formal style.

Formal institutions tend to inhibit displays of personal emotion. Understandably, the instiotional speech style has no exclamatory ending and can not be used with attitude suffixes like -지(요) -ci(yo), -네(요) -ney(yo), or -군(요) -kwun(yo).

Here are the nuts and bolts of how the endings of this style work:

Sentence Type	Sentence Ending	Example
For **statements** and **questions** • Consonant (C)-final roots	Use 습니다	읽습니다 *(Someone) reads*
	and 습니까	읽습니까? *Does (someone) read?*
• Vowel (V)-final roots	Use ㅂ니다	합니다 *(Someone) does*
	and ㅂ니까	합니까? *Does (someone) do it?*
• **Past** and **future tenses**	Use the past and future tense verb stems, and add appropriate endings	했습니다/했습니까? *(Someone) did it/* *Did (someone) do it?* 할 겁니다/ 할 것입니다. *(Someone) will do it* 할 겁니까?/할 것입니까? *Will (someone) do it?*
For **suggestions** • With peers	Use (으)ㅂ시다	합시다 *Let's do*
• With elders or people of a higher status	Use (으)십시다	읽으십시다 *Shall we read?*
For **commands**	Use (으)십시오	가십시오 *Please go* 앉으십시오 *Please have a seat*

Sentence Type	Sentence Ending	Example
If the verb root is ㄹ-**final**	Drop ㄹ when meeting (스)ㅂ니다, (스)ㅂ니까, and (으)십시오	살다 *to live:* 삽니다 *(Someone) lives* 삽니까 *Does (someone) live?* 사십시오 *Please live*

Here is a table demonstrating formal conjugation, going from the regular consonant-final verb 읽다 ilkta *to read*, to special class verbs, then regular and other vowel-final verbs:

Verbs / Suffixes	Statement (Present) -습니다/ㅂ니다 -supnita/pnita	Statement (Past) -습니다 -supnita	Statement (Future) -(으)ㄹ 겁니다 -(u)l kepnita
읽다 ilkta *to read*	읽습니다 ilksupnita	읽었습니다 ilkesssupnita	읽을 겁니다 ilkul kepnita
그렇다 kulehta *to be so*	그렇습니다 kulehsupnita	그랬습니다 kulaysssupnita	그럴 겁니다 kulel kepnita
돕다 topta *to help*	돕습니다 topsupnita	도왔습니다 towasssupnita	도울 겁니다 towul kepnita
듣다 tutta *to listen to*	듣습니다 tutsupnita	들었습니다 tulesssupnita	들을 겁니다 tulul kepnita
긋다 kusta *to draw a line*	긋습니다 kussupnita	그었습니다 kuesssupnita	그을 겁니다 kuul kepnita
밀다 milta *to push*	밉니다 mipnita	밀었습니다 milesssupnita	밀 겁니다 mil kepnita
가다 kata *to go*	갑니다 kapnita	갔습니다 kasssupnita	갈 겁니다 kal kepnita
크다 khuta *to be big*	큽니다 khupnita	컸습니다 khesssupnita	클 겁니다 khul kepnita
하다 hata *to do*	합니다 hapnita	했습니다 haysssupnita	할 겁니다 hal kepnita
부르다 pwuluta *to sing*	부릅니다 pwulupnita	불렀습니다 pwullesssupnita	부를 겁니다 pwulul kepnita

Verbs \ Suffixes	Questions -습니까/ㅂ니까? -supnikka/pnikka	Suggestion -(으)ㅂ시다 -(u)psita	-(으)십시다 -(u)sipsita	Command -(으)십시오 -(u)sipsio
읽다 ilkta *to read*	읽습니까? ilksupnikka?	읽읍시다 ilkupsita	읽으십시다 ilkusipsita	읽으십시오 ilkusipsio
그렇다 kulehta *to be so*	그렇습니까? kulehsupnikka?	--	--	--
돕다 topta *to help*	돕습니까? topsupnikka?	도웁시다 towupsita	도우십시다 towusipsita	도우십시오 towusipsio
듣다 tutta *to listen to*	듣습니까? tutsupnikka?	들읍시다 tulupsita	들으십시다 tulusipsita	들으십시오 tulusipsio
긋다 kusta *to draw a line*	긋습니까? kussupnikka?	그읍시다 kuupsita	그으십시다 kuusipsita	그으십시오 kuusipsio
밀다 milta *to push*	밉니까? mipnikka?	밉시다 mipsita	미십시다 misipsita	미십시오 misipsio
가다 kata *to go*	갑니까? kapnikka?	갑시다 kapsita	가십시다 kasipsita	가십시오 kasipsio
크다 khuta *to be big*	큽니까? khupnikka?	--	--	--
하다 hata *to do*	합니까? hapnikka?	합시다 hapsita	하십시다 hasipsita	하십시오 hasipsio
부르다 pwuluta *to sing*	부릅니까? pwulupnikka?	부릅시다 pwulupsita	부르십시다 pwulusipsita	부르십시오 pwulusipsio

<u>A word of caution</u>: While most other endings and suffixes in Korean strive to keep an alternation of consonant and vowel (CVCV), the -(스)ㅂ니다 -(s)pnita and -(스)ㅂ니까 -(s)pnikka pair is the opposite. The -ㅂ니다/까 -pnita/kka ending attaches to vowel-final and ㄹ-final verbs, and the -습니다/까 -supnita/kka ending attaches to consonant-final verbs, even though that puts two consonants in a row. (-읍니다 -upnita and -읍니까 -upnikka are outdated spellings of -습니다 -supnita and -습니까 -supnikka from before the 1980s, so older folks may still use them.)

Here are the typical situations where the institutional style may be used:

<1> At an organization with a rigid hierarchy

Company meetings, interactions with higher-ranked military officers, and traditional family situations can call for the institutional style. Note that the higher-ranking military officer and the grandmother in the examples below use a different speech style:

부장:
pwucang:
section chief: 질문 **있습니까?**
cilmwun isssupnikka?
Do you have any questions?

직원:
cikwen:
employee: 아니요. **없습니다.**
aniyo. epssupnita.
No, I don't.

부장:
pwucang:
section chief: 그럼 이것으로 회의를 **마치겠습니다.**
kulem ikesulo hoyuylul machikeyssssupnita.
Then, the meeting is adjourned with this.

병장:
pyengcang:
sergeant: 질문 있나?
cilmwun issna?
Do you have any questions?

일병:
ilpyeng:
private: 아닙니다! **없습니다.**
anipnita! epssupnita.
No, sir!

손주 며느리:
soncwu myenuli:
granddaughter-in-law: 안녕히 **주무셨습니까?**
annyenghi cwumwusyesssupnikka?
Did you sleep well?

시할머니:
sihalmeni:
grandmother-in-law: 그래. 너도 잘 잤니?
kulay. neto cal cassni?
Yes. Did you sleep well, too?

<2> When addressing strangers

When addressing strangers, certain expressions are frequently said in the formal style because they may sound more respectful when you do not know the person very well or when you have a reason to maintain formality:

처음 뵙겠**습니다.**
cheum poypkeyssssupnita.
Nice to meet you (It's my first time to see you).

잘 부탁**합니다.**
cal pwuthakhapnita.
I am obliged to you (Please take good care of me).

대단히 감사**합니다**/정말 고맙**습니다.**
taytanhi kamsahapnita/cengmal komapsupnita.
I/we greatly appreciate it/Thank you so much.

실례**합니다.**
sillyeyhapnita
Forgive me for intruding/forgetting my manners.

죄송**합니다**/미안**합니다.**
coysonghapnita/mianhapnita.
I am truly sorry/I'm sorry.

<3> Addressing the general public

News broadcasters and big department stores or hotel receptionists also use this style to emphasize that they are exalting the status of the TV viewers and customers:

내일은 날씨가 흐리고 춥겠**습니다.**
nayilun nalssika huliko chwupkeyssssupnita.
We project that it will be cloudy and cold tomorrow. (newscasting)

어서 오십시오. 친절히 도와드리겠**습니다.**
ese osipsio. chincelhi towatulikeyssssupnita.
Welcome/come in. We will be happy to assist you. (help counter)

새해 복 많이 받으**십시오.**
sayhay pok manhi patusipsio.
Happy New Year! (greeting card)

이곳에 주차하지 마**십시오.**
ikosey cwuchahaci masipsio.
Do not park here. (public sign)

오늘도 찾아주셔서 대단히 감사**합니다**.
onulto chacacwusyese taytanhi kamsahapnita.
We greatly appreciate your business. (department store)

다음 정류장은 이대앞**입니다**.
taum cenglyucangun itayaphipnita.
The next stop is Ewha University. (bus announcement)

내리실 문은 오른 쪽**입니다**.
naylisil mwunun olun ccokipnita.
The door to get off is on the right. (subway announcement)

(2) HUMBLE usage

The formal style 격식체 kyeksikchey was historically used by children, house servants, slaves, and untouchables (when they existed), but ever since the caste system was abolished, its usage bifurcated. Nowadays, it is used by lower-rung workers in a hierarchy, such as in a company, the military, or in other formal organizations, as you already know, when they assume a humble stance. The style is also (at one time, *uniquely*) adopted in children's stories in an effort to teach humility, although children's storybooks published since the '90s have continually moved towards polite ordinary "해요"체 "hayyo"chey narration. When it is used by adults in spoken Korean, the formal style gives a sense of a RIGID, hierarchical, institutional structure, expressing UPWARD distance and formality. When the same style is used in writing in children's books or newspaper and magazine advertisements, it gives the reader a sense of the GENTLE humility of the speaker—so we term it the **humble usage** (공손어법 kongson epep). Here are some examples from children's stories:

옛날 옛날 한 마을에 흥부라는 착한 동생과 놀부라는 욕심쟁이 형이 살았**습니다**.
yeysnal yeysnal han mauley hungpwulanun chakhan tongsayngkwa nolpwulanun yoksimcayngi hyengi salasssupnita.
A long, long time ago, a good younger brother, Heungbu, and a greedy older brother, Nolbu, lived in a village.

견우와 직녀가 일 년에 한번 만나 헤어질 때마다 흘리는 눈물이 7월 7석 날 내리는 큰비라고 **합니다**.
kyenwuwa ciknyeka il nyeney hanpen manna heyecil ttaymata hullinun nwunmwuli 7wel 7sek nal naylinun khunpilako hapnita.
The big rain falling on July 7th is said to be the tears Gyeonwoo and Jiknyeo shed every year they meet and part.

세종대왕은 조선왕조의 네 번째 왕으로 한글을 만드셨**습니다**.
seycongtaywangun cosenwangcouy ney penccay wangulo hankulul mantusyesssupnita.
King Sejong the Great, the fourth King of the Joseon Dynasty, created the Korean alphabet.

7.1.2 PLAIN speech style

The plain speech style, 일반체 ilpanchey, is one without formality or politeness suffixes. It is used toward children, and historically, toward those in lower social status or castes. It is also used in certain writings.

(1) Babysitter's usage

One usage of the plain style has different endings for questions, commands, and suggestions that sound very endearing (or be-littling) toward the listener because they are mainly used with young children. So, we termed it 유모 어법 ywumo epep, the baby-sitter's usage. (Traditional Korean grammar calls it "해라"체 "hayla"chey, using the style's command ending.)

This style is also used toward anyone who is the same age or younger whom you have known since childhood, such as a younger sibling or a grade school classmate. "Once a child, always a child" seems to be the case in this usage. It is NOT used by children toward OLDER children, or by adults toward their OLDER siblings, however.

Your grandparents can use this style to speak to your parents and to you, and your parents can use it to address you no matter how old you are; that is, it is used DOWN-WARDLY, toward someone who was known as a child when the speaker was the same age or older.

Parents use this style toward their friend's children and their children's friends when their children are still minors. Once these children grow to be adults, however, elders tend to switch to the ordinary -어 -e style to show respect for the adulthood of the younger person, especially when the child's adult friends or acquaintances are present. How old a person has to be to be considered an adult depends on the (grand)parents' judgment. If a grown-up child's friends are as close as family members, they may still be addressed with the plain style; if the (grand)children or their friends happen to be the heads of their respective households, even at a young age (having married in their late teens or being responsible for the livelihood of their family), they might be addressed with intimate or polite ordinary style, but probably NOT with the plain style.

The plain style is often thought of now as a "child-directed" speech style, but you can see it used in addressing adults of the lower castes in historical dramas.

Here are the nuts and bolts of how the endings of this style work:

Sentence Type	Sentence Ending	Example
For **statements** and **announcements**		
• Active verbs (C-final roots)	Use 는다	읽는다 (Someone) *reads*
• Active verbs (V-final roots)	Use ㄴ다	생각한다 (Someone) *thinks*
• Descriptive verbs	Use 다	예쁘다 (Someone) *is pretty*

For **questions**		
• To sound more intimate	Use 니	자니? *Are you asleep?*
• To sound tomboy ish	Use 냐	작냐? *Is it small?*
• For a more serious and old-sounding effect		
॰ Active verbs	Use 느냐	자느냐? *Are you asleep?*
॰ Descriptive verbs	Use (으)냐	작으냐? 크냐? *Is it small? Is it big?*
For **suggestions**	Use 자 (Active verbs only)	최선을 다하자! *Let's do our best!*
For **commands**		
• Positive	Use 어라 (Active verbs only)	조용히 해라! *Be quiet!*
• Negative	Use 지 마라 (or 지 말아라)	단념하지 마라/말아라! *Don't give up!*
For **exclamation**	Use 어라 (Descriptive verbs only)	예뻐라! *So pretty!*
For the **past tense**	Use the past tense suffix 었 plus endings	훌륭했다. *It was great.* 세탁했니? *Did you do the laundry?*
For the **future tense**	Use the future tense verb stem and add appropriate endings	갈 거냐? *Are they going to go?* 영특할 것이다 *She's probably brilliant*
If the verb root is ㄹ-final	Drop ㄹ when meeting ㄴ다, 는다, 니, (느)냐, and (으)냐	Active verbs: 살다 *to live* 산다, 사니?, 사냐? Descriptive verbs: 달다 *to be sweet* 다니?, 다냐?

Here is a table demonstrating plain conjugation, going from the regular consonant-final verb 읽다 ilkta *to read*, to special class verbs, and then other vowel-final verbs. Take note of the conjugation difference between active and descriptive verbs:

Verbs	Suffixes	Statement (Present) -ㄴ다/는다/다 -nta/nunta/ta	Statement (Past) -었다 -essta	Statement (Future) -(으)ㄹ 거다 -(u)l keta
읽다 ilkta *to read*		읽는다 ilknunta	읽었다 ilkessta	읽을 거다 ilkul keta
그렇다 kulehta *to be so*		그렇다 kulehta	그랬다 kulayssta	그럴 거다 kulel keta
돕다 topta *to help*		돕는다 topnunta	도왔다 towassta	도울 거다 towul keta
춥다 chwupta *to be cold*		춥다 chwupta	추웠다 chwuwessta	추울 거다 chwuwul keta
듣다 tutta *to listen to*		듣는다 tutnunta	들었다 tulessta	들을 거다 tulul keta
긋다 kusta *to draw a line*		긋는다 kusnunta	그었다 kuessta	그을 거다 kuul keta
달다 talta *to hang*		단다 tanta	달았다 talassta	달 거다 tal keta
달다 talta *to be sweet*		달다 talta	달았다 talassta	달 거다 tal keta
크다 khuta *to be big*		크다 khuta	컸다 khessta	클 거다 khul keta
일하다 ilhata *to work*		일한다 ilhanta	일했다 ilhayssta	일할 거다 ilhal keta
심하다 simhata *to be severe*		심하다 simhata	심했다 simhayssta	심할 거다 simhal keta
부르다 pwuluta *to sing*		부른다 pwulunta	불렀다 pwullessta	부를 거다 pwulul keta

	Question			Suggestion	Command
Suffixes **Verbs**	-니? -ni?	-냐? -nya?	-느냐/(으)냐? -nunya/(u)nya?	-자 -ca	-어라 -ela
읽다 ilkta *to read*	읽니? ilkni?	읽냐? ilknya?	읽느냐? ilknunya?	읽자 ilkca	읽어라 ilkela
그렇다 kulehta *to be so*	그러니? kuleni?	그러냐? kulenya?	그러냐? kulenya?	--	--
돕다 topta *to help*	돕니? topni?	돕냐? topnya?	돕느냐? topnunya?	돕다 topta	도와라 towala
춥다 chwupta *to be cold*	춥니? chwupni?	춥냐? chwupnya?	추우냐? chwuwunya?	--	--
듣다 tutta *to listen to*	듣니? tutni?	듣냐? tutnya?	듣느냐? tutnunya?	듣자 tutca	들어라 tulela
긋다 kusta *to draw a line*	긋니? kusni?	긋냐? kusnya?	긋느냐? kusnunya?	긋자 kusca	그어라 kuela
달다 talta *to hang*	다니? tani?	다냐? tanya?	다느냐? tanunya?	달자 talca	달아라 talala
달다 talta *to be sweet*	다니? tani?	다냐? tanya?	다냐? tanya?	--	--
크다 khuta *to be big*	크니? khuni?	크냐? khunya?	크냐? khunya?	--	--
일하다 ilhata *to work*	일하니? ilhani?	일하냐? ilhanya?	일하느냐? ilhanunya?	일하자 ilhaca	일해라 ilhayla
심하다 simhata *to be severe*	심하니? simhani?	심하냐? simhanya?	심하냐? simhanunya?	--	--
부르다 pwuluta *to sing*	부르니? pwuluni?	부르냐? pwulunya?	부르느냐? pwulununya?	부르자 pwuluca	불러라 pwullela

Descriptive verbs in -다 -ta plain style are usually in exclamations or ASSERTIONS, typically with a high-then-trailing intonation at the end:

와! 예쁘다!
wa! yeypputa!
Wow! How pretty!

와! 정말 **맛있다**!
wa cengmal masissta.
Wow! This is delicious!

For active verbs, the plain style statement ending is mainly reserved for announcement or slight warning, so in actual usage, the intimate ordinary style (ending in -어 -e) is regularly mixed with the plain style for regular statements. Also note that in the example below the younger sibling cannot use the babyitter endings to his older brother (except the command ending 줘라 cwela when the beneficiary is the younger brother himself).

형:
hyeng:
Older brother:

밥 먹었니?
pap mekessni?
Have you eaten?

동생:
tongsayng:
Younger brother:

아니, 아직. 형은 밥 먹었**어**?
ani, acik. hyengun pap mekesse?
No, not yet. Have you eaten, yet? (addressing the older brother)

~~아니, 아직. 형은 밥 **먹었니**?~~
ani, acik. hyengun pap mekessni?

형:
hyeng:

나도 아직 안 먹었**어**.
nato acik an mekesse.
Me, neither.

동생:
tongsayng:

그래? 그럼 저기 있는 피자 먹**어**.
kulay? kulem ceki issnun phica meke.
Is that right? Then, eat the pizza over there. (addressing the older brother)

~~그래? 그럼 저거 있는 피자 **먹어라**~~.
kulay? kulem ceki issnun phica mekela.

형:
hyeng:

그래. **먹는다**!
kulay. meknunta!
OK. I'm going to eat it~!

동생:
tongsayng:

나도 한 쪽만 **줘**.
nato han ccokman cwe.
Give me one piece, too. (addressing the older brother)

나도 한 쪽만 **줘라**.
nato han ccokman cwela.
Give me one piece, too. (addressing the older brother)

형:
hyeng:

그래, 이거 **먹어라**.
kulay, ike mekela.
OK. Take this.

Finally, when you see the -어라 -ela suffix at the end of DESCRIPTIVE verbs (especially after the idiomatic -기도 하다 -kito hata, which just adds emphasis), know that it is used for exclamation and NOT for command:

심하기도 해라!	춥기도 해라!	크기도 해라!	배불러라!
simhakito hayla!	chwupkito hayla!	khekito hayla!	paypwullela!
That's quite extreme!	*So cold!*	*How huge!*	*I'm so full!*

(2) Writer's usage

The plain speech style is also the style used in all sorts of writing that addresses a GENERAL audience. If you are writing a letter or email or are texting personal messages, you may choose to use some other speech style that fits your situation. It could be the polite or intimate ordinary style or the formal/humble style. But if you are writing a newspaper article or an editorial column, a magazine piece, or fiction or non-fiction book, you will likely follow this writer's usage of the plain style because you don't know who your readers are going to be and what their social rank will be. (Their social ranks would likely be diverse in any case, making it impossible to match the speech style for every reader.) So we name this 서면 어법 semyen epep, the **writer's usage**. (Traditional Korean grammar calls it "하라"체 "hala"chey, using the style's command ending.)

The writer's usage has the same endings as the babysitter's for statements and suggestions, except that the full form 것이다 kesita is usually used in the future ending. For questions, instead of -니 -ni or -냐 -nya, a more rhetorical question suffix is used, namely, -나 -na or -는가 -nunka (for active verbs) and -(으)ㄴ가 -(u)nka (for descriptive verbs), although -나 -na is frequently used for descriptive verbs nowadays. For the past tense, -는가 -nunka is used for both active and descriptive verbs. Of the two options for active verbs, the suffix -나 -na sounds a little friendlier and more youthful than -는가 -nunka, which reads with a more stern or distancing feel. For commands, -(으)라 -(u)la, instead of -어라 -ela, is used for this style, although in writings for and by young people, the -어라 -ela suffix is prevalent.

Here is a summary of the forms used in the writer's usage:

Verbs \ Suffixes	Statement (Present) -ㄴ다/는다/다 -nta/nunta/ta	Statement (Past) -었다 -essta	Statement (Future) -(으)ㄹ 것이다 -(u)l kesita
읽다 ilkta *to read*	읽는다 ilknunta	읽었다 ilkessta	읽을 것이다 ilkul kesita
그렇다 kulehta *to be so*	그렇다 kulehta	그랬다 kulayssta	그럴 것이다 kulel kesita
돕다 topta *to help*	돕는다 topnunta	도왔다 towassta	도울 것이다 towul kesita
춥다 chwupta *to be cold*	춥다 chwupta	추웠다 chwuwessta	추울 것이다 chwuwul kesita
듣다 tutta *to listen to*	듣는다 tutnunta	들었다 tulessta	들을 것이다 tulul kesita
긋다 kusta *to draw a line*	긋는다 kusnunta	그었다 kuessta	그을 것이다 kuul kesita
달다 talta *to hang*	단다 tanta	달았다 talassta	달 것이다 tal kesita
달다 talta *to be sweet*	달다 talta	달았다 talassta	달 것이다 tal kesita
크다 khuta *to be big*	크다 khuta	컸다 khessta	클 것이다 khul kesita
일하다 ilhata *to work*	일한다 ilhanta	일했다 ilhayssta	일할 것이다 ilhal kesita
심하다 simhata *to be severe*	심하다 simhata	심했다 simhayssta	심할 것이다 simhal kesita
부르다 pwuluta *to sing*	부른다 pwulunta	불렀다 pwullessta	부를 것이다 pwulul kesita

		Question		Suggestion	Command
Verbs	**Suffixes**	-는가/(으)ㄴ가? -nunka/(u)nka?	-나? -na?	-자 -ca	-(으)라 -(u)la
읽다 ilkta *to read*		읽는가? ilknunka?	읽나? ilkna?	읽자 ilkca	읽으라 ilkula
그렇다 kulehta *to be so*		그런가? kulenka?	그렇나? kulehna?	--	--
돕다 topta *to help*		돕는가? topnunka?	돕나? topna?	돕자 topca	도우라 towula
춥다 chwupta *to be cold*		추운가? chwuwunka?	춥나? chwupna?	--	--
듣다 tutta *to listen to*		듣는가? tutnunka?	듣나? tutna?	듣자 tutca	들으라 tulula
긋다 kusta *to draw a line*		긋는가? kusnunka?	긋나? kusna?	긋자 kusca	그으라 kuula
달다 talta *to hang*		다는가? tanunka?	다나? tana?	달자 talca	달라 talla
달다 talta *to be sweet*		단가? tanka?	다나? tana?	--	--
크다 khuta *to be big*		큰가? khunka?	크나 khuna?	--	--
일하다 ilhata *to work*		일하는가? ilhanunka?	일하나? ilhana?	일하자 ilhaca	일하라 ilhala
심하다 simhata *to be severe*		심한가? simhanka?	심하나? simhana?	--	--
부르다 pwuluta *to sing*		부르는가? pwulununka?	부르나? pwuluna?	부르자 pwuluca	부르라 pwulula

Conjugation is thus very similar to the babysitter's usage, but do be careful with the ㄹ-final verbs:

- If the verb root is ㄹ-final, remember to drop ㄹ when meeting -는가 -nunka, -(으)ㄴ가 -(u)nka, and -나 -na in addition to the other endings shared with babysitter's usage:

  e.g. 살다 salta *to live*: 사는가? sanunka?, 사나? sana?

  달다 talta *to be sweet*: 단가? tanka?

Here are some example sentences:

보라! 동해에 떠오르는 찬란한 태양을!
pola! tonghayey tteolunun chanlanhan thayyangul!
Behold, the splendid sun that is rising in the Eastern Sea!

간다 간다 나는 간다 사랑 찾아 나는 간다 산을 넘고 강을 건너 너를 향해 달려간다.
kanta kanta nanun kanta salang chaca nanun kanta sanul nemko kangul kenne nelul hyanghay tallyekanta.
I am going, I am going. Looking for love, I am going. Over the mountain, crossing the river, to you I am running.

버락 오바마 미국 대통령이 총기 규제를 촉구했다고 AFP 통신이 28일 보도했다.
pelak opama mikwuk taythonglyengi chongki kyuceylul chokkwuhaysstako AFP thongsini 28il potohayssta.
Agence France-Presse reported on the 28th that US President Barack Obama urged gun control.

누가 4 월을 잔인한 달이라 했는가?
nwuka 4 welul caninhan talila hayssnunka?
Who was it that called April a cruel month?

달마는 어디로 갔나?
talmanun etilo kassna?
Where has Dharma gone?

누구를 위해 좋은 울리나?
nwukwulul wihay congun wullina?
For whom does the bell toll?

7.1.3 MIDDLE AGE speech style

There is another speech style whose usage in the past was based on social classes but has now transformed to be more age-dependent. Korean grammarians call this style "하오"체 "hao"chey, referring to the command ending. You can only start using these forms once you become old enough. How old is old enough? To use "하오"체 "hao" chey (as established by Korean grammarians) or "하우"체 "hawu" chey (as is more often used in modern Korean), you should probably be past middle age and have a grown child or two, so we term it 중년체 cwungnyen chey "middle age speech style." People over 45 or 50 start using this style to speak to others of similar age to express age-based respect, recognizing some intimacy, yet socially positioning themselves in a little more formal place as adults or showing respect for each other than if they used the polite ordinary style. This might be because the polite ordinary style signals social distance, rather than age-based respect, and can be used toward younger strangers.

Older married couples can address each other with this style. Married daughters may use this style with their mothers (하우 hawu *do*), but will more often stick to the polite ordinary style with their fathers (해요 hayyo *do*). Married sons may use the polite ordinary style with their mothers (해요 hayyo *do*) and mix the polite ordinary and the institutional formal style with their fathers (해요 hayyo *do* ~ 하십시오 hasipsio *do*). Daughters' speech tends to emphasize their equal adult status with their mothers while showing respect towards them, while sons' speech tends to emphasize the hierarchical structure they are in with respect to their fathers. With the opposite-sex parents, they tend to use the more general ordinary style (해요 hayyo *do*). Depending on the family, 말 mal may be substituted with the honorific version 말씀 malssum:

딸:	엄마, 내 말 좀 들어 **보우**.
ttal:	emma, nay mal com tulepowu.
Daughter:	*Mom, can I say something?* Literally, *listen to my words.*

아들:	아버지, 제 말 좀 들어 **보십시오**.
atul:	apeci, cey mal com tuleposipsio.
Son:	*Father, can I say something?* Literally, *listen to my words.*

딸:	아빠, 제 말 좀 들어 **보세요**.
ttal:	appa, cey mal com tuleposeyyo.
Daughter:	*Dad, can I say something?* Literally, *listen to my words.*

아들:	엄마, 제 말 좀 들어 **보세요**.
atul:	emma, cey mal com tuleposeyyo.
Son:	*Mom, can I say something?* Literally, *listen to my words.*

Since the middle age speech style is used by older adults, the honorific suffix -(으)시 -(u)si is often used (to honor the subject) along with the ending, and contraction of the two (e.g., 하시오 hasio → 하쇼 hasyo or 하슈 hasyu) makes the style more casual. Men tend to stick to the more formal sounding vowel 오 o (e.g. 하시오 hasio or 하쇼 hasyo) while women tend to use 우 wu, which has the effect of bringing the listener and speaker closer together (e.g. 하시우 hasiwu or 하슈 hasyu).

어디 **가슈**?
eti kasyu?
Where are you going/
You going somewhere?

거, 연락 좀 자주 **하쇼**.
ke, yenlak com cacwu hasyo.
(You) keep in touch more often, eh?
(Literally, *contact me often.*)

The 오 o vowel, being more conservative and archaic-sounding, is the version that appears in written warnings or in dry, dramatic, and masculine-sounding poetry (with no contraction of the honorific suffix, if used):

이 곳에 쓰레기를 버리지 **마시오**.
i kosey ssuleykilul pelici masio.
No dumping on these premises.

내 마음은 호수요. 그대 노 저어 **오오**.
nay maumun hoswuyo. kutay no cee oo.
My heart is a lake; come to me, rowing on it.

Some native speakers feel that this style is dialectal or is a workers' style adopted by low-middle class speakers, perhaps because they feel as though, in formal and high-class situations, the formal style would be adopted. If we are considering older speakers only, you can think the formal style to be applied in strictly hierarchical situations (toward the company boss), while the middle age speech style is somewhere between formal and casual situations (toward acquaintances who are similarly older). The polite ordinary style will be used in more routine situations by older speakers (toward close neighbors you see everyday), and the intimate ordinary style will be used in familial situations (toward the children in the family or childhood friends).

A summary of this style can be found at the end of the chapter alongside the other remaining styles.

7.1.4 MOTHER-IN-LAW'S speech style

This style is basically an "I-respect-you-as-an-adult-in-this-formal-relationship-although-you-are-below-me" style, so we name it 장모체 cangmo chey, the mother-in-law's speech style, as a mnemonic device. (Traditional Korean grammar calls it "하게" 체 "hakey" chey, using the style's command ending.) This style is used by elders to address those who are on a lower rung of the social hierarchy due to age or rank. There are three typical formalistic situations in which you might hear this style of speech used: mothers-in-law 장모님 cangmonim and fathers-in law 장인 어른 cangin elun toward their sons-in-law 사위 sawi; professors 교수님 kyoswunim toward their (especially married or older) graduate students 대학원생 tayhakwensayng; and older company owners 사장님 sacangnim and section/department or whatever group chiefs (e.g. 부장님 pwucangnim *head of department*, 과장님 kwacangnim *section chief*, 실장님 silcangnim *office chief*, 팀장님 thimcangnim *team leader*, etc.) toward their young-adult employees. Peer employees normally mix the ordinary speech style "해요"체 "hayyo"chey and the formal style—institutional usage "하십시오"체 "hasipsio"chey.

You can think of the formal style 하십시오 hasipsio as being on the opposite end of the formality plane from this one. Here is an illustration of how the mother-in-law's speech style might be used in context:

우리랑 같이 **가세**.
wulilang kathi kasey.
Why don't you go with us/you go with us. (said by parents-in-law)

네. 그러겠**습니다**.
ney. kulekeysssupnita.
Yes, I will. (said by son-in-law)

자네, 오늘은 일찍 퇴근**하게**.
caney, onulun ilccik thoykunhakey.
You, go home early today. (said by the head of the department)

네. 그러겠**습니다**.
ney. kulekeysssupnita.
Yes, I will. (said by a younger, lower-rung employee)

For questions, this style makes use of the plain style writer's usage endings:

자네는 언제 졸업**하나/하는가**?
caneynun encey colephana/hanunka?
When are you graduating? (said by a thesis advisor)

이번 여름에 **합니다**.
ipen yelumey hapnita
(I am graduating) this summer. (said by the graduate advisee)

7.1.5 VASSAL'S speech style

This is a quite rare and exquisite, now an antiquated, style that expresses extreme reverence toward the addressee. We term it the "vassal's style" 신하체 sinhachey, an extreme exaltation style. (Korean grammarians call it "하소서"체 "hasose"chey.) It is used nowadays by anyone to his or her beloved (in poetry) but historically by mortals for the extreme exaltation of gods and by commoners to the King (when Korea was a caste society a century ago). This is why we call this "vassal's" speech style. You can still see the endings of this style in early translations of Buddhist Sutras and Christian Bibles and hear them frequently in historical dramas. In commands, the honorific suffix and the humble suffix often precede the ending (하-시-옵-소서 ha-si-op-sose). The following is an illustration of how the vassal's style might be used in sacred texts:

부처님, 부처님, 거룩하신 부처님, 저 이제 발원하**오니** 이 원을 들으**소서**.
pwuchenim, pwuchenim, kelwukhasin pwuchenim, ce icey palwenhaoni i wenul tulusose.
Buddha, oh Holy Buddha, now I turn to thee, mayst thou hear my wishes!

예수 그리스도는 십자가 위에서 "나의 하나님, 나의 하나님 어찌하여 나를
버리셨**나이까**?"라고 외쳤다.
yeyswu kulisutonun sipcaka wieyse "nauy hananim, nauy hananim eccihaye nalul
pelisyessnaikka?"lako oychyessta.
Jesus Christ cried out on the cross, "My Lord, My Lord, why hast thou forsaken me?"

7.1.6 MASTER'S speech style

If you are high and mighty, always ready to give the lowly your teachings, you may use
the master's speech style, or 상전체 sangcenchey. It is an archaic form of babysitter's style
that you may hear kings and high officials use. In modern days, you will only see this
written in religious writings or said by masters or kings in historical dramas. Typical
endings include -도다 -tota and -(니)라 -(ni)la both for statements with the latter ending only for the *be* verb. The first example below is from the Bible, and the second from
a Buddhist sutra.

누구든지 그리스도 안에 있으면 새로운 피조물이**라**. 이전 것은 지나갔으니,
보라! 새 것이 되었**도다**.
nwukwutunci kulisuto aney issumyen saylowun phicomwulila. icen kesun cinakassuni, pola! say kesi
toyesstota.
*If anyone is in Christ, he is a new creature; the old things passed away. Behold! New
things have come.*

생선을 묶었던 새끼줄에서는 비린 내가 나는**도다**. 이처럼 사람들은 무엇엔
가 점점 물들어 가면서도 그것을 깨닫지 못하노니 이것이 어리석음이**니라**.
sayngsenul mwukkessten saykkicwuleysenun pilin nayka nanuntota. ichelem salamtulun mwueseyn-
ka cemcem mwultule kamyenseto kukesul kkaytatci moshanoni ikesi elisekuminila.
*The twine that ties fish reeks of fish. Like so, mankind does not realize that he is becom-
ing steeped in something, and this is his folly.*

7.1.7 Summary of the styles

Here is a summary table of situational speech styles in order of increasing formality from left to right. Casual endings are shown between dotted lines, and formal endings between solid lines. The double solid line shows the high formality boundary. The antiquated endings (master's and vassal's styles) are left out. Details vary slightly between different versions of Korean grammarians' lists. Additional endings are provided for your amusement and future reference:

Ending type / Sentence type	Plain 해라	Polite Ordinary 해요	Middle Age 하우	Mother-in-law's 하게	Formal 하십시오
평서형 phyengsehyeng *indicative*	-ㄴ다/는다/다 -nta/nunta/ta	-어요 -eyo	-우/슈 -wu/syu	-네 -ney	-ㅂ니다/습니다 -pnita/supnita
의문형 uymwunhyeng *interrogative*	-(으)냐/(느)냐, 니 -(u)nya/(nu)nya, ni (babysitter's) -는/(으)ㄴ가, -나 -nun/(u)nka, -na (writer's)	-어요 -eyo	-우/슈 -wu/syu	-는/(으)ㄴ가, -나 -nun/(u)nka, -na	-ㅂ니까/습니까 -pnikka/supnikka
청유형 chengyuhyeng *propositive*	-자 -ca	-어요 -eyo	-우/슈 -wu/syu	-(으)세 -(u)sey	-(으)ㅂ시다/(으)십시다 -(u)psita/(u)sipsita
명령형 myenglyenghyeng *imperative*	-어라 -ela (babysitter's) -(으)라 -(u)la (writer's)	-어요 -eyo	-우/슈 -wu/syu	-게(나) -key(na)	-(으)십시오 -(u)sipsio
약속형 yaksokhyeng *promissory*	-(으)마 -(u)ma (babysitter's)	-(으)ㄹ게요 -(u)lkeyyo	-(으)리다 -(u)lita	-(으)ㅁ세 -(u)msey	-겠습니다 -keysssupnita
의도형 uytohyeng *intentional*	-(으)련다 -(u)lyenta	-(으)ㄹ래요 -(u)llayyo	-(으)려오 -(u)lyeo	-(으)려네 -(u)lyeney	-(으)렵니다 -(u)lyepnita
감탄형 kamthanhyeng *exclamatory*	-(는)구나 -nunkwuna	-네요; -(는)군요 -neyo; -nunkwunyo	-(는)구려 -(nun)kwulye	-(는)구먼 -(nun)kwumen	--

There are additional endings that are used only with a particular style, and those are typically not listed in a table like this but learned as individual endings as they are encountered. It is important that you remember that each system does NOT have a solid impenetrable wall around it. As you have seen, some of these styles are used alongside others in the same conversation. Here are some typically mixed style pairs:

<u>Polite ordinary style with formal style (young, similar age)</u>

직장동료 1:   일 다 **끝났어요**? 커피나 한 잔 **합시다**.
cikcangtonglyo 1:   il ta kkuthnasseyo? khephina han can hapsita.
Work colleague 1:   *Are you done with your work? Let's get some coffee.*

직장동료 2:   **좋습니다**. 지금 **갈까요**?
cikcangtonglyo 2:   cohsupnita. cikum kalkkayo?
Work colleague 2:   *Sure. Shall we go now?*

<u>Polite ordinary style with intimate ordinary style (age difference)</u>

직장선배: 일 다 **끝났어요**? 같이 커피나 한 잔 **하지**.
cikcangsenpay: il ta kkuthnasseyo? kathi khephina han can haci.
Older colleague: *Are you done with your work? Let's get some coffee.*

직장후배: **좋습니다**. 지금 **가실래요**?
cikcanghwupay: cohsupnita. cikum kasillayyo?
Younger colleague: *Sure. Do you want to go now?*

<u>Plain style with intimate ordinary</u>

아빠: 장미야, 비 **온다**. 우산 가지고 **가라**!
appa: cangmiya, pi onta. wusan kaciko kala!
Dad: *Jangmi, it's raining. Take an umbrella!*

장미: 네, 아빠!
cangmi: ney, appa!
Jangmi: *Yes, dad!*

As a final note, we want to remind you that different second-person pronouns for *you* should be used with the different styles. Here is an example:

Vassal's: **님이시여**! 지금 어디에 계시나이까?
    nimisiye! cikum etiey kyeysinaikka?
    Oh, lord/my love! Where art thou now?

Formal: **어르신**, 지금 어디에 계십니까?
    elusin, cikum etiey kyeysipnikka?
    Elder, where are you now?

Middle-age 1:   **당신** 지금 어디에 있소/계시오?
"hao"chey   tangsin cikum etiey issso/kyeysio?
    Where are you now?

Middle-age 2: "hawu"chey	**댁은** 지금 어디에 있수/계슈? taykun cikum etiey issswu/kyeysyu? *Where are you now?*
Mother-In-Law's:	**자네** 지금 어디에 있나? caney cikum etiey issna? *Where are you now?*
Ordinary polite:	**거기**는/**그쪽**은 지금 어디에 있어요? kekinun/kuccokun cikum etiey isseyo? *Where are you now?*
Ordinary intimate:	**민주 씨**/**민주야**, 지금 어디에 있어? mincwu ssi/mincwuya cikum etiey isse? *Minju, where are you now?*
Babysitter's:	**통일아**, 너 지금 어디에 있니?/있냐? thongila, ne cikum etiey issni?/issnya? *(Little) Tongil, where are you now?*
Writer's:	**그대**는 현재 어디에 있는가? kutaynun hyencay etiey issnunka? *Where are you now?*

Now you are ready to consort with kings or enter into babysitting jobs and married life in Korean!

7.2 Speaker Attitude Endings

Think of the different ways you might say "it's raining" if you were a) pleasantly surprised, b) waxing pensive, or c) warning someone who was about to go outside. Without changing the words at all, you could communicate these attitudes through different intonation patterns (changing the pitch of your voice in different ways). This is part of how you have learned to communicate in English—these intonation patterns are meaningful and, thus, linguistic.

Korean has several endings that express this kind of **speaker attitude**. These attitude endings come before speech style endings, but because they are full of emotion, they are NEVER used with the formal style. They are mainly used in the ordinary speech styles.

7.2.1 Assumed and not assumed knowledge

Three commonly used attitude endings have to do with shared or assumed knowledge; the first two assume some knowledge on the part of the listener and function like English **tag questions** (*right? isn't it? didn't you?*, etc.), and one marks the adding of information or reasoning that the listener is assumed NOT to know.

(1) -지 *as you know, right?*

The most versatile of these attitude suffixes is -지 -ci, whose basic function is to underscore the speaker's assumption that the addressee knows the stated facts. It has slightly different nuances in statements and questions and is said with different intonations.

<1> Confirmation

In QUESTIONS, -지 -ci underscores the speaker's assumption that the information is true and that the listener shares that knowledge. -지 -ci questions seek confirmation, and they function like English tag questions, *isn't it, didn't they, right?* With this meaning, there is a low tone on the penultimate (second from the last) syllable, then high-falling tone on the last syllable.

In answers, -지 -ci shows that the speaker assumes the information is known by the listener, meaning *as you know, of course,* or *indeed.* When you add -요 -yo at the end, -지요 -ciyo is usually pronounced [죠 -cyo]. In answers with -지 -ci, the last syllable tends to dip low.

선미: 그 책 **재미있지요**?
senmi: ku chayk caymiissciyo?
Sunmi: *The book is fun, isn't it?*

나: 네.
na: ney.
Me: *Yes.*

김: 오늘은 학교 안 **가죠**?
kim: onulun hakkyo an kacyo?
Kim: *You don't go to school today, right?*

이: 네, 주말이니까 안 **가죠**.
i: ney, cwumalinikka an kacyo.
Lee: *Right. I don't go to school because it's the weekend (as you know).*

추: 나 **사랑하지**?
chwu: na salanghaci?
Chu: *You love me, right?*

홍: **물론이지**!
hong: mwullonici!
Hong: *Of course!*

공: 일이 많아서 **힘들었지요**?
kong: ili manhase himtulessciyo?
Kong: *It was hard, all that work, eh?*

전: 괜찮아요.
cen: kwaynchanhayo.
Juhn: *I am OK.*

<2> Assumed knowledge

-지 -ci can also be used with a question word. Unlike a straightforward, information-seeking question, this has the effect of asking with the sense *I know you know the answer: you told me before, but tell me again,* or *it just occurred to me, but….* The English question would have a continually rising intonation all throughout the question, starting low and going rather high at the end. The Korean sentence also has a very high tone on the last syllable immediately following a prolonged low tone.

누구시지요?
nwukwusiciyo?

Do I know you?/Who are you?

이게 **뭐지**요?
ikey mweciyo?

What is this? *(You should know, so tell me.)*

너, 생일이 **언제지**?
ne, sayngili enceyci?

When is your birthday again?

지금 **몇 시지**?
cikum myech sici?

Wait – **what** time is it? *(sudden realization)*

여기가 **어디지**?
yekika etici?

Where are we? *(sudden realization)*

<3> Emphatic urging

Since it shows the assumption of shared knowledge, -지 -ci makes claims, recommendations, or commands sound extra coercive, with the sense that *you should know to…* or *you know better (not) to…*:

지영: 오늘 같이 영화 **보지요**.
ciyeng: onul kathi yenghwa pociyo.
Jiyoung: *We should watch a movie together.*

동호: 영화는. 집에 가서 공부나 **하지**.
tongho: yenghwanun. cipey kase kongpwuna haci.
Dongho: *What movie?? Why don't you go home and study!*

친구: 게임할 시간 더 **있지**?
chinkwu: keyimhal sikan te issci?
Friend: *You have more time for the game, right?*

나: 오늘 게임 너무 많이 했어. 이제 그만 **하지**.
na: onul keyim nemwu manhi haysse. icey kuman haci.
Me: *We played too much today. We'd better stop now.*

<4> Offer and agreement

While -지 -ci is used toward the second person *you* for exhortation, -지 -ci with the first person *I* is used when the speaker agrees to do something or makes an offer a little heartier than -(으)ㄹ게 -(u)lkey. Because these are polite offers, the intonation is not extreme.

하늘: 누가 이것 좀 들어 주세요.
hanul: nwuka ikes com tule cwuseyyo.
Haneul: *Somebody please carry this for me.*

원식: 제가 **들지요**.
wensik: ceyka tulciyo.
Won-Shik: *Sure, I'll get it.*

구: 여기 **앉으시지요**.
kwu: yeki ancusiciyo.
Ku: *Please sit here. (Why don't you sit here?)*

박: 네, **그러지요**.
pak: ney, kuleciyo.
Pak: *Certainly.*

<5> Blame -지 (그랬어요)

Since the second person *you* is supposed to be in the know, the -지 -ci suffix can also express blame for something that is NOT done (or not done correctly). Often, 그랬 어 kulaysse follows the -지 -ci suffix and means *why did(n't) you do that?* or *should have*. The intonation on -지 -ci can be whiny (low-high-low), as you might expect, or disappointed (with a sudden drop):

나한테 **말하지**!
nahanthey malhaci!
Why didn't you tell me?

그거 나를 **주지** (그랬어)!
kuke nalul cwuci (kulaysse)!
You should have given it to me!

(2) -잖아 *ya know? did you not know?*

-잖아 -canha is another tag question, originally built from -지 -ci + 않다 anhta *not, is it not (the case)?* It carries many of the same meanings as its component parts, confirming *isn't it the case?* and *don't you know?* but has a stronger sense of assertion that *you DO know this* than -지 -ci alone has. It can be used for any kind of assertion but is especially useful when answering a question about why and offering up a reason (that the other person is assumed to know). It is used in conversation, and we recommend that you use this ending cautiously because it could sound snappy or nagging:

정수:　　　오늘 오후에 같이 영화나 보자.
cengswu:　onul ohwuey kathi yenghwana poca.
Jeongsoo:　*Let's watch a movie or something this afternoon.*

현애:　　　오늘 오후에 치과 약속 **있잖아**.
hyenay:　　onul ohwuey chikwa yaksok isscanha.
Hyunae:　　*I have a dental appointment, don't you know?*

정수:　　　참, 치과 약속 있었지. 그럼 다음에.
cengswu:　cham, chikwa yaksok issessci. kulem taumey.
Jeongsoo:　*Right! You have a dental appointment. Some other time, then.*

재화:　　　우산은 왜 가지고 가세요?
cayhwa:　　wusanun way kaciko kaseyyo?
Jaehwa:　　*What's up with the umbrella?*

효순:　　　지금 비가 **오잖아요**.
hyoswun:　cikum pika ocanhayo.
Hyosoon:　*It's raining outside (don't you see?/didn't you know?).*

아버지:　　방 청소해라.
apeci:　　　pang chengsohayla.
Father:　　*Clean your room.*

아이:　　　지난 주에도 **했잖아요**.
ai:　　　　cinan cwueyto haysscanhayo.
Child:　　*But I did it last week, too (as you know)!*

아버지: 청소는 매주 해야지!
apeci: chengsonun maycwu hayyaci!
Father: *You should clean your room every week!*

(잠시 후) (camsi hwu) (*A moment later*)

아버지: 방 청소 안 하냐!
apeci: pang chengso an hanya!
Father: *Aren't you cleaning your room?*

아이: 지금 하고 **있잖아요**!
ai: cikum hako isscanhayo!
Child: *I am (don't you see?)!*

As a simple conversation starter, 있잖아(요) isscanha(yo) ... is equivalent to *guess what* or *you know what?* in English:

있잖아(요). 할 얘기가 있는데(요)···
isscanha(yo). hal yaykika issnuntey(yo)...
Guess what. I've got something to tell you...

(3) -거든 *because, you see...*

Whereas -잖아 -canha assumes that the listener has some knowledge about the information discussed and implies *you should know/why are you asking/saying this?*, the ending -거든 -ketun indicates that you are providing new information as an afterthought or a reason that the listener might or might not know. -거든 -ketun is similar to English *it's because* sentences when one has NOT been asked a question, or like *you see* added at the end of a sentence. Both -잖아 -canha and -거든 -ketun are used in casual speech, and we advise you to use them only with your friends and those close to you.

친구: 미팅 안 가?
chinkwu: mithing an ka?
Friend: *You're not going to the meeting?*

나: 취소**됐잖아**.
na: chwisotwaysscanha.
Me: *It got cancelled, dontcha know?*

친구: 아, 취소됐지.
chinkwu: a, chwisotwayssci.
Friend: *Right, it's cancelled. (I spaced out.)*

친구: 미팅 안 가?
chinkwu: mithing an ka?
Friend: *You're not going to the meeting?*

나: 취소**됐거든**.
na: chwisotwaissketun.
Me: *Well, (it's because) it got cancelled, you see.*

친구:　　아, 취소됐구나.
chinkwu:　　a, chwisotwaysskwuna.
Friend:　*Oh, it's cancelled! (I didn't know.)*

형:　　잠깐 얘기 좀 할 수 있을까?
hyeng:　　camkkan yayki com hal swu issulkka?
Older brother:　*Can I have a word with you now?*

동생:　　지금 **나갈 거거든**. 나중에 전화할게.
tongsayng:　　cikum nakal keketun. nacwungey cenhwahalkey.
Brother:　*I am going out now, you see. I will call you later.*

-거든 -ketun (pronounced 거텅 keteng or even 걸랑 kellang by some young people in colloquial speech) can also indicate information that offers a reason, justification, or clarification:

미나:　　오늘 진짜 피곤해 보인다.
mina:　　onul cincca phikonhay pointa.
Mina:　*You look really tired today.*

동현:　　오늘 시험 때문에 어젯밤에 못 **잤거든**.
tonghyen:　　onul sihem ttaymwuney eceyspamey mos cassketun.
Donghyun:　*I did not sleep last night because of the test today.*

은비:　　지금 가야 **되거든**.
unpi:　　cikum kaya toyketun.
Eunbi:　*I have to go now. I have an appointment, you see.*

시은:　　그래, 그럼 나중에 얘기해.
siun:　　kulay, kulem nacwungey yaykihay.
Shieun:　*I see. Let's talk later then.*

-거든 -ketun can also be used as a way to start a new conversation.

어제 내가 학교에 **갔거든**. 그런데 …
ecey nayka hakkyoey kassketun. kulentey …
So, yesterday, I went to school. And then….

요즘 내가 속이 **아프거든**. 그래서 …
yocum nayka soki aphuketun. kulayse …
You know my stomach is hurting recently. So…

7.2.2 Noticing, introspection, and retrospection

Two endings communicate the speaker's reaction when noticing something: -네 -ney and -군 -kwun. Another ending -더라 -tela communicates that the speaker is reflecting on her past experience to comment in reaction to what's going on now.

(1) -네 *I see that..., I notice that...*

The ending -네 -ney expresses an emotional reaction similar to English *Oh!, Wow!,* or *Hey!*

<1> Spontaneous reaction

-네 -ney indicates that the speaker is reacting SPONTANEOUSLY and IMMEDIATELY (on-site) with a slight degree of emotion and wonder to what was just noticed. In English, this sentiment is often conveyed in intonation or with interjections.

-네 -ney can be used with both active verbs and descriptive verbs; you simply add -네 -ney after the verb root. (Also, remember to drop ㄹ from ㄹ-final verbs before -네 -ney!)

머리가 아주 **기네요**!
melika acwu kineyyo!
Oh, wow! Your hair is quite long!

김치를 잘 **만드네요**!
kimchilul cal mantuneyyo!
You make really good kimchi!

벌써 금요일**이네요**! 시간 참 **빠르네요**.
pelsse kumyoilineyyo! sikan cham ppaluneyyo.
It's already Friday! Time flies!

소영: 비가 또 **오네요**.
soyeng: pika tto oneyyo.
Soyoung: Oh, It's raining again. (That's odd. How come?)

현진: 네, 이번 여름에는 정말 비가 많이 **오네요**.
hyencin: ney, ipen yelumeynun cengmal pika manhi oneyyo.
Hyunjin: Yes, it's been raining a lot this summer (indeed).

Notice that when the verb is conjugated in the -었 -ess form before -네 -ney, it is used for perfective not past tense. It indicates that the action has been completed and the speaker is experiencing it NOW, to which she is reacting. It cannot be used to comment on something experienced in the past because -네 -ney is an immediate reaction. (In this case, use -더라 -tela, which is coming up soon.)

와, 눈이 많이 **왔네요**!
wa, nwuni manhi wassneyyo!
Wow, it('s) snowed a lot!

한국, 그간 많이 **변했네요**!
hankwuk, kukan manhi pyenhayssneyyo!
Wow, Korea has changed a lot (since I saw it last).

그 식당 참 **맛있었네요**!
ku siktang cham masissessneyyo!
The food was really good at that restaurant!

Because of the subtle sense of emotion and wonder, -네 -ney is often used in song lyrics and poems:

그대 얼굴이 참 **예쁘네요**.
kutay elkwuli cham yeyppuneyyo.
Your face is so pretty!

들에는 오늘 또 불같은 꽃이 **피네**.
tuleynun onul tto pwulkathun kkochi phiney.
Flowers are ablaze in the field yet again today.

<2> Emotional bonding, agreeing

The -네 -ney ending is also used when the speaker (emotionally) agrees, usually when the other speaker seeks a confirmation with the -지 -ci ending. The first -네 -ney below is for what's noticed anew, and the second -네 -ney is used for agreeing with what is said for the purposes of emotional bonding with the other person:

은양: 어! 가방 **샀네요**.
unyang: e! kapang sassneyyo.
Eunyang: *Hey, (I see that) you bought a new bag!*

용재: 네, 어제 세일에서 샀는데 **괜찮지요**?
yongcay: ney, ecey seyileyse sassnuntey kwaynchanhciyo?
YongJae: *Yes, I bought it at the sale. It looks good, doesn't it?*

은양: 네, 아주 **괜찮네요**.
Eunyang: ney, acwu kwaynchanhneyyo.
Eunyang: *Yeah, it's really nice.*

<3> Empathetic guess

When you want to convey empathy or express your guess based on personal experience or knowledge, combine the -네 -ney ending with the conjecture ending -겠 -keyss as -겠네 -keyssney:

곧 비가 **오겠네**.
kot pika okeyssney.
(By the looks of it,) it's going to rain soon.

벌써 3시야! 아기가 금방 **일어나겠네**.
pelsse sesiya! akika kumpang ilenakeyssney.
Oh, it's already 3:00; the baby's going to wake up soon.

은이: 세 시간이나 차를 타고 왔어요.
uni: sey sikanina chalul thako wasseyo.
Euni: *I had to ride/drive three hours to get here.*

세영: 저런! 정말 **피곤하겠네**요!
seyyeng: celen! cengmal phikonhakeyssneyyo!
Seyoung: *Oh my! You must be really tired!*

현정: 지난 주에 매일 네 시간씩밖에 못 잤어요.
hyenceng: cinan cwuey mayil ney sikanssikpakkey mos casseyo.
HyunJung: *Last week, I only slept four hours per day.*

현기: 저런! 정말 **피곤했겠네**요.
hyenki: celen! cengmal phikonhaysskeyssneyyo.
Hyun-Gi: *Oh my! You must have been really tired!*

(2) -군 *I see! Oh...!*

-군 -kwun is another ending that can convey a reaction to what you observed or experienced. While -네 -ney signals that your response is emotional and instantaneous, -군 -kwun as an INTROSPECTIVE ending expresses that the newly acquired information has been reasoned through in your own head, more like talking to yourself and thinking *oh, I see!* That is, you realized something you hadn't known before by thinking through something you observed.

You can add the exclamatory ending -아 -a (-군아 -kwuna) to engage whoever is listening to you, although the standard spelling has changed to -구나 -kwuna nowadays. You may also add the -요 -yo ending to -군 -kwun to express appropriate politeness to your listener, but you cannot add the politeness marker to your exclamation (--구나요 -kwunayo)

엄마: 오늘 하늘이 참 **파랗구나**.
emma: onul hanuli cham phalahkwuna.
Mom: *Wow. The sky is so blue today!*

딸: 그렇지요?
ttal: kulehciyo?
Daughter: *Isn't it?*

이슬: 오늘 하늘이 참 **파랗군요**.
isul: onul hanuli cham phalahkwunyo.
Iseul: *The sky is really blue today.*

재화: 정말 그렇**군**.
cayhwa: cengmal kulehkwun.
Jae-Hwa: *Indeed (I hadn't noticed before).*

-군 -kwun and -구나 -kwuna can be used with descriptive verbs as well as past and future tenses, but -는 nun has to be inserted for present tense active verbs (-는군(요) -nunkwun(yo) and -는구나 -nunkwuna):

후배: 제가 거의 매일 영화를 한 편씩 봐요.
hwupay: ceyka keuy mayil yenghwalul han phyenssik pwayo.
Younger friend/under-classman: *I watch a movie almost everyday.*

선배: **영화 좋아하는구나**!
senpay: yenghwa cohahanunkwuna!
Older friend/upper-classman: *Oh, you like movies (I didn't know that).*

친구: 영훈이가 많이 아프대.
chinkwu: yenghwunika manhi aphutay.
Friend: *I hear that Younghoon is very sick.*

나: 그래서 영훈이가 오늘 수업에 못 **왔구나**.
na: kulayse yenghwunika onul swuepey mos wasskwuna.
Me: *I see. That's why he didn't come to class today.*

미진: 그간 너무 바빴어. 내일도 못 가.

micin: kukan nemwu pappasse. nayilto mos ka.
Mijin: I've been so busy; I can't come tomorrow, either.

찬진: **그랬구나.** 내일도 안 **올 거구나.**
chancin: kulaysskwuna. nayilto an ol kekwuna.
Chanjin: I see. You won't be coming tomorrow either, huh?

(3) -더라 That's what happened/that's what I saw

Korean also has a way to indicate that what you are talking about is something that you personally experienced, using a tiny, little ending -더 -te. When you are recalling something that you personally experienced to tell the other person about it, or recounting something from the past that's relevant now, you use the sentence ending -더라 -tela. (It is a combination of the **retrospective suffix** -더 -te and the **interjection/exclamation suffix** -라 -la.) For example, if your brother went out for a walk this morning and found that it was quite chilly, he would say this to you as you are about to head out:

형: 오늘 날씨가 **춥더라.** 코트 입고 가.
hyeng: onul nalssika chwuptela. khothu ipko ka.
Older brother: *Oof! It's cold today (I find)! Put on a coat before you go out.*

나: 알았어.
na: alasse.
Me: *Got it.*

Here is another example:

친구: 그 수업 신청해? 그 교수님 강의 **재미있더라.**
chingwu: ku swuep sinchenghay? ku kyoswunim kangui caymiisstela.
Friend: *Are you registering for that class? That professor's class was/is fun (I have taken it myself).*

나: 잘됐다.
na: caltoaysta.
Me: *Oh, good!*

Deducing or surmising about someone else requires the -겠 -keyss suffix:

형: 진우 보니까 공부하느라고 **힘들겠더라.**
hyeng: cinwu ponikka kongpwuhanulako himtulkeysstela.
          I saw Jinwoo, and it looked like/I feel that he was having a tough time with his studies (because he has too much).

If you use -더라 -tela in a *wh*-question with a high intonation at the end of the sentence, you are probably trying to remember something you did or knew earlier:

나:	어, 내 코트 어디 **있더라**?
na:	e, nay khothu eti isstela?
Me:	*Er, where is/did I put my coat (I can't remember/I saw it somewhere)?*

룸메이트:	거실에 있잖아.
lwummeyithu:	kesiley isscanha.
Roommate:	*It's in the living room.*

나:	가만있자... 약속이 몇 **시더라**?
na:	kamanissca... yaksoki myech sitela?
Me:	*Let me see/wait a minute... What time <u>was</u> that appointment (I can't recall)?*

동생:	일곱시야!
tongsayng:	ilkopsiya!
Younger sibling:	*It's at seven!*

If you say -지 -ci in place of -더라 -tela, you mean something a little different:

나:	어, 내 코트 어디 **있지**?
na:	e, nay khothu eti issci?
Me:	*Hmm, WHERE did I put my coat (do you know)?*

룸메이트:	거실에 있잖아.
lwummeyithu:	kesiley isscanha.
Roommate:	*It's in the living room. (Remember?)*

나:	오늘 약속 몇 **시지**?
na:	onul yaksok myech sici?
Me:	*WHAT time was that appointment again? (tell me 'cause you know.)*

동생:	일곱시야!
tongsayng:	ilkopsiya!
Younger sibling:	*At seven.*

Unlike -지 -ci or -네 -ney, you cannot directly add the politeness ending -요 -yo to -더라 -tela. You need to use another version (-더라고 -telako), which adds the meaning, *I am saying*, and then add -요 -yo: -더라고요 -telakoyo.

그 집 찌개가 **맵더라고요**.
ku cip ccikayka mayptelakkoyo.
The jjigae at that restaurant/of that family is spicy, I found out (by eating) (and I'm telling you that).

그곳은 응달도 **덥더라고요**.
kukosun ungtalto teptelakoyo.
It is hot even in the shade over there (I experienced) (so I'm telling you).

내가 들어가니까 울고 **있더라고요**.
nayka tulekanikka wulko isstelakoyo.
I'm saying he was crying when I walked in.

All of the examples above are events that one observed in the past, while the reporting is taking place here and now. It's important to remember that there is NO PAST TENSE MARKER before -더라 -tela (nor after) in these cases. The version with the past tense, -었 더라 -ess tela, can only be used if the action HAD ALREADY BEEN COMPLETED at the time one WITNESSED the situation:

내가 가니까 다 **떠났더라**.
nayka kanikka ta ttenasstela.
Everyone had left when I arrived. (So I saw no one.)

점심 먹자고 전화하니까 벌써 **먹었더라고요**.
cemsim mekcako cenhwahanikka pelsse mekesstelakoyo.
He had already eaten when I called to invite him to lunch.

You may combine the retrospective suffix -더 -te with the introspective suffix -군 -kwun because they are both about looking in your head. So, you get -더군(요) -tekwun(yo). There is NO such form as -더지(요) -teci(yo) because -지 -ci is about SHARED knowledge and -더 -te is about you recalling YOUR OWN PERSONAL experience. There is also NO such form as -더네(요) -teney(yo) because -네 -ney is for spontaneous and instantaneous reaction to what you have just found out while -더 -te is about reminiscing about an experience that you already had.

한국은 진짜 매력적인 **나라더군(요)**.
hankwukun cincca maylyekcekin nalatekwun(yo).
Korea is truly an enchanting country. I'm thinking this based on my experience, as I have visited it.

Compare this with another sentence with the same English translation:

한국은 진짜 매력적인 나라군(요).
hankwukun cincca maylyekcekin nalakwun(yo).
Korea is truly an enchanting country. I can see/understand why people are saying that.

7.2.3 Fine-tuning -지, -네, -군/구나, and -더라

Let's see how -지 -ci, -네 -ney, and -군 -kwun can work together in a conversation:

영옥: 가방 샀**네요**. **빨간색이군요**.
yengok: kapang sassneyyo. ppalkansaykikwunyo.
Young-Oak: *Oh, you bought a new bag! And (I see that) it's a red one.*

영미: 네. 세일에서 샀는데 **괜찮지요**?
yengmi: ney. seyileyse sassnuntey kwaynchanhciyo?
Young-Mi: *Yes. I bought it on sale. It looks good, doesn't it?*

영옥: 네, 아주 **괜찮네요**!
yengok: ney, acwu kwaynchanhneyyo!
Young-Oak: *Yes, not bad at all!*

영희: 아, **시끄럽네**! 왜 이렇게 **시끄럽지**?
yenghuy: a, sikkulepney! way ilehkey sikkulepci?
YoungHee: *Ugh, it's noisy! Why is it so noisy?*

하린: 옆집에서 오늘 파티한대.
halin: yephcipeyse onul phathihantay.
Harin: *The neighbors said they are having a party today.*

영희: 아, 그래서 이렇게 **시끄럽구나**!
yenghuy: a, kulayse ilehkey sikkulepkwuna!
YoungHee: *I see. That's why (it's noisy)!*

하린: 꼭 우리가 시험 있을 때만 **파티하더라**.
halin: kkok wulika sihem issul ttayman phathihatela.
Harin: *They always have to throw a party right when we have a test (as has been the case in the past).*

The endings -지 -ci, -네 -ney, and -군 -kwun come IN THE PLACE OF the ordinary ending -어 -e. The main function of the ordinary ending is to simply transmit information and not necessarily emotion or attitude. A natural Korean conversation is sprinkled with these attitude markers, however, and one stripped of them would sound at best odd, if not downright ungrammatical:

박: 송희 씨, 가방 샀어요. 빨간색이에요.
pak: songhuy ssi, sasseyo. ppalkansaykieyyo.
Pak: *Songhee, you bought a bag; it's red (I'm telling you this).*

송희: 네. 세일에서 샀어요.
songhuy: ney. seyileyse sasseyo.
Songhee: *Yes. I bought it on sale.*

The sentences above simply state facts (even though it's Songhee who bought her own bag!) and would sound really strange, like a robot talking with no intention of connecting emotionally. Can you imagine how awkward conversations would sound in Korean without the attitude endings!

In addition to playing the role of a bridge on which emotions can cross to meet the other person, attitude endings, when present, also compensate for missing subjects. For example, you can only understand 가방 샀군요 kapang sasskwunyo as (*I see that*) YOU *bought a bag!*

7.3 Helping Verbs

In this section, we will explore Korean endings that communicate helping verb information in Korean and English. Some express **modality**, that is, the meanings of English **modal verbs** such as *can, must, may,* and *should.* Others are comparable to English helping verbs such as *want to* or *seem like.* A final set of endings presented here use helping verbs in KOREAN (and NOT in English).

7.3.1 How modality is expressed in Korean

The first set of endings that we'll talk about are those that are expressed by **modal verbs** in English *can, may, must, might, could, would, will, shall,* and *should*. Most of these require added verbs in Korean, so, as before, we will refer to the ending using a dictionary form of that helping verb, and in example sentences, we will conjugate verbs for whatever tense, aspect, and speech style is appropriate. The endings are organized by their English meanings in the following sections. We'll start with the concepts *can* and *may*.

(1) CANs and MAYs

There are several ways to express ability and possibility in Korean, similar to the English *can, may,* and *might*. Most of them start with prospective -(으)ㄹ -(u)l to express the unknown or something yet to happen, which means that they are 으 u-type endings, as discussed in chapter 6.

<1> -(으)ㄹ 수 있다; -(으)ㄹ 수 없다 *can, be able to; cannot, not be allowed to*

You learned in chapter 6 how to say *can't* in Korean, which is 못 mos, but that only works for *can't*. For the POSITIVE sentence with *can*, you need to use -(으)ㄹ 수 있다 -(u)l swu issta. Its negative counterpart (*can't*) is -(으)ㄹ 수 없다 -(u)l swu epsta. They can express both (IN)ABILITY and PERMISSION/PROHIBITION:

이거 들 수 있어요?
i ke tul swu isseyo?
Can you lift this?

그럴 수 없어요.
kulel swu epseyo.
I/we can't do that.

여기에서 피아노를 **칠 수 없어요**.
yekieyse phianolul chil swu epseyo.
I/You can't play the piano here.

이 곳은 일반인이 들어**갈 수 없습니다**.
i kosun ilpanini tulekal swu epssupnita.
The general public may not enter this area.

The word 수 swu is a dependent noun, so it is written with a space before and after. It being a (dependent) noun also means that various particles may come with it for different nuances:

여기서 피아노를 칠 수**가** 없다.
yekise phianolul chil swunka epsta.
We can't play the piano here.

여기서 피아노를 칠 수**는** 없다.
yekise phianolul chil swunun epsta.
We can't play the piano here.
other activities or actions might be OK

여기서는 피아노를 칠 수**도** 없다.
yekisenun phianolul chil swuto epsta.
We can't do piano playing here. not to mention other forbidden things

여기서 피아노**는** 칠 수**가** 없다.
yekise phianonun chil swuka epsta.
We can't play the piano here. other instruments might be OK

여기서는 피아노**도** 칠 수**가** 없다.
yekisenun phianoto chil swuka epsta.
We can't even play the piano here.

<2> -(으)ㄹ 수 있다; -(으)ㄹ 리 없다 *can, could, may, might; cannot be*

With DESCRIPTIVE verbs, -(으)ㄹ 수 있다 -(u)l swu issta expresses POSSIBILITY (because it doesn't make much sense to talk about someone being ABLE to be *big* or *pretty*). To weaken the possibility, the particle -도 -to can be added. In this possibility-plausibility sense, the negative version is -(으)ㄹ 리 없다 -(u)l li epsta:

성인도 **즐길 수 있는** 동화
senginto culkil swu issnun tonghwa
children's stories that adults, too, may enjoy

일을 한꺼번에 하려면 **힘들 수도 있다.**
ilul hankkepeney halyemyen himtul swuto issta.
It might be difficult if you try to finish all of the work at once.

지금 안 떠나면 **늦을 수도 있어.** 빨리 가자.
cikum an ttenamyen nucul swuto isse. ppalli kaca.
If we don't leave right now, we could be late. Hurry up!

괜찮아. 지금 시간에 길이 **막힐 리 없어.**
kwaynchanha. cikum sikaney kili makhil li epse.
It's OK. There is no way the road is bad this time of the day.

정말 그럴 수도 있어요?
cengmal kulel swuto isseyo?
Could that actually be? (*Can something like that happen?*)

그럴 **리가 없습니다.**
kulel lika epssupnita.
It cannot be. (*It's not possible that that's the case.*)

<3> -(으)ㄹ 수밖에 없다 *cannot but, can't help doing, there's no choice but*

With the aid of the particle -밖에 -pakkey *only/nothing but,* -(으)ㄹ 수 없다 -(u)l swu epsta brings about an emphatic positive—*cannot but...* or *can only.* You can leave out the verb 없다 epsta in spoken Korean:

가기 싫었지만 **갈 수밖에 없었습니다.**
kaki silhessciman kal swupakkey epsesssupnita.
I didn't want to, but I could not but go.

어제 잠을 못 잤어. **피곤할 수밖에 없지.**
ecey camul mos casse. phikonhal swupakkey epsci.
I didn't get sleep last night! Obviously, I am tired. I could only be/couldn't not be tired.

할 수 있는 건 다 했다. 이제는 **기다릴 수밖에.**
hal swu issnun ken ta hayssta. iceynun kitalil swupakkey.
We have done everything we could. Now, we just wait/Now, we have (no choice) but to wait.

<4> -(으)ㄹ지(도) 모르다 *could, might, may*

The ending -(으)ㄹ지(도) -(u)l ci(to) moluta literally means *to not know whether (something will happen)*, and as *may* or *might*, it connotes a sense of gentle warning or foreboding, like *you never know*. It can be used with negative sentences as well. -(도) -to is optional.

내일은 비가 **올지 모릅니다**.
nayilun pika olci molupnita.
It may rain tomorrow.

태희는 안 **올지도 몰라**. 예약을 바꿔야 할까?
thayhuynun an olcito molla. yeyyakul pakkweya halkka?
Taehi might not come. Should we change the reservation?

<5> -(으)ㄹ 줄 알다; -(으)ㄹ 줄 모르다 *can, know how to; can't, not know how to*

In order to say more clearly that you know (or don't know) HOW TO DO SOMETHING, when talking about an acquired skill or knowledge, you say, -(으)ㄹ 줄 알다 -(u)l cwul alta or its negative counterpart, -(으)ㄹ 줄 모르다 -(u)l cwul moluta. While -(으)ㄹ 수 있다 -(u)l swu issta can indicate both capability and possibility, -(으)ㄹ 줄 알다 -(u)l cwul alta expresses capability (know-how) only:

김: 한국어 **읽을 줄 아세요**?
kim: hankwuke ilkul cwul aseyyo?
Kim: *Do you know how to read Korean?*

제니: 네, 한국어 **읽을 줄 압니다**.
ceyni: ney, hankwuke ilkul cwul apnita.
Jenny: *Yes, I know how to read Korean.*

토니: 아니요, 한국어 **읽을 줄 몰라요**.
thoni: aniyo, hankwuke ilkul cwul mollayo.
Toni: *No, I don't know how to read Korean.*

<6> 보이다, 들리다 *can, can't* with senses

When the sensory verbs like 보다 pota *to see, look* and 듣다 tutta *to hear, listen* are used in their passive forms (보이다 poita *to be seen* and 들리다 tullita *to be heard*, respectively), they take on the sense of ABILITY as in *visible* and *audible*. The adverb 잘 cal often accompanies these verbs. For the negative *can't*, you need to use 안 an (not 못 mos). Natural English translations turn the sentence around as (I) *can see* X and (I) *can hear* X, but note the Korean structure and particle usage.

제 방에서 남산이 잘 **보여요**.
cey pangeyse namsani cal poyeyo.
I can see Namsan well from my room.
(Namsam is visible/is seen from my room.)

여기서는 차 소리가 잘 **안 들려요**.
yekisenun cha solika cal an tullyeyo.
You can't hear the car noise much from here.
(The car noise is not audible/is not heard from here.)

(2) More MAYs and SHOULDs, MUSTs, HAVE TOs, NEED TOs

This section is about permission, prohibition, and obligation, expressed with a variety of modals in English such as *may*, *have to*, and *must* (with and without *not*). Many of the Korean expressions use the verb 되다 toyta.

<1> -어도 되다 *you may, it's okay to*

The verb 되다 toyta is used in the expression of permission -어도 되다 -eto toyta *you may, you can* where the particle -도 + 되다 -to + toyta attaches to the intimate ordinary -어 -e form of the verb. (It may be helpful to remember this as a single expression with the vowel incorporated, -어도 되다 -eto toyta.) You might have heard people talk about the difference between *can* and *may* in English; -어도 되다 -eto toyta ONLY works for *may*— for talking about PERMISSION, NOT about one's ability or a possibility. (You learned -(으)ㄹ 수 있다 -(u)l swu issta and -(으)ㄹ 줄 알다 -(u)l cwul alta for abilities, and -(으)ㄹ지 모르다 -(u)l ci moluta for possibility or likeliness.) -어도 되다 -eto toyta literally means, *even if (you do that), it's okay*, thus, it has come to mean *you may…*:

낯선 사람:	여기 **앉아도 돼요**?
nachsen salam:	yeki **ancato twayyo**?
Stranger:	*May I sit here?/Is it okay to sit here?*

나:	네, **앉아도 돼요**.
na:	ney, **ancato twayyo**.
Me:	*Yes, you may/can.*

친구:	이 물 **마셔도 돼**?
chinkwu:	i mwul **masyeto tway**?
Friend:	*May/can I drink this water?/Is it okay to drink this water?*

나:	응, **마셔도 돼**. 차를 **시켜도 돼**.
na:	ung, **masyeto tway**. chalul **sikhyeto tway**.
Me:	*Yes, you may/can drink it. It is also okay to order tea.*

Used with DESCRIPTIVE verbs, the original meaning of -어도 되다 -eto toyta becomes a little more transparent, as *it's okay (even) if ….*:

우리 농구팀에 들어 와. 키가 **작아도 돼**!
wuli nongkwuthimey tulewa. khika **cakato tway**!
Join our basketball team. It's OK if you are short/you can be short!

편지 봉투 하나 줘. **작아도 돼**.
phyenci pongthwu hana cwe. **cakato tway**.
Give me an envelope. It's OK if is small./It can be small.

<2> -(으)면 안 되다 *may not, should not*

Because -어도 되다 -eto toyta means *you may*, you may think that you just need to negate it as -어도 **안** 되다 -eto <u>an</u> toyta to mean *you may not*. This is NOT the case! -어도 **안** 되다 -eto <u>an</u> toyta means *even if you do, it's still not okay*. For *may not*, to deny permission, you need to say -(으)면 안 되다 -(u)myen an toyta, literally, IF (*you do it*) …, *it's not okay*.

집 안에서 신발을 **신으면 안 돼요**.
cip aneyse sinpalul sinumyen an twayyo.
You should not/are not supposed to wear shoes inside.

여기서 담배 **피우면 안 돼요**.
yekise tampay phiwumyen an twayyo.
You should not/are not allowed to smoke here.

안 되다 an toyta, without the conditional *if* clause -(으)면 -(u)myen can be used by itself to get someone to stop doing what they are doing or to say that whatever is under discussion does not work:

애들아! **안 돼**!
yaytula! an tway!
Hey, you kids! That's a no-no!

내일은 **안 돼요**.
nayilun an twayyo.
Tomorrow doesn't work.

아이:	엄마, 이거 먹어도 돼?
ai:	emma, ike meketo tway?
	Mom, may I eat this?
어머니:	**안 돼**! 상했어!
emeni:	antway! sanghaysse.
	No! Don't! It's rotten.

안되다 antoyta, without a space between 안 an and 되다 toyta, has an idiomatic sense *pitiful, unlucky* or *unsuccessful*:

그 사람 참 안됐다⋯
ku salam cham antwayssta...
What a pity/What a pitiful state he is in!

안될 때는 뒤로 넘어져도 코가 깨져.
antoyl tttaynun twilo nemecyeto khoka kkaycye.
When things don't go well, you break your nose even when you fall backwards.

잘되면 제 탓, 안되면 조상 탓이지.
caltoymyen cey thas, antoymyen cosang thasici.
We take credit for success and blame others for failure.
(Literally, *If it goes well, it's my own doing, if not, ancestors are to blame.*)

<3> -(만) -(으)면 되다 *only have to, only need to*

Playing on this *is okay* usage of 되다 toyta, the expression -(만) -(으)면 되다 -(man) -(u)myen toyta has come to mean *all you have to do is…* or *(you) just have to…* . It literally means, *if (you) only do this, it is all good*, and the *only* part, -만 -man, can be left out.

청소는 다 했고 이제 설거지(만) **하면 돼요**.
chengsonun ta hayssko icey selkeci(man) hamyen twayyo.
I've finished cleaning, and I just need to do the dishes.

A: 기말 시험하고 보고서 다 끝냈어?
kimal sihemhako pokose ta kkuthnaysse?
Have you finished your final test(s) and paper(s)?

B: 시험은 끝났고 이제 보고서(만) **쓰면 돼**.
sihemun kkuthnassko icey pokose(man) ssumyen tway.
Tests are done, and I only have the paper(s) to write.

이거**만 하면 돼요**.
ikeman hamyen twayyo.
You just need to do this (and then you will be done).

기다려! 마지막 두 페이지**만 읽으면 돼**!
kitalye! macimak twu pheyiciman ilkumyen tway!
Wait. I just need to read the last two pages.

You can also use a verb clause -기**만** -kiman and the helping verb 하다 hata before adding -으면 되다 -umyen toyta. Verb + -기 -ki makes a *doing* gerund out of the verb, so using verb + -기만 하다 -kiman hata *just doing X* in this expression puts extra emphasis on the ACTION that is needed. (You will learn about -기 -ki in chapter 10.)

모두 기다리니까 우리가 가**기만 하면 돼**요.
motwu kitalinikka wulika kakiman hamyen twayyo.
Everyone's waiting; all that needs to happen is us gettin' there.

이사는 다 끝났고 짐을 풀**기만 하면 돼**요.
isanun ta kkuthnassko cimul phwulkiman hamyen twayyo.
We're done moving; all we need to do is unpack.

Compare: 이사는 다 끝났고 짐**만 풀면 돼**요.
isanun ta kkuthnassko cimman phwulmyen twayyo.
We're done moving; we just need to unpack the boxes.

<4> -어야 되다/하다 *have (got) to, should, ought to, need to*

To express obligation in English, we don't use *must* as often as *have to*, and you may feel there is a ranking of *must* > *have (got) to* > *should* > *ought to* in terms of how insistent one is being or how required the action is. That is, *must* is stronger than *have to* and so on. In Korean, one expression covers most of these, with the fundamental meaning of NECESSITY or OBLIGATION: -어야 되다 -eya toyta (or -어야 하다 -eya hata, a more formal version). -어야 되다 -eya toyta is also composite: -야 -ya, which attaches to the intimate ordinary -어 -e form of the verb, means *not until* or *only when*, and 되다 toyta means *is okay*. So all together, the expression literally means, *only when (you do something), is it okay*, thus, *you have to ... .*

It can be softened with other endings, such as -겠 -keyss or one of the *seems like* expressions that come up in the next section, but -어야 되다/하다 -eya toyta/hata is not as strong as *must* is in English.

학생은 공부를 열심히 **해야 돼요**.
haksayngun kongpwulul yelsimhi hayya twayyo.
Students should study hard.

기내에서는 안전 벨트를 **착용해야 한다**.
kinayeysenun ancen peylthulul chakyonghayya hanta.
You have to wear a seatbelt on airplanes.

10월 17일까지 서류를 **제출하셔야 합니다**.
10wel 17ilkkaci selyulul ceychwulhasyeya hapnita.
You need to complete this paper by October 17th.

한국 문화에서는 어른을 **공경해야 됩니다**.
hankwuk mwunhwaeysenun elunul kongkyenghayya toypnita.
One should show respect to elders in Korean culture.

To soften the sense of *have to* to *really should, ought to,* or *had better,* you can add the suffix -겠 -keyss and even drop the verb (되다 toyta or 하다 hata). You can also add -지 -ci when you think the other person should know.

감기가 나으려면 좀 **쉬셔야 되겠어요**.
kamkika naulyemyen com swisyeya toykeysseyo.
It looks like you ought to rest to recover from your cold.

주말엔 집에서 좀 **쉬어야겠어요**.
cwumaleyn cipeyse com swieyakeysseyo.
I think I should rest at home this weekend.

여행가려면 돈을 **모아야겠어요**.
yehayngkalyemyen tonul moayakeysseyo.
I'd better save up money to travel.

여행가려면 돈을 **모아야지**.
yehayngkalyemyen tonul moayaci.
If you want to travel, you gotta save up money.

<5> -지 않으면 안 되다 *absolutely must*

Two negatives do not always make a positive in Korean. In fact, the double negative -지 않으면 안 되다 -ci anhumyen an toyta, the strongest on the obligation scale, is comparable to the English *must*. Based on the other expressions above, it's perhaps clear that its literal meaning is *if* (*you DON'T do that*), *it's NOT okay*, thus, *you must*.

지금 가**지 않으면 안 돼**.
cikum kaci anhumyen an tway.
We must go now.

서류는 내일까지 제출하**지 않으면 안 됩니다**.
selyunun nayilkkaci ceychwulhaci anhumyen an toypnita.
The document must be submitted by tomorrow.

<6> -지 않아야 되다/-지 말아야 되다 *you have to NOT...*

To talk about what is the right thing to NOT do, you can attach -어야 되다 -eya toyta to a NEGATIVE and get -지 않아야 되다 -ci anhaya toyta or -지 말아야 되다 -ci malaya toyta (말다 malta is a verb for *don't do* commands).

건강해지려면 담배를 피우지 않아야 합니다.
kenkanghaycilyemyen tampaylul phiwuci anhaya hapnita.
Not smoking is a good thing to do if you want to get healthy.

부자가 되려면 일단 돈을 쓰지 말아야 돼요.
pwucaka toylyemyen iltan tonul ssuci malaya twayyo.
If you want to get rich, firstly, you have to not spend money.

<7> -지 않아도 되다/안 -어도 되다 *you don't have to...*

If you think about the literal meanings of the last few of expressions above and remember back to the first one, -어도 되다 -eto toyta *you have to*, you can probably see why -지 않아도 되다 -ci anhato toyta means *you don't have to*. It is the negative counterpart to -어도 되다 -eto toyta and comes from the literal meaning *even if (you DON'T do that), it's okay.*

청소하지 않아도 돼요. 갈 시간이에요.
chengsohaci anhato twayyo. kal sikanieyyo.
You don't have to clean up. It's time to go.

보고서는 다시 쓰지 않아도 됩니다.
pokosenun tasi ssuci anhato toypnita.
You don't have to rewrite the report.

안 -어도 되다 an -eto toyta is used more colloquially.

아이:	피곤한데 이 **안 닦아도 돼요**?
ai:	phikonhantey i an takkato twayyo?
Child:	*I am tired. May I not brush my teeth?*

엄마:	아니, 이 닦고 자야지!
emma:	ani, i takkko cayaci!
Mother:	*No! You have to brush them before going to bed.*

틈틈이 열심히 공부하면 학기 말에 밤을 안 새워도 된다.
thumthumi yelsimhi kongpwuhamyen hakki maley pamul an sayweto toynta.
If you diligently study little by little (throughout the term), you don't have to stay up all night at the end of the term.

With descriptive verbs, the original composite meaning of -지 않아도 되다 -ci anhato toyta becomes a little more transparent, as *it's okay even if it isn't...*, just like the positive counterpart, -어도 되다 -eto toyta:

우리 농구팀에 들어와. 키가 **크지 않아도 돼**!
wuli nongkwuthimey tulewa. khika khuci anhato tway!
Join our basketball team. You don't have to be tall!

편지 봉투 하나 줘. 깨끗하지 **않아도 돼**.
phyenci pongthwu hana cwe. kkaykkushaci anhato tway.
Give me an envelope. It doesn't have to be clean.

<8> -(으)ㄹ 필요(가) 없다 there is no need to

You can express an idea similar to *you don't have to* with -(으)ㄹ 필요(가) 없다 -(u)l
philyo(ka) epsta, literally, *there is no need to.*

여기에서 시청은 가까우니까 지하철을 **타실 필요가 없어요**. 5분만 걸어가
세요.
yekieyse sichengun kakkawunikka cihachelul thasil philyoka epseyo. 5pwunman kelekaseyyo.
*To get to City Hall from here, you don't need to take the subway. You can just walk a
couple of blocks.*

김치 담글 때 배추를 밤새 **절일 필요가 없다**. 몇 시간만 절이면 된다.
kimchi tamkul ttay paychwulul pamsay celil philyoka epsta. myech sikanman celimyen toynta.
There is no need to salt the cabbage overnight to make kimchi; a couple hours will suffice.

The positive counterpart, -(으)ㄹ 필요가 있다 -(u)l philyoka issta *it is necessary to* or *there
is a need to*, is not as commonly used.

(3) SHOULD HAVE

Another expression that uses a modal verb (and an auxiliary) in English is *should have*.
The Korean version is a rather complex set of expressions that you can simply learn as
units.

<1> -(으)ㄹ 걸 그랬다 I should have

-(으)ㄹ 걸 그랬다 -(u)l kel kulaysssta is shortened from -(으)ㄹ 것을 그랬다 -(u)l kesul kulayssta. The main verb 그랬다 kulaysssta is optional in casual speech when you don't have
to worry about being polite. When it shows up, it is always in the past tense. It comes
with the sense of self-blaming *I wish I had done... but I didn't.* Take note that this expression can only be used with the first person subjects *I* or *we.*

공부를 더 열심히 **할 걸 (그랬어)**.
kongpwulul te yelsimhi hal kel (kulaysseyo).
I should have/I wish I had studied harder.

대학생 때 여행을 많이 **다닐 걸 그랬어요**.
tayhaksayng ttay yehayngul manhi tanil kel kulaysseyo.
I should have traveled a lot when I was in college.

You might have heard a similar-sounding expression -(으)ㄹ걸 -(u)lkel (with no space before 걸 kel). This one is different. -(으)ㄹ걸(요) -(u)lkel(yo) expresses the speaker's GUESS or SUPPOSITION and is shortened from -(으)ㄹ 거야 -(u)l keya or -(으)ㄹ 거예요 -(u)l keyeyyo:

변: 지훈이가 왜 안 왔지?
pyen: cihwunika way an wassci?
Byun: *Why is Jihoon not coming?*

주: 지훈이는 오늘 못 **올걸(요)**? 바쁘대(요).
cwu: cihwuninun onul mos ol kel(yo)? papputay(yo).
Ju: *I don't think he can come today. He/They said he is busy.*

<2> -지 그랬다 *you should have*

If the *should have* is turned to *you*, it takes on a scolding or blaming tone, and a different ending, -지 그랬다 -ci kulayssta, should be used:

공부 좀 더 열심히 하**지 그랬니**.
kongpwu com te yelsimhi haci kulayssni.
You should have studied harder/Why didn't you study harder?

회의 때 좀 참**지 그랬어요**.
hoyuy ttay com chamci kulaysse(yo).
You should have held your tongue in the meeting.

<3> -었어야 하다/되다 *he/she/they should have*

If the *should have* is turned to a third person *he/she/they*, yet another ending is used: -었어야 하다 -esseya hata (or in spoken Korean, -었어야 되다 -esseya toyta). This ending can be used for first and second person subjects, too. With the suffix -지 -ci added (-었어야지 -esseyaci), the sense becomes more like *you should have known better (not) to...*

정부는 정책을 오래 전에 실시**했어야 했다**.
cengpwunun cengchaykul olay ceney silsihaysseya hayssta.
The government should have instituted this policy long ago.

적신호에 길을 건너지 말**았어야 됐어**.
ceksinhoey kilul kenneci malasseya twaysse.
I/You/(S)he/They should not have crossed the street at a red light.

적신호에 길을 건너지 말**았어야지**.
ceksinhoey kilul kenneci malasseyaci.
You/(S)he/They should have known better not to cross the street at a red light.

(4) WILLs, SHALLs & WOULDs, COULDs

By now you know that English modal verbs don't line up perfectly with Korean endings. Some Korean endings cover multiple English meanings and vice versa. You have to get to the core meaning of the KOREAN endings as you add them to your repertoire of things you know how to express. Here are some sentences with Korean endings you already know that translate using a variety of modal verbs in English. Try to learn the different sense expressed by the Korean endings.

지금쯤은 집에 **있을 거야**.
cikumccumun cipey issul keya.
They'll be home by now.

옆자리로 좀 옮겨 **줄래요**?
yepcalilo com olmkye cwullayyo?
Will you please move to the next seat?

해줄게. 어렵지 **않을 거야**.
haycwulkey. elyepci anhul keya.
I'll do that for you. It won't be difficult at all.

할 수 있어. 어렵지 **않을 거** 같아.
hal swu isse. elyepci anhul ke kata.
I can do that. It shouldn't be difficult at all.

진짜 **좋겠다**!
cincca cohkeyssta!
She must be really happy!

이 책 꼭 **읽어야 돼**.
i chayk kkok ilkeya tway.
You must read this book/you gotta read this book.

아프겠다!
aphukeyssta!
That's gotta hurt!

차 좀 **드시겠어요**?
cha com tusikeysseyo?
Would you like some tea?

좀 깎아 **주시겠어요**?
com kkakka cwusikeysseyo?
Would you be able to give me a discount?

옆자리로 좀 옮겨 **주시겠어요**?
yephcalilo com olmkye cwusikeysseyo?
Could you please move to the next seat?

그럴 **리가** 없어.
kulel lika epse.
That couldn't happen.

학생들은 숙제를 제 시간에 **내야 한다**.
haksayngtulun swukceylul cey sikaney nayya hanta.
Students shall turn in assignments on time.

이 보고서를 부장님께 갖다 **드릴까요**?
i pokoselul pwucangnimkkey kacta tulilkkayo?
Shall I give the boss this report?

7.3.2 How English helping verbs are expressed in Korean

A few basic endings in Korean correspond to structures with what we'll call "helping verbs" in English. These are expressions like *want to* and *it seems like*, which make use of added verbs that have a meaning of their own. Korean has various ways of expressing each idea. Some use helping verbs like English does, others use verb suffixes. We have grouped them by shared meaning in this section so that their usages can be compared.

(1) WANT TO

There are two ways to express *want to*, one of which you already know from chapter 6. Let's compare them.

<1> -(으)ㄹ래 *I wanna; I feel like doing...*

You saw in chapter 6 that -(으)ㄹ래 -(u)llay can express what the speaker feels like doing now or in the fairly immediate future. It is **not** used for longer-term plans or hypothetical situations (e.g., *if I had a million dollars, I (would) want to...*). Although it can ask about the listener's (*your*) wishes in QUESTIONS, -(으)ㄹ래 -(u)llay can only talk about wants or desires from the first person's (*my*) point of view in statements:

남: 뭐 **읽을래**?
nam: mwe ilkullay?
Nam: *What do you wanna read?*

방: 역사 소설 **읽을래**.
pang: yeksa sosel ilkullay.
Bahng: *I feel like/I'm gonna read a historical fiction.*

손: 지금 도서관에 갈 건데 같이 **갈래**?
son: cikum tosekwaney kal kentey kathi kallay?
Sohn: *I am going to go to the library. Wanna come with me?*

한: 아니, 집에서 혼자 공부**할래**.
han: ani, cipeyse honca kongpwuhallay.
Han: *No, I wanna study at home alone.*

-(으)ㄹ래(요) -(u)llay(yo) is only used in ordinary speech styles and usually between family members and close acquaintances. For more formal situations, you can use the suffix -겠 -keyss instead:

나: 우리랑 커피 같이 **하겠어요**?
na: wulilang khephi kathi hakeysseyo?
Me: *Would you like to have coffee with us?*

나이 어린 직장 동료: 네, 감사합니다.
nai elin cikcang tonglyo: ney, kamsahapnita.
Younger co-worker: *Yes, thank you.*

나: 커피 드시러 같이 **가시겠습니까**?
na: khephi tusile kathi kasikeysssupnikka?
Me: *Would you like to go get some coffee with me?*

상사: 갔다 오세요. 일이 좀 밀려서요.
sangsa: kassta oseyyo. ili com millyeseyo.
Boss: *You go ahead. I am a bit swamped.*

<2> -고 싶다 *I want to, would like to; do you want to?*

While -(으)ㄹ래 -(u)llay expresses immediate desires, for longer-term wishes and to talk about other people's wants, you can use -고 싶다 -ko siphta:

졸업한 다음에 뭐 **하고 싶어요**?
colephan taumey mwe hako sipheyo?
What do you want to do after you graduate?

태권도 도장을 **열고 싶어요**.
thaykwento tocangul yelko sipheyo.
I want to start a Taekwondo studio.

Notice how -고 싶다 -ko siphta is for deeper hopes and wishes, while -(으)ㄹ래 -(u)llay is for immediate wants:

은이: 아, 심심해... 뭐 재미있는 거 **하고 싶다**.
uni:　a, simsimhay... mwe caymiissnun ke hako siphta.
Euni:　*I am bored... I want to do something fun.*

미나: 그럼 뭐 하러 **나갈래**?
mina:　kulem mwe hale nakallay?
Mina:　*Then, do you wanna go out and do something (with me now)?*

은이: 안돼. 지금 나가면 과제를 못 **끝낼 거야**.
uni:　antway. cikum nakamyen kwaceylul mos kkutlayl keya.
Euni:　*No, if I go out now, I won't be able to finish the assigned work.*

There is no difference between *want* and *wish* marked grammatically in Korean, but a different kind of distinction is important. If something is at your immediate disposal, you would use -(으)ㄹ래 -(u)llay because use -고 싶다 -ko siphta implies that what is mentioned is not an immediate possibility. This leaves room for the listener to respond with *but you can, if you really want(ed) to*:

나:　　아! 여행**가고 싶다**...
na:　　a! yehayngkako siphta...
Me:　　*Aaah, I want to/I wish I could travel (now)!*

친구:　가려면 갈 수 있잖아.
chinkwu:　kalyemyen kal swu isscanha.
Friend:　*You can/could (if you really want/wanted to).*

나:　　잠 좀 푹 **자고 싶어요**.
na:　　cam com phwuk cako sipheyo.
Me:　　*I want to/I wish I could get some good sleep!*

엄마:　지금 자.
emma:　cikum ca.
Mom:　　*Get some sleep now.*

If you want something to happen that you have no control over EVER, as in *I want him to ...* or *I wish he would...*, you would use -(으)면 좋겠다 -(u)myen cohkeyssta or -었으면 좋겠다 -essumyen cohkeyssta, literally meaning, *it would be nice if...* . The past-tense version makes it a little stronger wish for something that's not likely to happen in the foreseeable future.

룸메가 청소 좀 자주 **하면 좋겠어요**.
lwummeyka chengso com cacwu hamyen cohkeysseyo.
It would be nice if my roommate cleaned more often.

비가 이제 좀 **그쳤으면 좋겠어**.
pika icey com kuchyessumyen cohkeysse.
I wish the rain would stop already.

<3> -고 싶어하다 *he/she/they want to*

For talking about a THIRD PERSON's desires, add -어하다 -ehata as a way of saying that the other person ACTS AS THOUGH they want to, distancing yourself from asserting someone else's feelings: -고 싶어하다 -ko siphehata.

엄마:	그 집 아들은 졸업하고 뭐 **하고 싶어해**?
emma:	ku cip atulun colephako mwe hako siphehay?
Mother:	*What does your son want to do after he graduates?*

엄마 친구:	태권도장을 **차리고 싶어해**.
emma chinkwu:	thaykwentocangul chaliko siphehay.
Mother's friend:	*He wants to set up a Taekwondo studio.*

어머니께서는 은퇴하시고 나서 여행을 **다니고 싶어하신다**.
emenikkeysenun unthoyhasiko nase yehayngul taniko siphehasinta.
Mom wants to travel after she retires.

(2) IT SEEMS LIKE

The -겠 keyss suffix you learned in chapter 6 conveys your conjecture *it must be*, but there are other endings that can express your guess or interpretation of the world.

<1> -(으)ㄴ/는/(으)ㄹ 것 같다 *seems like, as if, as though*

As our first of the *seems like* series, we introduce the verb 같다 kathta to you. The word means *alike* or *similar*, and the closest English translation for this expression -는 것 같다 -nun kes kathta is *it seems to me like...* or *I think...* . The main function is to show that the speaker is non-committal. If you THINK something is the case, you can't be held accountable for the absolute truth of what you are saying, right? It is also used to soften the tone when the speaker shares his or her opinion, much like *I think* in English.

Use -(으)ㄴ것 같다 -(u)n kes kathta for descriptive verbs (*it seems pretty/big/fun*), -는 것 같다 -nun kes kathta for present tense active verbs (*it seems like she does X*), and -(으)ㄹ 것 같다 -(u)l kes kathta for future activities that seem likely (*it seems like she will do X*). For active verbs that are completed (*it seems like he did X, it seemed like she has done X*), use -(으)ㄴ것 같다 -(u)n kes kathta and do not include the past tense -었 -ess. The verb

같다 kathta itself can be put into any tense and speech style (*it seemed to me, it seems to me,* and *it will seem like*).

This ending is complex in a way different from the others so far. While the main meaning of this ending is *seems like*, the first part, -(으)ㄴ, -는 or -(으)ㄹ indicates the tense and aspect of the situation being talked about, for example, *it seems like they* WERE, *it seems like they* ARE..., or *it seems like they* WILL BE. We refer to these as the past, present and future forms of the ending. Notice that 이다 ita conjugates like a descriptive verb with this ending:

		seems like...		
	Examples	Past	Present	Future
Active Verb	쓰다 *write* sseta	쓴 것 같다 ssun kes kathta	쓰는 것 같다 ssunun kes kathta	쓸 것 같다 ssul kes kathta
	읽다 *read* ilkta	읽은 것 같다 ilkun kes kathta	읽는 것 같다 ilknun kes kathta	읽을 것 같다 ilkul kes kathta
	걷다 *walk* ketta	걸은 것 같다 kelun kes kathta	걷는 것 같다 ketnun kes kathta	걸을 것 같다 kelul kes kathta
	알다 *know* alta	안 것 같다 an kes kathta	아는 것 같다 anun kes kathta	알 것 같다 al kes kathta
	돕다 *help* topta	도운 것 같다 towun kes kathta	돕는 것 같다 topnun kes kathta	도울 것 같다 towul kes kathta
	낫다 *get better* nasta	나은 것 같다 naun kes kathta	낫는 것 같다 nasnun kes kathta	나을 것 같다 naul kes kathta
Descriptive Verb	크다 *big* khuta	N/A	큰 것 같다 khun kes kathta	클 것 같다 khul kes kathta
	작다 *small* cakta		작은 것 같다 cakun kes kathta	작을 것 같다 cakul kes kathta
	맵다 *spicy* maypta		매운 것 같다 maywun kes kathta	매울 것 같다 maywul kes kathta
	달다 *sweet* talta		단 것 갈다 tan kes kathta	달 것 같다 tal kes kathta
	하얗다 *white* hayahta		하얀 것 같다 hayan kes kathta	하얄 것 같다 hayal kes kathta
Noun 이다 ita	친구이다 chinkwuita *be friend*	N/A	친구인 것 같다 chinkwuin kes kathta	친구일 것 같다 chinkwuil kes kathta

In the following examples, pay close attention to the form of the ending and the tense of 같다 kathta with respect to how they are translated in English:

엄마: 정아 숙제 다 끝냈니?
emma: cenga swukcey ta kkuthnayssni?
Mom: *Has your sister finished her homework?*

나: 네, 다 **한 것 같아요**.
na: ney, ta han kes kathayo.
Me: *Yes, it _seems_ like she has _finished_ it.*

엄마: 정아 숙제 다 끝냈니?
emma: cenga swukcey ta kkuthnayssni?
Mom: *Has your sister finished her homework?*

나: 네, 다 **한 것 같았어요**.
na: ney, ta han kes kathasseyo.
Me: *Yes, it _seemed_ like she had _finished_ it.*

조: 준호는 오늘 안 **올 것 같네**.
co: cwunhonun onul an ol kes kathney.
Jo: *It doesn't seem to me like Junho is coming today.*

최: 그래. 아주 **피곤한 것 같아**.
choy: kulay. acwu phikonhan kes katha.
Choi: *Yeah. It _seems_ like he _is_ really tired.*

조: 준호는 오늘 안 **올 것 같네**.
co: cwunhonun onul an ol kes kathney.
Jo: *It doesn't seem to me like Junho is coming today.*

최: 그래. 아주 **피곤한 것 같았어**.
choy: kulay. acwu phikonhan kes kathasse.
Choi: *Yeah. He _seemed_ really tired.*

나는 그 소식을 듣고 세상이 무너지는 것 같았다.
nanun ku sosikul tutko seysangi mwunecinun kes kathassta.
Having heard the news, I _felt as though_ the world _was crumbling_ down.

Be careful with a sentence like the last where English doubles up the past tense, making both *seem* and the other verb. In Korean, the other verb is only past tense if it had been COMPLETED when *it seemed* as you can see in the next dialogue exchange.

나는 그 소식을 듣고 세상이 무너진 것 같았다.
nanun ku sosikul tutko seysangi mwunecin kes kathassta.
Having heard the news, I _felt as though_ the world _had crumbled_ down.

<2> -나 보다/(으)ㄴ가 보다/(으)ㄹ 건가 보다 *looks to me like, the evidence points to…*

When you want to express WHAT THE EVIDENCE POINTS TO, when you are a bit more objective or sure about how something seems, you can use -나 보다 -na pota with present tense active verbs, -(으)ㄴ가 보다 -(u)nka pota with descriptive verbs. For the past tense, use -었나 보다 -essna pota and future tense -(으)ㄹ 건가 보다 -(u)l kenka pota for both active and descriptive verbs.

-나/(으)ㄴ가 보다 -na/(u)nka pota demonstrates a bit more CERTAINTY based on what you can outwardly observe so it sounds more ASSERTIVE than -(으)ㄴ/는/(으)ㄹ 것 같다 -(u)n/nun/(u)l kes kathata, which indicates more SUBJECTIVITY in your interpretation of things (or non-committal-ness disguised as uncertainty). Since -나/(으)ㄴ가 보다 -na/(u)nka pota has the *look* verb in the expression, it makes sense that it is more about looking at the evidence. It is often rendered as "seems like" in English:

어머니: 옆집 앞에 이삿짐 트럭이 서 있네. **이사가나 보다**.
emeni: yephcip aphey isascim thuleki se issney. isakana pota.
Mother: *Hmm… I see a moving truck parked in front of the neighbor's house. Seems like they are moving.*

딸: 네, 플로리다로 간대요.
ttal: ney, phullolitalo kantayyo.
Daughter: *Yes, they are moving to Florida, I hear.*

박: 소영이 기분이 좋아 보이네. 시험을 **잘 봤나 봐**.
pak: soyengi kipwuni coha poiney. sihemul cal pwassna pwa.
Pak: *Soyoung looks happy. She seems to have done well on her test.*

주: **그런가 봐**.
cwu: kulenka pwa.
Ju: *It seems like it.*

최: 준호가 파티에 안 와서 섭섭했다!
choy: cwunhoka phathiey an wase sepsephayssta!
Choi: *I was disappointed to see Junho missing at the party.*

장: 준호가 요즘 일이 **많은가 봐**. 이번 주 내내 프로젝트 때문에 시달렸거든.
cang: cwunhoka yocum ili manhunka pwa. ipen cwu naynay phuloceykthu ttaymwuney sitallyessketun.
Jang: *He seems to be up to his ears these days. He has been swamped with the project work all week.*

The conjugation of this ending is a little trickier than others. You must remember that descriptive and active verbs take different versions of the ending for the present tense, but that all past tense forms use -나 보다 -na pota after the past tense marker -었 -ess. Here's a chart of examples to help you internalize the patterns:

	Examples	Past	Present	Future
Active Verb	쓰다 *write* ssuta	썼나 보다 ssessa pota	쓰나 보다 ssena pota	쓸 건가 보다 ssul kenka pota
	읽다 *read* ilkta	읽었나 보다 ilkessna pota	읽나 보다 ilkna pota	읽을 건가 보다 ilkul kenka pota
	걷다 *walk* ketta	걸었나 보다 kelessna pota	걷나 보다 ketna pota	걸을 건가 보다 kelul kenka pota
	알다 *know* alta	알았나 보다 alassna pota	노나 보다 nona pota	놀 건가 보다 nol kenka pota
	돕다 *help* topta	도왔나 보다 towassna pota	돕나 보다 topna pota	도울 건가 보다 towul kenka pota
	낫다 *get better* nasta	나았나 보다 naassna pota	낫나 보다 nasna pota	나을 건가 보다 naul kenka pota
Descriptive Verb	크다 *big* khuta	컸나 보다 khessna pota	큰가 보다 khunka pota	
	작다 *small* cakta	작았나 보다 cakassna pota	작은가 보다 cakunka pota	
	맵다 *spicy* maypta	매웠나 보다 maywessna pota	매운가 보다 maywunka pota	NA
	달다 *sweet* talta	달았나 보다 talassna pota	단가 보다 tanka pota	
	하얗다 *white* hayahta	하얬나 보다 hayayssna pota	하얀가 보다 hayanka pota	
Noun 이다 ita	친구이다 chinkwuita *be a friend*	친구였나 보다 chinkwuyessna pota	친구인가 보다 chinkwuinka pota	NA

<3> -나/-(으)ㄴ가/-(으)ㄹ까 I wonder...

When you take the verb 보다 pota away from -나 보다 -na pota/-(으)ㄴ가 보다 -(u)nka pota, you get -나 -na (for present tense active verbs and past tense verbs) and -(으)ㄴ가 -(u)nka (for descriptive verbs), endings that express a wondering-to-oneself question. (If you remember, this ending is also used in the mother-in-law's speech style as well as in the writer's usage of the plain speech style.)

옆집 앞에 이삿짐 트럭이 서 있네. **이사 가나**?
yephcip aphey isascim thuleki se issney. isakana?
Hmm... I see a moving truck parked in front of the neighbor's home. I wonder if they are moving.

소영이가 기분이 좋아 보이네. 시험을 잘 **봤나**?
soyengika kipwuni coha poiney. sihemul cal pwassna?
Soyoung looks happy. Did she do well on the test, I wonder?

정호가 왜 안 **오나**? **피곤한가**? 기분이 안 **좋은가**?
cenghoka way an ona? phikonhanka? kipwuni an cohunka?
Why isn't Junho coming? Is he tired? Is he upset? I wonder…

This ending, together with the politeness suffix -요 -yo, is handy for making questions less intrusive and more polite than a direct, information-seeking ordinary style. That's right! Even when you signal that you are being polite with the suffix -요 -yo, there is a yet more polite way to ask a question by sounding like you are wondering about something.

누가 한국어 **선생님이신가요**?
nwuka hankwuke sensayngnimisinkayo?
Who/Which one of you is the Korean teacher, might I ask?

Compare: 누가 한국어 **선생님이세요**?
nwuka hankwuke sensayngnimiseyyo?
Who/Which one of you is the Korean teacher?

소: 밖에 날씨가 **추운가요**?
so: pakkey nalssika chwuwunkayo?
So: *Is it cold outside, I wonder? (If you don't mind me asking…/Would you mind telling me?)*

송: 아니요. 오늘은 **따뜻해요**.
song: aniyo. onulun ttattushayyo.
Song: *No, it's warm today.*

정: 걔가 시험에 **붙었나요**?
ceng: kyayka sihemey pwuthessnayo?
Jeong: *I wonder if she made the cut on the test?*

유: 네, 그렇대요.
yu: ney, kulehtayyo.
Yu: *Yes, I was told so.*

In chapter 6, you learned the usage of -(으)ㄹ까(요) -(u)lkka(yo) for asking oneself *should I…?* This ending is on a continuum with -(으)ㄴ가(요) -(u)nka(yo), basically to express rhetorical questions or wondering to oneself. The prospective suffix -(으)ㄹ -(u)l highlights the sense of unknown/uncertainty, so -(으)ㄹ까(요) -(u)lkka(yo) is more unknowable while -(으)ㄴ가(요) -(u)nka(yo) and -나(요) -na(yo) reflect wondering about something that is happening or has happened. Be careful: the past tense version is NOT -(으)ㄴ가 -(u)nka, but rather -었나 -essna. The past tense of -(으)ㄹ까(요) -(u)lkka(yo) is -었을까(요) -essulkka(yo):

지금 밖에 비가 **오나**?
cikum pakkey pika ona?
Is it raining out, I wonder?
(self-talk: it doesn't seem bright and sunny, so…)

지금 서울에는 비가 **올까**?
cikum sewuleynun pika olkka?
Might it be that it's raining in Korea now?

소영이가 잘 **도착했나**?
soyengika cal tochakhayssna?
I wonder if Soyoung has arrived well.

소영이가 잘 **도착했을까**?
soyengika cal tochakhayssulkka?
I wonder if Soyoung was able to arrive safely.
(I have concerns/reason to doubt.)

정호가 왜 안 **오나**?
cenghoka way an ona?
Why isn't Jeongho coming, I wonder?

정호가 왜 안 **올까**?
cenghoka way an olkka?
I really wonder why Jeongho isn't here.
(He should already be here.)

<4> -어 보이다 *looks good/big/pretty*

When using a DESCRIPTIVE verb, it is possible to talk directly about how someone actually LOOKS and not just about what you surmise given some other kinds of evidence. This calls for the helping verb 보이다 poita *to be seen* or *visible* (the PASSIVE form of the verb 보다 pota *to look at; see*), used with the -어 -e form of the descriptive verb.

누나: 오늘 할아버지께서 **피곤해 보이시네**.
nwuna: onul halapecikkeyse phikonhay poisiney.
Sister: *Grandpa looks tired today.*

동생: **그래 보이시네**.
tongsayng: kulay poisiney.
Younger brother: *Yes, he looks that way.*

연: 머리 자르니까 **어려 보인다**!
yen: meli calunikka elye pointa!
Yeon: *Wow! You got your hair cut. You look young!*

정: 고마워.
ceng: komawe.
Jeong: *Thank you.*

그의 눈에는 주변의 모든 것이 **아름다워 보였다**.
kuuy nwuneynun cwupyenuy motun kesi alumtawe poyessta.
Everything around him looked beautiful to him.

When attached to an ACTIVE verb, 보이다 poita is used with its CAUSATIVE meaning, *to show*, so -어 보이다 -e poita here means SHOW (*off*) doing X:

그 남자가 배 근육을 **자랑해 보였다**.
ku namcaka pay kunyukul calanghay poyessta.
He showed off his abdomen muscles.

아이가 엄마한테 새로 배운 글자를 **써 보였다**.
aika emmahanthey saylo paywun kulcalul sse poyessta.
The child (proudly) wrote the new letter/character she had learned.

7.3.3 Fine-tuning conjugation

A key point to conjugating for many of these endings is to know which versions to use based on tense, aspect, and type of verb (descriptive or active). You have seen many variations on endings, including -ㄴ -n, -은 -un, -는 -nun, -을 -ul, -었 -ess, and -었을 -essul. So let's review them.

There are four basic patterns that you need to distinguish. We'll assign them names here so that we can refer back to them later when they come up again, but notice some key points. ALL FOUR PATTERNS DIFFERENTIATE ACTIVE AND DESCRIPTIVE VERBS IN THE PRESENT TENSE CONJUGATIONS. Whether to use -은 -un, -ㄴ -n, -는 -nun, and -∅ (nothing) is different between the four patterns. They also differ in the use of the PAST TENSE marker -었 -ess. We will show conjugations of the verbs 쓰다 sseuta to write, 읽다 ilkta to read, 작다 cakta to be small, and 하다 hata to do. The tricky or unexpected conjugations are shaded:

Conjugation Pattern:	Past	Present	Future
Plain style -는다 -nunta pattern	-었다: 썼다, 작았다 -essta: ssessta, cakassta	**ACTIVE VERB** **vowel-final** -ㄴ다: 쓴다 -nta: ssenta **consonant-final** -는다: 읽는다 -nunta: ilknunta **DESCRIPTIVE VERB** -∅다: 작다 -ta: cakta	-(으)ㄹ 거∅다: 할 거다 -(u)lketa: hal keta
-(는)군 -(nun)kwun pattern	-었군: 썼군, 작았군 -esskwun: ssekwun, cakasskwun	**ACTIVE VERB** -는군: 쓰는군 -nunkwun: ssununkwun **DESCRIPTIVE VERB** -∅군: 작군 -kwun: cakkwun	-(으)ㄹ거∅군: 할 거군 -(u)lkekwun: hal kekwun
Clause connector -는데 -nuntey pattern	-었는데: 썼는데, 작았는데 -essnuntey: ssessnuntey, cakassnuntey	**ACTIVE VERB** -는데: 쓰는데 -nuntey: ssenuntey **DESCRIPTIVE VERB** -(으)ㄴ데: 작은데 -(u)ntey: cakuntey	-(으)ㄹ 건데: 할 건데 -(u)l kentey: hal kentey
Noun modifier -는 것 같다 -nun kes katha pattern	**ACTIVE VERB** -(으)ㄴ: 쓴 것 -(u)n: ssen kes **DESCRIPTIVE VERB** -던: 작던 것 -ten: cakten kes	**ACTIVE VERB** -는: 쓰는 것 -nun: ssenun kes **DESCRIPTIVE VERB** -(으)ㄴ: 작은 것 -(u)n: cakun kes	-(으)ㄹ N: 할 것 -(u)l N: hal kes

You learned the plain speech style at the beginning of this chapter. Notice that present tense descriptive verb form looks like its dictionary form, taking only -다 -ta, but the past tense is indicated with -었 -ess. (Remember, this is only a shorthand for -었 -ess/-았 -ass). AND there is a distinction between vowel-final and consonant-final active verbs in the present tense conjugation - ㄴ다 -nta and -는다 -nunta.

The -(는)군 -(nun)kwun pattern is similar to the plain speech style pattern, except that the consonant-versus vowel-finality of active verbs is irrelevant. The ending for the present tense active verb is always -(는)군 -(nun)kwun.

You will learn the -는데 -nuntey connector in chapter 8. Its conjugation pattern is yet different from the others: Present and past tense active verbs take -는데 -nuntey but the past tense marker -었 -ess is also used. The present tense DESCRIPTIVE verb ending is -(으)ㄴ데 -(u)ntey.

In the noun modifier pattern, which you saw in the ending -(으)ㄴ/-는/-(으)ㄹ 것 같다 -(u)n/-nun/-(u)l kes kathta *it seems like*, present tense ACTIVE verbs take -는 -nun, while present tense DESCRIPTIVE verbs and PAST TENSE ACTIVE verb conjugations are the same, this time as -(으)ㄴ -(u)n but without any additional past tense marker (that is, no -었 -ess). PAST TENSE DESCRIPTIVE verbs are a bit special. You'll practice these more in chapter 10, where you'll see that these forms are used to modify (describe) any noun, not just 것 kes.

Try seeing which of these patterns applies to other, new conjugations you learn.

7.3.4 Korean helping verbs

This section looks at expressions that use helping verbs in Korean, which attach to the -어 -e form of the verb and a few other endings that are similar in meaning (though they do not have helping verbs).

When a verb is used as a helping verb, it takes on an abstract sense in Korean. 주다 cwuta literally means *to give*, and 보다 pota means *to see*, but when these verbs turn into helping verbs (coming after another verb in the -어 -e form), their core meaning is extended to something more abstract, namely doing FOR someone and TRYING doing something.

(1) FOR YOU!

While in English we use the preposition *for* to express doing something to benefit another, Korean uses a helping verb, 주다 cwuta *to give*, attached to a verb in the -어 -e form.

<1> -어 주다/어 드리다 *do something for someone*

-어 주다 -e cwuta means *do for someone* and the expression is often used to ask for a favor or help, or even to give a polite command (disguising it as a request that something be done "for me"). It is also used to talk about favors done by others for others.

드리다 tulita is the humble form of *give* for giving something to someone who should be honored, so -어 드리다 -e tulita is the humble form, *do something for someone honored.* The *for someone* part is often only IMPLIED in English and is sometimes expressed only as *please.*

할머니께 저녁 진지를 **만들어 드렸다**.
halmenikkey cenyek cincilul mantule tulyessta.
I made dinner for Grandma.

불 좀 **꺼 줘요**.
pwul com kke cweyo.
Turn off the lights for me/please.

아주머니, 제가 문 **열어 드릴게요**.
acwumeni, ceyka mwun yele tulilkeyyo.
I will open the door for you, Ma'am.

한국에서는 생일날에 친구들에게 밥을 **사 준다**.
hankwukeysenun sayngilnaley chinkwutuleykey papul sa cwunta.
In Korea the birthday boy/girl treats (buys food for) his/her friends.

Most requests need the helping verb -어 주다 -e cwuta. You may even say that what distinguishes a request from a command in Korean is the presence of -어 주다 -e cwuta at the end. Even in the same polite speech, the request can be further cushioned with sentence endings such as -(으)ㄹ래요 -(u)llayyo, -(으)세요 -(u)seyyo, and -겠어요 -keysseyo or a negative to avoid sounding blunt or abrasive:

잠깐 자리 좀 **봐 주세요**.
camkkan cali com pwa cwuseyyo.
(Would you) please keep an eye on my seat for me?

잠깐 자리 좀 **봐 주실래요**?
camkkan cali com pwa cwusillayyo?
Would you mind keeping an eye on my seat for me?

잠깐 자리 좀 **봐 주시겠어요**?
camkkan cali com pwa cwusikeysseyo?
Would you be so kind as to keep an eye on my seat for me?

잠깐 자리 좀 **봐 주지 않으시겠어요**?
camkkan cali com pwa cwuci anhusikeysseyo?
Wouldn't you be so kind as to keep an eye on my seat for me?

학생: 선생님, 이것 좀 **가르쳐 주시겠어요**?
haksayng: sensayngnim, ikes com kaluchye cwusikeysseyo?
Student: *Teacher, could you please teach me this?*

Compare: 선생님, 이것 좀 가르치세요.
           sensayngnim, ikes com kaluchiseyyo.
           Teacher, please teach me this.

(2) BEEN THERE, DONE THAT?

Korean has helping verb constructions to express *trying something* and having had an experience *ever before*. One is -어 보다 -e pota, and one is -(으)ㄴ 적이 있다 -(u)n ceki issta.

> The spacing (띄어쓰기) rules involving the suffix -어 can get quite complex, forcing even the most learned to be doubtful of their spelling. The rules do not merit much of our precious time. When in doubt, check your spelling and spacing by searching for "띄어쓰기 (spacing)" or "철자법 (spelling rules)."

<1> -어 보다/어 봤다 *try doing, have tried*

In Korean, *to try (doing something)* is -어 보다 -e pota, literally, *do (and) see*. If you make it past tense -어 봤다 -e pwassta, it expresses *have you ever done/tried*:

아빠:	이거 **먹어 볼래**?
appa:	ike meke pollay?
Older brother:	*Do you wanna try this?*

나:	전에 **먹어 봤는데** 그냥 그랬어요.
na:	ceney meke pwassnuntey kunyang kulaysseyo.
Me:	*I've tried it before, and it was so-so.*

진수:	캐나다에 **가 봤어요**?
cinswu:	khaynataey ka pwasseyo?
Jinsu:	*Have you (ever) been to Canada?*

소민:	네. 지난 봄 방학 때 **가 봤어요**.
somin:	ney. cinan pom panghak ttay ka pwasseyo.
Somin:	*Yes, I went last spring break.*

<2> -(으)ㄴ 적이 있다/없다 *have you ever*

-(으)ㄴ 적이 있다/없다 -(u)n ceki issta/epsta carries the classic sense of having had an experience *ever before*. 적 cek is a dependent noun referring to a time; thus, the expression literally means *there has (not) been a time when*.

The usage of -(으)ㄴ 적이 있다 -(u)n ceki issta and -어 봤다 -e pwassta *have tried* inevitably overlap, but -(으)ㄴ 적이 있다 -(u)n ceki issta can't be used to ask if someone WILL or WANTS TO try something as -어 보다 -e pota can; it has an inherent past tense in -(으)ㄴ 적 -(u)n cek. The two expressions are often COMBINED to talk about past experiences:

형무:	한국에 **가 본 적이 있어요**?
hyengmwu:	hankwukey ka pon ceki isseyo?
Hyung-Mu:	*Have you ever been to Korea?*

상무:	네, **가 봤어요**/네, 있어요.
sangmwu:	ney, ka pwasseyo/ney, isseyo.
Sang-Mu:	*Yes, I have.*

장: 스키 **타** 본 적은 있는데 스노보드 **타** 본 적은 없어.
cang: sukhi tha pon cekun issnuntey sunopotu tha pon cekun epse.
Jang: *I have skied before, but I have never tried snowboarding.*

정: 스노보드 한 번 **타 봐**. 정말 재미있어.
ceng: sunopotu han pen tha pwa. cengmal caymiisse.
Jeong: *(You should) try snowboarding. It is really fun.*

<3> -곤 하다 *used to...*

If you are reflecting back on an experience you had in the past and you want to say you *used to* do something, you can use -곤 하다 -kon hata (or -고는 하다 -konun hata as a fuller form) for some activities or events that happened REPEATEDLY OR HABITUALLY:

개는 하루에 다섯 잔 이상 커피를 **마시곤 했었다**.
kyaynun halwuey tases can isang khephilul masikon hayssessta.
He often used to drink five cups of coffee per day.

나는 여름이면 늘 할머니 댁에 **가곤 했다**.
nanun yelumimyen nul halmeni taykey kakon hayssta.
I would always go to Grandma's house during the summers.

Since it indicates a repeated occurrence, you cannot use the -곤 하다 -kon hata ending for verbs that express a one-time activity (e.g., 태어나다 thayenata *to be born*, 죽다 cwukta *to die*, 입학하다 iphakhata *to enter school*, 졸업하다 colephata *to graduate*, 취직하다 chwicikhata *to get a job*, 시작하다 sicakhata *to start*, or 끝나다 kkuthnata *to finish*):

내 친구는 뉴욕에 취직하곤 했다.
nay chinkwunun nyuyokey chwicikhakon hayssta.
~~My friend used to get a job in New York.~~

You cannot use the ending for an activity with duration, either (e.g., 살다 salta *to live*, 자라다 calata *to grow up*, 좋아하다 cohahata *to like*, or 싫어하다 silhehata *to dislike*). For such things that you used to do but don't do anymore, use the double past expression, -었었 -essess:

어렸을 때 시골에 살곤 했다.
elyessul ttay sikoley salkon hayssta.
~~I would (often) live in the countryside when I was young.~~

→ 어렸을 때 시골에 **살았었다**.
   elyessul ttay sikoley salassessta.
   I used to live in the countryside when I was young and don't now.

(3) GET IT DONE!

In this section, we'll talk about three expressions that have to do with ending or finishing: -어 놓다 -e nohta/-어 두다 -e twuta *to get something done (for future use)*, -어 버리다 -e pelita *to finish something up* or *to get it over with*, and -고 말다 -ko malta *to end up doing*.

<1> -어 놓다/어 두다 *get it done*

The two verbs 놓다 nohta and 두다 twuta mean *to put or let go (of something)* and *to leave (something)*, respectively. By extension, the helping verb expressions -어 놓다 -e nohta and -어 두다 -e twuta mean *get something done now (and let go of it in your mind)* and *get something done now and leave it (for future use)*:

아이:	엄마, 차고 문을 닫을까요?
ai:	emma, chako mwunul tatulkkayo?
Child:	*Mom, should I close the garage door?*

엄마:	아버지가 곧 오실 거니까 문을 **열어 놓아라/놔라**.
emma:	apecika kot osil kenikka mwunul yele nohala/nwala.
Mother:	*Dad is coming soon, so keep it open.*

강:	내일 눈이 정말 많이 올 거래요!
kang:	nayil nwuni cengmal manhi ol kelayyo!
Kang:	*I heard that it will snow a lot tomorrow.*

박:	네, 그래서 라면하고 물을 많이 **사 뒀어요**.
pak:	ney, kulayse lamyenhako mwulul manhi sa twesseyo.
Pak:	*Yes, so I bought lots of ramen and water (to stock up).*

김:	나중에 먹을 시간이 없을 테니까 지금 많이 **먹어 둬**.
kim:	nacwungey mekul sikani epsul theynikka cikum manhi meke twe.
Kim:	*We won't have time to eat later, so eat as much as you can now.*

이:	그래야겠어.
i:	kulayyakeysse.
Yi:	*Yes, I'd better.*

숙제는 미리 미리 **해 놓으면** 좋아.
swukceynun mili mili hay nohumyen coha.
It's good to get your homework done ahead of time.

모두에게 **전화해 놓는** 거 잊지 마!
motwueykey cenhwahay nohnun ke icci ma!
Don't forget to call everyone (before the event)!

외국어는 **배워 두면** 유용하다.
oykwukenun paywe twumyen yuyonghata.
It will be useful to learn foreign languages.

두다 twuta has a more long-term sense of *putting aside, putting away, or storing* so -어 두다 -e twuta has a slightly stronger sense that the result of the action now will be of use LATER. Younger speakers do not seem to make a great distinction between -어 놓다 -e nohta and -어 두다 -e twuta and tend to use -어 놓다 -e nohta more.

<2> -어 버리다 *finish it up; end up happening*

The concrete sense of 버리다 pelita is *to throw away* or *to ruin*—an irrevocable or finished state. Having inherited this meaning figuratively, -어 버리다 -e pelita is used to talk about something you want to *finish up* or something *that ended up happening* despite your wishes or efforts. It is used with either a positive or negative feeling, but a sense of finality either way.

숙제를 다 **해 버렸다**!
swukceylul ta hay pelyessta!
I got my homework all done (and out of the way)!

국이 조금 남았는데 다 **먹어 버리자**.
kwuki cokum namassnuntey ta meke pelica.
There's only a tiny bit of soup left. Let's eat it up.

짐을 다 **싸 버려서** 입을 옷이 없어요.
cimul ta ssa pelyese ipul osi epseyo.
I packed up all my clothes/I finished my packing, so I don't have anything to wear.

전기가 **나가 버렸다**.
cenkika naka pelyessta.
The power went out!

야구하다 창문을 **깨뜨려 버렸어요**.
yakwuhata changmwunul kkayttulye pelyesseyo.
I (up and) broke the window while playing baseball.

친구가 화가 나서 **집에 가 버렸다**.
chinkwuka hwaka nase cipey ka pelyessta.
My friend got mad, so he/she (up and) went home.

잊어버리다 icepelita *to forget* and 잃어버리다 ilhepelita *to lose* or *misplace something* are fixed as compound verbs, so you do not put a space before 버리다:

지갑을 **잃어버렸어요**!
cikapul ilhepelyesseyo!
I lost my wallet!

지갑을 **잊어버리지 마**!
cikapul icepelici ma!
Don't forget your wallet!

이제 **잊어버려**.
icey icepelye.
You can let it go now. (Forget about it.)

<3> -고 말다 *end up -ing*

Another "ending up" helping verb expression is -고 말다 -ko malta. The verb 말다 malta means *to not do (anything further)* or *to do something as the final act*. All together, -고 말다 -ko malta means *to do something and end (that way)*. It normally conveys a sense that this end is contrary to intentions, though not always undesirable.

> 그 가게는 장사가 안 되어서 문을 **닫고 말았다**.
> ku kakeynun cangsaka an toyese mwunul tatko malassta.
> *After struggling with low sales for some time, the store finally ended up closing.*

> 운동도 안 하고 일만 하면 건강을 **해치고 말 겁니다**.
> wuntongto an hako ilman hamyen kenkangul haychiko mal kepnita.
> *If you don't exercise and only work, you will end up ruining your health.*

> 배를 먹을 생각이 없었는데 동생이 먹는 배가 너무 맛있어 보여서 먹기 시작했다가 결국 두 개나 **먹고 말았다**.
> paylul mekul sayngkaki epsessnuntey tongsayngi meknun payka nemwu masisse poyese mekki sicakhaysstaka kyelkwuk twu kayna mekko malassta.
> *I wasn't going to have any, but my sister made them look so delicious that I ended up eating two pears!*

The intentional -겠- -keyss- is used with -고 말다 -ko malta to indicate the speaker's strong will or intention to finish or accomplish something:

> 오늘 안에 숙제를 다 **끝내고 말겠다**!
> onul aney swukceylul ta kkuthnayko malkeyssta!
> *I am determined to finish the homework today.*

-어 버리다 -e pelita can be used together with -고 말다 -ko malta:

> 저녁을 **태워 버리고 말았다**.
> cenyekul thaywe peliko malassta.
> *I ended up burning my dinner.*

(4) I'M DYING!

Lastly, let's look at a couple of fun, colloquial endings that are used for exaggerating. You will surely **hear** them often even if, for some reason, you don't happen to **use** them very often—but we think you will!

<1> -어 죽겠다 *so ... I could die*

-어 죽겠다 -e cwukkeyssta (built from the verb 죽다 cwukta *to die*) attaches to descriptive verbs to exaggerate how extreme something is:

> 배고파 **죽겠다**!
> paykopha cwukkeyssta!
> *I'm starving to death!*

> 와, 김치가 매워 **죽겠다**!
> wa, kimchika maywe cwukkeyssta!
> *Wow! This kimchi is killer spicy!*

The ending usually doesn't attach to active verbs unless the verb carries an overall descriptive meaning. (In the expression "*I'm dying to*" -고 싶어 죽겠다 -go siphe cwukkeyssta, 싶 siph, to which -어 죽겠다 -e cwukkeyssta attaches, is a descriptive verb.) Also, it only works to talk about one's own (first person) perspective:

발 **냄새나 죽겠다**!
pal naymsayna cwukkeyssta!
My/your feet stink terribly!

힘들어 죽겠다.
himtule cwukkeyssta.
This is so exhausting!/This is killing me!

아기가 **귀여워 죽겠다**.
akika kwiyewe cwukkeyssta.
The baby is so cute I could just die!

~~아기가 귀여워서 오빠가 죽겠다.~~
akika kwiyewese oppaka cwukkeyssta.
~~*The baby is so cute my older brother could just die.*~~

<2> -(으)ㄹ **뻔하다** *that was a close call!*
Another fun Korean ending, -(으)ㄹ 뻔하다 -(u)l ppenhata, is closest in meaning to the English idiom, *a close call*. It is made up of the prospective suffix -(으)ㄹ -(u)l (here, meaning *almost*) plus a dependent noun 뻔 ppen plus the verb 하다 hata. So, -(으)ㄹ 뻔하다 -(u)l ppenhata is used to emphasize (or exaggerate) a usually bad thing that ALMOST HAPPENED. The adverbs 하마터면 hamathemyen (*missed*) *by an inch* and 거의 keuy *almost, nearly* are frequently used with this ending:

경:	길을 건너다가 차에 **치일 뻔 했어. 죽을 뻔 했어**!
kyeng:	kilul kennetaka chaey chiil ppen haysse. cwukul ppen haysse!
Gyeong:	*I almost got hit by a car just now, crossing the street. I almost died!*

화숙:	하마터면 **큰일 날 뻔 했네요**!
hwaswuk:	hamathemyen khunil nal ppen hayssneyyo!
Hwasook:	*What a scare!/That was a close one!*

명희:	바닥이 미끄러우니 조심해!
myenghuy:	pataki mikkulewuni cosimhay!
MyoungHee:	*Watch out for the wet floor!*

영길:	억, **미끄러질 뻔 했어**!
yengkil:	ek, mikkulecil ppen haysse!
Young-Gil:	*Argh, I almost slipped!*

명희:	할머니께서도 거의 **넘어질 뻔 하셨어**.
myenghuy:	halmenikkeyseto keuy nemecil ppen hasyesse.
MyoungHee:	*Yeah, Gramma also almost fell.*

아버지께서 어머니 생신을 **잊어버릴 뻔 하셨다.**
apecikkeyse emeni sayngsinul icepelil ppen hasyessta.
Dad almost forgot Mom's birthday.

7.4 Pre-final and final endings

In this chapter we have looked at a number of endings, which as we said at the beginning may be single suffixes or compositionally complex.

Speech style endings and attitude endings are basically suffixes that come at the end of sentences. They are called **final endings.**

Korean also has **pre-final endings** that attach to verbs BEFORE the speech style and attitude endings. You learned about pre-final endings such as -었 -ess -, -(으)ㄹ -(u)l, and -겠- keys in chapter 6. Here are some examples in various speech styles with pre-final endings in bold.

그는 항상 같은 곳에 앉**는**다.
kunun hangsang kathun kosey ancnunta.
He always <u>sits</u> in the same spot.

그럼 벌써 가게 문을 닫**았겠**네.
kulem pelsse kakey mwunul tatasskeyssney.
They <u>must have</u> closed the store then!

새가 죽**었을**까요?
sayka cwukessulkkayo?
<u>Has</u> the bird di<u>ed</u>, you think?

무궁화 꽃이 피**었**습니다.
mwukwunghwa kkochi phiesssupnita.
The hibiscus flowers <u>have bloomed</u>.

In this chapter you also learned helping verb constructions which are, in a sense, not ENDINGS at all. They contain VERBS ready to get endings for tense, aspect, attitude, and speech style. It's true that they do come with suffixes that connect the helping verb to the rest of the sentence, but note that all together they are not the last part of the sentence, nor are they just suffixes.

Final and pre-final endings are kinds of suffixes that are recognized as such in traditional Korean grammar, while helping verbs are considered a different animal. The main take-away is that what is a helping verb and what is a suffix may not be the same in Korean and English, and in the end, you'll want to come to understand the KOREAN system, as in sentences like these:

가지 않으면 안 됐겠군요!
kaci anhumyen an twaysskeysskwunyo!
You must have had to go then, I gather.

갈 수밖에 없었을지도 모릅니다.
kal swupakkey epsessulcito molupnita.
It may be that there was no other choice but to go.

거기 가지 않아도 됐었겠군.
keki kaci anhato twayssesskeysskwun.
It appears that they didn't have to go.

먹어 본 적이 없었을 리 없지.
meke pon ceki epsessul li epsci.
There is no way they never tried this.

그거 할 줄 몰랐나 보네.
kuke hal cwul mollassna poney.
I guess they didn't know how to do it.

웃어버릴 뻔 한 적이 있었지.
wusepelil ppen han ceki issessci.
Sure there's been a time when I almost burst out laughing.

There are scores more endings in Korean. What we have covered in this chapter lays the foundation for you to continue to pick up more endings as you go along improving your Korean. 할 수 있겠지요! hal swu isskeyssciyo *You can do it!*

Exercises

7.1 Speech Style Endings

Exercise 1. Fill in the blanks with the appropriate formal -습니다 style of each verb in the tense given in the top row.

	Past	Present	Future
공부하다	공부했습니다		
읽다		읽습니다	
보다			볼 겁니다/볼 것입니다
재미있다		재미있습니다	
친구이다	친구였습니다		
동생이다		동생입니다	
—-final: **크다**			클 겁니다/클 것입니다
ㄹ-final: **물다**		뭅니다	
Special-ㄷ: **묻다**	물었습니다		
Special-르: **빠르다**		빠릅니다	
Special-ㅂ: **덥다**			더울 겁니다/더울 것입니다
Special-ㅅ: **짓다**		짓습니다	
Special-ㅎ: **까맣다**	까맸습니다		

Exercise 2. Change the underlined words to the formal -습니다 style.

1) 나는 지금 대학교 1학년이에요. 이름은 민지예요. 대학교 생활은 재미있어요. 친구들도 많고 룸메이트도 괜찮아요. 기숙사에는 부엌이 없어서 음식을 못 만들어요. 그래서 보통 학교 식당에서 아침하고 점심을 먹어요. 가끔 한국 식당에도 가요. 영화를 좋아해서 친구하고 영화도 자주 봐요. 그리고 테니스도 가끔 쳐요. 또 한국 음악도 자주 들어요.

2) 매일 공부 때문에 바빠요. 숙제도 매일 내요. 그리고 시험 때에는 하루 종일 도서관에서 살아요. 잠도 잘 못 자요. 저는 잠을 못 자면 얼굴이 부어요. 그래서 힘들어요. 그렇지만 시험이 끝나면 기숙사 방에서 쉬어요. 그리고 친구하고 같이 만나서 놀아요. 시내에 나가서 커피를 마셔요. 노래방에 가서 노래도 불러요.

3) 요즘 날씨가 아주 추워요. 그래서 어제 백화점에 가서 따뜻한 코트를 샀어

요. 코트가 색깔도 예쁘고 디자인도 괜찮아서 아주 마음에 <u>들었어요</u>. 오늘 새로 산 코트를 입고 친구가 선물로 준 모자도 <u>썼어요</u>. 부츠도 <u>신었어요</u>. 이제는 <u>따뜻해요</u>.

4) 다음 주말은 아주 <u>바쁠 거예요</u>. 학교 풋볼 시합이 있어서 경기를 보러 <u>갈 거예요</u>. 경기를 보고 나서 친구들하고 맥주 한 잔 <u>마실 거예요</u>. 그리고 같이 노래방에서 노래를 <u>부를 거예요</u>.

Exercise 3. Conjugate the verbs in parentheses for the formal -습니다 style.

어제는 11월 20일입니다. 겨울이지만 날씨가 별로 안 _____ (춥다). 그래서 친구하고 같이 시내에 나가서 쇼핑도 하고 영화도 봤습니다. 어젯밤에는 눈이 와서 온 세상이 _____ (하얗다). 추웠지만 기분이 좋아서 친구하고 계속 _____ (걷다). 그래서 감기에 걸렸습니다. 오늘 아침에 일어났는데 목이 많이 _____ (붓다). 그래서 아침의 음악 수업 시간에 노래를 못 _____ (부르다). 그리고 지금은 기침도 나고 열도 많이 _____ (나다). 지금 점심을 _____ (먹다). 그리고 나서 감기 때문에 오늘 오후에 병원에 _____ (가다). 병원이 학교에서 좀 _____ (멀다). 그래서 택시를 _____ (타다). 저녁에 약을 먹고 푹 _____ (자다). 약을 먹으면 감기가 다 _____ (낫다). 감기가 나으면 이번 주말에 친구하고 또 _____ (걷다). 그리고 같이 시내에 가서 _____ (놀다).

Exercise 4. Fill in the blanks with the appropriate plain style for each verb in the tense given in the top row.

	Past	Present	Future
공부하다	공부했다		
읽다		읽는다	
보다			볼 거다/볼 것이다
재미있다		재미있다	
친구이다	친구였다		
동생이다		동생이다	
—-final: **쓰다**			쓸 거다/쓸 것이다

	Past	Present	Future
—-final: **크다**		크다	
ㄹ-final: **길다**	길었다		
ㄹ-final: **물다**		문다	
Special-ㄷ: **묻다**			물을 거다/물을 것이다
Special-르: **부르다**		부른다	
Special-르: **빠르다**	빨랐다		
Special-ㅂ: **덥다**		덥다	
Special-ㅂ: **돕다**			도울 거다/도울 것이다
Special-ㅅ: **짓다**		짓는다	
Special-ㅎ: **까맣다**	까맸다		

Exercise 5. Change the underlined words to plain style.

1) 나는 지금 대학교 1학년<u>이에요</u>. 이름은 민지<u>예요</u>. 대학교 생활은 재미있어
 <u>요</u>. 친구들도 많고 룸메이트도 <u>괜찮아요</u>. 기숙사에는 부엌이 없어서 음식을
 못 <u>만들어요</u>. 그래서 보통 학교 식당에서 아침하고 점심을 <u>먹어요</u>. 가끔 한
 국 식당에도 <u>가요</u>. 영화를 좋아해서 친구하고 영화도 자주 <u>봐요</u>. 그리고 테
 니스도 가끔 <u>쳐요</u>. 또 한국 음악도 자주 <u>들어요</u>.

2) 매일 공부 때문에 <u>바빠요</u>. 숙제도 매일 <u>내요</u>. 그리고 시험 때에는 하루 종일
 도서관에서 <u>살아요</u>. 잠도 잘 못 <u>자요</u>. 저는 잠을 못 자면 얼굴이 <u>부어요</u>. 그래
 서 <u>힘들어요</u>. 그렇지만 시험이 끝나면 기숙사 방에서 <u>쉬어요</u>. 그리고 친구하
 고 같이 만나서 <u>놀아요</u>. 시내에 나가서 커피를 <u>마셔요</u>. 노래방에 가서 노래도
 <u>불러요</u>.

3) 요즘 날씨가 아주 <u>추워요</u>. 그래서 어제 백화점에 가서 따뜻한 코트를 <u>샀어
 요</u>. 코트가 색깔도 예쁘고 디자인도 괜찮아서 아주 마음에 들었어요. 오늘
 새로 산 코트를 입고 친구가 선물로 준 모자도 <u>썼어요</u>. 부츠도 <u>신었어요</u>. 이
 제는 <u>따뜻해요</u>.

4) 다음 주말은 아주 <u>바쁠 거예요</u>. 학교 풋볼 시합이 있어서 경기를 보러 갈 거
 <u>예요</u>. 경기를 보고 나서 친구들하고 맥주 한 잔 <u>마실 거예요</u>. 그리고 같이 노
 래방에서 노래를 <u>부를 거예요</u>.

Exercise 6. Conjugate the verbs in parentheses for the plain style, keeping in mind the tense.

어제는 11월 20일이었다. 겨울이지만 날씨가 별로 안 _____ (춥다). 그래서 친구하고 같이 시내에 나가서 쇼핑도 하고 영화도 봤다. 어젯밤에는 눈이 와서 온 세상이 _____ (하얗다). 추웠지만 기분이 좋아서 친구하고 계속 _____ (걷다). 그래서 감기에 걸렸다. 오늘 아침에 일어났는데 목이 많이 _____ (붓다). 그래서 아침의 음악 수업 시간에 노래를 못 _____ (부르다). 그리고 지금은 기침도 나고 열도 많이 _____ (나다). 지금 점심을 _____ (먹다). 그리고 나서 감기 때문에 오늘 오후에 병원에 _____ (가다). 병원이 학교에서 좀 _____ (멀다). 그래서 택시를 _____ (타다). 저녁에 약을 먹고 푹 _____ (자다). 약을 먹으면 감기가 다 _____ (낫다). 감기가 나으면 이번 주말에 친구하고 또 _____ (걷다). 그리고 _____ (놀다).

Exercise 7. Underline the appropriate speech style to complete the sentence. Some have more than one possible answer.

1) 동생: 언니, 주말에 뭐 (하니, 하냐, 해)?
   언니: 글쎄, 아직 모르겠는데.

2) 형: 텔레비전 좀 (봐라, 보라, 봐).
   동생: 왜? 뭐 재미있는 거 있어?

3) 성경 (Bible): 수고하고 짐 진 자들아, 다 내게로 (와라, 오라, 와).

4) 신하 (vassal): 마마, 말씀 드릴 것이 (있네, 있도다, 있사옵니다)
   왕 (king): (알겠도다, 알겠사옵니다).

5) 부장님 (department manager): 내일은 좀 일찍 (출근해라, 출근하게, 출근하구료).
   직원 (employee): 네, 알겠습니다.

6) 장모님 (mother-in-law): 자네, 언제 집에 (오느냐, 오는가, 오우)?
   사위 (son-in-law): 일곱 시쯤 (옵니다, 오네, 오소).

7.2 Speaker Attitude Endings

Exercise 8. Choose the appropriate expression to complete the dialogues. Be sure to conjugate the given verbs appropriately and use the same speech style as the questions.

-거든	-잖아	-지 (confirmation)	-지 (offer, agreement)

1) A: 커피 좀 더 갖다 주실래요?

   B: 네, 금방 _____. (갖다 드리다)

2) A: 어제 눈이 별로 안 _____? (오다)

   B: 응, 별로 안 왔네.

3) A: 일 그만 하고 나가자!

   B: 오늘 할 일이 _____. 건드리지 마. (많다)

4) A: 늦었다. 빨리 수업 가자.

   B: 기억 안 나? 지난 주에 교수님께서 오늘 수업은 취소한다고 _____. (하시다)

   A: 아, 참! 맞다! 깜빡 잊어 버렸네.

-겠네	-군(요)/구나	-네	-더라(고)	-지

5) A: 내 구두 어때? 새로 산 구두야. 예쁘지?

   B: 정말 _____. (예쁘다)

6) A: 다음 학기에 장학금을 받게 돼서 정말 기분이 좋아요.

   B: 와! 정말 _____. (좋다)

7) A: 지훈이가 아르바이트를 세 개나 한대.

   B: 아, 그래서 요즘 그렇게 지훈이 얼굴을 보기가 _____! (힘들다)

8) A: 스타워즈 영화를 좋아해?

   B: 그럼, 당연히 _____. 어렸을 때부터 스타워즈 팬이었잖아. (좋아하다)

9) A: 어제 친구는 만났어?

   B: 약속 시간에 좀 늦게 갔는데 _____. (기다리고 있다)

Exercise 9. Underline the most appropriate answer to complete the sentence.

1) A: 여보세요. 거기 최고 슈퍼(지요, 네요, 거든요, 잖아요)?

   B: 네, 그렇습니다.

2) A: 여기 (앉으시지요, 앉으시네요, 앉으시거든요, 앉으시잖아요).

   B: 네, 감사합니다.

3) A: 왜 아직도 집에 있어? 너 오늘 약속있다고 (말하잖아, 말했잖아).

   B: 약속이 (취소되잖아, 취소되거든, 취소됐잖아, 취소됐거든). 방금 전화 받았어.

4) A: 이 식당의 순두부찌개가 아주 맛있지요?

   B: 네, (맛있네요, 맛있잖아요, 맛있거든요).

5) A: 돈 좀 빌려 줄 수 있어?

   B: 미안, 지금 돈이 (없지, 없었지, 없거든, 없잖아). 은행에서 찾아서 빌려 줄게.

6) A: 넘어져서 팔을 다쳤어.

   B: 저런, 정말 (아프네, 아팠네, 아팠겠지, 아팠겠네). 좀 조심하지 그랬어.

7) A: 오늘은 날씨가 참 좋네요.

   B: 네, 아침에 나가 보니까 정말 (따뜻하군요, 따뜻하네요, 따뜻하더라고요)

8) A: 수민이가 감기에 걸렸대요.

   B: 아, 그래서 오늘 학교에 못 (왔지요, 왔군요, 왔거든요). 왜 안 왔는지 궁금했어요.

Exercise 10. Provide a proper response to what was just said using -겠네(요). Use the same speech style as the first sentence.

1) A: 이번 학기에 여섯 과목이나 들어요.

   B: 와! _____.

2) A: 피아노를 10년 동안 쳤어.

   B: 그럼 아주 잘 _____.

3) A: 이번 달에 쇼핑을 너무 많이 했네.

   B: 그럼 지금 돈이 _____. 돈을 아껴써야지!

4) A: 어젯밤에 1시간만 자고 시험 공부했어요.

5) B: 아이고, _____.

7.3 Helping Verbs

Exercise 11. Underline the most appropriate expression to complete the sentence.

1) A: 여기에서는 *휴대폰을 (쓸 수 없어요, 쓸 줄 몰라요).

   *휴대폰: cell phone

   B: 아, 그래요?

2) A: 내일 눈이 많이 올 수도 있대요.

   B: (그럴 수가 없어요, 그럴 리가 없어요). 일기 예보 봤는데 내일 날씨가 좋
   대요.

3) A: 왜 택시를 안 타고 지하철을 탔어요?

   B: 길이 너무 막혀서 지하철을 (탈 수 없었어요, 탈 수밖에 없었어요).

4) A: 한국어 (읽을 수 없어요, 읽을 줄 알아요)?

   B: 네. 잘 읽어요.

5) A: 차가 막혀서 (늦을 수도 없어요, 늦을지도 몰라요). 기다리지 마세요.

   B: 알았어요.

6) A: 내 목소리가 잘 (들을 수 있어요, 들려요)?

   B: 아니요!

Exercise 12. Choose the appropriate expression to complete the dialogues. Be sure to conjugate the given verbs appropriately and use the same speech style as the questions.

-지 말아야 하다	-어도 되다	-어야 되다	-지 않아도 되다

1) A: 실례합니다. 여기 _____? (앉다)

   B: 네, 그러세요.

2) A: 보고서는 내일까지 끝내야 합니까?

   B: 아니요. 내일까지 _____. (끝내다)

3) A: 한국에서는 집 안에서 신발을 신어도 돼요?

   B: 아니요. 신발을 _____. (벗다)

4) A: 건강을 위해서 술을 너무 많이 _____. (마시다)

   B: 알겠습니다.

-(으)ㄹ 필요가 없다	-(으)면 되다
-(으)면 안 되다	-지 않으면 안 되다

5) A: 숙제 다 했어?

   B: 응, 경제학 숙제하고 영어 숙제는 다 하고 한국어 숙제만 _____. (하다)

6) A: 실내에서는 담배를 _____. (피우다)

   B: 죄송합니다.

7) A: 오늘 생일 파티에 케이크 가져갈까?

   B: 내가 가져갈 테니까 _____. (가져오다)

8) A: 조금 더 있다가 가세요.

   B: 친구를 만나기로 해서 지금 _____. (가다)

Exercise 13. Underline the appropriate expression from the parentheses to complete the dialogues most naturally. Some have more than one possible answer.

1) A: 주영이한테 이 영화 같이 보자고 할까?

   B: 주영이는 아마 이 영화를 (볼 걸, 봤을 걸, 볼 걸 그랬어). 그러니까 다음에 같이 보자고 하자.

2) A: 아, 시험을 너무 못 봤어요.

   B: 공부를 좀 열심히 (할 걸 그랬어요, 하지 그랬어요, 했어야지요).

3) A: 또 지각했어. 좀 더 일찍 (나갈 걸그랬어, 나가지 그랬어, 나갔어야 했어).

   B: 내일은 일찍 일어나!

4) A: 어제 빨간 불이 길을 건너다가 차에 치일 뻔 했어.

   B: 저런, 그러니까 길을 건널 때 (조심하지 그랬어, 조심했어야지, 조심할 걸 그랬어).

Exercise 14. Use the provided information and express your ideas in less intrusive ways, or more indirectly, using -(으)ㄴ/는/(으)ㄹ 것 같다. Use the same speech style as the questions.

1) A: 밖에 날씨가 어때요?

   B: 좀 _____. (춥다)

2) A: 치마가 너무 길어요?

   B: 아니요. 별로 안 _____! (길다)

3) A: 지금 동생 뭐 해?

   B: 방에서 뭐 _____. (만들다)

4) A: 그 친구가 커피 선물을 좋아할까?

   B: 글쎄. 그 친구는 커피를 안 _____. (마시다)

5) A: 감기가 나았어요?

   B: 네, 다 _____. (낫다)

6) A: 지금 가면 안 늦겠지요?

   B: 글쎄. 택시 안 타면 _____. (늦다)

Exercise 15. Change the underlined parts to make these questions sound more polite using -(으)ㄴ가/-나.

1) A: 지금 비가 <u>와요</u>?

   → _____

   B: 아니요. 안 와요.

2) A: 어디 <u>가요</u>?

   → _____

   B: 학교에 가요.

3) A: 김치찌개가 <u>매워요</u>?

   → _____

   B: 좀 맵네요.

4) A: 방이 깨끗해요?

→ _____

B: 네, 깨끗합니다.

5) A: 어젯밤에 눈이 왔어요?

→ _____

B: 네, 많이 왔어요.

6) A: 가방이 많이 무거웠어요?

→ _____

B: 조금요.

7) A: 내일도 올 거예요?

→ _____

B: 네.

Exercise 16. Choose the appropriate expression to complete the dialogues using -어 보이다. Be sure to conjugate the given verbs appropriately.

따뜻하다	아프다	젊다	행복하다

1) A: 빨간 옷이 참 예쁘시네요. 빨간 색을 입으시니까 _____요.

B: 고마워요.

2) A: 무슨 일 있어? 얼굴이 _____네.

B: 어, 감기에 걸려서 좀 아팠어.

3) A: 해리하고 지니가 사귄대!

B: 응, 두 사람이 아주 _____더라.

4) A: 새 코트 샀네요. 아주 _____요.

B: 네, 정말 따뜻해요.

Exercise 17. Choose the appropriate expression to complete the dialogues. Be sure to conjugate the given verbs appropriately and use the same speech style as the questions.

-나/-(으)ㄴ가 보다	-나/-(으)ㄴ가/-(으)ㄹ까
-어 보이다	-(으)ㄹ 것 같다

1) A: 오늘 오후에 비가 _____. 우산 가져 가세요. (오다)

   B: 네, 그럴게요.

2) A: 이 옷 어때요?

   B: 까만 색 옷을 입으니까 _____. (날씬하다)

3) A: 정우씨가 기분이 아주 좋아 보여요.

   B: 네, 시험을 아주 잘 봐서 기분이 _____. (좋다)

4) A: 겨울인데 왜 이렇게 _____? (따뜻하다)

   B: 글쎄요.

Exercise 18. Fill in the blanks with the appropriate -어 주다/드리 form of the given verb.

1) A: 할머니 생신에 뭐 해 드렸어요?

   B: 케이크를 _____어요. (만들다)

2) A: 똑똑!

   B: 잠깐만 기다리세요. 금방 _____게요. (열다)

3) A: 선생님, 한국어를 _____서 감사합니다! (가르치시다)

   B: 그렇게 _____서 고마워요. (얘기하다)

4) A: 동생 집에 있지? 동생한테 이것 좀 _____. (전하다)

   B: 그럴게.

5) A: 책을 안 가져왔네. 책 좀 _____래? (빌리다)

   B: 네, _____게요. (빌리다)

Exercise 19. Choose the appropriate expression to complete the dialogues. Be sure to conjugate the given verbs appropriately and use the same speech style as the questions.

-어 보다	-어 봤다	-(으)ㄴ 적이 없다	-곤 하다

1) A: 감기에 걸려서 목이 아파요.

   B: 그럼 *생강차를 _____! (마시다)   *생강차: ginger tea

2) A: 김치 스파게티 먹어 봤어요?

   B: 아니요. 한 번도 _____. (먹어 보다)

3) A: 요즘도 테니스 자주 치세요?

   B: 대학교 때에는 자주 _____데 요즘은 시간이 없어서 못 쳐요. (치다)

4) A: 그 가수의 새 노래를 _____? (듣다)

   B: 네! 정말 좋던데요?

-고 말다	-어 놓다/두다	-어 버리다	-어 죽겠다	-(으)ㄹ 뻔하다

5) A: 왜 어제 파티에 안 왔어?

   B: _____! (잊다)

6) A: 여행 준비 다 했어요?

   B: 네, 비행기 표도 사고 가방도 _____. (싸다)

7) A: 울지 않으려고 했는데 _____? (울다)

   B: 네! 정말 좋던데요?

8) A: 어제 길을 건너다가 차에 _____. (치이다)

   B: 저런! 큰일날 뻔 했다!

9) A: 아! 목 _____! 물 좀 줘. (마르다)

   B: 여기 있어.

CHAPTER 8

Complex Sentences

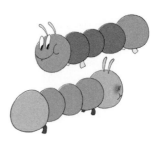

Now that you have all the basic building blocks of nouns and particles, verbs and conjugations, and sentence endings in hand and ready to wield, you can make all kinds of basic sentences! In this chapter, we expand on those powers and show how to make longer, more complex sentences by connecting two or more sentences into one.

One way to create a complex sentence is using a sentence, or **clause**, to modify a noun. (Once a sentence is inside the larger sentence, it is called a clause.) For example, you could say something like this to ask about a birthday present you received yesterday:

어제 생일 선물 받았어. 어디 갔지?
ecey sayngil senmwul patasse. eti kassci?
I got a birthday present yesterday. Where is it?

Or you can say it all in one sentence:

어제 **받은** 내 생일 선물 어디 갔지?
ecey patun nay sayngil senmwul eti kassci?
Where is the birthday present <u>that I received yesterday?</u>

Another way to make a complex sentence is by linking two clauses together with *and*, *but*, *because*, and so on. Korean uses suffixes we'll call **connectors** to do this. To take an example, suppose that you just found out it was raining. You could say:

지금 비가 와요. 테니스는 내일 칩시다.
cikum pika wayo. theynisunun nayil chipsita.
It's raining now. Let's play tennis tomorrow.

Or you can say this all in one sentence:

지금 비가 **오는데**, 테니스는 내일 칩시다.
cikum pika onuntey, theynisunun nayil chipsita.
<u>*It's raining now, so* let's play tennis tomorrow.</u>

In this chapter we will explore the useful and interesting world of complex sentences. We'll start with using clauses to modify nouns, then we'll move on to linking clauses together, end to end. Since verbs come at the end of clauses in Korean, both of these kinds of complex sentences involve endings on verbs to indicate how that clause connects to the rest of the sentence. The first kind needs a **modifier ending**, and the second kind a **connector**.

8.1 Adnominal Clauses

One of the ways to make a sentence complex and interesting is to use modifiers. *I listen to music* is a simpler sentence than *I listen to fun Korean music,* which is simpler than *I listen to fun Korean music that I was introduced to by my best friend from high school.*

In English, if you have just one adjective to describe a noun, it comes before the noun, as in *a great dancer;* if the adjective is "complex," it comes AFTER the noun: *the scholar interested in K-pop.* And if you want to describe the noun using a clause, it also comes AFTER the noun: *a pop idol I listen to daily.*

In Korean, all noun-modifiers come BEFORE the noun, and when the noun-modifier is sentence-sized, that is, a **clause** called an **adnominal clause,** the verb conjugates with special endings. The endings for this adnominal usage are different from the endings used on verbs at the ends of sentences. Let's take a look first at some adnominals that do NOT conjugate.

8.1.1 Inalterable adnominals

We mentioned **adnominals** in chapter 3 as modifiers that ONLY come before nouns, do not function as predicates, and aren't conjugated. They are called adnominals because they ADD some meaning to nouns (i.e. **nominals**) and they are sort of ADD-ed, being placed in front of the noun. These adnominals are short, but they are independent words in Korean, written with a space afterwards. Here are some useful adnominals and examples of their use:

Modifier	Examples	Modifier	Examples
첫 ches *first*	첫 만남 ches mannam *first encounter/meeting* 첫 시험 ches sihem *the first exam*	딴 ttan *different, irrelevant*	딴 사람 ttan salam *a changed man* 딴 말 ttan mal *irrelevant remarks*
옛 yeys *old*	옛 사랑 yeys salang *a bygone romance* 옛 친구 yeys chinkwu *old friends*	맨 mayn *the most, extreme*	맨 앞 mayn aph *the foremost* 맨 끝 mayn kkuth *the very end*
새 say *new*	새 가방 say kapang *new bag* 새 친구 say chinkwu *new friends*	고 ko *the late*	고 김광석 씨 ko kimkwangsek ssi *the late Mr. Kwang-seok Kim*
헌 hen *old*	헌 가방 hen kapang *old bag* 헌 책 hen chayk *old book*	만 man *full*	만 한 시간 man han sikan *one solid hour* 만 스무 살 man sumwu sal *(fully) 20 years old*

8.1.2 Descriptive verbs

Now let's move on to CONJUGATING noun-modifiers. This is a key place where descriptive verbs are treated differently from active verbs in Korean grammar.

(1) Adnominal clauses with present tense descriptive verbs

You know how to conjugate descriptive verbs as predicates at the end of the sentence, but descriptive verbs that come before a noun as adnominals take a different form. You will recall that for -(으)ㄴ/는/(으)ㄹ 것 같다 -(u)n/nun/(u)l kes kathta *it seems like*, descriptive verbs take the -(으)ㄴ 것 같다 -(u)n kes kathta version of the ending. And you know that 것 kes is a noun that means *thing*. What is happening structurally with this expression is that descriptive verbs are being conjugated with -(으)ㄴ -(u)n to modify the noun 것 kes. Indeed, descriptive verbs are marked with -(으)ㄴ -(u)n when they come before ANY noun to modify it. -은 -un is added after consonant-final roots and -ㄴ -n after vowel-final roots. Here are some examples of descriptive verbs in adnominal clauses compared to their predicate forms:

Descriptive verbs as adnominals		Descriptive verbs as predicates	
예쁜 꽃 yeyppun kkoch	a *pretty* flower	꽃이 예쁘다. kkochi yeypputa.	The flower is pretty.
작은 꽃 cakun kkoch	a *small* flower	꽃이 작아요. kkochi cakayo.	The flower is small.
대단한 사람 taytanhan salam	an *amazing* person	그 사람 대단하다! ku salam taytanhata!	She is amazing!
먼 길 men kil	the *long (far)* road	길이 멉니다. kili mepnita.	The road is long/far.

Descriptive verbs that are of special conjugation classes undergo their root changes, since the adnominal ending is an -으 type suffix.

이렇다 ilehta	이런 날 ilen nal	a day *like this*
맵다 maypta	매운 김치 maywun kimchi	*spicy* kimchi
낫다 nasta	더 나은 방법 te naun pangpep	a *better* solution

Some words that are simple adjectives in English, like *tall*, are complex descriptors in Korean. They look a little more like sentences in Korean, but when they end with a descriptive verb, it takes the -(으)ㄴ -(u)n suffix to modify a noun. The particles are often dropped in these modifying phrases:

키(가) 크다 khi(ka) khuta	*tall* Literally, *the height is tall*	키(가) 큰 아이 khi(ka) khun ai	the *tall* child

머리(가) 좋다	*smart*	머리(가) **좋은** 학생	*the smart students*
meli(ka) cohta	Literally, *the head is good*	meli(ka) cohun haksayng	
코(가) 높다	*snooty*	코(가) **높은** 사람들	*snooty people*
kho(ka) nophta	Literally, *the nose is high*	kho(ka) nophun salamtul	

Be careful of words that translate as adjectives in English, but are formed with 있다/없다 issta/epsta. 있다 issta and 없다 epsta are ACTIVE VERBS in Korean, grammatically speaking, so these verbs use a different ending, -는 -nun, when they modify a noun:

맛있는 식당	*a delicious restaurant*	**힘없는** 목소리	*a feeble voice*
masissnun siktang		himepsnun moksoli	
재미있는 수업	*a fun class*	**인기 있는** 가수	*a popular singer*
caymiissnun swuep		inki issnun kaswu	

Keep in mind that ANY descriptive verb could come at the end of a longer phrase, and it would still be conjugated with -(으)ㄴ -(u)n to make an adnominal:

내 생각에 진짜 **대단한** 사람
nay sayngkakey cincca taytanhan salam
a person who is truly amazing in my opinion

이거보다 **매운** 김치
ikespota maywun kimchi
kimchi that is spicier than this

여러 나라에서 **인기 있는** 가수
yele nalaeyse inki issnun kaswu
a popular singer in many countries = *a singer who is popular in many countries*

And, any of these complex noun phrases, with an adnominal clause modifying the noun, can then be used in a sentence as subject, object, complement, etc.

내 생각에 진짜 **대단한** 사람은 우리 이모야.
nay sayngkakey cincca taytanhan salamun wuli imoya.
{A person who is truly amazing in my opinion} is my aunt.

제가 이거보다 **매운** 김치를 못 먹어요.
ceyka ikespota maywun kimchilul mos mekeyo.
I can't eat {kimchi that is spicier than this}.

2NE1은 여러 나라에서 **인기 있는** 그룹이었다.
2NE1un yele nalaeyse inki issnun kulwupiessta.
2NE1 was {a group that was popular in many countries}.

(2) More than one descriptor

When there is more than one descriptive verb modifying a noun, they are connected using verbal connectors:

크고 예쁜 꽃을 샀어요.
khuko yeyppun kkochul sasseyo.
I bought a big, pretty flower.

조용하고 깨끗한 방으로 주세요.
coyonghako kkaykkushan pangulo cwuseyyo.
I would like to have a quiet, clean room.

맵고 짠 음식은 몸에 안 좋다.
maypko ccan umsikun momey an cohta.
Spicy and salty foods are not good for your health.

파랗지만 먹음직스러운 사과를 샀다.
ppalkahciman mekumciksulewun sakwalul sassta.
I bought green, yet delicious-looking, apples.

8.1.3 Active verbs

Just like descriptive verbs, ACTIVE verbs can be used to delineate a noun, in phrases like *people who sing* (or, *singing people*) or *the country that has a long and vibrant history from hermitdom to fame across six continents*, for example.

(1) Adnominal clauses with present tense active verbs

In Korean, clausal modifiers with active verbs go in front of the noun just like those with descriptive verbs. And if the verb is in the PRESENT TENSE, it gets the ending -는 -nun as the adnominal suffix.

한국어를 **가르치는** 선생님 hankwukelul kaluchinun sensayngnim	*a teacher who teaches Korean*
책을 많이 **읽는** 친구 chaykul manhi ilknun chinkwu	*a friend who reads a lot*
한국 문화를 잘 **아는** 사람 hankwuk mwunhwalul cal anun salam	*a person who knows a lot (about) Korean culture*
지금 선생님과 **이야기하는** 학생 cikum sensayngnimkwa iyakihanun haksayng	*the student who is talking with the teacher now*

This pattern works whether the person (or thing) being described is DOING the action or is the OBJECT of the action:

책을 **읽는** 아이 chaykul ilknun ai	*the child who is reading*
제가 **읽는** 책 ceyka ilknun chayk	*the book that I am reading*

내가 **만들 수 있는** 한국 음식
nayka mantul swu issnun hankwuk umsik
*the Korean **food** I am able to cook*

도서관에서 한국 역사에 대한 책을 **찾는** 사람
tosekwaneyse hankwuk yeksaey tayhan chaykul chacnun salam
*the **person** who is looking for Korean history books at the library*

The examples you just saw above contain a small sentence inside them, but they are not sentences themselves; they are noun phrases, talking about the noun noted in bold in English. Since they are noun phrases, they can be used as subjects and objects in a full sentence. We have put them in curly brackets:

{**제가 읽는** 책}이 참 재미있어요.
ceyka ilknun chayki cham caymiisseyo.
*{The **book** that I am reading} is really fun.*

{**내가 만들 수 있는** 한국 음식}이 몇 가지 안 돼요.
nayka mantul swu issnun hankwuk umsiki myech kaci an twayyo.
*{The number of Korean **foods** I am able to cook} is not too many.*

{**빵 굽는** 사람}이 누구예요?
ppang kwupnun salami nwukwuyeyyo?
*Who is {the **person** who bakes bread}?*

친구가 {**아파트를 짓는** 회사}에서 일해요.
chinkwuka aphathulul cisnun hoysaeyse ilhayyo.
*My friend works for {a **company** that builds apartments}.*

{**저기서 음악을 듣는** 사람}이 내 동생이에요.
cekise umakul tutnun salami nay tongseyngieyyo.
*{The **person** who is listening to music over there} is my brother.*

{**남을 생각할 줄 아는** 사람}이 되고 싶어.
namul sayngkakhal cwul anun salami toyko siphe.
*I want to be {someone **who is considerate of others**}.*

8.1.4 Active or descriptive verb?

We mentioned above that "adjectives" like *fun* (재미있다 caymiissta) use the -는 -nun ad-nominal suffix because their 있다/없다 issta/epsta component makes them ACTIVE VERBS. 이다 ita *to be* works like the descriptive verbs, however, and uses the -(으)ㄴ -(u)n suffix:

아주 **재미있는** 영화를 보고 싶다.
acwu caymiissnun yenghwalul poko siphta.
*I want to see a *really fun* movie.*

내 **룸메이트인** 그 친구
nay lwummeyithuin ku chinkwu
*that friend *who is a roommate of mine**

Remember to think twice about 하다 hata words—is it a descriptive verb or an active verb?—and choose the correct suffix -(으)ㄴ -(u)n or -는 -nun.

똑똑한 소녀　　　　　*the smart girl, the girl who is smart*
ttokttokhan sonye

등산하는 학생들　　　*the students who are hiking*
tungsan hanun haksayngtul

정직한 사람들　　　　*honest people, people who are honest*
cengcikhan salamtul

싫어하는 옷 (cf. **싫은** 옷)　*the clothes that I do not like* (cf. *the distasteful clothes*)
silhehanun os (cf. silhun os)

좋아하는 옷 (cf. **좋은** 옷)　*the clothes that I like* (cf. *the good clothes*)
coahanun os (cf. cohun os)

8.1.5 Adnominal clauses with past tense active verbs

When an active verb in an adnominal clause refers to a COMPLETED event, as in *the person who taught me Korean*, or *all the people I have met here*, its verb is conjugated with -(으)ㄴ -(u)n. (Yes, the same -(으)ㄴ -(u)n that is used for PRESENT TENSE DESCRIPTIVE verbs.)

{**어제 본** 영화}는 액션 영화였다.
ecey pon yenghwanun ayksyen yenghwayessta.
{The movie that I watched yesterday} was an action movie.

{**시험을 다 끝낸** 사람들}은 나가도 좋습니다.
sihemul ta kkuthnayn salamtulun nakato cohsupnita.
{People who have finished the test} may leave now.

{**내 피자를 먹은** 사람}이 누구야?
nay phicalul mekun salami nwukwuya?
Who ate my pizza?/Who is {the person who ate my pizza}?

{**그 회사가 지은** 아파트}는 아주 현대식이야.
ku hoysaka ciun aphathunun acwu hyentaysikiya.
{The apartment that company built} is very modern.

8.1.6 Adnominal clauses with future tense verbs

If the noun is described with a FUTURE TENSE adnominal clause (NOUN *who will* ..., NOUN *that (someone) will* ...), the connector to use is -(으)ㄹ -(u)l.

{**내가 부를** 노래}는 사랑 노래예요.
nayka pwulul nolaynun salang nolayyeyyo.
{The song I am going to sing} is a love song.

These future/prospective adnominal clauses sometimes translate with *to do* in English, as in *someone to do this, work to do, food to eat.*

{이 일을 해 줄 사람}을 찾았어?
i ilul hay cwul salamul chacasse?
Have you found {someone to do this job for you}?

{오늘 밤에 할 일}이 많아요.
onul pamey hal ili manhayo.
I have a lot of {work to do tonight}.

Descriptive verbs do not usually come with -(으)ㄹ -(u)l, but when they do, they either mean something verb-like or are used as part of a larger **set expression**:

그때가 **좋을 때**였지.
kuttayka cohul ttayyessci.
Those were the good times.

내일은 더 **추울지도** 몰라.
nayilun te chwuwulcito molla.
It may be colder tomorrow.

하얘도 **매울 수 있어**.
hayayto maywul swu isse.
It's white, but it could be spicy.

피곤할 짓을 왜 했어?
phikonhal cisul way haysse?
Why did you do stuff that will make you tired?

8.1.7 Retrospective adnominal suffix

One of the most famous children's songs in Korea is 나의 고향 nauy kohyang "*My Hometown*" and it begins with:

내가 살던 고향은 꽃 피는 산골···
nayka salten kohyangun kkoch phinun sankol...
The hometown I once lived in was in the woods where flowers bloom...

Note that 살던 salten is used instead of 산 san in this case to express (*the hometown*) *where I once lived*. -던 -ten is another adnominal ending that is a combination of the retrospective suffix -더 -te and the adnominal suffix -(으)ㄴ -(u)n. It is the adnominal ending for an action that happened IN THE PAST FOR A WHILE, as opposed to -(으)ㄴ -(u)n which expresses an action which was COMPLETED in the past. Here are the details of -던 -ten usage:

(1) Active verb + 던 *used to*

-던 -ten is a **durative** marker for adnominals with an event or activity that happened HABITUALLY or REPEATEDLY in the past:

내가 자주 **가던** 식당이 문을 닫았어요.
nayka cacwu katen siktangi mwunul tatasseyo.
The restaurant that I used to go to often closed.

여기가 어릴 때 내가 **살던** 동네예요.
yekika elil ttay nayka salten tongneyyeyyo.
Here is the place where I used to live when I was young.

이건 내가 자주 **마시던** 커피예요.
iken nayka cacwu masiten khephiyeyyo.
This is the (brand/kind of) coffee that I often drank/used to drink.

In this usage - 던 -ten is often paired with frequency adverbs such as 자주 cacwu *frequently* and 가끔 kakkum *occasionally* or 적 cek and 때 ttay phrases such as 어릴 적 elil cek *when I was young*, and 초등학교 때 chotunghakkyo ttay *when I was in elementary school.*

You might remember another expression from chapter 7 that means *used to*: -곤 하다 -kon hata. The difference is that - 던 -ten is an adnominal suffix that attaches to a verb that comes before a noun it modifies, whereas -곤 하다 -kon hata is an ending that can end a sentence.

(2) Active verb + 던 *was/were doing*
-던 -ten is also used for adnominals with an action that went on for a while in the past but was not necessarily completed. Compare the two coffee sentences:

내가 **마시던** 커피 어디 있어요?
nayka masiten khephi eti isseyo?
Where is the coffee that I was drinking?

내가 아까 **마신** 커피는 카페인이 없는 커피예요.
nayka akka masin khephinun khapheyini epsnun khephiyeyyo.
The coffee that I drank a while ago is decaf.

Adverbs that denote the past tense are often used with these -던 -ten clauses: 아까/좀 전에 akka/com ceney *a while ago*, 어제 ecey *yesterday*, 지난 주에 cinan cwuey *last week*, etc.

(3) Active verb + 었던 *had been...*
You will sometimes also hear -었던 -essten, with the past tense suffix AND -던 -ten. This stacked ending emphasizes the fact that an event or activity was going on for a while or was repeated but is NOT ANYMORE.

이 가수는 90년대에 인기 **있었던** 가수예요.
i kaswunun 90nyentayey inki issessten kaswuyeyyo.
This singer used to be popular in the 90s (but isn't anymore).

결혼하다 kyelhonhata is a good verb to show the differences between the three adnominal endings that mark a past event: **completive** -(으)ㄴ -(u)n, **durative past** -던 -ten, and **durative-completive** -었던 -essten:

저는 결혼한 사람입니다.
cenun kyelhonhan salamipnita.
I am underline{married}. (Literally, *I am a person* who got married.)

저는 **결혼하던** 사람입니다.
cenun kyelhonhaten salamipnita.
I am a person who used to get married.

제가 그날 **결혼하던** 사람입니다.
ceyka kunal kyelhonhaten salamipnita.
I am the person who was getting married *that day.*

저는 한번 **결혼했던** 사람입니다.
cenun hanpen kyelhonhayssten salamipnita.
I am a person who (has been) married once *(and am not anymore).*

(4) Descriptive verbs and 이다 with -던 *that was once (the case)*

For descriptive verbs and 이다 ita, -던 -ten is used for the regular ol' PAST state, though note that *used to be* is a good translation sometimes.

뜨겁던 사랑이 식어 버렸어.
ttukepten salangi sike pelyesse.
Our underline{once-passionate} *love has lost its fervor.*

어렵던 한국어가 쉬워졌어요.
elyepten hankwukeka swiwecyesseyo.
Korean, which was difficult for me, *has become easier./The Korean* that used to be difficult *has gotten easier.*

In colloquially spoken Korean -었던 -essten is frequently used in place of -던 -ten.

어려웠던 한국어가 쉬워졌어요.
nelyewessten hankwukeka swiwecyesseyo.
Korean, which used to be so difficult, *is so much easier now.*

10 년 전에 **초등학생이었던** 사촌 동생이 대학생이 됐어요.
10 nyen ceney chotunghaksayngiessten sachon tongsayngi tayhaksayngi twaysseyo.
My cousin who was an elementary school student 10 years ago *has become a college student.*

8.1.8 Summary of adnominal forms

For active verbs, -(으)ㄴ -(u)n indicates a completed (past) event, -는 -nun an ongoing (or an imminent) event, and -(으)ㄹ -(u)l a yet-to-happen event that describes the following noun. -던 -ten signals that the act was on- going for a while, and -었던 -essten emphasizes that it is no more so. Add -은 -un and -을 -ul after consonant-ending stems and add ㄴ and ㄹ after vowel-ending stems:

어제 **먹은** 샌드위치 ecey mekun sayntuwichi	*the sandwich that I ate yesterday*
어제 **먹었던** 샌드위치 ecey mekessten sayntuwichi	*the sandwich that I ate yesterday* (colloquially spoken)
전에 **먹던** 샌드위치 ceney mekten sayntuwichi	*the sandwich that I used to eat before/* *the sandwich that I was eating before*
내가 **먹는** 샌드위치 nayka meknun sayntuwichi	*the sandwich that I eat (everyday)/* *the sandwich that I am eating (now)*
나중에 **먹을** 샌드위치 nacwungey mekul sayntuwichi	*the sandwich that I am going to/will eat later*
어제 **마신** 커피 ecey masin khephi	*the coffee that I drank yesterday*
어제 **마셨던** 커피 ecey masyessten khephi	*the coffee that I drank yesterday* (colloquially spoken)
전에 **마시던** 커피 ceney masiten khephi	*the coffee that I used to drink before/* *the coffee that I was drinking before*
내가 **마시는** 커피 nayka masinun khephi	*the coffee that I drink (everyday)/* *the coffee that I am drinking (now)*
나중에 **마실** 거피 nacwungey masil kephi	*the coffee that I am going to/will drink later*

In a way, descriptive verbs and the **copula**, 이다 ita *to be*, assume that an action took place at some point in the past so that something has come to be in such-and-such present state (e.g. *It underlined{interested} me, and I now am underlined{interested}*). So the same connector -(으)ㄴ -(u)n expresses the PRESENT state with descriptive verbs (e.g., *interested, interesting, big, tired*) and PAST tense/PERFECTIVE aspect with active verbs (e.g., *to interest someone/to attract, to grow, to tire*).

8.1.9 No preposition-like particles

One important point to keep in mind: Even if a preposition is needed to describe a noun in English, you should lose the particle in Korean in the adnominal clause:

오늘 저는 한류에 대해서 발표하겠습니다.
onul cenun hanlyuey tayhayse palphyohakeysssupnita.
Today, I would like to present underline{on} Hallyu.

→ {오늘 제가 발표할 주제}는 한류입니다.
   onul ceyka palphyohal cwuceynun hanlyuipnita.
   {The topic underline{that I will be presenting on today}} is Hallyu.

미진이가 자주 동생한테 전화하곤 했다.
micinika cacwu tongsaynghanthey cenhwahakon hayssta.
Mijin used to frequently make a phone call underline{to} her younger sibling.

→ {미진이가 자주 전화하던 사람}은 동생이다.
micinika cacwu cenhwahaten salamun tongsayngita.
{The person that Mijin used to make frequent phone calls to} is her younger sibling.

Because those particles are dropped in Korean adnominal clauses and because PRO-NOUNS are often dropped in Korean, there is oftentimes ambiguity about the role of the noun being modified:

지금 이야기하는 사람 누구야?
cikum iyakihanun salam nwukwuya?
Who is the person who is talking now? OR *Who is the person you are taking to/about?*

If pronouns (and particles) are used for the subject or object of the adnominal clause, then it is possible to determine who is being described:

제가 찾는 사람 ceyka chacnun salam	*the person that I am looking for*
저를 찾는 사람 celul chacnun salam	*the person who is looking for me*
제가 본 사람 ceyka pon salam	*the person who I saw*
저를 본 사람 celul pon salam	*the person who saw me*

8.1.10 Adnominal complexity

That's just about all you need to learn about adnominal clauses, if you want to know how to make the past, present, future (or completive, durative, and prospective) and -던 -ten past forms of active and descriptive verb adnominals. There are just a couple more areas to watch out for.

First, note that the adnominal form of a verb often comes in a long, full, complex clause and ends up making a long noun phrase—just like in English (e.g., *the gentleman who gives me advice about my stamp collection*).

이건 {이따가 내가 친구하고 마실 커피}예요.
iken ittaka nayka chinkwuhako masil khephiyeyyo.
This is {coffee that I will drink with my friend later}.

남편이 {내가 싫어하는 옷}을 많이 선물로 줘.
namphyeni nayka ilhehanun osul manhi senmwullo cwe.
My husband often gives me {clothes that I do not like} as gifts.

There can also be two or more adnominal forms in the same noun phrase. When that happens, little elements like *the* or *that* appear in a position that is not so intuitive to English speakers:

{어제 **먹은** 그 **맛있는** 비빔밥}을 누가 만들었어요?
ecey mekun ku masissnun pipimpapul nwuka mantulesseyo?
Who made {the delicious bibimbap that I had yesterday}?

There can also be a complex noun phrase inside another complex noun phrase:

어제 우리가 집에서 **먹은** 그 **맛있는** 비빔밥을 **파는** 식당이 어디예요?
ecey wulika cipeyse mekun ku masissnun pipimpapul phanun siktangi etiyeyyo?

Where is the |restaurant| *that sells the* |delicious| *bibimbap that we ate at home yesterday?*

8.1.11 Summary chart

The following is a summary of adnominal clause endings in chart form.

Active Verbs		
Past	**Present**	**Future**
- (으)ㄴ -(u)n (completive past) -던 -ten (durative past)	- 는 -nun	- (으)ㄹ -(u)l
먹다 mekta *to eat*	어제 먹은 과자 ecey mekun kwaca *the cookie that I ate yesterday*	지금 먹는 과자 cikum meknun kwaca *the cookie that I am eating now*	나중에 먹을 과자 nacwungey mekul kwaca *the cookie that I will eat later*
	아까 먹던 과자 akka mekten kwaca *the cookie that I was eating a while ago*		
마시다 masita *to drink*	어제 마신 커피 ecey masin khephi *the coffee that I drank yesterday*	요즘 마시는 커피 yocum masinun khephi *the coffee that I drink nowadays*	나중에 마실 커피 nacwungey masil khephi *the coffee that I will drink later*
	아까 마시던 커피 akka masiten khephi *the coffee that I was drinking a while ago*		

Descriptive Verbs			
	Past	**Present**	**Future**
	-던 -ten	**-(으)ㄴ** -(u)n	**-(으)ㄹ** -(u)l
작다 cakta *small*	작던 꽃 cakten kkoch *the flower that was small*	작은 꽃 cakun kkoch *a small flower*	작을 수 있어 cakul swu isse *(it) can be small*
예쁘다 yeypputa *pretty*	예쁘던 얼굴 yeypputen elkwul *the face that used to be pretty*	예쁜 얼굴 yeyppun elkwul *a pretty face*	예쁠지 몰라 yeyppul ci molla *(it) might be pretty*
재미있다 caymiissta *fun*	재미있던 게임 caymiissten keyim *the game that used to be fun*	재미있는 게임 caymiissnun keyim *a fun game*	재미있을 거예요 caymiissul keyeyyo *(it)will be fun*

Nouns 이다 ita			
	Past	**Present**	**Future**
	-던 -ten (durative past) **-었던** -essten (durative completive past)	**-(으)ㄴ** -(u)n	**-(으)ㄹ** -(u)l
친구다 chinkwuta *be a friend*	친구였던 사람 chinkwuyessten salam *someone who was/used to be a friend*	친구인 사람 chinkwuin salam *the person who is a friend*	친구일 거예요 chinkwuil keyeyyo *(he) will be a friend*

Pay attention to the conjugation of special-ㄷ, -ㄹ, and -ㅂ class verbs. Again, active verbs and descriptive verbs conjugate differently.

Type	Dictionary Form	Past	Present	Future
special- ㄷ	듣다 tutta *to listen to*	내가 들은 음악 nayka tulun umak *music that I listened to*	내가 듣는 음악 nayka tutnun umak *music that I listen to/ am listening to*	내가 들을 음악 nayka tulul umak *music that I will listen to*
ㄹ	만들다 mantulta *to make*	내가 만든 김치 nayka mantun kimchi *kimchi that I made*	내가 만드는 김치 nayka mantunun kimchi *kimchi that I make/ am making*	내가 만들 김치 nayka mantul kimchi *kimchi that I will/ am going to make*
special- ㅂ	굽다 kwupta *to bake*	내가 구운 빵 nayka kwuwun ppang *bread that I baked*	내가 굽는 빵 nayka kwupnun ppang *bread that I bake/am baking*	내가 구울 빵 nayka kwuwul ppang *bread that I will bake*

Type	Dictionary Form	Past	Present	Future
special-ㅂ	춥다 chwupta *cold*	춥던 날씨 chwupten nalssi *weather that used to be cold*	추운 날씨 chwuwun nalssi *cold weather*	추울 거예요 chwuwul keyeyyo *it will be cold*
special-ㅅ	낫다 nasta *to get better*	다 나은 사람 ta naun salam *person who recovered*	잘 낫는 약 cal nasnun yak *medicine that cures well*	못 나을 병 mos naul pyeng *disease that cannot be cured*
special-ㅎ	빨갛다 ppalkahta *red*	빨갛던 코 ppalkahten kho *a nose that used to be red*	빨간 코 ppalkan kho *red color*	빨갈 거예요 ppalkal keyeyyo *it will be red*
special-르	부르다 pwuluta *to call*	노래를 부른 사람 nolaylul pwulun salam *person who sang a song*	노래를 부르는 사람 nolaylul pwulunun salam *person who sings a song*	노래를 부를 사람 nolaylul pwulul salam *person who will sing a song*
special-르	부르다 pwuluta *full (stomach)*	배가 부르던 날들 payka pwuluten naltul *times when (they) used to be full*	배가 부른 날들 payka pwulun naltul *times when (they) are) full*	배가 부를 거예요 payka pwulul keyeyyo *(they) will be full*

8.2 Coordinated and Subordinate clauses

Another way to put two sentences into one is to just connect them end to end. In these cases, they are either **coordinated clauses** on equal footing or one is a **subordinate clause** and one is the **main clause**, like this:

Coordinate clause + Coordinate clause:

I went to the store to get milk,   +   *but it was sold out.*

Main clause + Subordinate clause:

I bumped into a high-school friend   +   *when I went to the store to get milk.*

Which clauses are coordinated and which are subordinated doesn't matter much in Korean in terms of how they work, so we won't focus on the distinction. But do know that subordinate clauses provide a BACKGROUND of some sort for the main action, and that the order of the clauses is often different in Korean as compared to English. The key point is that THE MAIN CLAUSE IS ALWAYS THE LAST ONE IN A KOREAN SENTENCE.

Another tricky point is that while conjunctions in English usually come at the beginning of the clause, Korean connectors are, of course, at the end of the clause. Instead of *though X happened, Y happened*, Korean says *X happened-though*, … with the same meaning as the English. The connector works backwards, in a sense: it subordinates the PRECEDING clause. Keep an eye on the examples and translations, and it will all become clearer.

8.2.1 Warm-up: connector adverbs and clause connectors

You know these connector ADVERBS (연결부사 yenkyelpwusa) from previous chapters:

그렇지만 kulehciman *but*　　　　　그래서 kulayse *so*

그러면 kulemyen *if so then*　　　　그리고 kuliko *and*

그런데 kulentey *yeah but; by the way*　그러니까 kulenikka *that's why, so*

Perhaps then you can make out these useful **connectors** that are part of the connector adverbs:

-지만 -ciman　　　　　　　　-어서 -ese

-(으)면 -(u)myen　　　　　　-고 -ko

-(으)ㄴ데 -(u)ntey　　　　　-(으)니까 -(u)nikka

The **connectors** are the suffixes attached to the action verb 그러다 kuleta *to do like that*, the descriptive verb 그렇다 kulehta *to be like that*, or a variant form 그리(하)다 kuli(ha)ta. These verbs 그러- kule-, 그렇- kuleh-, and 그리- kuri- do not add much meaning, so the meanings of the connector adverbs pretty transparently reflect the meaning of the connectors themselves.

Connector adverb	Meaning	Verb + Suffix	Connecting Suffix	Meaning
그리고	*and*	그리(하)-고	-고	*and*
그렇지만	*but*	그렇-지만	-지만	*but*
그러다가	*do and then*	그러-다가	-다가	*was doing, when*
그러자	*upon that happening*	그러-자	-자	*upon doing*
그래서	*so*	그렇-어서	-어서	*so*
그래도	*even so*	그렇-어도	-어도	*even though*
그러면 그럼 (colloquial)	*if so*	그렇-(으)면	-(으)면	*if*
그러니까	*so*	그렇-(으)니까	-(으)니까	*so*

Connector adverb	Meaning	Verb + Suffix	Connecting Suffix	Meaning
그런데 근데 (colloquial)	*but, so, and, ";"*	그렇-(으)ㄴ데	-(으)ㄴ데	*but, so, and, ";"*
그러면서	*so and*	그러-(으)면서	-(으)면서	*and, while*

These connecting suffixes freely attach to other verbs, too, as we will see. You learned in chapter 6 that Korean suffixes fall into three categories of conjugation type: the consonant-type, the 어 e-type, and the 으 u-type. The preceding verbs conjugate accordingly. As we take a closer look at these and other connectors, you will start to internalize those conjugation patterns. We have organized the connectors for you below by their meanings.

8.2.2 Basic conjunctions: *and* and *or*

In this section we talk about four connectors that are, grammatically speaking, **coordinating** connectors because it is NOT the case that one clause is the background for the other; the two clauses are equal in "importance."

(1) -고 *and*

Remember that 그리고 kuliko means *and*, and it can be used at the beginning of a sentence to connect ideas:

학교에 갔다. 그리고 가게에도 들렀다.
hakkyoey kassta. kuliko kakeyeyto tulleyssta.
I went to school. And I also stopped by the store.

When it comes to connecting two or more VERBS (or clauses) into one sentence, you use the CONNECTOR -고 -ko, which you see at the end of 그리고 kuliko.

학교에 **가고** 가게에도 들렀다.
hakkyoey kako kakeyeyto tulleyssta.
I went to school and also stopped by the store.

나는 학교에 **가고** 아빠는 회사에 가.
nanun hakkyoey kako appanun hoysaey ka.
I go to school, and Dad goes to work.

어제 나는 학교에 **가고** 커피숍에서 아르바이트도 했습니다.
ecey nanun hakkyoey kako khephisyopeyse alupaithuto hayssupnita.
Yesterday I went to school and also worked my part-time job at the school coffee shop.

김치는 **맵고** 짜요.
kimchinun maypko ccayo.
Kimchi is spicy and salty.

내 여동생은 **작고** 귀엽다.
nay yetongsayngun cakko kwiyepta.
My sister is small and cute.

You see that -고 -ko can be used with both descriptive verbs and active verbs and that the connected clauses may have the same subject or different subjects.

The verb that -고 -ko is attached to may be in the past or future tense or may be used without a tense marker. The last verb of the sentence will determine the tense of both clauses, along with the speaker's attitude, politeness, and so on. So usually, tense marking on the last verb is sufficient, unless there is a reason to count the listed activities as SEPARATE events. In the second example below, the implication is stronger that the person did not go to the movies WITH the friend she met. (To make it clear that she went to the movies with that friend, a different connector would be used):

언니: 어제 뭐 했어?
enni: ecey mwe haysse?
Big sister: *What did you do yesterday?*

나: 친구 **만나고** 영화 봤어.
na: chinkwu mannako yenghwa pwasse.
Me: *I met a friend and watched a movie.*

언니: 어제 뭐 했어?
enni: ecey mwe haysse?
Big sister: *What did you do yesterday?*

나: 친구 **만났고** 영화 봤어.
na: chinkwu mannassko yenghwa pwasse.
Me: *I met a friend, and I watched a movie.*

(2) -(으)며 *and*

It gets boring if you list multiple clauses and repeat -고 -ko again and again. Clauses with -고 -ko are often mixed with some that have the -(으)며 -(u)mye connector, especially in formal Korean. -(으)며 -(u)mye connects after a present, past or future tense and works with both active and descriptive verbs:

내일은 눈이 **오고** 바람이 **불며** 매우 춥겠습니다.
nayilun nwuni oko palami pwulmye maywu chwupkeysssupnita.
It will be snowy, windy and cold tomorrow.

나는 서울에서 태어나고 **자랐으며** 10살 때 미국으로 왔다.
nanun sewuleyse thayenako calassumye 10sal ttay mikwukulo wassta.
I was born and raised in Seoul and came to the United States at the age of 10.

(3) -거나 *or*

Remember that -(이)나 -(i)na is used to list NOUNS as options to choose from:

커피**나** 차 드실래요?
khephina cha tusillayyo?
Would you like to have coffee or tea (or something else)?

When there is more than one option of ACTIVITIES or DESCRIPTIONS to choose from (that is, verbs), the connector -거나 -kena is used. As a consonant-type suffix, -거나 -kena connects to the dictionary-form root of the verb, and it indicates that *there are multiple options* and the listed options are just examples of the kind under discussion.

이번 주말에는 **쉬거나** 잘 거예요.
ipen cwumaleynun swikena cal keyeyyo.
I will either take a rest or sleep this weekend.

주말에는 보통 테니스 **치거나** 친구를 만나요.
cwumaleynun pothong theynisu chikena chinkwulul mannayo.
I usually play tennis or meet my friend on weekends.

맵거나 짠 음식은 건강에 좋지 않다.
maypkena ccan umsikun kenkangey cohci anhta.
Spicy or salty foods are not good for your health.

-거나 -kena can be used with the past tense marker if the action is completed.

벌써 떠났**거나** 오늘 오지 않을 거야.
pelsse ttenasskena onul oci anhul keya.
Either he already left or he's not going to come today.

이 약은 체**했거나** 배탈이 났을 때 드세요.
i yakun cheyhaysskena paythali nassul ttay tuseyyo.
Take this medicine when you have gotten indigestion symptoms or (developed) a stomachache.

Here are a couple more usages of -거나 kena:

<1> -거나 whether A or B

When -거나 -kena connects two CONTRASTING ideas, it means *whether A or B* or *whether … or not*, emphasizing *the choice is irrelevant; it doesn't matter which*. -거나 -kena is attached to BOTH verbs in these cases:

비가 **오거나** 눈이 **오거나** 매일 운동했어요.
pika okena nwuni okena mayil wuntonghaysseyo.
Whether it rained or snowed, I exercised every day.

그 사람이 돈이 있**거나** 없**거나** 상관 없다.
ku salami toni isskena epskena sangkwan epsta.
I don't care whether that person is rich or not.

그러**거나** 말**거나** 관심 없다.
kulekena malkena kwansim epsta.
I don't care whether (he) does that or not.

<2> -거나 *any time/anywhere/anything, etc.*

When -거나 -kena is used with a *wh*-question word in the sentence, the meaning is *X-ever* as in *wherever, whatever, whenever…etc.* (*is okay*).

넌 어디에 가**거나** 잘 할 거야.
nen etiey kakena cal hal keya.
Wherever you go, you will do just fine.

언제 오시**거나** 환영합니다.
encey osikena hwanyenghapnita.
Whenever you come, you are always welcome.

(4) -든지 *whether A or B*

-든지 -tunci, which is often pronounced [던지 tenci], also connects verbs to choose from, but has a sense of *either way is* FINE. It attaches to each of the choices. The more collo-quial version is -든가 -tunka [-등가 -tungka/-덩가 -tengka].

내일 오**든지** 모레 오**든지** 마음대로 해.
nayil otunci moley otunci maumtaylo hay.
Come tomorrow or the day after tomorrow, as you like.

피곤하면 목욕하**든지** 자**든지** 하세요.
phikonhamyen mokyokhatunci catunci haseyyo.
If you are tired, take a bath or sleep.

내가 가**든지** 네가 가**든지** 중요하지 않다.
nayka katunci neyka katunci cwungyohaci anhta.
It is not important whether I go or you do.

키가 **크든지 작든지** 상관 없다.
khika khutunci caktunci sangkwan epsta.
I don't care if (she) is tall or short.

가든지 말든지 관심 없다.
katunci maltunci kwansim epsta.
Whether (you) go or not, I am not interested.

먹든지 말든지 마음대로 해라.
mektunci maltunci maumtaylo hayla.
Eat or not, do as you like.

-든지 -tunci is used interchangeably with -거나 -kena, but -든지 -tunci focuses usually on the will of the chooser, whereas -거나 -kena on the irrelevance and insignificance of the given options.

8.2.3 Setting up contrast: *but*

Sentences can also be connected with a sense of contrast: *A but B*. The next set of connectors link clauses where the ideas contrast with each other, the event in the main clause often being UNEXPECTED. Remember! The main clause is always the last one in the sentence in Korean.

(1) -지만 *but, however, although*

The connector -지만 -ciman works pretty straightforwardly like English *but*, with the same order of clauses. It can follow present, past, or more rarely, future tense verbs with -(으)ㄹ 거 -(u)l ke, and the subjects of the two clauses need not be the same.

배가 **고프지만** 아무것도 먹고 싶지 않아.
payka kophuciman amwukesto mekko siphci anha.
I'm hungry, but I don't want to eat anything.

배가 **고팠지만** 아무 것도 먹지 않았다.
payka kophassciman amwu kesto mekci anhassta.
Although I was hungry, I did not eat anything.

슈퍼에 **갈 거지만** 과자는 안 살 거야.
syupheey kal keciman kwacanun an sal keya.
I'm going to go to the market, but I am not going to buy chips!

날씨는 **맑지만** 좀 추워요.
nalssinun malkciman com chwuweyo.
It's clear, but it's a little bit chilly.

어제는 비가 **왔지만** 내일은 안 올 거예요.
eceynun pika wassciman nayilun an ol keyeyyo.
Although it rained yesterday, it is not going to rain tomorrow.

(2) -(으)나 *but, although*

You may encounter the connector -(으)나 -(u)na *but* in writing or formal speech. It can follow a tense or aspect suffix (-었 -ess, -겠 -keyss, etc.):

그는 열심히 공부하였**으나** 공부로 동생을 이길 수 없었다.
kunun yelsimhi kongpwuhayessuna kongpwulo tongsayngul ikil swu epsessta.
He worked hard, but he could not beat this younger brother at studying.
내일은 맑겠**으나** 바람이 불고 춥겠습니다.
nayilun malkkeyssuna palami pwulko chwupkeysssupnita.
Although it will be clear, it will be windy and cold tomorrow.

(3) -(으)ㄴ데/-는데 *yeah, but; but then; and; so*

-(으)ㄴ데 -(u)ntey/-는데 -nuntey is a multi-purpose subordinator and probably the most frequently used connector in Korean. It is distinctly a spoken-language connector, and its meaning depends on what comes after it to complete the sentence; *and*, *so*, and *yeah but* may all make good translations of this connector. In all cases, the -(으)ㄴ데 -(u)ntey/-는데 -nuntey clause provides some sort of background, often followed by a clause that is opposite of or UNEXPECTED in relation to what is said in the first clause.

It is also a suffix that recognizes active versus descriptive verbs: -(으)ㄴ데 -(u)ntey comes after descriptive verbs, 이다 ita and -(으)ㄹ 것이다 -(u)l kesita, while -는데 -nuntey comes after active verbs or any past tense verb with -었 -ess. (Be careful with a 하다 hata word to determine whether it is an active or descriptive verb and choose the correct suffix form.) Also, ㄹ is dropped from ㄹ-final verbs before this connector.

비가 **오는데** 우산이 없어.
pika onuntey wusani epse.
It's raining <u>and</u> I don't have an umbrella.

비가 **오는데** 나가야 돼.
pika onuntey nakaya tway.
It's raining <u>but</u> I have to go out.

비가 **오는데** 오늘 나가지 말자.
pika onuntey onul nakaci malca.
It's raining, <u>so</u> let's not go out today.

머리가 **긴데** 좀 잘라라.
melika kintey com callala.
Your hair is a bit long; why not get a hair-cut?

얼굴은 **아는데** 이름은 몰라.
elkwulun anuntey ilumun molla.
I know the face, but not the name.

월요일인데 학교에 안 가요?
welyoilintey hakkyoey an kayo?
It's Monday; aren't you going to school?

돈은 **있는데** 시간이 없어요.
tonun issnuntey sikani epseyo.
I have money but not time.

피곤한데 좀 쉬세요.
phikonhantey com swiseyyo.
You are tired—get some rest.

공부하는데 자꾸 방해하지 마.
kongpwuhanuntey cakkwu panghayhaci ma.
I'm studying; stop disturbing me.

어제는 비가 **왔는데** 오늘도 올 건가?
eceynun pika wassnuntey onulto ol kenka?
It rained yesterday; will it today, too, I wonder?

사무실에 **전화할 건데** 아무도 받지 않을 거야.
samwusiley cenhwahal kentey amwuto patci anhul keya.
I will call the office, but nobody will answer it.

8.2.4 Conditionals: *if, only if, even if*

Korean has different connectors for *if*, ONLY *if*, and EVEN *if/even though*. In English, these clauses sometimes come after the main clause and sometimes before, but in Korean, of course, the connector always comes at the end of the first clause, which is the CONDITION-background (subordinate clause).

(1) -(으)면 *if*

-(으)면 -(u)myen is your basic *if*. It can be used after a past tense verb, and with 이다 ita, both 이면 imyen and 이라면 ilamyen are used. ㄹ of ㄹ-verbs DOES NOT DROP OUT before -(으)면 -(u)myen, but the 으 is not needed.

> Here is a review of the rule for dropping final ㄹ: When BoNuS comes, ㄹ drops out, and it will NEVER need the vowel 으 in a following suffix (so, you won't hear [르 lu].) Since the suffix -(으)면 -(u)myen does not begin with ㅂ, ㄴ, or ㅅ, you keep the ㄹ in the verb!

너무 **싱거우면** 소금을 넣어요.
nemwu singkewumyen sokumul neheyo.
If it's too bland, put some salt in it.

이게 **싫으면** 다른 걸로 골라라.
ikey silhumyen talun kello kollala.
If you don't like this, pick something else.

너무 **길면** 좀 자르세요.
nemwu kilmyen com caluseyyo.
If it's too long, cut it a little bit.

이게 네 펜**이라면** 왜 내 가방에 있어?
ikey ney pheynilamyen way nay kapangey isse?
If this is your pen, why is it in my bag?

어제 못 **잤으면** 오늘은 일찍 자.
ecey mos cassumyen onulun ilccik ca.
If you didn't get a good sleep last night, go to bed early today.

바람이 조금 덜 **불면** 더 좋겠다.
palami cokum tel pwulmyen te chgkeyssta.
If it were a little less windy, it would be nice.

Take note, though, that -(으)면 -(u)myen is also used where we might say *when* in English for FUTURE actions:

집에 **도착하면** 전화해.
cipey tochakhamyen cenhwahay.
Call me when you get home.

졸업하면 어디에서 살고 싶어?

colephamyen etieyse salko siphe?.

Where do you want to live when you graduate?

(2) -어야 only if/when (can you); have to X in order to Y

Another basic and highly useful connector is -어야 -eya as in -어야 되다 -eya toyta *you have to*. -어야 -eya is a nifty connector that means ONLY IF/*only when*. *You have to* will often be in natural translations of these sentences.

오늘 **쉬어야** 내일 또 일을 할 수 있어요.

onul swieya nayil tto ilul hal swu isseyo.

Only if I get good rest tonight, can I work tomorrow.

돈이 **있어야** 차를 사지요.

toni isseya chalul saciyo.

Only if you have money, can you buy a car, ya know/You have to have money to buy a car.

산에 **가야** 범을 잡지.

saney kaya pemul capci.

Only when you go to the mountain can you catch a tiger, right?/You have to go to the mountains to catch a tiger.

(3) -어도 even if; even though; despite

-어도 -eto means both *even if* (for hypothetical conditions) and *even though* (for factual conditions), but it's a connector that works "backwards" from English: -어도 -eto attaches at the END of the *even if/even though* clause (the subordinate clause).

    -어도 -eto has the -어 -e conjugation built in; that is, verbs are conjugated for the -어 -e (intimate ordinary) form and then -도 -to *also, even* is attached to make up this connector. 이다 ita plus this connector becomes 이라도 ilato in spoken Korean. (이어도 ieto sounds somewhat stilted.) To emphasize the COMPLETION of an action, the past tense -었 -ess suffix can be used.

날씨가 **추워도** 매일 운동해야 돼요.

nalssika chwuweto mayil wuntonghayya twayyo.

Even if it is cold, you have to exercise every day.

밖이 **추워도** 지금 운동할 거예요.

pakki chwuweto cikum wuntonghal keyeyyo.

Even though it is cold, I'm going to exercise now.

죽어도 못 잊어요.

cwuketo mos iceyo.

I cannot forget even if/though/when I die. (I'll never forget.)

친구**라도** 봐 줄 수 없을 것이다.

chinkwulato pwa cwul swu epsul kesita.

Despite the fact that he is my friend, I still won't be able to bend the rules for him.

관광지에 **살아도** 관광을 잘 못 해요.
kwankwangciey salato kwankwangul cal mos hayyo.
Even though I live in a site known for tourism, I don't get to do a lot of sightseeing.

키는 **작아도** 힘은 장사네요!
khinun cakato himun cangsaneyyo!
He is short but he is like Hercules!/Even though he is short, ...

열 번이나 **봤어도** 얼굴을 기억 못 해.
yel penina pwasseto elkwulul kiek mos hay.
Although I saw/have seen him ten times, I can't remember his face.

8.2.5 Reasons, causes and consequences: *because, since, so*

There are several clausal suffixes that indicate the reason or cause for what happens in the main clause, like English *because, so* and *since*.

-(으)ㄴ데/-는데 -(u)ntey/-nuntey, which you saw earlier as a contrast connector, can also introduce a reason clause, typically involving a command or a suggestion.

내일이 시험**인데** 공부하세요.
nayili sihemintey kongpwuhaseyyo.
Tomorrow's the test, so study.

Other *because* connectors differ in their nuanced meanings and usages, and sometimes also in their degree of formality.

(1) -(으)니까/(으)니 *since, as*

One of the most useful connectors in the reason-cause category is probably -(으)니까 -(u)nikka. It attaches to the reasoning clause, which comes FIRST in Korean:

내일은 일요일**이니까** 좀 시간이 있다.
nayilun ilyoilinikka com sikani issta.
Since tomorrow is Sunday, I judge that I have some time.

너무 **바쁘니까** 그건 내일 할게요.
nemwu pappunikka kuken nayil halkeyyo.
As I'm super busy now, I'll do that tomorrow, OK?

이제 3월이 **됐으니까** 날씨가 따뜻해질 거야.
icey samweli twayssunikka nalssika ttattushaycil keya.
Since it is now March, (I think) the weather should get warmer.

When the main clause is a suggestion, command, request or recommendation, you will need to use -(으)니까 -(u)nikka to provide justification (and not one of the other *because* connectors below). This is because -(으)니까 -(u)nikka has a sense of PERSONAL REASON-ING (*I have thought this through and feel this is a reason*), which is needed to back up a command or suggestion. Thus the -(으)니까 -(u)nikka clause typically offers a SUBJEC-

TIVE REASONING for the main clause. Likewise, it will sound weird if the -(으)니까 -(u) nikka clause is used to offer an excuse or apology.

미안해. 버스가 안 **왔으니까** 늦었어.
mianhay. pesuka an wassunikka nucesse.
I am sorry. I am late because the bus did not come.

The following chart shows the main clause endings (those for suggestions, commands, recommendations and requests) with which your reason clause will typically appear with the -(으)니까 -(u)nikka connector.

Suggestions	-자 -ca, -(으)ㅂ시다 -(u)psita, -(으)까요? -(u)kkayo, -(으)ㄹ래요? -(u)llayyo, -으면 어때요? -umyen ettayyo?	길이 모두 **막혔으니까** 다른 길로 돌아가**자**. kili motwu makhyessunikka talun killo tolakaca. *Since the road is all blocked up, let's take another route.*
Commands & Recommendations	-어라 -ela, -(으)세요 -(u)seyyo, -어 보세요 -e poseyyo	추울지 모르니까 옷 잘 입고 **나가**(**세요**). chwuwulci molunikka os cal ipko naka(seyyo). *It may be cold; put on a good layer when you go out.*
Requests	-어 주세요 -e cwuseyyo, -어 주시겠어요? -e cwusikeysseyo?, -어 주시겠습니까? -e cwusikeysssupnikka?	더우니까 창문 좀 **열어 주시겠어요**? tewunikka changmwun com yele cwusikeysseyo? *It's hot; would you please open the window a bit?*

In written and formal Korean, -(으)니 -(u)ni is used instead of -(으)니까 -(u)nikka:

내일부터 기온이 **떨어지겠으니**, 감기 조심하시기 바랍니다.
nayilpwuthe kioni ttelecikeyssuni, kamki cosimhasiki palapnita.
Given that the temperature will drop starting from tomorrow, take care not to catch a cold.

(2) -어서 *so, consequently, as a result*

Another frequently used connector is -어서 -ese. It expresses a NATURAL CAUSE for the following action or state to ensue. That is, the main clause expresses a logical and NATURAL CONSEQUENCE of the first, unlike -(으)니까 -(u)nikka, which involves personal reasoning. The past tense -었 -ess is not used before -어서 -ese (that is, NEVER -었어서 -essese, except in highly colloquial speech to emphasize the completion of the previous event, which is not so any more in the present).

길이 모두 **막혀서** 다른 길로 돌아갔다.
kili motwu makhyese talun killo tolakassta.
The road was all blocked up, so we took another route.
(Not under our control but a natural consequence.)

머리가 **아파서** 집중할 수 없어요.
melika aphase cipcwunghal swu epseyo.
I have a headache so I can't really concentrate.
(Not under my control but a natural consequence)

This one is a backward-facing connector when translated as *because* (as are the others in this section), but forward-facing if translated as *so, consequently*. It might be good to think of it as *consequently*, because its core meaning is logical cause and natural consequence. With 이다 ita, 이라서 ilase is a common form, while 이어서 iese is a bit more bookish.

내일은 일요일**이라서** 오늘 좀 여유가 있다.
nayilun ilyoililase onul com yeyyuka issta.
Tomorrow is Sunday so I have some free time.

이제 3월이 **돼서** 날씨가 따뜻해질 거야.
icey 3weli twayse nalssika ttattushaycil keya.
It is now March, so (naturally) the weather is going to get warmer.

Very colloquially, -어 가지고(서) -e kaciko(se) (sloppily pronounced [가꼬 kakko] or [가꾸서 kakkwuse]) can be used in place of -어서 -ese:

표가 다 **팔려 가지고** 영화를 못 봤어요.
phyoka ta phallye kaciko yenghwalul mos pwasseyo.
The tickets were sold out so we couldn't see the movie.

아기가 **아파 가지고** 계속 울고 있다.
akika apha kaciko kyeysok wulko issta.
The baby's sick so she's been crying a while.

(3) -기 때문에 *because of, on account of, due to*

때문에 ttaymwuney is used to mark a NOUN cause, and -기 때문에 -ki ttaymwuney is the connector for VERBS (or clauses). -기 때문에 -ki ttaymwuney can be used after a past tense -었 -ess. The 때문에 ttaymwuney clause often names a specific and direct cause for an undesirable result or an event that prevents something from happening.

시험 **때문에** 못 간다.
sihem ttaymwuney mos kanta.
I can't go because of the test.

돈이 **부족하기 때문에** 살 수 없다.
toni pwucokhaki ttaymwuney sal swu epsta.
I can't buy it because I don't have enough money. (because of not having enough money)

감기에 **걸렸기 때문에** 안 가기로 했어.
kamkiey kellyesski ttaymwuney an kakilo haysse.
I decided not to go due to a cold.

(4) Fine-tuning -어서 vs. -으니까 vs. -기 때문에

The two connectors -어서 -ese and -(으)니까 -(u)nikka are similar, but they are not always interchangeable. As we pointed out, -어서 -ese is more objective, fact-based, thus authoritarian than -(으)니까 -(u)nikka, which provides one's subjective reasoning.

Here is the rule of thumb to follow:

- -(으)니까 -(u)nikka is used when the speaker provides a reason based on his or her personal judgment
- -어서 -ese is used to express logical causes for the following clause; think *consequently, naturally*

나:	오늘은 거리에 사람들이 별로 없네요?
na:	onulun keliey salamtuli pyello epsneyyo?
Me:	*There are not many people on the street today, huh?*

엄마:	날씨가 **추워서**.
emma:	nalssika chwuwese.
Mother:	*It's cold, so... (naturally, people don't want to be out and about).*

엄마':	날씨가 **추우니까**.
emma':	nalssika chwuwunikka.
Mother':	*Well, 'cause the weather is cold, (I figure) that's why.*

동생:	아직 안 나갔어?
tongsayng:	acik an nakasse?
Younger brother:	*Have you not left yet?/You are still here.*

형:	**추우니까** (나가기 싫다).
hyeng:	chwuwunikka (nakaki silhta).
Older brother:	*'Cause it's cold (I don't feel like going out).*
	(giving an excuse, personal reason)

형':	**추워서** (나가기 싫다).
hyeng':	chwuwese (nakaki silhta).
Older brother':	*It's cold (so, naturally, I don't feel like going out).*

The key difference is that -으니까 -unikka marks your personal thoughts about why, sometimes an excuse or a justification, often in response to a question about why.

엄마:	5시인데 벌써 자니?
emma:	tasessiintey pelsse cani?
Mother:	*It's five o'clock; are you sleeping already?*

딸:	피곤**하니까요**!
ttal:	phikonhanikkayo!
Daughter:	*'Cause I'm tired! (I have good reason to sleep!)*

Even if the cause is personal or even emotional (or a STATE of hunger, fatigue, etc.), it can be a LOGICAL PRECURSOR marked with -어서 -ese. That is, one can do (or not do) something as a natural consequence of a feeling.

너무 **바빠서** 그건 이따 할 거예요.
nemwu pappase kuken itta hal keyyo.
I'm too busy, so I'm going to do that later.
(Me working on it later is a consequence of me being busy now.)

어제는 너무 **피곤해서** 그냥 잤어요.
eceynun nemwu phikonhayse kunyang casseyo.
I was too tired yesterday (that/so) I just slept.
(Sleeping as a logical consequence of being tired.)

언니가 의사**라서** 아프면 항상 물어 봐요.
ennika uysalase aphumyen hangsang mwule pwayo.
My older sister is a doctor, so (naturally) I always ask her when I am sick.

Because, -어서 -ese entails a logical or natural CONSEQUENCE, it CANNOT be used for a suggestion, command, and request as these are not consequences. They are the result of your reasoning, and only -으니까 -unikka can be used to provide reasoning:

이 길이 **멀어서** 다른 길로 **갈 거예요.**
i kili melese talun killo kal keyeyyo.
This route is long (far), so I am going to go another way.

이 길은 **멀어서** 다른 길로 **가자.**
i kilun melese talun killo kaca. (X)
This route being long, let's go another way.

이 길은 **머니까** 다른 길로 **가자.**
i kilun menikka talun killo kaca.
Since this route is long, let's go another way.

추우니까 재킷 **입어라.**
chwuwunikka caykhis ipela.
It's cold—wear a jacket. (I think you should)

추워서 재킷 **입어라.**
chwuwese caykhis ipela.
It being cold, wear a jacket.

-기 때문에 -ki ttaymwuney and -어서 -ese are similar in meaning and usage, but in nuance, -기 때문에 -ki ttaymwuney is more matter-of-fact and marks a more direct cause than -어서 -ese.

비가 **왔기 때문에** 나무가 살아났다.
pika wasski ttaymwuney namwuka salanassta.
Because of the rain, the shrub revived.
(direct cause →기 때문에 ki ttaymwuney is better here.)

비가 **와서** 정원이 생기에 차 보인다.
pika wase cengweni sayngkiey cha pointa.
It rained/it's rainy, so the garden looks vibrant and healthy.
(natural consequence, though there may be other causes, too)

-어서 -ese is a connector for "natural" emotional responses as well:

도와주셔서 감사합니다.
towajwusyese kamsahapnida.
Thank you for helping (me).

시험이 끝나서 너무 시원해!
sihemi kketnase nemwu siwenhay!
Good riddance—the test is over!

(5) -(으)므로 *so*
-(으)므로 -(u)mulo is a formal version of -어서 -ese and is used in formal and written Korean. Unlike -어서 -ese, -(으)므로 -(u)mulo can be used with -었 -ess:

사랑**하였으므로** 행복하였다.
salanghayessumulo hayngpokhayessta.
I was happy for I loved.

전쟁이 **끝났으므로** 평화가 찾아왔다.
cencayngi kkuthnassumulo phyenghwaka chacawassta.
The peace set in for the war had ended.

(6) -느라고 *because (one) was -ing*
-느라고 -nulako combines the meanings *while (doing something)* and *because*. It is used when the action in the -느라고 -nulako clause prevents the other action or has some other typically negative result. It usually introduces volitional action verbs—things one chooses to do (not verbs like *resemble* or descriptive verbs like *big*).

숙제를 **하느라고** 영화 보러 못 갔어요.
swukceylul hanulako yenghwa pole mos kasseyo.
Because I was doing homework, I could not go to the movies.

음악을 **듣느라고** 전화 소리를 못 들었어요.
umakul tutnulako cenhwa solilul mos tulesseyo.
Because I was listening to music, I could not hear the phone ringing.

오래 **일하느라고** 피곤했지?
oray ilhanulako phikonhayssci?
You must have been (so) tired working long hours.

스프를 **먹느라고** 비행기를 놓칠 뻔 했다.
suphulul meknulako pihayngkilul nohchil ppen hayssta.
While finishing up my soup, I almost missed my plane!

너무 크느라고 사지 않았다.
nemwu khunulako saci anhassta.
Because/While it was being big, I didn't buy it.

8.2.6 Sequences of actions: *before, after, while* and *as soon as*

Another way you might want to make your sentences longer and richer is to link actions in their time sequence, telling what happened before what and what happened after what, etc. First we'll talk about -고 -ko, -어서 -ese and -어 가지고 -e kaciko.

(1) -고 and -고 나서 *and; and then*

You can get a sequential *and then* sense from -고 -ko in Korean, just like you can from *and* in English.

어제는 저녁을 **먹고** 산책을 했어요.
eceynun cenyekul mekko sanchaykul haysseyo.
Yesterday, I ate dinner and (then) took a walk.

As mentioned earlier, when it comes after the past tense -었 -ess, though, it doesn't have the sequential meaning.

저녁을 **먹었고** 산책을 했어요.
cenyekul mekessko sanchaykul haysseyo.
I ate dinner, and (at some point) I took a walk.
(I did these two things, but not necessarily in that order or one right after the other.)

A related connector, -고 나서 -ko nase makes it clear that the first clause's action comes first. -고 나서 -ko nase literally means *and having come out (of that first action)*, so it indicates that the first action is done before the second. Since the connector itself implies that the first action is completed first, this connector cannot attach to a verb in the past tense.

어제는 저녁을 **먹고 나서** 산책을 했어요.
eceynun cenyekul mekko nase sanchaykul haysseyo.
Yesterday, I ate dinner and then took a walk.

~~어제는 저녁을 **먹었고 나서** 산책을 했어요~~.
eceynun cenyekul mekessko nase sanchaykul haysseyo.
Yesterday, I ate dinner and then took a walk.

오늘은 청소를 **하고 나서** 빨래도 할 거예요.
onulun chengsolul hako nase ppallayto hal keyeyyo.
Today, I will clean my place and then do laundry.

이것 **끝내고 나서** 저것도 좀 해 주세요.
ikes kkuthnayko nase cekesto com hay cwuseyyo.
Could you please do that after you finish this?
(*Could you please finish this and <u>then do</u> that?*)

(2) -어서 *and then/there; having done something (and with that)*

Related to the NATURAL CONSEQUENCE meaning, clauses in -어서 -ese can be translated as *X being the case* or *(someone) having done X*. A sequential usage comes into play when -어서 -ese is used on physical-direction verbs (e.g., 오다 ota *to come*, 가다 kata *to go*, 들어오다 tuleota *to come in*, 들어가다 tulekata *to go in*, 나오다 naota *to come out*, 나가다 nakata *to go out*, 올라가다 ollakata *to go up*, 올라오다 ollata *to come up*, 내려가다 naylyekata *to go down*, 내려오다 naylyeota *to come down*, 앉다 ancta *to sit*, 눕다 nwupta *to lie down*, and 일어나다 ilenata *to get up*.) The idea is *having gone some place* (or *having sat down, gotten up*, etc.) *you do something* THERE. The subject of the two clauses must be the same for -어서 -ese to have a sequential meaning. This connector is also often used with life-cycle verbs such as 태어나다 tayenata *be born*, 자라다 calata *grow up*, and 죽다 cwukta *die*.

여기 **와서** 잠깐 앉아요.
yeki wase camkkan ancayo.
Come here 'n sit down for a minute (here).

아침에 **일어나서** 이를 닦았어요.
achimey ilenase ilul takkasseyo.
I got up and (then) brushed my teeth.

친구를 **만나서** 영화 볼 거예요.
chinkwulul mannase yenghwa pol keyeyyo.
I will meet my friend and go watch a movie (with her).

호랑이는 **죽어서** 가죽을 남기고 사람은 죽어서 이름을 남긴다.
holanginun cwukese kacwukul namkiko salamun cwukese ilumul namkinta.
While tigers leave their skin after death, people leave their names.
(Through one's achievements a human's name lives on.)

The sequential usage of -어서 -ese also works with MAKING something that you then do something with. Thus, it suffixes onto verbs like 만들다 mantulta *to make*, 씻다 ssista *to wash*, 썰다 sselta *to chop*, 자르다 caluta *to cut*, 깎다 kkakkta *to trim*, 갈다 kalta *to sharpen*, and 쓰다 ssuta *to write*:

내일 편지를 **써서** 부칠 거예요.
nayil phyencilul ssese pwuchil keyeyyo.
I will write a letter and then send it tomorrow.

선물로 케이크를 **사서** 가지고 갔어요.
senmwullo kheyikhulul sase kaciko kasseyo.
I bought a cake and took it as a gift.

칼을 **갈아서** 토마토를 써세요.
khalul kalase thomatholul sseseyyo.
Sharpen the knife first and then cut the tomatoes.

In both of these uses, *having done X* is a good translation for an -어서 -ese clause, as there is a sequencing and also a trace of cause and natural consequence. The first action is done FOR THE PURPOSE OF doing the second.

-어 가지고 -e kaciko can be used as a very colloquial version of sequential -어서 -ese. The subject of the two clauses must be the same for -어 가지고 -e kaciko to have a sequential meaning.

표를 예매**해 가지고** 오세요.
phyolul yeymayhay kaciko oseyyo.
Please book a ticket and (then) come/Come with your ticket purchased.

돈을 **모아 가지고** 집을 살 거예요.
tonul moa kaciko cipul sal keyeyyo.
I will save money and buy a house.

한국어를 **배워 가지고** 한국 드라마를 자막 없이 보고 싶다.
hankwukelul paywe kaciko hankwuk tulamalul camak epsi poko siphta.
Having learned Korean, I want to watch Korean dramas without captions.
(I want to learn Korean and then (be able to) watch Korean dramas without captions.)

선희:	컴퓨터 왜 껐어?
senhuy:	khemphyuthe way kkesse?
Sunhee:	*How come you turned off the computer?*

태우:	숙제가 **끝나 가지고**.
thaywu:	swukceyka kkuthna kaciko.
Taewoo:	*My homework is finished.*

(3) -(으)ㄴ 후에/-(으)ㄴ 다음에 *after doing*

후 hwu is a Sino-Korean root that means *after*, as in 오후 ohwu *afternoon*, and 다음 taum is a little more colloquial version of *after* (literally, *next*). The connector part, -(으)ㄴ -(u)n is the past tense adnominal suffix, which makes sense in this connector, since the first action has to be completed for the second to come after. This also means that -(으)ㄴ -(u)n attaches to the verb root, without -었 -ess. -에 -ey is used after either -(으)ㄴ 후 -(u)n hwu or -(으)ㄴ 다음 -(u)n taum, but can also be dropped.

숙제를 **한 다음에** 나가 놀 수 있어.
swukceylul han taumey naka nol swu isse.
You can go out to play after you have done your homework.

빨래를 **한 다음** 청소를 했어요.
ppallaylul han taumey chengsolul haysseyo.
After I did laundry, I cleaned the house.

여권을 **만든 후에** 비자를 신청하십시오.
yekwenul mantun hwuey picalul sinchenghasipsio.
Get a passport and then apply for a visa/After you get a passport, apply for a visa.

(4) Fine-tuning -고 나서 vs. -어서 vs. -(으)ㄴ 후에

So which sequence connector should you use when? The rule of thumb is, for it to be a sequence connector, -어서 -ese should be used for actions that are carried out FOR THE PURPOSE OF the next action. And the first action is being used as a tool, in a sense. Otherwise the clause containing the -어서 -ese-marked verb is interpreted as a REASON, like the first usage we talked about for -어서 -ese. In the following example, having dinner is one event, and taking a walk is another, separate event.

> 저녁을 **먹어서** 산책을 했어요.
> cenyekul mekese sanchaykul haysseyo.
> *I ate dinner and (then) took a walk.*
> *cf. I had dinner so I took a walk.* (this interpretation is okay)

For simple temporal sequences (one thing after another), you must use -고 -ko, -고 나서 -ko nase or -(으)ㄴ 후/다음에 -(u)n hwu/taumey, and the meanings are straightforward.

> 어제는 저녁을 **먹고** 산책을 했어요.
> eceynun cenyekul mekko sanchaykul haysseyo.
> *Yesterday, I ate dinner and (then) took a walk.*

> 어제는 저녁을 **먹고 나서** 산책을 했어요.
> eceynun cenyekul mekko nase sanchaykul haysseyo.
> *Yesterday, I ate dinner, and then took a walk.*

> 어제는 저녁을 **먹은 후에** 산책을 했어요.
> eceynun cenyekul mekun hwuey sanchaykul haysseyo.
> *Yesterday, after I had eaten dinner, I took a walk.*

(5) -기 전에 *before doing*

전 cen is a Sino-Korean root that means *before* as in 오**전** ocen *before noon*. It can be used after nouns referring to times, like 점심 전 cemsim cen *before lunch*. To say *before* DOING X, a connector, -기 전에 -ki ceney is needed, which consists of a -기 -ki suffix (that makes a verb into an *-ing* gerund) and 전에 ceney. Since the clause with -기 전에 -ki ceney hasn't or hadn't happened, there is NEVER a past tense suffix before -기 전에 -ki ceney. It attaches to the verb root.

> 시험 **전에** 밤을 새웠어요.
> sihem ceney pamul saywesseyo.
> *Before the test, I stayed up all night.*

> 시험 **보기 전에** 밤을 새웠어요.
> sihem poki ceney pamul saywesseyo.
> *Before taking the test, I stayed up all night.*

> 밥 **먹기 전에** 손을 씻어라.
> pap mekki ceney sonul ssisela.
> *Before you eat, wash your hands.*

더 **늦기 전에** 하고 싶은 일이 있다.
te nucki ceney hako siphun ili issta.
Before it gets too late/any later, there's something I want to do.

8.2.7 Concurrent actions

There are several options for connecting clauses that express simultaneous actions in Korean.

(1) -(으)면서/(으)며 *while doing*

To show that two actions happen simultaneously, -(으)면서 -(u)myense (colloquial) or -(으)며 -(u)mye (written) is used with an active verb. The clause that has the connector on it is the background action. (So this is also a backward-facing connector, if translated as *while*.) You may also simply use the *-ing* participle in English translations:

운전하면서 문자 보내면 위험해요.
wuncenhamyense mwunca ponaymyen wihemhayyo.
It's dangerous to send texts while driving.

무슨 음악 **들으면서** 운동할 거예요?
mwusun umak tulumyense wuntonghal keyeyyo?
What kind of music will you be listening to when you exercise?

일하고 **공부하며** 바쁘게 살았다.
ilhako kongpwuhamye pappukey salassta.
I lived a busy life, working and studying.

The subject of the -(으)면서 -(u)myense verb and the subject of the main clause verb have to be IDENTICAL. If you want to say two different people are doing something at the same time, use -고 -ko instead (simultaneity is implied), or you can use the expression coming up in the next section, -는 동안에 -nun tonganey.

언니는 음악 **들으면서 나**는 운동했어요.
enninun umak tulumyense nanun wuntonghaysseyo.
I exercised while my sister listened to music.

언니는 음악 **듣고** 나는 운동을 했어요.
enninun umak tutko nanun wuntongul haysseyo.
My older sister listened to music and I exercised.

When -(으)면서 -(u)myense is used with DESCRIPTIVE VERBS, it doesn't mean *while* in a temporal sense of *at the same time*, but in setting up a contrast or unexpected situation, and it is translated as *even though* in some cases, and as *in addition* or *on top of that* in others. This meaning also works with active verbs when the action has been completed or is cast as background, serving the typical function of a descriptive verb.

우리 언니는 **똑똑하면서** 운동도 잘 한다.
wuli enninun ttokttokhamyense wuntongto cal hanta.
My sister is smart and athletic.

차가 가격이 **저렴하면서도** 연비가 좋다.
chaka kakyeki celyemhamyenseto yenpika cohta.
This car is cheap, and also fuel-efficient.

그는 나의 친구**이면서** 멘토이다.
kunun nauy chinkwuimyense meynthoita.
He is my friend and simultaneously my mentor.

돈도 **없으면서** 차를 샀어요?
tonto epsumyense chalul sasseyo?
How come you bought a car when/even though you don't have money?

공부도 안 **했으면서** 성적을 잘 받기를 기대했어?
kongpwuto an hayssumyense sengcekul cal patkilul kitayhaysse?
Did you expect to get a good grade when/even though you didn't even study much?

너는 안 **가면서** 나는 가라고 해?
nenun an kamyense nanun kalako hay?
Why are you telling me to go while you are not going?

(2) -는 동안 *during*, -는 사이 *between*, -는 중 *in the middle of*

Whereas clauses connected with -(으)면서 -(u)myense must have the same subject, the trio -는 동안 -nun tongan, -는 사이 -nun sai, and -는 중 -nun cwung may be used with different subjects, all meaning *while (something else is going on)*. The nuance difference between the three is based on the nouns 동안 tongan, 사이 sai, and 중 cwung, which refer to *duration*, an *interval* or *gap*, and *middle*, respectively. They are all used with a present tense adnominal -는 -nun and with ACTIVE verbs. These endings cannot be used with descriptive verbs. The -에 -ey (locative-CONTACT particle) is optional after these words.

같이 **여행하는 동안** 동생이 사진을 많이 찍었어요.
kathi yehaynghanun tongan tongsayngi sacinul manhi ccikesseyo.
My sister took many pictures during our trip/while we were travelling.

내가 **없는 사이에** 친구가 왔다 갔다.
nayka epsnun saiey chinkwuka wassta kassta.
My friend stopped by while I was out.

회의하는 중에 전화가 왔다.
hoyuyhanun cwungey cenhwaka wassta.
I got a phone call while I was in the meeting.

기다리시는 동안 차라도 한 잔 하실래요?
kitalisinun tongan chalato han can hasillayyo?
Would you like to have a cup of tea while waiting?

자는 **동안** 문자가 왔다.
canun tongan mwuncaka wassta.
The text message arrived while I was sleeping.

The three nouns 동안 tongan, 사이 sai, and 중 cwung can also come after a time or event
NOUN:

한 시간 동안 han sikan tongan	*for an hour*	회의중 hoyuycwung	*meeting in progress*
방학 동안 panghak tongan	*during vacation*	통화중 thonghwacwung	*the line is busy*
수업 사이에 swuep saiey	*between classes*	방송중 pangsongcwung	*on air*
휴식 시간 사이에 hyusik sikan saiey	*between breaks*	공사중 kongsacwung	*under construction*

(3) -는 길에 *on my way to ...*

길 kil means *road* or *way*. With the noun-modifier suffix -는 -nun and together with 가
다 kata *to go* or 오다 ota *to come*, it makes the expression 가는/오는 길에 kanun/onun kiley,
which means *on the way (to/from somewhere)*.

집에 **오는 길에** 슈퍼에 잠깐 들렀어요.
cipey onun kiley syupheey camkan tullesseyo.
I stopped by a grocery store on my way home.

사무실에 **가는 길에** 우체국에 들러서 이것 좀 보내 줘.
samwusiley kanun kiley wucheykkwukey tullese ikes com ponay cwe.
Please drop this off at the post office on your way in to the office.

(4) -는 김에 *while you're at it*

To get the broader sense *while you're at it*, you can use the connector -는 김에 -nun kimey.
김 kim means *steam*, and metaphorically refers to effort, so the expression says *using the
same steam* or *while you're at it, as long as you are ...* and then the main clause can be
about *why don't you/you might as well....* The actions are not necessarily simultaneous,
as they are with -(으)면서 -(u)myense or -는 동안 nun tongan, and unlike 가는/오는 길
에 kanun/onun kiley, the person does not have to be on an actual route going or coming.

슈퍼 **가는 김에** 약국에도 좀 들러.
syuphe kanun kimey yakkwukeyto com tulle.
While/since you are going to the grocery store, please also stop by the pharmacy for me.

비옷을 **사는 김에** 장화도 사기로 했어요.
piosul sanun kimey canghwato sakilo haysseyo.
I decided to buy boots, too, while I was shopping for a raincoat.

네 방 청소하는 **김에** 내 방도 좀 청소해 줄래?
ney pang chengsohanun kimey nay pangto com chengsohay cwullay?
While you're cleaning your room, do you want to clean mine, too?

8.2.8 More temporal and sequence-related connectors

Four more very useful sequencing connectors are -다가 -taka *was -ing when (suddenly)*, -자(마자) -ca(maca) *as soon as*…, -(으)ㄹ 때 -(u)l ttay *when (I did)*…, and -(으)ㄴ 지 -u(n) ci *since*. There is also an interesting usage of -(으)니까 -(u)nikka as temporally relating the actions in two clauses (rather than providing a reason for the main clause).

(1) -다가 *was doing X when*

-다가 -taka basically marks the background action for another abrupt or unexpected happening, but the nuance is slightly different when used on present versus past tense verbs. The 가 ka part of -다가 -taka is frequently dropped.

<1> Present tense + 다가 *was doing X when*

With a present tense verb, a -다가 taka clause means *(someone) was in the middle of -ing, and* THEN *(something else happened to interrupt it)*. -다가 -taka attaches at the end of a clause talking about the activity that got interrupted by the event in the main clause. The past tense suffix is not in the -다가 taka clause because the action is still going on when the action in the main clause happens, interrupting it.

지우는 집에 **가다가** 친구를 만났다.
ciwunun cipey kataka chinkwulul mannassta.
Jiwoo was going/on his way home, when he ran into his friend.

전화가 와서 **자다** 깼다.
cenhwaka wase cata kkayssta.
I woke up in the middle of sleeping because the phone rang.

스키를 **타다** 다리를 다쳤다.
sukhilul thata talilul tachyessta.
I hurt my leg (while/in the middle of) skiing.

친구하고 **문자하다가** 자 버렸다.
chinkwuhako mwuncahataka ca pelyessta.
I was texting my friend, but then I fell asleep.

-다가 -taka can also be repeated on two different verbs, followed by 하다 hata *to do*, to show a flip-flopping between two actions:

그 여자는 너무 기뻐서 **울다가 웃다가** 했다.
ku yecanun nemwu kippese wultaka wustaka hayssta.
The woman was so happy she laughed and cried, cried and laughed.

There is another connector that is easily confusable with this one: -어다가 -etaka. It is a colloquial version of sequential -어서 -ese *having done X* that emphasizes CONTACT with the object (holding it and putting it somewhere) and it has the -어 -e form built in.

이걸 **가져다(가)** 저기 놓아 주세요.
ikel kacyeta(ka) ceki noha cwuseyyo.
Please take this and put it over there.

그걸 **빌려다(가)** 뭣에 쓰게?
kukel pillyeta(ka) mwesey ssukey?
What will you do with that (having borrowed it)?

<2> Past tense + 다가 *I did X briefly and then unexpectedly...; no sooner did I X when I...*

-다가 -taka can be used on a past tense verb as well, and when it is, it means that the first action is COMPLETED, not interrupted, and the following action happens abruptly, unexpectedly, or immediately following the first action.

나는 학교에 **가다가** 친구를 만났다.
nanun hakkyoey kataka chinkwulul mannassta.
I ran into my friend on my way to school.

vs.

나는 학교에 **갔다가** 친구를 만났다.
nanun hakkyoey kasstaka chinkwulul mannassta.
I went to school and bumped into my friend (there).

앉았다가 가세요.
ancasstaka kaseyyo.
Please sit down (for a minute) and then go.

컴퓨터를 **껐다가** 켜세요.
khemphyuthelul kkesstaka khyeseyyo.
Please turn off the computer and then turn it (back) on.

The subjects of the two clauses must be the same whether -다가 -taka appears in the present or the past tense:

내가 집에 **가다가** 친구가 나타났다.
nayka cipey kataka chinkwuka nathanassta.
When I was going home, my friend appeared.

나는 집에 **가다가** 친구를 만났다.
nanun cipey kataka chinkwulul mannassta.
While I was going home, I ran into my friend.

(2) -자마자, -자 *as soon as, (up)on*

-자마자 -camaca means *as soon as* and is used when the action in the main clause happens right after the action in the -자마자 -camaca clause. The -마자 -maca part of -자마자 -camaca can be dropped for a slightly less immediate sense, used mainly in written Korean.

동생은 전화를 **받자마자** 웃기 시작했다.
tongsayngun cenhwalul patcamaca wuski sicakhayssta.
My younger sister started to laugh as soon as she got on the phone.

정 **들자** 이별이다.
ceng tulca ipyelita.
We are parting just when we became friends.

그런 생각이 **나자** 눈물이 쏟아졌다.
kulen sayngkaki naca nwunmwuli ssotacyessta.
When that occurred to me, tears came.

(3) -(으)ㄹ 때 *when*

때 ttay means *a specific time when*, and it can be used after a noun that refers to a certain time period:

점심 **때**쯤에 만납시다.
cemsim ttayccumey mannapsita.
Let's meet around lunchtime.

방학 **때** 학교에 안 가요.
panghak ttay hakkyoey an kayo.
I do not go to school during school break/at vacation time/when it's break time.

The following nouns that denote events or time periods are frequently used with 때 ttay:

방학 panghak *school vacation*, 휴가 hyuka *vacation*, 명절 myengcel *holiday*, and 생일 sayngil *birthday*.

때 ttay is also used after the meal time words such as 점심 cemsim *lunch* and 저녁 cenyek *dinner*, but NOT 밤 pam *night*.

-(으)ㄹ 때 -(u)l ttay (notice the space before 때 ttay) is used as a clause connector to link the time when the main clause activity takes place to a time when something else is happening. When the action in the -을 때 -ul ttay phrase is completed, the past tense suffix, -었 -ess, and not -(으)ㄴ -(u)n, should be used.

시간이 **날 때** 보통 뭐 하세요?
sikani nal ttay pothong mwe haseyyo?
What do you usually do when you have spare time?

뉴욕에 갔을 때 어디에서 묵었어요?
nyuyokey kassul ttay etieyse mwukesseyo?
Where did you stay when you went to NY?

The "tense" marking before -(으)ㄹ 때 -(u)l ttay is of note. This is a case where the distinction between **aspect** (COMPLETION) and **tense** is important:

한국에 **갈 때** 한국 항공사 비행기를 탔어요.
hankwukey kal ttay hankwuk hangkongsa pihayngkilul thasseyo.
I took a plane operated by a Korean airline when I went/was going to Korea.

한국에 **갔을 때** 날씨가 아주 더웠어요.
hankwukey kassul ttay nalssika acwu tewesseyo.
It was very hot when I went/got to Korea. (I went to Korea and found it was very hot.)

In the first sentence, the action of going to Korea was not completed by the time the person took the airplane, so 갈 때 kal ttay is used. In the second sentence, on the contrary, the action of going to Korea was completed before (she found that) it was hot in Korea, so 갔을 때 kassul ttay is used. Let's see more examples:

책을 **읽(고 있)을 때** 친구가 들어왔다.
chaykul ilk(ko iss)ul ttay chinkwuka tulewassta.
My friend came in when I was reading.

책을 다 **읽었을 때** 친구가 들어왔다.
chaykul ta ilkessul ttay chinkwuka tulewassta.
My friend came in when I had finished reading.

어렸을 때 우리는 코딱지만한 셋방에 살았었다.
elyessul ttay wulinun khottakcimanhan seyspangey salassessta.
When I was a child, we lived in a tiny mother-in-law apartment.

할아버지께서 **건강하셨을 때는** 주말에 하이킹을 가곤 했다.
halapecikkeyse kenkanghasyessul ttaynun cwumaley haikhingul kakon hayssta.
When my grandfather was healthy, we used to go hiking on the weekends.

When -(으)ㄹ 때 -(u)l ttay is used for a future sense, it picks out a starting point.

오늘 춥다. **나갈** 때 코트 입어.
onul chwupta. nakal ttay khothu ipe.
It's cold today. Put on a jacket when you go out.

들어올 때 과일 좀 사 와라.
tuleol ttay kwail com sa wala.
Get (buy and bring) some fruit when you come home.

영화가 **시작할 때** 나 불러!
yenghwaka sicakhal ttay na pwulle!
Call me as the movie starts!

To refer to a future event's ending point or its entirety, -(으)면 -(u)myen is used.

나가면 전화해라.
nakamyen cenhwahayla.
Call me when you are out.

포틀랜드에 **오면** 연락하세요.
phothullayntuey omyen yenlakhaseyyo.
Once you are in Portland, contact me.

영화가 **시작하면** 나 불러!
yenghwaka sicakhamyen na pwulle!
Call me once the movie has started!

(4) -(으)ㄴ 지 *since*

Another temporal connector is -(으)ㄴ 지 -(u)n ci, which means *since* in its TEMPORAL sense, as in *it's been a long time since (some other event)*. The main clause ends with 됐다 twayssta (되다 toyta in the past tense) to mean literally, *it has become X amount of time since…* . And since the event in the -(으)ㄴ 지 -(u)n ci clause took place in the past, this connector has the past tense adnominal -(으)ㄴ -(u)n built in, and the past tense -었 -ess is not needed. 지 ci is a (dependent) noun in this structure, so you should leave a space between -(으)ㄴ -(u)n and 지 ci.

한국어 **공부한 지** 얼마나 됐어요?
hankwuke kongpwuhan ci elmana twaysseyo?
How long has it been since you (first) started studying Korean?

한국에 **가본 지** 3년 됐어요.
hankwukey kapon ci sam nyen twaysseyo.
It's been 3 years since I went to Korea (last time).

테니스 **친 지** 한 달 됐어요.
theynisu chin ci han tal twaysseyo.
I have been playing tennis for a month./It's now a month that I have been playing tennis.

Sentences like the last example, 테니스 친 지 한 달 됐어요 theynisu chin ci han tal twaysseyo, can be interpreted two different ways. One is about how long it's been since the time you first STARTED playing tennis, (which is the translation given above), and the other is since the LAST TIME you played tennis:

(마지막으로) 테니스 **친 지** 한 달 됐어요.
(macimakulo) theynisu chin ci han tal twaysseyo.
It's been a month since (the last time) I played tennis.

The first example sentence can be also interpreted differently:

한국어 **공부한 지** 얼마나 됐어요?
hankwuke kongpwuhan ci elmana twaysseyo?
How long has it been since you (last) studied Korean?

It's just a quirk of this structure that interpretation depends on the context.

(5) -(으)니까/(으)니 *when ... I find that; upon doing...*

In addition to expressing reasoning as you saw earlier, -(으)니까 -(u)nikka also carries a sequential sense: *upon doing X, one* EXPERIENCES *something else*. In this usage, -(으)니까 -(u)nikka can only be in the PRESENT TENSE, and the grammatical subjects of the subordinate and the main clause are different (except very colloquially). The 까 kka part is left out in more formal writing.

신문을 **펼치니까** 친구 사진이 있었어요.
sinmwunul phyelchinikka chinkwu sacini issesseyo.
I opened the newspaper and (found that) my friend's photo was there.

집에 **가니까** 친구가 와 있었어요.
cipey kanikka chinkwuka wa issesseyo.
I went home and (I found) my friend was there.

여자가 문서를 **여니** 글자가 모두 깨져 있었다.
yecaka mwunselul yenikka kulcaka motu kkaycye issessta.
The woman opened the document and (found that) all the text was garbled.

봄이 **오니** 여기저기 새소리가 들린다.
pomi oni yekiceki say solika tullinta.
The spring has come, (and I find that) birds' chirping can be heard here and there.

In this usage, -(으)니까 -(u)nikka can be combined with -다(가) -ta(ka) *in the middle of doing* to get -다(가)... 보니(까) -ta(ka) ... poni(kka), which expresses *having been at something for a while and losing track of time or suddenly realizing something*:

얼마를 **걷다 보니** 큰 건물이 나왔다.
elmalul ketta poni khun kenmwuli nawassta.
I walked for some time and came across a big building. (Literally, *a big building showed up.*)
게임하다 보니 시간 가는 줄도 몰랐다.
keyimhata poni sikan kanun cwulto mollassta.
I was so lost in the game, I didn't realize how much time had passed.

일하다 시계를 **보니까** 점심 시간이 지났다.
ilhata sikyeylul ponikka cemsim sikani cinassta.
I looked up from work and saw the clock and it was past lunchtime.
(Literally, *lunch time had passed.*)

자다가 들으니까 너희들 내 욕하던데.
cataka tulunikka nehuytul nay yokhatentey.
I heard while sleeping that you guys were trashing me (and that sort of woke me up).

While -자(마자) -ca(maca) highlights the immediacy of the event in the main clause, -(으)니(까) -(u)ni(kka) emphasizes the subject's personal experience:

가방을 열자 편지 한 통이 떨어졌다.
kapangul yelca phenci han thongi ttelecyessta.
A letter dropped out when I opened the bag.

가방을 여니 편지 한 통이 보였다.
kapangul yeni phyenci han thongi poyessta.
I spotted a letter when I opened the bag.

8.2.9 Intents and purposes: *in order to do; trying to do*

The subordinate clauses in this section may not feel like clauses at all because they translate to verb phrases with *to* infinitives in English, like *while trying to make kimbap*—there's no subject in them. But the connectors here act like other connectors in Korean by linking two actions. This section covers three ways to talk about the intentions behind the actions in the main clause.

(1) -(으)러 *(go/come) in order to do*

To express a purpose for coming or going somewhere, -(으)러 -(u)le is the connector to use, with the verb 가다 kata *to go* or 오다 ota *to come* or their relatives 들어가다 tulekata, 나가다 nakata, 들어오다 tuleota, 나오다 naota in the main clause.

아내:	지금 어디 가?	
anay:	cikum eti ka?	
Wife:	*Where are you going?*	

남편:	쌀 **사러** 슈퍼 가.	
namphyen:	ssal sale syuphe ka.	
Husband:	*I am going to the store to buy rice.*	

고:	어떻게 오셨습니까?	
Ko:	ettehkey osyesssupnikka?	
Ko:	*What brought you here? (May I help you?)*	

한:	김지훈씨 **만나러** 왔습니다.	
Han:	kimcihwunssi mannale wasssupnita.	
Han:	*I came to see Mr. Jihoon Kim.*	

내일 이태원에 인도 음식 **먹으러** 가요.
nayil ithayweney into umsik mekule kayo.
Tomorrow I am going to Itaewon to eat Indian food.

도대체 여기에 뭐 **하러** 왔어?
totaychey yekiey mwe hale wasse?
What the heck did you come here for?

(2) -으려고 *intending to do; trying to do; about to do*

-(으)려고 -(u)lyeko expresses the subject's INTENTION to do something and means *(while) trying to/intending to do X*. It can also express the immediacy of an action:

세일 때 **사려고** 기다리고 있어.
seyil ttay salyeko kitaliko isse.
I'm waiting to buy (it) when it goes on sale.

밤샘을 **하려고** 낮잠을 자 놓았다.
pamsaymul halyeko naccamul ca nohassta.
Thinking that I would pull an all-nighter (later), I took a nap.

버스가 **떠나려고** 한다.
pesuka ttenalyeko hanta.
The bus is about to take off.

The main clause is often not needed to complete the thought in -(으)려고 -(u)lyeko sentences. 하다 hata sometimes makes a courtesy appearance instead.

백:	졸업하고 뭐 할 생각이야?
Payk:	colephako mwe hal sayngkakiya?
Paek:	*What are you thinking of doing after graduation?*

최:	대학원에 **가려고** (해).
Choi:	tayhakweney kalyeko (hay).
Choi:	*I'm considering graduate school.*

어머니:	그 칼로 뭐 **하려고**?
emeni:	ku khallo mwe halyeko?
Mother:	*What are you going/trying to do with that knife?*

딸:	뚜껑 **따려고요**.
ttal:	ttwukkeng ttalyekoyo.
Daughter:	*I was trying/about to pry off the lid.*

-(으)려고 -(u)lyeko without the -고 -ko part also combines with -(으)니까 -(u)nikka to mean *when I tried to do X, (I found Y)* and with -(으)면 -(u)myen to mean *if (you) are trying to do X, if you want to do X*. They are contracted versions of -(으)려고 하니까 -(u)lyeko hanikka and -(으)려고 하면 -(u)lyeko hamyen, which you may also hear. You can add more shortened connectors to this list. The -(으)려 -(u)lye part of these connectors is often pronounced as [-(으)ㄹ라 -(u)lla] or [-(으)ㄹ래 -(u)llay] in casual speech, but it is still different from -(으)러 -(u)le *in order to* that you just learned in the last section.

돈을 **내려(고 하)니까** 지갑이 없었다.
tonul naylye(ko ha)nikka cikapi epsessta.
When I was trying/about to pay, there was no wallet. (I found I had no wallet.)

용서를 **하려(고 하)면** 다 잊어야지.
yongselul halye(ko ha)myen ta iceyaci.
If you are (trying/intending) to forgive, you gotta forget everything.

집중하려는데 더 딴생각이 났어요.
cipcwunghalyenuntey te ttansayngkaki nasseyo.
When I meant/tried to concentrate, I got more distracted.

(3) Fine-tuning -(으)려고 vs. -(으)러

Remember that -(으)러 -(u)le *in order to...* is only used with movement verbs such as 가다 kata *go*, 오다 ota *come*, 들어오다 tuleota *enter*, and 나가다 nakata *go out*, whereas -(으)려고 -(u)lyeko does not have that kind of restriction.

할아버지 **뵈려고** 오늘 세 번이나 왔는데.
halapeci poylyeko onul sey penina wassnuntey.
I've been here three times today, hoping to see the old man.

할아버지 **뵈러** 오늘 세 번이나 왔는데.
halapeci poyle onulsey penina wassnuntey.
I've been here three times today to see the old man.

친구를 **주려고** 선물을 샀어요.
chinkwulul cwulyeko senmwulul sasseyo.
I bought a present to give to my friend.

친구를 **주러** 선물을 샀어요.
chinkwulul cwule senmwulul sasseyo.
I bought a present to give to my friend.

(4) -고자 *trying to do; intending to do*

-고자 -koca is a more formal way of expressing your intention, and it can replace -(으)려고 -(u)lyeko in formal speech and writing. There is more hope and intention in the meaning of -고자 -koca and less control and immediacy than in -(으)려고 -(u)lyeko.

한국에 가서 한국어를 **배우려고** 해요.
hankwukey kase hankwukelul paywulyeko hayyo.
I am thinking of going to Korea (soon) and learning Korean.

한국에 가서 한국어를 **배우고자** 합니다.
hankwukey kase hankwukelul paywukoca hapnita.
I intend/hope to go to Korea and learn Korean.

8.2.10 Other kinds of background

This last set of clause connectors is harder to translate into English. We can find comparable idiomatic constructions in English for some of them, but others are uniquely Korean expressions.

(1) -(으)면 -(으)ㄹ수록 *the more X, the more Y*

English sentences such as *the more I sleep, the more tired I become* are expressed in Korean with one connector: -(으)ㄹ수록 -(u)l swulok.

지훈:	피곤해 보이는데 낮잠 좀 자지 그래?
cihun:	phikonhay poinuntey naccam com caci kulay?
Jihun:	*You look tired. Why don't you take a nap?*

여자친구: **잘수록 더** 피곤해져.
yeca chinku: calswulok te phikonhaycye.
Girlfriend: *The more I sleep, the more tired I become.*

The clause can be embellished by repeating the verb with -(으)면 -(u)myen and using 더 te *more* for emphasis:

채소는 많이 **먹으면** (많이) **먹을수록** 몸에 좋아요.
chaysonun manhi mekumyen (manhi) mekulswulok momey cohayo.
The more vegetables you eat, the better it is.

다이어트를 하면 **할수록** 살이 **더** 찐다.
taiethulul hamyen halswulok sali te ccinta.
The more I diet, the more weight I gain.

(2) -어 봤자 *it's no use doing; might as well not do*
-어 봤자 -e pwassca attaches to a clause that *is no use doing*. This ending CANNOT connect to a past tense verb, and there should be a space between the first verb in -어 -e form and 봤자 pwassca.

외워 봤자 또 잊어버릴 거야.
oywe pwassca tto icepelil keya.
I might as well not memorize (it); I will forget it again.

지금 택시 **타 봤자** 늦었어.
cikum thayksi tha pwassca nucesse.
It's no use taking a taxi; we're late.

지금 표 사러 **가 봤자**, 좋은 좌석은 다 팔렸을 거야.
cikum phyo sale ka pwassca, cohun cwasekun ta phallyessul keya.
There's no point in going to buy tickets now; all the good seats will be sold out.

When -어 봤자 -e pwassca is attached to a DESCRIPTIVE verb, it means *to whatever degree it might be* (*it won't be* THAT *much*), or *be that as it may*, (*I'm not too concerned/I'm not totally convinced*), and when it is used as a sentence ending, the verb 이다 has to be used: -어 봤자다 -e pwasscata.

카레가 **매워 봤자** 얼마나 맵겠어요?
khaleyka maywe pwassca elmana maypkeysseyo?
Well, the curry won't be that spicy./ How spicy could it possibly be?

멀어 봤자야.
mele pwasscaya.
It can't be that far.

(3) -더니 *I recall X but now I find Y*
-더니 -teni is a distinctively Korean ending. It is used to express that the speaker observed something in the past that is somehow relevant to or in contrast with what is the

case currently, as expressed in the main clause. It's a "flashback" connector: it indicates that the speaker is (thinking) back to the moment when she observed or experienced something and contrasting it with the current situation. -더 -te of -더니 -teni shows that the speaker experienced or witnessed what she is talking about, and -니 -ni of -더니 -teni is related to the usage of -(으)니까 -(u)nikka for *upon doing X, I find that*....

<1> Present tense + 더니: the speaker's recollection of her surroundings

If -더니 -teni is used with a PRESENT TENSE verb and a SECOND or THIRD person subject, the speaker *I* is recalling something she observed about the other person, next to something that is different enough to comment on at the present moment.

오늘 바쁘다고 **그러더니** 어떻게 왔어?
onul papputako **kuleteni** ettehkey wasse?
I heard you saying you were busy today; how come you are here?

친구가 집에 **가더니** 안 온다.
chinkwuka cipey **kateni** an onta.
I saw my friend go home but (I noticed that) he never came back.

어제는 날씨가 **춥더니** 오늘은 따뜻해졌다.
eceynun nalssika **chwupteni** onulun ttattushaycyessta.
It was cold yesterday, I recall, but it's gotten warm today.

어렸을 때에는 아주 **작더니** 지금은 빌딩이네!
elyessul ttayeynun acwu **cakteni** cikumun piltinginey!
I remember you being really short when you were young, but you are a building now!

은미 어디 갔어? 방금까지 여기 **있더니**.
unmi eti kasse? pangkumkkaci yeki **issteni**.
Where is Eunmi? She was just here. (I just saw her here.)

친구가 매일 운동을 **하더니** 건강해졌다.
chinkwuka mayil wuntongul **hateni** kenkanghaycyessta.
My friend exercised everyday, and I see that he has gotten healthy.

친구가 한국 음악을 자주 **듣더니** 한국어가 늘었다.
chinkwuka hankwuk umakul cacwu **tutteni** hankwukeka nulessta.
I noticed my friend listens to Korean music a lot, and (now I see that) her Korean has improved.

그 친구는 축의금 많이 하겠다고 **하더니** 내 결혼식에 오지도 않았어.
ku chinkwunun chwukuykum manhi hakeysstako **hateni** nay kyelhonsikey ocito anhasse.
He said he'd give me a big gift of money, but he didn't even attend my wedding, I noticed.

<2> Past tense + 더니: the speaker's recollection about herself

When -더니 -teni attaches to a verb in the PAST TENSE, it expresses a combination of three things about the speaker: *I* completed an action, *I* am recalling it, and *I* find out something upon that action being completed. -었더니 -essteni only works with the first person *I*:

집에 **갔더니** 친구가 와 있었다.
cipey kassteni chinkwuka wa issessta.
When I went home, I saw my friend waiting for me there.

매일 운동을 **했더니** 건강해졌다.
mayil wuntongul hayssteni kenkanghaycyessta.
I exercised everyday, and (I see that) my health has improved.

If we think again about -었 -ess as PERFECTIVE (aspect not tense), we can imagine that present tense + 더니 teni works for observing OTHERS' activities because they are observed IN ACTION, not after the action is completed. For the first person, however, one is not observing one's own action in progress, but is observing the fact that, having completed the action, something changed. One may describe one's own experience using the suffix -더니 -teni in the present tense if she is speaking of her out-of-body experience or seeing herself in her own dream:

내가 버스에서 뛰어내리더니 막 뛰는 거야.
nayka pesueyse ttwienayliteni mak ttwinun keya.
I saw myself jump off the bus and run, you know.

(4) -던데 *I found*

You'll recall that -(으)ㄴ데 -(u)ntey/-는데 -nuntey is used to provide background information of various kinds, often conflicting with the current situation. -던데 -tentey is used when the speaker wants to express her OBSERVATION or EXPERIENCE, which could be presented as a disagreement. This meaning comes from the retrospective suffix -더 -te that we just saw in -더니 -teni.

걔는 **갔던데** 너는 왜 안 가니?
kyaynun kasstentey nenun way an kani?
He went (I heard/I saw him there), so then, why are you not going?

시험이 **쉽던데** 잘 못 봤어?
sihemi swiptentey cal mos poasse?
I found the exam easy/the (professor's) exams were easy (in my experience)… and you bombed it?

(5) -(으)ㄹ 텐데 *I cautiously project, I reservedly imagine*

Don't confuse -던데 -tentey with -(으)ㄹ 텐데 -(u)l theyntey, which is a combination of 테 (터 + 이) they (the + i) and -(으)ㄴ데 -(u)ntey/-는데 -nuntey that introduces mild concern:

비가 **올 텐데** 우산 가지고 가지?
pika ol theyntey wusan kaciko kaci?
It's going to rain; why not take an umbrella?

배고프실 텐데 뭣 좀 먹고 하세요.
paykophusil theyntey mwes com mekko haseyyo.
I imagine you are hungry; eat something before continuing on.

8.2.11 Ending a sentence with a connector

Although connectors normally link two clauses to yield one larger sentence, sometimes when the main clause is too obvious or seems unnecessary, it is left unsaid. This leaves the connector clause as the ONLY clause in the sentence, with the connecting suffix as the sentence-ender. When this happens, which is usually in spoken Korean, the correct assumption to make is that there is more than meets the ear.

김: 그 식당 어땠어요?
kim: ku siktang ettaysseyo?
Kim: *How was the restaurant?*

정: **맛있던데요.**
ceng: masisstenteyyo.
Jang: *I found their food yummy.*

송: 오늘 시험이 너무 어려웠지?
song: onul sihemi nemwu elyewessci?
Song: *Today's test was very difficult, wasn't it?*

민: 그래. 항상 **공부해 봤자야.**
min: kulay. hangsang kongpwuhay pwasscaya.
Min: *Right. No point in studying (since the result is always the same).*

박: 전화 안 해?
pak: cenhwa an hay?
Pak: *Aren't you calling them?*

유: 전화번호가 **바뀌었을 텐데요.**
yu: cenhwa penhoka pakkwiessul theynteyyo.
Yu: *Their number has probably changed.*

소영: 어디 **가는데?**
soyeng: eti kanuntey?
Soyoung: *Where are you going (dressed so pretty/at this time of night)?*

룸메이트: 친구가 **전화해서.**
lwummeythu: chinkwuka cenhwahayse.
Roommate: *A friend of mine just called (so I am going out to see her).*

최: 오늘 수업에 늦었어.
choi: onul swuepey nucesse.
Choi: *I was late for class today.*

우주: 그렇게 늦장을 **부리더니.**
wucwu: kulegkey nuccangul pwuliteni.
Woojoo: *Yup. I saw you dawdling, so.... (I knew you'd be late).*

엄마: 밤에 커피는 왜 마셔?
emma: pamey khephinun way masye?
Mom: *Why are you drinking coffee at night?*

나: 오늘 밤 **새우려고**요.
na: onul pam saywulyekoyo.
Me: *I am trying to stay up all night.*

제 이름은 김영진**이고**요.
cey ilumun kimyengcinikoyo.
My name is Youngjin Kim (and I have more to say about myself.)

8.2.12 Adnominals in connectors

At the beginning of this chapter, you learned about adnominals, and by now you know a number of connectors as well as sentence endings that are composite, which are made up of several parts that may include suffixes, dependent nouns, helping verbs, and in fact, adnominals.

When first learning these endings, it may be easiest to simply memorize them as single units, but if you can understand their make-up (and now you can), you can deepen and expand on your knowledge of how Korean works. For example, when an ending has an adnominal followed by a noun, there is a space between them (e.g. -는 김에 -nun kimey). But when an ending consists only of suffixes, there is no space (e.g., -(으)ㄴ데/-는데 -(u)ntey/-nuntey). This is an important distinction in learning how to form the past tense (-(으)ㄴ 김에 -(u)n kimey vs. -었는데 -essnuntey). Knowing about this basic structure also makes it easier to learn new expressions.

To close this chapter, let's look at expressions that include adnominals plus nouns in Korean. Some are endings we have talked about before but will review here, and others are new, but with your knowledge of adnominals, easily understandable.

Some of the sequential connectors are made up of nouns with past-tense adnominals. With each of them, the action is completed, so it makes sense that the adnominal ending is PAST TENSE -(으)ㄴ -(u)n. Here are the nouns, followed by some example sentences.

다음 taum *after*	뒤 twi *behind, after*	후 hwu *after*
적 cek *experience/time when*	지 ci *(time) since*	

스키 타 본 적은 있는데 **스노보드 타 본 적**은 없다.
sukhi tha pon cekun issnuntey sunopotu tha pon cekun epsta.
I have skied before, but I have never tried snowboarding.

졸업한 다음에 대학원에 진학하고 싶다.
colephan taumey tayhakweney cinhakhako siphta.
I want to advance to graduate school after I graduate (have graduated).

탁구를 친 지 몇 년 됐다.
thakkwulul chin ci myech nyen twayssta.
It's been several years since I played ping-pong.

We also mentioned that some connectors make use of present tense modifying clauses:

-는 길에 -nun kiley *on the way*   -는 김에 -nun kimey *while you're at it*
-는 동안/중 -nun tongan *while/during*

With these connectors, the action is ongoing, so the PRESENT TENSE -는 -nun is used.

Finally, endings that use -(으)ㄹ -(u)l: Not all of these endings have nouns that are translatable or usable outside of the ending itself, but they all have something to do with a future or prospective action. Here is a list of nouns that are frequently used with -(으)ㄹ -(u)l modifying clauses. Some of them have been talked about as endings. Others are simply how things are said in Korean using adnominals plus nouns. This is a chance to expand on what you know!

계획 kyeyhoyk *plan*, 예정 yeyceng *schedule*, 기회 kihoy *opportunity*, 생각 sayngkak *thought/ idea*, 가능성 kanungseng *possibility*, 수 swu *possibility*, 리 li *possibility*, 줄 cwul *capability* and 뻔 ppen a *close call*, etc.

Here are some examples:

졸업하고 대학원에 **진학할 예정이다**.
colephako tayhakweney cinhakhal yeycengita.
I am scheduled to advance to graduate school after I graduate.

졸업하고 대학원에 **진학할 가능성**이 높다.
colephako tayhakweney cinhakhal kanungsengi nophta.
There's a good chance that I will advance to graduate school after I graduate.

무단횡단을 하다가 차에 **치일 뻔 했다**.
mwutanhoyngtanul hataka chaey chiil ppen haysta.
I almost got hit by a car just now, jaywalking.

태권도를 배워 **볼 생각**입니다.
thaykwentolul paywe pol sayngkakipnita.
I am thinking of taking up Taekwondo.

한국어 **읽을 줄 압니다**.
hankwuke ilkul cwul apnita.
I know how to read Korean.

You can see that making interesting sentences in Korean usually has to do with finding the right verb ending. This is the case for sentence endings, clause connectors, and adnominals.
Keep reading to see what else can be accomplished through verb endings in Korean!

Exercises

8.1 Adnominal Clauses

Exercise 1. Fill in the blanks with the appropriate adnominal.

첫	옛	새	헌	딴	맨	고	만

1) 나는 _____ 스무 살입니다.

2) _____ 눈이 오니까 _____ 사랑이 생각나요.

3) 공부하면서 _____ 생각하지 마세요.

4) 제일 먼저 오셨으니까 _____ 앞에 서세요.

5) 오늘은 새 학기 첫날이니까 _____ 신발 신지 말고 _____ 신발을 신고 가.

6) _____ 김광석 씨의 노래는 언제 들어도 좋다.

Exercise 2. Fill in the cells with the appropriate noun-modifying forms.

	Past	Present	Future
치마를 입다	치마를 입은 사람	사람	사람
안경을 쓰다	사람	안경을 쓰는 사람	사람
매일 걷다	사람	사람	매일 걸을 사람
침대에 눕다	사람	침대에 눕는사람	사람
얼굴이 붓다	얼굴이 부은 사람	사람	사람
노래를 부르다	사람	노래를 부르는 사람	사람
김치를 만들다	사람	사람	김치를 만들 사람
머리가 좋다		사람	
피곤하다		사람	
맵다		음식	
하얗다		집	
배가 부르다		사람	

	Past	Present	Future
머리가 길다		사람	
발이 아주 크다		사람	

Exercise 3. Rewrite the phrases on the left as noun-modifying forms.

1) 차가 따뜻해요. → _____ 차

2) 얼굴이 하얘요. → _____ 얼굴

3) 아기가 아주 귀여워요. → _____ 아기

4) 친구가 목이 말라요. → _____ 친구

5) 오늘 바람이 많이 불어요. → _____ 오늘

6) 룸메이트가 수업에 매일 늦게 와요. → _____ 수업

7) 친구가 커피를 마셔요. → _____ 커피

8) 언니가 요리 학교에 다녀요. → _____ 요리 학교

9) 친구가 차를 타요. → _____ 차

10) 저 슈퍼에서 김치를 팔아요. → _____ 김치

Exercise 4. Rewrite the phrases on the left as noun-modifying forms.

1) 남자가 결혼했어요.

→ _____ 남자

2) 동생이 잘 생겼어요.

→ _____ 동생

3) 언니가 빵을 구웠어요.

→ _____ 빵

4) 동생이 이 음악을 지난 주에 들었어요.

→ _____ 음악

5) 제가 김밥을 만들었어요.

→ _____ 김밥

6) 어제 아침에 신문을 읽었어요.

→ _____ 신문

7) 동생이 이 모자를 쓸 거예요.

→ _____ 동생

8) 언니가 빵을 구울 거예요.

→ _____ 빵

9) 이 음악을 곧 들을 거예요.

→ _____ 이 음악

10) 다음 학기에 이 아파트에서 살 거예요.

→ _____ 아파트

11) 내일 아침에 신문을 읽을 거예요.

→ _____ 신문

Exercise 5. Underline the appropriate answer to complete the sentence most naturally.

1) 이 식당에 대학교 때 자주 갔어요.

→ 대학교 때 자주 (간, 가던) 식당이에요.

2) 어제 이 식당에 갔어요.

→ 어제 (간, 가던) 식당이에요.

3) 아까 커피를 마시고 있었어요.

→ 아까 (마신, 마시던) 커피 어디 있어요?

4) 차를 다 마셨어요.

→ 다 (마신, 마시던) 찻잔은 어디에 둘까요?

5) 내가 어렸을 때 이 나무가 작았어요.

→ 어렸을 때 (작던, 작은) 나무가 커졌어요.

6) 5년 전에 사촌이 초등학생이었어요.

→ 5년 전에 (초등학생이던, 초등학생이었던) 사촌이 지금은 고등학생이에요.

8.2 Coordinated and Subordinate Clauses

Exercise 6. Fill in the blanks with the most appropriate connector adverbs. Use each one no more than once.

그래서	그러면	그렇지만	그리고

1) 요즘은 날씨가 참 이상합니다. 12월인데 날씨가 아주 따뜻합니다. _____ 비가 많이 옵니다. _____ 나는 눈이 오는 날을 좋아합니다. _____ 빨리 눈이 오기를 기다립니다. 눈이 오면 공원에 가서 눈사람도 만들고 친구하고 같이 *군고구마도 사 먹을 겁니다. _____ 너무 재미있을 것 같습니다.   *군고구마: broiled sweet potato

그러니까	그러다가	그래도	그런데

2) 언니: 날씨가 춥다. 코트 입고 나가.

동생: 괜찮아. 스웨터 입었어.

언니: _____ 코트 안 입으면 춥다!

동생: 코트 입으면 너무 더운데. 그냥 갈게.

언니: 아이고! _____ 감기 걸려.

동생: 알았어! 코트 입을게. _____ *잔소리 그만해! _____ 언니는 왜 코트 안 입어?

언니: 나는 안 춥거든.   *잔소리: nagging

Exercise 7. Rewrite the underlined parts in the appropriate connector forms.

1) 저는 평일에는 무척 바쁩니다. <u>그런데</u> 주말에는 시간이 좀 여유가 있습니다. 그래서 주말에는 운동하러 헬스클럽에 <u>갑니다. 그러거나</u> 자전거를 타러 한강 공원에 갑니다.

운동은 힘들지만 음악을 듣습니다. 그러면서 운동을 하면 운동하는 것이 즐거워집니다.

a. _____

b. _____

c. _____

2) 어제는 눈이 왔어요. 그리고 날씨가 정말 추웠어요. 그렇지만 바람은 오늘처럼 안 불었어요. 오늘 날씨는 추워요. 그런데 바람도 많이 불어요. 날씨 때문에 벌써 며칠째 집에만 있었어요. 그래서 너무 답답해요. 빨리 날씨가 좋아져서 밖에 나가고 싶어요.

a. _____

b. _____

c. _____

3) 나는 매일 커피를 다섯 잔씩 마셔요. 그래도 잠은 잘 자요. 그런데 어제는 커피를 열 잔이나 마셨어요. 그래서 잠을 잘 수가 없었어요. 오늘부터는 커피를 좀 줄일 거예요. 그리고 대신 카페인 없는 차를 마실 거예요.

a. _____

b. _____

c. _____

4) 내일은 오전에는 날씨가 맑겠습니다. 그러나 오후부터 비가 오겠습니다. 그리고 추워지겠습니다. 모레에는 날씨가 흐리겠습니다. 그리고 춥겠습니다. 또 바람도 많이 불겠습니다.

a. _____

b. _____

c. _____

Exercise 8. Choose the appropriate connector to complete the dialogues most naturally. Be sure to conjugate the given verbs appropriately. Use each connector only once.

-든지	-(으)ㄴ/는데	-(으)면서	-지만

1) A: 음악을 _____ 공부할 수가 있어? (듣다)

   B: 그럼. 나는 항상 그러는데.

2) A: 내일 바빠? 내가 잠깐 들러도 될까?

   B: 아침에는 _____ 저녁 때는 시간이 괜찮을 것 같아. 저녁에 와. (바쁘다)

3) A: 날씨가 _____ 왜 집에 있어? 나가자! (좋다)

   B: 미안, 지금 할 일이 좀 있어서. 오후에 _____ 내일 아침에 나가자. (나가다)

   A: 좋아!

-거나	-(으)며	-(으)ㄴ/는데	-(으)나

4) A: 어제 *건강검진을 _____ *위가 많이 안 좋아졌대. (받다)

   *건강검진: physical examination   *위: stomach

   B: 저런! 그러니까 앞으로 _____ 짠 음식은 많이 먹지 마. (맵다)

5) *일기 예보: 일기예보를 말씀드리겠습니다. 내일 낮 *기온은 3도로 낮지는 _____ 바람이 많이 불어서 춥겠습니다. (않겠다) 밤부터는 _____ 눈도 오겠습니다. (추워지겠다)

   *일기예보: weather forecast   *기온: temperature

Exercise 9. Choose the appropriate connector to complete the dialogues most naturally. Be sure to conjugate the given verbs appropriately.

-(으)면	-어도	-어야

1) A: 건강해지려면 운동을 열심히 해야지!

   B: 시간이 _____ 운동을 하지. 요즘 너무 바빠! (있다)

2) A: 수현이가 달리기 대회에서 일등을 했대!

B: 수현이가 키는 _____ 운동을 잘 해. (작다)

3) A: 지금 슈퍼 가려고 하는데 뭐 부탁할 거 있어?

B: 슈퍼에서 김치를 _____ 김치 좀 사다 줘. (팔다)

-느라고	-어 가지고	-(으)니까	-(으)므로

4) A: 주말에 너희 집에 놀러 가도 돼?

B: 토요일에는 내가 시간이 _____ 일요일에 우리 집에 와
서 같이 점심 먹자. (없다)

5) A: 오늘 피곤해 보이네.

B: 지난 주말에 아버지를 _____ 하나도 못 쉬었어. (도와 드
리다)

6) A: 어제는 날씨가 너무 _____ 밖에서 얼어 죽을 뻔 했어. (춥다)

B: 요즘 날씨가 좀 이상하지?

7) *당뇨병은 치료가 _____ *예방에 힘써야 한다. (어렵다)
*당뇨병: diabetes   *예방: prevention

Exercise 10. Choose the answer(s) that completes the sentence appropriately. Circle
ALL that apply.

1) A: 비가 (오는데, 와서, 오니까) 집에 있을까?

B: 글쎄, 어제도 집에 (있었는데, 있어서, 있으니까) 오늘은 나가자.

2) A: 4월이 (되는데, 됐는데, 돼서, 됐으니까) 아직 눈이 오네!

B: 글쎄 말이야. 올해는 봄이 너무 늦게 오는 거 같아.

3) A: 오늘은 축구하러 안 나가요?

B: 날씨가 너무 (추워서, 추운데) 안 나가기로 했어요.

4) A: 공사 때문에 길이 다 (막혀서, 막혔기 때문에, 막혔으니까) 다른 길로 가세요.

B: 네, 그렇게요.

5) A: 아니, 아프다면서요? 괜찮아요?

B: 감기에 (걸려서, 걸리기 때문에, 걸리느라고, 걸리니까) 좀 아팠어요. 이제는
괜찮아요.

6) A: 집에 있으면서 왜 전화를 안 받았어요?

B: (청소하기 때문에, 청소하느라고, 청소했는데, 청소하니까) 못 받았어요.

Exercise 11. Choose the answer(s) that completes the sentence appropriately. Circle
ALL that apply.

1) 내릴 사람이 다 (내리고, 내려서, 내린 후에) 타세요.

2) 여기 (오고, 와서, 온 후에) 앉으세요.

3) 저녁을 (먹고, 먹어서, 먹은 다음에) 영화를 볼 거예요.

4) 김치를 (먹고 나서, 먹기 전에) 이를 닦아야 해요.

5) 나는 서울에서 (태어나고, 태어나서, 태어난 다음에) 자랐어요.

Exercise 12. Choose the appropriate connector to complete the dialogues most naturally. Be sure to conjugate the given verbs appropriately.

-고 나서	-는 동안에	-어서 (sequential)	-(으)면서

1) A: 내일 뭐 해?

B: 친구를 _____ 경영학 발표 프로젝트를 같이 하기로 했어.
너는? (만나다)

A: 나는 내일 집에서 영화나 _____ 쉬려고 해. (보다)

2) A: 내 문자 못 받았어? 몇시간 전에 보냈는데.

B: 어, 미안! 내가 수업을 _____ 네가 문자를 보냈나 봐. (듣다)

수업이 _____ 확인하려고 했는데 잊어버렸네. (끝나다)

-기 전에	-는 길에	-는 김에	-(으)ㄴ 후에

3) 나는 이번 학기가 _____ 한국에서 여름에 영어를 가르치

는 일을 하기로 했다. (끝나다) 그래서 한국에 _____ 여행도

많이 하고 한국어도 열심히 공부하기로 결심했다. (가다) 그리고 한국에

_____ 일본하고 중국에도 들를 것이다. (가다) 그래서 여름이

_____ 일본어와 중국어를 좀 공부해 두려고 한다. (오다) 이번

여름이 정말 기대가 된다!

Exercise 13. Choose the appropriate connector to complete the dialogues most naturally. Be sure to conjugate the given verbs appropriately.

-다가	-(으)ㄴ 지	-자 마자

1) 오늘 학교에 _____ 고등학교 동창인 은지를 만났다. (가다) 은

지하고 내가 마지막으로 _____ 거의 5년이 지났지만 우리는 한

눈에 서로를 알아 보았다. (만나다) 은지는 고등학교를 _____

미국에 유학을 갔기 때문에 졸업한 후에 서로 만날 기회가 없었다. (졸업하

다) 나는 고등학교 때 은지하고 꽤 친했기 때문에 은지를 만나서 무척 반가

웠다.

-(으)ㄹ 때	-(으)니까

2) A: 김 교수님께서 연구실에 계실까?

B: 아까 내가 김 교수님 연구실에 _____ 계시던데. 빨리 가 봐.
   (가다)

(An hour later)

A: 교수님 만나 뵈었어?

B: 글쎄, 안 계시더라고. 금방 나가셨대.

A: 다음에 _____ 에는 이메일을 먼저 드리고 가 봐. (뵈러 가다)

Exercise 14. Choose the answer(s) that completes the sentence appropriately. Circle ALL that apply.

1) 오늘 학교에 (오다가, 왔다가) 가벼운 *교통사고를 당했어요.
   *교통사고를 당하다: get into a car accident

2) 학교에 (가다가, 갔다가) 올게요!

3) 컴퓨터가 잘 안 되면 (끄다가, 껐다가) 켜세요.

4) 영화를 (보다가, 봤다가) 잠이 들었어.

5) 동생이 스키를 (타다가, 탔다가) 다리를 다쳤다.

6) 버스를 (타다가, 탔다가) 우연히 고등학교 때 친구를 만났다.

7) 신발을 (사다가, 샀다가) 마음에 안 들어서 다른 신발로 바꿨다.

8) 어머니께 예쁜 구두를 (사다가, 샀다가) 드렸다.

9) *재활용품을 (가져다가, 가졌다가) 집에서 사용했다. *재활용품: recycled material

Exercise 15. Underline the answer(s) that best completes the sentence.

1) A: 학교 (시작하는 지, 시작한 지) 벌써 4주가 됐네.

   B: 정말 시간이 빨리 가지?

2) A: 한국에서는 뜨거운 음식 (먹을 때, 먹었을 때) 소리를 내도 괜찮아.

   B: 그렇구나.

3) A: 어제 진영이를 (만날 때, 만났을 때) 무슨 일 있었어? 진영이가 화가 났던데.

   B: 글쎄, 별 일 없었는데 왜 그러지?

4) A: 왜 이렇게 늦었어요?

   B: 이제 (오니까, 왔으니까) 화 내지 마세요.

5) A: 어제 집에 (가니까, 갔으니까) 중학교 친구가 와 있더라고요.

   B: 어머, 반가웠겠어요.

Exercise 16. Choose the appropriate connector to complete the dialogues most naturally. Be sure to conjugate the given verbs appropriately. Use each connector only once.

-더니	-(으)러	-(으)려고	-(으)면 을수록

1) A: 어떻게 오셨습니까?

   B: 김 부장님을 _____ 왔습니다! (뵈다)

2) A: 졸업한 다음에 계획이 어떻게 되세요?

   B: 네, 대학원에 _____ 생각하고 있습니다. (진학하다)

3) A: 운동 시작한 지 한 달 됐지? 할 만 해?

   B: 처음에는 너무 _____ 이제는 운동을 안 하면 몸이 더 피곤한 것 같아. (힘들다)

   A: 그렇지? 운동은 _____ 더 기운이 생기는 것 같아. (하다)

-고자	-던데	-어 봤자	-(으)ㄹ텐데

4) A: 저희 회사에 왜 *지원하셨습니까? *지원하다: apply

   B: 저는 이 회사에서 마케팅 전문가로서의 꿈을 _____ 합니다. (펼치다: unfold, follow)

5) A: _____ 이것 좀 먹어 봐. (배고프다)

   B: 네, 잘 먹겠습니다.

6) A: 아까 보니까 한국어를 꽤 잘 _____ 언제부터 한국어를 공부하셨어요? (하시다)

   B: 대학교 1학년때부터 배웠으니까 4년쯤 배웠습니다.

7) A: 내일이 시험인데 공부 안 해?

   B: 지금부터 _____ 얼마나 하겠어? 그냥 포기할래. (공부하다)

Exercise 17. Choose the answer(s) that completes the sentence appropriately. Circle ALL that apply.

1) 어제는 날씨가 (춥더니, 추웠더니) 오늘은 따뜻하다.

2) 매일 삼십분씩 (걷더니, 걸었더니) 건강해졌다.

3) 친구가 매일 삼십 분씩 (걷더니, 걸었더니) 건강해졌다.

4) 친구가 집에 (가더니, 갔더니) 안 오네.

5) 친구 집에 (가더니, 갔더니) 아무도 없었다.

6) 소파에서 좀 (졸더니, 졸았더니) 덜 피곤하다.

7) 강아지가 아까부터 (졸더니, 졸았더니) 이제는 잔다.

Exercise 18. Underline the appropriate word from the parentheses to complete the sentence most naturally.

1) 구름은 좀 (끼지만, 꼈지만) 날씨는 괜찮다.

2) 어제는 몸이 안 좋아서 집에서 텔레비전을 (보면서, 봤으면서) 쉬었어요.

3) 너는 어제 시험도 잘 (보면서, 봤으면서) 왜 그렇게 기분이 안 좋아?

4) 어제 너무 (추워서, 추웠어서) 집에 있었다.

5) 동생이 감기에 심하게 (걸리기 때문에, 걸렸기 때문에) 학교에 못 갈 거 같아요.

6) 내가 학교에 (가니까, 갔으니까) 아무도 안 와 있었다.

7) 어제 한국 음식을 (먹으니까, 먹었으니까) 오늘은 중국 음식을 먹을까요?

8) 한국에 (갈 때, 갔을 때) 아시아나 비행기를 타고 갔다.

9) 영화가 다 (끝날 때, 끝났을 때) 친구가 왔다.

10) 동생이 길을 (건너다가, 건넜다가) 교통사고가 났어요.

11) 학교에 (가다가, 갔다가) 올게요.

12) 동생한테서 전화가 (오는데, 왔는데) 나중에 집에 들를 거라고 했어요.

13) 지금 밖에 비가 (오는데, 왔는데) 약속을 취소할까요?

14) 동생이 매일 (운동하더니, 운동했더니) 살이 많이 빠졌다.

15) 건강해지려고 매일 (운동하더니, 운동했더니) 살이 많이 빠졌다.

Exercise 19. Underline the appropriate word from the parentheses to complete the sentence most naturally.

1) 오늘은 비가 (와서, 오니까) 내일 테니스 칩시다.

2) 집에 (오고, 와서) 같이 저녁 먹을래?

3) 길이 (복잡해서, 복잡한데) 지하철 타는 게 어때요?

4) (지각하느라고, 지각해서) 죄송합니다.

5) 10인분 불고기를 (만들어서, 만드느라고) 힘들어서 죽을 뻔 했어요.

6) 내가 청소를 (하면서, 하는 동안에) 동생은 빨래를 했다.

7) 나는 음악을 (들으면서, 듣는 동안에) 공부를 한다.

8) 저는 졸업하고 대학원에 (가러, 가려고) 합니다

9) 주말에는 친구를 (만나고자, 만나러) 뉴욕에 갈 거예요.

10) 형은 법대를 졸업하고 나서 변호사로서 (성공하러, 성공하고자) 한다.

Exercise 20. Choose the appropriate formal version of the connector to replace the underlined parts.

어서	(으)며	-(으)ㄴ 후에	-고자	-(으)나

1) 어제 너무 <u>아파 가지고</u> 수업에 결석했습니다. 죄송합니다.

2) 사업가로서 <u>성공하려고</u> 하는 꿈이 있습니다.

3) <u>사용하신 다음에</u> 반납하여 주십시오.

4) 요즘은 <u>일하면서</u> 공부하는 학생들도 많다.

5) <u>노력했지만</u> 결과가 좋지 않았다.

CHAPTER 9

Verb Derivations

You are truly becoming an expert in manipulating verb conjugations and verbal suffixes—the core of Korean grammar. Thus far, all of them have been **inflectional suffixes**, serving grammatical or functional purposes such as marking tense, aspect, sentence type, speech style, speaker's intention, and logical or temporal connection between clauses. In this chapter we'll focus on **derivational suffixes**, specifically, those that convert regular verb roots into new honorific, passive and causative verb **stems** (which are then ready for inflectional suffixes) and those that derive adverbs from descriptive verbs.

As you have seen, attitudes, formality, and politeness are all GRAMMATICALLY marked on verbs in Korean. This means you can't just choose ways to be polite to someone when you feel like it. Having learned speech styles, it is high time we talk about **honorifics**, since they are another very important linguistic manifestation of culture and society. Passives and causatives are also very useful in Korean.

After the three verb derivations in 9.1, we will show you how to derive an adverb from a verb in 9.2, some intensifying verb prefixes in 9.3, and then we'll wrap up with a demonstration of how verb suffixes can be stacked up.

9.1 Deriving New Kinds of Verbs

There are three kinds of verbs created with derivational suffixes in Korean: **honorifics**, **passives**, and **causatives**. Let's begin with honorifics.

9.1.1 Honorifics

Obviously, honorifics, known as 존댓말 contaysmal or 높임말 nophimmal, have something to do with honor, but what exactly is this **honorific system** and how is it different from speech styles?

In the Korean language, using honorifics is about recognizing and respecting someone in a higher or honored social position like your elders. **Honorifics** refers to the ways of talking about someone in that honored position, while speech styles have to do with whom you are talking TO. If you are talking about AND to an honored person (e.g., *Are you cold, Grandma?* or, *Please make yourself comfortable, Sir*), you use honorifics AND polite or formal speech style at the same time. If you are talking TO your cousin ABOUT your grandparents, you would use an ordinary speech style but honorific words to refer to your grandparents' actions and items that belong to them. For example, in the sentence *Grandmother-(particle) is eating dinner*, the underlined words have honorific versions.

Honorifics take the form of special honorific verbs to talk about what honored people do, honorific nouns to refer to certain things that "belong" to honored people (like the house they live in or the meals they eat), and honorific particles on nouns referring to honored people. The honorific system also includes **humble** forms that refer to one's own self with respect to an honored person. That is, you honor the other by humbling yourself.

Who is worth expressing deference to? Grandparents, teachers, customers, your boss, doctors and other professionals. In general, adults who are older than you and people you encounter who are in their late 30s and above (unless they are your customers, in which case they may be in their late teens) begin to receive linguistically honorific treatment. In a highly hierarchical organization (e.g., college, a company, the military, gangs), adults in their upper teens start using 존댓말 contaysmal to their 선배 senpay (class seniors) and upper-rung people who may be only a year or two older.

Do be cautious, however, because you may insult the listener or bring about a comical effect by over-using honorific words in some cases. Also, you use honorific expressions to talk about people you are PERSONALLY connected to; no matter how grand the person is, you do NOT honor public figures or celebrities.

Let's look at some examples. The first of the pair is talking ABOUT a young person, and the second ABOUT someone to be honored. The verbs are different, depending on who is doing the action.

너, 어디 **가**?
ne, eti ka?
Where are you going?

아빠, 어디 **가세요**?
appa, eti kaseyyo?
Dad, where are you going?

너희 누나 오후에 집에 **있어**?
nehuy nuna ohwuey cipey isse?
Is your sister home in the afternoon?

부모님 오후에 댁에 **계셔**?
pwumonim ohwuey taykey kyeysye?
Are your parents home in the afternoon?

Now, let's see how to derive this kind of honorific verb.

(1) Deriving -(으)시 honorific verbs

An honorific verb expresses deference to the person doing the action or being described by the verb, namely, the SUBJECT. To make an honorific verb, add the suffix -(으)시 -(u) si to the verb root.

쓰다 ssuta *to write:* 쓰- ssu- + (으)시 -(u)si + 다 ta
→ 쓰시다 ssusita *to write-honorific* (dictionary form)

읽다 ilkta *to read:* 읽- ilk- + (으)시 -(u)si + 다 ta
→ 읽으시다 ilkusita *to read-honorific* (dictionary form)

가다 kata *to go:* 가- ka- + (으)시 -(u)si + 다 ta
→ 가시다 kasita *to go-honorific* (dictionary form)

Once the honorific suffix -(으)시 -(u)si is attached to the verb root, *voilà!* You now have a new verb **stem**, ready for other suffixes and conjugation. Since you know how to conjugate vowel-final verbs in the various tenses, modalities, and speech styles, any newly derived honorific verbs with -(으)시 -(u)si should be straightforward.

One thing to note is that the verb 있다 issta has two honorific forms. When it means *exist* (or *to be at/stay at a location*), its honorific version is 계시다 kyeysita (as you probably know from the farewell greeting 안녕히 계세요 annyenghi kyeyseyyo *Stay well*). When 있다 issta expresses someone HAVING something, thus its honorific version talks about an honored person having something, the form is 있으시다 issusita. In a sense, with the special honorific verb 계시다 kyeysita, the PERSON('s EXISTENCE) is honored, whereas with the derived verb 있으시다 issusita, the the PERSON('s OWNERSHIP) is honored but not the item itself. The honorific verb 계시다 kyeysita is used for the progressive as well: -고 계시다 -ko kyeysita instead of -고 있다 -go issta.

The honorific form of the *be* verb 이다 ita works as expected, becoming 이시다 isita in the dictionary form.

Here are two example dialogues where these honorific verbs are used to talk about someone honored. In the second set, the father is talked about honorifically, although speech styles change. The mother is using honorifics because she is addressing what the son brought up. She may or may not use honorifics when she talks to her husband face to face.

이웃: 저 분이 누구**세요**?
iwus: ce pwuni nwukwuseyyo?
Neighbor: *Who is that person?*

나: 저희 어머니 친구분**이세요**.
na: cehuy emeni chinkwupwuniseyyo.
Mother: *He/she is my mom's friend.*

아들: 아버지 지금 어디 **계세요?**
atul: apeci cikum eti kyeyseyyo?
Son: *Where is Father now?*

아버지가 현금이 좀 **있으실까요?**
apecika hyenkumi com issusilkkayo?
Do you think Father has some cash?

어머니: 글쎄. 아마 **없으실 거야.**
emeni: kulssey. ama epsusil keya.
Mother: *Well. I don't think so* (Literally, *he probably won't have cash*)

Let's look more closely at the conjugation of honorific verbs for the formal, plain, and ordinary speech styles.

<1> Conjugation of honorific -(으)시 verbs for the formal style

There are many situations in which you would use honorifics in the formal style. If you are talking to someone in the formal style, you will likely use honorific forms for that person's doings as well as for those of colleagues. There will inevitably be people to be honored in the formal, hierarchical institutions and situations where formal speech style is used.

Here is a context where the formal style might be used with honorifics: you are interacting with an elder next door. Notice that the speaker does not use honorifics to talk about his or her own actions.

이웃 할아버지: 할아버지 어디 **가셨니?**
iwus halapeci: halapeci eti kasyessni?
Elderly neighbor: *Has your grandfather gone somewhere?*

나: 네. 매일 뒷산에 **올라가십니다.** 저는 안 갑니다. 곧 **오실 겁
니다.** 아, 저기 **오(시)고 계십니다.**
na: ney. mayil twissaney ollakasipnita. cenun an kapnita. kot osil kepnita. a, ceki o(si)ko kyeysipnita.
Me: *Yes. He climbs the hills out back every day. I don't go. He will be back soon. Oh, there he is coming.*

Below is an overview of verb conjugation with -(으)시 -(u)si in the formal style. Remember that 이다 ita *to be* + -(으)시 -(u)si works as expected, becoming 이시다 isita in the dictionary form; 계시다 kyeysita replaces 있다 issta when it means *to exist* (or *to be at/stay at a location*), but 있으시다 issusita is used when talking about the honored person *having something*; and the progressive ending is -고 계시다 -ko kyeysita instead of -고 있다 -ko issta. You will sometimes hear the honorific -(으)시 -(u)si used redundantly on the main verb as well, for example, 가시고 계시다 kasiko kyeysita *is-honorific going-honorific*, but this is not a "standard" usage.

Dictionary Form	Honorific Dictionary Form	Present	Past	Future	Progressive
앉다 ancta *to sit*	앉으시다 ancusita	앉으십니다/ 까 ancusipnita/kka	앉으셨습니다/ 까 ancusyesssupnita/ kka	앉으실 겁니다/ 까 ancusil kepnita/kka	앉고 계십니다/ 까 ancko kyeysipnita/ kka
가다 kata *to go*	가시다 kasita	가십니다/ 까 kasipnita/kka	가셨습니다/ 까 kasyesssupnita/kka	가실 겁니다/까 kasil kepnita/kka	가고 계십니다/ 까 kako kyeysipnita/kka
알다 alta *to know*	아시다 asita	아십니다/ 까 asipnita/kka	아셨습니다/ 까 asyesssupnita/kka	아실 겁니다/ 까 asil kepnita/kka	알고 계십니다/ 까 alko kyeysipnita/kka
이다 ita *to be*	이시다 isita	이십니다/ 까 isipnita/kka	이셨습니다/ 까 isyesssupnita/kka	이실 겁니다/ 까 isil kepnita/kka	--
있다 issta *to have*	있으시다 issuisita	있으십니다/ 까 issusipnita/kka	있으셨습니다/ 까 issusyesssupnita/ kka	있으실 겁니다/ 까 issusil kepnita/kka	--
있다 issta *to exist, stay*	**계시다** kyeysita	계십니다/ 까 kyeysipnita/kka	계셨습니다/ 까 kyeysyesssupnita/ kka	계실 겁니다/ 까 kyeysil kepnita/kka	--

\<2\> Conjugation of honorific -(으)시 verbs for the plain style

Honorifics are used in the plain style in personal writings (e.g. journals and letters), where the subject is an honored person with whom the writer has a personal relationship. They are also used in the babysitter's usage talking about parents or grandparents and older acquaintances. Remember—honorifics are not used just because the person is old, famous or has a high social status. To use honorifics, you have to have a PERSONAL relationship with the person. You don't use honorifics for K-Pop stars and the President.

Here is a context where the plain style might be used with and without honorifics. The writer's age does not matter:

오늘의 일기 중
onuluy ilki cwung
An excerpt from today's journal entry

할아버지는 매일 뒷산에 **올라가신다**. 오늘도 **가셨다**. 나는 안 간다. 오늘 옆
집에서 할아버지를 찾아 **오셨다**. 그 옆집 할아버지는 매일 **오신다**. 내일도
오실 거다. 아, 지금 다시 **오(시)고 계신다**.

halabecinun mayil twissaney ollakasinta. onulto kasyessta. nanun an kanta. onul yephcipeyse halapecil-ul chaca osyessta. ku yephcip halapecinun mayil osinta. nayilto osil keta. a. cikum tasi o(si)ko kyeysinta.

Grandfather climbs the hills out back every day. He went today as well. I don't go. The old man neighbor came for Grandfather today. He comes every day. He'll come tomorrow as well. Oh, he is coming again now.

In the plain style present tense, active and descriptive verbs are differentiated, and (이)
시다 (i)sita uses the same ending as descriptive verbs. 계시다 kyeysita *to exist-honorific*
works either way.

Dictionary Form	Honorific Dictionary Form	Present	Past	Future	Progressive
앉다 ancta *to sit*	앉으시다 ancusita	앉으신다 ancusinta	앉으셨다 ancusyessta	앉으실 거다 ancusil keta	앉고 계신다/ 계시다 ancko kyeysinta/ kyeysita
가다 kata *to go*	가시다 kasita	가신다 kasinta	가셨다 kasyessta	가실 거다 kasil keta	가고 계신다/ 계시다 kako kyeysinta/ kyeysita
알다 alta *to know*	아시다 asita	아신다 asinta	아셨다 asyessta	아실 거다 asil keta	알고 계신다/ 계시다 alko kyeysinta/ kyeysita
이다 ita *to be*	이시다 ita	이**시다** isita	이셨다 isyessta	이실 거다 isil keta	— —
있다 issta *to have*	있으시다 issusita	있으시다 issusita	있으셨다 issusyessta	있으실 거다 issusil keta	— —
있다 issta *to exist, stay*	**계시다** kyeysita	**계신다/계시다** kyeysinta/kyeysita	계셨다 kyeysyessta	계실 거다 kyeysil keta	— —

<3> Conjugation of honorific -(으)시 verbs for the intimate ordinary style

Similarly to the plain style, you would use honorifics to talk about your or another's
parents and grandparents, your boss or teachers, and so on, and use the intimate ordinary style when talking to a child, or to a sibling or a best friend.

Here is a context where the intimate ordinary style might be used with honorifics:
You are in your upper teens and are interacting with your close friend.

친구: 할아버지 어디 **가셨어**?
chinkwu: halapeci eti kasyesse?
Friend: *Has your grandpa gone somewhere?*

나: 응. 매일 뒷산에 **올라가셔**. 나는 안 가. 곧 **오실 거야**. 아, 저기 오(시)
고 계셔.
na: ung. mayil twissaney ollakasye. nanun an ka. kot osil keya. a, ceki o(si)ko kyeysye.
Me: *Yes. He climbs the hills out back every day. I don't go. He will be back soon.*
Oh, there he is coming.

Conjugations are regular and expected, including the present tense forms ending in
-(으)셔 -(u)sye from -(으)시 + 어 -(u)si + e. (Vowel harmony dictates the default -어 -e
vowel after the 이 i of -(으)시 -(u)si.)

Dictionary Form	Honorific Dictionary Form	Present	Past	Future	Progressive
앉다 ancta *to sit*	앉으시다 ancusita	앉으셔 ancusye	앉으셨어 ancusyesse	앉으실 거야 ancusil keya	앉고 계셔 ancko kyeysye
가다 kata *to go*	가시다 kasita	가셔 kasye	가셨어 kasyesse	가실 거야 kasil keya	가고 계셔 kako kyeysye
알다 alta *to know*	아시다 asita	아셔 asye	아셨어 asyesse	아실 거야 asil keya	알고 계셔 alko kyeysye
이다 ita *to be*	이시다 isita	이셔 isye	이셨어 isyesse	이실 거야 isil keya	--
있다 issta *to have*	있으시다 issusita	있으셔 issusye	있으셨어 issusyesse	있으실 거야 issusil keya	--
있다 issta *to exist, stay*	계시다 kyeysita	계셔 kyeysye	계셨어 kyeysyesse	계실 거야 kyeysil keya	--

<4> Conjugation of honorific -(으)시 verbs for the polite ordinary style
The honorific form is often used for commands in the polite ordinary style. Of course it
would also be used to talk about any honored person with colleagues or other acquaintances with whom you use the polite ordinary style.

Here is a context where the intimate ordinary style might be used with honorifics:
you are in your 30s and are interacting with your neighbor also in their 30s.

이웃: 할아버지 어디 **가셨어요**?
iwus: halapeci eti kasyesseyo?
Neighbor: *Has your grandpa gone somewhere?*

나: 네. 매일 뒷산에 **올라가세요**. 저는 안 가요. 곧 **오실** 거예요. 아, 저
기 오(시)고 계세요.
na: ney. mayil twissaney ollakaseyyo. cenun an kayo. kot osil keyeyyo. a, ceki o(si)ko kyeyseyyo.
Me: *Yes. He climbs the hills out back every day. I don't go. He will be back soon.*
Oh, there he is coming.

Honorific verbs with -(으)시다 -(u)sita conjugate irregularly in the present tense polite ordinary style, unlike the intimate ordinary -(으)셔 -(u)sye. Similiarly to how the verb 이다 ita becomes 이에요 ieyyo, honorific verbs in the polite present tense style use the ending -(으)세요 -(u)seyyo. The National Institute of the Korean Language does allow the regular, expected form -(으)셔요 -(u)syeyyo, and you may see it in older printed materials or those published in North Korea, but most South Korean speakers use -(으)세요 -(u)seyyo. You hear this ending in greetings like 안녕하세요 annyenghaseyyo and 안녕히 계세요 annyenghikyeyseyyo.

Dictionary Form	Honorific Dictionary Form	Present	Past	Future	Progressive
앉다 ancta *to sit*	앉으시다 ancusita	앉으세요 ancuseyyo	앉으셨어요 ancusyesseyo	앉으실 거예요 ancusil keyeyyo	앉고 계세요 ancko kyeyseyyo
가다 kata *to go*	가시다 kasita	가세요 kaseyyo	가셨어요 kasyesseyo	가실 거예요 kasil keyeyyo	가고 계세요 kako kyeyseyyo
알다 alta *to know*	아시다 asita	아세요 aseyyo	아셨어요 asyesseyo	아실 거예요 asil keyeyyo	알고 계세요 alko kyeyseyyo
이다 ita *to be*	이시다 isita	이세요 iseyyo	이셨어요 isyesseyo	이실 거예요 isil keyeyyo	_ _
있다 issta *to have*	있으시다 issusita	있으세요 issuseyyo	있으셨어요 issusyesseyo	있으실 거예요 issusil keyeyyo	_ _
있다 issta *to exist, stay*	계시다 kyeysita	계세요 kyeyseyyo	계셨어요 kyeysyesseyo	계실 거예요 kyeysil keyeyyo	_ _

<5> Conjugation of honorific verbs derived from regular and special-class verbs

When honorific verbs are derived from special-class verbs, the root shapes change to the special form because the honorific suffix -(으)시 -(u)si begins with a vowel. The following chart compares regular and special-class verbs in their honorific forms:

Class	Dictionary Form	Meaning	Honorific Dictionary Form	Present Intimate Ordinary	Present Polite Ordinary
regular	앉다 ancta	*to sit*	앉으시다 ancusita	앉으셔 ancusye	앉으세요 ancuseyyo
regular	알다 alta	*to know*	아시다 asita	아셔 asye	아세요 aseyyo
irregular	하다 hata	*to do*	하시다 hasita	하셔 hasye	하세요 haseyyo
special-르	모르다 moluta	*to not know*	모르시다 molusita	모르셔 molusye	모르세요 moluseyyo

Class	Dictionary Form	Meaning	Honorific Dictionary Form	Present Intimate Ordinary	Present Polite Ordinary
regular	좋다 cohta	*to be good*	좋으시다 cohusita	좋으셔 cohusye	좋으세요 cohuseyyo
special-ㅎ	그렇다 kulehta	*to be so*	그러시다 kulehta	그러셔 kulesye	그러세요 kuleseyyo
regular	잡다 capta	*to hold*	잡으시다 capusita	잡으셔 capusye	잡으세요 capuseyyo
special-ㅂ	춥다 chwupta	*to be cold*	추우시다 chwuwusita	추우셔 chwuwusye	추우세요 chwuwuseyyo
regular	닫다 tatta	*to close*	닫으시다 tatusita	닫으셔 tatusye	닫으세요 tatuseyyo
special-ㄷ	걷다 ketta	*to walk*	걸으시다 kelusita	걸으셔 kelusye	걸으세요 keluseyyo
regular	웃다 wusta	*to smile*	웃으시다 wususita	웃으셔 wususye	웃으세요 wususeyyo
special-ㅅ	짓다 cista	*to make*	지으시다 ciusita	지으셔 ciusye	지으세요 ciuseyyo

Here are some example sentences:

그분을 아세요, 모르세요?
kupwunul aseyyo, moluseyyo?
Do you know her or not?

좋으시면 그러세요.
cohusimyen kuleseyyo.
If you like (that idea), please do so.

추우시면 문을 닫으세요.
chwuwusimyen mwunul tatuseyyo.
If you are cold, do close the door.

좀 더 걸으시겠어요?
com te kelusikeysseyo?
Would you like to walk some more?

이 약을 어디에서 지으셨어요?
i yakul etieyse ciusyesseyo?
Where did you get the prescription filled?

두 분 다 이쪽에 앉으실 거예요.
twu pwun ta iccokey ancusil keyeyyo.
Both of them will sit on this side.

(2) Inherently honorific words

The suffix -(으)시 -(u)si works to convert most verbs into honorific counterparts, but a few verbs do not get converted by the addition of -(으)시 -(u)si. There are some **inherently honorific verbs** such as 드시다 tusita *to eat* and 주무시다 cwumwusita *to sleep*. These are ready-made honorific verbs that have special verb roots and -(으)시 -(u)si built in. When an inherently honorific verb exists, the regular verb counterpart is normally not converted to honorific via the -(으)시 -(u)si suffix. For example, since there is an inherently honorific verb for *sleep,* 주무시다 cwumwusita, the verb 자다 cata *to sleep* is not converted into an honorific (자시다 casita).

The choice of honorific verb also depends on whether the subject or the object of the sentence is honored. There are also inherently honorific NOUNS and PARTICLES. Luckily the list of these inherently honorific words is not too long.

<1> Verbs for an honored subject

Here is the list of inherently honorific verbs to use, instead of adding -(으)시 -(u)si, when the SUBJECT is to be honored (that is, when an honored person is doing the action and is the subject of the sentence). You see 계시다 kyeysita *to exist* here among the inherently honorific verbs, and you know that it is used instead of 있다 issta in the progressive and also when it means *to exist* (while 있으시다 issusita is used for *to have*). All of the other inherently honorific verbs listed here straightforwardly take the place of the regular forms for talking about the doings of an honored person:

General	Honorific
있다 issta	계시다 kyeysita *to exist, to be (at, in, -ing)*
있다 issta	있으시다 issusita *to have*
배고프다 paykophuta	시장하시다 sicanghasita *to be hungry*
먹다 mekta	잡수시다 capswusita, 자시다 casita, 드시다 tusita *to eat*
자다 cata	주무시다 cwumwusita *to sleep*
늙다 nulkta	연로하시다⁺ yenlohasita *to be old*
아프다 aphuta	편찮으시다 phyenchanhusita , 아프시다 aphusita *to be ill*
죽다 cwukta	돌아가시다⁺ tolakasita *to pass away*
(말)하다 (mal)hata	말씀하시다 malssumhasita *to speak, say*

The words marked with a plus (⁺) should be used *only for the elderly*—that is, people who are in their late 50s or over. (This age threshold may change depending on how old YOU are and as the life expectancy becomes longer. A few decades ago, age forty, for example, was considered "old age" when one would have grandchildren, but people in their 40s are now regarded as too young to be considered middle-aged or elderly.)

Here are some example sentences with inherently honorific verbs. Heed who is doing the action or being described by the verb in each sentence.

아빠 집에 **계시니**?
appa cipey kyeysini?
Is your father at home?

할아버지, **시장하세요**?
halapeci, sicanghaseyyo?
Grandpa, are you hungry?

안녕히 **주무세요**!
annyenghi cwumwuseyyo!
Good night! (Sleep well.)

할머니, 신분증 **있으세요**?
halmeni, sinpwuncung issuseyyo?
Ma'am, do you have your ID card?

맛있게 **드세요**!
masisskey tuseyyo!
Please enjoy your meal!

할아버지 어디 **편찮으셔**?
halapeci eti phyenchangusye?
Is your grandfather not well?

그 나이 드신 선생님**께서는 돌아가셨다**.
ku nai tusin sensayngnimkkeysenun tolakasyessta.
That old teacher has passed away.

As for the honorifc verbs for 먹다 mekta *eat*, all of the following are said. They all exalt the grandmother you are speaking of. 잡수시다 capswusita may sometimes be shortened to 잡숫다 capswusta or 자시다 casita. (Remember, you can't use 자시다 casita to mean *sleep*!)

할머니, **진지 드시고** 주무세요. *Gramma, eat before you sleep.*
halmeni, cinci tusiko cwumwuseyyo.

할머니, **진지 잡수시고** 주무세요. *Gramma, eat before you sleep.*
halmeni, cinci capswusiko cwumwuseyyo.

할머니, **진지 잡숫고** 주무세요. *Gramma, eat before you sleep.*
halmeni, cinci capswusko cwumwuseyyo.

할머니, **진지 자시고** 주무세요. *Gramma, eat before you sleep.*
halmeni, cinci casiko cwumwuseyyo.

<2> Honorific particles

Before we go much further with honorifics, let's learn the particles which will appear in sentences along with honorific verbs and other expressions. There are only three honorific particles, and the forms are easy to memorize. The object-focus particle -을/를 -ul/lul does not have a corresponding honorific particle:

	General	Honorific
subject-focus particle	-이/가 -i/ka	-께서 -kkeyse
topic-contrast particle	-은/는 -un/nun	-께서는 -kkeysenun
recipient particle *to (a person)*	-에게 -eykey, -한테 -hanthey	-께 -kkey
animate source particle *from (a person)*	-에게서 -eykeyse, -한테서 -hantheyse	-께 -kkey

Honorific particles only attach to nouns referring to honored PEOPLE, not their possessions. See how the honorific particles attach to the honored subject of honorific verbs (and not to non-honored subjects) in these sets of examples:

친구가 전화를 했어요.
chinkwuka cenhwalul haysseyo.
A friend called.

할머니**께서** 전화를 하셨어요.
halmenikkeyse cenhwalul hasyesseyo.
Grandma called.

친구는 지금 한국에 있어요.
chinkwunun cikum hankwukey isseyo.
My friend is in Korea now.

교수님**께서는** 지금 한국에 계세요.
kyoswunimkkeysenun cikum hankwukey kyeyseyyo.
The professor is in Korea now.

친구가 병이 나서 아파요.
chinkwuka pyengi nase aphayo.
A friend got ill and is sick.

할아버지**께서** 병환이 나셔서 편찮으세요.
halapecikkeyse pyenghwani nasyese phyenchanhuseyyo.
Grandpa has taken ill and is sick.

These are highly deferential particles, and, right or wrong, many native speakers opt for the non-honorific versions in casual situations when the person to be honored is not present. Honorific particles are also not often used when referring to one's close family members (especially within the household), even when honorific verbs are used. Let's now move to honored objects.

<3> Verbs for an honored object

There are verbs to use to express deference to the **grammatical object** of the sentence, whether direct or indirect, when it is a person to be honored. When you say that you can *take your grandmother* somewhere, your grandmother is the **direct object**. When you say that you *give your teacher* an apple or *ask her* a question, your teacher is the recipient of the object (or the action), so she is the **indirect object**, and the correct honorific particle here is -께 -kkey. In these cases, different honorific VERBS are used from when the SUBJECT is honored. That is, there are special inherently honorific VERBS to use to encode honor for the grammatical OBJECT, direct or indirect, when it is a person to be honored. These honorific verbs are only used when the object noun refers to an honored PERSON, not their possessions.

Here are the verbs that express deference to their grammatical objects. We include the SUBJECT-honorific forms on the right for comparison—notice that they are different! (The recipient particle -한테 -hanthey is not given here, but don't forget that it is the spoken version of non-honorific -에게 -eykey.)

General	Direct Object Honorific	Subject Honorific
-을/를 데려가다/오다 -ul/lul teylyekata/ota	-을/를 모셔가다/오다 -ul/lul mosyekata/ota *to take/bring an honored person*	-을/를 데려가시다/오시다 -ul/lul teylyekasita/osita *honored person takes/brings someone*
-을/를 만나다 -ul/lul mannata	-을/를 (만나)뵙다/뵈다 -ul/lul (manna)poypta/poyta *to meet an honored person*	-을/를 만나시다 -ul/lul mannasita *honored person meets someone*
Ø	-을/를 모시다 -ul/lul mosita *to bring in/take care of an honored person in one's house*	

General	Indirect Object (Recipient) Honorific	Subject Honorific
-에게 -을/를 말하다 -eykey -ul/lul malhata	-께 -을/를 말씀드리다 -kkey -ul/lul malssumtulita *to say to an honored person*	-에게 -을/를 말씀하시다 -eykey -ul/lul malssumhasita *honored person says*
-에게 -을/를 주다 -eykey -ul/lul cwuta	-께 -을/를 드리다 -kkey -ul/lul tulita *to give to an honored person*	-에게 -을/를 주시다 -eykey -ul/lul cwusita *honored person gives*
-에게 전화/연락/ 편지하다 -eykey cenhwa/yenlak/ phyencihata	-께 전화/연락/편지 드리다 -kkey cenhwa/yenlak/phyenci tulita *to give a call/contact/send a letter to an honored person*	-에게 전화/연락/편지 주시다 -eykey cenhwa/yenlak/phyenci cwusita *honored person calls/contacts/ sends a letter*
-에게 -을/를 묻다/ 물어보다 -eykey -ul/lul mwutta/ mwulepota	-께 -을/를 여쭙다/여쭈다/ 여쭤보다 -kkey -ul/lul yeccwupta/yeccwuta/ yeccwepota *to ask an honored person*	-에게 -을/를 물으시다/ 물어보시다 -eykey -ul/lul mwulusita/mwuleposita *honored person asks*

Here are some examples to put the OBJECT-HONORIFIC VERBS in context. In each set of sentences, find the object that is being honored and the verb that does that (we'll underline it in the English). Also, pay attention to how the particles agree with the doer and the recipient of the action (but remember that the object-focus particle -을/를 -ul/lul does not have a corresponding honorific particle):

내일 숙제를 **가져와라**.
nayil swukceylul kacyewala.
Bring your homework tomorrow.

내일 동생을 **데려와라**.
nayil tongsayngul teylyewala.
Bring your younger brother tomorrow.

내일 부모님을 **모셔와라**.
nayil pwumonimul mosyewala.
Bring your <u>parents</u> tomorrow.

그거 동생한테 **물어 봤어**?
kuke tongsaynghanthey mwule pwasse?
Did you ask that of the younger brother?

그거 할아버지께 **여쭤 봤어**?
kuke halapecikkey yeccwe pwasse?
Did you ask that <u>of Grandpa</u>?

동생한테 밥 먹으라고 **말해**.
tongsaynghanthey pap mekulako malhay.
Tell your younger brother to eat.

할머니께 진지 드시라고 **말씀드려**.
halmenikkey cinci tusilako malssumtulye.
Tell <u>Grandma</u> to eat.

한국에서 누구 누구를 **만났니**?
hankwukeyse nwukwu nwukwulul mannassni?
Who all did you see in Korea? (people met are young and close)

한국에서 누구 누구를 **뵈었니**?
hankwukeyse nwukwu nwukwulul poyessni?
<u>Who all</u> did you see in Korea?

제가 친구한테 이메일을 **썼어요**.
ceyka chinkwuhanthey imeyilul ssesseyo.
I wrote my friend an email.

제가 할아버지께 편지를 **드렸어요**.
ceyka halapecikkey phyencilul tulyesseyo.
I wrote/sent <u>my Grandpa</u> a letter.

딸:	그거 누구한테 **주실 거예요**?
ttal:	kuke nwukwuhanthey cwusil keyeyyo?
Daughter:	*Who will you be giving that to?*

아버지:	할머니께 **드릴 거야**.
apeci:	halmenikkey tulil keya.
Dad:	*I'm going to give (this) <u>to Grandma</u>.*

나: 아주머니, 누구를 **만나러** 오셨어요?
na: acwumeni, nwukwulul mannale osyesseyo?
Me: *Ma'am, who are you here for?/Who do you want to see?*

이웃: 이 댁 할머니를 좀 (만나)**뵈러** 왔어요.
iwus: i tayk halmenilul com (manna)poyle wasseyo.
Neighbor: *I'm here to see <u>the grandmother of this family</u>.*

Here is some extra practice with the verbs for *give*, -어 주다 -e cwuta and -어 드리다 -e tulita, talking about lending someone a book. If the giver is higher than or equal to the receiver, use 주다 cwuta. If the giver is lower, use 드리다 tulita. If the giver is someone to be honored, then use -(으)시 -(u)si:

내가 친구에게 책을 빌려 **줬어요**. nayka chinkueykey cheykul pillye cwesseyo. *I lent my friend a book.*	I lent it, so NO -(으)시 -(u)si From me to a friend, so 주다 cwuta
친구가 나에게 책을 빌려 **줬어요**. chinkuka naeykey cheykul pillye cwesseyo. *My friend lent me a book.*	My friend lent it, so NO -(으)시 -(u)si From my friend to me, so 주다 cwuta
아버지께서 저에게 책을 빌려 **주셨어요**. apecikkeyse ceeykey cheykul pillye cusyesseyo. *Father lent me a book.*	Father lent it, so -(으)시 -(u)si From Father to me, so 주다 cwuta
할아버지께서 아버지께 책을 빌려 **주셨어요**. halapecikkeyse apecikkey cheykul pillye cusyesseyo. *Grandpa lent Father a book.*	Grandpa lent it, so -(으)시 -(u)si From Grandpa to me, so 주다 cwuta
내가 아버지께 책을 빌려 **드렸어요**. nayka apecieykey cheykul pillye tulyesseyo. *I lent Father a book.*	I lent it, so NO -(으)시 -(u)si From me to a Father, so 드리다 tulita
아버지께서 할아버지께 책을 빌려 **드리셨어요**. apecikkeyse halapecikkey cheykul pillye tulisyesseyo. *Father lent Grandpa a book.*	Father lent it, so -(으)시 -(u)si From Father to Grandpa, so 드리다 tulita

<4> Honorific nouns

Korean also has some honorific nouns that are used when the item belongs to an honored person. There is no suffix to change regular nouns into honorific ones, and not all nouns have an honorific form. In fact, not many do. But the following honorific nouns exist and need to be used appropriately. The words marked with a plus should be used ONLY FOR ELDERLY people (who are in their late 50's or over).

Regular	Honorific
이름 ilum	성함 sengham, 함자⁺ hamca [함짜 hamcca] *name*
생일 sayngil	생신⁺ sayngsin *birthday*
나이 nai	연세⁺ yensey *age*

Regular	Honorific
집 cip	댁 tayk *house*
사람 salam, 명 myeng	분 pwun *person* (for both 사람 and 명)
술 swul	약주⁺ yakcwu *alcoholic drinks*
말 mal	말씀 malssum *word, speech*
병 pyeng	병환⁺ pyenghwan *illness*
밥 pap	진지 cinci *meal*
아내 anay	부인 pwuin *wife*
남편 namphyen	바깥분 pakkathpwun *husband*
부모 pwumo	부모님 pwumonim *parents*
딸 ttal	따님 ttanim *daughter*
아들 atul	아드님 atunim *son*
자녀 canye	자제분 caceypwun *children, off-spring*
(시)아버지 (si)apeci	아버님 apenim *father(-in-law)*
(시)어머니 (si)emeni	어머님 emenim *mother(-in-law)*
할아버지 halapeci	할아버님 halapenim *grandfather*
할머니 halmeni	할머님 halmenim *grandmother*
이모 imo	이모님 imonim *maternal aunt*
고모 komo	고모님 komonim *paternal aunt*

Let's see some of the words in context. Remember that only honored people get honorific particles. Be sure you understand who (that is, what honored person) "owns" each item in bold.

할머님께서 **병환**이 나셨다.
halmenimkkeyse pyenghwani nasyessta.
Grandma has fallen ill.

방금 할머니께서 뭐라고 **말씀**하셨어?
pangkum halmenikkeyse mwelako malssumhasyesse?
What did Grandma say just now?

부모님 **연세**가 어떻게 되세요?
pwumonim yenseyka ettehkey toyseyyo?
How old are your parents?

손님, 여기에 **성함**을 써 주세요.
sonnim, yekiey senghamul sse cwuseyyo
Please write your name here.

이 음료수 어느 **분**이 시키셨습니까?
i umlyoswu enu pwuni sikhisyesssupnikka?
Which of you ordered these drinks?

Now have a look at these next sentences. Can you figure out the difference in meaning between the first two sentences that is not obvious in the English?

할아버지 **집**에 계시냐?
halapeci cipey kyeysinya?
Is your Grandfather at home?

할아버님 **댁**에 계세요?
halapenim taykey kyeyseyyo?
Is your Grandfather at home?

방학 때 할아버지 **댁**에 갔었어요.
panghak ttay halapeci taykey kassesseyo.
I visited my grandfather during the vacation.

The person saying 할아버지 집에 계시냐? halapeci cipey kyeysinya? did not use 댁 tayk, and from this we know that the grandpa is staying at the house of the person who is being asked the question, and that person is not someone to be honored (so neither is their house). Also, since the ending is -냐 -nya, we know that the house of the listener should not be called 댁 tayk. The same sentence can be said with 댁 tayk if the house is assumed to be the grandpa's house and not the peer/younger-person listener's. So, the second sentence, 할아버님 댁에 계세요? halapenim taykey kyeyseyyo? is probably said by a neighbor who is much younger than the grandfather (and about the same as the listener, or a bit younger), looking for the grandfather at his own house. The third sentence, 방학 때 할아버지 댁에 갔었어요 panghak ttay halapeci taykey kassesseyo is about your own experience, but since it is your grandpa's house, you correctly used 댁 tayk. (And you are reporting this to someone you should be polite to, so you used -요 yo.)

Let's see some more. The following sentences all mean *How old is (someone)?* but notice that, in addition to the honorific noun for *age*, the question word and verb are also different in the honorific. This expression (어떻게 되세요 ettehkey toyseyyo) is common when asking about an honored person's age and name (and occasionally birthday as well, in spoken Korean).

나이가 몇이에요? (or 몇 살이에요?)
naika myechieyyo? (myech salieyyo?)
How old are you? (to a young adult who is your peer)

연세가 어떻게 되세요?
yenseyka ettehkey toyseyyo?
How old are you? (to an elder)

할머니 연세가 어떻게 되세요?
halmeni yenseyka ettehkey toyseyyo?
How old is your/the grandmother? (to someone older)

The word 말씀 malssum *word, speech, speaking* is used both when the honored person is speaking and when one is speaking to an honored person:

교수님, **말씀**하세요.
kyoswunim, malssumhaseyyo.
Professor, please speak. (Go ahead, professor.)

주문하신 상품이 도착하지 않았다는 **말씀**이지요?
cwumwunhasin sangphwumi tochakhaci anhasstanun malssumiciyo?
You are saying that the order did not arrive. Is that correct?

어제 부장님과 **말씀** 나누었습니다.
ecey pwucangnimkwa malssum nanwuesssupnita.
I spoke with your department chief yesterday.

부모님께 미팅에 대해 **말씀** 드려라.
pwumonimkkey mithingey tayhay malssum tulyela.
Tell your parents about the meeting.

Are honorifics all clear now? It never hurts to practice. Here are a few more more examples for you.

몇 **분**이세요?
myech pwuniseyyo?
How many? (to customers in a restaurant)

자제분께서 어느 학교에 **다니시나요?**
caceypwunkkeyse enu hakkyoey tanisinayo?
Where are your kids attending school? (to a boss)

부군께서도 여기에서 일**하세요?**
pwukwunkkeyseto yekieyse ilhaseyyo?
Is your husband working here as well? (to a colleague)

식사도 **하실** 건가요 아니면 음료수만 **드실** 건가요?
siksato hasil kenkayo animyen umlyoswuman tusil kenkayo?
Will you be having a meal or just drinks? (to customers)

<5> Humble pronouns

This is a good place to review the humble first person pronouns, compared to pronouns that are used in the plain and intimate ordinary speech styles. The humble pronouns are sensitive to the LISTENER, that is, whom you are speaking TO, and not whom you are talking ABOUT. As such, they are more aligned with politeness and formality than honorifics; however, in cases where you are talking with an honored person, you will need to use polite (or formal) speech style, honorifics to talk about the honored person, and humble pronouns about yourself. Some example sentences follow the chart of pronouns.

	First Person Singular *I*		First Person Plural *we*	
	Plain	Humble	Plain	Humble
With the subject-focus marker	내가 nayka	제가 ceyka	우리가 wulika	저희가 cehuyka
With the topic marker	나는 nanun	저는 cenun	우리는 wulinun	저희는 cehuynun
With the object-focus marker	나를 nalul	저를 celul	우리를 wulilul	저희를 cehuylul
With the possessive marker	나의 = 내 nauy = nay	저의 = 제 ceuy = cey	우리의 wuliuy	저희의 cehuyuy

See if you can figure out the age hierarchy before reading the translation for these examples. The person being spoken to is indicated in small letters after each translation:

민우야, **내**가 해 줄게.
minwuya, nayka hay cwulkey.
Minu, I'll do it for you. (to a peer or someone younger)

할아버지, **제**가 해 드릴게요.
halapeci, ceyka hay tulilkeyyo.
Grandpa, I'll do it for you. (to Grandfather)

내가 할머니께 선물을 드렸어.
nayka halmenikkey senmwulul tulyesse.
I gave my grandmother a present. (to a peer or someone younger)

제가 동생한테 선물을 줬어요.
ceyka tongsaynghanthey senmwulul cwesseyo.
I gave my younger sibling a present. to someone older

제가 할머니께 선물을 드렸어요.
ceyka halmenikkey senmwulul tulyesseyo.
I gave my grandmother a present. (to someone older)

할머니께서 **나**한테 선물을 주셨어.
halmenikkeyse nahanthey senmwulul cwusyesse.
My grandmother gave me a present. (to a peer or someone younger)

할머니께서 **저**한테 선물을 주셨어요.
halmenikkeyse cehanthey senmwulul cwusyesseyo.
My grandmother gave me a present. (to someone older)

어머니께서 할머니께 선물을 드리셨어요.
emenikkeyse halmenikkey senmwulul tulisyesseyo.
My mother gave my grandmother a present. (to someone older)

할머니께서 어머니께 선물을 주셨어요.
halmenikkeyse emenikkey senmwulul cwusyesseyo.
My grandmother gave my mother a present. (to someone older)

Honorifics are very important in Korean lingua-culture; you must bear in mind whom you are talking ABOUT and use honorifics appropriately. The most important time to use honorifics, so as to not make huge social blunders, is when you are face-to-face with the honored person. That is, when you are speaking TO someone to be honored and also ABOUT them, so you need to use both polite or formal speech style AND honorifics. The hardest to remember is probably when talking ABOUT someone to be honored when you are talking TO someone you can be casual with. **Don't let down your ~~guard~~ honor!**—use the right honorifics, or you are violating social code.

And do be careful NOT to talk about yourself with honorific terms!

Waiter: 몇 분이세요? myechpwuniseyyo? *How many of you?*
You: 세 명이에요. sey myengieyyo. *There are three of us.*

Host: 뭐 더 **드시겠어요**? mwe te tusikeysseyo? *What more would you like to have?*
Guest: 맛있네요. 국 좀 더 **먹어도 돼요**? masissneyyo. kwuk com te meketo twayyo?
It's good! May I have a little more soup?

The honorific system is the apex of the Korean language. Mastering it is a great indication that you are way past the beginner level. You can do it!

9.1.2 Passives

Another way to derive new verbs using suffixes in Korean is to make them **passive**. We are talking about how to change a sentence around from **active voice** (*A kissed B*) to **passive voice** (*B was kissed by A*). You have to rearrange the sentence and, in Korean, change the verb to a passive in one of three ways. The first is to derive a passive verb by adding a suffix 이 i, 히 hi, 리 li, or 기 ki to the root of a **transitive** verb. This makes a **short-form passive**. Only a limited number of native Haan Korean verbs convert via these suffixes. The second way is to add the longer ending -어지다 -ecita to the verb root. The third way is to add the structural suffix -게 -key to the verb root and use 되다 toyta as the main verb.

Before we go into detail about how to convert active verbs into passive verbs using these methods, let's talk first about what the passive is and why and how passive sentences are made. Along the way, keep an eye out for passive verbs with each kind of ending in the passive sentence examples. We'll indicate in parentheses which ending is used for each passive verb.

(1) When the passive might be preferred in Korean

There are several situations in which you would use a passive sentence in Korean even when the equivalent does not look like a passive in English. Let's explore.

<1> Focusing on the experiencer

You can think of a passive structure as a way to focus on the person or the thing that UNDERGOES what the verb "does." That experiencer is made the SUBJECT of the sentence.

차가 사슴을 쳤어요.
chaka sasumul chyesseyo.

The car hit the deer.

사슴이 차에 **치였어요**. (passive suffix: 이)
sasumi chaey chiyesseyo. (i)

The deer was hit by the car.

<2> De-emphasizing the agent

Another reason to use the passive is if we DON'T want to emphasize the **agent** (the doer of the action). Perhaps we want to avoid blaming or bragging. Passive sentences allow us to move the doer further back in the sentence or even leave it out:

우리 개가 도둑을 물었어요.
wuli kayka totwukul mwulesseyo.

Our dog bit the thief.

도둑이 (개한테) **물렸어요**. (리)
totwuki (kayhanthey) mwullyesseyo. (li)

The thief was bitten (by our dog).

내가 컵을 깼어요.
nayka khepul kkaysseyo.
I broke a cup.

컵이 **깨졌어요**. (-어지다)
khepi kkaycyesseyo. (-ecita)
The cup is broken.

내가 내일 갈 준비를 했어.
nayka nayil kal cwunpilul haysse.
I prepared for tomorrow's departure.

내일 갈 **준비가 됐어**. (하다 → 되다)
nayil kal cwunpika twaysse. (hata → toyta)
I am ready to go. (Literally, *the preparation to go got done.*)

<3> Unknown or general agent

Sometimes why something happens or who does it is not known, is not important, or is general (*whoever, everyone, people,* etc.). You will want to use the passive in those cases:

한국은 남과 북으로 **나뉘었다**. (이)
hankwukun namkwa pwukulo nanwiessta. (i)
Korea is/was/got divided into South and North.

막걸리는 쌀로 **만들어진다**. (-어지다)
makkellinun ssallo mantulecinta. (-ecita)
Makgeolli is made from rice.

내일부터 도서관에서 **일하게 됐다**! (-게 되다)
nayilpwuthe tosekwaneyse ilhakey twayssta! (-key toyta)
It has come to be that I work at the library starting tomorrow.
(*I get to start my work at the library tomorrow.*)

<4> What's natural in Korean

There are also some sentences in Korean that just sound much more natural in the passive voice, especially those that involve the senses. The first option in each pair below is much more natural than the second one:

내 목소리(가) **들려**? (리)
nay moksoli(ka) tullye? (li)
Can you hear me? (Literally, *Is my voice heard?*)

내 목소리를 들을 수 있어?
nay moksolilul tulul swu isse?
Are you able to hear me?

여기서는 경치가 안 **보인다**. (이)
yekisenun kyengchika an pointa. (i)
(I) can't see the scenery from here. (Literally, *The scenery is not seen/visible from here.*)

여기서는 경치를 볼 수 없다.
yekisenun kyengchilul pol swu epsta.
I am not able to see the scenery from here.

<5> What might be expressed as English "middle verbs"

When you are translating your thoughts from English to Korean, be careful of verbs that are used in a subtly passive way in English, which are called **middle verbs**. They look just like their active counterparts in English but have a passive meaning. They are straightforwardly passive verbs in Korean:

그 책이 잘 **팔린다**. (리)
ku chayki cal phallinta. (li)
The book sells well. (The book is sold well.)

펜이 잘 **써져요**. (-어지다)
pheyni cal ssecyeyo. (-ecita)
The pen writes well. (Literally, *The pen gets written well. i.e., The ink is made to come out.*)

<6> Simple mismatch

Finally, some English intransitive verbs simply are expressed with passive verbs in Korean:

문자가 안 **보내져**. (-어지다)
mwuncaka an ponaycye. (-ecita)
The text message doesn't go. (is not getting sent)

불이 **꺼졌다**. (-어지다)
pwuli kkecyessta. (-ecita)
The light went out. (got turned off)

(2) Particles in passive structures

Now that you have a good sense of why and when to use passives, let's look more carefully at the sentence structures and particles. The key point is that PARTICLES have to do with GRAMMATICAL subjects and objects, regardless of the underlying meaning relationships of who is doing what to whom. (This basic meaning doesn't change, it's just that in a passive sentence, the **experiencer** is the subject.) Let's see what particles they are marked with.

<1> Experiencer marked with -이/가

As we reviewed, in passive sentences, the experiencer (the one that something is done to) is the subject, so it is marked with the subject particle -이/가 -i/ka:

전화**가** 끊겼어요. (passive suffix: 기)
cenhwaka kkunhkyesseyo. (ki)
The phone got hung up.

음악 소리**가** 들려요. (려)
umak solika tullyeyo. (li)
Music is heard/audible. ((I) hear music.)

친구**가** 안 보여요. (이)
chinkwuka an poyeyo. (i)
My friend is not seen/visible. (I can't see my friend. (She is not here.))

Consider this example:

친구**가** 강도에게 돈을 빼앗겼어요. (기)
chinkwuka kangtoeykey tonul ppayaskyesseyo. (ki)
My friend had his money stolen by a robber.

In the last example sentence above, what gets directly affected by the verb (that is, what is stolen) is the "money," but we want to talk about the FRIEND and his ordeal, so 친구 chinkwu *friend* goes in the subject position and is marked with -이/가 -i/ka, while 돈 ton *money* is marked as the object of the verb with -을/를 -ul/lul. Although the money can be the subject of the passive sentence in English, it is not natural to do so in Korean.

~~돈**이** 친구에게서 도둑**한테**~~ 빼앗겼어요. (기)
toni chinkwueykeyse totwukhanthey ppayaskyesseyo. (ki)
The money was stolen from my friend by a thief.

~~친구의 돈**이** 도둑**에게**~~ 빼앗겼어요. (기)
chinkwuuy toni totwukeykey ppayaskyesseyo. (ki)
My friend's money was stolen by a thief.

<2> Animate agent marked with -한테 or -에게

The ANIMATE doer of the action is marked with -한테 -hanthey or -에게 -eykey if the doer is stated overtly in the passive sentence:

도둑이 경찰**에게** 쫓기고 있어요. (기)
totwuki kyengchaleykey ccochkiko isseyo. (ki)
The thief is being chased by the police.

Certain verbs in Korean are inherently experiencer-oriented. That is, they are not actually passive in FORM, but they have a passive-like meaning. For those verbs, the ANI-MATE doer of the action can also be marked with -한테 -hanthey or -에게 -eykey.

누나가 아빠**한테** 크게 혼났어요. (혼나다)
nwunaka appahanthey khukey honnasseyo. (honnata)
My older sister got a long lecture from Dad.
혼나다 honnata: *to get scolded*

우리 팀이 캐나다 팀**한테/에** 졌어요. (지다)
wuli thimi khaynata thimhanthey/ey cyesseyo. (cita)
Our team lost to the Canadian team.
지다 cita: *to lose, be defeated*

내가 동생**한테** 또 속았어요. (속다)
nayka tongsaynghanthey tto sokasseyo. (sokta)
I got one pulled over on me by my younger brother again.
속다 sokta: *to get deceived*

그 군인이 적군**에게** 총을 맞았어요. (맞다)
ku kwunini cekkwunhanthey chongul macasseyo. (macta)
The soldier was hit by an enemy ('s gunshot).
맞다 macta: *to get hit*

내가 사기꾼**한테** 돈을 사기당했어요. (당하다)
nayka sakikkunhanthey tonul sakitanghaysseyo. (tanghata)
I got my money swindled out of me by a con-artist.
당하다 tanghata: *to suffer, undergo (something negative)*

<3> Inanimate agent marked with -에 and instruments with -(으)로

When the doer (or cause) is an INANIMATE thing, it is marked with -에 -ey or -(으)로 -(u)lo. If the inanimate thing has more agency or control, like perhaps *the wind*, -에 -ey is better. These are often translated with *by* in English. If the inanimate thing is more like an INSTRUMENT with no will, power or agency of its own, -(으)로 -(u)lo is preferred, and the appropriate translation for that would be *with*. Here are some examples to compare and see what we mean by instrument and agency:

그의 업적은 아버지의 명성**에** 덮여 버렸다. (리)
kuuy epcekun apeciuy myengsengey tephye pelyessta. (li)
His accomplishment was covered/overshadowed by his father's fame.

온 산이 눈**에** 덮여 있다. (이)
on sani nwuney tephye issta. (i)
The whole mountain got covered by the snow.

온 산이 눈**으로** 덮여 있다. (이)
on sani nwunulo tephye issta. (i)
The whole mountain is covered with snow.

은의 얼룩은 치약**으로** 잘 닦인다. (이)
unuy ellwukun chiyakulo cal takkinta. (i)
Toothpaste removes stains on silver well. (Literally, Silver stains are wiped well with toothpaste.)

(3) How passive verbs are formed

Finally, let's talk about how to turn a verb into a passive. As mentioned in the introduction, there are three ways this can be done. The first is to add a short-form passive suffix 이 i, 히 hi, 리 li, or 기 ki to the root of a **transitive** verb to derive a passive verb. The choice of the particular suffix depends on the shape of the verb root. This is a tricky option, as not every transitive verb can be converted in this way. Only a handful of native Haan Korean verbs have these short-form passive versions. The second way is to add the suffix -어지다 -ecita to the verb root. This suffix is also used only for Haan Korean verbs, but it works with more verbs and is not limited to just a few. The third way is to add the structural suffix -게 -key to the verb root and use 되다 toyta as the main verb. Let's first see what short-form passives are.

<1> Deriving short-form passives with suffixes 이, 히, 리, and 기

Short-form passives are passive verbs that are formed by adding 이 i, 히 hi, 리 li, or 기 ki to the root of a transitive verb.

Here's how it works.

a. 이

-이 -i can be considered the default passive suffix. There is no predicting what roots -이 -i is attached to because, unlike with the other passive suffixes, the shapes of the roots that take -이 -i are so widely varied. We'll show you which verbs go with this suffix and recommend that you learn them all. If you feel like you can't remember them all, it's better to memorize the passive version because then you can always figure out the active verb based on the passive. That is, if you know 놓이다 nohita *to be put* (*down*), you can figure out that it is derived from the verb 놓다 nohta *to put* (*down*) (놓 noh + 이 i).

Since there are only a few verbs that take each suffix, and you basically have to memorize them, we have devised a mnemonic story for each suffix to help you. The title of the mnemonic story will have the passive suffix in it, and the storyline uses the base verbs that take that suffix to become passive. For the mnemonic to work for you, you need to learn the KOREAN words used in the story, of course (e.g. *change*: 바꾸다 pakwuta). And remember that the **transitivity** of the verbs won't necessarily match between English and Korean verbs. The verbs in capital letters are the ones that form 이 i passives, and they are also in the chart following.

A mnemonic device for verbs that convert to passive using 이 i is "A table too tomato-Y (i.e., TOMATO-이 i)":

A tomato **HIT** the table. **USE** a cloth to **WIPE** it. If you can still **SEE** the stain, **COVER** it up by **PUTTING DOWN** a placemat. Or, **CHANGE** the table cloth. **DIVIDE** up the work with someone.

Here are the verbs that use -이 -i to make a passive:

Active	Passive	Example
놓다 nohta *release/put down*	놓이다 nohita *be placed*	여기 **놓여** 있던 책 못 봤어요? yeki nohye issten chayk mos pwasseyo? *Did you not see the book that was (placed) here?*
닦다 takkta *wipe*	닦이다 takkita *be wiped*	이 치약은 이가 잘 **닦여요**. i chiyakun ika cal takkyeyo. *This toothpaste cleans teeth well. (teeth get cleaned well)*
덮다 tephta *cover*	덮이다 tephita *be covered*	눈 **덮인** 산 nwun tephin san *a mountain covered with snow*
보다 Pota *see, watch*	보이다 poita *be seen, visible*	여기서 경치가 잘 **보여요**. yekise kyengchika cal poyeyo. *You can see the view well from here.*
쓰다 ssuta *use*	쓰이다 ssuita *be used*	미국에서는 미터가 안 **쓰여요**. mikwukeysenun mitheka an ssuyeyo. *The metric system is not used in the U.S.*
치다 chita *hit*	치이다 chiita *be hit*	사슴이 차에 **치였어요**. sasumi chaey chiyesseyo. *The deer was hit by a car.*
나누다 nanwuta *divide*	나뉘다 nanwita *be divided*	한국은 남한과 북한으로 **나뉘었다**. hankwukun namhankwa pwukhanulo nanwiessta. *Korea is divided into South Korea and North Korea.*
바꾸다 pakwuta *change*	바뀌다 pakwita *be changed*	밤새 그 사람 마음이 **바뀌었다**. pamsay ku salam maumi pakkwiessta. *His mind has been changed overnight.*

b. 히

The passive suffix -히 -hi is usually attached to verb roots that have a hard final consonant (e.g. ㄱ, ㄷ, ㅂ).

The mnemonic we suggest is "<u>HE (히 hi) scraped my car</u>":

Someone didn't **CLOSE** the gate so it **BLOCK**ed the path. As I drove through the narrow alley, the gate **SCRATCH**ed my car. So I left them a note to **READ** and **TOOK A PICTURE**, hoping to **CATCH** the person who left the gate open. I want to make them **EAT** the bill.

Here are the -히 -hi -passive verbs and examples:

Active	Passive	Example
닫다 tatta *close*	닫히다 tathita *be closed*	도서관 문이 **닫혔어**요. tosekwan mwuni tathyesseyo. *The library is closed.*
막다 makta *block*	막히다 makhita *be blocked*	길이 **막혔어**요. kili makhyesseyo. *The road that is blocked.*
먹다 mekta *eat*	먹히다 mekhita *be eaten*	배가 고파서 잘 **먹혀**요. payka kophase cal mekhyeyo. *I am hungry so the food is well-eaten.*
읽다 ilkta *read*	읽히다 ilkhita *be read*	이 책이 요즘 많이 **읽혀**요. i chayki yocum manhi ilkhyeyo. *This book is read by many people nowadays.*
잡다 capta *catch*	잡히다 caphita *be caught*	도둑이 **잡혔어**요. totwuki caphyesseyo. *The thief was caught.*
찍다 ccikta *imprint*	찍히다 ccikhita *be imprinted*	이 사진에 친구가 **찍혔어**요. i saciney chinkwuka ccikhyesseyo. *My friend was pictured in this photo.*

c. 리

The passive suffix -리 -li is the easiest to remember, as it attaches to verb roots that are ㄹ-related one way or another. The original root can be any old ㄹ-verb that has a passive counterpart. It can also be a special-ㄷ class verb, whose final consonant alternates with ㄹ before vowel-initial suffixes. It can also be a 르-verb requiring special conjugation, doubling up the final ㄹ. Since the verb can have many different shapes, it would be best if you memorize the base verbs that take the -리 -li suffix.

The mnemonic we have come up with for the -리 -li suffix is "<u>the unfriend-LY (리 li) dog</u>":

> As soon as the dog **HEAR**d me **OPEN** the door, he was trying to **BITE** and **CUT OFF** my finger. We have to **SELL** this vicious dog.

Here are the -리 -li -passive verbs and examples:

Active	Passive	Example
듣다 tutta *listen*	들리다 tullita *be heard, audible*	한국 음악이 **들려요**! hankwuk umaki tullyeyo! *Korean music is heard. (I can hear Korean music.)*
물다 mwulta *bite*	물리다 mwullita *be bitten*	옆집 개한테 **물렸어요**. yephcip kayhanthey mwullyesseyo. *I was bitten by the dog next door.*
열다 yelta *open*	열리다 yellita *be opened*	창문이 **열려** 있어요. changmwuni yellye isseyo. *The window is open.*
자르다 caluta *cut (short)*	잘리다 callita *be cut*	회사에서 **잘렸어요**. hoyseeyse callyesseyo. *I got fired. (Literally, I got cut from the company.)*
팔다 phalta *sell*	팔리다 phallita *be sold*	김치가 다 **팔렸어요**. kimchika ta phallyesseyo. *Kimchi is sold out.*

d. 기

Finally, the suffix -기 -ki attaches mainly to verb roots that end in a nasal consonant (like ㄴ or ㅁ) and to those that end in ㅅ and ㅊ. This probably seems like a random coincidence, so it's probably best just to memorize them.

One pronunciation note is that, although -다 ta is pronounced as tense [ㄸ] in the dictionary form of nasal-final words like 젊다 cemta [점따 cemtta] and 감다 kamta [감따 kamtta], the consonant in the passive suffix is pronounced lax: 담기다 tamkita [담기다 tamkita] and 잠기다 camkita [잠기다 camkita] and **not** [담까다 tamkkita] and [잠까다 camkkita].

The mnemonic we offer for the -기 -ki suffix is "the yuc-**KY** (기 ki) situation":

> I got a phone call from my friend who went to the bank to withdraw money. My friend said: 'I was **HOLD**ing a bag that **CONTAIN**ed the money, and someone started **CHAS**ing me to **ROB** me of it! I see a door, but it's **LOCK**ed!' Then the phone got **DISCONNECT**ed.

Here are the -기 -ki -passive verbs and examples:

Active	Passive	Example
빼앗다 ppayasta *steal, rob*	빼앗기다 ppayaskita *be robbed of*	동생한테 내 과자를 **빼앗겼어요**. tongsaynghanthey nay kwacalul **ppayaskyesseyo**. *I was robbed of my cookies by my younger siblings.*
안다 anta *hug, hold in arms*	안기다 ankita *be held*	엄마에게 **안긴** 아기 emmaeykey **ankin** aki *the baby who was held by the mother*
쫓다 ccochta *chase*	쫓기다 ccochkita *be chased*	지금 경찰한테 **쫓기고** 있어요! cikum kyengchalhanthey **ccochkiko** isseyo! *I am being chased by the police now!*
끊다 kkunhta *cut (off)*	끊기다 kkunhkita *be cut (off)*	전화가 **끊겼어요**. cenhwaka **kkunhkyesseyo**. *The phone was hung up.*
담다 tamta *contain*	담기다 tamkita *be filled*	사랑이 **담겼어요**. salangi **tamkyesseyo**. *There is love (in it).*
잠그다 camkuta *lock*	잠기다⁺ camkita *be locked*	창문이 **잠겼어요**. changmwuni **camkyesseyo**. *The window is locked.*

+Note an extra change in the passive verb: it is not 잠그기다 camkukita.

As you've seen, there is a pattern to which suffix fits with which verb to make a passive, but it is not a simple rule, and it is rather tricky to remember them all. It is also easy to confuse the rules for making passive verbs with those for making causative verbs, as you will see later on. So your best bet is to memorize the most common passives laid out here paired with their base active verbs in sentences or phrases, and then do the same for causatives on another day. If memorizing gets tough, it's better to remember the passive version because then you can always figure out the active verb root. Memorizing 끊기다 kkunhkita will give you both 끊기다 kkunhkita *to get cut off (passive)* and 끊다 kkunhta *to cut/hang up (active)*. Now let's move on to the longer passive forms.

<2> Long-form passive 1: active verb + 어지다

As we mentioned, not every verb has a passive form that uses the 이 i, 히 hi, 리 li, or 기 ki suffix. How then is one to express passive ideas with other verbs? A sure way is to use the suffix -어지다 -ecita.

You may already know the -어지다 -ecita suffix from somewhere else. Namely, when it is attached to descriptive verbs, it adds the sense *become*:

날씨가 추워요.	vs.	날씨가 **추워졌어요**.
nalssika chwuweyo.		nalssika chwuwecyesseyo.
It's cold.		*It's gotten cold.*

일이 힘듭니다.	vs.	일이 **힘들어졌습니다**.
ili himtupnita.		ili himtulecyesssupnita.
This work is hard.		*The work has become hard.*

Here are a few more *become* + descriptive verb examples:

너무 추워서 얼굴이 **파래졌다**.
nemwu chwuwese elkwuli phalaycyessta.
She was so cold that her face turned blue.

새 학기가 시작돼서 **바빠졌어요**.
say hakkika sicaktwayse pappacyesseyo.
I've gotten busy, as the new semester began.

방이 아주 **깨끗해졌다**.
pangi acwu kkaykkushaycyessta.
The room has gotten very clean.

젊어지는 비결이 뭐예요?
celmecinun pikyeli mweyeyyo?
What is your secret to becoming younger?

When -어지다 -ecita is attached to TRANSITIVE active verbs, it makes a passive by way of this *become* (or *get*) meaning:

내가 컵을 **깼어요**.	컵이 **깨졌어요**.
nayka khepul kkaysseyo.	khepi kkaycyesseyo.
I broke a cup.	*The cup is/got broken.*

The suffix -어지다 -ecita works with native Haan Korean transitive verbs and ONE-syllable Sino-Korean transitive verbs like 정하다 cenghata *to decide* and 향하다 hyanghata *to head to*. Here are some more verbs that are frequently used in the -어지다 construction. Pay attention to the translation as well as the particle uses. The passive examples are those with a verb in bold. The object-focus particle is also put in bold in the active sentence for your comparison.

Base	-어지다 Form	Examples
켜다 khyeta *turn on, light*	켜지다 khyecita *come on*	내가 촛불을 켰다. nayka chospwulul khyessta. *I lit the candle.* 가로등 불이 **켜졌다.** kalotung pwuli khyecyessta. *Street lamps came on.*
끄다 kkuta *turn off, put out*	꺼지다 kkecita *go out, go off*	내가 발등의 불을 껐다. nayka paltunguy pwulul kkessta. *I put out the fire on my foot.* 불이 **꺼졌다.** pwuli kkecyessta. *The light/fire went out.*
끊다 kkunhta *hang off, cut, disconnect*	끊어지다 Kkunhecita *get cut off*	내가 전화를 끊었다. nayka cenhwalul kkunhessta. *I hung up the phone.* 전화가 **끊어졌다.** cenhwaka kkunhecyessta. *The phone got disconnected.*
만들다 mantulta *make*	만들어지다 mantulecita *turn out*	만두를 꽤 잘 만들었다. mantwulul kkway cal mantulessta. *I made the dumplings pretty well.* 만두가 잘 **만들어졌다.** mantwuka cal mantulecyessta. *The dumplings turned out well.*
쓰다 ssuta *write*	써지다 ssecita *write, get written*	내가 편지를 썼다. nayka phyencilul ssessta. *I wrote a/the letter.* 오늘은 글이 잘 **써진다.** onulun kuli cal ssecinta. *Today, my thoughts are flowing.* 이 펜이 잘 **써진다.** i pheyni cal ssecinta. *This pen writes well.*

Base	-어지다 Form	Examples
지우다 ciwuta *erase*	지워지다 ciwecita *get erased*	낙서를 지웠다. nakselul ciwessta. *I erased the graffiti.* 녹음이 **지워졌다.** nokumi ciwecyessta. *The recording got deleted.*
미루다 milwuta *postpone*	미뤄지다 milwecita *be put off*	바빠서 미팅을 미뤘다. pappase mithingul milwessta. *Being busy, I put off the meeting.* 날씨 때문에 미팅이 **미뤄졌다.** nalssi ttaymwuney mithingi milwecyessta. *The meeting got postponed due to weather.*
기다리다 kitalita *wait*	기다려지다 kitalyecita *look forward to*	애타게 그 날을 기다린다. aythakey ku nalul kitalinta. *I yearn for the day.* 그 날이 **기다려진다.** ku nali kitalyecinta. *I look forward to that day.*
정하다 cenghata *set, decide*	정해지다 cenghaycita *be decided*	내가 날짜를 정했다. nayka nalccalul cenghayssta. *I have decided on the date.* 날짜가 **정해졌다.** nalccaka cenghaycyessta. *The date is set./The date has been set.*
깨다 kkayta *break*	깨지다 kkaycita *break, get broken*	내가 창문을 깼다. nayka changmwunul kkayssta. *I broke the window.* 창문이 **깨졌다.** changmwuni kkaycyessta. *The window broke.* 약속이 **깨졌다.** yaksoki kkaycyessta. *The promise was broken.*

<3> Long-form passive 2: 되다

되다 toyta is a highly useful verb in Korean grammar. Its basic meaning is *to become*, but it also makes a kind of passive when it replaces 하다 hata in Sino-Korean Noun + 하다 hata TRANSITIVE verbs:

나:	왜 그래? 무슨 걱정 있어?
na:	way kulay? mwusun kekceng isse?
Me:	*What's up? Are you worried about something?*

친구:	시험을 못 볼까 봐 **걱정돼**.
chinkwu:	sihemul mos polkka pwa kekcengtway.
Friend:	*I am worried I might not do well on the test.* (Literally, *it has become a worry.*)

나:	너무 **걱정하지** 마. 공부 많이 했잖아.
na:	nemwu kekcenghaci ma. kongpwu manhi haysscanha.
Me:	*Don't worry too much. You studied a lot.*

동생:	내일 여행 갈 **준비** 다 **했어**?
tongsayng:	nayil yehayng kal cwunpi ta haysse?
Brother:	*Did you prepare your trip for tomorrow?*

나:	**준비** 다 **됐어**.
na:	cwunpi ta twaysse.
Me:	*I am ready.* (Literally, *preparation has been completed.*)

In the dialogues where 되다 toyta is used, there is a sense that the situation CAME TO BE: in the first instance, 동생 tongsayng has become worried, or worries have come about. In the second conversation, the situation has come to be that 나 na is ready for the trip—it has all come together. The cause of *my* worrying and the brother's being prepared are attributed to some unnamed external forces, thus these sentences are passive.

Here are some of the frequently used 하다-되다 hata-toyta pairs. Note the change of particles between sentences:

하다 Hata Verb	되다 Toyta Verb	Example
준비하다 cwunpihata *prepare*	준비되다 cwunpitoyta *get prepared*	준비를 다 했다. cwunpilul ta hayssta. *I have prepared everything.* 준비**가** 다 **됐다**. cwunpika ta twayssta. *All is prepared.*
시작하다 sicakhata *start, begin*	시작되다 sicaktoyta *get started*	영화를 시작했다. yenghwalul sicakhayssta. *They started the movie.* 영화**가** 시작**됐다**. yenghwaka sicaktwayssta. *The movie (got) started.*

하다 Hata Verb	되다 Toyta Verb	Example
취소하다 chwisohata *cancel*	취소되다 chwisotoyta *get cancelled*	약속을 취소했다. yaksokul chwisohayssta. *I cancelled the appointment.* 강의가 **취소됐다.** kanguyka chwisotwayssta. *The class got cancelled.*
이해하다 ihayhata *understand*	이해되다 ihaytoyta *be able to understand*	네가 이해를 해라. neyka ihaylul hayla. *You, be more understanding.* 상황이 **이해돼요.** sangwhangi ihaytwayyo. *I see.* *(I can understand the situation.)*

In spoken Korean, particles can get copied and appear attached to the roots:

하다 Hata Verb	되다 Toyta Verb	Example
걱정하다 kekcenghata *worry*	걱정되다 kekcengtoyta *be worried*	걔에 대해 걱정을 하지 마. kyayey tayhay kekcengul haci ma. *Don't worry about him.* 그 일이 걱정이 **된다.** ku ili kekcengi toynta. *I am worried about it.*

Some Sino-Korean verbs allow EITHER the 하다 hata or the 되다 -toyta verb with the same animate subject. The meaning difference is, then, that the 하다 hata version implies **agency** on the part of the subject, and the 되다 -toyta version offers a report of WHAT HAPPENED TO THE SUBJECT:

하다 Hata Verb	되다 Toyta Verb	Example
취직하다 chwicikhata *get a job*	취직되다 chwiciktoyta *get hired*	내가 회사에 취직을 **했다.** nayka hoysaey chwicikul hayssta. *I (looked for and) got a job.* 내가 회사에 취직이 **됐다.** nayka hoysaey chwiciki wayssta. *(I) got hired.*

<4> Long-form passive 3: -게 되다

The last passive construction to introduce to you is made up of an active verb and -게 되다 -key toyta, which literally means *to become such that....* A more natural translation is *be made to/allowed to* or *get to*. It is used when something comes to be that is not the subject's will or intention, again, attributing the control to an external force or situation:

피곤해서 수업 시간에 자꾸 **자게 된다**.
phikonhayse swuep sikaney cakkwu cakey toynta.
I am so tired, so I end up falling asleep during class.

시험 기간에는 종종 밤을 **새우게 된다**.
sihem kikaneynun congcong pamul saywukey toynta.
I often end up pulling all-nighters during the exam period.

한국에 **가게 됐어**!
hankwukey kakey twaysse!
I get to go to Korea!

무슨 일을 하게 **됐어**?
mwusun ilul hakey twaysse?
What kind of work will you be doing? (*What work has it come to be that you (will) do?*)

내일도 **일하게 될 거야**.
nayilto ilhakey toyl keya.
I reckon that I'll (need to) work tomorrow.

The -게 되다 -key toyta expression is also used to deliver news in a softened tone, since it places the control of the opportunity in someone else's hands. 거기 가게 됐어요 keki kakey twaysseyo *I get to go there/It turned out that I'm going there*, for example, sounds more like a humble report of a happy (or upsetting) coincidence or long-awaited (or dreaded) result. Compare that to 거기 가요 keki kayo *I'm going there*, which can sound like a straightforward declaration of a sure plan.

내일부터 **일하게 됐다**!
nayilpwuthe ilhakey twayssta!
(It turns out that) I am going to work starting tomorrow.

그 사람을 마음에 **들어하게 될 거야**.
ku salamul maumey tule hakey toyl keya.
You will come to like her.

장학금을 **받게 될 거예요**.
canghakkumul patkey toyl keyeyyo.
You'll be getting a/the scholarship. You'll see.

The -게 되다 -key toyta part only delivers the meaning of *to come to be that*, so, if 되다 toyta is in the perfective aspect/past tense, the opportunity or need has arisen, or it arose in the past. As in the last example above, if you think the opportunity or need (to do something) WILL arise, 되다 toyta should be in the future tense. Since there is no indication of tense on the verb that -게 되다 -key toyta attaches to, WHEN the activity takes place, whether it is yet to begin or has already been completed, is open to interpretation based on the context.

내일도 **일하게 됐어**.
nayilto ilhakey twaysse.
It has come to be that I (need to) work tomorrow, too.
(So I will work tomorrow.)

내일도 **일하게 될 거야**.
nayilto ilhakey toyl keya.
I figure (it will turn out that) I (will need to) work tomorrow.
(So I will work tomorrow, probably.)

In the past tense, -게 되다 -key toyta can also show a change over time:

전에는 파를 싫어했는데 이제는 잘 **먹게 됐다**.
ceneynun phalul silhehayssnuntey iceynun cal mekkey twaysta.
I used to not like green onions, but I have come to be able to eat them.

전엔 수영을 잘 못 했는데 이젠 잘 **하게 됐다**.
ceneyn swuyengul cal mos hayssnuntey iceyn cal hakey twaysta.
I wasn't good before, but now I have come to be a good swimmer.

\<5\> Fine-tuning -어지다 and -게 되다

Some grammarians may say that the -어지다 -ecita suffix is to be used with descriptive verbs, and the -게 되다 -key toyta ending is used with active verbs. Native speakers, however, use either ending on either type of verb depending on the *meaning*: -어지다 -ecita indicates an incremental change usually not immediately discernible, while -게 되다 -key toyta reports a stark change of state, typically as a result of a particular (external) event.

날씨가 **따뜻해졌어**.
nalssika ttattushaycyesse.
The weather has gotten warm.

소금을 너무 넣어서 국이 **짜졌어**.
sokumul nemwu nehese kwuki ccacyesse.
I put in too much salt, so the soup has become salty.

간장 대신 소금을 넣었더니 국이 **짜게 됐다**.
kancang taysin sokumul nehessteni kwuki ccakey twaysta.
The soup turned out salty, as I put in salt instead of soy sauce.

그 사건으로 일이 더 **복잡하게 됐다**.
ku sakenulo ili te pokcaphakey twaysta.
The matter got more complicated due to that incident.

(4) Translation of Korean passives into English

Apart from the general tendency for passives to express events that happen by accident or of their own accord, Korean passive verbs are often better translated into English as middle verbs, as noted above. That is, they are often translated into active sentences. Compare the translations below and when passives are used in Korean versus English:

불이 **꺼졌어요**.
pwuli kkecyesseyo.
The light went out (~~became turned off~~).

불이 **꺼져 있어요**.
pwuli kkecye isseyo.
The light is turned off.

펜이 잘 **써져요**.
pheyni cal ssecyeyo.
The pen writes well (~~is written well~~).

빨간 펜으로 **써져 있어요**.
ppalkan pheynulo ssecye isseyo
It is written in red.

문이 **열렸어**.
mwuni yellyesse.
The door opened (~~was opened~~).

문이 **열려 있어**.
mwuni yellye isse.
The door is open.

Some Korean passive sentences are best translated with an animate subject and the verb *can* or *can't*, as noted earlier:

여기서 그 빌딩이 **보인다**.
yekise ku piltingi pointa.
I can see that building from here.

옆방의 음악이 **들린다**.
yephpanguy umaki tullinta.
I can hear the music from next door.

누룽지가 잘 안 **긁혀**.
nwulwungcika cal an kulkhye.
I can't scrape the burnt rice (off the pot).

오늘은 글이 잘 안 **써진다**.
onulun kuli cal an ssecinta.
I can't write well today.

벌써 그 날이 **기다려진다**.
pelsse ku nali kitalyecinta.
I can't wait for that day already.

It's safe to say that passives are used much more often in Korean than in English. Try a web search on some passive verb forms and see how they are used. It's likely you'd translate into English with an active sentence in many cases. Then, try translating some of your English thoughts into passive sentences in Korean, and see what your Korean friends think.

Or, for a simpler approach, read back through the examples to find some of the most useful Korean passive expressions, such as

이 도시락에는 사랑이 담겼어요.
i tosilakeynun salangi tamkyesseyo.
There is love in this lunch box.
(Literally, *Love has been put into this lunch box.*)

9.1.3 Causatives

The last kind of verb derivation we'll talk about is **causative** verbs. Making causatives is like making *eat* into *feed,* *see* into *show,* and so on, except that in Korean the base and causative verbs always look similar—they are derived with a simple suffix in the simplest short-form version, similarly to how passive verbs are derived.

They are called causatives because deriving them adds the meaning CAUSE *someone/ something to do such-and-such* or MAKE *someone/something be such-and-such.* In making a causative, you add a new player, the CAUSER of the action, into the sentence as the subject. In terms of structure, it turns an intransitive verb, be it active or descriptive, into a transitive verb (e.g. *wide* → *widen, sleep* → *make someone sleep, put someone to sleep*). It can also turn a transitive verb into a **ditransitive** verb (that has two objects, e.g., *see something* → *show someone something* or *make someone see something*).

When verbs have causative counterparts in English, they often don't resemble each other (e.g. *eat* → *feed, die* → *kill*). For most English verbs, though, there is no causative version, and one of the helping verbs *make, let, have, help,* or *get* has to be used (e.g., *She made him leave*). Have these structures in mind when thinking about Korean causatives.

In Korean, there are two ways to make causatives. The first is by attaching a causative suffix to the verb root. We call this the **short-form causative**, and like passives, the choice of suffix depends on the base verb. The other way is to make use of a helping verb causative construction: -게 하다 -key hata/-게 만들다 -key mantulta. We call this the **long-form causative**. Let's get started with the causative derivations and then we'll do a quick check-up on particle usage in causative constructions.

(1) How causatives are formed

As with passives, only Native Korean verb roots can be made into **short-form causatives**, and there are patterns to which suffix to use to make a verb into a causative. These patterns are, in fact, VERY similar to the passive-forming patterns. Also, not all verbs have a short-form causative counterpart, and you will ultimately need to memorize the causative verbs that do exist. It will be good to remember the causative verbs because then you can always figure out the non-causative root. That is, 높이다 nophita *to raise* is derived from the verb 높다 nophta (높 noph +이 i) *to be high.*

<1> Deriving short-form causatives with suffixes 이, 히, 리, 기, ㅣ우, 추

Short-form causatives are formed by adding 이 i, 히 hi, 리 li, 기 ki, ㅣ우 iwu, or 추 chwu to the root of a transitive or intransitive verb.

We provide mnemonic stories for the causatives, too. Again, do note that the storyline will only help you memorize the BASE verbs as the ones that can become causative with the particular suffix emphasized in the title of the mnemonic story. Also, recall that the transitivity won't necessarily match in English and Korean.

Here's how it works.

a. 이

Just like for passives, -이 -i attaches to the most varied verb root shapes. And as it happens, 보다 pota *to see*, for example, has the same shape for both the passive and causative verbs: 보이다 poita *to be visible* and *to show*.

Your mnemonic device for 이 i causatives is "The story of a little bird-ie (bird-이 i)":

> I **SAW** a bird flying **HIGH**, then it fell so I thought it **DIED**. It **FOOL**ed me because it wasn't dead. I brought it in, **BOIL**ed some gruel and **FED** it. The porridge was **STICK**ing all around its beak.

Here are the verbs that become causatives through the -이 -i -suffix, along with example sentences:

Verb	Causative	Example
보다 pota *see, watch*	보이다 poita *show*	친구에게 사진을 **보여** 줬어요. chinkwueykey sacinul poye cwesseyo. *I showed a picture to my friend*
높다 nophta *high*	높이다 nophita *make high, raise*	담을 **높였어요**. tamul nophyesseyo. *I raised a wall.*
죽다 cwukta *die*	죽이다 cwukita *kill*	석유회사가 전기 자동차**를 죽였다**. sekyuhoysaka cenki catongchalul cwukyessta. *Gas companies killed the electric car.*
속다 sokta *get duped*	속이다 sokita *deceive*	친구를 **속이면** 안 되지. chinkwulul sokimyen an toyci. *You shouldn't really take advantage of your friends, you know.*
끓다 kkulhta *boil*	끓이다 kkulhita *boil s.t.*[+]	물 좀 **끓일까요**? mwul com kkulhilkkayo? *Shall I boil some water?*
먹다 mekta *eat*	먹이다 mekita *feed*	아기에게 우유를 **먹였어요**. akieykey wuyulul mekyesseyo. *I fed the baby milk.*
붙다 pwuthta *stick*	붙이다 pwuthita *stick s.t.*	벽에 사진을 **붙였어요**. pyekey sacinul pwuthyesseyo. *I attached a picture to the wall*

[+] "s.o." means *someone* and "s.t." means *something*, as in "make s.o. do something" or "cause s.t. to happen."

b. 히

The causative suffix -히 -hi tends to attach to verb roots that have a hard final consonant (e.g. ㄱ, ㄷ, or ㅂ or complex finals, just like for the passive -히 -hi). Note that 읽다 ilkta *to read* has the same shape for both passive and causative forms: 읽히다 ilkhita *to be read* and *to make s.o. read*.

The mnemonic we suggest is "HE (히 hi) can read on the sofa-bed":

> We WIDEned the room and BRIGHTened it so that we could LAY DOWN our sofa-bed and have our son PUT ON his pajamas and READ there.

Here are the -히 -hi-causative verbs and examples:

Verb	Causative	Example
넓다 nelpta *wide*	넓히다 nelphita *widen*	가게를 **넓혔다**. kakeylul nelphyessta. *I expanded the store.*
밝다 palkta *bright*	밝히다 palkhita *brighten*	촛불로 방을 **밝혔다**. chospwullo pangul palkhyessta. *I brightened up the room with a candle.*
눕다 nwupta *lie down*	눕히다 nwuphita *have s.o. lie down; lay s.o. down*	아기를 침대에 **눕혔어요**. akilul chimtayey nwuphyesseyo. *I laid my baby in the crib.*
입다 ipta *put on*	입히다 iphita *have s.o. wear; put clothes on s.o.*	강아지한테 옷을 **입혀요**. kangacihanthey osul iphyeyo. *I dress my dog in clothes.*
읽다 ilkta *read*	읽히다 ilkhita *have s.o. read*	아이에게 책을 **읽힌다**. aieykey chaykul ilkhinta. *I have my child read books.*

c. 리

The causative suffix -리 -li is the easiest to remember, as it attaches to verb roots that are ㄹ-related one way or another. The original root can be any old ㄹ-verb that has a causative counterpart. It can be a ㄹ-final verb or a special-ㄷ class verb whose final consonant alternates with ㄹ before vowel-initial suffixes. It can also be a 르- lu- verb, requiring special conjugation and doubling up the final ㄹ. Since the verb can have many different shapes, it would be best if you memorize the base verbs for the -리 -li suffix. Again, this is the same as for the passive -리 -li suffix.

The mnemonic we have come up with for the -리 -li causative suffix is "friend-LY (리 li) advice":

If you **KNOW** I have **SAVE**d you from drowning when you **DOZE**d off and that your clothes will **DRY**, then there is no need to **CRY**.

Here are the -리 -li-causative verbs and examples:

Verb	Causative	Example
알다 alta *know*	알리다 allita *inform, notify*	빨리 친구들한테 이 소식을 **알려줘**. ppalli chinkwutulhanthey i sosikul allyecwe. *Let my friends know this news quickly.*
살다 salta *live*	살리다 sallita *save s.o.*	**살려** 주세요! sallye cwuseyyo! *Save me!*
졸다 colta *doze off*	졸리다 collita *make someone fall asleep, sleepy*	아, **졸려**… a, collye… *Oh, I'm sleepy…*
마르다 maluta *dry*	말리다 mallita *dry something*	옷을 **말리자**. osul mallica. *Let's dry the clothes.*
울다 wulta *cry, ring*	울리다 wullita *make s.o. cry; ring a bell*	종을 **울려라**! congul wullyela! *Ring the bell!*

d. 기

The suffix -기 -ki attaches mostly either to verb roots that end in a nasal consonant (like ㄴ or ㅁ) or those that end in ㅅ or ㅌ. 안다 anta *to hold/hug* is one verb that has the same shape for both the passive and causative verbs, 안기다 ankita.

Also, like the passive suffix -기 -ki, the causative suffix is pronounced lax as 안기다 ankita [안기다 ankita] and 남기다 namkita [남기다 namkita] and NOT [안끼다 ankkita] and [남끼다 namkkita], even though the 다 ta is tense in the dictionary form of nasal-final words like 안다 anta [안따 antta] and 남다 namta [남따 namtta].

The mnemonic we offer for causative verbs derived with the -기 -ki suffix is "a chee-KY (기 ki) plan":

TAKE OFF your clothes, and **LEAVE** them here. **ENTRUST** them to me. **PUT ON YOUR SHOES** and leave. I will **LAUGH**, **FOIST** your clothes on my brother, and **WASH** my hands of your problem.

Here are the -기 -ki-causative verbs and examples:

Verb	Causative	Example
벗다 pesta *take off (clothes)*	벗기다 peskita *have s.o. take off (clothes)*	**젖은 옷을 빨리 벗기세요** cecun osul ppalli peskiseyyo *Please take those wet clothes off (of s.o.) quickly.*
남다 namta *remain*	남기다 namkita *leave s.o./s.t.*	**남기지** 말고 다 먹어. namkici malko ta meke. *Don't leave any; eat it up.*
맡다 mathta *take on*	맡기다 mathkita *entrust s.o. with s.t.*	그 일 나한테 **맡기지** 마! ku il nahanthey mathkici ma! *Don't put me in charge of/make me do that job.*
신다 sinta *put on*	신기다 sinkita *make s.o. put on shoes*	아기 신발을 좀 **신겨라**. aki sinpalul com sinkyela. *Put the shoes on the baby.*
웃다 wusta *laugh, smile*	웃기다 wuskita *make s.o. laugh; be funny*	**웃기는** 친구 wuskinun chinkwu *A funny friend (= a friend that makes me laugh)*
떠안다 tteanta *shoulder s.t.*	떠안기다 tteankita *foist s.t. on s.o.*	팀장이 나머지 일을 다 나한테 **떠안겼다**. thimcangi nameci ilul ta nahanthey tteankyessta. *The team leader foisted all the remaining work on me.*
씻다 ssista *wash*	씻기다 ssiskita *have s.o. wash; wash s.o.*	아기 얼굴을 **씻기세요**. aki elkwulul ssiskiseyyo. *Please wash the baby's face.*
안다 anta *hold, hug*	안기다 ankita *make s.o. hold (a baby)*	그 사람은 나한테 아기를 **안기고** 사라졌다. ku salamun nahanthey akilul ankiko salacyessta. *He gave the baby to me and disappeared.*

e. ㅣ우

The suffix - ㅣ우 -iwu is NOT used in making passives, only causatives. It attaches to vowel-final verb roots. If the root ends in ㅣ or ㅐ, simply add the vowel 우 wu; if the verb root ends in any other vowel, add - ㅣ우 -iwu. In all cases, the causative form will ultimately look like it has a version of - ㅣ우 -iwu. You will see that 크다 khuta is the only exception.

The mnemonic we offer for the - ㅣ우 -iwu suffix is "<u>Eeww (ㅣ우 iwu), that smells bad (or Oooo (우 wu), that smells good)</u>":

I **PUT ON** my hat, went to the bus stop, and **STOOD** there. The bus **STOP**ped, so I **GOT ON**. It was **EMPTY**, so I decided to **SLEEP**. When I **WOKE UP**, the bus was **FULL**. I had **BURN**t my coat on the heater, and it smelled bad. The woman next to me had a **BIG** flower that was in full **BLOOM**, and it smelled good.

Here are the -ㅣ우 -iwu-causative verbs and examples:

Verb	Causative	Example
쓰다 ssuta *wear (a hat, glasses)*	씌우다 ssuywuta *cover s.t. up*	아이한테 모자를 **씌웠어요**. aihanthey mocalul ssuywesseyo. *I put a hat on the kid's head.*
서다 seta *stop, stand*	세우다 seywuta *stop, stand s.t./s.o.*	경찰이 차를 **세웠어요**. kyengchali chalul seywesseyo. *The police stopped a car.*
타다 thata *ride; burn*	태우다 thaywuta *give a ride to s.o.;* *burn s.t.*	차에 **태웠어요**. chaey thaywesseyo. *I gave (s.o.) a ride in a car.* 과자를 **태웠어요**. kwacalul thaywesseyo. *I burned the cookies.*
비다 pita *empty*	비우다 piwuta *empty something*	쓰레기통을 **비우세요**. ssuleykithongul piwuseyyo. *Please empty the trash can.*
자다 cata *sleep*	재우다 caywuta *put s.o. to sleep*	아기를 **재웠다**. akilul caywessta. *I put the baby to sleep.*
깨다 kkayta *wake up*	깨우다 kkaywuta *wake s.o. up*	7시에 **깨우세요**. ilkopsiey kkaywuseyyo. *Please wake me up at 7.*
차다 chata *fill up*	채우다 chaywuta *fill s.t. up, out*	욕조에 물을 **채웠다**. yokcoey mwulul chaywessta. *I filled the tub (with water).*
크다 khuta *big*	키우다 kKhiwuta *raise (child, pet)*	강아지를 한 마리 **키워요**. kangacilul han mali khiweyo. *I am raising a puppy.*
피다 phita *bloom*	피우다 phiwuta *make s.t. bloom*	한 송이 국화꽃을 **피우기** 위해 han songi kwukhwakkochul phiwuki wihay *To help one meager chrysanthemum bloom…*

f. 추

The last (regular) causative suffix -추 -chwu (also not used for passives, only causatives) attaches to verb roots that end in ㅈ. Do remember that you cannot just add these suffixes willy-nilly to derive causative verbs; thus, you cannot derive 잊추다 icchwuta from 잊다 icta *to forget* and expect it to mean *make s.o. forget*. Below are some that actually work.

A short mnemonic story for -추 -chwu-causative verbs is: "<u>won'tchu</u> (won't -추 -chwu) <u>please?</u>":

> You are **LATE** for the meeting, so stay **LOW** as you enter—and won't you please **SET** your alarm!

Here are the -추 -chwu-causative verbs and examples:

Verb	Causative	Example
낮다 nacta *low*	낮추다 nacchwuta *lower*	목소리를 **낮춰요**. moksolilul nacchweyo. *Please lower your voice.*
늦다 nucta *late*	늦추다 nucchwuta *push back, postpone*	약속 시간을 **늦췄어요**. yaksok sikanul nucchwesseyo. *I pushed back an appointment time.*
맞다 macta *fit, be correct*	맞추다 macchwuta *adjust, tune, guess, make s.t. fit*	느린 시계를 **맞췄어요**. nulin sikyeylul macchwesseyo. *I corrected the slow clock.*

g. Unpredictable pairs

Words like 없다 epsta *to not exist*, 젖다 cecta *to be wet*, and 돋다 totta *to sprout* have causative counterparts, but their derivation is not predictable. You will simply need to memorize them:

Verb	Causative	Example
없다 epsta *not exist*	없애다 epsayta *remove s.t.*	얼룩을 **없앴다**. ellwukul epsayssta. *(I) removed the stain.*
젖다 cecta *wet*	적시다 ceksita *wet s.t.*	수건을 **적셔서** 뜨거운 이마에 놓아 주었다. swukenul ceksyese ttukewun imaey noha cwuessta. *I wet the towel and put it on her feverish forehead.*
돋다 totta *sprout, come out*	돋구다 totkwuta *make s.t. sprout, come out*	떨어진 식욕을 **돋구는** 음식 ttelecin sikyokul totkwunun umsik *food that stimulates one's lost appetite*

<2> Fine-tuning short-form causatives

As you have witnessed, causatives add a causer to the sentence, and passives take away an agent and move the object into the subject position. They both shift the alignment of players with respect to subject and object. They both use suffixes 이 i, 히 hi, 리 li, or 기 ki with, additionally, ㅣ우 iwu and 추 chwu for causatives, such that for verbs that have both passive and causative counterparts, the two may look the same. But the derivation of passives and causatives depends on the transitivity of the base verb; for many verbs, it is not possible to make a passive or causative counterpart.

Now that you have learned that 이 i, 히 hi, 리 li, and 기 ki can function to make both passives and causatives, when you meet a new verb, your job is to memorize not just the pronunciation, spelling, and vague meaning of it, but also its exact transitivity (including passive- or causative-ness) and its active-descriptive category. Is it a descriptive verb? Does it need an object?

So, if you have just learned a new word, say, 깨다 kkayta, it's not enough to memorize that it means *to break*, especially because the English word *break* can be transitive or intransitive. It would be best to learn a new word in a whole sentence with the exact context it might be used in in real life. (창문 깨지마! changmwun kkaycima! *Don't break the window* (has an object), thus 깨다 kkayta is a TRANSITIVE verb, *s.o. breaks s.t.*)

Even better if you can look up and memorize a word's transitivity AND passive and causative forms, if any. Let's see how your knowledge of transivity should guide you:

깨다 kkayta *to break s.t.* is a transitive verb that needs an object (and all transitive verbs are active verbs). Since the base verb is transitive, it will likely go in the direction of being made passive if it's going to undergo a derivation. Sure enough, a related word is 깨지다 kkaycita *to break (intransitive), to get broken.*

동생이 접시를 **깼다**.
tongsayngi cepsilul kkayssta.
My sister broke the plate.

접시가 **깨졌다**.
cepsika kkaycyessta.
The plate broke. (got broken)

Be aware that words can have multiple meanings. 깨다 kkayta is also an intransitive verb, *to wake up*, that needs no object. Since the base verb is intransitive, it will likely go toward the direction of getting a "causer." Sure enough, a related word is 깨우다 kkaywuta *to wake someone up*:

아기가 또 **깼다**.
akika tto kkayssta.
The baby woke up again.

누나 **깨우지** 마.
nwuna kkaywuci ma.
Don't wake your sister up.

Let's examine a few other words. The two different meanings of 쓰다 ssuta *to wear on the head* and *to be bitter* derive counterparts the same way. Similarly for 차다 chata *to kick* and *to be full* and 타다 thata *to burn* and *to ride on*:

설탕 없이는 커피가 **쓰다**.
Selthang epsinun khephika ssuta.
Coffee without sugar is bitter.

그 말을 듣고 입맛이 **써졌다**.
ku malul tutko ipmasi ssecyessta.
Hearing it left a better aftertaste in my mouth.
(Literally, *my mouth-taste was made bitter.*)

학교에 빨간 털모자를 **쓰고** 갈 거야.
hakkyoey ppalkan thelmocalul ssuko kal
I'm going to wear a red stocking cap to school.

아이한테 모자 **씌우지** 마.
aihanthey moca ssuywuci ma. keya.
Don't put a/the hat on the child.

공, 이 쪽으로 **차**!
kong, i ccokulo cha!
Kick the ball this way!

개 **차였대**.
kyay chayesstay.
He got dumped, I hear.

고급 과정은 인원이 다 **찼어**.
kokup kwacengun inweni ta chasse.
The advanced-level course is already full.

내 잔 좀 **채워** 줘!
nay can com chaywe cwe!
Fill my glass, please.

버스에 몇 명 안 **탔네**.
pesuey myechmyeng an thassney.
The bus is near empty.
(Literally, *Not too many got on the bus.*)

목말 **태워** 줘!
mokmal thaywe cwe!
Give me a ride on your shoulders!

해변에서 잠들어서 얼굴이 까맣게 **탔어**.
haypyeneyse camtulese elkwuli kkamahkey thasse.
I fell asleep on the beach, and my face was tanned black.

고기 좀 너무 **태우지** 마!
koki com nemwu thaywuci ma!
Don't keep burning the meat!

The practice of paying attention to the transitivity of a verb is also a good idea because the transitivity of a Korean verb does not always match that of the English verb. Let's look at a couple of mis-match cases: 속다 sokta *to be duped* → 속이다 sokita *to dupe s.o.* (causative) and 비다 pita *empty* → 비우다 piwuta *to empty s.t.*:

동생한테 **속았다**.
tongsaynghanthey sokassta.
I got the wool pulled over my eyes by my sister.

그 장사꾼이 나를 **속였다**.
ku cangsakkwuni nalul sokyessta.
The salesman pulled one over on me.

그 때는 잠깐 사무실이 **빌 거예요**.
ku ttaynun camkkan samwusili pil keyeyyo.
The office will be empty for a short while then./There will be nobody in the office then.

쓰레기 통 **비우고** 왔어.
ssuleyki thong piwuko wasse.
I've come back from emptying the trash can.

Also, the English word *dry* can mean *dry* as in *not wet any more* or *to dry s.t. else* as in *drying meat for jerky.* Since Korean verbs usually come with only ONE base **voice** (and transitivity), you need to learn the two DIFFERENT words 마르다 maluta *be dry* and 말리다 mallita *to dry s.t.* (the causative of 마르다 maluta):

머리가 이제 다 **말랐어**.
melika icey ta mallasse.
My hair is all dry now.

수건을 햇볕에 **말려**.
swukenul hayspyethey mallye.
Dry the towel in the sun.

Another pair you need to be extra careful about is 끓다 kkulhta *(something) boils* and 끓이다 kkulhita *(you) boil something*:

찌개가 다 **끓었어.**
ccikayka ta kkulhesse.
The stew is done boiling/cooking.

라면 끓여 먹게 물 좀 **끓여.**
lamyen kkulhye mekkey mwul com kkulhye.
Boil some water so we can cook ramen noodles.

Along these lines, some expressions come in pairs of verbs that are grammatically intransitive and transitive but have a sense of passivity and intention, respectively:

형이 화가 **났어요.**
hyengi hwaka nasseyo.
My elder brother is mad.
(anger came out; the anger is in charge, not him)

형이 화를 **냈어요.**
hyengi hwalul naysseyo.
My elder brother got mad.
(showed his anger; with some volition)

초인종 소리가 **났어요.**
choincong solika nasseyo.
The doorbell rang.

소리 **내지** 마!
soli nayci ma!
Don't make a sound.

수업이 **끝났어요.**
swuepi kkuthnasseyo.
The class ended.

수업을 **끝냈어요.**
swuepul kkuthnaysseyo.
I (the teacher) finished the class.

컴퓨터가 **고장났어요.**
khemphyutheka kocangnasseyo.
The computer is broken.

누가 컴퓨터를 **고장냈어요.**
nwuka khemphyuthelul kocangnaysseyo.
Someone broke the computer.

Occasionally you will see that the addition of a derivational suffix creates an oddball that doesn't seem to fit in the transitivity scale. 웃기다 wuskita, for example, means *funny* and is very much just an adjective in most usages, though we can see that it came from the causative of laugh: 웃다 wusta → 웃-기-다 wus-ki-ta *to make someone laugh.* Here are some similar verb pairs:

소리 없이 **웃는** 건 미소라고 해.
soli epsi wusnun ken misolako hay.
Laughing silently is called a smile.

그 친구 아주 **웃겼어.**
ku chinkwu acwu wuskyesse.
That fella was really funny.

나를 그렇게 **웃기지** 마!
nalul kulehkey wuskici ma!
Don't make me laugh so much!

고양이 **우는** 소리가 들린다.
koyangi wunun solika tullinta.
I hear a cat meowing ("crying").

선생은 강당이 쩌렁쩌렁 **울리게** 고함을 쳤다.
sensayngun kangtangi ccelengcceleng wullikey kohamul chyessta.
The teacher yelled so loud the auditorium shook.
(Literally, *the auditorium was made to resound.*)

수업이 재미없어서 **졸았다.**
swuepi caymiepsese colassta.
The class was no fun, so I dozed off.

저녁 8 시가 되면 벌써 **졸리다.**
cenyek yetelpsika toymyen pelsse collita.
I'm already sleepy at 8:00 in the evening.

Finally, remember that some causative verbs are the same as their passive counterparts:
보이다 poita, 들리다 tullita, 읽히다 ilkhita, and 씻기다 ssiskita. Usually, you can tell which
is the causative verb and which is the passive verb by taking a look at the particle used
right before the verb as shown in the first set of examples below. In addition, the helping verb structure -어 주다 -e cwuta is often added to the causative version, and -어지
다 is redundantly used on some passives.

나: 내 친구 사진을 **보여 줄게.**
na: nay chinkwu sacinul poye cwulkey.
I will show you my friend's picture.

너: 사진이 너무 작아서 얼굴이 안 **보여.**
ne: sacini nemwu cakase elkwuli an poye.
I cannot see the face because the picture is too small.

나: 이 책이 요즘 애들한테 많이 **읽혀진대.**
na: i chayki yocum aytulhanthey manhi ilkhyecintay.
This book is read by many children nowadays, I'm told.

너: 그럼 그 책을 내 동생한테 **읽혀야겠다.**
ne: kulem ku chaykul nay tongsaynghanthey ilkhyeyakeyssta.
Then I will have my younger sibling read it.

<3> Long-form causative: -게 하다/게 만들다

The constructions -게 하다 -key hata and -게 만들다 -key mantulta, added to a verb root,
make **long-form causatives**, another way to introduce a causer into a sentence who
makes it so that someone does/is... .

Take a look at the following two sentences. In both, the younger sibling is being
caused to eat broccoli, but can you tell who's putting broccoli in the younger sibling's
mouth?

누나가 동생한테 브로컬리를 **먹였다**.
nwunaka tongsaynghanthey pulokhellilul mekyessta.
The older sister fed broccoli to her younger brother.

누나가 동생한테 브로컬리를 **먹게 했다/만들었다**.
nwunaka tongsaynghanthey pulokhellilul mekkey hayssta/mantulessta.
The older sister had/made her younger brother eat broccoli.

The first sentence above uses a short-form causative, and it is clear that the older sister did the feeding. The second uses a long-form causative, and it is not quite as clear who did the actual feeding motions. Short-form causatives imply more direct action on the part of the causer, with both physical and temporal proximity.

With long-form causatives, particles get shifted around. If there is already an object marked with -을 -ul/-를 -lul, you should mark the doer of the action with -한테 -hanthey/-에게 -eykey. If the original verb is intransitive (and there is no object marked with -을 -ul/-를 -lul), you should mark the doer of the action as the object of the causative verb (the person being made to do something) with the OBJECT particle -을 -ul/-를 -lul. Or, you CAN mark the doer with the subject particle -이 -i/-가 -ka if the causer is marked with the topic marker -은 -un/-는 -nun. The choice of particles ultimately depends on what other particles are being used in the sentence. The bottom line is that you want to avoid using the same particle twice:

새 언니들**이** 신데렐라**를** 울게 만들었다.
say ennituli sinteyleyllalul wulkey mantulessta.
The stepsisters made Cinderella cry.

새 언니들**은** 신데렐라**가** 울게 만들었다.
say ennitulun sinteyleyllaka wulkey mantulessta.
The stepsisters made Cinderella cry.

형이 나**한테** 형 방**을** 치우게 만들었다.
hyengi nahanthey hyeng pangul chiwukey mantulessta.
My older brother made me clean his room.

형은 내**가** 형 방을 치우게 만들었다.
hyengun nayka hyeng pangul chiwukey mantulessta.
My older brother made me clean his room.

교수님**께서** 나**에게** 장학금을 받게 해 주셨다.
kyoswunimkkeyse naykey canghakkumul patkey hay cwusyessta.
The professor helped me to get a scholarship.

교수님**께서는** 내가 장학금을 받게 해 주셨다.
kyoswunimkkeysenun nayka canghakkumul patkey hay cwusyessta.
The professor helped me to get a scholarship.

This long-form causative structure can also apply to descriptive verbs. The person who is "put into the particular state" is usually marked by -을 -ul/-를 -lul.

동생은 나를 힘들게 만든다.
tongsayngun nalul himtulkey mantunta.
My younger brother wears me out.

Due to the vagueness of the verb 하다 hata *to do*, as you can imagine, -게 하다 -key hata can also be interpreted as PERMISSION: *let someone do something.* The subject particle -이 -i/-가 -ka tends to express more agency on the part of the actual doer (the subject of the base verb), as opposed to -을 -ul/-를 -lul or -한테 -hanthey/-에게 -eykey, but either interpretation is possible:

형이 내가 파티에 가게 했다.
hyengi nayka phathiey kakey hayssta.
My older brother <u>let/made</u> me go to the party.

형이 나를 파티에 가게 했다.
hyengi nalul phathiey kakey hayssta.
My older brother <u>made/let</u> me go to the party.

형이 나한테 파티에 가게 했다.
hyengi nahanthey phathiey kakey hayssta.
My older brother <u>let/made</u> me go to the party.

Again, the helping verb -어 주다 -e cwuta *give; do for someone* helps to clarify that it's a favor, and therefore, the interpretation is *let* or *help*:

형이 내가 파티에 가게 했다.
hyengi nayka phathiey kakey hayssta.
My older brother made me go to the party.

형이 나를 파티에 가게 해줬다.
hyengi nalul phathiey kakey haycwessta.
My older brother let/helped me go to the party.

Finally, learn the useful verb 시키다 sikhita *to order.* It works as a shorthand for causative constructions. 시키다 sikhita takes a NOUN object, so it is useful with Sino-Korean nouns (from noun + 하다 hata active verbs).

공부하다 — 공부시키다
kongpwuhata — kongpwusikhita
study — to make (someone) study

운동하다 — 운동시키다
wuntonghata — wuntongsikhita
exercise — to make (someone) exercise

청소하다 — 청소시키다
chengsohata — chengsosikhita
clean — to make (someone) clean

이해하다 — 이해시키다
ihayhata — ihaysikhita
understand — to make (someone) understand

발전하다 — 발전시키다
palcenhata — palcensikhita
develop — to make (something) develop

실망하다 (active verb) — 실망시키다
silmanghata (active verb) — silmangsikhita
be disappointed — to make (someone) disappointed

행복하다 (descriptive verb) — **행복시카다**, 행복하게 하다
hayngpokhata — hayngpoksikhita, hayngpokhakey hata
be happy — to make (someone) happy

Here are some examples. Notice the particles at work:

막내(한테) 집(을) **청소시키자**.
maknay(hantey) cip(ul) chengsosikhica.
Let's make the little one clean the house.

나(를/한테) **운동시키지** 마.
na(lul/hantey) wuntongsikhici ma.
Don't make me work (so hard/much).

나(를) **실망시키지** 마.
na(lul) silmangsikhici ma.
Don't disappoint me. (Don't make me disappointed.)

쟤(를) 좀 **이해시켜** 줘라.
cyay(lul) com ihaysikye cwela.
Help him understand (this).

(2) Particles in causative structures

As in passives, the positions of different players and elements in the sentence change in causatives. Instead of *my sibling read a book*, we might want to say *someone made my sibling read a book*. Now *my sibling*, which is the subject of the verb *read* in the non-causative sentence, becomes the OBJECT of the causative verb (*make* or *have/let (someone) read*). So there will be some differences in the particles used in causatives versus their base sentences in Korean. Let's clarify how the particles work.

<1> Subjects in causative structures: add a noun with -이/가

As you know, with causatives, we want to add another player to the sentence—the one who causes someone to do the action (whereas with passives, we want to hide or remove the doer). This new player is the SUBJECT of the sentence, marked with -이 -i/-가 -ka (or -은/는 -un/nun in the right cases):

누나**가** 동생한테 브로컬리를 먹였다.
nwunaka tongsaynghanthey pulokhellilul mekyessta.
<u>*The older sister*</u> *fed her younger brother broccoli.*

새엄마는 콩쥐를 울게 만들었다.
sayemmanun khongcwilul wulkey mantulessta.
The stepmother made Kong Jwi cry.

<2> Subjects of intransitives become OBJECTS in short-form causatives: -이/가 → -을/를

When an intransitive verb, like *laugh* or *be high*, is made into a causative, the subject of the intransitive verb (marked with -이/가 -i/ka) becomes the object of the (short-form) causative verb, marked with -을/를 -ul/lul because that person is MADE to do the action or be in the new state.

Here are some examples. The second sentence of each pair, marked with →, is the causative (which is transitive).

옷이 말랐다.
osi mallassta.
The clothes are dry./The clothes have dried.

→ 옷을 말리자.
osul mallica.
Let's dry the clothes/make the clothes dry up.

벽에 사진이 붙어 있어요.
pyekey sacini pwuthe isseyo.
There is a picture stuck on the wall.

→ (누가) 벽에 사진을 붙였어요.
(nwuka) pyekey sacinul pwuthyesseyo.
(Someone) stuck a picture on the wall.

그 사람은 목소리가 무척 깊고 낮다.
ku salamun moksolika mwuchek kiphko nacta.
His voice is very deep and low.

→ 목소리를 낮추세요.
moksolilul nacchwuseyyo.
Please lower your voice.

욕조가 찼어요.
yokcoka chasseyo.
The bathtub is full.

→ (누가) 욕조를 채웠어요
(nwuka) yokcolul chaeywesseyo.
(Someone) filled the tub.

아기**가** 울었어요.
akika wulesseyo.
The baby cried.

→ (누가) 아기를 울렸어요.
(nwuka) akilul wullyesseyo.
(Someone) made the baby cry.

It is important to know which base verbs are intransitive in Korean, such as 마르다 maluta *to dry up* and 붙다 pwuthta *to stick to*, especially when the English counterpart works as either intransitive or causative/transitive (like *dry* and *stick*). This will just have to be learned when you learn a new verb in Korean, but be aware that far fewer verbs in Korean work with more than one kind of transitivity.

<3> Subjects of intransitive verbs: -이/가 → -이/가 or -을/를 in long-form causatives
The subject of an intransitive verb made into a long-form causative with -게 하다/만들다 -key hata/mantulta can be marked either with -이/가-i/ka as the doer of the action or with -을/를 -ul/lul as the one BEING MADE TO do it.

신데렐라**가** 울었다.
sinteyleyllaka wulessta.
Cinderella cried.

→ 새 언니들은 신데렐라**가** 울게 만들었다.
say ennitulun sinteyleyllaka wulkey mantulessta.
Cinderella's stepsisters made <u>her cry</u>.

→ 새 언니들은 신데렐라**를** 울게 만들었다.
say ennitulun sinteyleyllalul wulkey mantulessta.
Cinderella's stepsisters made <u>her</u> cry.

**<4> Subjects of transitive verbs become INDIRECT OBJECTS in short-form causatives:
-이/가 → -한테/에게**
The subject of a transitive verb (that is, the doer in the base sentence) becomes the object of causative verbs (because he or she is the person who is MADE *to do the action*), but because there is already an object (of the base action—the transitive verb), it is common to mark these (usually animate) nouns with -한테 -hanthey or -에게 -eykey:

아기**가** 당근을 먹었어요.
akika tangkunul mekesseyo.
The baby ate carrots.

→ 아기**에게** 당근을 먹였어요.
akieykey tangkunul mekyesseyo
(I) fed the baby carrots./ I fed carrots to <u>the baby</u>.

아이**가** 바지를 입었어요.
aika pacilul ipesseyo.
The child put on pants.

→ 아이**에게** 바지를 입혔어요.
aieykey pacilul iphyesseyo
(I) put the pants on the child.

걔**가** 이 음악을 들었어요.
kyayka i umakul tulesseyo.
That child listened to this music.

→ 걔**한테** 이 음악을 들려 주세요.
kyayhanthey i umakul tullye cwuseyyo.
Play this music for that child. (Literally, *Have this music be listened to by that child.*)

<5> Subjects of transitive verbs: -이/가 → -이/가 or -한테/에게 in long-form causatives

The subject of a transitive verb made into a long-form causative with -게 하다 -key hata can be marked either with -이/가 -i/ka as the doer of the action or with -한테/에게 -hanthey/eykey as the one being made to do it:

내**가** 형 방을 치웠다.
nayka hyeng pangul chiwessta.
I cleaned my brother's room.

→ 형은 내**가** 자기 방을 치우게 만들었다.
hyengun nayka caki pangul chiwukey mantulessta.
My brother made me clean his room.

→ 형은 나**한테** 자기 방을 치우게 만들었다.
hyengun nahanthey caki pangul chiwukey mantulessta.
My older brother made me clean his room.

내**가** 장학금을 받았다.
nayka canghakkumul patassta.
I got a/the scholarship.

→ 교수님께서는 내**가** 장학금을 받게 해 주셨다.
kyoswunimkkeysenun nayka canghakkumul patkey hay cwusyessta.
The professor allowed/helped me to get a scholarship.

→ 교수님께서는 나**에게** 장학금을 받게 해 주셨다.
kyoswunimkkeysenun naeykey canghakkumul patkey hay cwusyessta.
The professor allowed/helped me to get a scholarship.

<6> Objects of transitive verbs: -을/를 remains -을/를 in causative structures

If a verb already has a direct object marked with -을/를 -ul/lul in the base form, that object is still marked with -을/를 -ul/lul in the causative structure as well:

아이가 신을 신었어요.
aika sinul sinesseyo.
The child put on his shoes.

→ 아이한테 신을 신겼어요
   aihanthey sinul sinkyesseyo
   (I) put the shoes on the child.

9.2 Suffixes to Derive Adverbs from Verbs

We have been talking about how a verb can be extended to become a related type of verb. In another kind of **derivation**, some verbs can be converted into adverbs, similar to how, in English, adding the suffix *-ly* turns adjectives (e.g., *I am calm*) into adverbs (e.g., *She handled the matter calmly*). We introduce below four ways to derive Korean adverbs, mainly from descriptive verbs.

9.2.1 Native Haan Korean adverb maker -이/애

Many native Haan Korean, mostly descriptive verbs, become adverbs with the addition of the suffix -이 and in some cases -애. Verbs that end in ㄹ or that are of the special-르 -lu category double up the ㄹ. Not all verbs can do this, but here are the most common ones:

Native Korean Verb	-이/애 Adverb Example
많다 manhta *plentiful*	**많이** 드세요. manhi tuseyyo. *Enjoy your food!* (Literally, *Eat a lot.*)
높다 nophta *high*	공을 너무 **높이** 던졌어. kongul nemwu nophi tencyesse. *You threw the ball too high.*
같다 kathta *same, alike*	**같이** 왔어요? kathi wasseyo? *Did you come together?*
깨끗하다 kkaykkushata *clean*	**깨끗이** 다 치워라. kkaykkusi ta chiwela. *Clean it all up (cleanly)!*
멀다 melta *far*	**멀리** 가지 말자. melli kaci malca. *Let's not go too far.*

Native Korean Verb	-이/애 Adverb Example
빠르다 ppaluta *fast*	**빨리** 오세요. ppalli oseyyo. *Come quick!*
모르다 moluta *not know*	어제 밤에 **몰래** 나갔어. ecey pamey mollay nakasse. *I snuck out (secretly) last night.*

The suffix -이 -i can also be attached to certain reduplicated nouns (some one-syllable Sino-Korean roots) to make adverbs with the meaning *every* or *each and every*. (Also observe how ㄹ disappears before ㄴ or ㄷ):

Base Noun	-이 "Each And Every" Example
집 cip *house*	저녁 5 시면 **집집이** 불이 들어온다. cenyek 5 simyen cipcipi pwuli tuleonta. *Lights come on in every household at 5:00.*
일 il *one*	**일일이** 다 보지는 못 했어요. ilili ta pocinun mos haysseyo. *I wasn't able to check every single item.*
겹 kyep *layer*	추울까 봐 **겹겹이** 껴 입고 나갔다. chwuwulkka pwa kyepkyepi kkye ipko nakassta. *I was afraid of the cold and put on layers to go out.*
곳 kos *place*	원유가 폭등으로 **곳곳이** 난리다. wenyuka phoktungulo koskosi nanlita. *It's mayhem everywhere because of the skyrocketing crude oil prices.*
틈 thum *crack, gap, interval*	**틈틈이** 공부하면 뒤처지지 않아. thumthumi kongpuhamyen twichecici anha. *You won't get behind if you use scrap time to study.*
샅 sath *crotch*	**샅샅이** 뒤져라! sathsathi twicyela! *Search! Leave no corners unturned!*
낱 nath *individual item*	밀고자는 들은 것을 **낱낱이** 보고했다. milkocanun tulun kesul nathnathi pokohayssta. *The squealer ratted out every single detail he heard.*
날 nal *day*	**나날이** 새롭다 nanali saylopta. *Everything is new every day.*
달 tal *month*	그는 **다달이** 부모님 용돈을 부친다. kunun tatali pwumonim yongtonul pwuchinta. *He never fails to send money to his parents every month.*

Base Noun	-이 "Each And Every" Example
번 pen *time*	그는 **번번이** 약속을 해 놓고 취소한다. kunun penpeni yaksokul hay nohko chwisohanta. *Every time he makes an appointment, he cancels.*
산 san *scatter*	떨어진 손거울이 **산산이** 조각나고 말았다. ttelecin sonkewuli sansani cokaknako malassta. *The portable mirror that dropped broke into a jillion pieces.*
층 chung *layer*	창고에 반품이 **층층이** 쌓여 있다. changkoey panphwumi chungchungi ssahye issta. *Returned goods are stacked high in the warehouse.*

9.2.2 Native Haan Korean adverb maker -오/우

Another pair of adverbial suffixes is -오 -o and -우 -wu. They used to be attached to (descriptive or active) native Haan Korean verbs somewhat freely but they are just vestigial traces found in fixed forms in modern Korean. Here are some examples. Notice the changes in spelling, e.g., 넘다 nem.ta → 너무 ne.mwu not 넘우 nem.wu:

Native Korean Verb	-오/우 Adverb Example
넘다 nemta *to exceed*	**너무** 먹었다. nemwu mekessta. *I ate too much.*
맞다 macta *to face*	**마주** 보고 앉아라. macwu poko ancala. *Sit facing each other.*
고르다 koluta *even*	**고루** 나눠 줬어요? kolwu nanwe cwesseyo? *Did you distribute (them) evenly?*
밭다 pathta *at close intervals*	손톱을 너무 **바투** 깎지 마. sonthopul nemwu pathwu kkakkci ma. *Don't cut your fingernails too short/close.*
잦다 cacta *frequent*	**자주** 오세요. cacwu oseyyo. *Come often!*
맵다 maypta *severe*	**매우** 맵네요. maywu maypneyyo. *It's awfully spicy.*
돌다 tolta *to turn*	그거 **도로** 줘. kuke tolo cwe. *Give that back to me.*

9.2.3 Sino-Korean adverb maker -히

For Sino-Korean DESCRIPTIVE VERBS, -히 -hi is the key to the adverb-hood. You can think of it as replacing 하다 hata:

Sino-Korean Descriptive Verb	-히 Adverb Example
편하다 phyenhata *comfortable*	**편히** 주무세요. phenhi cwumwuseyyo. *Have a good sleep.*
공손하다 kongsonhata *polite*	할머니께 **공손히** 인사드려. halmenikkey kongsonhi insatulye. *Give a polite greeting to Grandma.*
분명하다 pwunmyenghata *clearly*	어느 거야? **분명히** 말해! enu keya? pwunmyenghi malhay! *Which one is it? Say it clearly!*
확실하다 hwaksilhata *surely*	그 사람을 거기서 **확실히** 봤어요. ku salamul kekise hwaksilhi pwasseyo. *I am certain I saw him there.*
당연하다 tangyenhata *just, natural*	나도 **당연히** 가야지. nato tangyenhi kayaci. *I should of course go as well.*
굉장하다 koyngcanghata *magnificent*	**굉장히** 크다! koyngcanghi khuta! *It's colossally huge!*
조용하다 coyonghata *quiet*	**조용히** 해주세요. coyonghi haycwuseyyo. *Please keep quiet!*

9.2.4 Functional adverb maker -게

The final adverb suffix to introduce to you is -게 -key. You can think of this as a function marker that tells you a DESCRIPTIVE VERB is "temporarily" being used as an adverb. Adverbs usually tell you the **manner** in which things are done or the **degree** to which something is/has become; functional adverbs can tell you the **result**, the **manner**, or how the action is **experienced**. The -게 -key adverbs do not always translate as adverbs in English, but they are very common and useful in Korean:

Descriptive Verb	-게 Adverb Example
크다 khuta *big*	음악 좀 더 **크게** 틀어 줘. umak com te khukey thule cwe. *Please play the music louder/more loudly.*

Descriptive Verb	-게 Adverb Example
작다 cakta *small*	사진에 얼굴이 너무 **작게** 나왔다. saciney elkwuli nemwu cakkey nawassta. *The face came out too small in the picture.*
빨갛다 ppalkahta *red*	**빨갛게** 익었다. ppalkakey ikessta. *It has ripened "red" (well).*
재미있다 caymiissta *fun*	**재미있게** 읽었다. caymiisskey ilkessta. *That (book) was fun! (Literally, I read fun-ly.)*
맛있다 masissta *delicious*	**맛있게** 먹었다. masisskey mekessta. *That (food/meal) was good! (Literally, I ate deliciously.)*
하얗다 hayahta *white*	집을 **하얗게** 칠했다. cipul hayahkey chilhayssta. *We painted the house white.*
예쁘다 yeypputa *pretty*	**예쁘게** 입으세요. yeyppukey ipuseyyo. *Enjoy your (new) clothes! (Literally, Wear them prettily.)*
바쁘다 papputa *busy*	요즘 **바쁘게** 지내고 있다. yocum pappukey cinayko issta. *I am quite busy these days. (Literally, I am spending time busily these days.)*
쉽다 swipta *easy*	일을 너무 **쉽게** 생각했어. ilul nemwu swipkey sayngkakhaysse. *I underestimated the job. (Literally, I thought of the work too easily.)*
어렵다 elyepta *difficult*	직장을 **어렵게** 구했다. cikcangul elyepkey kwuhayssta. *He procured a job with great difficulty. (Literally, He got the job difficultly.)*
뜨겁다 ttukepta *hot*	그 둘은 서로를 **뜨겁게** 사랑한다. ku twulun selolul ttukepkey salanghanta. *They love each other passionately.*
차갑다 chakapta *cold*	그녀는 그를 **차갑게** 대했다. kunyenun kulul chakapkey tayhayssta. *She gave him a cold reception.*
편하다 phyenhata *comfortable*	**편하게** 계세요. phyenhakey kyeseyyo. *Make yourself comfortable.*
익숙하다 ikswukhata *familiar*	사진으로 많이 봐서 **익숙하게** 느껴져. sacinulo manhi pwase ikswukhakey nukkyecye. *I've been seeing them in photos, so they feel familiar to me.*

When the -게 -key suffix is attached to an ACTIVE VERB, the construction takes on a **goal** meaning *so that*. This is the basic structure used in long-form passives and causatives as you saw, but it also works with verbs other than 되다 toyta and 하다 hata /만들다 mantulta:

라면 **먹게** 물 좀 끓여 줘.
lamyen mekkey mwul com kkulhye cwe.
Please boil some water for me so I can make myself some ramen.

한국어를 더 잘 할 수 **있게** 열심히 공부하자.
hankwukelul te cal hal swu isskey yelsimhi kongpwu haca.
Let's study hard to get better at Korean.

9.3 Intensifying Verbal Prefixes

The Korean language makes use of all kinds of verbal suffixes, but there is a small number of PREFIXES as well. They attach to certain native Haan Korean verbs and add color, vigor, candor, and a degree of boorishness to your language. As such, they are mainly used in less formal situations. Here is a list of intensifying adverbs (and related NOUNS in parentheses):

들- tul- *excessive*

들끓다 tulkkulhta *to boil over*   들볶다 tulpokkta *to harass, pester*
들추다 tulchwuta *to lift up, divulge*   들뜨다 tulttuta *excited*

엇- es-/빗- pis- *askew*

엇나가다 esnakata *to go astray*   엇갈리다 eskallita *to miss each other*
빗맞다 pismacta *to miss the target*   빗금 piskum *diagonal lines*
빗나가다 pisnakata *to mis-aim, miss the target*

짓- cis- *crush*

짓누르다 cisnwuluta *to oppress*   짓이기다 cisikita *to mash*
짓뭉개다 cismwungkayta *to squash*   짓밟다 cispalpta *to stomp down, trample*

덧- tes- *double up*

덧나다 tesnata *to worsen*   덧니 tesni *snaggle tooth*
덧신 tessin *footies, overshoes*

엿- yes- *stealthy*

엿보다 yespota *to peep*   엿듣다 yestutta *to eavesdrop*

헛- hes- *empty*

헛듣다 hestutta *to mishear*

헛살다 hessalta *to waste one's life*

헛짚다 hesciphta *to miscalculate, make a wrong guess*

헛보다 hespota *to (wrongly) see what is not there*

헛되다 hestoyta *vain, meaningless*

새- say- / 샛- says- (emphatic)

새빨갛다 sayppalkahta *bright red*

새파랗다 sayphalahta *bright/very blue*

새하얗다 sayhayahta *bright/sparkling/snow white (new)*

샛노랗다 saysnolahta *bright yellow*

새까맣다 saykkamahta *pitch black*

치- ch- *upward*

치밀다 chimilta *to flare up, surge*

치뜨다 chittuta *to lift up (eyes)*

치솟다 chisosta *to soar*

치키다 chikhita *to pull/hike up (pants)*

뒤- twi- *rough*

뒤틀다 twithulta *to warp, twist*

뒤섞다 twisekkta *to mix roughly*

뒤흔들다 twihuntulta *to shake up*

되- toy- *back, return, again*

되돌이키다 toytolikhita *to undo, go back*

되묻다 toymwutta *to ask in return, ask again*

휘- hwi- *whirl*

휘감다 hwikamta *to wrap around*

휩쓸다 hwepssulta *to sweep away/across*

휘두르다 hwitwuluta *to swing, brandish*

휘날리다 hwinallita *to flap, flutter, whirl around (flying)*

휩싸다 hwipssata *to engulf, cover*

휘젓다 hwicesta *to stir up*

And here are some example sentences:

아이가 지루해서 몸을 **뒤틀고** 있다.
aika cilwuhayse momul twithulko issta.
The child is so bored that he is twisting his body.

그걸 보고 있자니 화가 **치민다.**
kukel poko issacani hwaka chiminta.
Watching that really ticks me off. (Literally, *While watching it, anger flares up.*)

또 덧니가 **났어?**
tto tesnika nasse?
You got another snaggle tooth?

밖에는 눈이 **휘날리고** 있어.
pakkeynun nwuni hwinalliko isse.
It's blizzardy out. (Literally, *the snow is whipping around.*)

나 좀 **들볶지** 말고 나둬!
na com tulpokkci malko natwe!
Stop pestering me and leave me alone!

9.4 Categories of Verb Suffixes and Their Ordering

We close this FOURTH chapter on Korean's dynamic and abundant verb suffixes with a quick note on the TYPES of suffix and how they are ordered in a long and complex verb, such as deriving an honorific passive verb and then making it a past tense question in the formal style. Categories of verb suffix help us talk about how all those suffixes get stacked up.

9.4.1 Inflection and derivation

As we mentioned at the beginning of the chapter, verb suffixes (actually ANY suffixes or prefixes) are categorized as **derivational** or **inflectional**. You learned a number of inflectional suffixes for **tense** and **aspect** and the ordinary speech style in chapter 6, and for **modality**, speaker attitudes, and other **speech styles** in chapter 7. Inflectional suffixes don't change the BASIC MEANING of verbs. They add only grammatical or **functional** information. (English has only a few inflectional suffixes, including past tense *-ed*, perfective aspect *-en*, and progressive aspect *-ing* for verbs, and plural *-s* for nouns.)

On the other hand, DERIVATIONAL suffixes (and prefixes) make new words that you could say merit being listed in a dictionary. You learned three kinds of Korean verb **derivations** in this chapter: honorific verbs, passives, and causatives. Most Korean grammarians consider the honorific suffix, -(으)시 -(u)si to be inflectional because it is so predictable, like the past tense or speech style endings, but for our purposes, it functions as derivational. Converting verbs into adverbs with the suffixes -이 -i, -애 -ay, -오 -o, -우 -u, and -히 -hi is also considered derivational while using -게 -key is considered inflectional because it feels temporary and on-the-fly, dependent on the grammatical structure of the sentence and less like creating a new word.

It may feel like Korean passive and causative suffixes are inflectional because passive and causative verbs look and sound similar to their base verbs, but they are considered different enough in meaning and usage to be considered derivation. Also, not all verbs can be made into a passive, causative, or honorific verb using a suffix. This limited usage is a common trait of derivational suffixes and unlike inflectional suffixes that can be attached to any verb across the board.

Categorizing verbs as inflectional or derivational allows us to understand that DERIVATIONAL SUFFIXES COME BEFORE INFLECTIONAL SUFFIXES in terms of ordering the many suffixes a verb might have on it. First, the passive or causative suffix creates a new verb stem; then, the honorific -(으)시 -(u)si can be added; finally, this new **stem** (root + derivational suffixes) can be **inflected** for tense, aspect, modality, speaker attitude, and sentence type, along with whatever speech style is required.

The distinction also allows us to generalize that KOREAN HAS A VERY LARGE NUM-
BER OF INFLECTIONAL SUFFIXES.

9.4.2 Order of suffixes

All these derivational and inflectional suffixes can stack up to make a very long verb,
but there is order to all these suffixes—generalizations we can make about what comes
first and next, just like derivational suffixes coming before inflectional.

Basically, the order of the suffixes is as follows, where slashes are used to indicate
that some pairings are incompatible (such as attitude endings + certain speech styles,
or tense + certain aspects), whereby if one shows up, the other can't. What is presented here may be somewhat different from traditional grammar, but hopefully you will
find it useful. (Only the short-form causative and passive suffixes are indicated here.
Long-form causative and passive suffixes may come in either order, depending on the
intended meaning):

> VERB ROOT–causative/passive–honorific] ^{STEM}–tense–aspect–modality–attitude*
>
> *Following the attitude suffix are sentence type and speech style suffixes

To close the chapter, we'll show you a few sentences with complex verbs that exemplify this ordering, using suffixes that you have learned thus far. Do not worry too
much about the specific terminology for each suffix; but do note that derivational
suffixes (causative/passive/honorific) come first, then **pre-final** inflectional suffixes
in a particular order (as above), modality, and then **final** inflectional suffixes at the
end of the sentence. Modality is a tricky animal and overlaps with the tense and aspect to a large degree.

We'll use a bracket to mark the end of derivational suffixes (the verb **stem**) and the
beginning of inflectional suffixes here as well.

높-이-시]-었-겠-습니다.
noph-i-si]-ess-keyss-supnita.
root (*high*)-causative-honorific]-perfective (tense/aspect)-conjecture (modality)-formal (speech
style)/statement (sentence type)
The honorable person raised (something), I'm guessing and telling you this humbly.

잡-히-시]-었-을-까-요?
cap-hi-si]-ess-ul-kka-yo?
root (*catch*)-passive-honorific]-perfective (tense/aspect)-probability (modality)-question (sentence
type)/polite ordinary (speech style)
I ask myself whether the honorable person was caught, and I say this politely to you.

When there is more than one aspect marker, the order is also fixed (e.g. -었-겠-더 -ess-keyss-te):

먹-이-시]-었-겠-더-군-요.

mek-i-si]-ess-keyss-te-kwun-yo.

root (*eat*)-causative-honorific]-perfective (tense/aspect)-conjecture-retrospective (modality)-realization (attitude)-politeness

The honorable person seems to have fed (someone), I realized as I reflected on what had happened.

If you can memorize and understand these complex verbs, you can use them as a model for creating similarly complex verbs yourself when you speak Korean. You have learned plenty of suffixes and are ready to string them together to express yourself fully. That's an amazing skill in an intricate and fascinating language!

Exercises

9.1 Deriving New Kinds of Verbs

Exercise 1. Fill in the cells with the appropriate honorific verb forms.

	-(으)시다	-(으)세요	-(으)셨어요
이다	이시다		
있다 *(to have)*		있으세요	
있다 *(there is)*			계셨어요
주문하다		주문하세요	
오다	오시다		
치다		치세요	
쓰다			쓰셨어요
부르다		부르세요	
입다	입으시다		
걷다		걸으세요	
돕다			도우셨어요
만들다		만드세요	
짓다	지으시다		
그렇다		그러세요	

Exercise 2. Rewrite the underlined parts using appropriate honorific expressions if needed.

1) 우리 할아버지 <u>이름</u>은 박준영이에요. 우리 할아버지는 <u>나이</u>가 예순 살이에 요. 할아버지는 작년까지 한국에 <u>살았어요</u>. 그래서 나는 할아버지를 자주 못 <u>만났어요</u>. 그렇지만 작년에 할머니가 <u>죽어서</u> 지금은 할아버지가 우리하 고 같이 <u>살아요</u>. 그래서 좋아요.

2) 지난 주 수요일은 할아버지 <u>생일</u>이었어요. 그래서 나하고 동생은 할아버지 <u>한테</u> 멋있는 모자하고 신발을 <u>사 줬어요</u>. 우리 부모님은 할아버지<u>한테</u> <u>생일</u> 선물로 새 컴퓨터를 <u>줬어요</u>. 할아버지가 아주 <u>좋아했어요</u>. 할아버지가 오래 <u>살면 좋겠어요</u>.

3) 작년에 할아버지가 많이 <u>아팠어요</u>. 그렇지만 이제 할아버지가 아주 건강해 <u>져서</u> 다행이에요. 요즘 할아버지는 하루에 여덟 시간 <u>자고</u> 매일 <u>운동해요</u>. 음식도 채소와 과일을 잘 <u>먹어요</u>. 나는 평일에는 자주 할아버지한테 전화를 <u>하고</u> 주말에 할아버지를 <u>만나러</u> 할아버지 집에 가요. 할아버지와 함께 텔레 비전도 <u>보고</u> 나가서 외식도 <u>해요</u>.

Exercise 3. Underline the appropriate expression from the parentheses to complete the sentence.

1) 학생:　　　선생님, 점심 (먹었어, 드셨어, 먹었어요, 드셨어요)?
　 선생님:　　아니, 아직 안 (먹었어, 드셨어, 먹었어요, 드셨어요).

2) 아들:　　　아버지, (얘기해, 말씀하셔, 얘기하세요, 말씀하세요).
　 아버지:　　아니야. 네가 먼저 (얘기해, 말씀하셔, 얘기하세요, 말씀하세요).

3) 동생:　　　할머니, 안녕히 (자, 주무셔, 자요, 주무세요).
　 할머니:　　그래, 너도 잘 (자, 주무셔, 자요, 주무세요).

4) 종업원:　　모두 몇 (명이에요, 명이세요, 분이에요, 분이세요)?
　 친구와 나: 두 (명이에요, 명이세요, 분이에요, 분이세요).

5) 동생:　　　할머니, 컴퓨터가 (있어, 계셔, 있으세요, 계세요)?
　 할머니:　　아니. (없어, 안 계셔, 없으세요, 안 계세요).

6) 동생:　　　지금 할머니 뭐 하고 (있어, 계셔, 있으세요, 계세요)?
　 언니:　　　책을 읽고 (있어, 계셔, 있으세요, 계세요).

Exercise 4. Underline the appropriate expression from the parentheses to complete the sentence.

1) 학생:　　　안녕하세요? (내, 제) 이름은 김유정이라고 합니다.
　 선생님:　　반가워요. (나, 저) 는 박명훈이에요.

2) 학생:　　　똑똑! 김선생님을 (만나러, 뵈러) 왔는데요.
　 김선생님: 아, 나를 (만나러, 뵈러) 왔다고요?

3) 가: 어제 뭐 했어?

  장: 부모님을 (데리고, 모시고) 노래방에 갔어.

  가: 나는 콘서트에 갔어.

  장: 혼자?

  가: 아니, 여자 친구를 (데리고, 모시고) 갔는데 재미있었어.

4) 학생 1: 이거 잘 모르겠는데? 박선생님께 (물어, 물으셔, 여쭤, 여쭈셔) 볼까?

  학생 2: 그러는 게 좋겠다.

Exercise 5. Underline the appropriate form of the verb to complete the sentence.

1) 동생이 저한테 꽃을 (줬어요, 주셨어요, 드렸어요, 드리셨어요).

2) 저는 할머니께 생신 카드를 (줬어요, 주셨어요, 드렸어요, 드리셨어요).

3) 어머니께서 동생한테 용돈을 (줬어요, 주셨어요, 드렸어요, 드리셨어요)

4) 할머니께서 아버지께 용돈을 (줬어요, 주셨어요, 드렸어요, 드리셨어요).

5) 아버지께서 할아버지께 옷을 (줬어요, 주셨어요, 드렸어요, 드리셨어요).

6) 저는 동생한테 전화를 (했어요, 하셨어요, 드렸어요, 드리셨어요).

7) 할머니께서 동생한테 전화를 (했어요, 하셨어요, 드렸어요, 드리셨어요).

8) 어머니께서 할머니께 전화를 (했어요, 하셨어요, 드렸어요, 드리셨어요).

Exercise 6. A student is meeting her teacher for the first time. Make her sentences more polite.

1) 처음 만나요.   _____

2) 이름이 뭐예요?   _____

3) 나이가 몇 살이에요?   _____

4) 집이 어디예요?   _____

5) 만나서 반가워요.   _____

6) 또 만나요.   _____

Exercise 7. Fill in the cells with the appropriate passive forms.

Active	Passive	Active	Passive
보다	보이다	팔다	
닦다		먹다	
듣다		빼앗다	
읽다		나누다	
쓰다		찍다	

Exercise 8. Underline the active or passive verb appropriate for each context.

1) 아이가 강아지를 (봐요, 보여요).

2) 여기서 경치가 잘 안 (봐요, 보여요).

3) 경찰이 길을 (막았어요, 막혔어요).

4) 공사 때문에 길이 (막았어요, 막혔어요).

5) 문이 (닫아서, 닫혀서) 못 들어가요.

6) 가게 문을 (닫았어요, 닫혔어요).

7) 도둑이 개한테 (쫓고 있어요, 쫓기고 있어요).

8) 경찰이 도둑을 (쫓고 있어요, 쫓기고 있어요).

9) 집을 (팔아요, 팔려요).

10) 요즘 이 책이 잘 (팔아요, 팔려요).

11) 불이 (껐어요, 꺼졌어요).

12) 텔레비전을 (껐어요, 꺼졌어요).

13) 준비가 다 (됐어요, 했어요). 나갑시다!

14) 너무 (걱정하지, 걱정되지) 마세요. 다 잘 될 거예요.

Exercise 9. Fill in the blanks with the appropriate passive form using -어 있다, -어지다, -되다 or -게 되다.

1) 강아지가 동생한테 _____ 다. (안다)

2) 친구 집에 갔는데 문이 _____고 아무도 없었다. (닫다)

3) 내 책상 위에는 가족 사진이 _____ 다. (놓다)

4) 갑자기 불이 안 _____ 다. (켜다)

5) 펜이 오래 돼서 잘 안 _____ 다. (쓰다)

6) 창문이 _____ 서 바람이 들어온다. (깨다)

7) 친구가 아파서 약속이 _____ 다. (미루다)

8) 교수님께서 *학회에 가셔서 수업이 _____ 다. (취소하다)   *학회: conference

9) 친구한테서 연락이 없어서 _____ 다. (걱정하다)

10) 전에는 한국어를 못 했는데 열심히 연습해서 _____ 다. (잘하다)

11) 인터넷을 통해서 한국 문화를 많이 _____ 다. (알다)

Exercise 10. Fill in the cells with the appropriate causative forms.

Verb	Passive	Verb	Passive
보다	보이다	쓰다	
눕다		낮다	
마르다		먹다	
벗다		입다	
타다		신다	
끓다		울다	
없다		넓다	

Exercise 11. Fill in the blanks with the appropriate CAUSATIVE version of a verb from the box.

읽다	쓰다	없다	먹다	씻다

1) 아이를 아침 여덟 시에 _____세요.

2) 아이에게 아침하고 점심을 _____세요.

3) 아이에게 책을 _____세요.

4) 밥 먹기 전에 손을 _____세요.

5) 밖에 나갈 때 모자를 _____세요.

깨다	울다	없다	낮다	눕다

6) 아기를 _____지 마세요.

7) 아이를 9시에 침대에 _____세요.

8) 아기가 잘 때 목소리를 _____세요.

9) 아기 옷의 *얼룩을 _____ 주세요.   *얼룩: stain

9.2 Suffixes to Derive Adverbs from Verbs

Exercise 12. Fill in the blanks with the appropriate adverb form. Do <u>not</u> use -게 forms.

1) _____ 드세요. (많다)

2) 버스 시간 다 됐어요. _____나오세요. (빠르다)

3) 누가 내 과자를 _____ 먹었어? (모르다)

4) 공을 너무 _____던지지 마세요. (멀다)

5) 책을 _____ 많이 읽어서 머리가 아파요. (넓다)

6) _____앉으세요. (편하다)

7) _____ 해 주세요. (조용하다)

8) 영화가 _____ 재미있네요. (굉장하다)

Exercise 13. Fill in the blanks with the appropriate -게 form of a descriptive verb from the box.

예쁘다	작다	편하다	힘들다	하얗다

1) 시끄러워요. 음악을 _____ 하세요.

2) 사진 찍을게요. _____ 웃으세요.

3) 너무 놀라서 얼굴이 _____ 됐어요.

4) 할 일이 많아서 _____ 공부했어요.

5) _____ 앉아 계세요.

뜨겁다	행복하다	크다	맛있다	재미있다

6) 그 둘은 서로 _____ 사랑했어요.

7) 방학 때 가족들하고 _____ 지냈어요.

8) 안 들려요. 좀 _____ 말씀하세요.

9) 차린 건 없지만 _____ 드세요.

10) 신데렐라는 왕자님과 _____ 살았어요.

9.3 Intensifying Verbal Prefixes

Exercise 14. Choose the prefix that is commonly used for the given active and descriptive verbs.

짓	헛	치	되	엇/빗	새/샛

1) 빨갛다, 노랗다, 파랗다, 까맣다 _____

2) 나가다 _____

3) 밀다, 솟다 _____

4) 돌이키다, 묻다 _____

5) 살다, 되다 _____

6) 누르다, 밟다 _____

들	덧	엿	뒤	휘

7) 보다, 듣다 _____

8) 감다, 젓다 _____

9) 흔들다, 섞다 _____

10) 끓다, 볶다 _____

11) 나다 _____

9.4 Categories of Verb Suffixes and Their Ordering

Exercise 15. Fill in the blanks using the verb and verbal suffixes provided in parentheses. Pay attention to the order of the verb suffixes.

1) A: 동생이 교통사고가 나서 입원했어요.

   B: 아이고, 걱정이 _____. (많다: 겠, 네, 요, (으)시)

2) A: 네 동생이 시험 공부를 다 했는지 모르겠네.

   B: 다 _____. 너무 걱정 마세요. (하다: 겠, 요, 었, 지)

3) A: 누가 여기에 이걸 놔뒀을까요?

   B: 내 생각에는 선생님께서 _____. (놔두다: 요, 었, (으)ㄹ, (으)시, 것 같다)

4) A: 아직 아무 것도 못 드셨다고요? 뭐라도 좀 _____. (들다: 어야, 요, (으)시, 지)

   B: 생각이 없어요. 나중에 먹을게요.

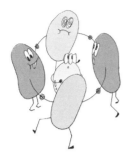

CHAPTER 10

Embedded Sentences

In this final chapter, we'll do more manipulating of verbs, this time to put sentences inside sentences. In chapter 8 you learned how to use a sentence to modify a noun and how to link two sentences end to end, which can also be viewed as sentence embedding. In this chapter we'll be doing two other things: first, changing sentences into noun phrases, and secondly, using sentences, that is, **clauses**, as the objects of verbs like *say*, *think*, *know*, and *wonder*.

By changing sentences into noun phrases we can make sentences like *Eating your vegetables is important* or *The fact that you can sing and chew gum at the same time is interesting to me*, where the underlined portion is a sentence being used as a noun phrase. In Korean, the verb at the end of the embedded sentence needs to be turned into a noun so that we are able to talk about the activity as a THING. And, in order to use a sentence (clause) as the object of verbs like *say* and *think,* the verb at the end of the clause also needs a connector. In both cases we are embedding a sentence by doing something to its verb.

So, the last step of our journey through Korean grammar fundamentals is juggling sentences inside sentences. Without further ado, let's see how that works.

10.1 Making Sentences into Nouns

Verbs can be turned into nouns or they can be used as "temporary" nouns in a sentence to talk about an activity. In English, you can use what's called a **to** **infinitive**: *To do that would be to give up*. Or, you can get an *-ing* **gerund** to do the same work: *Ahhh! Resting helps!* An entire clause can also function as the subject or the object of the larger sentence: *It's comforting that you are my friend* or I forget *that life is as meaningful as you make it*.

There are three suffixes that can make verbs function as nouns in Korean: -는 것 -nun kes, -기 -ki, and -음 -um. Each one has its special usage and nuance.

10.1.1 -는 것 phrases

The most on-the-fly way to make verbs into nouns is with -는 것 -nun kes. (We'll call them -는 거 -nun ke phrases from here on, since you will generally only see 것 kes in formal writings.) The -는 -nun part is an adnominal suffix as you learned about in chapter 8, and 거 ke means *thing*. So, the phrase 네가 읽는 거 neyka ilknun ke means *the thing that you are reading*, or, *what you are reading*. As you know, modified nouns like these can be used as any regular noun would be in a sentence. And you know that the past and future adnominals are expressed with -(으)ㄴ -(u)n and -(으)ㄹ -(u)l, respectively, and descriptive verbs also need -(으)ㄴ -(u)n before adding 거 ke:

네가 보는 거 내 일기장이야.
neyka ponun ke nay ilkicangiya.
The thing that/What you are looking at is my diary.

소영이가 색칠한 것이 예뻐요.
soyengika saykchilhan kesi yeyppeyo.
The thing that/What Soyoung (has) painted is pretty.

은비가 만들 게 뭔지 알아요?
unpika mantul key mwenci alayo?
Do you know what Eunbi is going to make?

> Recall that 것 kes is reduced to 거 ke in spoken Korean (just as in 이거 ike, 그거 kuke, and 저거 ceke), and that it contracts with a following particle:
>
> 거 ke + 은/는 un/nun → 건 ken
> 거 ke + 이/가 i/ka → 게 key
> 거 ke + 을/를 ul/lul → 걸 kel

In fact, 거 ke can be abstract or basically meaningless, functioning just as a place-holder so that the -는 거 -nun ke phrase can be interpreted as (THE FACT) THAT *someone did X*, or just *(the act of) doing X*. Then it can be used as a noun and we can comment on THE ACTION of someone doing something.

날씨가 좋은 게 다행이에요.
nalssika cohun key tahayngieyyo
It's a good thing the weather is nice.

동현이가 똑똑한 것이 확실해요.
tonghyen ttokttokhan kes-i hwaksilhayyo.
I am certain that Donghyun is smart.

네가 책 쓰는 거 몰랐어.
neyka chayk ssunun ke mollasse.
I didn't know about you writing a book./I didn't know that you write books.

우리 아들이 손톱을 **물어 뜯는 것** 때문에 걱정이다.
wuli atuli sonthopul mwule ttutnun kes ttaymwuney kekcengita.
It makes me worry that my son bites his fingernails./My son biting his nails worries me.

(우리) 거기 **가는 거** 어떻게 생각해?
(wuli) keki kanun ke ettehkey sayngkakhay?
What do you think of (us) going there?

문을 **잠그는 걸** 잊어 버렸다.
mwunul camkunun kel ice pelyessta.
I forgot to lock the door.

The activity can be in any tense. You just have to change the adnominal ending before 거 ke:

동생이 엄마한테 자주 **전화하는 게** 확실해.
tongsayngi emmahanthey cacwu cenhwahanun key hwaksilhay.
I am certain that my little brother calls Mom often.

동생이 엄마한테 **전화한 게** 확실해.
tongsayngi emmahanthey cenhwahan key hwaksilhay.
I am certain that my little brother called Mom.

동생이 엄마한테 **전화할 게** 확실해.
tongsayngi emmahanthey cenhwahal key hwaksilhay.
I am certain that my little brother will call Mom.

And, besides specific actions, -는 거 -nun ke phrases can stand for an activity in general:

비타민을 너무 많이 **먹는 건** 안 좋아.
pithaminul nemwu manhi meknun ken an coha.
It is not good (for you) to take too many vitamins./Taking too many vitamins is not good.

말보다 **실천하는 게** 중요하다.
malpota silchenhanun key cwungyohata.
It is more important to act than just to talk. (Literally, *Acting is more important than words.*)

As you can see, -는 거 -nun ke is a composite expression, rather than a simple noun-making suffix, and its function is to make sentences into nouns that we can then comment on, all in one big sentence. It is common to use -는 거 -nun ke phrases with descriptions, like *it is good to*, or *it is odd that* or as objects of verbs like 보다 pota *see* and 잊어버리다 icepelita *forget to*. Also notice that they translate sometimes with infinitives (*to do*) and sometimes with gerunds (*doing*).

In addition, there are idiomatic usages of -는 거 -nun ke phrases, some of which we introduce below.

(1) Witnessing the act

-는 거 -nun ke phrases are used as the object of sense verbs, like 보다 pota *see* and 듣다 tutta *hear* to talk about seeing or hearing something happen. When the present tense -는 거 -nun ke is used in these cases, the action is seen or heard IN PROGRESS. If a past tense -은 거 -un ke is used, it means *that someone HAD DONE X.*

동생이 **넘어지는 거** 봤어?
tongsayngi nemecinun ke pwasse?
Did you see your brother fall down?

동생이 **넘어진 거** 못 봤어?
tongsayngi nemecin ke mos pwasse?
Didn't you see that your brother had fallen down?

네가 **노래 부르는 거** 들었어.
neyka nolay pwulunun ke tulesse.
I heard you singing.

(2) Clarifying what exactly it is that is happening

-는 거 -nun ke phrases are used with 이다 ita to ask for and offer CLARIFICATION of what is being done, something like *what is it that …?* or, with more emotion, *excuse me, but what exactly (are you doing??).* It can be in any style with any attitude ending:

코트는 왜 **벗는 거**예요? 지금 나가는데.
khothunun way pesnun keyeyyo? cikum nakanuntey.
Why are you taking your coat off? We're leaving now.

내 방에서 뭐 **하는 거야**?
nay pangeyse mwe hanun keya?
What exactly is it that you are doing in my room?

내 책 **찾는 건데**.
nay chayk chacnun kentey.
I'm looking for my book. (Is there a problem?)

(3) Explaining what you're supposed to do, the way it's done

-는 거다 -nun keta can also mean *you're supposed to.* You can think of this usage as meaning *it's the done thing* (that is, *the thing that is done*) or, you can think of it as an extension of the clarification usage (*what you do is* or *what you're supposed to do is*).

집에 들어갈 때 신발을 **벗는 거**예요.
cipey tulekal ttay sinpalul pesnun keyeyyo.
You are supposed to take your shoes off as you enter a home.

장: 이거 어떻게 **하는 거야**?
cang: ike ettehkey hanun keya?
Chang: *How is one supposed to do this? (Clarify it for me.)*

최: **그렇게 하는 거** 아냐. 나한테 좀 줘 봐.
choy: kulehke hanun ke anya. nahanthey com cwe pwa.
Choi: *That is not how you do it/how it is done. Give it to me/let me see.*

팀: 한국 배는 껍질도 **먹는 거야**?
thim: hankwuk paynun kkepcilto meknun keya?
Tim: *Can I eat a Korean pear with the skin on? (Clarify it for me.)*

민: 아니야. 배 껍질은 **먹는 게** 아니야.
min: aniya. pay kkepcilun meknun key aniya.
Min: *No, you're not supposed to eat pear skin.*

10.1.2 Turning verbs into nouns with -기

Another way to make verbs into nouns is by suffixing -기 -ki onto a verb root: for example, 듣기 tutki *listening* and 읽기 ilkki *reading*. The same suffix -기 -ki can also be found in nouns such as 크기 khuki *size* from 크다 khuta *big* and concrete item nouns such as 쓰레받기 ssuleypatki *dustpan* and 돋보기 totpoki *magnifying/reading glasses*.

Here are some more examples of -기 -ki nouns.

Dictionary Form	-기 -ki Form
읽다 ilkta *to read*	읽기 ilkki *reading*
쓰다 ssuta *to write*	쓰기 ssuki *writing*
듣다 tutta *to listen*	듣기 tutki *listening*
말하다 malhata *to speak*	말하기 malhaki *speaking*
달리다 tallita *to run*	달리기 talliki *running*
뛰다 ttwita *to hop, jump*	뛰기 ttwiki *jumping*
더하다 tehata *to add*	더하기 tehaki *addition*
빼다 ppayta *to take out*	빼기 ppayki *subtraction*
크다 khuta *to grow; big*	크기 khuki *size*
밝다 ppalkta *bright*	밝기 ppalkki *brightness*
빠르다 ppaluta *fast*	빠르기 paluki *speed*
세다 seyta *strong*	세기 seyki *strength*

While both -기 -ki and -는 거 -nun ke phrases are sometimes translated as *doing* X, -는 거 -nun ke phrases are more often used to talk about a WHOLE EVENT. Nouns derived via -기 -ki suffixation, on the other hand, are more noun-like; they refer to activities as THINGS in a sense, and they are not always translated with *-ing*, as you can see in the chart above.

Here are some example sentences to give you a sense of how the activities are talked about as nouns when suffixed with -기 -ki:

집의 **크기**는 위치에 비해 중요하지 않다.
cipuy khukinun wichiey pihay cwungyohaci anhta.
The size of a house is not as important as its location.

외국어를 배우려면 **쓰기**와 **말하기**를 연습해야 합니다.
oykwukelul paywulyemyen ssukiwa malhakilul yensuphayya hapnita.
To learn a foreign language, you need to practice writing and speaking.

더하기, 빼기, 곱하기, 나누기를 배운다.
tehaki, ppayki, kophaki, nanwukilul paywunta.
We learn <u>addition</u>, <u>subtraction</u>, <u>multiplication</u>, and <u>division</u>.

밥 먹고 바로 **달리기**를 시작하는 건 힘들 거예요.
pap mekko palo tallikilul sicakhanun ken himtul keyeyyo.
It will be difficult to start with <u>running</u> right after you eat.

걷기부터 해 보세요.
ketkipwuthe hay poseyyo.
You should start with <u>walking</u>.

While -는 거 -nun ke clauses often refer to activities that take place in the real world (e.g. *that someone does/did something*), -기 -ki nouns focus on an activity IN THE ABSTRACT (*doing X*) or with a PROSPECTIVE sense (*to do X*). For example, -기 -ki nouns are used in making lists of activities, especially in planning. Suppose that you are writing a To-Do list or your resolutions for the New Year; in Korean, the list would look like this:

1. 하루에 30분씩 운동하기   *(to) Exercise 30 minutes per day*
   halwuey 30pwunssik wuntonghaki

2. 매일 한국어 연습하기   *Practice Korean*
   mayil hankwuke yensuphaki

3. 몸에 좋은 음식 먹기   *Eat healthy food*
   momey cohun umsik mekki

There are also a number of ready-made -기 -ki expressions that are common and easy to use. Many of them show the prospective feel of -기 -ki nouns. You saw -기 전에 -ki ceney *before* and -기 때문에 -ki ttaymwuney *because* as set expressions in a previous chapter, for example. Since the -기 -ki suffix usually ANTICIPATES, it does not tend to attach after the past tense -었 -ess (except for the idiomatic -었기 때문에 -esski ttaymwuney).

(1) -기(가) + FEELING: *It is easy to do; doing is easy*

-기 -ki phrases are used with several descriptive verbs that denote the subject's emotion or opinion about the activity: *...ing is easy/hard/important* or *It is easy/hard/important to ...*. In these cases, the subject particle -이/가 -i/ka can be used after the -기 -ki phrase.
    The most common descriptive verbs used in these constructions are:

-기 쉽다 -ki swipta *easy*	-기 편하다 -ki phyenhata *comfortable*
-기 어렵다/힘들다 -ki elyepta/himtulta *difficult*	-기 싫다 -ki silhta *don't like/want*
-기 좋다 -ki cohta *good*	-기 편리하다 -ki phyenlihata *convenient*
-기 나쁘다 -ki napputa *bad, inconvenient*	
-기 불편하다 -ki pwulphyenhata *uncomfortable/inconvenient*	

Here are some -기 -ki examples in sentences:

여기가 **살기(가)** 좋은 동네예요.
yekika salki(ka) cohun tongneyyeyyo.
This is a neighborhood that is good to live in.

한글은 **배우기 쉽다.**
hankulun paywuki swipta.
It is easy to learn the Korean alphabet.

헬멧을 안 쓰면 **다치기 쉽다.**
heylmeysul an ssumyen tachiki swipta.
It is easy to get hurt if you don't wear a helmet.
(You are likely to get hurt if you don't wear a helmet.)

이런 거 요즘 **보기 어려워요.**
ilen ke yocum poki elyeweyo.
It's hard to spot stuff like this these days.

신기 편하면 그 신발 가져도 좋아.
sinki phyenhamyen ku sinpal kacyeto coha.
If you find them comfortable to wear, you can have those shoes.

채소 **먹기 싫어?**
chayso mekki silhe?
You don't want to eat vegetables?

-기 -ki phrases can also be used with the active verbs 좋아하다 cohahata *like* and 싫어하다 silhehata *dislike*. The object particle -을/-를 -ul/-lul is used on the -기 -ki phrase in these cases.

동생은 **노래하기(를) 좋아해요.**
tongsayngun nolayhaki(lul) cohahayyo.
My younger sibling likes to sing.

저 친구는 **물에 들어가기(를) 싫어해서** 수영 안 해.
ce chinkwunun mwuley tulekaki(lul) silhehayse swuyeng an hay.
He does not like (to get in the) water, so he does not swim.

(2) -기 위해(서)/위하여 *in order to; for the purpose of*

Remember -을/-를 위해(서) -ul/-lul wihay(se) *for* that you learned in chapter 4?

너를 위해 준비했어.
nelul wihay cwunpihaysse.
I prepared (this) for you.

It can be used with a -기 -ki clause as well.

건강해지기 위해 하는 운동
kenkanghayciki wihay hanun wuntong
Exercise that I do for becoming healthy

먹기 위해 삽니까, **살기 위해** 먹습니까?
mekki wihay sapnikka, salki wihay meksupnikka?
Do we live in order to eat or eat to live?

(3) -기(를) 시작하다 *start to, begin to*

-기(를) 시작하다 -ki(lul) sicakhata means *start to/begin to*:

친구가 갑자기 **울기 시작했다.**
chinkwuka kapcaki wulki sicakhayssta.
My friend suddenly started to cry.

열다섯 살 때부터 커피를 **마시기 시작했어요.**
yeltases sal ttaypwuthe khephilul masiki sicakhaysseyo.
I started drinking coffee when I was fifteen years old.

(4) -기(를) 바라다/원하다 *hope that; someone wishes to; want someone to*

-기(를) 바라다 ki(lul) palata and -기(를) 원하다 -ki(ul) wenhata mean *hope that* or *wish to*. Unlike -(으)면 좋겠다 -(u)myen cohkeyssta, which can only express the speaker's own wishes that are beyond her control, -기(를) 바라다 -ki(lul) palata and -기(를) 원하다 -ki(ul) wenhata express someone else's desires as well:

건강하시기(를) 바랍니다.
kenkanghasiki(lul) palapnita.
I wish for your health/I hope you are well.

저희 결혼식에 참석해 **주시길 바랍니다.**
cehuy kyelhonsikey chamsekhay cwusikil palapnita.
I hope that you can come to our wedding.

나는 내 남동생이 미국에서 **공부하길 원한다.**
nanun nay namtongsayngi mikwukeyse kongpwuhakil wenhanta.
I want my younger brother to study in the United States.

내 남동생은 영국에서 **공부하길 원한다/바란다.**
nay namtongsayngun yengkwukeyse kongpwuhakil wenhanta/palanta.
My younger brother wants to/hopes to study in the U.K.

The past tense suffix -었 -ess can be used with -기 바라다 -ki palata to express hopes for another person's recent/past states.

행복했기(를) 바란다.
hayngpokhaysski(lul) palanta.
I hope that you have been happy.

좋은 시간 **보내셨기(를) 바랍니다.**
cohun sikan ponaysyesski(lul) palapnita.
I hope you (have) had a good time.

(5) -기로 하다 *decide to*

-기 -ki phrases are also used to talk about deciding and promising to do something: -기로 하다 -kilo hata, -기로 결심하다 -kilo kyelsimhata, and -기로 정하다 -kilo cenghata mean *to decide to do something*, where -기로 (정)하다 -kilo (ceng)hata emphasizes an agreed upon decision, and -기로 결심하다 -kilo kyelsimhata a personal determination. -기로 약속하다 -kilo yaksokhata means *to promise to do something*.

그럼 다음 주에 여기서 **만나기로 해요**.
kulem taum cwuey yekise mannakilo hayyo.
Let's (decide to) meet here next week.

내일부터 열심히 **운동하기로 결심했어요**.
nayilpwuthe yelsimhi wuntonghakilo kyelsimhaysseyo.
I have made up my mind/am determined to exercise hard starting from tomorrow.

친구와 주말에 등산 **가기로 약속했다**.
chinkwuwa cwumaley tungsan kakilo yaksokhayssta.
I promised my friend that we will go on a hike this weekend.

(6) -기에 *this is (too …) to do*

Another -기 -ki expression allows you to describe a noun as *too big/small/old/difficult*, or *just right*, etc. *to do*:

지금 시험 공부 **시작하기에** 너무 늦었다! 시험이 한 시간밖에 안 남았잖아.
cikum sihem kongpwu sicakhakiey nemwu nucessta! sihemi han sikanpakkey an namasscanha.
It (now) is too late <u>to start studying</u> for the exam; the exam is in an hour.

이 재킷은 결혼식에 **입고 가기에는** 너무 낡았다.
i caykhisun kyelhonsikey ipko kakieynun nemwu nalkassta.
This jacket is too old and tatty <u>to wear</u> to the wedding.

여섯 살이면 집에 **혼자 두기에** 너무 어려.
yeses salimyen cipey honca twukiey nemwu elye.
A six year old kid is too young <u>to leave</u> alone at home.

이 숟가락은 아이스크림 **먹기에** 딱 맞아.
i swutkalakun aisukhulim mekkiey ttak maca.
This spoon is just right <u>for eating</u> ice cream with.

(7) -기는 -지만/는데 *well, it is like that/does do that, but*

One last expression to introduce here that uses a -기 -ki clause is one that gives a concession (*well, that's true*), before proceeding with a counterpoint (*but…*). It is often used in response to a question or challenge. The verb first shows up with -기 -ki and topic marker -는 -nun and then repeated again with either -지만 -ciman or -(으)ㄴ데/-는데 -(u)ntey/-nuntey. With active verbs, it means something like, *as for doing that, (I)* DID *it but*. -기 -ki always attaches to a present tense verb, while the verb with -지만 -ciman or -(으)ㄴ데/는데 -(u)ntey/nuntey can be in any tense.

영재: 그 안내서를 읽었어, 안 읽었어?
yengcay: ku annayselul ilkesse, an ilkesse?
Youngjae: *Did you read the instructions or not??*

준호: **읽기는 읽었는데** 되게 복잡하더라.
cwunho: ilkkinun ilkessnuntey toykey pokcaphatela.
Junho: *Well, I* DID READ *them, but they were very complicated.*

With descriptive verbs, it translates better as, *well, it* IS *(pretty), but*:

내가 준 선물 괜찮아? 예쁘지?
nayka cwun senmwul kwaynchanha? yeyppuci?
Do you like my gift? It's pretty, isn't it?

예쁘기는 예쁜데 내 스타일이 아니야. 미안.
yeyppukinun yeyppuntey nay suthaili aniya. mian.
Yes, it IS *pretty, but it's not my style. Sorry.*

하다 hata can be used before -지만 -ciman or -(으)ㄴ데/-는데 -(u)ntey/-nuntey instead of repeating the same verb:

선물 걔한테 줬어?
senmwul kyayhanthey cwesse?
Did you give him/her the gift?

주기는 했는데 걔가 안 열어 보더라.
cwukinun hayssnuntey kyayka an yele potela.
I gave it to him/her, but she/he didn't open it.

10.1.3 Turning verbs to nouns with -(으)ㅁ

There is one more suffix, -(으)ㅁ -(u)m, that is used to convert verbs into nouns. This pattern is more restricted. You can think of it as mainly a name-maker, as -(으)ㅁ -(u)m nouns are the MOST NOUN-Y and LEAST VERB-LIKE of the three noun-maker endings. -(으)ㅁ -(u)m nouns often name the PRODUCT of an action as opposed to talking about an event or activity itself:

Verb Dictionary Form	-(으)ㅁ Noun
살다 salta *to live*	삶 salm *life*
죽다 cwukta *to die*	죽음 cwukum *death*
웃다 wusta *to laugh*	웃음 wusum *a smile, a laugh*
울다 wulta *to cry*	울음 wulum *a cry*
믿다 mitta *to trust*	믿음 mitum *trust*
얼다 elta *to freeze*	얼음 elum *ice*

Verb Dictionary Form	-(으)ㅁ Noun
자다 cata *to sleep*	잠 cam *sleep*
꾸다 kkwuta *to dream*	꿈 kkwum *a dream*
추다 chwuta *to dance*	춤 chwum *a dance*
기쁘다 kipputa *happy*	기쁨 kippum *joy, happiness*
슬프다 sulphuta *sad*	슬픔 sulphum *sadness*
아프다 aphuta *to hurt*	아픔 aphum *pain*

Here are some examples with a little more context:

삶과 **죽음** *life and death*
salmkwa cwukum

믿음, 사랑, 소망 *faith, love, and hope*
mitum, salang, somang

아이들의 **웃음** 소리 *the sound of children's laughter*
aituluy wusum soli

아기가 **잠**이 들었다.
akika cami tulessta.
The baby fell asleep.

아이의 **울음** 소리가 크게 들렸다.
aiuy wulum solika khukey tullyessta.
I could hear the child's loud crying.

Redundant as it may seem, some of these nouns are used doubled up with their base verbs:

잠을 **잤**어요.
camul casseyo.
I slept.

꿈을 **꾸**었습니다.
kkwumul kkwuesssupnita.
I dreamed (a dream).

그림을 **그렸**어요.
kulimul kulyesseyo.
I drew a picture.

얼음이 **얼**었어요.
elumi elesseyo.
Ice has frozen up.

그림자가 촛불에 **춤**을 **추**고 있다.
kulimcaka chospwuley chwumul chwuko issta.
The shadow is dancing in the candlelight.

In written and somewhat bookish Korean, the -(으)ㅁ -(u)m suffix may also mark a clause whose nature is "truth revealing." In this usage, the function of -(으)ㅁ -(u)m is more verbal and the verb can be marked with -었 -ess:

그가 말한 모든 것이 **거짓이었음**이 들통났다.
kuka malhan motun kesi kecisiessumi tulthongnassta.
It has been revealed that everything he said was a lie.

그가 **떠났음**이 확실했다.　＝　그가 **떠난 것**이 확실했다.
kuka ttenassumi hwaksilhayssta.　　　kuka ttenan kesi hwaksilhayssta.
It was clear that he had left.　　　*It was clear that he had left.*

10.1.4 Fine-tuning -기 vs. -(으)ㅁ

The reason a -기 -ki noun could not have been used in the previous set of examples is that -기 -ki nouns typically have a prospective or future sense to them. If you think back on the expressions from this section, you might see that nuance (e.g., -기 전에 -ki ceney *before doing*, -기로 하다 -kilo hata *decide to do*, -기(를) 바라다 ki(lul) palata *hope to do*). We also mentioned that -기 -ki clauses are about the ACTIVITY and -(으)ㅁ -(u)m clauses about the PRODUCT. One manifestation of that nuance distinction is that -기 -ki forms are used to talk about actions that should be done or are planned for the future, whereas -(으)ㅁ -(u)m forms are used for actions that have been completed when making lists. Remember that a To-Do list would use -기 -ki words, like this:

1. 30 분 **운동하기** *Exercise 30 minutes*
   30 pwun wuntonghaki

2. 한국어 **연습하기** *Practice Korean*
   hankwuke yensuphaki

3. 방 청소**하기** *Clean the room*
   pang chengsohaki

Suppose that, in the evening, you reflect on your day. You would write a note or diary entry like this:

1. 아침에 30분 **운동함** *Exercised 30 minutes in the morning*
   achimey 30 pwun wuntongham

2. 한 시간 동안 한국어 **연습함** *Practiced Korean for an hour*
   han sikan tongan hankwuke yensupham

3. 방 **청소함** *Cleaned the room*
   pang chengsoham

Note that there is no past tense in the -(으)ㅁ -(u)m forms, they just have a more completed or product-like connotation.

In sum, -는 거 -nun ke clauses are the most verb-like, as if making a sentence into a noun on-the-fly just so that it can be used as the object of a verb or subject of the sentence, referring to an event. -기 -ki nouns are more noun-like ways of talking about an activity to engage in, and -음 -um nouns are the most noun-like, most permanent and concrete in referring to the PRODUCT of actions in many cases.

10.2 Sentences as Objects of Saying and Thinking Verbs

The content of what someone *says, thinks, knows, wonders,* or *assumes* is usually a sentence introduced by *that* in English. It works the same way for all these verbs: *I said that I will be going to the party, I know that there was a lot of food, and I doubted that his reputation would hold up forever.* In Korean, these embedded sentences (the underlined parts) are said quite differently.

In the first section below, we'll talk about quoting what someone says. These are called **reportative** forms. Then we'll get into thinking, knowing and assuming, which are all a bit different. The last section will be about embedded questions, where someone wonders, knows or doesn't know *who, what,* or *where.* Let's see how it all works.

10.2.1 Direct quotation: *She said, and I quote, "..."*

When you want to relay information that you have heard or read, one way to do this is by repeating it exactly, as a **direct quotation**. The original sentence the person said or wrote is transferred AS IS with its punctuation marks and all. In Korean, the quoted part is connected via -(이)라고 -(i)lako to a verb of saying, telling, etc.

그 사람은 "누가 방에 있어요?" 라고 물었습니다.
ku salamun "nwuka pangey isseyo?" lako mwulesssupnita.
That person asked, "Who is in the room?"

나는 "아무도 없습니다" 라고 대답했습니다.
nanun "amwuto epssupnita" lako taytaphaysssupnita.
I answered, "There is nobody."

소년은 심심하면 "늑대야!" 라고 소리치곤 했어요.
sonyenun simsimhamyen "nuktayya!" lako solichikon haysseyo.
The boy would cry out "Wolf!" whenever he was bored.

메모에는 "여섯 시 도착" 이라고 쓰여 있었다.
meymoeynun "yeses si tochak" ilako ssuye issessta.
It said on the memo, "Six o'clock arrival."

이 i of -(이)라고 -(i)lako is used when the quoted part ends in a consonant, and it is dropped if the quoted part ends in a vowel. Although -(이)라고 -(i)lako is usually used after the quoted sentence, 하고 hako is another option especially after onomatopoeia (words that mimic a sound or movement, like *whoosh*). There is no space before -(이)라고 -(i)lako, but there is a space before 하고 hako, which can only appear in the present tense (not 했고 hayssko):

옆 방에서 "쾅!" 하고 소리가 났어요.
yeph pangeyse "khwang!" hako solika nasseyo.
There was a loud "bang!" in the next room.

아이는 "엉엉" 하고 울었습니다.
ainun "engeng" hako wulesssupnita.
The kid wept loudly with a "boo-hoo."

The main verbs used in direct quotation should be about saying and writing, right? The most common ones include the following verbs:

> 하다 hata *to say*, 말하다/얘기하다 malhata/yaykihata *to talk/speak*, 묻다/물어 보다 mwutta/mwule pota *to ask*, 대답하다 taytaphata *to answer*, 듣다 tutta *to hear*, 소리치다 so-lichita *to shout/cry*, 쓰다 ssuta *to write*, 쓰여 있다 ssuye issta *to be written*, and 그러다 kuleta *to say so*.

10.2.2 Communicating what is said or heard

You can also choose to transmit information without directly quoting, and using words somewhat different from what the original speaker or writer used. By doing so, you are **indirectly quoting** the person, using **reportative** forms:

그 사람은 누가 방에 있느**냐고** 물었습니다.
ku salamun nwuka pangey issnunyako mwulesssupnita.
That person asked who was in the room.

나는 아무도 없**다고** 대답했어요.
nanun amwuto epstako taytaphaysseyo.
I answered that nobody was there.

When you indirectly quote someone in Korean, the connector to use depends on whether the original utterance was a statement, question, command or suggestion (the parts in bold in the examples above). There are also **contracted (shortened)** forms for the end of the sentence, the *he said* part. Let's look at the full, uncontracted forms first.

(1) Indirect quotation: full forms

Imagine the following chat message.

친구: 숙제 했어?
chinkwu: swukcey haysse?
Friend: *Did you finish your homework?*

나: 아니, 아직 못 했는데.
na: ani, acik mos hayssenuntey.
Me: *No, I didn't yet.*

친구: 그럼 같이 숙제하자.
chinkwu: kulem kathi swukceyhaca.
Friend: *If that's the case, let's do it together.*

나: 저녁에 전화해.
na: cenyekey cenhwahay.
Me: *Call me this evening.*

친구: 8시쯤 전화할게.
chinkwu: 8siccum cenhwahalkey.
Friend: *I will call you around eight o'clock.*

Then this is how "나" would write a journal entry reporting on the chat:

…친구가 숙제를 다 했냐고 물어서 나는 아직 못 했다고 대답했다. 그랬더니 같이 숙제하자고 했다. 그래서 친구보고 저녁에 전화하라고 했다. 친구는 8시쯤 전화하겠다고 했다…

…chinkwuka swukceylul ta hayssnyako mwulese nanun acik mos haysstako taytaphayssta. kulaysseni kathi swukceyhacako hayssta. kulayse chinkwupoko cenyekey cenhwahalako hayssta. chinkwunun yetelpsiccum cenhwahakeysstako hayssta…

My friend <u>asked if</u> I had finished my homework, so I <u>said that</u> I had not finished it yet. Then, he <u>suggested that</u> we do homework together, so <u>told him to</u> call me tonight. My friend <u>said he would</u> call me around eight.

Did you notice the different connectors used and how the TENSE of the quoted part stays the same? Where the friend asked 숙제했어? swukcey haysse?, the indirect quotation is 숙제 했냐고 swukcey hayssnyako, and where the friend said 전화할게 cenhwahalkey, the indirect quote says 전화하겠다고 cenhwahakeysstako. (Here, the form changes from -(으)ㄹ게 -(u)lkey to -겠다 -keyssta, but the tense is still future.)

Any endings that express speaker attitudes, such as -지 -ci, -네 -ney and -군 -kwun, -(으)ㄹ게 -(u)lkey and -(으)ㄹ래 -(u)llay, and formality endings such as -어요 -eyo and -습니다 -supnita, are NOT included in indirect quotation.

If the subject of the quoted sentence is first person, then the reflexive pronoun 자기 caki *oneself, one's own* will be used in the indirect quotation. Also, although there are more specific verbs of speaking (and writing) that can be used as the main verb in these sentences, the verb 하다 hata *to say* is the most convenient one:

내 친구가 "제 이름은 세영이에요"라고 말했다.
nay chinkwuka "cey ilumun seyyengieyyo"lako malhayssta.
My friend said, "My name is Seyoung."

→ 내 친구가 **자기** 이름은 세영**이라고 했다**.
nay chinkwuka caki ilumun seyyengilako hayssta.
My friend said that her name was Seyoung.

To get started on the how-to, let's preview the connector forms:

- **Statements** connect with -ㄴ다고/-는다고/-다고 -ntako/-nuntako/-tako
- **Questions** connect with -(느)냐고 -(nu)nyako
- **Commands** connect with -(으)라고 -(u)lako
- **Suggestions** connect with -자고 -cako
- **Requests** for something use a special verb 달라고 하다 tallako hata; requests for a service or favor: use -어/아 달라고 하다 -e/a tallako hata

The statement connectors are the plain speech style endings plus -고 -ko. The connector for commands is the writer's usage command ending plus -고 -ko, and the others are the same as the babysitter's usage. We add **requests** to this list because they require a special verb when quoting them.

Now let's look more closely at each sentence type.

<1> Reporting statements with -(ㄴ/는)다고

When reporting statements, the verb is conjugated for the -ㄴ다/는다/다 -nta/nunta/ta form you learned as the plain style sentence ending in chapter 7, and then -고 -ko completes the connector as -ㄴ다고/는다고/다고 -ntako/nuntako/tako. Like the sentence ending pattern, -ㄴ다고 -ntako is used after active verbs that end in vowels, -는다고 -nuntako after active verbs that end in consonants, and -다고 -tako after descriptive verbs and the past tense -었 -ess. Any verb of saying or telling a statement can be used as the main verb.

Like they do with other suffixes, 이다 ita becomes -(이)라고 -(i)lako, and -(으)ㄹ 거 다 -(u)l keta becomes -(으)ㄹ 거라고 -(u)l kelako. Also, don't forget that ㄹ drops out before -ㄴ다고 -ntako and -는다고 -nuntako. Let's look at some examples of indirect quotation:

학생: "죄송합니다. 보고서를 다 끝내지 못 했습니다."
haksayng: "coysonghapnita. pokoselul ta kkuthnayci mos haysssupnita."
Student: *"I'm sorry, I have not been able to finish my report."*

→ 학생이 보고서를 다 끝내지 못 **했다고 대답했다**.
haksayngi pokoselul ta kkuthnayci mos haysstako taytaphaysta.
The student answered that he could not finish his report.

교수님: "월요일에 시험을 볼 거예요."
kyoswunim: "welyoiley sihemul pol keyeyyo."
Professor: *"Yes, there will be a test on Monday."*

→ 교수님께서 월요일에 시험을 **볼 거라고 말씀하셨습니다**.
kyoswunimkkeyse welyoiley sihemul pol kelako malssumhasyesssupnita.
The professor told me there will/would be a test on Monday.

소개팅에서 만난 사람: "저는 고기를 잘 먹습니다."
sokaythingeyse mannan salam: "cenun kokilul cal meksupnita."
Blind date: *"Yes, I do eat meat."*

→ 소개팅에서 만난 사람이 나한테 자기는 고기를 잘 **먹는다고 말했다**.
sokaythingeyse mannan salami nahanthey cakinun kokilul cal meknuntako malhaysta.
My blind date said that she/he did eat meat.

소개팅에서 만난 사람: "우리 집은 아주 큽니다."
sokaythingeyse mannan salam: "wuli cipun acwu khupnita."
Blind date: *"My house is quite large."*

→ 소개팅에서 만난 사람이 나한테 자기 집이 아주 **크다고 말했어**.
sokaythingeyse mannan salami nahanthey caki cipi acwu khutako malhaysse.
My blind date said his/her house was very big.

As we mentioned, the tense of what was said remains the same in quoting, and tense is indicated in the connector. But attitude endings like -지 -ci, -네 -ney, -군 -kwun, and speech style endings are not communicated; that is, **final endings** are not quoted. **Prefinal endings**, however, are included.

어머니: "제주도는 경치가 정말 아름답**네**."
emeni: "ceycwutonun kyengchika cengmal alumtapne."
Mother: *"The scenery on Jeju Island is beautiful!"*

→ 어머니께서 제주도는 경치가 정말 **아름답다고 말씀하셨다**.
emenikkeyse ceycwutonun kyengchika cengmal alumtaptako malssumhasyessta.
My mother said that the scenery on Jeju Island is really beautiful.

이웃집 사람: "그 고양이가 제 고양이가 아니었**군요**."
iwuscip salam: "ku koyangika cey koyangika aniesskwunyo."
Neighbor: *"I see that that cat was not mine."*

→ 이웃집 사람이 그 고양이가 자기 집 고양이가 **아니었다고 했다**.
iwuscip salami ku koyangika caki cip koyangika aniesstako hayssta.
The neighbor said the cat was not hers.

친구: "소개팅에서 만난 사람이 그 대학에 다니**던데**."
chinkwu: "sokaythingeyse mannan salami ku tayhakey tanitentey."
Friend: *"I found out the person I met at the blind date goes to that university."*

→ 친구가 나한테 자기가 소개팅에서 만난 사람이 그 대학에 **다니더라고
했습니다**.
chinkwuka nahanthey cakika sokaythingeyse mannan salami ku tayhakey tanitelako haysssupnita.
My friend told me she found out that the person she met at the blind date goes to that university.

<2> Reporting questions with -(느)냐고/(으)냐고

When reporting someone's question, -느냐고 -nunyako or, more commonly, -냐고 -nya-ko is added to the dictionary form root of active verbs, and -(으)냐고 -(u)nyako to the dictionary form root of descriptive verbs; ㄹ drops out of any ㄹ-final verbs. For past tense, -었(느)냐고 -ess(nu)nyako and for future, -(으)ㄹ 거냐고 -(u)l kenyako is used.

소개팅에서 만난 사람: "고기 드십니까?"
sokaythingeyse mannan salam: "koki tusipnikka?"
Blind date: *"So, do you eat meat?"*

→   소개팅에서 만난 사람이 나한테 고기를 먹**냐고 물었어**.
sokaythingeyse mannan salami nahanthey kokilul meknyako mwulesse.
My blind-date asked me if I eat meat.

나: "연세 대학교 근처에 살지요?"
na: "yensey tayhakkyo kuncheey salciyo?"
Me: *"Don't you live near Yonsei University?"*

→   나는 소개팅에서 만난 사람에게 연세대학교 근처에 사**냐고 물었다.**
nanun sokaythingeyse mannan salameykey yenseytayhakkyo kuncheey sanyako mwulessta.
I asked my blind date if he lived near Yonsei University.

교수님: "보고서를 언제 낼 거예요?"
kyoswunim: "pokoselul encey nayl keyeyyo?"
Professor: *"When will you submit your report?"*

→   교수님께서 학생에게 보고서를 언제 낼 거**냐고 물으셨다.**
kyoswunimkkeyse haksayngeykey pokoselul encey nayl kenyako mwulusyessta.
The professor asked the student when she would submit her report.

Quotation also works even if what you want to quote has not yet been said—that is, when asking questions or talking about things to be said in the future with the main verb conjugated in the future tense.

어머니께 제주도는 경치가 어떠**냐고 여쭤봐야겠다.**
emenikkey ceycwutonun kyengchika ettenyako yeccwe pwayakessta.
I should ask Mother what the scenery on Jeju Island is like.

이웃집 사람에게 저 고양이가 누구 고양이**냐고 물어 볼래.**
iwuscip salameykey ce koyangika nwukwu koyanginyako mwule pollay.
I wanna ask my neighbor whose cat that is.

<3> Reporting suggestions & proposals with -자고

To report a *let's* suggestion someone made, attach -자고 -cako to the dictionary form root of the verb they used. Of course, this connector doesn't work with past or future forms—it wouldn't make sense (*Let's went? Let's will go?*). If you think about it, there are many other ways to express suggestions or proposals in English. That means that the Korean connector may work for more cases than you may first think.

언니: "오늘 밤 영화 보자."
enni: "onul pam yenghwa poca."
Older sister: "Let's see a movie tonight!"

→ 언니가 오늘 밤에 영화를 보**자고 했습니다.**
ennika onul pamey yenghwalul pocako haysssupnida.
Older sister suggested that we go see a movie tonight.

부장님: "이제 회의를 끝냅시다."
pwucangnim: "icey hoyuylul kkuthnaypsita."
Manager: "Let's wrap up the meeting."

→ 부장님은 사원들에게 이제 그 사안에 관한 회의를 끝내**자고 제안하셨습니다.**
pwucangnimun sawentuleykey icey ku saaney kwanhan hoyuylul kkuthnaycako cheyanhasyesssupnida.
The manager proposed to the employees that they wrap up the meeting on that issue.

소개팅에서 만난 남자: "같이 걸을까요?"
sokaythingeyse mannan namca: "kathi kelulkkayo?"
Blind date: "*Shall we walk?*"

→ 소개팅에서 만난 사람이 나한테 같이 걷**자고 했어**.
   sokaythingeyse mannan salami nahanthey kathi ketcako haysse.
   My blind date wanted to walk together.

어머니: "이번 주말에 캠핑 가지 말자!"
emeni: "ipen cwumaley khaymphing kaci malca!"
Mother: "*Let's not go camping this weekend.*"

→ 어머니께서 이번 주말에 캠핑 가지 말**자고 하셨어요**.
   emenikkeyse ipen cwumaley khaymphing kaci malcako hasyesseyo.
   Mom says we should not/suggests that we not go camping this weekend.

<4> Reporting commands with -(으)라고

To report about how someone told someone else to do something, or made a command, you can use the connector -(으)라고 -(u)lako on the dictionary form root (be careful not to get the -(으)라고 -(u)lako form confused with the -어라 -ela ending), and then finish with the main verb (이야기)하다 (iyaki)hata or 말하다 malhata *to say*, 명령하다 myenglyenghata *to order*, 요구하다 yokwuhata *to demand*, or 권하다 kwenhata *to gently urge, recommend*. Of course, commands do not have past or future tense. To indicate who was told the command, you have the option to use the particles -더러 -tele and -보고 -poko in addition to -한테 -hanthey and -에게 -eykey:

언니: "이 영화 봐라."
enni: "i yenghwa pwala."
Older sister: "*Watch this movie!*"

→ 언니가 나**보고** 그 영화를 보**라고 했다**.
   ennika nahapoko ku yenghwalul polako hayssta.
   Older Sister told me to watch that movie.

부장님: "이제 회의를 끝내세요."
pwucangnim: "icey hoyuylul kkuthnayseyyo."
Manager: "*Now, wrap up the meeting.*"

→ 부장님은 사원들**에게** 이제 회의를 끝내**라고 지시하셨다**.
   pwucangnimun sawentuleykey icey hoyuylul kkuthnaylako cisihasyessta.
   The manager instructed the employees to wrap up the meeting.

소개팅에서 만난 남자: "커피 좀 드세요."
sokaythingeyse mannan namca: "khephi com tuseyyo."
Blind date: "*Please have some coffee.*"

→ 소개팅에서 만난 사람이 나**한테** 커피를 마시**라고 권했다**.
   sokaythingeyse mannan salami nahanthey khephilul masilako kwenhayssta.
   My blind date urged me to have some coffee.

어머니: "이번 주말에는 캠핑 가지 말아라!"
emeni: "ipen cwumaleynun khaymphing kaci malala!"
Mother: "Don't go camping this weekend."

→ 어머니께서는 이번 주말에는 캠핑 가지 말**라고 하셨다.**
emenikkeysenun ipen cwumaleynun khaymphing kaci mallako hasyessta.
My mother asked me not to go camping this weekend.

English speakers often say *someone* ASKED *someone to do something* as a way of talking about a polite command. It is nevertheless a command, not a question, so you'd need to use -(으)라고 -(u)lako. In Korean, we can only INFER the politeness of the original conversation, since politeness and other sentence endings are not included in indirect quotations. (Look at the manager and the blind-date example above.)

<5> Reporting about requests or asking FOR something with 달라고/-어 달라고

In Korean, ASKING FOR something also has nothing to do with asking a question. When you ask someone for something, you are REQUESTING the thing. This takes a special verb in Korean: 달라고 하다 tallako hata *to ask for, to request*. This expression is used whether you are telling someone to ask for something, repeating that you yourself asked for something, saying that you are planning to ask someone for something, and so on.

어머니: 승무원이 지나가면 물 좀 **달라고 부탁해라.**
emeni: sungmwuweni cinakamyen mwul com tallako pwuthakhayla.
Mother: If the flight attendant comes by, ask him for some water.

아들: 저기요. 물 좀 주실 수 있어요?
atul: cekiyo. mwul com cwusil swu isseyo?
Son: Excuse me. Could you please give me some water?

<잠시 후 camsi hwu>   (a little later)

→ 아들: 아까 물 좀 **달라고 말씀드렸는데요.**
atul: akka mwul com tallako malssumtulyessnunteyyo.
Son: I asked for water a while ago...

You can also talk about requesting an ACTION as a favor. When someone uses -**어** 주다 -e cwuta *to do for someone* to ask for a favor (for themselves), it is transmitted as -**어** 달라고 하다 -e tallako hata in indirect quotation.

"창문 좀 열어 줘."
changmwun com yele cwue.
"Open the window for me, please."

→ 창문을 **열어 달라고 부탁했어.**
changmwunul yele tallako pwuthakhaysse.
I asked him to open the window.

의자를 세워 주시기 바랍니다.
uycalul seywe cwusiki palapnita.
"Please put your seat in the upright position."

→ 승무원은 나에게 의자를 **세워 달라고 했다**.
sungmwuwenun naeykey uycalul seywe tallako hayssta.
The flight attendant asked me to put my seat in the upright position.

We use the word *give* in English whether we are asking the action to be given to (that is, done for the benefit of) ourselves or someone else, but be careful of the distinction between talking about requesting something for one's OWN BENEFIT with -어 **달라고** 하다 -e tallako hata *to request*, and talking about telling someone to do something FOR SOMEONE ELSE, which uses -어 **주라고** 하다 -e cwulako hata. You can use special reportative particles -더러 tele and -보고 -poko, instead of -에게 -eykey, for the person who does either type of "giving":

어머니께서 **나한테** 동생 방 좀 **청소해 달라고 하셨다**.
emenikkeyse nahanthey tongsayng pang com chengsohay tallako hasyessta.
Mom asked <u>me</u> to clean my younger brother's room (<u>for her</u>, otherwise she will have to clean that room).

Cf. 어머니께서 **나더러** 동생 방 좀 **청소해 주라고 하셨다**.
emenikkeyse natele tongsayng pang com chengsohay cwulako hasyessta.
Mom told <u>me</u> to clean my younger brother's room (<u>for him</u>).

내 여자친구는 **나보고** 마사지를 **해 달라고 했다**.
nay yecachinkwunun napoko masacilul hay tallako hayssta.
My girlfriend asked <u>me</u> to give <u>her</u> a massage. = My girlfriend <u>asked for</u> a massage.

Cf. 내 여자친구는 **나한테** 마사지를 **해 주라고 했다**.
nay yecachinkwunun nahanthey masacilul hay cwulako hayssta.
My girlfriend asked <u>me</u> to give (<u>someone else</u>) a massage.

그 친구는 항상 돈을 **빌려 달라고 부탁해**.
ku chinkwunun hangsang tonul pillye tallako pwuthakhay.
That friend is always asking to borrow money.

<6> Review and summary

Here is a grand summary chart of indirect quotation. *She* could be replaced by any pronoun in these examples, and the main verb (at the end of sentence) could be put in any tense.

Statement		
Tense	Example	Translation

Active verb-는/ㄴ다고 하다 -nuntako hata

Present	공부한다고 한다. kongpwuhantako hanta. 나를 믿는다고 한다. nalul mitnuntako hanta.	*She says that she is studying.* *She says that she believes in me.*
Past	공부했다고 한다. kongpwuhaysstako hanta. 나를 믿었다고 한다. nalul mitesstako hanta.	*She says that she studied.* *She says that she believed in me.*
Future	공부할 거라고 한다. kongpwuhal kelako hanta. 나를 믿을 거라고 한다. nalul mitul kelako hanta.	*She says that she is going to study.* *She says that she is going to believe in me.*

Descriptive verb-다고 하다 -tako hata

Present	바쁘다고 한다. papputako hanta.	*She says that she is busy.*
Past	바빴다고 한다. pappasstako hanta.	*She says that she was busy.*
Future	바쁠 거라고/것이라고 한다. pappul kelako/kesilako hanta.	*She says that she will be busy.*

Noun-이라고 하다 -ilako hata

Present	한국 사람이라고 한다. hankwuk salamilako hanta.	*She says that she is (a) Korean.*
Past	한국 사람이었다고 한다. hankwuk salamiesstako hanta.	*She says that she was (a) Korean.*
Future Conjecture	한국 사람일 거라고/것이라고 한다. hankwuk salamil kelako/kesilako hanta.	*She says that she will/might be (a) Korean.*

Question		
Tense	Example	Meaning

Active verb-(느)냐고 하다/묻다

Tense	Example	Meaning
Present	매일 책을 읽(느)냐고 묻는다. mayil chaykul ilk(nu)nyako mwutnunta.	*She asks if he reads books every day.*
Past	자기 블로그를 읽었(느)냐고 묻는다. caki pullokulul ilkess(nu)nyako mwutnunta.	*She asks if he read her blog post.*
Future	신문을 읽을 거냐고 묻는다. sinmwunul ilkul kenyako mwutnunta.	*She asks if he will read the newspaper.*

Descriptive verb-(으)냐고 하다/묻다 -(u)nyako hata/mwutta

Tense	Example	Meaning
Present	바쁘냐고 묻는다. pappunyako mwutnunta.	*She asks if he is busy.*
Past	바빴냐고 묻는다. pappassnyako mwutnunta	*She asks if he was busy.*
Future	바쁠 거냐고 묻는다. pappul kenyako mwutnunta.	*She asks if he will be busy.*

Command		
Tense	Example	Meaning

Active verb only -(으)라고 하다 -(u)lako hata, -지 말라고 하다 -ci mallako hata

Tense	Example	Meaning
Present	아침 먹으라고 한다. achim mekulako hanta.	*She tells him to eat breakfast.*
	공부하지 말라고 한다. kongpwuhaci mallako hanta.	*She tells him not to study.*

Proposal		
Tense	Example	Meaning

Active verb only -자고 하다 -cako hata, -지 말자고 하다 -ci malcako hata

Tense	Example	Meaning
Present	아침 먹자고 한다. achim mekcako hanta.	*She suggests that we eat breakfast.*
	공부하지 말자고 한다. kongpwuhaci malcako hanta.	*She suggests that we not study.*

Request		
Tense	Example	Meaning

-어 달라고 하다 -e tallako hata

Tense	Example	Meaning
Present	나한테 자기 숙제를 해 달라고 한다. nahanthey caki swukceylul hay tallako hanta.	*She asks me to do her homework.*

And to review how it all works in a real-life situation, suppose that it is dinner time, and a girl (let's say her name is Seyoung) just heard her mom saying "세영아! 와서 저녁 먹어라! seyyenga! wase cenyek mekela! *Seyoung! Come and eat!*" And right at that moment, Seyoung's friend texted her to ask if she could talk about the homework with her. Seyoung will probably want to tell her friend that she was called to the dinner table so she can't talk.

To text her friend about what her mom said (using indirect quotations), she FIRST has to choose the right connector to match the kind of sentence her mom said—was it a statement, a command, a question, or a suggestion?

- Since "저녁 먹어라 cenyek mekela" is a command, she will use -으라고 -ulako.
- Then she can choose a main verb to be specific, or just use 하다 hata.
- Finally, she needs to indicate who was told the command with -한테 -hanthe, -더러 -tele, or -보고 -poko.

Putting it all together, Seyoung would send her friend a message like this:

엄마가 나보고 저녁 먹으라고 하셨어. 나중에 문자하자.
emmaka napoko cenyek mekulako hasyesse. nacwungey mwuncahaca.
Mom told me to eat dinner. Let's chat later.

(2) Indirect quotation: shortened forms

Get ready for high-speed Korean! Now that you know how indirect quotation forms are made, you are ready to learn the shortened forms of indirect quotation that are most often used in colloquial speech. There are two ways of shortening: one for *you* and *I* and one for others and indefinite *they say* (or, *I hear*).

The first shortened form is very simple. When asking what the other person just said and answering with an indirect quotation (only for *you* and *I*), choose the right connector for the sentence type, tense and verb-type (active or descriptive) and then just stop after -고 -ko. That is, there is no need to use the verb 하다 hata or any other speaking verb. Since we are talking about colloquial speech, you can assume that this is for the ordinary style, so if you want to be polite, you can simply add -요 -yo:

아는 언니: 좀 도와 줄래?
anun enni: com towa cwullay?
A female acquaintance: Can you help me with this?

나: **뭐라고**(요)?
na: mwelako(yo)?
Me: What? (What did you say?)

아는 언니: 도와 **달라고**.
anun enni: towatalako.
A female acquaintance: I asked for help/I'm asking for help.

남자친구: 배고파. 빨리 먹자.
namcachinku: paykopha. ppalli mekca.
Boyfriend: *I'm hungry. Let's eat soon!*

나: **배고프냐고**?
na: paykophunyako?
Me: *Am I hungry? (Are you asking if I am hungry?)*

남자친구: 빨리 **먹자고**!
namcachinku: ppalli mekcako!
Boyfriend: *I said let's eat soon!*

Even if "*I*" hadn't asked for clarification of what my boyfriend said, in the last example, the boyfriend could still have said 빨리 **먹자고** ppalli mekcako *I said let's eat soon* if I didn't respond and he wanted to repeat himself.

When talking about what someone else (*he, she, they*) said, 하- ha- or 해- hay- gets contracted with the connector so that the ㅎ disappears, and -고 -ko drops out. The sentence ending is as fits the situation (formal or ordinary, past tense, etc.). The contracted endings look like this:

	Full Form	Contracted Form
Statements	-(ㄴ/는)다고 해(요) -(n/nun)tako hay(yo)	-(ㄴ/는)대(요) -(n/nun)tay(yo)
	-(ㄴ/는)다고 합니다 -(n/nun)tako hapnita	-(ㄴ/는)답니다 -(n/nun)tapnita
	-(ㄴ/는)다고 한다 -(n/nun)tako hanta	-(ㄴ/는)단다 -(n/nun)tanta
Questions	-(느)냐고 해(요) -(nu)nyako hay(yo)	-내(요) -nyay(yo)
	-(느)냐고 합니다 -(nu)nyako hapnita	-냡니다 - nyapnita
	-(느)냐고 한다 -(nu)nyako hanta	-냔다 -nyanta
Commands	-(으)라고 해(요) -(u)lako hay(yo)	-(으)래(요) -(u)lay(yo)
	-(으)라고 합니다 -(u)lako hapnita	-(으)랍니다 -(u)lapnita
	-(으)라고 한다 -(u)lako hanta	-(으)란다 -(u)lanta

	Full Form	Contracted Form
Suggestions	-자고 해(요) -cako hay(yo)	-재(요) -cay(yo)
	-자고 합니다 -cako hapnita	-잡니다 - capnita
	-자고 한다 -cako hanta	-잔다 - canta
Requests	-(어) 달라고 해(요) -(e) tallako hay(yo)	-(어) 달래(요) -(e) tallay(yo)
	-(어) 달라고 합니다 -(e) tallako hapnita	-(어) 달랍니다 -(e) tallapnita
	-(어) 달라고 한다 -(e) tallako hanta	-(어) 달란다 -(e) tallanta

Let's see how this flies by in conversation:

사람들이 내가 송중기하고 **사귀냬다**!
salamtuli nayka songcwungkihako sakwinyaynta!
People ask if I am dating Song Joongki! (question)

수민이가 영빈 씨더러 **전화하랍니까**?
swuminika yengpin ssitele cenhwahalapnikka?
Did Soomin ask Youngbin to call him? (command)

엄마, 누나가 내일 같이 **외식하재요**.
emma, nwunaka nayil kathi oysikhacayyo.
Mom, Sis is asking us to eat out with her tomorrow. (suggestion)

The indirect quotation, in reduced or full forms, is greatly useful because it can be generalized to veiled or vague sources (*they say*) or when there is no particular person in mind (*I hear*):

수민이하고 영빈이가 **사귄답니다**!
swuminihako yengpinika sakwintapnita!
I hear/they say that Soomin and Youngbin are dating!

감자가 눈가의 주름을 줄여 **준단다**.
kamcaka nwunkauy cwulumul cwulye cwuntanta.
They say potatoes reduce eye wrinkles.

(3) Reportative adnominals

When certain nouns are modified with a clause, it must include the (typically shortened) reportative in Korean. For example, instead of -는 소문 -nun somwun *a rumor that*, it has to be REPORTATIVE -**다**는 소문 -tanun somwun *a rumor SAYING that*.

네가 **약혼했다는 소문**을 들었어.
neyka yakhonhaysstanun somwunul tulesse.
I heard a rumor that you got engaged.
(Literally, *I heard a rumor that said you got engaged.*)

네가 **약혼한 소문**을 들었어.
neyka yakhonhan somwunul tulesse.
I heard a rumor that you got engaged.

김교수님께서 **은퇴하신다는 이야기**를 들었다.
kimkyoswunimkkeyse unthoyhasintanun iyakilul tulessta.
I heard that Professor Kim is retiring.
(Literally, *I heard a story that said Professor Kim is retiring.*)

김교수님께서 **은퇴하시는 이야기**를 들었다.
kimkyoswunimkkeyse unthoyhasinun iyakilul tulessta.
I heard that Professor Kim is retiring.

택시 운전사들이 파업**할 거라는 소리**를 들었어?
thayksi wuncensatuli phaephal kelanun solilul tulesse?
Did you hear the news that (said) taxi drivers were on strike?

택시 운전사들이 파업**할 거인 소리**를 들었어?
thayksi wuncensatuli phaephal kein solilul tulesse?
Did you hear the news that taxi drivers were on strike?

Here are some more nouns that you will hear with REPORTATIVE modifying clauses. Notice that they are all related to communicating or thinking.

이야기 iyaki *story*, 말 mal *story*, 글 kul *writing*, 전화 cenhwa *call*, 소문 somwun *rumor*, 소식 sosik *news*, 소리 soli *rumor/news*, 방송 pangsong *broadcast*, 질문 cilmwun *question*, 기사 kisa *newspaper article*, 보고 poko *report*, 연락 yenlak *contact*, 이메일 imeyil *email*, 요청 yocheng *request*, 명령 myenglyeng *order* , 생각 sayngkak, 의심 uysim

Modifying clauses are also used with questions, suggestions, commands, and request quotation forms if the modified noun is one of the communicating nouns in the box above:

한국에 **언제 오느냐는 질문**을 하셨다.
hankwukey encey onunyanun cilmwunul hasyessta.
She asked me (the question of) when I will come to Korea.

그가 나에게 같이 사업을 **해 보자는 요청**을 했다.
kuka naeykey kathi saepul hay pocanun yochengul patassta.
He suggested that we start business together. (Literally, *he made the suggestion that....*)

내일까지 보고서를 **제출하라는 이메일**을 받았다.
nayilkkaci pokoselul ceychwulhalanun imeyilul patassta.
I received an email saying that I need to submit the report by tomorrow.

"Mental" nouns don't have to have the reportative in the modifier, but they do frequently show up with it. Some examples are 이유 iyu *reason*, 느낌 nukkim *feeling*, and 사실 sasil *fact*.

친구가 벌써 **떠났다는 사실**을 알았다.
chinkwuka pelsse ttenasstanun sasilul alassta.
I found that my friend had already left.
(Literally, *I learned the fact that my friend had already left.*)

친구가 벌써 **떠난 사실**을 알았다.
chinkwuka pelsse ttenan sasilul alassta.
I found that my friend had already left.
(Literally, *I learned the fact that my friend had already left.*)

네가 **거기에 가고 싶다는 이유**를 난 모르겠다.
neyka kekiey kako siphtanun iyulul nan molukeyssta.
I don't understand why you want to go there.
(Literally, *I don't know the reason that you want to go there.*)

네가 **거기에 가고 싶은 이유**를 난 모르겠다.
neyka kekiey kako siphun iyulul nan molukeyssta.
I don't understand why you want to go there.
(Literally, *I don't know the reason that you want to go there.*)

겨울이 다 **갔다는 느낌**이 들어요.
kyewuli ta kasstanun nukkimi tuleyo.
I have a feeling that winter has left.
(Literally, *the thought comes to me that winter left.*)

겨울이 다 **간 느낌**이 들어요.
kyewuli ta kan nukkimi tuleyo.
I have a feeling that winter has left.
(Literally, *the thought comes to me that winter left.*)

10.2.3 Communicating what is thought or assumed

Now let's move on to talking about what people think, know, and think they know.

While in English *saying that…*, *thinking that…*, and *knowing that…* are all said similarly, they need different connectors in Korean. You learned the various ways to report on what someone said, commanded, asked, suggested, or requested in the previous section. Here we'll see how to express different kinds of *thinking* and *knowing* in Korean.

(1) REPORTATIVE FORM -고 생각하다 *(Here is what) I think*

When you have an OPINION to express on what you think about a situation, you may simply use the adverbial 내/제 생각에는 nay/cey sayngkakeynun *in my opinion* and perhaps end the sentence with -(으)ㄴ 것 같다 -(u)n kes kathta *it seems like*. You can also "quote" your own thought and say -(ㄴ/는)다고 생각하다 -(n/nun)tako sayngkakhata *to think that…*. (This works like an indirect quotation.) Let's look at a few examples:

서울의 대중교통은 **훌륭하다고 생각합니다**!
sewuluy taycwungkyothongun hwullyunghatako sayngkakhapnita!
In my opinion, Seoul public transportation is great!

사랑이 **뭐라고 생각하세요**?
salangi mwelako sayngkakhaseyyo?
What do you think love is?

내가 나이를 **먹었다고 생각될 때**
nayka nailul mekesstako sayngkaktoyl ttay
When I feel that I am too old

In English, we normally move a negative word, when there is one, OUT OF THE THOUGHT and put it on the main verb, saying *I don't think she is going* instead of *I think she is not going* (unless we want to really emphasize it). Korean can do this, but the negative usually stays inside the "quoted" (thought) sentence.

한국어 공부가 그렇게 어렵지 **않다고 생각합니다**.
hankwuke kongpwuka kulehkey elyepci anhtako sayngkakhapnita.
I don't think studying Korean is that difficult.
= *I think studying Korean is not that difficult.*

세상에 불가능한 것은 **없다고 생각한다**.
seysangey pwulkanunghan kesun epstako sayngkakhanta.
I don't think there is anything that's impossible.
= *I think there is not anything that is impossible.*

However, you CAN assert (*I*) DON'T *think that* in Korean by putting a negative on the *think* verb:

(저는) 그렇게 **생각하지 않아요**.
(cenun) kulehkey sayngkakhaci anhayo.
I don't think that is the case/I don't agree.

English "*I think*" is used in many ways that do not naturally translate to Korean 생각하다 sayngkakhata, as this Korean verb indicates reflection or perspective on a situation. See how Koreans may express similar ideas:

비가 올 거라고 생각한다.
pika ol kelako sayngkakhanta.
I do think/I predict that it's going to rain.

비가 올 거 같다.
pika ol ke kathta.
I think it's going to rain.

서울의 대중 교통은 대단하다고 생각한다.
sewuluy taycwung kyothongun taytanhatako sayngkakhanta.
I think Seoul's public transportation is truly great.
= *I feel that Seoul's public transportation is truly great.*

서울의 대중 교통은 대단한 거 같다.
sewuluy taycwung kyothongun taytanhan ke kathta.
I think Seoul's public transportation is great. (it seems to me)

(2) Reportative form -고 알(고 있)다 *as far as I know, I am thinking that...*

If you are expressing what you think you know to be true, that is, what you know based on information you have collected at this point, then you "quote" the information (using the reportative form) and use the verb 알고 있다 alko issta *to know*. You can also just use the adverbial 내가 알기에는 nayka alkieynun *to my knowledge*.

> 에펠 탑이 서울 타워보다 **크다고 알고 있다.**
> eypheyl thapi sewul thawepota khutako alko issta.
> *(If I'm not wrong) I think the Eiffel Tower is bigger than Seoul Tower.*

> = **내가 알기에는** 에펠 탑이 서울 타워보다 크다.
>   nayka alkieynun eypheyl thapi sewul thawepota khuta.
>   *To my knowledge, the Eiffel Tower is bigger than Seoul Tower.*

> 판다는 죽순을 주식으로 **먹는다고 알고 있다.**
> phantanun cwukswunul cwusikulo meknuntako alko issta.
> *(If I'm not wrong) I think panda bears eat bamboo shoots as their main staple.*

> = **내가 알기에** 판다는 죽순을 주식으로 먹는다.
>   nayka alkiey phantanun cwukswunul cwusikulo meknunta.
>   *To my knowledge, panda bears eat bamboo shoots as their main staple.*

(3) Adnominal form + 것으로 알(고 있)다 *as far as I know, I am thinking that...*

The same, more or less UNCONFIRMED THINKING can be expressed with a noun-modifier form plus 것으로 알다 kesulo alta or 것으로 알고 있다 kesulo alko issta. The expression all together communicates *I am thinking that* or *as far as I know*, but is just a little more certain than reportative -고 알다 -ko alta. (With the future tense, you can use 믿다 mitta as well). -는/-(으)ㄴ/-(으)ㄹ 것으로 -nun/-(u)n/-(u)l kesulo can be reduced to -는/-(으)ㄴ/-(으)ㄹ 걸로 -nun/-(u)n/-(u)l kello in spoken Korean:

> 누나는 엄마가 오늘 **오시는 것으로 알고 있다.**
> nwunanun emmaka onul osinun kesulo alko issta.
> *Sis thinks that Mom is coming today. (She might or might not.)*

> 그 시합은 우리 팀이 **이긴 걸로 알고 있어.**
> ku sihapun wuli thimi ikin kello alko isse.
> *I think we won that game, (although I can't be 100 percent sure).*

> 결혼식에 사람들이 많이 **올 걸로** 믿고 있어.
> kyelhonsikey salamtuli manhi ol kello mitko isse.
> *I think there will be a lot of people at the wedding.*

(4) Adnominal form + 것을 알(고 있)다 *I know...*

If you know the information you are expressing is a CONFIRMED FACT that you are sure of, then you say *I know (the fact) that*, using the abstract noun 것 kes with the OBJECT marker -을/-를 -ul/-lul and the verb 알다 alta or 알고 있다 alko issta *to know*. This is just like the previous expression but with 것을 kesul instead of 것으로 kesulo.

-는/-(으)ㄴ/-(으)ㄹ 것을 -nun/-(u)n/-(u)l kesul can be reduced to -는/-(으)ㄴ/-(으)ㄹ 걸 -nun/-(u)n/-(u)l kel in spoken Korean:

나는 에펠 탑이 서울 타워보다 **큰 걸** 알고 있습니다.
nanun eypheyl thapi sewul thawepota khun kel alko issupnita.
(I have the factual information) I know that the Eiffel Tower is bigger than Seoul Tower.

아빠가 오늘 **한국에서 오시는 걸** 알아.
appaka onul hankwukeyse osinun kel ala.
I know (for a fact) that Dad is coming from Korea today.

(5) ADNOMINAL FORM + 줄 알았다 *I thought..., I was assuming..., I knew...*

When your thinking is an ASSUMPTION not based on information or facts, it can turn out to be right or wrong. To express this kind of *thinking*, you don't use the verb 생각하다 sayngkakhata *to think*. Surprisingly, you use the verb 알았다 alassta *I knew it to be...* with a dependent noun 줄 cwul, which indicates an ASSUMPTION. This treats the information as valid knowledge at the time speaker had it, although it may turn out false.

엄마 아빠 어디 계셔? 집에 **계시는 줄 알았는데**.
emma appa eti kyeysye? cipey kyeysinun cwul alassnuntey.
Where are Mom and Dad? I thought/assumed they were home. (but they are not)

한라산이 백두산보다 **높은 줄 알았어**.
hanlasani payktwusanpota nophun cwul alasse.
I thought Mt. Halla was bigger than Mt. Baekdu. (but it is not)

네가 밥 먹고 **온 줄 알았어**.
neyka pap mekko on cwul alasse.
I thought you had eaten/ate before you came.

시험이 **어려울 줄 알았는데** 쉬웠다.
sihemi elyewul cwul alassnuntey swiwessta.
I thought the test would be difficult, but it was easy.

If you knew something *was going to be* the case and it was borne out you can say exactly that with -(으)ㄹ 줄 -(u)l cwul and 알았다 alassta (in the past tense): *I knew it!*

그렇게 뛰어 다니더니 **넘어질 줄 알았다**!
kulehkey ttwie taniteni nemecil cwul alassta!
You run around all the time, I knew that you would fall!

그럴 줄 알았다!
kulel cwul alassta!
I knew that would happen!

걔가 내 생일 **잊어 버릴 줄 알았어**!
kyayka nay sayngil ice pelil cwul alasse!
I knew he would forget my birthday!

Because the assumption connector 줄 cwul plays double duty for when you are right OR wrong, it can bring about ambiguous interpretations. The only way to differentiate the two meanings is by a pause followed by a dip in the intonation before 알다 alta for the meaning *I knew it*. The pause and low-tone emphasize the verb 알다 alta. Otherwise, the low tone comes before the verb in the embedded clause. The location is marked with ᵥ below:

개가 내 생일 잊어 버린 줄 ᵥ 알았어!
kyayka nay sayngil ice pelin cwul alasse!
I KNEW he had forgotten my birthday! (and he did)

개가 내 생일 ᵥ 잊어 버린 줄 알았어!
kyayka nay sayngil ice pelin cwul alasse!
I thought he had forgotten my birthday! (but he hadn't)

개가 내 생일 잊어 버릴 줄 ᵥ 알았어!
kyayka nay sayngil ice pelil cwul alasse!
I KNEW he was going to forget my birthday! (and he did)

개가 내 생일 ᵥ 잊어 버릴 줄 알았어!
kyayka nay sayngil ice pelil cwul alasse!
I thought he would forget my birthday! (but he didn't)

(6) ADNOMINAL FORM + 줄 몰랐다 *I didn't know that... Who knew... Who'd have thought...*

If you had the wrong information and DIDN'T KNOW the facts that you just found out, then you use noun modifier form with 줄 cwul and the verb 몰랐다 mollassta *didn't know*.

서울 타워가 그렇게 **높은 줄 몰랐어요**.
sewul thaweka kulehkey nophun cwul mollasseyo.
I didn't know that Seoul Tower was so big!

선생님께서는 우리가 **가는 줄 모르셨다**.
sensayngnimkkeysenun wulika kanun cwul molusyessta.
The teacher didn't know that we were going.

우리 부모님 **오실 줄 몰랐어**?
wuli pwumonim osil cwul mollasse?
You didn't know that my parents would come?

여보! 나 왔어. 아이구, 자기가 오늘 **저녁한 줄 모르고** 피자 사 왔는데.
yepo! na wasse. aikwu, cakika onul cenyekhan cwul moluko phica sa wassnuntey.
Hi honey! I'm home. Oh, I didn't know you had made dinner so I bought pizza...

여보! 나 왔어. 아이구, 자기가 오늘 **저녁할 줄 모르고** 피자 사 왔는데.
yepo! na wasse. aikwu, cakika onul cenyekhal cwul moluko phica sa wassnuntey
Hi honey! I'm home. Oh, I didn't know you'd be making dinner so I bought pizza...

The last two examples above highlight the use of Korean tenses: they indicate when the event happens with respect to when the thought happens.

In sum, the adnominal form + 줄 cwul is used when there is some assumption that you then find out about; it can turn out to be correct or not.

10.2.4 Communicating what is wondered about

The last kind of sentence-in-a-sentence is **embedded questions**. These are sentences that communicate what one wonders about, like *I don't know why they keep wanting more*. There is some unknown information, indicated by a *wh*-question word (or *if* or *whether*) in a sentence that is not overall a question.

(1) CONNECTOR FORM + 지 알다/모르다 *know/not know and wonder WH-*

If you remember how to conjugate -는데 -nuntey, you'll have no problem with **embedded questions** because they use the connector -는지 -nunci, which conjugates just like -는데 -nuntey: -는지 -nunci for present active verbs, -(으)ㄴ지 -(u)nci for present descriptive verbs, -(으)ㄹ지 -(u)lci for future tense, and -었는지 -essnunci for past tense.

Verbs that are used with embedded questions include:

> 알다 alta *know*, 모르다 moluta *not know*, 생각나다 sayngkaknata *recall*, 기억나다 kieknata *remember*, 듣다 tutta *hear*, 보다 pota *see*, 배우다 paywuta *learn*, 가르치다 kaluchita *teach*, 궁금(해)하다 kwungkum(hay)hata *to be curious about, want to know, wonder*, 이상(해)하다 isang(hay)hata *(find) it strange*, 신기(해)하다 sinki(hay)hata *(find it) curious, odd*.

This is how it works. You have a question and you want to know the answer to it, then you combine the two ideas into one:

그 일이 **언제 해결됐어요**? 알고 싶어요.
ku ili encey haykyeltwaysseyo? alko sipheyo.
When was that resolved? I want to know.

→ 그 일이 **언제 해결됐는지** 알고 싶어요.
ku ili encey haykyeltwayssnunci alko sipheyo.
I want to know when that was resolved.

지금 **몇 시야**? 알아?
cikum myech siya? ala?
What time is it? Do you know?

→ 지금 **몇 신지** 알아?
cikum myech sinci ala?
Do you know what time it is now?

거기 **누구랑 가게 될 거 같아요**? 궁금해요.
keki nwukwulang kakey toyl ke kathayo? kwungkumhayyo.
Who does it look like you'll go there with? I'm curious.

→ 거기 **누구랑 가게 될지** 궁금해요.
keki nwukwulang kakey toylci kwungkumhayyo.
I'm curious about who you'll get to go there with.

Here are examples that show various tenses and *wh*-words:

친구가 **언제 올지** 알아요?
chinkwuka encey olci alayo?
Do you know <u>when</u> your friend <u>will come</u>?

친구가 **언제 오는지** 알아요?
chinkwuka encey onunci alayo?
Do you know <u>when</u> your friend <u>is coming</u>?

친구가 **언제 왔는지** 알아요?
chinkwuka encey wassnunci alayo?
Do you know <u>when</u> your friend <u>came</u>?

열쇠가 **어디 있을지** 모르겠어요.
yelsoyka eti issulci molukeysseyo.
I don't know <u>where</u> the key <u>would be</u>.

열쇠가 **어디 있는지** 모르겠어요.
yelsoyka eti issnunci molukeysseyo.
I don't know <u>where</u> the key <u>is</u>.

열쇠가 **어디 있었는지** 모르겠어요.
yelsoyka eti issessnunci molukeysseyo.
I don't know <u>where</u> the key <u>was</u>.

저게 **얼만지** 진짜로 궁금해요.
cekey elmanci cinccalo kwungkumhayyo.
I sure wonder <u>how much</u> that is.

걔가 아까 **왜 화났는지** 들었어요.
kyayka akka way hwanassnunci tulesseyo.
I heard <u>why s/he was</u> upset then.

한글을 **누가 만들었는지** 배웠어요.
hankulul nwuka mantulessnunci paywesseyo.
I learned <u>who created</u> Hangul.

뭐가 더 **예쁜지** 얘기해 주세요.
mweka te yeyppunci yaykihay cwuseyyo.
Let me know <u>which is</u> prettier.

왜 이렇게 **피곤한지** 모르겠어요.
way ilehkey phikonhanci molukeysseyo.
I don't know <u>why</u> I <u>am</u> so tired.

이 문제를 **어떻게 풀어야 할지** 모르겠어요.
i mwunceylul ettehkey phwuleya halci molukeysseyo.
I don't know <u>how</u> to (how one <u>would</u>) solve this problem.

When there is no overt question word such as 왜 way *why* or 몇 myech *how many*, the sentence is interpreted as wondering *if* or *whether*. For *whether or not*, the verb and its negative or opposite can both be included, both with the connector.

그 집에 금송아지가 **있는지 (없는지)** 누가 **알아**.
ku cipey kumsongacika issnunci (epsnunci) nwuka ala.
Who knows whether they have a golden calf (or not).

오늘 친구가 **올지 안 올지** 몰라요.
onul chinkwuka olci an olci mollayo.
I don't know if my friend will come today or not.

Even when there is no knowledge verb, the clause with the -지 ci connector carries a strong sense of *wondering about something*:

이 시간에 어디에 **있는지** 전화도 안 하고…
i sikaney etiey issnunci cenhwato an hako...
(You gotta wonder) where on earth he is at this hour, not even calling...

정태가 감기에 **걸렸는지** 계속 기침을 했어.
cengthayka kamkiey kellyessnunci kyeysok kichimul haysse.
(It's not clear) whether ChungTae caught a cold, but he continuously coughed.

방이 **추운지** 모두 움츠리고 있었어.
pangi chwuwunci motwu wumchuliko issesse.
Perhaps (I don't know if) the room was cold; everyone was hunching their shoulders.

(2) Fine-tuning indirect questions vs. embedded questions

Indirect questions, or questions indirectly quoted, are questions that have been said, that is, they have been asked by someone and are reported by someone else. On the other hand, embedded questions are questions that someone conceived of and are being communicated for the first time in a statement form:

선생님께서 우리가 **가냐고 물으셨다**.
sensayngnimkkeyse wulika kanyako mwulusyessta.
The teacher underline{asked whether} we were going to go.

선생님께서 우리가 **가는지 모르셨다**.
sensayngnimkkeyse wulika kanunci molusyessta.
The teacher underline{didn't know whether} we were going to go.

As you can imagine, native Korean speakers mix them mix them up in actual use.

선생님께서 우리가 **가는지 물으셨다**.
sensayngnimkkeyse wulika kanunci mwulusyessta.
The teacher (wondered about it so) underline{asked whether} we were going to go.

(3) Fine-tuning 알다/모르다 *know how to*

Our final note on embedded sentences is about the expression "knowing HOW TO DO something." In a sense, there is really no QUESTION since this is about having a skill or not, being able or not. In Korean, this is basically an idiom, as we introduce in chapter 7, and it is expressed with -(으)ㄹ 줄 알다 -(u)l cwul alta *know how to* and -(으)ㄹ 줄 모르다 -(u)l cwul moluta *not know how to*.

우리 할머니께서는 김치를 맛있게 **담글 줄 아신다.**
wuli halmenikkeysenun kimchilul masisskey **tamkul cwul asinta.**
My grandmother knows how to make delicious kimchi.

정말 타이어 **갈 줄 몰라요**?
cengmal thaie **kal cwul mollayo**?
You really don't know how to change a tire?

감사할 줄 아는 사람이 되자.
kamsahal cwul anun salami toyca.
Let's be grateful. (Literally, *let's become people who know how to be thankful.*)

If you are truly wondering about the METHOD, then you use an embedded question 어떻게 …-는지 ettehkey …-nunci *how one does X* or 어떻게 …-는 건지 ettehkey …-nun kenci *how it is that one is to do X*. Or you can use the noun 방법 pangpep *method* with a noun-modifying clause:

서울역에 **어떻게 가는지** 아세요?
sewulyekey **ettehkey kanunci** aseyyo?
Do you know how to get to Seoul Station?

타이어를 **어떻게 가는지** 인터넷에서 봤다.
thaielul **ettehkey kanunci** intheneyseyse pwassta.
I saw online how to change a tire.

타이어를 **가는 방법**을 인터넷에서 배웠다.
thaielul **kanun pangpep**ul intheneyseyse paywessta.
I found out online how to change a tire.

어머니께 떡볶이 **어떻게 만드는 건지** 여쭤 보자.
emenikkey ttekpokki **ettehkey mantunun kenci** yeccwe poca.
Let's ask Mom how to make dukkbokki.

어머니께 떡볶이 **만드는 방법**에 대해 여쭤 보자.
*emenikkey ttekpokki **mantunun pangpep**ey tayhay yeccwe poca.*
Let's ask Mom how to make dukkbokki.

축하합니다!

이 책을 마치셨네요!

계속 한국어 공부에 정진하시기 바랍니다!

Exercises

10.1 Making Sentences into Nouns

Exercise 1. Complete the dialogues with the appropriate -(으)ㄴ/-는 거 form.

1) A: 일하면서 _____에 대해 어떻게 생각해? (대학교에서
   수업을 듣다)

   B: 그건 좀 힘들지 않을까?

2) A: 지금 내 방에서 뭐 _____야? (하다)

   B: 보면 몰라? _____지. (청소하다)

3) A: 김치볶음밥은 어떻게 _____예요? (만들다)

   B: 별로 안 어려워. 김치랑 밥을 넣고 이렇게 볶으면 _____야.
   (되다)

4) A: 내 김치 볶음밥을 누가 다 _____야? (먹다)

   B: 미안! 내가 너무 배고파서 먹었어.

5) A: 어제 집 앞 사거리에서 차 사고가 _____ 알아요? (나다)

   B: 정말요? 몰랐어요!

6) A: 내 노트북이 사라졌다! 동생한테 다시 가져오라고 해야겠어!

   B: 네 동생이 _____ 확실해? 누가 훔쳐 갔을 수도 있잖아.
   (가져가다)

Exercise 2. Choose the appropriate expressions to complete the dialogues most naturally. Be sure to conjugate the given verbs appropriately.

-기로 하다	-기 바라다	-기 시작하다

1) A: 한국어를 참 잘 하시네요! 언제부터 한국어를 _____?
   (배우다)

   B: 고등학교 때부터요. 그리고 요즘은 한국 드라마를 보면서 많이 배워요.

   A: 그럼 저랑 같이 한국 드라마 보실래요?

   B: 좋아요. 이번 주말에 같이 _____. (보다)

2) A: 안녕하세요? 이제 곧 김교수님 말씀이 있겠습니다. 모두 여기를
   _____. (봐 주다)

-기 때문에	-기에	-기 위해서	-기는 하지만

3) A: 지금 형이 집에 있어?

   B: 집에 _____ 자는 것 같아. (있다)

   A: 어, 형하고 얘기해야 하는데. 내일은 내가 _____ 못 만나는
   데…. (바쁘다)

   B: 그럼 깨울게.

4) A: _____ 어떻게 해야 할까? (건강해지다)

   B: 매일 조금씩 운동하는 것이 좋지. 자, 나가서 같이 좀 걸을까?

   A: 음... 오늘은 밖에서 _____는 좀 추운 것 같아. 내일부터 걷자.
   (걷다)

Exercise 3. Convert the verbs to -(으)ㅁ nouns.

1) 자다   →   _____

2) 믿다   →   _____

3) 꾸다   →   _____

4) 아프다   →   _____

5) 웃다   →   _____

6) 울다   →   _____

7) 살다   →   _____

8) 얼다   →   _____

Exercise 4. Underline the appropriate expression from the parentheses to complete
the sentence.

1) 오늘 약속이 (있기, 있는 것)을/를 잊어 버렸다.

2) 지금 뭐 (함, 하기, 하는 거)예요/이에요?

3) 우리 동생은 책 (읽음, 읽기, 읽는 것)을/를 좋아해요.

4) 오늘은 추워서 밖에서 (걸음, 걷기, 걷는 것)은/는 힘들어요.

5) 내일 친구와 (만남, 만나기, 만나는 것) (으)로 했어요.

6) 옆집 아기의 (울음, 울기, 우는 것) 소리에 잠을 깼다.

7) (잠, 자기, 자는 것) 전에 이를 닦으세요.

8) 그의 갑작스런 (죽음, 죽기, 죽는 것)은/는 많은 사람을 놀라게 했다.

9) 오늘은 날씨가 너무 (추움, 춥기, 추운 것) 때문에 거리가 한산했다.

10) 그럼 편안히 (쉬시기, 쉬심, 쉬시는 것)을/를 바랍니다.

10.2 Sentences as Objects of Saying and Thinking Verbs

Exercise 5. Fill in the blanks with the appropriate indirect quotation forms.

	-다고 하다	-냐고 하다	-(으)라고 하다	-자고 하다
보다	본다고 하다			
잡다		잡(느)냐고 하다		
하다			하라고 하다	
(모자를) 쓰다				쓰자고 하다
돕다			도우라고 하다	
듣다		듣(느)냐고 하다		
팔다	판다고 하다			
(노래를) 부르다		부르(느)냐고 하다		
예쁘다	예쁘다고 하다		N/A	N/A
춥다		추우냐고 하다	N/A	N/A
달다	달다고 하다		N/A	N/A
빠르다		빠르냐고 하다	N/A	N/A
그렇다	그렇다고 하다		N/A	N/A

Exercise 6. Tell your Mom what Jiwoo said in his text message, using indirect quotation forms.

> *Jiwoo's text message:*
> 오늘 아침에 바빠서 연락을 못 했어. 나도 토요일에 시간이 괜찮아.
> 토요일 오전 열시에 시간이 있어? 시간 있으면 그 때 도서관 앞에서
> 만나자. 지훈이랑 같이 갈 거야. 지금 동아리 모임에 가. 그러니까 저
> 녁 때 연락해 줘.

(예) 지훈이가 오늘 아침에 바빠서 연락을 <u>못 했다고 해요</u>.

1) 지훈이도 토요일에 시간이 ＿＿＿＿＿＿＿＿＿고 해요.

2) 토요일 오전 열시에 시간이 ＿＿＿＿＿＿＿＿＿고 해요.

3) 시간 있으면 그 때 도서관 앞에서 ＿＿＿＿＿＿＿＿＿고 해요.

4) 지훈이랑 같이 ＿＿＿＿＿＿＿＿＿고 해요.

5) 지금 동아리 모임에 ＿＿＿＿＿＿＿＿＿고 해요.

6) 그러니까 저녁 때 ＿＿＿＿＿＿＿＿＿고 해요.

Exercise 7. Pass on the same text message to your friend using <u>shortened</u> indirect quotation forms.

(예) 지훈이가 오늘 아침에 바빠서 연락을 <u>못 했대</u>.

1) 지훈이도 토요일에 시간이 ＿＿＿＿＿＿＿＿.

2) 토요일 오전 열시에 시간이 ＿＿＿＿＿＿＿＿.

3) 시간 있으면 그 때 도서관 앞에서 ＿＿＿＿＿＿＿＿.

4) 지훈이랑 같이 ＿＿＿＿＿＿＿＿.

5) 지금 동아리 모임에 ＿＿＿＿＿＿＿＿.

6) 그러니까 저녁 때 ＿＿＿＿＿＿＿＿.

Exercise 8. Underline the correct expression from the parentheses to complete the sentence.

1) 아버지 → 언니: "수진아! 신문 좀 갖다 줘."

   아버니께서 언니더러 신문을 갖다 (주라고, 달라고, 주시라고, 드리라고) 하셨다.

2) 아버지 → 언니: "수진아! 할머니께 열쇠 좀 갖다 드려라."

   아버니께서 언니더러 할머니께 열쇠를 갖다 (주라고, 달라고, 주시라고, 드리라고) 하셨다.

3) 언니 → 아버지: "아빠! 정우 용돈 좀 주세요."

   언니가 아버지께 정우 용돈을 좀 (주라고, 달라고, 주시라고, 드리라고) 했다.

4) 누나 → 동생: "수현아! 내 친구한테 신문 좀 갖다 줘."

   누나가 동생더러 자기친구한테 신문을 갖다 (주라고, 달라고, 주시라고, 드리라고) 했다.

Exercise 9. Fill in the blank as shown in the example.

(예) 친구: 내일 강의가 취소됐어.

   → 친구한테서 내일 강의가 <u>취소됐다는</u> 이야기를 들었어요.

1) 이메일: 다음 학기의 경제학 101 수업 시간이 바뀌었습니다.

   → 다음학기의 경제학 101 수업 시간이 _____ 이메일을 받았다.

2) 친구의 문자: 오늘 저녁에 우리 집에 들러.

   → 친구한테서 오늘 저녁에 자기 집에 _____ 문자를 받았다.

3) 뉴스: 내일부터 날씨가 따뜻해지겠습니다.

   → 내일부터 날씨가 _____ 뉴스를 들었다.

4) 학생의 질문: 보고서 마감은 언제입니까?

   → 학생들에게서 보고서 마감은 _____ 질문을 받았다.

5)   아버지의 메세지: 저녁 7시에 식당에서 만나자.

→ 아버지께 저녁 7시에 식당에서 _____ 메시지가
와 있었다.

6)   동생의 부탁: 100달러만 빌려 줘.

→ 동생한테서 100달러만 _____ 부탁을 받았다.

Exercise 10. Underline the appropriate connector to complete the dialogues most
naturally.

1)   비서: 사장님, 오늘 회의가 (있는 것을, 있는 것으로) 알고 계십니까?

사장: 아, 그렇지. 몇 시부터 시작이지?

비서: 10시부터 (시작하는 것을, 시작하는 것으로) 알고 있습니다.

2)   팀장: 우리*신제품과 비슷한 제품이 시장에 있습니까?
*(신)제품: (new) product

컨설턴트: 아닙니다. 아직 (없다고 생각합니다, 없다고 알고 있습니다).

팀장: 그럼 신제품 *판매 전망에 대해 어떻게 보십니까?
*판매 전망: sales projection

컨설턴트: 네, 비슷한 제품이 없기 때문에 (희망적이라고 생각합니다, 희망적
이라고 알고 있습니다).

Exercise 11. Seyoung did not know much about Eunji, her friend. Fill in the blanks
with a noun-modifier 줄 (+ 알았다/몰랐다) form to complete the sentences.

(예)   은지: 오늘 내 생일이에요.

세영: 오늘 은지 씨의 <u>생일인줄 몰랐어요</u>. <u>내일인줄 알았어요</u>.

1)   은지: 저는 필라델피아에서 태어났어요.

세영: 아, 그래요? 은지씨가 서울에서 _____ 알았어요.

2)   은지: 저는 학교 앞 아파트에 혼자 살아요.

세영: 아, 그래요? 은지씨가 기숙사에서 룸메이트들이랑 _____
알았어요.

3)   은지: 그 영화는 벌써 봤어요. 다른 영화 봐요.

세영: 그렇군요! 은지씨가 이 영화를 벌써 _____ 몰랐어요.

4)   은지: 저는 키가 작지만 동생은 키가 아주 커요.

세영: 은지 씨 동생이 키가 _____ 몰랐어요.

5)   은지: 이번 학기에 수업을 여섯 과목을 들어요.

세영: 은지씨가 이번 학기에 수업을 여섯 과목을_____ 몰랐어요.

6)   은지: 저는 이번 가을 학기에 한국에 유학갈 거예요.

세영: 어, 저는 은지씨가 내년에 _____ 알았어요.

Exercise 12. Jiwoo has lots of questions about college life. Complete Jiwoo's questions as shown in the example.

(예) 진우: 브라운 교수님 연구실이 <u>어디 있는지</u> 아세요?

나: 컬리지 홀 빌딩 2층에 있어요.

1)   진우: 동아리 모임에 가려고 하는데 동아리 모임을 어디에서 _____ 아세요?

나: 학생회관 지하의 동아리 방에서 해요.

2)   진우: 학생회관이 어디에 _____ 아세요?

나: 기숙사 옆에 있어요.

3)   진우: 컴퓨터를 사려고 하는데 어떤 컴퓨터가 _____ 아세요?

나: 삼성 컴퓨터가 좋은 것 같아요.

4)   진우: 세영 씨가 컴퓨터를 아주 싸게 샀대요. 세영 씨가 어디에서 컴퓨터를 _____ 아세요?

나: 온라인으로 샀대요.

5)   진우: 브라운 교수님 수업의 숙제를 언제까지 _____ 아세요?

나: 내일 오후 2시까지 내야 돼요.

6)   진우: 브라운 교수님께서 오늘 학교에 안 나오셨대요. 왜 학교에 안 _____ 아세요?

나: 브라운 교수님께서 *학회에 가셔서 안 나오셨대요.
      *학회: academic conference

7)   진우: 브라운 교수님께서 언제 다시 학교에 _____ 아세요?

나: 다음 주 월요일에 나오실 거래요.

Answer Key

Chapter 1: The Korean Alphabet

Exercise 1.

아, 애, 오, 어, 우, 야, 에, 으, 이, 요

Exercise 2.

아, 야, 어, 여, 오, 요, 우, 유, 으, 이

Exercise 3.

1) 와	4) 워	7) 의
2) 왜	5) 웨	
3) 외	6) 위	

Exercise 4.

가, 나, 다, 라, 마, 바, 사
아, 자, 차, 카, 타, 파, 하

Exercise 5.

차, 해, 코, 표, 더, 무, 혀, 네, 띠, 그

Exercise 10.

1) 1 – 10 (Native number)
2) 1 – 10 (Sino-Korean number)
3) Monday, Tuesday, Wednesday, Thursday, Friday, Saturday, Sunday
4) Hello! My name is Eunji Kim.
5) Good-bye! (to someone who is leaving) Good-bye. (to someone who is staying)
6) Thank you. Thank you. (a little more formal)
7) Excuse me.
8) Sorry. I am so sorry. (an apology for a more grave mistake)

Exercise 11.

1) 애	6) 세	11) 언제
2) 개	7) 새	12) 찌개
3) 얘	8 위	13) 의사
4) 예	9) 왜	14) 의자
5) 네	10) 가게	15) 가위

16) 가세요	19) 네 이름
17) 어때요	20) 세 사람
18) 내 이름	21) 새 사람

Exercise 12.

1) pie	6) radio
2) banana	7) opera
3) yoga	8) love
4) tire	9) Switzerland
5) coffee	10) stress

Exercise 13.

1) bag	6) dryer
2) pop	7) ice cream
3) film	8) jazz
4) island	9) quiz
5) lunch	10) bus

Exercise 14.

1) 스타	6) 바닐라
2) 코트	7) 컴퓨터
3) 포크	8) 텔레비전
4) 샌드위치	9) 뉴욕
5) 퀴즈	

Chapter 2: Pronunciation Rules & Spelling

Exercise 1.

섞, 다
먹, 는다
먹, 섞
먹, 읽

Exercise 2.

1) b	3) b	5) b
2) c	4) c	6) c

Exercise 4.

1) a	3) a	5) b
2) a	4) a	6) b

Exercise 5.

1) a-c	3) a-b	5) a-b
2) a-c	4) b-c	6) a-b

Exercise 11.

1) c	2) b	3) a

Exercise 12.

1) b	3) b	5) b
2) b	4) b	6) b

Exercise 13.

1) c	3) a	5) d
2) c	4) b	6) d

Exercise 14.

1) a-b-c	3) a-b
2) a-b	4) a-b-c

Exercise 15.

1) b	3) b	5) b
2) a	4) b	6) a

Exercise 17.

1) a-b in fast speech
2) a-b
3) a-b
4) a-b-c in fast speech, otherwise b-c
5) a-b-c

Exercise 20.

1) 감사합니다	7) 없는데요
2) 의	8) 몇 학년
3) 한국어	9) 못
4) 같이	10) 반가워요
5) 백화점	11) 며칠
6) 없어요	

Chapter 3: Parts of Speech & Sentence Structure

Exercise 1.

1) adjective	6) pronoun
2) noun	7) numeral
3) adverb	8) particle
4) adnominal	9) interjection
5) verb	

Exercise 2.

1) 전공합니다	5) 했습니다
3) 좋아해요	6) 찾았습니다
4) 여깁니다	

Exercise 3.

1) subject: 김치, no object
2) no subject, no object
3) subject: 내일, no object
4) no subject, object: 김치
5) subject: 낚시, no object
6) subject: 엄마, object: 지갑

Exercise 4.

1) 나는 학생이 아니에요.
2) 친구가 지금 방에 없어요.
3) 나는 오늘 학교에 안 가요.
4) 비빔밥이 맛없어요.
5) 날씨가 안 좋아요.

Exercise 5.

1) 오늘 집에서 친구하고 공부했습니다.
2) 친구하고 오늘 집에서 공부했습니다.
3) 친구하고 집에서 오늘 공부했습니다.
4) 집에서 오늘 친구하고 공부했습니다.
5) 집에서 친구하고 오늘 공부했습니다.

Exercise 6.

2) 2020년 1월
3) 2010년 5월 5일
4) 김연아
5) 워싱턴주 킹카운티 시애틀시
6) 서울시 종로구

Exercise 7.

1) 아기가 <u>정말</u> 예뻐요.
2) 공원에서 <u>큰</u> 나무가 넘어졌어요.
3) 인터넷에서 산 신발이 <u>빨리</u> 왔어요.
4) 선생님께서 나한테 <u>무척</u> 잘 해 주세요.
5) <u>꽤</u> 좋은 소식이네요.
6) 오늘도 날씨가 <u>아주</u> 추워요.

Exercise 8.

1) C, S	3) Q, S
2) P, Q	4) C, C

Exercise 9.

1) 언니가 뭐 해요?

2) 누가 지금 자요?

3) 언니가 어디에서 자요?

4) 언니가 언제 자요?

Exercise 10.

2) 저는 열아홉 살이고 대학교 삼학년입
니다.

3) 제 동생 이름은 진아예요.

4) 진아는 대학생이 아니에요.

5) 동생은 고등학교에 다닙니다.

6) 저는 동생하고 친해서 매일 전화합니다.

7) 우리 가족은 플로리다에 삽니다

8) 저는 우리 가족이 보고 싶습니다.

9) 그래서 이번 방학에 플로리다에 갈
겁니다.

Chapter 4: Particles

Exercise 1.

1) 가

2) 이, 을

3) 이, 가, 이

4) 이, 이, 를, 가

5) 이, 를

6) 가, 을, 을, 가

Exercise 2.

1) 에

2) 에, 에, 에서

3) 에, 에서

4) 에서, 에서, 에

5) 에서, 에서

Exercise 3.

1) 를, 로, 에서, 으로   4) 에서

2) 으로, 으로   5) 으로

3) 에   6) 이랑, 랑

Exercise 4.

1) ∅

2) 한테/에게

3) 한테/에게

4) 에서

5) ∅, 한테서/에게서

6) ∅, 부터, 까지

7) 에서, 까지

Exercise 5.

1) 은, 는, 는, 는, 도

2) 는

3) 를, 만, 도, 도

4) 이, 만

5) 를, 는, 가

6) 은

7) 는, 는

8) 이, 은

Exercise 6.

은, 는, 도, 는, 만

Exercise 7.

1) 밖에, 이나   3) 만큼, 보다

2) 짜리, 쯤

Exercise 8.

1) 마다, 보다   3) 끼리, 나

2) 와, 과   4) 씩

Exercise 9.

1) 이   3) 까지

2) 부터

Exercise 10.

1) 에 대해   4) 에 비해

2) 를 통해   5) 에 의해

3) 를 위해   6) 에 따르면

Exercise 11.

1) 에(는), 에만

2) 을, 도

3) 을, 에서만

4) 하고만, 하고는

5) 에, 에도

6) 한테서(는)/에게서(는),
한테서는/에게서는

7) 로, 로도

Chapter 5: Nouns

Exercise 1.

1) 인간   4) 식사   7) 금일

2) 정문   5) 상점   8) 성명

3) 연령   6) 가격

Exercise 2.

1) country
2) learning
3) week
4) male
5) eating
6) water

Exercise 3.

1) cleaning
2) choosing
3) taking a walk
4) calling
5) greeting

Exercise 4.

1) customer service
2) lemon lime soda
3) group blind dating
4) cell phone
5) window shopping
6) steering wheel
7) studio apartment
8) selfie

Exercise 5.

1) 아이들이 자요.
2) 친구들하고 같이 바닷가에 갔어요.
3) 여기들 앉으세요.
4) 너희들, 거기서 뭐 하고 있어? Or: 너
희, 거기서들 뭐 하고 있어? Or: 너희,
거기서 뭐 하고들 있어?
5) X

Exercise 7.

1) 시, 구
2) 이삼사의 오구일공
3) 열두, 사십오, 한, 삼십
4) 이십사/스물네, 삼백육십오
5) 이천십오
6) 이만삼천
7) 사천팔백만
8) 삼억이천만

Exercise 8.

1) b. 삼
   c. 삼공오/삼백오
   d. 스무
   e. 여덟
   f. 삼십
   g. 오십

2) h. 두
   i. 한
   j. 오십오
   k. 열
   l. 오
   m. 이
   n. 세
   o. 한
   p. 스물한

Exercise 6.

0	1	2	3	4	5	6	7	8	9	10
공/영	하나	둘	셋	넷	다섯	여섯	일곱	여덟	아홉	열
	일	이	삼	사	오	육	칠	팔	구	십

10	20	30	40	50	60	70	80	90	100	1,000
열	스물	서른	마흔	쉰	예순	일흔	여든	아흔	N/A	N/A
십	이십	삼십	사십	오십	육십	칠십	팔십	구십	백	천

10,000	1 million
N/A	N/A
만	백만

Exercise 9.

1) a. 층   f. 켤레
   b. 호   g. 잔
   c. 명/사람   h. 등
   d. 그릇   i. 대
   e. 시간

2) j. 곡   l. 편   n. 권
   k. 장   m. 번

Exercise 10.

1) 이   2) 그   3) 저

Exercise 11.

1) 제 (responding to the teacher)
2) 저, 나
3) 우리, 나   5) 저희
4) 우리   6) 네, 내

Exercise 12.

1) 자신   3) 자기
2) 스스로   4) 자체

Exercise 13.

1) 무슨   8) 얼마나
2) 누구   9) 어떤
3) 어디   10) 몇
4) 언제   11) 뭐
5) 어떻게   12) 얼마
6) 어느   13) 왜
7) 누가

Exercise 14.

1) 누군가
2) 아무도
3) 아무것도
4) 뭐든지, 아무거나
5) 언제든지, 아무 때나
6) 누구든지, 아무나
7) 언제든지, 아무 때나
8) 아무 데서도
9) 언젠가

Exercise 15.

1) 모두   3) 어떤   5) 더
2) 몇   4) 좀   6) 다른

Exercise 16.

1) 절대로   3) 항상
2) 한번도   4) 전혀

Exercise 17.

1) 대부분   3) 전부
2) 몇몇   4) 다소

Chapter 6: Verbs

Exercise 1.

1) 예요, 이에요, 이에요, 이에요
2) 이에요, 아니에요, 이에요
3) 있어요, 없어요, 있어요
4) 있어요, 있어요, 예요

Exercise 2.

1) A   4) D   7) D   10) D
2) D   5) D   8) A
3) A   6) A   9) A

Exercise 3.

1) 좋아해요, 슬퍼해요, 귀여워요
2) 즐거워해요, 좋은데, 만나고 싶어해요,
   친해요

Exercise 4.

1) 말라요, 말랐어
2) 찼어
3) 꼈어
4) 닫았어, 열었어 for present,
   닫아, 열어 for future
5) 닮았어요   7) 생겼어
6) 늦었어요   8) 걸렸어요

Exercise 5.

버스를 타
점심을 먹어, 버스가 서
이를 닦아, 커피를 마셔
친구하고 놀아, 테니스를 쳐
저녁을 만들어, 돈을 내
선물을 줘, 집에서 쉬어
학교에 와, 친구가 돼
동생이야, 이메일을 써
친구야, 머리가 아파

Exercise 6.

1) 이에요, 예요, 재미있어요, 괜찮아요,
   넓어요, 좋아요
2) 만들어요, 먹어요, 가요, 봐요, 쳐요
3) 바빠요, 내요, 살아요, 자요, 쉬어요, 놀아
   요, 마셔요
4) 푸르러요, 돼요, 좋아해요

Exercise 7.

먹었어요, 먹을 거예요
닦아요, 닦을 거예요
놀았어요, 놀아요
만들어요, 만들 거예요
줬어요, 줄 거예요
와요, 올 거예요
마셨어요, 마셔요
내요, 낼 거예요
썼어요, 쓸 거예요
쉬어요, 쉴 거예요
되었어요/됐어요, 되어요/돼요
친구예요, 친구일 거예요
동생이었어요, 동생일 거예요

Exercise 8.

1) 살았어요, 싫어했어요, 시켰어요,
   청소했어요, 갔어요, 없었어요,
   많았어요, 울었어요
2) 끝났어요, 췄어요, 애기 했어요,
   먹었어요, 만났어요, 돌아왔어요
3) 바쁠 거예요, 갈 거예요, 마실 거예요,
   할 거예요, 있어요/있을 거예요, 갈
   거예요, 샀어요, 줄 거예요, 좋아할
   거예요
4) 갔어요, 들었어요, 샀어요, 입었어요,
   썼어요, 예뻐요, 써요
5) 생겼어요, 좋아요, 결혼했어요, 있어요,
   갈 거예요, 만날 거예요, 보고 싶어요

Exercise 9.

1) 먹었어요
2) 살았어요
3) 죽었어요, 죽어요
4) 컸어요, 커요
5) 일어나, 일어났어
6) 시작해요, 시작했어요

Exercise 10.

1) 맑았었는데
2) 생겼어, 생겼었어
3) 왔었어, 갔어
4) 아팠었는데

Exercise 11.

1) 자고 있어요
2) 일어나 있어요
3) 서 있어요
4) 살고 있어요, 살아 계세요
5) 들어 있어요
6) 열려 있어서
7) 입고 있어요, 끼고 있어요

Exercise 12.

1) 매울
2) 매웠을
3) 올
4) 왔을
5) 있었을 거예요
6) 있을 거예요

Exercise 13.

1) 마실게요   4) 올 거예요
2) 빌려줄게요   5) 탈 거예요
3) 힘들 거예요   6) 볼래요

Exercise 14.

1) 청소할게요   4) 닦을게요
2) 갈게요   5) 만들게요
3) 걸을게요

Exercise 15.

1) 어떨까요   3) 마실래요
2) 끝날까요   4) 도착했을까

Exercise 16.

1) 뵙겠습니다
2) 먹겠습니다
3) 주문하시겠습니까
4) 묻겠습니다
5) 드리겠습니다
6) 오겠습니다

Exercise 17.

1) 가져갈게요   3) 만날까요
2) 먹을래   4) 할 거야

Exercise 18.

1) 나는 학생이 아니에요. 그래서 안
   바빠요. 숙제가 없어요. 시험도 없어요.
2) 내 방은 안 커요. 그리고 안 조용해요.
   그래서 나는 내 방이 안 좋아요.
3) 나는 운동을 안 좋아해요. 그래서 매일
   아침에 운동(을) 안 해요. 그리고
   샤워(를) 안 해요.
4) 주말에 학교에 안 가요. 그리고
   친구들을 안 만나요. 같이 점심을 안
   먹어요.
5) 나는 일본어를 몰라요. 중국어도
   몰라요.
6) 밤에는 기숙사에 보통 없어요. 12
   시까지 공부(를) 안 해요. 그리고 안
   자요.

Exercise 19.

1) 못 봐요
2) 못 해요
3) 못 가요
4) 못 먹어요
5) 공부(를) 못 해요

Exercise 20.

1) 가지 않아요
2) 가지 못했어요
3) 가지 못할 거예요
4) 쉬지 못해요
5) 연락하지 않아요
6) 조용하지 않아요

Exercise 21.

닭고 있어요, 닭아요, 닭을 거예요
치고 있어요, 쳐요, 칠 거예요
주고 있어요, 줘요, 줄 거예요
뛰고 있어요, 뛰어요, 뛸 거예요
재고 있어요, 재요, 잴 거에요
공부하고 있어요, 공부해요, 공부할 거
  예요

Exercise 22.

A, A, B, A, A, C, C, A, C, B, B

Exercise 23.

크지 않아요, 클까요, 커요
놀지 않아요, 놀까요, 놀아요
그렇지 않아요, 그럴까요, 그래요
덥지 않아요, 더울까요, 더워요
묻지 않아요, 물을까요, 물어요
짓지 않아요, 지을까요, 지어요
빠르지 않아요, 빠를까요, 빨라요

Exercise 24.

1) 들어, 든   6) 까맣, 하얘
2) 걸을, 걸어   7) 지으
3) 구울, 구워   8) 나았어
4) 춥, 추워   9) 부르, 불러
5) 어때, 빨갈   10) 마를

Exercise 25.

살아요, 살 거예요, 삽니다, 사세요
만들고 있어요, 만들 거예요, 만듭니다,
  만드네요
달아요, 다세요, 다네요

Exercise 26.

1) 들을   4) 물   7) 닫아
2) 들   5) 걸을   8) 달아
3) 묻   6) 걸

Exercise 27.

1) 불러요   4) 길어요
2) 불어요   5) 말았어요
3) 길렀네요   6) 말랐어요

Exercise 28.

추웠어요, 하얬어요, 걸었어요, 부었어요,
  불렀어요, 나요, 멀어요, 나을 거예요,
  걸을 거예요, 놀 거예요

Chapter 7: Sentence Endings

Exercise 1.

공부합니다, 공부할 겁니다/공부할
  것입니다
읽었습니다, 읽을 겁니다/읽을 것입니다

봤습니다, 봅니다
재미있었습니다, 재미있을 겁니다/
　재미있을 것입니다
친구입니다, 친구일 겁니다/친구일
　것입니다
동생이었습니다, 동생일 겁니다/동생일
　것입니다
컸습니다, 큽니다
물었습니다, 물 겁니다/물 것입니다
묻습니다, 물을 겁니다/물을 것입니다
빨랐습니다, 빠를 겁니다/빠를 것입니다
더웠습니다, 덥습니다
지었습니다, 지을 겁니다/지을 것입니다
까맣습니다, 까말 겁니다/까말 것입니다

Exercise 2.

1) 입니다, 입니다, 재미있습니다,
　괜찮습니다, 만듭니다, 먹습니다,
　갑니다, 봅니다, 칩니다, 듣습니다
2) 바쁩니다, 냅니다, 삽니다, 잡니다,
　붓습니다, 힘듭니다, 쉽니다, 놉니다,
　마십니다, 부릅니다
3) 춥습니다, 샀습니다, 들었습니다,
　썼습니다, 신었습니다, 따뜻합니다
4) 바쁠 겁니다/바쁠 것입니다, 갈
　겁니다/갈 것입니다, 마실 겁니다/마실
　것입니다, 부를 겁니다/ 부를 것입니다

Exercise 3.

추웠습니다, 하얬습니다, 걸었습니다,
　부었습니다, 불렀습니다, 납니다,
　먹습니다, 갈 겁니다/갈 것입니다,
　멉니다, 탈 겁니다/탈 것입니다, 잘
　겁니다/잘 것입니다, 나을 겁니다/나을
　것입니다, 걸을 겁니다/걸을 것입니다,
　놀 겁니다/놀 것입니다

Exercise 4.

공부한다, 공부할 거다/공부할 것이다
읽었다, 읽을 거다/읽을 것이다
봤다, 본다
재미있었다, 재미있을 거다/재미있을
　것이다
친구(이)다, 친구일 거다/것이다
동생이었다, 동생일 거다/것이다
썼다, 쓴다

컸다, 클 거다/클 것이다
길다, 길 거다/길 것이다
물었다, 물 거다/물 것이다
물었다, 묻는다
불렀다, 부를 거다/부를 것이다
빠르다, 빠를 거다/빠를 것이다
더웠다, 더울 거다/더울 것이다
도왔다, 돕는다
지었다, 지을 거다/지을 것이다
까맣다, 까말 거다/ 까말 것이다

Exercise 5.

1) 이다, (이)다, 재미있다, 괜찮다,
　만든다, 먹는다, 간다, 본다, 친다,
　듣는다
2) 바쁘다, 낸다, 산다, 잔다, 붓는다,
　힘들다, 쉰다, 논다, 마신다, 부른다
3) 춥다, 샀다, 들었다, 썼다, 신었다,
　따뜻하다
4) 바쁠 거다/바쁠 것이다, 갈 거다/
　갈 것이다, 마실 거다/마실 것이다,
　부를 거다/부를 것이다

Exercise 6.

추웠다, 하얬다, 걸었다, 부었다, 불렀다,
　난다, 먹는다, 갈 거다/갈 것이다, 멀다,
　탈 거다/탈 것이다, 잘 거다/잘 것이다,
　나을 거다/나을 것이다, 걸을 거다/걸을
　것이다, 놀 거다/놀 것이다

Exercise 7.

1) 해
2) 봐라, 봐
3) 오라
4) 있사옵니다, 알겠도다
5) 출근하게
6) 오는가, 옵니다

Exercise 8.

1) 갖다 드리지요
2) 왔지
3) 많거든
4) 하셨잖아
5) 예쁘네
6) 좋겠네요
7) 힘들구나

8) 좋아하지
9) 기다리고 있더라고

Exercise 9.
1) 지요
2) 앉으시지요
3) 말했잖아, 취소됐거든
4) 맛있네요
5) 없거든
6) 아팠겠네
7) 따뜻하더라고요
8) 왔군요

Exercise 10.
Possible answers are:
1) 힘들겠네요
2) 치겠네
3) 없겠네
4) 피곤하겠네요 or 힘들겠네요

Exercise 11.
1) 쓸 수 없어요
2) 그럴 리가 없어요
3) 탈 수밖에 없었어요
4) 읽을 줄 알아요
5) 늦을지도 몰라요
6) 들려요

Exercise 12.
1) 앉아도 돼요
2) 끝내지 않아도 됩니다
3) 벗어야 돼요
4) 마시지 말아야 합니다
5) 하면 돼
6) 피우면 안 됩니다
7) 가져올 필요가 없어
8) 가지 않으면 안 돼요

Exercise 13.
1) 봤을걸
2) 하지 그랬어요/했어야지요
3) 나갈 걸 그랬어/나갔어야 했어
4) 조심하지 그랬어/조심했어야지

Exercise 14.
1) 추운 것 같아요

2) 긴 것 같아요
3) 만드는 것 같아
4) 마시는 것 같아
5) 나은 것 같아요
6) 늦을 것 같아

Exercise 15.
1) 오나요
2) 가나요
3) 매운가요
4) 깨끗한가요
5) 왔나요
6) 무거웠나요
7) 올 건가요

Exercise 16.
1) 젊어 보여
2) 아파 보이
3) 행복해 보이
4) 따뜻해 보여

Exercise 17.
1) 올 것 같아요
2) 날씬해 보여요
3) 좋은가 봐요
4) 따뜻할까요/ 따뜻한가요

Exercise 18.
1) 만들어 드렸
2) 열어 드릴
3) 가르쳐 주서, 얘기해 줘
4) 전해 줘
5) 빌려 줄, 빌려 드릴

Exercise 19.
1) 마셔 보세요
2) 먹어 본 적이 없어요
3) 치곤 했는
4) 들어 봤어요
5) 잊어버렸어요
6) 싸 놨어요/싸 뒀어요
7) 울고 말았어요
8) 치일 뻔 했어
9) 말라 죽겠다

Chapter 8: Complex Sentences
Exercise 1.
1) 만
2) 첫, 옛
3) 딴
4) 맨
5) 헌, 새
6) 고

Exercise 2.
치마를 입는, 치마를 입을
안경을 쓴, 안경을 쓸
매일 걸은, 매일 걷는
침대에 누운, 침대에 누울
얼굴이 붓는, 얼굴이 부을
노래를 부른, 노래를 부를
김치를 만든, 김치를 만드는
머리가 좋은
피곤한
매운
하얀
배가 부른
머리가 긴
발이 아주 큰

Exercise 3.
1) 따뜻한
2) 하얀
3) 아주 귀여운
4) 목이 마른
5) 바람이 많이 부는
6) 수업에 매일 늦게 오는
7) 친구가 마시는
8) 언니가 다니는
9) 친구가 타는
10) 저 슈퍼에서 파는

Exercise 4.
1) 결혼한
2) 잘 생긴
3) 언니가 구운
4) 동생이 지난 주에 들은
5) 제가 만든
6) 어제 아침에 읽은
7) 곧 들을
8) 이 모자를 쓸
9) 언니가 구울
10) 다음 학기에 살
11) 내일 아침에 읽을

Exercise 5.
1) 가던   4) 마신
2) 간   5) 작던
3) 마시던   6) 초등학생이었던

Exercise 6.
1) 그리고, 그렇지만, 그래서, 그러면
2) 그래도, 그러다가, 그러니까, 그런데

Exercise 7.
1) 바쁜데, 가거나, 들으면서
2) 오고/왔고, 추웠지만, 추운데, 있어서
3) 마셔도, 마셔서, 줄이고
4) 맑겠으나, 오고, 흐리고

Exercise 8.
1) 들으면서
2) 바쁘지만
3) 좋은데, 나가든지
4) 받았는데, 맵거나
5) 않겠으나, 추워지겠으며

Exercise 9.
1) 있어야   5) 돕느라고
2) 작아도   6) 추워 가지고
3) 팔면   7) 어려우므로
4) 없으니까

Exercise 10.
1) 오는데/오니까, 있었는데
2) 됐는데
3) 추워서
4) 막혔으니까
5) 걸려서
6) 청소하느라고

Exercise 11.
1) 내리고, 내린 후에
2) 와서
3) 먹고, 먹은 다음에
4) 먹고 나서
5) 태어나고, 태어나서

Exercise 12.
1) 만나서, 보면서
2) 듣는 동안에, 끝나고 나서
3) 끝난 후에, 가는 김에, 가는 길에,
   오기 전에

Exercise 13.

1) 가다가, 만난 지, 졸업하자 마자
2) 가니까, 뵈러 갈 때

Exercise 14.

1) 오다가   6) 탔다가
2) 갔다가   7) 샀다가
3) 껐다가   8) 사다가
4) 보다가   9) 가져다가
5) 타다가

Exercise 15.

1) 시작한 지   4) 왔으니까
2) 먹을 때   5) 가니까
3) 만났을 때

Exercise 16.

1) 뵈러
2) 진학하려고
3) 힘들더니, 하면 할수록
4) 펼치고자
5) 배고플텐데
6) 하시던데
7) 공부해 봤자

Exercise 17.

1) 춥더니   5) 갔더니
2) 걸었더니   6) 졸았더니
3) 걷더니   7) 졸더니
4) 가더니

Exercise 18.

1) 겪지만   9) 끝났을 때
2) 보면서   10) 건너다가
3) 봤으면서   11) 갔다가
4) 추워서   12) 왔는데
5) 걸렸기 때문에   13) 오는데
6) 가니까   14) 운동하더니
7) 먹었으니까   15) 운동했더니
8) 갈 때

Exercise 19.

1) 오니까   5) 만드느라고
2) 와서   6) 하는 동안에
3) 복잡한데   7) 들으면서
4) 지각해서   8) 가려고

9) 만나러
10) 성공하고자

Exercise 20.

1) 아파서   4) 일하며
2) 성공하고자   5) 노력했으나
3) 사용하신 후에

Chapter 9: Verb Derivations

Exercise 1.

이세요, 이셨어요
있으시다, 있으셨어요
계시다, 계세요
주문하시다, 주문하셨어요
오세요, 오셨어요
치시다, 치셨어요
쓰시다, 쓰세요
부르시다, 부르셨어요
입으세요, 입으셨어요
걸으시다, 걸으셨어요
도우시다, 도우세요
만드시다, 만드셨어요
지으세요, 지으셨어요
그러시다, 그러셨어요

Exercise 2.

1) 성함, 이세요, 께서는, 연세, 이세요,
   께서는, 사셨어요, 를, 뵈었어요, 께서,
   돌아가셔서, 께서, 사세요
2) 생신, 께, 사 드렸어요, 께서는, 께,
   생신, 드리셨어요, 께서, 좋아하셨어요,
   께서, 사시면 좋겠어요
3) 께서, 편찮으셨어요, 께서,
   건강해지셔서, 께서는, 주무시고,
   운동하세요, 드세요/잡수세요, 께,
   드리고, 를, 뵈러, 댁, 보고, 해요

Exercise 3.

1) 드셨어요, 먹었어
2) 말씀하세요, 얘기해
3) 주무세요, 자
4) 분이세요, 명이에요
5) 있으세요, 없어
6) 계세요, 계셔

Exercise 4.
1) 제, 나
2) 뵈러, 만나러
3) 모시고, 데리고
4) 여쭤

Exercise 5.

1) 줬어요	5) 드리셨어요
2) 드렸어요	6) 했어요
3) 주셨어요	7) 하셨어요
4) 주셨어요	8) 드리셨어요

Exercise 6.
1) 처음 뵙겠습니다.
2) 성함이 어떻게 되세요?
3) 연세가 어떻게 되세요?
4) 댁이 어디세요?
5) 만나 뵈어서 반갑습니다.
6) 또 뵙겠습니다.

Exercise 7.
팔리다
닦이다, 먹히다
들리다, 빼앗기다
읽히다, 나뉘다
쓰이다, 찍히다

Exercise 8.

1) 봐요	8) 쫓고 있어요
2) 보여요	9) 팔아요
3) 막았어요	10) 팔려요
4) 막혔어요	11) 꺼졌어요
5) 닫혀서	12) 껐어요
6) 닫았어요	13) 됐어요
7) 쫓기고 있어요	14) 걱정하지

Exercise 9.

1) 안겨 있	7) 미뤄졌
2) 닫혀 있	8) 취소됐
3) 놓여 있	9) 걱정된
4) 켜진	10) 잘하게 됐
5) 써진	11) 알게 됐
6) 깨져	

Exercise 10.
씌우다
눕히다, 낮추다
말리다, 먹이다
벗기다, 입히다
태우다, 신기다
끓이다, 울리다
없애다, 넓히다

Exercise 11.

1) 깨우	4) 씻기	7) 눕히
2) 먹이	5) 씌우	8) 낮추
3) 읽히	6) 울리	9) 없애

Exercise 12.

1) 많이	5) 너무
2) 빨리	6) 편안히
3) 몰래	7) 조용히
4) 멀리	8) 굉장히

Exercise 13.

1) 작게	6) 뜨겁게
2) 예쁘게	7) 재미있게
3) 하얗게	8) 크게
4) 힘들게	9) 맛있게
5) 편하게	10) 행복하게

Exercise 14.

1) 샛	5) 헛	9) 뒤
2) 엇/빗	6) 짓	10) 들
3) 치	7) 엿	11) 덧
4) 되	8) 휘	

Exercise 15.
1) 많으시겠네요
2) 했겠지요
3) 놔두셨을 것 같아요
4) 드셔야지요

Chapter 10: Embedded Sentences
Exercise 1.
1) 대학교에서 수업을 듣는 거
2) 하는 거, 청소하는 거
3) 만드는 거, 되는 거
4) 먹은 거

5) 난 거
6) 가져간 거

Exercise 2.
1) 배우기 시작하셨어요, 보기로 해요
2) 봐 주시기 바랍니다
3) 있기는 하지만, 바쁘기 때문에
4) 건강해지기 위해서, 걷기에

Exercise 3.
1) 잠	5) 웃음
2) 믿음	6) 울음
3) 꿈	7) 삶
4) 아픔	8) 얼음

Exercise 4.
1) 있는 것	6) 울음
2) 하는 거	7) 자기
3) 읽기/읽는 것	8) 죽음
4) 걷기/걷는 것	9) 춤기
5) 만나기	10) 쉬시기

Exercise 5.
보냐고 하다, 보라고 하다, 보자고 하다
잡는다고 하다, 잡으라고 하다, 잡자고 하자
한다고 하다, 하(느)냐고 하다, 하자고 하다
쓴다고 하다, 쓰(느)냐고 하다, 쓰라고 하다
돕는다고 하다, 돕(느)냐고 하다, 돕자고 하다
듣는다고 하다, 들으라고 하다, 듣자고 하다
파(느)냐고 하다, 팔라고 하다, 팔자고 하다
부른다고 하다, 부르라고 하다, 부르자고 하다
예쁘냐고 하다
춥다고 하다
다냐고 하다
빠르다고 하다
그러냐고 하다

Exercise 6.
1) 괜찮다	4) 올 거라
2) 있(느)냐	5) 간다
3) 만나자	6) 연락해 달라

Exercise 7.
1) 괜찮대	4) 올 거래
2) 있내	5) 간대
3) 만나재	6) 연락해 달래

Exercise 8.
1) 달라고	3) 주시라고
2) 드리라고	4) 주라고

Exercise 9.
1) 바뀌었다는
2) 들르라는
3) 따뜻해지겠다는/따뜻해질 거라는
4) 언제냐는
5) 만나자는
6) 빌려 달라는

Exercise 10.
1) 있는 것을, 시작하는 것으로
2) 없다고 알고 있습니다, 희망적이라고 생각합니다

Exercise 11.
1) 태어난 줄
2) 사는 줄
3) 본 줄
4) 큰 줄
5) 듣는 줄
6) 유학갈 줄/유학가는 줄

Exercise 12.
1) 하는지
2) 있는지
3) 좋은지
4) 샀는지
5) 내야 되는지
6) 나오셨는지
7) 나오실지/나오실 건지

Index

Chapter 1: The Korean Alphabet

Chapter 2: Pronunciation Rules & Spelling

Chapter 3: Parts of Speech & Sentence Structure

Chapter 4: Particles

Chapter 5: Nouns

Chapter 6: Verbs

Chapter 7: Sentence Endings

Chapter 8: Complex Sentences

Chapter 9: Verb Derivations